SYMPOSIUM

ON

SOCIOLOGICAL THEORY

Editor

LLEWELLYN GROSS

University of Buffalo

HARPER & ROW, PUBLISHERS

New York, Evanston, and London

Library of Congress "Cataloguing in Source" data follows the index.

ACKNOWLEDGMENTS

In this book there is ample evidence of devotion to scholarly exploration, and to the difficult art of expressing ideas in a style that is proportionate to the purposes at hand. The sensibilities and good temper of those who wrote the book are also evident, even though there are differences of perspective among the authors—as one would expect in a symposium of this kind. The editor is grateful to the individual authors for their consideration of his suggestions, and for their integrity and intrepidity.

Without the encouragement of F. Stuart Chapin, a pioneer in both theory and research, this book might not have been launched. I am further indebted to colleagues, here and elsewhere, who by their interest, enthusiasm, or counsel lessened the burden of what could have been a tedious task. I wish to mention, in particular, Leonard Broom, Alvin Gouldner, Jacob Hyman, William Parry, Harry Raulet, George Theodorson, and Constantine Yeracaris.

I would be ruefully remiss if I did not mention the faithful assistance of my secretaries, Barbara Ainsworth and Frances K. Dietz. That my wife, Genevieve, and my son, Franz, played a part in this endeavor needs no telling to those who know them.

LLEWELLYN GROSS

Buffalo, New York
January, 1959

TABLE OF CONTENTS

PART IV: SOCIAL CHANGE

PART V: FUNCTIONAL THEORY

PART VI: MODELS IN SOCIAL SCIENCE

PART VII: FORMALIZATION OF THEORY

EDITOR'S INTRODUCTION

What Samuel Johnson said of literature is truer still of sociology. "It is amazing how little there is in the world." We are faced with a vast and unbounded domain of ignorance. Sober is the thought that if we could say nothing in sociology but what could be proved conclusively there would be no sociology. Our darkness appears to stem less from the shortage of time or talent than from the prevalent run of intellectual folk-ways, beliefs that set the course of academic thinking and tend, in some instances, to shut out the ill born and the institutionally unsponsored. There is little cause to wonder then that scarcely a dozen sociologists of those now alive are establishing the design of sociological theory in our time. If the metaphor can be forgiven, the lacement of sociological theory is as large as a fish net capable of capturing the grandest denizens of the Pacific. How now can a dozen anglers grasp any more than a small part of it? No handful of men, competent though they be, can hope to control a skein so massive. Clearly, a more sagacious allocation of professional resources is urgently needed. In harmony with this thought, the present volume is offered as a review and as a promise of the kinds of theoretical considerations that warrant examination in the immediate future.

Robert K. Merton is undoubtedly correct in stating that "a large part of what is now called sociological theory consists of generalized orientations towards data . . . rather than clear, verifiable statements of relationships between specified variables." But we hasten to add that between generalized orientations on the one hand and verifiable statements on the other is an intermediate area of high significance for the youthful science of sociology. This is the area of the procedurally informed approach, one which attempts, however sketchily, to present itself in a manner best calculated to negotiate the passage to clear and verifiable statements. It is an approach which strives to examine questions that bear directly on the character of scientific theories, through the careful ordering of *statement forms* that have essential human content. Of this

1

kind of approach, disciplined in nature, problematically sensitive, and conceptually corrigible, there is surely too little. And for understandable reasons.

Sociological theory, like any other active enterprise, has its master architects who, after designing a pattern, move on through the accumulation of new materials to the consolidation of their positions. Inevitably, they are supported by a corps of loyal co-workers who execute, apply, and perpetuate conceptual structures to which they are heirs, but not without alterations. These scholars constitute the majority of workmen in every science, including sociology. To complement the achievements of this group, there is another corps, which is usually less noticeable and often less well received than the first group, but is every bit as essential to the scientific enterprise. This second group is comprised of the intellectually unconstrained, those who search for unexplored horizons in human knowledge, with a desire to precipitate some novel perspective. Ever ready to compose anew, they champion the cause of radical innovations in social science. A third group stands somewhere between these two. Dependent on the heritage of learning bequeathed to them by their predecessors and contemporaries, those in the third group attempt by judicious study and thoughtful creation to enlarge the perimeter of human knowledge. They are more self-conscious of their intellectual beginnings than the others, and are sensitive to early preconceptions. They work with care and patience, so that what they do, though incomplete, will mark a fundamental social gain. It is in the latter two groups, we believe, that most of the contributors to this volume belong. The "missing link" between general orientations and the clear and verifiable statement will probably be found in the kind of considerations which they put forth and dissect here.

To provide common ground for the present endeavor, the editor prepared a list of general objectives that contributors might use as guide lines in writing their essays. The following were suggested as worthy of consideration:

1. To reconstruct, co-ordinate, and integrate existing contributions by introducing previously unrecognized insights, observations, and interpretations or by creating original schemes of analysis (assumption: sociology needs not only precise formulations that are close to the facts but also bold conceptions that extend somewhat beyond them).

2. To emphasize and develop further methodological approaches, strategies and procedures by explicating what is implicit in present theories and by inventing conceptual schemes or devices that will point the way toward new theories (assumption: deliberative methods can be discovered for building theories, and these methods can be described and taught).

3. To highlight the possibilities of theoretical advance through the development of logical and quasi-logical forms of exposition that will com-

plement the present drift toward informal prose and mathematical formulas. The latter are already sturdy movements in sociology (assumption: the next most significant advance in sociology may well occur on this level).

4. To offset somewhat the preeminence of "structural-functional" theory, fruitful though it is, by discovering variations within its main themes and, when possible, by formulating alternative analytical frameworks (assumption: a wider degree of differentiation among theories than now exists is a necessary condition for sociological maturity).

5. To facilitate comprehension by arranging statements in sequential or spatial patterns or by adopting the "If, then" and "Since, therefore" modes of analysis.

6. To establish relevance by avoiding discussion of the general nature of theory apart from empirical samples and by avoiding discussion of specific theories apart from some larger analytical framework.

Within the broad confines of these general expectations, it was hoped that contributors would have sufficient interest and ingenuity to explore anew such central concepts as "postulates," "explanations," "models," "types," "levels," "dispositions," "transactions," "functional relations," "processes," "probability," "causality," "verification," "confirmation," and "normative propositions." The editor assumed that a careful assessment of the relevance of these concepts for sociology could possibly precipitate a new phase in sociological science.

Aside from the question of whether every contributor had the above objectives in mind while writing his essay, it will be apparent to the serious reader that each has attempted to delineate new areas of thought and exploration. Each, we believe, has made a signal effort to present more fully certain lines of inquiry that the majority of sociologists has largely neglected or overlooked. If new discoveries belong to the scholar who thinks boldly, they also belong to those who have reconciled themselves to human frailty, their own in particular. Any human who nurtures his capacity to think outside and beyond the conventional circle of ideas must expect to compose many errors. The wisest of his interpretations will be subject not only to ignorance and oversight but also to the conduct of historical judgment, for the best known error is ever more supportable than one that is new and untried. Yet, no human can calculate the end of knowledge. The scholar's solemn task is therefore to speak as much of the "truth" as he dares and as little of "error" as he must. Beyond this he can only wait and hope that the outcome will prove to be significant.

In symposiums such as this, it is usually the contributors' duty to build the fires and the editor's duty to see that the flames are properly attended. However, any full-scale attempt to attend properly to the central threads of illumination that rise above the idiomatic details of each collaborator's effort would require a volume nearly as large as this one. Moreover, such a task would be pretentious for the ablest of editors. The interpretations of any editor are bound to involve some measure of selective perception and the imposition of ideas that maintain ascendancy by virtue of previous learning. For this reason, the particular construction placed upon the work of contributors to this symposium should be recognized for what it really is. It represents certain selectively perceived lines of convergence and divergence that are in some degree antecedently imposed by the editor. Since other kinds of comparisons than those mentioned can be found to characterize the essays, our introduction fails to do justice to the magnitude and subtlety of each contributor's efforts. It is believed, however, that experienced readers will recognize that the range and significance of a competent scholar's position can best be presented by him. These readers are encouraged to search for interrelationships among the essays in whatever terms and along whatever avenues may be most meaningful to them. By taking such steps, they may accumulate a fund of systematic information, an intellectual storehouse of orderly knowledge which will serve them well should they wish to advance their understanding of this subject.

Here then are what appear to be leading convergences in assumptions, principles, and aims of the contributors to this volume:

Values play a significant role in the process of creating social science.

For Werkmeister, social science is valued because it satisfies man's curiosity and can serve as an instrumental basis for rational decisions and actions. "The conditions under which values arise, the specific values accepted by particular groups, the ways in which values become modified, the effects of valuations on human behavior—all these matters belong to the legitimate domain of facts with which the social scientists are concerned." Knowledge of such facts suggests, as Werkmeister puts it, the value *of* science. Knowledge of this kind is useful insofar as it is in accord with the norms and ideals that are established outside of science. In addition to the value *of* social science, there are values *in* social science. These values appear as data or facts for study and as premises or explanatory categories attributable to the social group under investigation. The question of values as an explanatory category arises simply because, consciously and deliberately, human beings pursue ends which they value. Explanation and prediction in the social sciences are impossible without reference to the basic value commitments of the agents involved, since a change in these commitments may alter the whole series of events studied by the social scientist. Finally, Werkmeister speaks of values *for* science, the commitments that a scientist must make as a scientist. These commitments are important in the selection of problems for inquiry and are bound up with such standards of research as exactitude, intellectual integrity, and objectivity. From this viewpoint, the personal values of the individual scientist are part of the nonscientific framework within which science develops as an aspect of culture and society.

Furfey's analysis is largely in accord with Werkmeister's position. However, he examines more fully the connection between the criteria of scientific evaluation and the individual scientist's values, as determined by personal, group, and cultural influences. He suggests that criteria of relevance and scientific quality are influenced by humanitarian values and finds evidence for this in the sociologist's treatment of majority-minority group relations, crime, and delinquency. Such values, Furfey holds, should be made explicit. They should be derived from definite principles that serve to justify the working sociologist's choice of possible scientific criteria. This becomes the task of the "metasociologist."

Of similar concern is Hart's assertion that most invention is goal-directed and that therefore valuational aspects cannot be excluded. Social changes and their accompanying lags can be explained only when valuational behavior is dispassionately and fully understood. Present sociologists have concluded, says Hart, that it is entirely proper, scientifically, for applied sociology, having discovered what human purposes are most fundamental or widely accepted as ideal, to seek and disseminate knowledge as to how these purposes may be more adequately fulfilled. In a different but related vein, Sjoberg suggests that even though sociologists are no longer seeking to remake society, sociology, together with other social sciences, seems much more concerned with reinforcing certain values and beliefs in the social system. He documents the thesis that society's values and beliefs strongly influence scientists' techniques and modes of analysis. Contemporary American bureaucracy, Sjoberg finds, encourages the development of homogeneous operational procedures that are empiristic and particularistic. As a consequence, serious efforts to establish generalizations on the basis of cross-cultural comparisons are largely neglected. Social power then operates to restrict the kinds of materials that can be collected, analyzed, and reported. Thus, real doubt is cast on the representativeness of samples and on the significance of the results of sociological research.

Theoretical and methodological analyses must be anchored to recognized human problems.

Though the present essayists are not always explicit on questions concerning the essential nature of scientific problems, contextual examination reveals that many believe methodological proposals must pay their way in terms of results that increase our basic understanding of social behavior. Some of the contributors openly declare that patterns of explanation and prediction must be rooted in actual events, the knowledge of which will advance mankind in its resolution of human problems.

Edel strongly emphasizes the necessity of grounding abstract concepts in clearly recognized problems and purposes. He suggests that "there are at least three conditions that would warrant extending credit to a general or abstract high-level category for structuring an area of social inquiry: (1) when there is a promise of the development of greater theoretical knowledge by its use, in reference to some specific set of theoretical problems already articulated; (2) when there are definite institutional forms or practices which it expresses, so that it has at least an anchored meaning whose extension is being proposed for a wider field; (3) when there is some set of unified purposes that the concept can help articulate."

Wolff, on the other hand, speaks of the central problem of the sociology of knowledge as the relations between society and intellectual life. He points out that for Manheim these were existential problems which were eminently historical in character. That is to say, the fundamental factors constituting the "problem constellation" of the sociology of knowledge spring from the question of what happens when intellectual processes are viewed as the expression of historical circumstance and thus no longer are taken for granted. In a separate context, Wolff defends the thesis that "methodological problems, on the one hand, and volitional and metaphysical problems, on the other, have different criteria of confirmation or truth." The sociology of knowledge being "applied" theory in the service of changing the world is, by his interpretation, alien to the formalism of our time. Tangentially related to the same point is Timasheff's declaration that the postulate of order is at least a tacit assumption of every purposive activity. The major activities of everyday life, technological, economic, legal and medical, for instance, would be meaningless if the effects of action were not in some respects orderly. This is not the same thing as saying that the postulate of order would be meaningless without grounding it in everyday activity, but the emphasis upon empirical tests of verification in nearly all of the essays leads to a similar idea.

Consistent with his orientation toward values, Hart postulates that every social theory must be evaluated in terms of the practical aid which it promises to provide toward the solution of social problems. He holds that a valid science of social life is the most promising instrument for speeding up desirable social developments. Akin to Hart's assumptions is Bierstedt's view that while substantive theory is lagging behind methodological theory the former is vastly more significant for sociology even when its conclusions fall short of fulfilling the canons of scientific inquiry. Since Bierstedt regards the major achievements of the latter as coming frequently from novelists, journalists, and publicists—men who are close to the problems of daily living—his views seem largely consistent with those essayists to whom present reference is made.

Finally, of all the essayists, Mills expresses the issue most uncompromisingly. "Methods are methods for some range of problems; theories are theories of some range of phenomena." To be mastered entirely by one or the other is to be kept from trying to find out something that is going on in the world. Any really useful method then must be anchored in the actual work of study and must spring from the sense of a significant problem and the passion to solve it.

The basic character of a scientific theory is determined by the set of concepts or principles that are chosen as central to its formulation.

This theme appears with varying degrees of explicitness in almost all of the papers included in the volume. As Edel points out, the question "What is society?" raises the problem of selecting basic units or objects according to the social and cultural traits or properties which are to be referred or analyzed. Thus, social theory may be centered around concepts of individual consciousness, behavioral acts, interpersonal relations, or group relations. Complementing Edel's interpretation is Bendix and Berger's clarification of Simmel's focus on the concept of interaction, Durkheim's stress on collective coercion, and Weber's emphasis on the meaning which individuals in society attach to their own and others' actions. Bendix and Berger note, moreover, that Parsons takes the concept of system as indispensable in sociological theory. Of direct bearing then is Gouldner's examination of Parsons' contributions, which rest largely on the use of this very same concept. Relevant too is Werkmeister's insistence on the necessity of including key valuations in the set of definitions and postulates from which the set of laws governing social phenomena can be derived.

From a different but related perspective, Rapoport suggests that one of the basic problems of social science hinges on the extent to which social events can be identified and assigned numerical values. A science of social behavior becomes possible when such values enter into the variables of mathematical equations that lead to verifiable deductions. It is evident therefore that the assumptions we make about the counting and measurement of key events will largely determine the future success of social science.

Mills' contribution dovetails with the position of the preceding authors. He contends that good work in social science is composed of many studies which at key points anchor general statements about the shape and trend of the subject. He speaks of locating pivotal assertions and hunches in the process of shuttling back and forth between theory and the existing materials gathered in various stages of investigation. In looking over notes on other writers, Mills finds it helpful to use their general principles as a center from which to make his own elaborations and develop his own projects. Other useful approaches, varying in subtlety and detail, are found to tie in to this principle.

Common to all essays is a core vocabulary of basic concepts and methods that are often accepted without analysis. Words like "theory," "generalization," "empirical," and "fact" must usually be taken for granted in order to get on with the work at hand. Without the common universe of understanding implied by such words, the essayists could not move rapidly to new boundaries of knowledge and understanding.

Central concepts in sociology are placed or located in a theoretical framework through their linkage with one or more other concepts.

This linkage is frequently one of complementation, contrast, or polarity. When two concepts represent opposite extremes of the same quality or variable and, at the same time, possess overlapping referents, the area of overlap may be treated as though it referred to an independent quality. Hence, there exists the seemingly paradoxical situation in which we find polar concepts suggesting antithetical or contradictory meanings. In Gouldner's analysis, for example, functional autonomy and functional reciprocity are clarified through their relationship to postulated degrees of interdependence among the parts of a system. Between the social system's attempt to integrate the parts and the part's attempt to maintain relative independence, the overarching concepts of equilibrium and system tension emerge to symbolize what is problematic. "Organization is seen then as shaped by a conflict, particularly by the tensions between centripetal and centrifugal pressures, as limiting control over parts as well as imposing it, as establishing a balance between their dependence and independence, and as separating as well as connecting the parts."

The questions raised by Bendix and Berger in their discussion of the perspective of dual tendencies and in their numerous references to the role of paired concepts can be joined to the present principle. Under certain conditions, group forces strengthen the individual; under other conditions, they threaten his integration. Thus, the concept of individualization seems to require reference to the concept of socialization, primary relations to secondary relations, and status to contract. The authors' emphasis upon the reciprocity of social life wherein every action leads to reaction, together with the interpretation that conflict and strain help to maintain the adaptation of the social structure, parallels Gouldner's analysis in certain important respects. As the authors indicate, there are limitations in using paired concepts, and the reader is warned against assuming that such concepts when established in an analytic or definitional manner are identical with historically grounded hypotheses.

Closely related to Bendix and Berger's discussion is Wolff's reference to the presence of numerous dichotomies articulated by social scientists during the last hundred years. He mentions Maine's contrast between societies based on status and societies based on contract, Spencer's distinction between military and industrial societies, and Tonnies' analysis of Gemeinschaft and Gesellschaft types of societies. More recently we have Becker's sacred and secular societies and Redfield's folk and urban societies, to mention only a few of those known to the sociological reader. Wolff construes such "civilizational-historical" dichotomies as attempts at coming to terms with the emerging one world. He believes that they were not only intended by their authors as scientific hypotheses but also claim to express existential truth. "In other words, the existential element in these dichotomies is the mixture of faith and doubt that liberalism, increasing rationalization, reasonableness, progress are indeed true."

Much the same procedure is evident in Mills' habit of casting general ideas into types by the technique of cross-classifying them. As Mills ably demonstrates, the range and relationships of terms are more clearly brought out and one is then in position to write more explicitly about them. He states that some of the best insights are gained from considering extreme types—"from thinking of the opposite of that with which you are directly concerned." Such polar types, Mills finds, have the additional advantage of enabling one to sort out the dimensions in terms of which comparisons among materials can be made. In the absence of statistical samples, the range and major types of phenomena are thereby provided, and one may get some grasp of the variety of possible perspectives from which different specialties approach a problem. Mills' discussion of the release of the imagination, based as it is on Burke's famous phrase, "perspective by incongruity," and his development of the distinction between theme and topic are facets of this same general point.

Metaphors and analogies ranging from loose correspondences to near isomorphisms are pervasive features of every scientific theory.

In some cases, the burden of a particular essay rests entirely upon the fruitfulness of a complex and familiar analogy. In other cases, analogies and metaphors are merely supporting or auxiliary devices for enhancing the plausibility of a theoretical position. Without the search for similarities and parallelisms of form, new insights could not be readily transferred to the nonspecialist. Moreover, serious limitations would be placed on any attempt to integrate the sciences, for such integration is built on significant resemblances.

Resemblances and parallelisms between interrelated methods reappear time and again in the paper by George. Models are shown to stand in some kind of structural relationship to the natural and symbolic languages of their corresponding theories. A model may be pictorial or symbolic. Or it may be of some other form, as long as it is capable of interpretation in terms of simple observational facts and in terms of the language used to describe them. George points out that the syntax of the propositional calculus can be given an interpretation as propositions and functions. And the propositional calculus coupled with a part of the lower functional calculus, all suffixed for time, is isomorphic with neural nets which are structurally very much like the nervous system. From such a general model, it may then be possible to provide an interpretation of the behavior of the human organism and perhaps even of the physiological and biochemical language sometimes used to describe it. This general model, known as a finite automaton, is divisible into three systems, a Motivation system, an Emotional system, and a Control or Cognitive system. The latter is interpretable as sets of sets, or properties, representing the ultimate subdivisions of sensory discrimination, such as colors and shapes. This line of analysis leads to a theory of perception based on elaboration of sensory input and of beliefs aroused as a result of the categorizing process that perception serves. The Motivation and Emotional systems are constructed in a manner analogously similar to the Cognitive system.

On other occasions, George indicates that the same model can be used for interpreting theories at many levels. Thus, the various classical calculi can be mapped onto the calculus of probability, giving languages powerful enough for empirical descriptions. Such languages, we would add, must contain analogical relations with one another by virtue of their common descent from the same general model. Speaking metaphorically, as George does, "the collection of marks called calculi have certain structural properties like maps of anywhere at all, and the problem is to select a map that fits the country the scientist is interested in at any time." However, the precise relations of logical calculi cannot be precisely produced in the natural language other than by analogy. Therefore, approximations in respect to structural similarities and interdependencies are the most that can be hoped for in the near future.

Correspondence of pattern or structure, some of which are only implicit, appear in Greenberg's paper on "An Axiomatization of the Phonologic Aspect of Language." One may notice from this author's presentation that the observational truth of axioms and theorems depends upon the possibility of establishing co-ordinating definitions which relate the meanings of the primitive terms and relations of a calculus with specific objects or events subsumed under it. These definitions, sometimes operational in nature, serve to identify logical terms with descriptive terms. In instances where this identification or correspondence breaks down, we have evidence of gaps or weaknesses in the theory and empirical data of a particular subject matter. Greenberg holds that opinions concerning the methodological superiority of linguistics among the social sciences appears to rest upon the presence of units of universal occurrence that permit comparability between statements about different linguistic subsystems. If differences in definitions and analytic procedures among linguists could be overcome, the way would lie open, it seems, to statements of universal scope referring to all languages.

Greenberg's account suggests still other kinds of questions pertaining to relationships between structures based on identities or similarities of form. What are the constraints in respect to form placed by a metalanguage upon its object language and vice versa? How close is the correspondence between metalanguage and object language in the three basic aspects of any system of significant symbols: phonology, grammar, and semantics? Upon what bases can comparisons be made in dialect geography, historical linguistics, or typological linguistics? In Greenberg's approach to phonetics, the metalanguage is interpreted by means of co-ordinating definitions which refer to symbols that are largely articulatory rather than perceptual or acoustic. It is inevitable then that his axiomatization should be confined primarily to articulatory types of symbols.

When appraising conceptual schemes, one must display by detailed analysis their essential qualities and requirements, what they can and cannot do logically and factually, and where their implications lead in respect to both promise and accomplishment.

In Hempel's thorough assessment of functional analysis, this theme is amply illustrated. We are told that explanation by functional analysis requires reference to general laws of universal or statistical form. But the familiar argument for functionalism falls short of fulfilling criteria of nomological explanation, whether deductive or inductive.

As a deductive argument, functional analysis fails to explain why a given trait rather than one of its alternatives can satisfy a certain necessary condition for the functioning of a system in its setting. In all concrete cases of application, there do seem to exist alternatives. Yet the question of whether there are functional alternatives to a given trait has definite meaning only if the internal state and environment of the system are clearly specified. Without such specifications, the interpretation could be made that an alternative trait so modified the basic characteristics of the system that it was no longer the original system. This interpretation would safeguard the postulate of the functional indispensability of every culture trait against any empirical disconfirmation by turning it into a covert tautology.

As an inductive argument, functional analysis might be construed as showing that the occurrence of a trait is highly probable in the circumstances described by the premises. But this course is not promising, since in most cases it is not possible to specify with any precision the range of alternative traits satisfying a given functional requirement. Even if such a range of traits could be found there is no method for dividing this range into some finite number of cases and assigning a probability to each of these.

After showing that functional analysis does not provide either deductively or inductively adequate grounds for expecting the occurrence of a given trait rather than one of its alternatives, Hempel examines the possibility of utilizing a less ambitious kind of functional explanation, viz., that the necessary condition of a system must be fulfilled in some way or other by one of the alternatives in a class of traits. He holds that this kind of inference is trivial without additional knowledge of the characteristics of the alternative traits and such knowledge is not generally available. In a similar vein, the predictive use of functional analysis and the character of hypotheses of self-regulation are discussed in respect to their logical and empirical consequences. Full recognition is given to their limitations and accomplishments, deficient though the latter is. The author concludes that functional analysis may be conceived, at least ideally, as a program for research guided by certain heuristic maxims or "working hypotheses."

The same process of searching for the implications of a conceptual scheme or pattern of analysis, for the consequences of such implications, and for the consequences of these consequences is evident in much of Hochberg's contribution. In discussing the origins of axiomatization in Euclidian geometry, Hochberg indicates that the Greeks proved their theorems by taking various propositions for granted and defining introduced terms. Statements once proved were in turn used in proving further theorems. Thus, they made the foundations of geometry explicit. By showing what depended logically on what, they unified the various areas of geometry. However, the axioms of Euclid's geometry are not analytic truths and hence cannot serve as the theoretical basis for derived theorems. Although the Greeks attempted to justify their axioms on the grounds that they were self-evidently true, they were bothered by the thought that the "parallel postulate" was not as self-evident as the other so-called postulates and axioms. Perhaps the latter could be derivable then as a theorem. At this point, Hochberg goes on to explore the outcomes that followed from various unsuccessful attempts to "derive" the parallel postulate from the other axioms and postulates.

Again, in discussing a linguistic system called 'L,' Hochberg states that meaningful axioms are dependent upon meaningful terms. A meaningful term is one which is either a descriptive term of L or a logical word. Descriptive terms of L are either defined or undefined. Thus, if the axioms of L containing the word 'point' are meaningful propositions, that word must be one of the defined or undefined descriptive terms of L. If 'point' is an undefined term in L, this does not mean that it is an undefined term of the language in which the axioms of L are stated. If 'point' is a defined term in *L,* one must guard against the complaint that it inadequately represents the geometrician's term. This may be done by substituting some letter symbol that does not carry familiar associations. Much of Hochberg's paper is devoted to showing in great detail how certain lines of reasoning sometimes lead to fruitful, sometimes futile, results.

Additional cases of "follow through" in respect to logical or factual consequences are clearly evident in the contributions by Bierstedt and Timasheff. From Bierstedt's analysis, we find that there are different kinds of definitions, that different definitions perform different functions, and that as a consequence certain definitional terms can or cannot operate in specific ways. It follows from Bierstedt's interpretations that the theories containing these terms will have either utility or truth value. The larger part of Timasheff's paper revolves around a discussion of the meaning of the central terms of order, causality, and conjuncture. These terms are based on certain assumptions and conceptions that imply particular kinds of consequences and particular types of concrete application. Thus, causality is regarded as a particular aspect of order, and order is distinguished from conjuncture. Throughout, both authors implement their abstract distinctions by supplying illustrations from the sociological literature.

Though social science seeks to use language that is clear and correct, the current goal of analytic or procedural purity is questioned.

At the present stage of social science, the liberal recognition of and tolerance for alternative perspectives in the formulation of every kind of method is the only sensible approach. This would mean, for example, that objective observations, operational definitions, functional analyses, typological constructions, or logical axiomatizations, taken singly and separately, are not sufficient for a sprawling, ill-defined subject such as sociology. Any unilinear approach of this kind is premature in view of the many areas of fresh growth providing wide opportunities for discovery.

Rapoport is consistent with this viewpoint. He stresses the necessity of achieving understanding among physical and social scientists on the basis of mutual tolerance. For genuine co-operation, it is necessary that both groups learn a great deal of each other's languages, methods, and problems. As matters stand now, objective criteria for evaluating the pertinence of a sociomathematical theory are lacking because unambiguous criteria of predictive power are not entirely applicable. According to Rapoport, some mathematicians assume that their methods are directly translatable so as to apply to the content of social science. Others assume that the social scientist should have a ready-made list of definitions, relations, axioms and postulates, so that the mathematician can deduce theorems and conclusions. Both approaches have led to some gains, but they have definite and often unrecognized limitations. In respect to the first approach, it may be said that mathematicians have rarely succeeded in penetrating to the core of social problems, to the essential elements of the latter's field of inquiry. In regard to the second approach, it must be emphasized that the social scientist does not have any list of the kind referred to, though he does sometimes try to invent one. In doing so, he is confronted with the sizable problem of selecting the fundamental events of his field and clearly exhibiting the relationship of his terms to a system of referents. As a consequence, he becomes preoccupied with definitions and never gets to the stage of deriving theorems and applying these in the form of predictions. Rapoport discusses with wisdom and wide sympathy these and other forms of misunderstanding, many of which apply to social scientists.

From a different angle of vision, Edel challenges the notion that analytic categories need not exhibit empirical content or maintain a material status. He proposes that locus candidates be treated as empirical or material categories descriptive of level qualities, rather than as abstract categories structuring the inquiry prior to beginning it. To Edel, the emergence of a high-level concept or category is a real event in the natural world and requires not merely logical examination but also psychological, social, and historical description. A similar idea reappears in Gouldner's interpretation of Merton's middle-range theories. Gouldner sees in Merton's analysis the insistence that theoretical considerations alone cannot provide scientifically legitimate grounds for the admission of elements to a social system. From this vantage point, he criticizes Parsons' conception of the social system on the grounds that elements in the biological constitution and physiological functioning of man are excluded, as well as features of the physical and ecological environment.

By following Hochberg's comparisons between an ideal language and a language like English, we may conclude that each has its own merits and limitations. An ideal language is no substitute for ordinary language, since it cannot perform the functions of the latter. Elsewhere, we are told that what goes for logic does not necessarily go for social science. The formalization of certain statements in science is not tantamount to introducing quantification. Akin to the same general viewpoint is Martindale's thought that until quantification and allied methods are found in social science we should not scorn the significant function of classificatory and extreme types in promoting description and establishing the limits of relations that may later be quantified. Since the social sciences are in a less developed state than the physical sciences, a larger burden of their elementary work is carried on by types. This means that it will probably be a long time before sociology reaches the stage where one theory can be presented as a special case of a more comprehensive theory. At the present time, sociology can only institute methods compatible with the most possible precise comparisons. And this, says Martindale, is what ideal types were intended to do. The reader may wish to consider, in this connection, the appropriateness of Werkmeister's warning regarding the need to realize that "the complexities of human relations and the ever changing dynamics of cultural interactions may create problems for the social scientist that should caution us against a too hasty emulation of the natural sciences." Werkmeister states that the difficulties encountered in the social sciences arise not only because of the immense complexity of social phenomena but because human actions are conscious and deliberate and therefore subject to modification on the basis of insights and comprehension.

Further comments suggestive of the reasonableness of accepting compromises in regard to analytic or procedural purity can be found in the writings of Hart, Sjoberg, and Bierstedt. Hart contends that, "intermediate between causal, common-sense generalizations and rigorously verified conclusions from controlled experiments, it is useful and necessary to employ informal induction from instances. One of the weaknesses of books and articles about social research has been their failure to describe adequately this intermediate method." Although Sjoberg champions rigor, he believes that generality should not always be sacrificed for rigor's sake. "The fact is that when sociologists attempt to generalize, not only cross-culturally but also within their social system, they must rely upon the mental operational procedures which the physical operationalists view with disfavor." Complementing the views of the other contributors is Bierstedt's contention that substantive theory is vastly more significant for sociology even when its conclusions fall short of the confirmation that is ordinarily required by the canons of scientific inquiry.

That all of the principles stated in our introduction have been recognized in one sense or another by earlier theorists can be gleaned from a careful reading of this symposium. From Martindale's essay alone, we can construe Weber's view that types are not used to separate history from science but to mediate the use of historical materials for scientific purposes, as related to the issue of analytic purity in social science. Martindale's remarks on the conceptions of Comte and other early sociologists that society was an organism indicates some of the limitations to which analogies and metaphors are heir. His analysis of the consequences of their position in respect to the idea of progress, the search for social origins, and the use of historical data is further testimony to the relevance of our principle regarding the appraisal of scientific schemes. Again, Nagel's tests for estimating and weighing causal factors, as reviewed by Martindale, may be construed as criteria for separating central concepts from more peripheral ones. Even Parsons' critique of ideal types on the grounds that they concentrate on extreme or polar situations can be immediately recognized as pertinent to the principle loosely referred to in this volume as the linking of concepts through polarities. In such a manner, Martindale's essay, which is devoted largely to interpreting the writings of earlier theorists, reflects the nearly universal relevance of the general principles listed here.

For reasons previously mentioned, a well balanced account of the respects in which the contributors to this volume diverge in philosophic or social orientation is not possible. Such differences as exist among essayists are frequently a reflection of variations in choice of problems and vocabularies of analysis. Any essayist who attempts to reconstruct or reconceive familiar ideas by casting them in new contexts must take many words for granted. Thus, one author will take as his purpose the clarification of concepts A, B and C, but in doing this will usually find it necessary to use ancillary concepts X, Y and Z, with whatever ambiguity they commonly possess in the professional literature. Another author will choose to work in a different direction, perhaps to clarify concepts X, Y and Z, but in doing so will find it necessary to adapt concepts A, B and C, as they are presently understood. That each author should choose to set the stage for his writing by explicating certain terms at the expense of others is no more than can be expected in independent minds. We should also assume that each will differ in his prefaces, problems, and runs of attention.

Among the present group of authors, variations in terminological emphasis are more noticeable than fundamental disagreements in viewpoint. Brodbeck, for instance, has much to say about the terminological uses and misuses of "mathematical model," whereas some of the other contributors adopt these words because they have conventional facets of meaning that can be put to use in developing their special problems. To Brodbeck, the phrase "mathematical model" is ambiguous because it may be used to refer to a set of quantified empirical laws or a set of analytic (tautological) truths about numbers or a formalized set of indeterminate expressions. To escape this ambiguity, Brodbeck prefers the second usage just mentioned and labels it "arithmetic." Arithmetic representations of empirical theories are explained by illustrations from measurement, analytic geometry, probability theory, and the theory of games.

Brodbeck further suggests that the general term "model" has still greater ambiguity and vagueness than it has when qualified by the adjective "mathematical." Apart from the unambiguous usage of model as an isomorphism between theories, the word has been used to refer to quantified social theories, to any untested or untestable theory, to abstract theories in which certain variables are necessarily omitted, and to abstract theories that merely make use of perfect or ideal entities. Thus, by careful exposition and apt selection of illustrations, Brodbeck's paper lends precision to certain key terms in science.

Allowing for differences in conceptual emphasis, though not necessarily in basic conception, it can be said that Rapoport stresses the firm connection between mathematics and physics: "The deductive reasoning used in physical theory *is* the process of mathematical deduction." He finds, moreover, that physical events are described in mathematical language with very little methodological discussion or polemic. Viewing the unification of mathematics and physical science as an accomplished fact and recognizing the utility of mathematical models in providing a semblance of quantitative social science, we are not surprised that Rapoport fails to introduce some of the distinctions developed by Brodbeck. He has reasons for doubting that the term "mathematical model" can be given a strict interpretation in the social sciences. The parameters assumed in mathematical theories of mass behavior, for instance, are operationally definable only in principle. Hence, they cannot now be used with empirical exactness, but must serve as merely theoretical constructs or tools of mental experimentation.

Rapoport shows that in the behavior sciences the term "model" often refers to an analogical or metaphorical explanation. With such analogical constructs, mathematical models share the property of "as-if-ness": events act "as if" they were structured in certain ways. Beyond this, however, the similarity ends, since the mathematical model leads to specific relations among specific variables. From specific postulates, relations among quantitative variables can be deduced and in principle verified. This does not mean that the predictive power of the model is the sole test of its usefulness. Rapoport insists that mathematical models can have heuristic value. Most models are too simple to fit the involved interplay of variables associated with human behavior; opportunities for controlled experiment are extremely rare; parameters are difficult to estimate independently of each other. Nevertheless, crude models can be constructed that provide a means of unifying relevant observations and of creating an underlying framework, from which new observations in all their rich variety are consequences.

When we compare the essays of Brodbeck and Hochberg, differences in emphasis appear amidst basic similarities in point of view. Hochberg suggests that we establish a mathematical "identity" between two theories or interpretations of an axiomatic system when they can be shown to have equations of the same form, apart from whether or not their constants differ. This, he states, is one way of achieving a theoretical unification of different areas of science. Another way of achieving unification is to establish the correspondence of two theories, say 'M_1' and 'N_1' in accordance with certain specified criteria, called "co-ordination rules." When it can be shown by these criteria that 'M_1' predicts all that 'N_1' predicts, then 'N_1' is said to be reduced to 'M_1.' According to Hochberg, 'co-ordination' in terms of two interpreted theories can cover three somewhat different situations. In some instances, the co-ordination rules may be empirical laws, as when certain physiological states are asserted to correspond to certain behavioral states. Such laws are called "cross-sectional." In other instances, the co-ordinating rules may consist of a set of definitions of the terms of the reduced theory. In these instances, the laws of the reduced theory follow from those of the reducing theory and the analytically true definitions. Finally, co-ordination may consist of the partial interpretation of an abstract calculus and can be achieved by manipulating either the co-ordination or the calculus until successful two-way predictions are obtained.

So brief a résumé ignores many interesting details of Hochberg's paper but will be sufficient to contrast his interpretations with related themes in Brodbeck's paper. Brodbeck holds that it is all too easy to overestimate the significance of structural isomorphisms; the fact that laws of one area have the same form as those of another need not signify that they are connected in any way. She goes on to discuss three types of connections between theories by virtue of which one theory is sometimes mistakenly called a model for another. There is, first, that connection among two theories about apparently different phenomena which leads to the identification of one area with another. Such identification requires laws of the same form, constants of the same value in these laws, and interchangeability of the empirical concepts. When two theories are thus identified, they amount to two different ways of talking about the same thing. She concludes, therefore, that there is clearly no sense in which one is a model for the other.

A second type of connection between two areas is by means of empirical cross-connection laws. One illustration would be the joint occurrence of a psychological and physiological event when expressed by a psychophysiological law. By means of such laws, Brodbeck believes, psychology may, in principle, be "reduced" to physiology. But since this kind of reduction has nothing to do with similarity of structure, use of the term "model" in this context serves no good purpose.

A third type of connection between two areas involves the reduction of one area to another by means of definition. But definition alone is not sufficient for the reduction of sociology to psychology, for instance. "In addition there must be laws within psychological theory stating how the individuals *in* the group interact with each other to give the resultant behavior *of* the group. Such laws about the connections among the elements of a complex interaction are called composition laws. If these psychological composition laws exist, then the laws of group behavior are derivable from the definitions of the group concepts and the laws about the behavior of individuals in groups."

The reader will note that both Hochberg and Brodbeck discuss procedures for establishing the "identity" of two theories. However, while Hochberg views this identity as a basis for establishing a theoretical unification of science, Brodbeck sees it as a basis for rejecting the interpretation that one theory is a "model" for the other. Hochberg and Brodbeck seem to differ not only in the significance they attach to structural isomorphism but also in their view of the role of mathematical constants. Though directed toward different ends, their analyses of the bearing of definition and empirical laws on the reduction of one theory to another have many points in common. For instance, the role of "cross-sectional" laws in Hochberg's analysis appears to serve the same purpose as "cross-connection" laws in Brodbeck's formulation. To do full justice to these authors' essays, the reader should examine them in their entirety.

Returning to Hochberg's essay, it is interesting to note how his divergence from Greenberg's approach amounts to a kind of complementation of it. Hochberg points out that an axiomatic system is formalized when its descriptive signs are replaced by mere marks and that it is "completely" formalized when all terms, logical and descriptive, are replaced by such marks. The logician takes the latter step when he studies the nature of logical inference and logistic systems. It might be said that he attempts to construct an ideal language by using syntactical tools that will provide rigor and clarity. Such formalizations, Hochberg adds, do not amount to scientific discoveries. For this reason, he believes that any scientist "who calls for the complete formalization of scientific theories asks at best for a needless repetition of what the logician has already accomplished." Wiser, it would seem, for the empirical scientist to take such logical systems for granted and simply proceed to make deductions in conformity with them.

By characterizing the axiomatic method as "the most explicit possible application of a logico-mathematical model to a specific subject matter," Greenberg seems to differ from Hochberg in his use of the term "axiomatic." Nevertheless, Greenberg's views of the axiomatization process are in most respects closely similar to those advanced by Hochberg. In common with Hochberg and other logicians, he refers to two classes of terms, subject-matter interpretations (descriptive terms) and logico-mathematical interpretations (logical terms). And in agreement with Hochberg, he states that purely logico-mathematical theorems may be applied whenever required, without being proved in the system.

However, since Greenberg is more concerned with applications to a specific subject matter than he is with the problem of how a system should be ideally axiomatized, he takes a more liberalized view of the axiomatization process. Most everyone would agree with Greenberg that linguistics does not at present have a general theory, or a set of empirical generalizations of universal scope, on which to base lawful statements that are mutually connected in a single deductive structure. For this reason, Greenberg's efforts must of necessity be confined to the descriptive methodology of linguistics. In Greenberg's words, "Linguistics shares with other social-cultural sciences the peculiarity that its data are provided in terms of a universe of subsystems, individual languages, cultures, and societies, and its lowest-level generalizations are not of universal scope, but refer to the existence of certain phenomena within such particular subsystems."

As we have seen, both Brodbeck and Hochberg are concerned with the conditions under which one theory or area of phenomena can or cannot be reduced to another. Throughout their discussion, there is little reference to a closely related topic: the question which deals with the possible occurrence and function of both reductive and nonreductive levels. Whether this omission reflects a specialized goal or merely indicates certain preferences in language need not be settled here. The point is made only to indicate that the problem of reduction as presented by Edel and Werkmeister is not brought up for discussion. To Edel, this problem is primary. He suggests that some social phenomena may turn out to have considerable internal autonomy on their own level, while other phenomena may require constant explanation "from below." Again, the levels concept "insists on the search for continuity, for causal conditions under which novel phenomena come into existence. But whether such determination will come from a single preponderant source or a shifting source is not settled antecedently." Questions concerning stages of development and the major factors comprising them have to be taken as theses or hypotheses or investigatory principles in a *specific* levels theory in the social sciences. On a larger canvas, Edel considers level-producing processes in the perspective of evolution and the historical development of mankind. He suggests that clearer social description and sharper formulation of research problems may come about by placing the levels concept within a framework that is qualitative and emergent.

Pertinent to Edel's contribution are Werkmeister's views regarding the controversy between reductionism and nonreductionism in the social sciences. Werkmeister holds that the task of science does not imply the reduction of one level to another. The facts of higher levels cannot contradict the facts of lower levels, but must allow the latter to be preserved within the former as "limiting" cases. In this way, the uniqueness of the various levels of reality and the principle of the unity of science will both be maintained. In what is perhaps Werkmeister's strongest passage, he writes, "No explanation really explains if it is not adequate to the facts to be explained; and since man stands committed to values and consciously and deliberately pursues even ideational goals, a reductionism which neglects these aspects of human behavior in favor of a value-free and nonpurposive 'natural explanation' is in effect a falsification of the social events. Social events are *sui generis* and so are the laws governing them."

We will not attempt to set forth the many respects in which the essays by Gouldner and Hempel can be seen at certain points to reinforce, to supplement, or even to contradict one another. Taken together, the two essays give rise to numerous questions. For instance, what connections can be found between Hempel's delineation of the basic pattern of functional analyses and Gouldner's view of a social system, including as it does varying degrees of interdependence and equilibrium? In what respects, if any, can Gouldner's concept of functional reciprocity be taken as a sociological equivalent of universal law when this reciprocity is symmetrical? Is it possible to express Gouldner's idea of degrees of functional autonomy for system parts in the language of statistical laws, as Hempel describes them?

Both Hempel and Gouldner are in accord on the need to specify clearly the kind of system to which functional hypotheses refer. Hempel insists that the key concepts of functional analysis be explicitly construed as relative to some standard of survival or adjustment. He points out that this standard will vary from case to case and will be indicated by specifying a certain class or range of possible states of a system within which a given system remains or to which it returns. It would be fruitful to contrast this formulation of functionalism with Gouldner's theses concerning tension and conflict between a part and its system, between functional reciprocity and functional autonomy, between "cosmopolitans" and "locals," and between exogenous and endogenous factors. We might also compare Hempel's remarks on empirical hypotheses of self-regulation with Gouldner's several hypotheses of strategies for the maintenance of systems and for the functional autonomy of parts within them. Viewed in the large, both Hempel and Gouldner place differential emphasis on problems of explanation, teleology, system change, and stability. No doubt a careful study of both essays with an eye toward examining diverse conceptual usages will well repay the time and effort required. The same is probably true for many of the other essays. To mention a final example, the industrious reader would profit by defining in his own terms the numerous respects in which Hart, Mills, Timasheff, and Wolff differ from one another and the other contributors in conceptual orientation, vocabulary, and choice of problems.

So much for a brief statement on some few of the threads of convergence and divergence to be found in the essays of this volume. The reader who chooses to peruse each essay carefully will find other areas of both agreement and disagreement than those we have mentioned. For instance, we have not attempted to trace through the manner in which words such as "realism" and "nominalism," or "operational" and "empirical," are used in the contexts of each author's analysis. Moreover, we have not examined the equivalents of the phrase "levels of analyses" as they appear in the contributions of each author. By judicious selection of suitable portions of each essay, the ingenious reader could garner a host of useful insights on this subject. Again, one could, from these essays, put together an intelligent account of the main ingredients of a scientific theory, including suggestions and even rules on how to proceed in constructing such theories. Readers in search of specific avenues of exploration might concentrate on analysis of the more or less tangible assumptions made by each author in regard to the applicability of inductive processes and the extent to which generalizations drawn therefrom approximate universality. Finally, numerous minor differences in conceptual preferences will be apparent to those who read with an eye open to variations in discourse and the subtler nuances of meaning. These, too, should be noted for what they are worth in assessing the present state of sociological theory.

Outside critics of this volume, and we hope they are legion, may have an exciting time searching for unpalatable fruit within the leaves of its pages. They will tell us that a certain author erred in having said what he said or even in having implied something that indeed was not implied at all. Perhaps the author omitted something that should never have been omitted or accented certain ideas that need not be given serious attention. All this, most scholars would probably agree, is for the general welfare of science, as long as it leads to further developments of a "constructive nature." Even though the best ideas have a general quality of permanence, any idea is good enough if it can prove to be a necessary way station along some durable route to future knowledge. The stature of the present volume, then, can be gauged in full only through its role in advancing the sociology of tomorrow. If its major contributions are not neglected but rather outmoded for reasons that can be clearly determined, it will have achieved as much as any reasonable editor can expect.

I

ORIENTATION

1

On Intellectual Craftsmanship

C. WRIGHT MILLS

Columbia University

ONE

Useful discussions of method and of theory usually arise as marginal notes on work-in-progress or work about to get under way. "Method" has to do with how to ask and to answer questions with some assurance that the answers are more or less durable. "Theory" has to do with paying close attention to the words one is using, especially their degree of generality and their logical relations. What both method and theory amount to is clarity of conception and economy of procedure, and, most importantly just now, the release rather than the restriction of the sociological imagination.

To have mastered "theory" and "method" is to have become a self-conscious thinker, a man at work and aware of the assumptions and the implications of whatever he is about. To be mastered by "method" or "theory" is simply to be kept from working, from trying, that is, to find out about something that is going on in the world. Without insight into the way it is done, the results of study are infirm; without a determination that study shall come to significant results, all method is meaningless pretense.

For the working social scientist, neither method nor theory is an autonomous domain. Methods are methods for some range of problem; theories are theories of some range of phenomena. They are like the

25

language of the country you live in: having the ability to speak the language is nothing to brag about, but it is a disgrace, as well as an inconvenience, if you cannot speak it.

Method and theory must not only occur at the beginning of study, but also in the middle and at the end. They are built-in parts of the process of study itself. Of course, it is possible, and sometimes useful, to interrupt your work and to examine how several others have gone about theirs. As one begins his studies of some problem, he naturally turns first to studies that have already been done, and as he examines them, he certainly notices the methods their authors have used. He would be a fool if he did not do so. But once he goes beyond such an examination of the methods used in one area or another, and once he tries to transform methods into "methodology," he often becomes quite abstracted. He loses firm connection with the kinds of problems for which given methods have been devised, and, in the end, makes quite formal, and often even useless, his examination of methods. Although not necessarily the case, this is surely a very real danger.

In view of it, there are several cautions which might well be observed in any general attempts to "codify procedures." One must always keep uppermost a full sense of the problem at hand. This obviously means that one must be very well acquainted in a substantive way with the state of knowledge of the area with which the studies being examined are concerned. It also means, to an extent which I do not think can be made explicit, that such work is best done when the several studies examined are concerned with a similar area of study. Finally, such work is not best done as the sole speciality of any one person, much less of a young man who has in fact done little if any actual work, or who may have taken part only in studies done in one or another particular style.

When we pause in our studies to reflect on theory and method, the greatest yield is a restatement of our problems. Perhaps that is why, ultimately, in actual practice, every working social scientist must be his own methodologist and his own theorist, which means only that he must be an intellectual craftsman. Every craftsman can of course learn something from over-all attempts to codify methods, but it is often not much more than a general kind of awareness. That is why "crash programs" in methodology are not likely to help social science to develop. Really useful accounts of methods cannot evolve from a slapdash attack. If such accounts are not firmly anchored in the actual working of social study, the sense of a significant problem and the passion to solve it cannot be allowed full play in the mind of the working social scientist.

Advance in methods, then, is most likely to occur as modest generalizations out of actual work in progress. Accordingly, we should maintain in our individual practice, and in the organization of our discipline, a close state of interaction between method and work. Serious attention should be paid to general discussions of methodology only when they are in such reference to actual work. Such discussions of method do occur among social scientists; and I shall presently try to demonstrate one way in which they may be carried on, I hope, usefully.

If all students of man and society practiced this obvious and straightforward statement, how much further along the work of social science would be! At least all of us would then be at work on the problems of these disciplines. But everyone, alas, does not agree, not really. That other views of method and other views of theory are mistaken alleyways to curious destinations does not remove our need to examine them, because, for sundry reasons—mainly philosophical, academic, and temperamental—they are wordily proclaimed; often, I am afraid, they disturb people who are at work.

Statements of method and arguments about them—distinctions of concept and further distinctions—may all be very stimulating and even entertaining. But surely there will be no disagreement that by themselves they are merely promises. Statements of method promise to guide us to better ways of studying something, often in fact to studying almost anything. Elaborations of concepts, systematic and unsystematic, promise to alert us to distinctions in what we may see, or of what we may make of it, when we come to interpret it. Neither by itself can be taken as part of the actual work of the social studies.

In fact, both are often just the opposite: they are statesmanlike withdrawals from the problems of social science. Usually, they are based on some grand model of inquiry with which other people are beaten on the head. That this grand model is not capable of altogether full use is not, perhaps, too important, for it may still be used ritualistically. Usually, it is made up out of some philosophy of natural science, and quite usually, of all things, from a philosophical gloss on physics, perhaps always necessarily somewhat out of date. This little game, and others having similar rules, leads less to further work than to what may be called the methodological inhibition.

In a quite general way nowadays, such a philosophy serves to rationalize a kind of scientific know-nothingism, of which Max Horkheimer has written: "The constant warning against premature conclusions and foggy generalities implies, unless properly qualified, a possible taboo against all thinking. If every thought has to be held in abeyance until it has been completely corroborated, no basic approach seems possible and we would limit ourselves to the level of mere symptoms." [1] The young, it has frequently been noticed, are often corruptible, but in addition to them, it is curious to see older scholars of social science made

uneasy by the pretensions of certain methodologists among us. How
much more sensible and enlightening than the loud proclamations of
some American sociologists is the conversational statement of a Swiss
and an English economist: "Many authors instinctively set about tackling
these problems in the right way. But after studying the methodology
they become conscious of the numerous pitfalls and other dangers which
are waiting for them. The result is that they lost their former sure touch,
and are led astray or in unsuitable directions. Scholars of this type are
warned off methodology and advised especially not to read the following
treatise." [2]

Of method-and-theory-in-general, I do not here need to say any
more. Frankly, I am nowadays quickly made weary by it; so much discussion of it interrupts our proper studies. I feel the need to say that I
should much rather have one account by a working student of how he
is going about his work than a dozen "codifications of procedure" by
specialists who as often as not have never done much work of consequence. Better still: if sometimes in our professional forum we wish to
discuss method and theory rather than the substance of our studies, let
us ask each man whom we believe to be doing good or superior work
to give us a detailed account of his ways of work.

Only by conversations in which experienced thinkers exchange information about their actual ways of working can a useful sense of
method and theory be imparted to the beginning student. Since I do believe this, I want to continue practicing it. Accordingly, it is proper that
I try to contribute to the kind of conversation of which I have spoken.
That is why I am now going to report something of how I have gone
about my studies. I know that to do this is to run the risk of failing in
modesty and perhaps even to claim some peculiar virtue for my working
habits. But no matter. Any attentive reader of what I have written above
will surely know that I intend no such claims. It happens, at this writing,
that the studies I am going to discuss are completed, and the books I
have made out of them published, but I am going to write from notes
made during the course of this work, and as if I were still in the
middle of it.

Here, then, is a letter to a man just beginning independent work in
social science: [3]

TWO

You will know that this letter is neither a statement of formal
method nor an attempt to inspire. There are already too many formal

discourses on method, and certainly too many inspirational pieces on how to think. Neither would seem to be of much use to you. The first does not usually touch the realities of your most urgent problems; the second is usually vulgar and often nonsense.

It is best to begin, I think, by talking to you just a bit about how your choice of intellectual work is linked with the kind of life you are going to have. This is important because the intellectual and the human context of work in social science are inevitably of one piece of cloth. Moreover, presumption and verbiage are the two major vices of your chosen field, and no intellectual technique alone can cause you to avoid them completely, for they are human as well as intellectual qualities. To conceal that, out of politeness to my colleagues, would be of no service to you. Presumption and verbiage are indeed such powerful currents that they can only be overwhelmed by firm possession of one seminal quality: the passion for confronting problems of importance. And that too is a human as well as an intellectual quality.

You must have already discovered this, for in joining the scholarly community you must have realized that the most admirable thinkers within it do not split their work from their lives. They seem to take both too seriously to allow such dissociation, and they want to use each for the enrichment of the other. Of course, such a split is the prevailing convention among men in general, deriving, I suppose, from the hollowness of the work which men in general now do. But you will have recognized that as a scholar you have the exceptional opportunity of designing a way of living which will encourage the habits of good workmanship. Scholarship is a choice of how to live as well as a choice of career; whether he knows it or not, the intellectual workman forms his own self as he works toward the perfection of his craft; to realize his own potentialities and any opportunities that come his way, he constructs a character which has as its core the qualities of the good workman.

What this means is that you must learn to use your life experience in your intellectual work. In this sense, craftsmanship is the center of yourself, and you are personally involved in every intellectual product upon which you may work. To say that you can "have experience," means, for one thing, that the past plays into and affects the present, and that it limits the capacity for future experience. As a social scientist, you have to control this rather elaborate interplay, to capture experience and sort it out; only thus can you hope to use it to guide and test your reflection and in the process shape yourself as an intellectual craftsman. But how can you do this? One answer is: you must set up a file.

A personal file increases the continuity between life and work. It permits a continuity in the work itself, and in the planning of the work.

In such a file as I am going to describe, personal experience, professional activities, and actual work all come together. In this file, as an intellectual craftsman, you will try to get together what you are doing intellectually and what you are experiencing as a person. Here you will not be afraid to use your experience and directly to relate it to various projects which you have under way. In such a file, life and work become one.

By serving as a check on repetitious work, your file also enables you to conserve whatever energy you have. It also encourages you to capture "fringe-thoughts": various ideas occur, which may be by-products of everyday experience, snatches of conversation overheard on the street, or, for that matter, dreams. Once noted, these may lead to more systematic thinking, as well as lend intellectual relevance to more directed experience.

You will have often noticed how carefully accomplished thinkers treat their own minds, how closely they observe their development and organize their experience. They treasure their smallest experiences because, in the course of a lifetime, a modern man has so very little personal experience, and they recognize that experience is indispensable as a source of original intellectual work. To be able to trust your own experience even if it often turns out to be inadequate, I have come to believe, is one mark of the mature workman. Without such confidence, there can be little originality in an intellectual pursuit, and the file is one tool by which you can develop and justify this necessary assurance.

If the intellectual workman is a man who has become self-confidently aware of himself as a center of experience and reflection, the keeping of a file is one way of stabilizing, as it were, this confidence. By the keeping of an adequate file and through the self-reflective habits it fosters, you learn how to keep awake your inner world. Whenever you feel strongly about events or ideas, you must try not to let them pass from your mind. Instead, formulate them for your files. In so doing, draw out their implications, and show yourself either how foolish these feelings or ideas are, or how they might be articulated into productive shape. The file also maintains the habit of writing. You cannot "keep your hand in" if you do not write something at least every week. In the file, you can experiment as a writer and thus, as they say, develop your powers of expression.

Under various topics in your file there are ideas, personal notes, and excerpts from books; there are bibliographical items and outlines of projects. It is, I suppose, a matter of arbitrary habit, but I think you will find it best to sort all these items into a master file of "projects," with many subdivisions. The topics, of course, change. In fact, they sometimes change quite frequently. For instance, as a student working toward the preliminary examination while you are writing a thesis and, at the same time, doing term papers, your files will be arranged in these three areas of endeavor. But, after a year or so of graduate work, you will begin to reorganize the whole file in relation to the main project of your thesis. Then, as you pursue your work you will notice that no one project ever dominates it, or ever sets the master categories in which it is arranged. In fact, the use of this file encourages an expansion of the categories with which you are actively thinking. And the way in which these categories change—some being dropped out and others being added—is an index of your intellectual progress and breadth. Eventually, the file will come to be arranged according to several larger projects, having many subprojects, which change from year to year.

All this involves the taking of notes. You will have to acquire the habit of taking a very large volume of notes from any worth-while book which you read, although I have to say you often get better stuff out of yourself when you read really bad books. But enough of this. The first step in translating experience, either of other men's symbols, or of your own life, into the intellectual sphere, is to give it form. Merely to name an item of experience often invites you to explain it; the mere taking of a note from a book is often a prod to reflection. At the same time, of course, the taking of a note is a great aid in comprehending what you are reading.

Your notes may turn out, as mine do, to be of two sorts: in reading certain very important books you try to grasp the structure of the writer's argument, and take notes accordingly. But more frequently, and after a few years of independent work, rather than reading entire books, you will very often read parts of many books, from the point of view of some particular theme or topic in which you are interested, and concerning which you have plans in your file. Therefore, you will take notes which do not fairly represent the books you read. You are *using* this particular idea, this particular fact, for the realization of your own projects.

THREE

But how is this file, which so far must seem to you more like a curious sort of journal, used in intellectual production? The maintenance of such a file *is* intellectual production, one step removed from daily speculation, and one step removed from the library and "the field." It is a continually growing store of facts and ideas, from the most vague to the most finished.

For example, the first thing I did upon deciding on a study of the elite was to make a crude outline based on a listing of the types of people which I wished to understand.[4] The next step was to examine my entire file, not only those parts of it which obviously bore on the topic but also other portions which seemed to have no relevance whatsoever. Imagination and "the structuring of an idea" are often exercised by putting together hithertofore isolated items. This leads to the discovery of unsuspected connections. I made new units in the file for this particular range of problems, which, of course, led to a new arrangement of other parts of the file.

As you rearrange a filing system, you often find that you are, as it were, loosening your imagination. Apparently this occurs as a result of your attempt to combine various ideas and to correlate notes on different topics. It is a sort of logic of combination, and "chance" sometimes plays a curiously large part in it. In a relaxed way, you apply your intellectual resources, as exemplified in the file, to the new themes.

In the present case, I also began to use my observations and daily experiences. I thought first of experiences I had had which bore upon such problems, and then I went and talked with those who might have experienced or considered the issues. As a matter of fact, I began now to alter the character of my routine so as to include in it (1) people who *were* among those whom I wanted to study (for example, I accepted invitations to lecture to such groups as "The American Management Association" and "The Air War College"), (2) people in close contact with them (for example, servants) and (3) people interested in them (usually in some professional way; for example, lawyers). I do not know the full social conditions of the best intellectual workmanship, but certainly surrounding oneself by a circle of people who will listen and talk —and at times they have to be imaginary characters—is one of them. At any rate I try to surround myself with all the relevant environment which I think might lead me into thinking well along the lines of my work. That is one meaning of my remarks above about the fusion of personal and intellectual life.

Good work in social science today is not, and cannot usually be, made up of one clear-cut empirical "research." It is, rather, composed of a good many studies which at key points anchor general statements about the shape and the trend of the subject. So the decision—what are these anchor points?—cannot be made until existing materials are reworked and general hypothetical statements constructed.

Now, of "existing materials," I found in the files three relevant types: several theories having to do with the topic; materials already worked up by others as evidence for *those* theories; and materials already gathered and in various stages of accessible centralization, but not yet made theoretically relevant. Only after completing a first draft of a theory with the aid of such existing materials as these can I efficiently locate my own pivotal assertions and hunches and to design researches to test them—and maybe I will not have to, although of course I know I will later have to shuttle back and forth between existing materials and my own research.

I make it a rule—picked up, I suppose, from early philosophical reading which led me into the sociology of knowledge—that any final statement must not only "cover the data" so far as the data is available and known to me, but also in some way, positively or negatively, take into account the available theories. (This is of course one of the active meanings, if you'll forgive me please, of "the methodological consequences of the sociology of knowledge.") Sometimes this "taking into account" of an idea is easily done by a simple confrontation of the idea with overturning or supporting fact; sometimes a detailed analysis or qualification is needed. Sometimes I can arrange the available theories systematically as a range of alternatives, and so allow their range to organize the problem itself.[5] But sometimes I allow such theories to come up only in my own arrangement, and in various contexts. At any rate, in the book on the elite I will have to take into account the work of such men as Mosca, Schumpeter, Veblen, Marx, Lasswell, Michel, and Pareto. I am now at work on them.

In looking over some of the notes on these writers, I find that they fall into three general types of statement: (*a*) I learn directly, by restating systematically, what the man says on given points or as a whole. (*b*) I accept or refute these statements, giving reasons and arguments. (*c*) I also use the book as a source of suggestions for my own elaborations and projects. This involves grasping a point and then asking: How can I put this into testable shape and how can I test it? How can I use this as a center from which to elaborate, or use it as a perspective from which descriptive details will become relevant? It is in this handling of existing ideas, of course, that you feel yourself in continuity with previous work. Here are two excerpts from preliminary notes on Mosca, which may illustrate what I have been trying to describe:

In addition to these historical anecdotes, Mosca backs up his thesis with this assertion: It's the power of organization that enables the minority always to rule. There are organized minorities and they run things and men. There are unorganized majorities and they are run.[6] But: why not also consider the apparent opposite? In fact, why not the full scale of possibilities, as shown in the following chart?

	Elite (Minority)	Mass (Majority)	
Organized	1	2	1 the organized minority
			2 the organized majority
Unorganized	3	4	3 the unorganized minority
			4 the unorganized majority

This is worth full-scale exploration. The first thing has to be straightened out: just what is the meaning of "organized"? I think Mosca means: capable of more or less continuous and co-ordinated policies and actions. If so, his thesis is right by definition. He would also say, I believe, that an "organized majority" is impossible because all it would amount to is that new leaders, new elites, would be on top of these majority organizations, and he is quite ready to pick up these leaders in his "The Ruling Class." He calls them "directing minorities," all of which is pretty flimsy stuff alongside his big statement.

One thing that occurs to me is the use of the chart (I think it is the core of the problems of definition Mosca presents to us) as a model for trend analysis: Try this: from the nineteenth to the twentieth century, we have witnessed a shift from a society organized as 1 and 4 to a society established *more* in terms of 3 and 2. We have moved from an elite state to an organization state, in which the elite is no longer so organized or so unilaterally powerful, and the mass is more organized and more powerful. Some power has been made in the streets, and around it whole social structures and their "elites" have pivoted. And what selection of the ruling class is more organized than the farm bloc? That's not a rhetorical question: I can answer it either way at this time; it's a matter of degree; all I want now is to get it out in the open.

Mosca makes one point that seems to me excellent and worth elaborating further. There is often in "the ruling class," according to him, a top clique and there is this second and larger stratum, with which (*a*) the top is in continuous and immediate contact, and with which (*b*) it shares ideas and sentiments and hence, he believes, policies. (page 430) Check and see if anywhere else in the book he makes other points of connection. Is the clique recruited largely from the second level? Is the top, in some way, responsible for, or at least sensitive to, this second stratum?

Now forget Mosca: in another vocabulary, we have, (*a*) the elite, by which we here mean that top clique, (*b*) those who count, and (*c*) all the others. Membership in the second and third, in this scheme, is defined by the first, and the second may be quite varied in its size and composition and relations with the first and the third. (What, by the way, is the range of variations of the relations of *b* to *a* and to *c*? Examine Mosca for hints and further extend this by considering it systematically.)

This scheme may enable me more neatly to take into account the different elites, which are elites according to the several dimensions of stratification. Also, of course, to pick up in a neat and meaningful way the Paretian distinction of governing and nongoverning elites, in a way less formal than Pareto. Certainly many top status people would at least be in the second. So would the big rich. The Clique or The Elite would refer to power, or to authority, as the case may be. The elite in this vocabulary would always mean the power elite. The other top people would be the upper classes or the upper circles.

So in a way, maybe, we can use this in connection with two major problems: the structure of the elite; and the conceptual—later perhaps, the substantive—relations of stratification and elite theories. (Work this out.)

From the standpoint of power, it is easier to pick out those who count than those who rule. When we try to do the first we select the top levels as a sort of loose aggregate and we are guided by position. But when we attempt the second, we must indicate in clear detail how they wield power and just how they are related to the social instrumentalities through which power is exercised. Also we deal more with persons than positions, or we at least have to take persons into account.

Now power in the U. S. involves more than one elite. How can we judge the relative positions of these several elites? Depends upon the issue and decisions being made. One elite sees another as among those who count. There is this mutual recognition among the elite, that other elites count; in one way or another they are important people to one another. Project: select 3 or 4 key decisions of last decade—to drop the atom, to cut or raise steel production, the G. M. strike of '45—and trace in detail the personnel involved in each of them. Might use "decisions" and decision-making as interview pegs when you go out for intensives.

FOUR

There comes a time in the course of your work when you are through with other books. Whatever you want from them is down in your notes and abstracts. On the margin of these notes, as well as in a separate file, are still further ideas for empirical studies.

Now I do not like to do empirical work if I can possibly avoid it. It means a great deal of trouble if one has no staff, and, if one does employ a staff, then the staff is often more trouble than the work itself. Moreover, and quite properly, members of the staff often leave as soon as they have been trained and made useful. Besides, and more seriously, in the social sciences there is so much to do by way of initial "structuring" (let the word stand for the kind of work I am describing) that much "empirical research" is bound to be thin and uninteresting.

In our situation, empirical work as such is for beginning students and for those who aren't able to handle the complexities of big problems; it is also for highly formal men who do not care what they study so long as it appears to be orderly. All these types have a right to do as they please or as they must; they have no right to impose in the name of science such narrow limits on others. Anyway, you ought not to let them bother you.

Although you will never be able to get the money to finance all the empirical studies you design, it is necessary that you continue designing them. For once you lay out an empirical study, even if you do not follow it through, it leads you to a new search for data which often turns out to have unsuspected relevance to your problems. Just as it is foolish to design a field study if the answer can be got from a library, so it is foolish to think you have exhausted the books before you have translated them into appropriate empirical studies, which means merely into questions of what facts are needed.

Empirical projects necessary to my kind of work must promise: First, to have relevance for the first draft, of which I wrote above; they have to anchor it in its original form or they have to cause its modification, or to put it more pretentiously they must have implications for theoretical constructions. Second: the projects must be efficient and neat and, if possible, ingenious. By this, I mean that they must promise to yield a great deal of material in proportion to the time and effort they involve.

Now, I have not decided upon the studies necessary for the present job, but here is the beginning of a larger design within which various small-scale studies have begun to arise. Again I excerpt from the files:

I am not yet in a position to study the upper circles as a whole in a systematic and empirical way. So what I do is set forth some definitions and procedures that form a sort of ideal design for such a study. I can then attempt, *first,* to gather existing materials that approximate this design; *second,* to think of convenient ways of gathering materials, given the existing indices, that satisfy it as crucial points; and *third,* as I proceed, to make more specific the full-scale, empirical researches that would in the end be necessary.

(1) The upper circles must, of course, be defined systematically in terms of specific variables. Formally—and this is more or less Pareto's way—they are the people who "have" the most of whatever is available of any given value or set of values. So I have to make two decisions: What variables shall I take as the criteria, and what do I mean by "the most"? After I've decided on my variables, I must construct the best indices I can, if possible, quantifiable indices, in order to distribute the population in terms of them; only then can I begin to decide what I mean by "the most." For this should, in part, be left for determination by empirical inspection of the various distributions, and their overlaps.

My key variables should, at first, be general enough to give me some latitude in the choice of indices, yet specific enough to invite the search for empirical indices. As I go along, I'll have to shuttle between conceptions and indices, guided by the desire not to lose intended meanings and yet to be quite specific about them. Here are the four Weberian variables with which I will begin:

I. Class refers to sources and amounts of income. So I'll need property distributions and income distributions. The ideal material here (which is very scarce, and unfortunately dated) is a cross-tabulation of source and amount of annual income. Thus, we know that X per cent of the population received during 1936 Y millions or over, and that Z per cent of all this money was from property, W per cent from entrepreneurial withdrawal, Q per cent from wages and salaries. Along this class dimension, I can define the upper circles—those who have the most—either as those who receive given amounts of income during a given time—or, as those who make up the upper 2 per cent of the income pyramid. Look into treasury records and lists of big taxpayers. See if TNEC tables on source and amount of income can be brought up to date.

II. Status refers to the amounts of deference received. For this, there are no simple or quantifiable indices. Existing indices require personal interviews for their application, are limited so far to local community studies, and are mostly no good anyway. There is the further problem that, unlike class, status involves social relations: at least one to receive and one to bestow the deference.

It is easy to confuse publicity with deference—or rather, we do not yet know whether or not volume of publicity should be used as an index to status position, although it is the most easily available: (For example: On one of three successive days in mid-March 1952, the following categories of people were mentioned by name in the *New York Times*—or on selected pages—work this out).

III. Power refers to the realization of one's will even if others resist. Like status, this has not been well indexed. I don't think I can keep it a single dimension, but will have to talk (*a*) of formal authority—defined by rights and powers of positions in various institutions, especially military, political, and economic. And (*b*) power known informally to be exercised but not formally instituted—pressure group leaders, propagandists with extensive media at their disposal, and so on.

IV. Occupation refers to activities that are paid for. Here, again, I must choose just which feature of occupation I should seize upon. (*a*) If I use the average incomes of various occupations, to rank them, I am of course, using occupation as an index, and as a basis of, class. In like manner, (*b*) if I use the status or the power typically attached to different occupations, then I am using occupations as indices, and bases, of power and skill or talent. But this is by no means an easy way to classify people. Skill—no more than status—is not a homogeneous something of which there is more or less. Attempts to treat it as such have usually been put in terms of the length of time required to acquire various skills, and maybe that will have to do, although I hope I can think of something better.

Those are the types of problems I will have to solve in order to define analytically and empirically the upper circles, in terms of these four key variables. For purposes of design, assume I have solved them to my satisfaction, and that I have distributed the population in terms of each of them. I would then have four sets of people: those at the top in class, status, power, and skill. Suppose further, that I had singled out the top 2 per cent of each distribution, as an upper circle. I then confront this empirically answerable question: How much, if any, overlap is there among each of these four distributions? One range of possibilities can be located within this simple chart: (+ = top 2%; − = lower 98%):

			Class			
			+		−	
			Status		Status	
			+	−	+	−
+ Skill	+	1	2	3	4
Power		−	5	6	7	8
− Skill	+	9	10	11	12
		−	13	14	15	16

This diagram, if I had the materials to fill it, would contain major data and many important problems for a study of the upper circles. It would provide keys to many definitional and substantive questions.

I don't have the data, and I shan't be able to get it—which makes all the more important that I speculate about it, for in the course of such reflection, if it is guided by the desire to approximate the empirical requirements of an ideal design, I'll come upon important areas, on which I might be able to get materials that are relevant as anchor points and guides to further imaginative reflection.

There are two additional points which I must add to this general model in order to make it formally complete. Full conceptions of upper strata require attention to duration and mobility. The task here is to determine positions (1-16) between which there is typical movement of individuals and groups—within the present generation, and between the last two or three generations.

This introduces the temporal dimension of biography or career-lines, and of history into the scheme. These are not merely further empirical questions; they are also definitionally relevant. For (a) we want to leave open whether or not in classifying people in terms of any of our key variables, we should define our categories in terms of how long they, or their families, have occupied the position in question. For example, I might want to decide that the upper 2 per cent of status—or at least one important type of status rank—consists of those up there for at least two generations. Also (b), I want to leave open the question of whether or not I should construct "a stratum" not only in terms of an intersection of several variables, but also, in line with Weber's neglected definition of "social class," as composed of those positions between which there is "typical and easy mobility." Thus, the lower white-collar occupations and middle- and upper-wage worker jobs in certain industries seem to be forming, in this sense, a stratum.

In the course of the reading and analysis of others' theories, the design of ideal research, and the perusal of the files, you will begin to draw up a list of special studies. Some of them are too big to handle, and will in time be regretfully given up; some will end as materials for a paragraph, a section, a sentence, a chapter; some will become pervading themes to be woven into the entire book. Here again are initial notes for several such special projects:

(1) A time-budget analysis of a typical working day of ten top executives of large corporations, and the same for ten federal administrators. These observations will be combined with detailed "life history" interviews. The aim here is to describe the major routines and decisions, partly at least in terms of time devoted to them, and to gain an insight into the factors relevant to the decisions made. The procedure will naturally vary with the degree of co-operation secured, but ideally will involve first, an interview in which the life history and present situation of the man are made clear; second, observations of the day, actually sitting in a corner of the man's office, and following him around; third, a longish interview that evening or the next day in which we go over the whole day and probe the subjective processes involved in the external behavior we've observed.

(2) An analysis of upper-class weekends, in which the routines are closely observed and followed by probing interviews with the man and other members of the family on the Monday following.

For both these tasks I've fairly good contacts and of course good contacts, if handled properly, lead to better ones. (Added 1957: this turned out to be an illusion.)

(3) A study of the expense account and other privileges which, along with salaries and other incomes, form the standard and the style of living of the top levels. The idea here is to get something concrete on "the bureaucratization of consumption," the transfer of private expenses to business accounts.

(4) Bring up to date the type of information contained in such books as Lundberg's *America's Sixty Families,* which is dated as of the tax returns for 1923.

(5) Gather and systematize, from treasury records and other government sources, the distribution of various types of private property by amounts held.

(6) A career line study of the Presidents, all cabinet members, and all members of the Supreme Court. This I already have on IBM cards from the constitutional period through Truman's second term, but I want to expand the items used and analyze it afresh.

There are other—some 35 so far—"projects" of this sort (for example, comparison of the amounts of money spent in the presidential elections of 1896 and 1952, detailed comparison of Morgan of 1910 and Kaiser of 1950, and something concrete on the careers of "Admirals and Generals"). But, as I go along, I must of course adjust my aim to what is accessible. I hope that the above list will make clear the kind of thing I want to do.

My sense of form—unskilled though it is—begins to tempt me into concealment. I feel the tendency to leave my fragmentary notes and to round all this out, so as to make my ways of working seem more effective than they are. In short, I am tempted to draw your attention away from my limited discoveries and toward the ways in which I try to persuade. I want to guard against doing this. So I must tell you that during the last several months I have been doing a great deal of writing; to be sure it has been writing along the general lines of the big model and in terms of the theories examined, but still it has at times seemed entirely free of all that. I cannot say for sure whether my imagination has been prompted by having these larger designs before me, although I am aware that I can easily make it look that way. Maybe these designs are a sort of professional ritual I go through; maybe they are more than that, more than psychologically necessary. At any rate, some of this writing leads me to feel uneasy about the assumption that all the skills required to do social research and to put a book together are explicit and teachable, as are the deadbeat methods of much orthodox social science today.

Anyway, after these designs were written down, I began, with a clearer conscience, and I must say considerable zest, to read historical works on top groups, taking random (and unfiled) notes and interpreting the reading. You do not really have to *study* a topic you are working on; for, as I have said, once you are into it, it is everywhere. You are sensible to its themes; you see and hear them everywhere in your experience, especially, it always seems to me, in apparently unrelated areas. Even the mass media, especially bad movies and cheap novels and picture magazines and daytime radio, are disclosed in fresh importance to you.

From existing sources as well as those that you have fashioned, trying to remain open, as it were, on all sides, you slowly go forward, continually outlining and reoutlining the whole, specifying and elaborating and getting on with the anchor projects, refining and trying to index parts of the master design, writing this and editing that, bringing intellectual neatness for a day or a week or a month to this section or to that part.

FIVE

But, you may ask, how do ideas come? How is the imagination spurred to put all the images and facts together, to make images relevant and lend meaning to facts? I do not think I can really answer that; all I can do is talk about the general conditions and a few simple techniques which have seemed to increase my chances to come out with something.

When it is all read and some of it is being used, the social-science tradition of the last hundred years amounts to this: in the mind that has hold of it, in the mind that has been formed by it, there sometimes comes about a kind of sociological imagination. In brief, it is the capacity to shift from one perspective to another, and in the process to build up an adequate view of a total society and of its several components. I suppose it is this imagination that sets off the social scientist from the mere technician. I make no apologies for the "mere": adequate techniques can be trained in a few years. The sociological imagination can also be trained; certainly it seldom occurs without a great deal of work. Yet there is an unexpected quality about it, perhaps because its essence is the combination of ideas that no one expected were combinable. We might consider, for example, a mess of ideas from German philosophy and British economics. There is a playfulness of mind back of such combining, as well as a truly fierce drive to make a sense of the world, which the technician as such usually lacks. Perhaps he is too well trained, too precisely trained. Since one can be *trained* only in what is already known, training sometimes means that one is incapacitated by it from learning new ways. His training rebels against what is bound to be at first loose and even sloppy. I feel the need to say that I at least have rarely had an idea that later seemed to turn out rather well which was not in its beginning more than quite foggy and tenuous. Often ideas have at first seemed almost like nonsense, and fleeting nonsense at that; certainly they were often embarrassing to discuss with anyone who was not a proven colleague and friend. But you must cling to such vague images and notions, if they are yours, and you must work them out. For it is in such forms that original ideas almost always first appear.

I hope that you do not feel that what I have said means that the sociological imagination is something given to one as a gift of grace. I do not pretend to understand how it comes about as a capacity of an individual mind, but I do believe that you have got to work in order to call it forth. When you are really in the middle of some set of problems, you are working for it all the time, even when you do not realize it. You have to develop and nurse it, and you must live as well as work in such a way as to allow it to occur.

I believe that there are definite ways of stimulating it. Although I do not want to acquire or promulgate any technique of work that might limit the play of individual fancy, there are several ways I should like to tell you about that I have found useful to invite the sociological imagination:

I. Let me begin on the most concrete level. The rearranging of the file, as I have already said, is one way to invite imagination. You simply dump out heretofore disconnected folders, mixing up their contents, and then re-sort them. You try to do it in a more or less relaxed way, and I have always found a glass of Irish whiskey quite helpful. How often and how extensively you rearrange the files will of course vary with different problems and with how well they are developing. But the mechanics of it are as simple as that. Your own file is only a little one; the library is much larger. And part of the intellectual workman's way of life consists of a kind of relaxed browsing in libraries, letting his mind play over books and periodicals and encyclopedias. Of course, you will have in mind the several problems on which you are actively working, but you will also try to be passively receptive to unforeseen and unplanned linkages. A library, you know, is an enormously exciting place.

II. An attitude of playfulness toward the phrases and words with which various issues are defined often loosens the imagination. Look up synonyms for each of your key terms in dictionaries as well as in technical books, in order to know the full range of their connotations. This simple procedure will prod you to elaborate the terms of the problem and hence to define them less wordily and more precisely. For only if you know the several meanings which might be given to terms or phrases can you select the exact ones with which you want to work. But such an interest in words goes further than that.

In all work, but especially in examining more theoretical statements, you will try to keep close watch on the level of generality of every key term, and you will often find it useful to take a high-level statement and break it down to more concrete meanings. When that is done, the statement often falls into two or three components, each lying along different dimensions. You will also try to move up the level of generality; to remove the specific qualifiers and examine the re-formed statement or inference more abstractly, to see if you can stretch it or elaborate it. So from above and from below, you will try to probe, in search of clarified meaning, into every aspect and implication of the theory.

III. Many general ideas you come upon will, as you think about them, be cast into some sort of types. A new classification is the usual beginning of fruitful developments. The skill required to make up types and then to search for the conditions and consequences of each type will, in short, become an automatic procedure with you. Rather than rest content with existing classifications, you will search for their common denominators and for differentiating factors within and between them. For good types require that the criteria of classifications be explicit and systematic. To make them so you must develop the habit of cross-classification.

The technique of "cross-classifying" is of course not limited to quantitative materials; as a matter of fact, it is the best way to imagine and to get hold of *new* types as well as to criticize and clarify old ones. Charts, tables, and diagrams of a qualitative sort are not only ways to display work already done: they are very often genuine tools of production. They clarify the "dimensions" of the types which they also help you imagine and build. As a matter of fact, in the past fifteen years, I do not believe I have written more than a dozen pages first-draft without some little cross-classification, although, of course, I do not always or even usually display them. Most of them flop, in which case you have still learned something. When they work, they help you to think more clearly and to write more explicitly. They enable you to unfold the range and the full relationships of the very terms with which you are thinking and of the facts with which you are dealing.

For a working sociologist, cross-classification is what making the sign of the cross is for a good Catholic, or diagramming a sentence is for a diligent grammarian. In many ways, the cross-classification is the very grammar of the sociological imagination.

I want to give a silly little example, for in this way perhaps you will come to see how really deep-going this habit of mind can become. Yesterday afternoon I was very depressed. Someone had left a recent copy of a certain magazine in the house and I had thumbed it. As it always does, the thing disgusted me so that I came to the edge of melancholy. I took a little walk and overheard someone on a street corner say, "Well, things are not always as bad as they seem." Immediately I heard myself saying, "Yes, sometimes they are not so bad as they always seem." That's a confused piece of a cross-classification. I took out a notebook and played with the thing: "Always vs. sometimes vs. never," I wrote. "Is vs. seems," "bad vs. not bad." Those are the dimensions, which yield of course nine statements:

	Is 'bad'		
Seems 'bad':	*Always*	*Sometimes*	*Never*
Always	1	2	3
Sometimes	4	5	6
Never	7	8	9

Isn't that a fascinating little business? It is a way "to objectify" some moods. In playing with it, I got over the slump and began to write an essay on that magazine for the files. I called the piece "Seeing Is Not Believing." So now you understand that cross-classification, as a persistent habit of mind, is, among other things, a prime means of personal therapy.

IV. You will find that you often get the best insights by considering extreme types, or from thinking of the opposite of that with which you are directly concerned. If you think about despair, then also think about elation; if you study the miser, then also the spendthrift. That is also a general characteristic of anchor projects, which, if it is possible, ought to be designed in terms of "polar types." The hardest thing in the world is to study one object, but when you try to contrast objects, you get a sort of grip on the materials and you can then sort out the dimensions in terms of which the comparisons are made. You will find that the shuttling between attention to these dimensions and to the concrete types is very illuminating. This technique is also logically sound, for without a sample, you can only guess about statistical frequencies anyway: what you can do is to give the range and the major types of some phenomenon, and for that it is more economical to begin by constructing "polar types," opposites along various dimensions. This does not mean of course that you will not strive to gain and to maintain a sense of proportion, with the hope of obtaining some lead on the frequencies of given types. One continually tries, in fact, to combine this quest with the search for indices for which one might find or collect statistics.

The idea is to use a variety of perspectives: you will, for instance, ask yourself how would a political scientist whom you have recently read approach this, and how would that experimental psychologist or this historian? You try to think in terms of a variety of perspectives which, as an example, are represented here by different specialties. You will try in this way to let your mind become a moving prism catching light from as many angles as possible. In this connection, the writing of dialogues is often useful.

You will frequently find yourself opposing an idea or an opinion. In trying to understand a new intellectual field, you might first isolate the major arguments and examine them closely. One of the things meant by "being soaked in the literature" is being able to locate the opponents and the friends of every available viewpoint.[7]

V. The fact that in cross-classification you first work, for simplicity, in terms of yes-or-no encourages you to think of extreme opposites. And that is generally good, for qualitative analysis cannot of course provide you with frequencies or magnitudes. Its technique and its end is to give you the range of types. For many purposes, you need no more than that, although for some of course you do need to get a more precise idea of the proportions involved.

The release of imagination can sometimes be achieved by deliberately inverting your sense of proportion.[8] If something seems minute, imagine it to be enormous, then ask yourself: what difference might that make? And vice-versa, for gigantic phenomena. Nowadays, at least, I would never think of actually counting or measuring anything before I had played with each of its elements, conditions, and consequences in a make-believe world in which I control the scale of everything. This is one thing statisticians ought to mean, but never seem to mean, by that horrible little phrase about "knowing the universe before you sample it."

VI. On almost any problem with which you are concerned, you will try to get a *comparative* grip on the materials. The search for comparable cases either in one civilization or in several historical periods gives you leads. You would never think of describing an institution in twentieth-century America without trying to bear in mind similar institutions in other types of structure and epoch. And that is so even if you do not make explicit comparisons. In time, you will also come almost automatically to put historical depth into your reflection. One reason for doing so is that often what you are examining is limited in number, so to get a comparative grip on it, you have got to place it inside a frame with historical depth. To put it another way, the contrasting type approach often requires the examination of historical cases. This sometimes results in points useful for a trend analysis, or it leads to a typology of stages. You will use historical materials, then, because of the desire for a fuller range, or for a more convenient range of some phenomena, by which I mean one that includes the variations along some known set of dimensions. Some knowledge of world history is indispensable to the sociologist. Without such knowledge, no matter what else he knows, he is simply crippled.

VII. There is, finally, a point which has more to do with the craft of putting a book together than with the release of the imagination. Yet these two are often one: how you go about arrangements of materials for presentation always affects the content of your work. The idea I have in mind I learned from a great editor, Lambert Davis, who, I suppose, after seeing what I have done with it, would not want to acknowledge it as his child. It is the distinction of theme and topic.

A topic is of course a subject, like "the careers of corporation executives," or "the increased power of military officials," or "the decline of society matrons." Usually, most of what you have to say about a topic can readily be put into one chapter or into a section of a chapter. But the order in which all your topics are arranged often brings you into the realm of themes.

A theme is an idea, usually of some signal trend or of some master conception. In working out the construction of a book, you will know that you are on top of the job when you come to realize the two or three, or as the case may be, the six or seven, themes. You will recognize these themes because they insist upon being dragged into all sorts of topics. Perhaps you will feel they are mere repetitions, and sometimes that is all they are. They often show up in badly written sections of your manuscript, breaking your flow of words and detracting from the clarity of your prose.

What you must do is sort them out and state them in a general way as clearly and briefly as you can. Then, quite systematically you must cross-classify them with the full range of your topics. All this means that you will ask of each topic: just how is it affected by each of these themes? And again: just what, if any, is the meaning for each of these themes of each of the topics?

Sometimes a theme requires a chapter or a section for itself, perhaps when it is first introduced or perhaps in an accumulation towards the end. In general, most writers, as well as most systematic thinkers, would agree, I believe, that at some point all the themes ought to appear together, in relation to one another. Often, it is possible to do this at the beginning of a book. But it must usually be done near the end in any well-constructed book. And, of course, all the way through one should attempt to relate the themes to each topic. It is easier to write about this than to do it, for it is ordinarily not so mechanical a matter as it might appear. But sometimes it is, at least after the themes are properly sorted out and clarified. Of course, that is the rub. For what I have here called themes, in the context of literary craftsmanship, is referred to as ideas, in the context of intellectual work.

Sometimes, you may find that a book you are reading does not really have any themes. It is just a string of topics. Such a string of topics is indeed indispensable to the writing of books by men without ideas. So is lack of intelligibility.

SIX

I know you will agree that you should present your work in as clear and simple a language as your subject matter and your thought permit. But, as you may have noticed, a turgid and polysyllabic prose does seem curiously to prevail in the social sciences. It has in fact been said with authority that there is "a serious crisis in literacy"—a crisis in which social scientists are very much involved.[9] Is this peculiar language due to the fact that profound and subtle issues, concepts, and methods are being discussed? If not, then what are the reasons for what Mr. Malcolm Cowley aptly calls "socspeak"?[10] Is it really necessary to your proper work? If it is, there is nothing you can do about it; if it is not, then how can you avoid it?

Such lack of ready intelligibility, I believe, has little or nothing to do with the complexity of subject matter; certainly, nothing at all with profundity of thought. It has to do almost entirely with certain confusions of the academic writer about his own status.

In many academic circles today, anyone who tries to write in a widely intelligible way is liable to be condemned as a "mere literary man" or, worse still, a "mere journalist." Perhaps you have already learned that, as commonly used, these phrases mean: superficial because readable. The academic man in America is trying to carry on a serious intellectual life in a social context that often seems firmly set against it. His prestige must make up for many of the dominant values he has sacrificed by choosing an academic career. And his claims for prestige readily become tied to his self-image as a "Scientist." To be called a "mere journalist" makes him feel undignified and shallow. It is, I think, this situation that is often at the bottom of the elaborate vocabulary and the involved manner of speaking and writing. It is less difficult to learn this manner than to avoid learning it. For it has become a convention: those who do not use it are subject to moral disapproval. And to more than that. Since there is a premium upon its use, those who avoid it do so at their own risk. It may also be that it is the result of an academic closing of the ranks on the part of the mediocre, who understandably wish to exclude those who win the attention of academic men in other fields, as well as of intelligent people in general.[11]

To write is to raise a claim for the attention of readers. That is part of *any* style. To write is also to claim for oneself at least status enough to be read. The young academic man is very much involved in both claims, and because he feels his lack of public position, he often puts the claim *for* his own status before his claim for the attention of the reader *to* what he is saying. In fact, in America, even the most accomplished men of knowledge do not have much status among wide circles and publics. That is one reason why academic men slip so readily into unintelligibility. In turn, this very intelligibility is another explanation for why they lack the status they desire. This is truly a vicious circle, but one from which any individual scholar can attempt to escape. For here indeed: "style is the man."

To overcome the academic *prose,* if you will forgive me, you have first to overcome the academic *pose.* And to do so, it is much less important to study grammar and Anglo-Saxon roots than to get clear your own answers to these three questions: (1) How difficult and complex after all is my subject? (2) When I write, what status am I claiming for myself? (3) For whom am I trying to write?

The usual answer to the first question is: not so difficult and complex as the way in which you are writing about it. Proof of that is everywhere available, and is revealed by the ease with which ninety-five per cent of the books of social science can be translated into English. Sometimes it takes more space to say it plainly: usually it takes much less.[12]

But, you may ask, do we not sometimes need technical terms? [13] Of course we do, but "technical" does not necessarily mean "difficult." If such terms are really necessary and also clear and precise, which is what "technical" means, it is not difficult to slip them into a context of plain English and thus introduce them to the reader.

Perhaps you may object that the ordinary words of common use are often loaded with feelings and values and that accordingly it might be well to avoid them in favor of newly made-up words or technical terms. Here is my answer: it is true that ordinary words are often so loaded. To write clearly is to control these loads, to say exactly what you mean in such a way that this meaning and only this meaning will be understood by others. Assume that your intended meaning is circumscribed by a six-foot circle in which you are standing; assume that the meaning understood by your reader is another such circle, in which he is standing. The circles, let us hope, do overlap. The extent of that overlap is the extent of your communication. The part of the reader's circle that does not overlap is an area of uncontrolled meaning. In your circle, the part that does not overlap is a token of your failure. You fail to put the meaning across. The skill of writing is to get the reader's circle of meaning to coincide exactly with yours. You should write in such a way that both you and the reader stand in the same circle of controlled meaning.

Remember these horrible circles the next time you are writing. Remember too: the reader is free to run away. All this is why writing and talking are such unnatural things for a man to do. Better that he should go into a cave and remain silent. But do not technical words give us a better chance to make the circles coincide, at least among the scientific fraternity? The answer, I think, must be a flat no. Most of the technical terms in common use in social science are as value loaded, if not more so, as the words in good English usage. Apart from mathematical symbols, of which I am ignorant, any words (technical or not) used in attempted communication set up those two circles, and those two circles very seldom if ever perfectly coincide. That, I suppose, is what puts the tension in writing.

My first point, then, is that by far the most of "socspeak" is in no way due to any complexity of subject matter or of thought. It certainly cannot reasonably be due to any attempt to secure attention to what is being said. It is due, almost entirely, I believe, to claims for one's academic self. To write in this way is to say to the reader, often perhaps without knowing it: "I know something that is so difficult you can understand it only if you first learn my difficult language. In the meantime, you are merely a journalist, a layman, or some other sort of underdeveloped type, and so to hell with you." The first sentence is usually rubbish; the second always a silly impertinence. But "socspeak" rests, in the first place, upon just such claims. It rests, in the second place, upon confusions about: who one really might be.

Let us now consider the second question—the question of status.

Two ways of presenting the work of social science may be distinguished according to the idea the writer has of himself: (1) One is the idea that he is a man, who may shout, whisper, or chuckle, but who is always there. It is also clear what sort of a man he is: he is a confident center of experience and reasoning; he has found out something, and now he is telling us about it and how he has found it out. This is the voice behind the best expositions available in the English language.

(2) The other idea is not that of any voice of any man. In fact it is not a "voice" at all. It is an autonomous sound. It is a prose manufactured by a machine turned god. That it is full of jargon is not as important a feature of it as that it is very strongly mannered: it is not only impersonal; it is pretentiously impersonal. Government bulletins are sometimes written in this way. So are business letters, and a great deal

of social science. Any writing (I do not see how it can be denied) not imaginable as human speech is bad writing.

But, thirdly, there is not only the voice or its absence; there are also those who are to hear it. That, too, leads to characteristics of style. It is very important for any writer to have in mind just what kinds of people he is trying to speak to—and also what he really thinks of them. To try to write well, it now seems to me, I must know who I am and to whom I am speaking. I feel the need to confess that for a long time—far too long after I had begun to publish—I did not know the answer to either question; in fact I did not really know of either question. Nowadays, I am usually aware of the questions and of their importance, but often I do not know their proper answers, or I forget them. They are not easy questions: to answer them well requires decisions about oneself, as well as knowledge of reading publics. To write is to raise a claim to be read, but by whom?

One answer has been given by my colleague, Mr. Lionel Trilling, who has given me permission to pass it on. You are to assume that you have been asked to give a lecture on some subject you know well before an audience of students, university faculty members, and interested people from a nearby city. It is as simple as this: assume that such an audience is before you and that they have a right to know; assume that you want to let them know. Now write.

Such a choice of public by a social scientist assumes that anything he is doing and anything he finds out by doing it can be presented in an intelligible English, with no loss of meaning. The ease of translation makes this assumption, nine times out of ten, the only reasonable one. To write plainly may of course require more space, although I do not think that is usually so, and I am certain that it requires less space than the standard sociological prose.

Are there not some four broad possibilities available to the social scientist as a writer? (1) If he recognizes himself as a voice and assumes that he is speaking to some such public, as I have indicated, he will try to produce a readable prose. (2) If he assumes he is a voice but is not altogether aware of any public, he may easily fall into unintelligible ravings. Such a man had better be careful. (3) If he considers himself less a voice than an agent of some impersonal sound, then his public, should he find one, will most likely be a cultlike grouping of people who are hardly specialists of anything beyond this language, for to maintain it is surely a full-time job. (4) If without knowing his own voice, he should not find any public, but speaks solely for some record kept by no one, then I suppose we have to admit that he is a true manufacturer of the standardized prose: an autonomous sound in a great empty hall. It is all rather frightening, as in a Kafka novel, and it ought to be: we have been talking about the edge of reason.

The line between profundity and verbiage is often delicate, even perilous. No one should deny the curious charm of those who, like Whitman, beginning their studies, are so pleased and awed by the first step that they hardly wish to go further. Of itself, language does form a wonderful world, but, entangled in that world, we must not mistake the confusion of beginnings with the profundity of finished results. As a member of the academic community, you should think of yourself as a representative of a truly great language, and you should expect and demand of yourself the ability to carry on the discourse of civilized men when you speak and when you write.

There is one last point, which has to do with the interplay of writing and thinking. If you write solely with reference to the context of discovery, you will be understood by very few people; moreover, you will tend to be quite subjective in statement. To make more objective whatever you think, you must work in the context of presentation. At first, you "present" your argument or dissertation to yourself, which is often called "thinking clearly." Then when you think you have got it straight, you present it to others, and often discover that you have not been as logical and as articulate as you had assumed. Now you are in the context of presentation. Sometimes you will notice that as you try to present your subject, you will modify it, not only in form of statement but often in its content as well. You will get new ideas as you work in the context of presentation. In short, it will become a new context of discovery, different from the original one, and on a higher level, I think, because it will become more socially presentable and more objective. Here again: you cannot divorce how you think from how you write. You have to move back and forth between these two contexts, and whenever you move, it is well to know where you might be going. You need a signpost. Perhaps this will do:

In the end try to make your context of presentation reveal your context of discovery. Do not believe that you can ever do this fully and yet be understood. It is as much a mannerism, an art, a style, as is the most complete hiding of the context of discovery. But the ideal of presentation for expository writing is the clear revelation of what you have found out in terms of how you have found it out, and hence why you think it is so.

I wish I had known of this ideal ten years ago and had been practicing it. I have only got hold of it firmly this year (1956–57), and I have not worked with it long enough to know what kinds of exceptions, if any, must be made.

SEVEN

From what I have said, you will understand that in a way you never "start working on a project"; you are already "working," either in a more personal vein, in the files, in taking notes after browsing, or in more guided endeavors. Following this way of living and working, you will always have many topics which you want to work out further. After you decide on some "release," you will try to use your entire file, your browsing in libraries, your conversation, your selections of people—all for this topic. You are trying, you see, to build a little world containing all the key elements which enter into the work at hand, to put each in its place in a systematic way, to readjust continually this framework around developments in each part of it. Merely to live in such a little world is to know what is needed: ideas, facts, ideas, figures, ideas.

So you will discover and describe, setting up types for the ordering of what you have found out, focusing and organizing experience by distinguishing items by name. This search for order will cause you to seek patterns and trends, to find relations that may be typical and causal. You will search, in short, for the meanings of what you come upon, for what may be interpreted as visible tokens of something else that is not visible. You will make an inventory of everything that seems involved in whatever you are trying to understand; you will pare it down to essentials; then carefully and systematically you will relate these items to one another in order to form a sort of working model. And then, you will relate this model to whatever it is you are trying to explain. Sometimes it is that easy; often it just will not come.

But always, among all the details, you will be searching for indicators that might point to the main drift, to the underlying forms and tendencies of the range of society in the middle of the Twentieth Century. For, in the end, that is what you are always writing about.

Thinking is of course a struggle for order and at the same time for comprehensiveness. You must not close it up too soon, or you will fail to see all that you should; you cannot leave it open forever, or you yourself will burst. Perhaps it is this dilemma that makes reflection, on those rare occasions when it is more or less successful, the most passionate endeavor of which the human being is capable.

NOTES

1. Hadley Cantril, ed., *Tensions That Cause Wars* (Urbana: University of Illinois Press, 1950), p. 297.

2. W. A. Johr and H. W. Singer, *The Role of the Economist as Official Adviser* (London: George Allen & Unwin, 1955), pp. 3-4. This book, by the way, is a model of the proper way of going about discussions of method in social science. Significantly, it was written out of a kind of conversation between two experienced craftsmen.

3. First drafted spring 1952; rewritten spring 1956.

4. Just how and why I decided to do such a study does not seem altogether relevant here, but for what it may be worth: I forget how I became technically concerned with "stratification," but I think it must have been by reading Veblen. He had always seemed to me very loose, even vague about his "business" and "industrial" employments, which are a kind of translation of Marx for the academic American public. Marx himself, I think you must agree, is quite unfinished and much too simple about classes; he did not write a theory of classes, although Max Weber finished one version which I believe Marx would have liked. Anyway, I wrote a book on labor organizations and labor leaders, a politically motivated task; then a book on the middle classes, a task primarily motivated by the desire to articulate my own experience in New York City since 1945. It was thereupon suggested by friends that I ought to round out a trilogy by writing a book on the upper classes. I think the possibility had been in my mind; my plans have always run far ahead of my energies; I had read Balzac off and on, especially during the 'forties, and had been much taken with his self-appointed task of "covering" all the major classes and types in the society of the era he wished to make his own. I had also written a paper on "The Business Elite," and had collected and arranged statistics about the careers of the topmost men in American politics since the Constitution. These two tasks were primarily inspired by seminar work in American history.

In doing these several articles and books and in preparing courses in stratification, I uncovered, of course, a residue of ideas and facts about the upper classes. Especially in the study of social stratification is it difficult to avoid going beyond one's immediate subject, because "the reality" of any one stratum is in large part its relations to the rest. Accordingly, I began to think of a book on the elite.

And yet that is not "really" how "the project" arose; what really happened is (1) that the idea and the plan came out of my files, for all projects with me begin and end with them, and books are simply organized releases from the continuous work that goes into them; (2) that after a little while, the whole set of problems involved came to dominate me. When you keep waking up in the middle of the night to scribble a note, always about one topic, you may as well realize it: you are writing a book.

5. See, for example, *White collar,* ch. 13. I am now trying to do this with Lederer and Gasset vs. "elite theorists" as two reactions to 18th and 19th century democratic doctrine.

6. There are also statements in Mosca about psychological laws supposed to support his view. Watch his use of the word "natural." But this isn't central, and, in addition, it's not worth considering.

7. On this point, see, for instance, the book on John Dewey's technique of thought by Bogoslovsky: *The Logic of Controversy* (New York: Harcourt Brace & Co., 1928).

8. By the way, some of this is what Kenneth Burke, in discussing Nietzsche, has called "perspective by incongruity." See, by all means, Burke: *Permanence and Change* (New York: New Republic Book, 1936).

9. By Edmund Wilson, widely regarded as the best critic in the English-speaking world, who writes: "As for my experience with articles by experts in anthropology and sociology, it has led me to conclude that the requirement, in my ideal university, of having the papers in every department passed by a professor of English might result in revolutionizing these subjects—if indeed the second of them survived at all." *A Piece of My Mind* (New York: Farrar, Straus and Cudahy, 1956), p. 164.

10. Malcolm Cowley, "Sociological Habit Patterns in Linguistic Transmogrification," *The Reporter* (September 20, 1956), pp. 41 ff.

11. Cf. Robert Lekachman, "Economics for Everybody?" *Commentary* (January 1956) pp. 76 ff., who I think confuses the clarity of John Galbraith's prose with such inadequacies as may mark his analysis.

12. By the way, on various techniques of writing, the best book of which I know is: Robert Graves and Alan Hodge, *The Reader Over Your Shoulder* (New York: The Macmillan Company, 1944). See also G. E. Montague, *A Writer's Notes on His Trade* (London: Pelican Books, 1930–1949) and Bonamy Dobree, *Modern Prose Style* (Oxford, England: The Clarendon Press, 1934–1950).

13. Mathematical language, by the way, is of course not "socspeak": on the contrary, those who understand it tell me that it is precise, economical, clear. That is why I am so suspicious of many social scientists who claim a central place for mathematics among the methods of social study but who write prose imprecisely, uneconomically, and unclearly. They should take a lesson from Professor Paul Lazarsfeld, who believes in mathematics, very much indeed, *and* whose prose, while not at all "literary," always reveals, even in first draft, the mathematical qualities indicated. When I cannot understand his mathematics, I know that it is because I am too ignorant; when I disagree with what he writes in nonmathematical language, I know it is because he is mistaken, for one always knows just what he is saying and hence just where he has gone wrong.

II

SOCIAL TYPES

2

Sociological Theory and the Ideal Type

DON MARTINDALE

University of Minnesota

The degree of ambiguity surrounding the concept of "ideal types" in sociology may be seen by the fact that while some students have found them to be rather inadequate theories others have found them to be inadequate models of a mathematical type. Disregarding the common estimate of inadequacy, there is no consensus between these two positions as to whether ideal types are theories or methodological devices, for very different criteria are relevant to each case. Understandably, in interest of clarity, some students have been inclined to reject ideal types altogether, for even the most zealous exponent of their use seems to find it necessary to apologize for them. On the other hand, the most ardent critics of ideal types usually feel forced to admit, lamely, that they do have a place after all. Taken together all the diverse characterizations lend the problem of the ideal type in sociology the properties of a major mystery story. In reconstructing the scene of the crime, it is useful to go back to the state of sociology at the time the conscious formulation of ideal type occurred. We thus can attempt to uncover the motives and conditions that called it forth.

The present discussion will trace in rough outline the career of the ideal type in sociology, in order to clarify some of the problems posed by it and to locate some of the interpretations given to the ideal type. Particular attention will be devoted to Max Weber's concept of the ideal type, since the great bulk of modern discussion stems from it. Some of the contemporary revisions of Weber's type concepts and various substitutes and alternatives for the ideal types will be briefly sketched. Finally, a few of the more important criticisms of the ideal type will be examined.

In what follows I assume that a scientific theory is a logically interrelated body of empirical laws. Is the ideal type a theory? In the most recently published statement on the ideal type that I have been able to find (June, 1957), this is maintained. It is said that the ideal type "has the character of a *theoretical model*. As such, the type functions as an *explanatory schema* and as an implicit theory. The drawing out of this theory results in the explicit statement of hypotheses about the type." [1]

I assume that if anything has the character of a theory, if it functions as a theory functions, if it can be drawn out as a theory can be drawn out to produce hypotheses, then it is a theory. I do not, however, believe that ideal types are theories, for they are not logically interrelated bodies of empirical laws. McKinney is not alone in conceiving ideal types as theories; Watkins, Talcott Parsons, and others also have done so. Hempel accepted their conclusions but decided that as theories ideal types are scientifically unacceptable. On the other hand, in not treating ideal types as theories, I find myself in agreement with Max Weber, Robert MacIver, Robert Merton, and many others. All this is treated later.

Scientific method consists in the systematic procedures that institute an empirical proof. A hypothesis deduced from one's theory is tested and either confirmed, disconfirmed, or left in doubt. There are three general kinds of such systematic procedure for instituting a proof: experimental method, statistical method, and comparative method. The "logic of method" is the same in all cases. These subdistinctions arise in terms of the degree of precision of the theory and the amount and kind of control possible over the data to which a theory is addressed. In experimental method, procedure consists in instituting a controlled situation, the conduct of observation under controlled conditions, and the confirmation or disconfirmation of hypotheses in terms of the occurrence or nonoccurrence of predicted results. Statistical method deals with data arising from a repetitive operation (as, for example, from experiments, assembly lines, or recurrent natural facts such as births and deaths). Hypotheses are instituted with regard to quantitative data on the basis of mathematical models. The application of relevant statistical tests serves to confirm or disconfirm hypotheses. The oldest procedure of science is comparison. Comparison is an act intended to establish an item of empirical knowledge about which one is uncertain. Some idea guides the comparisons, and there is some theory, however crude, in the background.

The fundamental position taken in the present essay is that ideal types are neither experiments, mathematical models, nor theories but *devices intended to institute comparisons as precise as the stage of one's theory and the precision of his instruments will allow.* Just as one's theory determines the kind of situations set up in experimental procedure, or the kind of mathematical models selected in statistical procedure, so it determines the kind of ideal types developed in comparative procedure. Comparative procedure occurs most frequently in new sciences and on the frontiers of old sciences. Very often the success of comparative procedure leads to an increased precision of theory and method, gradually providing the basis for statistical and experimental procedures. If ideal types often give the impression of being provisional and jerry-built, it must be remembered that without the pioneers, civilization would not come to the wilderness. The evolution of the ideal type in sociology was determined by the attempts to transform comparative method into a more precise procedure. The place occupied by ideal types (and various alternatives for them) in current sociology is a testimony to the amount of sociological method still remaining on a comparative level.

TYPE CONSTRUCTION OF EARLY SOCIOLOGISTS

Sociology arose in the nineteenth century with the attempt to combine an organismic concept of society with a positivism of procedure. Its basic theory was evolutionary; its materials were historical; its method was comparative.

Sociology was invented by thinkers with very special inclinations and talents: men with imagination, varied interests, wide information, and conservative temperaments. Comte, for example, was haunted all his life by the terror of disorder. He dreamed of a castelike society that would bring conflict to an end, and he even proposed a special technique of "mental hygiene" to secure individual peace of mind. Herbert Spencer was proud of the England of his day and suspicious of all elements in his society that tended to bring about change. As for Comte and Spencer, the source of social disorder was differently conceived, but the conservative temperament of each was all too clear. Each in his way carved out spheres from the old intellectual disciplines which they appropriated for sociology—a defensive image, in each case, against the forces of disorder.

Under the circumstances in which the nineteenth century sociological synthesis occurred, it is not difficult to see why the new field depended on a comparative method. The idea that society was an organism discouraged the use of experimental methods by the new science. Society was conceived as a vague superbiological organism often (as with Comte) thought to be coextensive with humanity itself. Comte largely rejected the notion of sociological experiments. Consistently with his theory. he argued that to change anything meant to change everything in the societal organism. But it is impossible to observe everything. Thus, sociological experiments are almost out of the question. Spencer, who conceived all artificial interference with society as a change for the worse, was even opposed to sociological experiments on ethical grounds. The theories of the early sociologists, thus, ruled out experiment as an important sociological method. They could hardly turn to statistical method since it had not been devised.

Their theories and their reliance on historical materials reduced method to a comparison of cases. Society was conceived as an organism that had evolved, developed, or progressed. The task of the new science was to trace this evolution, development, or progress. The facts that one studied were initially and primarily historical.

But if the first source materials studied by sociology were historical, new materials were soon added by ethnographic reports on non-Western peoples. The early reports were quite unscientific. However, they aroused immediate and great curiosity because of contrasts they presented to social phenomena familiar to the European. As early as Comte, the possibility was seen of systematically utilizing such data for sociological purposes. However, Comte steadfastly maintained that the materials for sociology were primarily historical. "To indicate the order of importance of the forms of society which are to be studied by the Comparative Method, I begin with the chief method, which consists in a comparison of the different coexisting states of human society on the various parts of the earth's surface. . . . By this method, the different states of evolution may be observed at once. . . . But we must beware of the scientific dangers of ending the process of comparison by this method. . . . It can give us no idea of the order of succession. . . . The historical comparison of the consecutive states of humanity is not only the chief scientific device of the new political philosophy. Its rational development constitutes the substratum of the science, in whatever is essential to it." [2]

If the method of the new science was comparative, the fundamental methodological questions that would sooner or later have to be faced had to do with the employment of this method in a manner which would give standard, verifiable results. What was the unit of comparison? How was it to be set up? How could one be sure that different thinkers were comparing the same things? What are the criteria of a scientifically adequate comparison?

Early sociologists and ethnographers proceeded in blithe disregard of most of these questions. With rather smug ethnocentrism, the unilinear evolutionists assumed that their own societies and social circles (Victorian England, the Society of the Eastern Seaboard of the United States, The Society of Paris) [3] represented the pinnacle toward which world evolution was progressing. The latest ethnographic reports usually supplied the notion of what society had been in ancient times (the society of the Australian Bushman was a favorite). One then arbitrarily assumed that society had moved through successive stages from primitive beginnings to a high state of civilization occupied by the student. Such stages were often arrived at arbitrarily on the basis of quite extraneous considerations. Ethnographic and historical evidence was strung together like beads on a tenuous string of theory. When the thin thread of theory snapped, there was hardly anything to hold the miscellaneous "facts" together.

The collapse of the early theoretical formulations of positivistic organicism had a number of major and minor consequences familiar to all students of recent social thought: 1. The concept of "progress" and most forms of the concept of "social evolution" were abandoned by most social theorists. 2. Sociology broke most of its ties with anthropology. To many thinkers, the association seemed meaningless with the abandonment of the search for social origins and stages of precivilizational social change. 3. Sociology became apologetic of its dependence on history, showing increasing embarrassment in the use of historical data. 4. The comparative method was brought under critical review, and substitutes for it were sought. 5. Sociologists became increasingly sensitive about using large-scale concepts such as "culture," "civilization," and "society." The idea that these were superorganisms was dropped by almost everybody. The idea that "society" is the basic unit of sociological analysis was generally abandoned.

The naive and heedless enthusiasm of the early social scientists in constructing their pictures of social origins and development and the shocking way in which their creations were tumbled into ruins can easily obscure the nature of their conceptual activity. However, their problem, their data, and their method inevitably launched them upon programs of conscious and unconscious type construction. They assumed that mankind had undergone a regular and ordered development. Their problem was to discover what this was and what sequence of changes characterized it. Their data was ethnographic and historical; their method was "comparative." Specifically, they sought to establish the existence of certain types of society, types of social structure (particularly institutions) of smaller scope than society, and types of development or change. The names of many of the early social scientists are closely associated with the types they invented or used: Comte visualized society as developing through three basic types, Theological, Metaphysical, and Positivistic, which followed each other in sequence; Henry Sumner Maine traced social development from a patriarchal type of ancient society resting on social relations of status to modern types of political society resting on a contractual relation of the individual to the social whole; J. M. Bachofen thought one could discover an early universal prehistorical type of matriarchal family and society precedent to modern stages and types; Herbert Spencer thought that one could trace social development from an ancient militaristic-theological type of society to modern peaceable and industrial types; Tönnies traced the general development of civilization from *Gemeinschaft* (societies resting on psychological relations determined by friendship, kinship, and neighborliness) to *Gesellschaft* (societies resting on psychological relations determined by political administration and the trading of the market place); Durkheim traced social change from a type of society resting on mechanical solidarity to a type of society resting on organic solidarity (ties of interdependence due to social division of labor rather than similarity due to friendship, neighborliness, or what not).

It is evident, thus, that a large part of the intellectual effort of early social scientists went into the setting up of types of society, institution, and civilization sequence. Although much of this type construction was methodologically unconscious (that is, not an aspect of deliberate procedure), it was not completely random and accidental. Comte thought his broad types of humanity were composed of more specific subtypes. Maine was of the opinion that although Ancient society resting on Status was a widely distributed social type found from India to Ancient Rome its details varied from place to place. Maine and Bachofen both utilized legal materials in the conduct of their analyses and employed the principle of survivals to explain otherwise anomalous legal residues. Both Spencer and Durkheim were of the opinion that, in fact, societies existed in many forms more complex than their respective theological-militaristic, industrial peaceable, and mechanical and organic types. This automatically turned their types into generalized descriptions. Durkheim explicitly argued that comparison of societies only made sense when societies of the same type or at the same stage of development were compared. He had also advanced the idea that the type of legal relation found in a given society could be utilized as an index of its solidarity, distinguishing the problem of indices from causes. Tönnies recognized his societal types to be conceptual abstractions and simplifications. In all such respects, the type construction of the early sociologists was more intellectually responsible than may appear on the surface. Their ideal types were recognized to be conceptualizations rather than realities. Some of the problems of concepts formation were seen.

TYPE CONSTRUCTION UNDER THE INFLUENCE OF THE NEO-KANTIAN AND NEO-HEGELIAN MOVEMENTS IN MODERN SOCIAL SCIENCE

The theoretical crisis in which early sociology found itself with the collapse of organismic positivism precipitated a heightened interest in the problems of methodology and theory construction. A not illogical form of the reaction to the crisis of the social sciences was the rejection of the positivism of early sociology. The "reasonableness" of this reaction was evident in the attempt by its agents to clarify the "organismic" elements of early sociology in terms of idealistic philosophy and the retention, in fact the strengthening, of the ties between sociology and history which had supplied the new field with its data. The rejection of positivism called into question the relation between the natural and social sciences. The neo-Hegelian movement, however, instead of trying to re-unite the natural and social sciences sought to sharpen the differences between them. This in turn led to the question of the capacity of the social sciences to establish general knowledge. Hence, there evolved the sequence of discussions between the neo-Hegelians and neo-Kantians.

This is not the place to review all the details of the transition from positivistic organism to neo-Hegelianism and from there to neo-Kantianism. Some aspects of the thought of Dilthey and Rickert may serve to illustrate the manner in which the concept of "ideal types" was pressed into the service of the new points of view and given special interpretations.

A. Wilhelm Dilthey [4]

To Dilthey (1833–1911) the mind is teleological, pursuing its purposes and realizing its ends by the manipulation of the objects of the world. Man is the ultimate unit of social life and the social sciences which study man have quite a different relation to this unit than the natural sciences to their final units. In contrast to natural science, which arrives at its ultimate units by a process of analytical abstraction, Dilthey believed that the mind of man is given as an immediate reality. The conditions and states of society are understood directly from the inside.

The lines between social and natural science were sharply drawn. Natural-science knowledge is external and analytical; social-sciences knowledge is internal and synthetic. The basis for understanding the social world is found only in one's own experience. Only through "reliving" the experiences of the persons about us can we understand them. The devices and products of understanding fall into a number of groups:

(1) Concepts and judgments, for example, have properties independent of the context in which they occur. Distinguishable from these are (2) behaviors flowing from and revealing the purposes that activate them. Finally, (3) there are expressions, written expressions, for example, or creative works which reveal to the understanding the totality of life. We know the physical world; we understand the social world.

Understanding consists in the selection of the significant. Meaningful types are the basic instruments of understanding. They may be types of society, social structure, institution or of some subinstitutional element such as law or art, even types of personality. Meaningfulness or significance depends on the relation of the individual to the milieu in which everything is in living relationship to the ego. An occurrence is significant to the extent to which it reveals the nature of life. Significance is immanent in life—it is a category of life—it is an ultimate fact beyond which reason cannot extend. The type is the significantly representative form relating the greatest number of possible facts to the whole.

So far as the social scientist or cultural historian is concerned with the establishment of actual facts, his procedure corresponds to that of the natural scientist. This, however, for Dilthey, is only the beginning of his true task of establishing the conditions and circumstances for understanding. The social scientist's task is accomplished only when he "relives" the experience of which the "facts" were conditions and external content, penetrating thereby its significance.

At this point, one touches the fundamental idealism of Dilthey's argument. One understands anything including the past only by penetrating its inner relation to the "I" of the present. Difference may be perceived only in terms of and against a background of similarity. The substratum of understanding in the social sciences is provided by the unity of human nature beyond time and place. The final court of appeal in determining human meaning is the ideal human type. Understanding of society and history is an endless process leading to ever new discoveries of the variety of the human spirit on ever higher levels of experience: in every person, every community, every system of culture, in the spiritual whole of history.

Dilthey's solution of the problems of social science took the form of an identification of the social sciences and history. The social sciences and history together were placed in contrast to the physical sciences; each had a peculiar object of investigation, the psychical and physical respectively. The method of the two types of disciplines was also different, for the social sciences and history were thought to have immediate and direct contact with their objects while the objects of natural science could only be arrived at by external analysis. The break with positivism is evident. Natural science is a science of externals. Dilthey has nothing but pity for the social scientist who would imitate it.

Dilthey's solution to the problem of the social sciences was in one respect empirically motivated. The early materials for social science had, to considerable degree, been supplied by historical research. In identifying the social sciences and history, Dilthey was preserving at the time the sources of social-science data. However, with its implied devaluation of natural scientific knowledge and its separation of the various forms of knowledge into distinct kinds (rather than treating items of empirical knowledge as different only in degree) Dilthey could be expected to encounter opposition.

B. Heinrich Rickert [5]

The rationalistic tradition in Western thought takes the empirical world to be a unit, and scientific knowledge to be empirical conceptualization at its best. The neo-Kantianism of Rickert (1863–1936) illustrates both the opposition to Dilthey and the attempt to find an alternative solution to the problems of the social sciences.

As a Kantian, Rickert held that all empirical-scientific knowledge is based on experience. It is incorrect to set up a distinction in kind between knowledge of the psychical and knowledge of the physical, the one known directly, the other indirectly. Empirical knowledge regardless of its contents is knowledge of what is given in experience [6] whether of physical events or mental events. One may know one's own self empirically only in so far as it is given in one's experience. Psychology is a natural science and psychological events are explained in terms of general laws of psychological phenomena established by the same manner as physical events—the same kind of methods as natural science.[7] The difference between psychology and the natural sciences is only a matter of the degree of exactness and precision of its concepts.

Dilthey combined history and social science. He sharpened the distinction between natural and social science, and rested the distinction ultimately on a difference in knowledge, direct and external. Empirical knowledge for Rickert was all of a piece; items of it differ only in degree. Although the natural and social sciences were in Rickert's perspective combined as a single kind of enterprise, both were sharpened in their distinctness from history.

For Rickert, both science and history are empirical disciplines. However, science is treated as one kind of explanation of experience; history as quite another. Science works with abstract concepts and attempts to explain the general or recurrent; history operates with individual concepts and attempts to explain the unique. The ultimate generalizing concepts of science represent objects in simplest form possible; the individualizing concepts of history represent a potentially heterogeneous array of significant elements.[8] History and nature represent two kinds of interest in empirical reality, two kinds of abstraction from it. As intellectual disciplines, both history and science utilize general concepts, but they are concepts of a different kind.

History and science, thus, represent two contrasting analyses of nature. The most general concepts of natural science, for Rickert, concern objects in the simplest possible form, while the most general concepts of history represent nature in complex integrated structure. Hence in the materials of history the concepts of science have passed beyond their utility. The problem remains to determine the nature of historical individuality. Though the causal laws of natural science do not apply to historical individuals, this is not because they are uncaused. The peculiarity of historical materials lies in the individual uniqueness of the historical complex. Historical individuals receive this irreplaceable uniqueness from their relation to some value. The change or destruction of the value destroys the historical individual itself. The task of the historian consists in determining the value which constitutes the historical individual. This is not the same as evaluating historical individuals—passing moral censure or distributing praise and blame. Rather, the historian's purpose is to locate the historical individual in a more comprehensive whole.[9] In determining historical change, for example, the task of the historian lies precisely in isolating the significantly new, the teleological element which informs the totality of the development. Rickert rejected the concept of evolution, so central to the crisis of the social sciences, precisely because he felt that it tended to eclipse all historial stages but the last, shifting attention away from the estimate of each element or stage of historical development by referring it to a general value.

It may be seen that those aspects of social science activity accounted for by Dilthey as determinations of typicality and "meaningfulness" were accounted for by Rickert as characterizations of individual uniqueness in respect to a general value. Dilthey tends to assimilate social science and history to each other, separating them from natural science. Rickert fused the sciences into a single conceptual unit and excluded history from the circle.

In the course of the discussions of Dilthey and Rickert and their colleagues, the concept of "ideal types" tended to acquire connotations which in some quarters are still retained: devices for determining individual historical significance or "meaningfulness" as a part of a procedure of reliving, introspection, or *verstehen*.

CONTEMPORARY FORMULATIONS OF THE IDEAL TYPE DERIVING FROM MAX WEBER

Among contemporary sociological theorists there is by no means equal receptivity to the use of ideal types. However, the thinkers who have made basic use of the concept of "social action" for the analysis of social life have been not only most sympathetic to the use of ideal types but have consciously attempted to improve them. Social action, of course, is only one concept of contemporary sociology. The study of social action is concerned with but one area of sociology. Neither the concept nor the area is the exclusive property of any single sociologist or group of sociologists. Some of the sociologists utilizing the concept of social action as a basic one have been described by Sorokin as forming a school of sociology he calls "sociologistic"; some others using the concept have recently designated themselves as "functionalists." Ideal types are not the exclusive property of any single school of sociological theory. It was more the properties of the area covered by social action than a special theory that led to use of ideal types in connection therewith. These contemporary formulations go back primarily to Max Weber, who more than any other sociologist approached sociology by way of the concept of "social action."

Weber's discussion was cast in terms of the formulations by Dilthey as well as those of members of the neo-Kantian Marburg philosophers such as Windelband and historians such as Eduard Meyer. Weber not only attempted to avoid the semimystical conception of types as natural forms but reduced some of the presumed abstract theories of his day to mere ideal types. In Weber's opinion, for example, classical economic theory actually provided an illustration of the kind of "synthetic constructs" that have been conceived as "ideas of historical phenomena." [10] Classical economic theory presented not an abstract theory but an idealized picture of events in the commodity market under conditions of exchange operating in terms of free competition and rigorously rational conduct. Relations and events of historical life were selected and formed into an internally consistent system. Classical economics presented an idealization of certain elements of historical reality. Its "theory" was actually a utopia-like construct.

Weber went to some lengths to distinguish the ideal type in his sense from other notions with which it could presumably be confused. He urged that it was not an hypothesis, though it could be useful in formulating hypotheses. It is not a description of reality, though it aims, in part, at permitting unambiguous descriptions. The ideal type is not to be confused with ethical imperatives. "The idea of an ethical imperative,

of a 'model' of what 'ought' to exist is to be carefully distinguished from
the analytical construct, which is 'ideal' in the strictly logical sense of the
term." [11] Ideal types are not stereotypes, averages, or abstract concepts.
"An ideal type is formed by the one-sided *accentuation* of one or more
points of view and by the synthesis of a great many diffuse, discrete,
more or less present and occasionally absent concrete individual phenomena, which are arranged according to those one-sidedly emphasized
viewpoints into a unified *analytical* construct. In its conceptual purity,
this mental construct cannot be found anywhere in reality." [12]

In the contexts in which Max Weber's fullest formal discussions of
the ideal type are found, the problems of the neo-Kantians seem to have
been uppermost in his mind. He urged that the basic purpose of the
type is "to analyze historically unique configurations or their individual
components in terms of genetic concepts." [13] Weber illustrates this with
the concepts of the "church" and "sect." If we are interested in some
historical phenomena such as Christianity in the Middle Ages, Weber
urges, we must be prepared to admit that there exists in fact an infinitely
varied mass of details with most varied forms and nuances of clarity and
meaning. Study proceeds, Weber maintains, by asking what are the
"Christian" elements of the Middle Ages. A combination of articles of
faith, norms, church law, custom, maxims of conduct are fused into an
'idea.' The ideal types of the *sect* and *church* represent two idealized
types of arrangement of the critical elements of religious institutions which
may assist the student in the analysis of Christianity in the Middle Ages.
Weber insists all expositions of the "essence of Christianity" are ideal
types of only relative and problematic validity. Such presentations, however, are of basic value for research and systematic exposition. "They
are used as conceptual instruments for *comparison* with and the *measurement* of reality. They are indispensable for this purpose." [14]

The argument is interesting for its similarities and contrasts to the
conceptualizations of Rickert. The type is offered as a device for the
study of nature as history; it is, in this respect, like Rickert's historical
individual. However, it is not conceived as resting on a general value
on the basis of which all subelements derive "significance." A further
illustration from Weber's argument brings the contrast even more clearly
into focus. The ideal type, Weber says, is composed of both generic and
ideal typically constructed elements.[15] The concept of "exchange," for
instance, is a simple class concept. However, when this concept is related
to that of "marginal utility" and the idea of "economic exchange" is
offered one has left the field of pure class concepts for the type in which
typical conditions of exchange are assumed. Generic concepts merely
summarize common features of empirical phenomena, but the ideal type

is designed to aid the analysis of actual situations.[16] The critical element of the type is not—as for Rickert—a general value.

When Weber saw the main function of the ideal type in the analysis of historical materials and circumstances, he again was apparently following the neo-Kantians. However, there is no evidence that he accepted the dichotomization of history and science which would transform these two disciplines into opposites, each finding its boundaries in the other. Rather, with the neo-Hegelians, Weber seems to have felt that ideal type constructions represented the procedure by which historical materials were utilized by the social sciences. At the same time, in contrast to neo-Hegelians like Dilthey, Weber does not seem to have been willing to distinguish *in kind* between the knowledge of the social sciences and that of the natural sciences. In this last respect, Weber represents the partial return to the positivistic tradition of the founders of sociology. In sum: for Weber, ideal types were procedures by which historical materials were made useful for the general purposes of science. As applied to historical materials, he characterized ideal types as devices for description, as implements for comparison and measurement, and, under special circumstances, as procedures for instituting and testing hypotheses. The component elements of the type and the criteria for constructing them are particularly important. For Weber has also argued that the ideal type is not a description, not a general concept, not a law, not a moral or ethical judgment.

As noted, for Weber the ideal type contains both conceptual and observational materials, both being required for the type. Such conceptual and observational materials are not put together arbitrarily. The relationships expressed in a type are such as "our imagination accepts as plausibly motivated and hence as 'objectively possible' and which appear as *adequate* from the nomological standpoint." [17] Objective possibility and adequate causation are the criteria for forming conceptual and observational materials into a type.

The ideal type is a conceptual tool. Items and relations actually found in historical and social life supply the materials. These are selected, fused, simplified into the ideal type on the basis of some idea of the student as to the nature of social reality. Weber's discussion of the criteria for this selection and formation of elements into the type is not as unambiguously clear as it might be. It is unfortunate that the fullest statement of it occurs in the course of his critique of Eduard Meyer's historical methodology rather than in connection with his positive statements about ideal types. However, *objective possibility* seems to refer to the logical status of the items organized by the type.

In forming an ideal type, the student has in some sense extended his conceptions beyond the social reality presented to him. He has abstracted, sharpened, and extended relations actually perceived. Objective possibility as a guiding criterion of such conceptualization requires that the conceptual form so produced represent an empirically possible state of affairs. The ideal type is an imagined world. The criterion of objective possibility applied to this imagined world requires that it be an empirically possible world in the sense that it should not contradict any of the known laws of nature. An empirically possible world is *ipso facto* a logically possible world (the converse is not true). The terminology may be strange but the same could be said of every hypothesis of science. If it were not possible to test materially false hypotheses, science could not exist. The hypothesis is a conceptual formulation that guides investigation. No one knows for sure whether it is "true" until it has been tested. If one did, it would not be necessary to test it. However, to be capable of test at all it must express a material possibility. Similarly, the application of the criterion of objective possibility to ideal-type construction attempts to draw the line between science and metaphysics.

The second criterion for the selection of elements for the ideal type is that they be such as "appear adequate from the nomological standpoint." That is, the items should be "adequate" in terms of the causal laws of science. The special problems faced by the historian in making his estimates of events to include in his narrative is involved in this second criterion of the ideal type and its components. The historian often deals with complex situations resulting from the conjoint operation of a number of factors. The question is quite legitimate as to the extent to which some total given effect rests upon any one. "What is meant, . . . if correctly formulated logically, is simply that we can observe causal 'factors' and can conceptually isolate them, and that expected rules must be *thought* of as standing in a relation of *adequacy* to those facts, while relatively few combinations are *conceivable* of those conceptually isolated 'factors' with other causal 'factors' from which another result could be 'expected' in accordance with *general empirical rules.*" [18] Despite ambiguities, this seems to mean the historian, for his purposes, makes estimates of the combined factors that contribute to major events of interest. The laws of the science as established at the moment are the basis for his assignment of significance to some factors rather than others. If, on the other hand, historical materials are to be utilized for the purposes of science, the problem becomes a bit more complex. The causal laws of the science are employed to establish the significance of special items. Once established, these in turn may eventually help to reconstruct the laws of science.

The problems formulated by Weber in the concept of "adequate causation" have been taken up by Ernest Nagel. Ideally, Nagel maintains, explanation in history and science ascertain the necessary and sufficient conditions for the occurrence of a phenomenon. In fact, historical and scientific practice rarely achieves the ideal with any fullness. Historians particularly are often so removed from the full circumstances of an event that they can cite only the main, principal, or primary causal factors. Nagel rejects the notion that the "weighing" of causal factors in terms of their degree of importance is arbitrary and meaningless. He isolates a series of cases where such estimates are valuable: [19] (1) Two factors may be necessary for the occurrence of a third but not equally so; (2) Two factors may be necessary for a third, but a change in magnitude of one may have very different results from changes in the magnitude of another. (For example, industrial production may vary both with the supply of coal and the labor force but a given percentage change in the labor force may be far more significant.) (3) A variety of factors may be causally significant to event, but some may act as catalysts on others; (4) The frequency of total events may vary with items that do not exclusively determine them. In a whole series of such ways, it is Nagel's opinion, estimates of causal adequacy form a legitimate aspect of scientific and historical explanation.

In outlining the primary interpretation of the ideal type by Max Weber, a whole series of suggestions and interpretations distributed throughout his work must be ignored, however regretfully. The contexts containing Weber's fullest discussions were dominated by the neo-Kantian distinction between science and history. Some elements of the Kantian dichotomization seem to have brushed off onto Weber. The various passages in which such implications appear, as well as others which apparently suggest that the ideal type has relevance only for historical purposes, must for want of space, be by-passed here. Such passages can be matched by others on the other side. At times, when social science interests were uppermost, Weber speaks of the appearance of types in almost pure form. For example, in his *Religionsoziologie* (Vol. 1, pp. 436 ff., published in the *Archiv* 1915) in his discussion of various motives for religious rejection of the world, a series of types was outlined. Of them, Weber states, "The theoretically constructed types of conflicting 'life orders' are . . . intended to show that at certain points such and such internal conflicts are possible and 'adequate' . . . They can appear . . . in reality and in historically important ways, and they have. Such constructs make it possible to determine the typological loss of a historical phenomena." Here the context suggests that types are used not for historical ends but that historical materials are to be used for scientific purposes.

There are other problems in Weber's account touching the problem of "adequacy." If one central and unambiguous meaning of adequacy is causal adequacy—that is in accord with causal laws—there are other discussions of "adequate at the level of meaning." This, at times, in some passages, seems to refer to adequacy of an explanation in terms of ordinary common sense notions which may or may not be adequate in terms of the requirements of science. At times, however, a meaningfully adequate explanation is contrasted to a causally adequate one, in a way suggesting Dilthey's distinction.

However, the investigation of these and certain other passages to discern whether they are true or only apparent contradictions is of only incidental interest. More important is the status of the type in its most sound interpretation.

CURRENT USES OF THE IDEAL TYPE AND PARALLEL CONCEPTUAL FORMATIONS

Despite the many possible ambiguities of Weber's account, the sober and intellectually responsible character of his formulation of the ideal type is evident. He pointed out the fact that one did not eliminate ideal types from science by ignoring them—one merely withheld them from critical analysis. His own treatment was marked by the attempt to extract what he felt were the sound points from early positivism, neo-Hegelianism and neo-Kantianism. Types were used not to separate history from science but to mediate the use of historical materials for scientific purposes. Moreover, over-ambitious theoretical pretensions in social science and premature claims at having achieved abstract scientific formulations were denied, and their formidable structures revealed to be ideal types. Whatever the limitations, this bears the clear marks of intellectual honesty, and it is not surprising that many current sociologists whose point of approach to their problems is somewhat similar to Weber's have been inclined to employ their revised versions of the ideal type or obvious conceptual substitutes for it. A brief review of a few of these revisions of and substitutes for ideal types may illustrate the current state of thinking.

A. R. M. MacIver's Imaginative Reconstruction

The basic task of sociology, like all science, MacIver maintains, is to establish the existence of causal relations. These are to be established within the limits and on a "causal level" peculiar to the particular science. The basic procedure is to identify a situation in which the phenomenon occurs as against a comparable one where it does not, then to analyze out the cause. This is not always easy and may proceed by way of successive investigations with an ever more refined isolation of causes. A science performs its task most effectively where experimental control of the relevant situations is possible. In social science, where it is not, we often have to rest content with unrefined estimates of causes. Special interest attaches to procedure in social science precisely because we are so often unable to experiment.

The social scientist tries to follow a procedure very similar to the experiment setting up situations C and C_1, in one of which the particular cause (x) is present, in the other not. In the case of the social sciences, one of our situations C_1 is an *imaginative reconstruction*.

The very samples used by MacIver were drawn from those employed by Max Weber, Eduard Meyer, and others of the time when the problems of the ideal type were first discussed. "Where we cannot experiment we still follow the same process of analysis, but now one of our situations, C and C_1, usually remains hypothetical, a mental construct. We ask: what *would* have happened if the Persians had won the battle of Marathon? The alternative situation is not presented, cannot be reproduced in the world of reality. In the great majority of investigations into social causation, we must use what evidence we can muster, with whatever skill or comprehension we possess, to construct imaginatively an alternative situation that is never objectively given." [20]

Without the slightest ambiguity, MacIver's *imaginative reconstruction* may be treated as identical with the process of setting up ideal types.

B. Talcott Parsons' Use of Pattern Variables and the Production of Imaginary Societies

Parsons is certainly one of the most careful students of Max Weber among American sociologists. Parsons has been quite critical of Weber's use of the ideal type. As he saw it, for Weber, "The ideal type . . . is not merely an abstraction, but a peculiar kind of abstraction. It states the case where a normative or ideal . . . is perfectly complied with." [21] Moreover, Parsons maintains "ideal types call attention to extreme or polar" situations. The only system in which they fit is a limiting type of a kind "least likely to be found in reality even in at all close approximations," and this, according to Parsons, tends to shift attention away from the concept of a system as a balance of forces in equilibrium. "It leads to a kind of 'type atomism.' " [22] Parsons interprets Weber's ideal types in a manner that would bring them close to the formulations of Dilthey, a fact of which he seems heartily to approve. He does not, however, have much sympathy with Weber's use of types in a manner which would minimize the claims of abstract theory. Generally, Parsons' sympathies

are more for than against Weber. At the same time, in view of his objections, one could expect Parsons to try to improve on the type as a
conceptual tool.

Parsons seems to have found in the concept of "pattern variables"
the device for securing the generalized abstract theory he felt Weber
ideal types could not obtain. A pattern variable is not a variable; it is,
presumably, the schematization of directions or dimensions of some
possible variation. In *The Social System,* for example, he attempted to
establish "the pattern alternatives of value orientation as definitions of
relation role expectation patterns." [23] If one may be permitted to translate this, Parsons is raising the question as to the ways in which the relations between two or more persons may be arranged or limited. For
example, any person in a social relation, Parsons assumes, gets all he can
out of it. In Parsons' inimitable language, "In motivation terms it may
be presumed that the 'ultimate' interest of any actor is in the optimization
of gratification." [24] However, it is also clear that in any social relation
one person cannot get everything. "The polarity of affectivity-neutrality
formulates the patterning of action with respect to his basic alternative
in direction orientations to the social objects with whom an actor inter-
acts in a role, and in its relevance to the structure of the expectations of
his action in that role." [25] Again to translate: any relation between two
or more persons may be limited in terms of the interest or lack of interest of the parties involved.

Without tracing through all the steps of the argument, Parsons argues that any social relation is describable in terms of five pairs of pattern variables of role definition:

I. The Gratification-Discipline Dilemma
   Affectivity vs. Affective Neutrality

II. The Private vs. Collective Interest Dilemma
    Self-Orientation vs. Collectivity-Orientation

III. The Choice between Types of Value-Orientation Standard
     Universalism vs. Particularism

IV. The Choice between "Modalities" of the Social Object
    Achievement vs. Ascription

V. The Definition of Scope of Interest in the Object
   Specificity vs. Diffuseness

To translate again: in any relation between two or more persons, one or
other of the parties may be (I) interested or relatively disinterested,
(II) selfish or unselfish, (III) interested in some immediate end or in a
category of ends defined by a principle. The other party to the social
act may be valued because of (IV) what he can do (achievement—for
example, because he's a great football player) or what he is (ascription

—for example, because he comes from one of the "best" families in town). Finally, (V) one may be interested in the other person in a social relationship for a very specific reason (a carnival barker wants nothing more from the sucker but his money) or in a general way (as when a young man loves everything about the girl). Parsons maintains that "If the derivation of these five alternative pairs from possibilities of the combination of the basic components of the action system has been correct, if they are . . . on the same level of generality and are exhaustive of the relevant logical possibilities . . . they may be held to constitute a system. Then, on the relevant level, which, as we shall see, is the *only one* which needs to be considered, their permutations and combinations should yield a system of types of possible role-expectation pattern, on the relational level, namely defining the pattern of orientation to the actors in the role relationship. This system will consist of thirty-two types." [26]

Parsons does not seem to have received all the credit he deserves for his handling of the ideal type. He seems to have done for the type what Henry Ford did for the automobile when he took it out of the bicycle shops and put it on the assembly line of the modern factory. Parsons, similarly, seems to have indicated the way to mass produce ideal types on an assembly-line basis, for he appears to have invented no less than a machine for their production. In this case, a set of five dichotomous action alternatives are set up. These are cross-tabulated. Certain permutations and combinations are counted. By the simple turn of the crank, thirty-two types of social systems are turned out.

Lest it be thought for one moment that Parsons has in any way escaped the problem so often raised as to the relation between the idealization involved in the type and the empirical reality, his comments on his application of the thirty-two types of possible social systems may be considered. When we examine actual social life he states "we do not find that empirically observable structures cover anything like the whole range of theoretically possible variability, that is, according to purely logical permutations and combinations of structural components." [27] The discovery that actual social systems are not as rich as the imagined ones is said to "serve a two-fold purpose for the sociologist." It not only permits him to short-cut investigation "of the whole range of structural possibilities and concentrate on a fraction of them" but "it can serve as a highly important lead into the formulation, and hence, testing, of fundamental dynamic generalizations, of laws of social process, since the explanation of why the logically possible range of variability is empirically restricted can only be found in terms of them." [28]

There is a curious turn to these arguments. Apparently Parsons' assembly-line production of ideal types is so effective that, like the recent secretaries of agriculture, he is embarrassed by his surplus. The two main functions of actually looking at the facts are stated to be (1) to permit one to ignore some of the types and (2) to develop laws to explain why all the types cannot be found in fact. It is quite in accord with this surrealist atmosphere that Parsons permits himself to be startled by the fact that kinship has so much prominence in social structure,[29] which, he states, one would never expect from the thirty-two types. In explaining this surprise, Parsons is led to assign importance to all sorts of factors not even mentioned in his set of pattern variables such as the dependency of the human infant, the importance of sex to people, and the significance of child care, breast feeding, and the disabilities of women during pregnancy.

C. Howard P. Becker's Constructed Types

Although somewhat more explicit than Parsons, who employed the older terminology, Howard P. Becker has also been interested in the use of the type only after it has been purified.

The first innovation suggested to Becker is the renaming of "ideal" types as "constructed" types. This was in the interest of obtaining a vocabulary free from negative connotations of the term "ideal." Secondly, Becker suggests a breakdown of types into dated and localized, thought to be important for the historian, and undated and nonlocalized, being especially useful to sociologists.[30] Thirdly, Becker suggests a procedure for the setting up and use of types not quite paralleled in Weber's discussion.

If a sociologist is interested in some such phenomenon as revolution, Becker suggests, he must recognize the fact that no one revolution is ever quite duplicated by another. Hence, he proposes that the student examine as many revolutions as he conveniently can. On the basis of these, one may set up a series of types: revolutionary personality, processes, structures. This is after the student has formed a "highly provisional hypothesis" with the aim of developing a "constructed type" which can be employed as a tool. In social science "experimentation must be mental or selectively comparative. The process begins with a vaguely defined problem, the framing of a hypothesis, selective observation . . . with reference to it, and eventual construction of a type, or a battery of them . . ."[31]

This is all quite different from Weber, who had assigned ideal types to a much more provisional stage of theory construction and empirical investigation. Constructed types in Becker's formulation appear as the end products or goals of research rather than as early and tentative formulations. Similarly, Becker suggests that constructed types either are hypotheses or together with an hypothesis they acquire direct predictive power. "The constructed type, in conjunction with an appropriate hypothesis . . . may have predictive power. . . . We can say . . . that if and when these typical factors are given in this typical relation, these will probably be the typical consequences." This is somewhat qualified, however, for "All the constructive typologist ever says is that 'if and when certain factors, which have been isolated as significant, recur in configurations which can be regarded as identical for the purpose in hand, then this in turn will probably occur.' " [32]

Weber, of course, had insisted that his types were not hypotheses or made up of hypotheses. The moment one treats them as such, rather novel consequences occur. The ideal type is never found in reality, being ideal precisely in the sense that it is an abstraction, accentuation, and extension of relations found in social life. If one takes the position that "if and when the factors" idealized in the type are found, certain other presumably idealized consequences follow, the result seems rare indeed. It would appear that the sociologist wishes to play "What's My Line?" with nature. He imagines a nonexistent state of affairs and defies nature to reproduce it.[33] This sounds like a social scientist who knows his own mind and is inclined to accept no nonsense, least of all from nature.

D. Merton's Paradigms

Still another device employed under similar circumstances and in much the same manner as the ideal type is Robert Merton's paradigm. Merton's brilliant study of the rise of the scientific attitude in 17th century England, using Weber's typology of the inner-worldly asceticism and Protestant rationality, reveals Merton's familiarity with and skill in employing ideal-type procedures. In view of this, Merton's use of the term "paradigm" rather than "ideal type" seems to represent an unwillingness to quibble over minor issues and to find a neutral terminology. In any case, he has not only urged the utility of paradigms which he finds to have great propaedeutic value but has employed them as a device to interpret material felt essential for functional analysis, as a device for analyzing deviant social behavior, as an implement for isolating the problems in the sociology of knowledge, and as devices for investigating problems of intermarriage, social structure, and discrimination.

Precisely what Merton understands by the paradigm is not stated. Traditionally, of course, in grammatical analysis a paradigm was a set of forms containing some particular language element. The term also has been used to refer to a display in fixed order, to a pattern or to an example. The last of these seem closest to Merton's intention, for among the functions explicitly assigned to paradigms are the following: (1) bring into the open assumptions, concepts, and propositions used in sociological analysis; (2) isolate the skeleton of fact, inference, and theoretic conclusion; (3) provide an economical arrangement of concepts and their interrelations for description, having a notational function; (4) require that each new concept be logically derivable from previous terms of the paradigms or explicitly incorporated in it; (5) promote cumulative theoretic interpretation; (6) suggest systematic cross-tabulation of basic concepts; (7) assist codification of methods of qualitative analysis in a manner approximating the rigor of quantitative analysis.[34]

In terms of the various meanings of paradigm, pattern or model seems most nearly to approximate Merton's intention. However, there are various references to "formal" paradigms, "analytic" paradigms, "theoretic" paradigms, and "plain" paradigms. Whether all these have all the functions of paradigms is not noted. The various statements and examples leave much undetermined. Some statements suggest that the paradigm is merely an outline of the basic ideas of some particular study. At the other extreme, some statements suggest that the paradigm is a system of theory in which every concept is logically derivable, the paradigm being in fact a completed system of theory reduced to its most economical axiomatic structure, a calculus of concepts. Between these extremes, there are other statements suggesting that the paradigm is no more ambitious than a device for instituting systematic description.

Merton's paradigm for functional analysis, for example, seems to represent little more than a provisional outline of items that it is advisable for the functional sociologist to study. These are even phrased in the form of a mnemonic set of questions to ask oneself:

1. To what items are functions imputed?

2. What situations can be adequately analyzed on the basis of observed motivations?

3. What are the sources of function and disfunction?

4. What is assumed to be functional?

5. How is the intervening variable to be validly established as a functional requirement in a situation where one cannot experiment?

6. By what mechanisms are functions fulfilled?

7. How can we most accurately determine functional alternatives?

8. How does a structural contact limit functional variation?

9. How is one to account for structural strains in the social system?

10. To what degree is functional analysis limited by the difficulty of locating adequate samples of social systems? [35]

This particular paradigm, which was described as a provisional codified guide for adequate and fruitful functional analysis, was said to lead directly to the postulates and assumptions underlying functional analysis. It was also stated to sensitize the sociologist to the scientific implications and ideological aspects of functional analysis. The paradigm consists of a list of items felt to be crucial and a set of questions to be asked at an early stage of study. The paradigm, in this case, is certainly not a systematic description or an axiomatic theory.

A much more interesting paradigm is present in Merton's essay on social structure and anomie. The provocative general proposition is advanced that social structures themselves may exert a pressure on individuals to engage in nonconformist or conformist conduct.[36] Developing this idea, Merton isolates two elements of social structure felt to be important for conformist and nonconformist behavior. Every social structure holds out to its members goals defined as legitimate; at the same time it regulates and defines the means and modes of reaching these goals. Merton urges that in a society where there is a very strong emphasis on the goals (success) without a corresponding emphasis on the means of achieving institutionally prescribed conduct, the latter can shift into the background. In this case, the society itself contains the pressures that lead to the breaking of its own norms. This, he maintains, is actually the case of American culture which "enjoins the acceptance of three cultural axioms; first, all should strive for the same lofty goals; . . . second, present seeming failure is but a way station to ultimate success; and third, genuine failure consists only in the lessening or withdrawing of ambition." [37] On the basis of this, Merton outlines a typology of individual adaptation. It may be noted that both presumed empirical laws and a set of specific historical conditions are present in the paradigm.

A TYPOLOGY OF MODES OF INDIVIDUAL ADAPTATION [38]

Modes of Adaptation	Culture Goals	Institutionalized Means
I. Conformity	+	+
II. Innovation	+	−
III. Ritualism	−	+
IV. Retreatism	−	−
V. Rebellion	±	±

One may accept the cultural goals and the institutional means (conform), accept the goals but not the means (innovate), reject the goals but accept the means (be a ritualist), passively reject both goals and means (retreat), or rebel actively toward both goals and means.

In this second paradigm, Merton has all the elements and has conformed to the requirements of the ideal type as set down by Weber. A set of concepts was used to extrapolate from some relations found in actual social life. He analytically simplified and drew out the implications of certain selected tendencies. As far as our knowledge goes, three of his types—conformist, innovator, ritualist—are objectively possible. Undoubtedly, examples of a dyed-in-the-wool, simon-pure conformist or retreatist in everything could not be easily found—a fact in no way lessening the analytical clarification of possible combinations of social relations.

I am not familiar, from Merton's work, with any cases of paradigms which would fulfill the requirements of a closed system of concepts formed into an axiomatic theory. In view of this, it may be assumed that Merton's paradigms are, perhaps intentionally, a more loose version of what Weber intended by the ideal type.

JOHN McKINNEY'S CONSTRUCTED TYPES

John McKinney's statement may be taken to illustrate the fact that ideal types have not gone out of fashion even with the youngest writers and thinkers at present. McKinney primarily follows Howard P. Becker's conceptualizations, but his formulations have a strongly individualized property. It is argued that all concepts are constructs and creative "due to their abstract genesis." Since this is the case, it is urged "the way is often to move one step further and create the constructed type." Such constructed types are characterized as being "a little more out of touch with perceptual reality than other constructs are." Moreover, a constructed type is said to be "a devised system of characteristics (criteria, traits, elements, attributes, aspects, etc.) not experienced directly in this form." The constructed type is said to be used for "comparison and measurement of empirical approximations" during which employment it reveals "nothing but deviations from the construct." This, it seems, is highly desirable, serving the purpose of "quantification in terms of the degree of deviation." [39]

Exactly why McKinney wants a quantitatively precise measure of the degree of deviation of types from reality is not clear to me. The point, however, seems to be important, for McKinney develops it further in a recent major volume on sociological theory. "Although examination of empirical cases never reveals anything more than 'approximations' or 'deviations' from the constructed type, it is essential that the type be formulated on the basis of empirical evidence. . . . Obviously, any variation or deviation must be a variation or deviation *from something*. To identify that something is necessarily to determine uniformity represented by the type." [40] Since the "uniformity represented by the type" is an imagined one, the intriguing suggestion of quantifying degree of fictitiousness remains.

THE CRITIQUE OF THE IDEAL TYPE

It is evident that sociologists have been constructing ideal types consciously and unconsciously since the origins of the science. They have invented types of society, social change, family, religion, economy, politics, state, social movements, revolution, personality—the list is as extensive and varied as sociology itself. It is important to keep this in mind if one is to avoid some kinds of pitfalls. Schumpeter, for example, makes what he conceives to be a crushing criticism of Weber's use of types. "Some economists, among whom it must suffice to mention Max Weber, have felt the need of explaining the rise of capitalism by means of a special theory. But the problem such theories have been framed to solve is wholly imaginary and owes its existence to the habit of painting unrealistic pictures of a purely feudal and a purely capitalistic society, which then raises the question what it was that turned the tradition-bound individual of one into the alert profit-hunter of the other." [41] Schumpeter then proceeded to advance a scheme of ideal-typical forms of capitalism: early capitalism; mercantilist capitalism; intact capitalism; modern capitalism. If, under any circumstances, ideal types are going to be developed, scientifically responsible behavior would seem better served by recognizing this fact and bringing them under critical control. To withdraw such activities from scientific review reserves these areas for irrational activity. Moreover, the criticism of the ideal type on the grounds that it is unrealistic—that is, ideal—is the least rewarding form of criticism directed at the type.

The chief criticism of the ideal types in the earliest and most unreflective stage is that they were too vague to give consistent results. Some contributed to the development of sociology by making observation, description, or conceptualization a bit more precise than it had been previously. Some served their purpose and disappeared as they should have. Later developments in sociology provided the best criticism of early forms of ideal-typical procedure. They were ambiguous, inconsistent, and untrustworthy. From this standpoint, the assemblage and sharpening of the theoretical and methodological problems bound up with the type which occurred with neo-Hegelianism and neo-Kantianism represented a distinct advance.

The formulations of Dilthey, which would turn ideal types into configurations of "meaningfulness" guiding emphatic reliving of cultural and historical experience, and those of Rickert, which would make of them devices for assigning significance to aspects of historical individuals by referring these to some general value—such formulations have lost their interest for modern students. Even the most tender minded of contemporary students is inclined to see science as all of one piece. The insights produced by intuition, empathy, or some method of *verstehen* are to the modern student mere untested hypotheses. The funeral oration of the *verstehen* point of view was gracefully and ceremoniously performed by Abel in his *Operation Called Verstehen* [42] with his review of the claims of empathy to methodological standing and his disposal of it as an exercise in imagination that may, at times, be of secondary use in the sober tasks of proof. The positive values of the neo-Hegelian and neo-Kantian studies of the ideal type were: (1) pulling the various aspects of the problem of the ideal type together into one context; (2) focusing attention on the importance of social-psychological materials for sociology, paving the way for the appearance of a vigorous subdivision of sociology; (3) bridging the gap that was tending to grow up between history and social science, thus maintaining a relation that would permit social-science findings to bear on historical materials and historical data to become grist for the sociological mills. However, for the modern student the interpretation of ideal types as "meaningful *Gestalts*" is unacceptable. Whenever ideal types are given a significance similar to that assigned by Dilthey or Rickert, the modern student reacts in alarm.

An interesting type of criticism of the ideal type, at least of Weber's, has been advanced by Talcott Parsons. It will be recalled that Parsons interpreted the ideal type in a manner strongly suggesting the Dilthey-Rickert discussions, as a special kind of abstraction, one stating the case "where a normative or ideal pattern is perfectly complied with." Weber, of course, had observed that there may be ideal types of brothels as well as ideal types of religions. However, this was not the grounds on which Parsons was critical of Weber's use of the ideal type.

Parsons urges that ideal types tend to concentrate on extreme or polar situations, tending thus to shift analysis away from the social system as a balance of forces in equilibrium. The ideal type is stated to be of utility only in analyzing a "limiting type" of system. Furthermore, Parsons argues, ideal types tend to lead to a "type atomism." The use of ideal types forms an obstacle to the formation of abstract theory. "Ideal type theory is . . . perhaps the most difficult level on which to develop a coherent generalized system. The concepts can readily be formulated *ad hoc* for innumerable purposes and can have a limited usefulness. . . . This, however, does not suffice for a generalized system. For this purpose, they must be arranged and classified in a definite order of relationship. Only then will they have highly generalized significance on either a theoretical or empirical level." [43]

The criticism that the ideal type concentrates only on polar or extreme situations and hence is adequate only for the analysis of a "limiting type" of system seems to entail a confusion between the analytical sharpening of relations in the type with extreme social situations. W. I. Thomas and F. Znaniecki, for example, in *The Polish Peasant* advanced a series of types to express the adaptation of the individual to changing social organization. They distinguished between the Bohemian, the Philistine, and the Creative Man. The Bohemian had so weakly internalized the social norms that he tended to overrespond to every social situation —to bend and twist, as it were, with every wind. The Philistine had taken over the conventional pattern in a narrow inflexible manner. The Creative Man had achieved a progressive, flexible, and responsive relation to his social order. These were types—analytical simplifications of adjustment possibilities. However, far from permitting the analysis only of extreme or polar types of individual adjustment to social organization and change they proved to be an elastic system of possibilities ranging from individual disorganization to mastery of one's life situation.

On the other hand Parsons' criticisms that Weber's ideal types tend to result in a kind of type "atomism" standing in the way of the development of abstract theory seems to be well taken. To be sure, this criticism holds only for those instances in which ideal types are mistaken for abstract theory. When theory is taken to be a logically interrelated body of empirical laws, types cannot be theories. Weber, unfortunately, did not formulate his conception of social-science theory, but he did object to the notion that ideal types are theories. In fact, Weber believed that many social scientists had raised premature claims of having achieved abstract general theory. Classical economic theory provided Weber with an example of a presumed abstract theory which, he maintained, was merely an ideal type. Parsons and Weber were actually in agreement, but the criticism applies to anyone who does mistake ideal types for theory. When classical economics confused an ideal type for an abstract general theory, it was started on a course toward a metaphysics of ideal forms. Being strongly nominalistic and rather positivistic in inclination, Weber was decidedly suspicious of a kind of generalization he thought tended to become metaphysical. Weber's concept of ideal types, in part, represented the claims of empiricism against hasty overgeneralization.

Of particular interest in connection with Parsons' criticism of Weber's ideal types is the criticism advanced by J. W. N. Watkins.[44] Watkins claims to find two kinds of ideal types in Weber's work which he calls "holistic" and "individualistic." Ideal types are constructed, on the one hand, by abstracting and expanding the outstanding features of a historical situation. These are organized into a coherent picture emphasizing traits of a situation as a whole. They are "holistic." On the other hand, some ideal types are constructed in a way similar to the modes in deductive economics, by formalizing the results of close analysis of some significant details of economic or social life considered in isolation. Such "individualistic" ideal types are constructed by inspecting the situations of actual individuals and abstracting such things as schemes of personal preference, kinds of knowledge of the situation or types of relation between individuals. The ideality of the type lies in simplifying the initial situation and expressing in abstract and formal ways the properties of the selected elements.

Watkins' criticism is simple and unambiguous and directed exclusively toward what he calls "holistic" ideal types. He argues that such holistic types involve one in the assumption that we somehow apprehend the over-all characteristics of social situations before learning about the parts.

On the contrary, Watkins argues, general knowledge of a social situation is always derivative. The basic principle of "methodological individualism" is that social processes and events should be explained in terms of the principles governing the behavior of individuals and descriptions of their situations. The methodological "principle of holism" would deduce behavior of individuals from microscopic laws which are *sui generis,* applying to the system as a whole. The fundamental reasons, according to Watson, for accepting the principle of "methodological individualism" are:

1. While physical things can exist unperceived, social things (laws, princes, prime ministers, ration books) are created by personal attitudes. If social objects are formed by individual attitudes, explanation of them must be individualistic.

2. The social scientist has no direct access to the structure and behavior of a system of interacting individuals, though he can arrive at reliable opinions about the dispositions and situations of individuals. Thus abstract social structures are best understood from more empirical beliefs about individuals.[45]

Watkins, of course, is not objecting to the use of ideal types as a conceptual procedure but to the use of ideal types in the service of a certain kind of sociological theory. Modern sociological functionalism appears to be precisely the kind of social theory that Watkins most opposes.

Talcott Parsons as one of the modern functionalists was impatient of Weber's actual typologies for precisely the opposite reason:

In formulating his classification of the four types of action, Weber neglected to develop the analysis of the structure of the total social system which is a logically necessary prerequisite of such a classification.[46]

By and large, Weber's work gives far more comfort to Watkins than to Parsons, for he had strong nominalistic reactions against prevalent forms of social realism. The extent to which Weber is both a comfort and source of despair to Watkins and Parsons transcends the problems of the ideal type.

A somewhat different type of criticism of ideal types has been advanced by Hempel,[47] not, in this case, confined to Weber alone. Hempel's criticism has been methodological, and it advanced from the standpoint of the methodological practice of the natural science.

The most general criticism Hempel has of typological concepts in the social sciences is that they tend to use the concepts and principles of classical logic, a logic of properties of classes. As a result, Hempel believes, they are incapable of adequately dealing with relations and quantitative concepts.

Hempel distinguished a variety of types: classificatory types, extreme types, and models. He urges that classificatory types tend always in time to be supplanted by precise formulations in statistical terms. To function legitimately, extreme types which are not class concepts must set up criteria for comparisons of more or less. They are destined to disappear as soon as operational criteria are found for proper judgment of "more or less" in a continuum. A scale of temperatures eventually replaces judgments of hot and cold, for example. It follows, Hempel maintains, that classificatory and extreme types are displaced as soon as statistical studies and operations are refined. They belong to the early stages of the growth of a scientific discipline. This brings us to models which are the basis for Hempel's discussion of Weber's types.

Hempel found in Weber's ideal types a good deal that was methodologically sound. For example, Weber saw ideal types as devices for the grasp of causal relations and meaning in concrete social and historical phenomena. The principles expressing connections were seen by Weber as "general empirical rules." Meanings discovered by emphatic understanding were admitted by Weber to be neither universally applicable nor always dependable. Weber conceived of the imaginary experiment as a dangerous and an uncertain procedure to be used only with caution in the absence of adequate experimental and observational data. Weber's discussion showed that he was aware of the close connection between contrary-to-fact conditionals and general laws. For Weber, the ideal type was an explanatory scheme embodying a set of "general empirical rules" which prompted conceptual grasp of concrete social and historical phenomena. By and large, Hempel found this to be a sophisticated and responsible set of ideas. He admits that imaginary experiments are also found in natural science where they may be intuitive or theoretical. Hempel's objection to Weber is due to his apparent reduction of the explanatory principles of sociology to meaningful rules of intelligible behavior and the reliance on imaginary experiments of an intuitive character.

Hempel is much more critical of Becker's reformulation of the type than he seems to have been of the statements by Weber. He noted that Becker argued that types function as hypotheses in the form of "if *P* . . . then *Q*" where *P* is the type evoked and *Q* is some more or less complex characteristic. However, in the nature of type construction, the consequence seldom, if ever, follows empirically, and the antecedent is then empirically false. From the occurrence *Q,* we can infer either that *P* was not realized or that the hypothesis "if *P* then *Q*" is false. Thus, when Becker has argued that all other factors being equal or irrelevant *Q* will be realized whenever *P* is realized, evidently no empirical evidence can ever refute the hypothesis, since unfavorable findings can always be attributed to a violation of the *ceteris paribus* clause. By contrast, in the formulation of a physical hypothesis, this clause is never used.

Hempel finds that in the physical sciences, too, there are ideal structures—ideal gases, perfectly electric bodies, and the like. Such concepts refer to extreme conditions which cannot be met in full. Their scientific value lies in the laws governing the behavior of ideal systems which are deductible from more comprehensive theoretical principles and confirmed by empirical evidence. Such types of models are of great value to physical science. On the other hand, perhaps the nearest approach to them is the kind of type concept found in analytical economics, such as the idea of a perfectly free competition, or of economically rational behavior. However, in contrast to the natural-science idealizations, the principles are intuitive rather than theoretical idealizations. The class of empirical evidence to which they refer is not always clearly specified. Only when operational meaning is attached to such theoretical parameters as "money," "profit," "utility," and the like, will the presuppositions of the theory acquire empirical meaning and become capable of test.

IDEAL TYPES AND SOCIOLOGICAL THEORY

Hempel's treatment of the type is one of the most promising contributions of the recent discussions. Basically, he distinguishes three kinds of types: classificatory types, extreme or polar types, and the models of interpreted systems. The peculiar value of the classification is that it distinguishes between types on the basis of their methodological function, rather than in terms of some extraneous consideration such as whether they are going to be used by historians or by sociologists. There is little doubt that among the many concept formations described as types these subdistinctions apply.

Hempel separated the problems represented by classificatory and extreme types from models. Classificatory types, which it should be noted

are not ideal types, are dismissed rather cavalierly as representing an old fashioned logic of properties and attributes not well adapted to study quantities and relations. Hempel's judgments are made from the standpoint of the natural sciences. The argument that classificatory types are destined to be replaced by formulations in statistical terms and that extreme or polar types are destined to disappear as soon as operational criteria are found for judgments of "more or less" in a continuum is indisputable. This, however, is no reason to scorn the significant (even if provisional) function of classificatory and extreme types in promoting description and establishing the limits of relations that may later be quantified. Precisely because the social sciences are in a less developed state than the physical sciences a larger burden of their elementary work is carried on by types. The moment adequate statistical conceptions are established and operational criteria for quantification are found, the types supplanted ought to be scrapped without further ado. One would hardly persist in distinguishing only hot and cold when a thermometer is available.

More important is Hempel's distinction between legitimate and illegitimate idealized models. Idealized models representing interpreted theories, such as are found in the physical sciences, were in Hempel's mind valuable applications of scientific theories. Ideal types were, he thought, illegitimate models, even though the principles expressing connections in ideal types for Weber were "general empirical tools." The idealizations expressed in the theoretical models of physical science were legitimate because they are deduced from general principles. By contrast, the principles of the ideal type were viewed as illegitimate, because they were intuitive rather than theoretical and often addressed to an only vaguely specified body of data. In any case, the model does not represent an axiomatic system explaining a body of tested empirical materials.

If the only types of legitimate models are those representing interpreted theoretical systems, one can only conclude that it will be long before the social sciences can achieve them. The long-range objective of presenting a theoretical system as a special case of a more comprehensive theory may be fine, but it will be a long time before sociology reaches this stage. Meanwhile, once again, invidious comparisons are introduced between sociology and the physical sciences. Wherever statistical and experimental methods have not been developed to a point adequate to its needs, sociology can only institute the most precise comparisons possible. This is precisely what ideal types were intended to do. In areas where quantification is incomplete and inadequate, mathematical models are, as yet, unavailable and where one, on the other hand, is not able to experiment, there is no choice but to find bases on which one can compare cases. It goes without saying that if one's comparison is between some actual state

of affairs and the type, about all that can be predicted is nonsense. Rather, one compares two or more actual sets of affairs. The function of ideal types is to isolate the factors on which the comparison becomes critical. The degree to which the relations involved in the type are intuitive seriously curtails the extent to which one can generalize on the basis of them. However, in the early stages of science, one accepts help from whatever quarter.

Obviously, if one is looking for a permanent fixture in the achievements of science, the ideal type—at least any given one—can only be a disappointment. Whenever the ideal type is compared to the model representing an interpreted theory, the ideal type comes off a poor second best. This is inevitable, for the two are not comparable. Ideal types are not interpreted theories; they are devices intended to institute precise comparisons. Unless one wishes to assume that ideal types are not methodological expedients but transempirical forms constituting a kind of heaven of Platonic ideals in which actual events participate, one must assume that any given ideal type is destined to be surpassed. It must also be assumed, however, that ideal types will continue to be employed as long as sociology or any science relies upon the comparative method.

NOTES

1. John C. McKinney, "Methodology, Procedures, and Techniques in Sociology," pp. 186-235 in Howard Becker and Alvin Boskoff, eds., *Modern Sociological Theory* (New York: Dryden Press, 1957), p. 226.

2. Auguste Comte, *Positive Philosophy,* trans. by Harriet Martineau, Vol. 2, pp. 103-05.

3. The works of Herbert Spencer, Lewis H. Morgan, and Emile Durkheim illustrate this.

4. Wilhelm Dilthey's *Gesammelte Schriften* (Leipzig and Berlin: B. B. Tuebner, 1936) particularly *Einleitung in die Geisteswissenschaften: Versuch einer Grundlegung für das Studium der Gesellschaft und der Geschichte,* I, and "Der Aufbau der geschichtlichen Welt in den Geisteswissenschaften," *Gesammelte Schriften,* III. Reviews of Dilthey's position for social science and for history may be found in Maurice Mandelbaum, *The Problem of Historical Knowledge* (New York: Liveright Publishing Corporation, 1938), pp. 59 ff., and Alexander Goldenweiser, "The Relation of the Natural Sciences to the Social Sciences" in *Contemporary Social Theory,* Harry Elmer Barnes, Howard Becker, and Frances Bennett Becker, eds. (New York: D. Appleton-Century, 1940), pp. 93-98.

5. Heinrich Rickert, *Die Grenzen der Naturwissenschaftlichen Begriffsbildung* (Tübingen: J. C. B. Mohr, 1920). Summaries are also found in Mandel and Goldenweiser.

6. *Ibid.,* p. 100.

7. *Ibid.,* pp. 93 ff.

8. *Ibid.,* p. 281.

9. *Ibid.,* p. 272.

10. Max Weber, *The Methodology of the Social Sciences,* trans. by Edward A. Shils and Henry A. Finch (Glencoe, Ill.: Free Press, 1949), p. 89.

11. *Ibid.,* pp. 91-92.

12. *Ibid.,* p. 90.

13. *Ibid.,* p. 93.

14. *Ibid.,* p. 97.

15. *Ibid.,* p. 100.

16. *Ibid.,* p. 101.

17. *Ibid.,* p. 92.

18. *Ibid.,* p. 187.

19. Ernest Nagel, "The Logic of Historical Analysis" in *Readings in the Philosophy of Science,* Herbert Feigl and May Brodbeck, eds. (New York: Appleton-Century-Crofts, Inc., 1953), pp. 688 ff.

20. R. M. MacIver, *Social Causation* (New York: Ginn and Company, 1942), pp. 258-59.

21. Talcott Parsons, *Essays in Sociological Theory Pure and Applied* (Glencoe, Ill.: Free Press, 1949), p. 76.

22. *Ibid.,* p. 78.

23. Talcott Parsons, *The Social System* (Glencoe, Ill.: Free Press, 1951), p. 58.

24. *Ibid.,* p. 59.

25. *Ibid.,* p. 60.

26. *Ibid.,* p. 66.

27. *Ibid.,* p. 152.

28. *Ibid.*

29. *Ibid.,* p. 153.

30. Howard Becker, *Through Values to Social Interpretation* (Durham, N.C.: Duke University Press, 1950), p. 90.

31. *Ibid.,* p. 109.

32. *Ibid.,* p. 108.

33. In addition to the statement in *Through Values* others are contained in "Constructive Typology in the Social Sciences" in *Contemporary Social Theory, op. cit.,* pp. 17-46, and "Interpretive Sociology and Constructive Typology" in *Twentieth Century Sociology* (New York: The Philosophical Library, 1945), pp. 70-95.

34. Robert K. Merton, *Social Theory and Social Structure* (Glencoe, Ill.: Free Press, 1949), pp. 12-16.

35. *Ibid.,* pp. 49 ff.

36. *Ibid.,* pp. 133 ff.

37. *Ibid.,* p. 132.

38. *Ibid.,* p. 133.

39. John C. McKinney, "Constructive Typology and Social Research" in *An Introduction to Social Research* (Harrisburg: The Stackpole Co., 1954), pp. 144-45.

40. In Howard Becker and Alvin Boskoff, *op. cit.,* pp. 226-27.

41. Joseph R. Schumpeter, "Capitalism," *Encyclopaedia Britannica* (1958), IV, 801-07.

42. Theodore Abel, "The Operation Called Verstehen," *American Journal of Sociology,* 54 (Chicago: University of Chicago Press, 1948), reprinted in *Readings in the Philosophy of Science, op. cit.,* pp. 677 ff.

43. Talcott Parsons, *Essays, op. cit.,* p. 91.

44. J. W. N. Watkins, "Ideal Types and Historical Explanation," *The British Journal for the Philosophy of Science,* 3 (1952), reprinted in an expanded version in Feigl and Brodbeck's *Readings in the Philosophy of Science, op. cit.,* pp. 723 ff.

45. *Ibid.,* p. 729.

46. Talcott Parsons, *Essays, op. cit.,* p. 78.

47. Carl G. Hempel, *Symposium: Problems of Concept and Theory Formation in the Social Sciences, Language and Human Rights* (Philadelphia: University of Pennsylvania Press, 1952), pp. 65-86.

BIBLIOGRAPHY

ABEL, THEODORE. "The Operation Called Verstehen," *American Journal of Sociology,* 54 (1948).

BECKER, HOWARD. "Constructive Typology in the Social Sciences," *American Sociological Review,* V (Feb., 1940), 40-55.

————. "Constructive Typology in the Social Sciences" in H. E. Barnes, Howard Becker, and F. B. Becker (eds.), *Contemporary Social Theory.* New York: D. Appleton-Century Company, 1940.

DILTHEY, WILHELM. *Gesammelte Schriften.* Leipzig and Berlin: B. B. Tuebner, 1936.

HEMPEL, C. G. "Typological Methods in the Natural and Social Sciences," *Proceedings, American Philosophical Association: Eastern Division,* I (1952), 65-86.

MACIVER, R. M. *Social Causation.* Boston: Ginn and Co., 1942.

MCKINNEY, JOHN C. "Constructive Typology and Social Research" in *An Introduction to Social Research.* Harrisburg: The Stackpole Co., 1954, 139-94.

————. "Methodology, Procedures, and Techniques in Sociology" in *Modern Sociological Theory*. New York: Dryden Press, 1957, 186-235.

MERTON, ROBERT K. *Social Theory and Social Structure*. Glencoe, Ill.: Free Press, 1949.

NAGEL, ERNEST. "The Logic of Historical Analysis" in *Readings in the Philosophy of Science,* eds., Herbert Feigl and May Brodbeck. New York: Appleton-Century-Crofts, Inc., 1953, 688-700.

PARSONS, TALCOTT. *Essays in Sociological Theory: Pure and Applied*. Glencoe, Ill.: Free Press, 1949.

RICKERT, HEINRICH. *Die Grenzen der Naturwissenschaftlichen Begriffsbildung*. Tübingen: J. C. B. Mohr, 1920.

WATKINS, J. W. N. "Ideal Types and Historical Explanation," reprinted in Feigl and Brodbeck, *Readings in the Philosophy of Science,* 723-43.

WEBER, MAX. *The Methodology of the Social Sciences*. Translated by Edward A. Shils and Henry A. Finch. Glencoe, Ill.: Free Press, 1949.

3

Images of Society
and Problems of Concept Formation
in Sociology

REINHARD BENDIX

University of California

and

BENNETT BERGER

University of California

To explain the known facts of society, sociological theories require some orderly framework of concepts. But, like historians who find it necessary to "rewrite" or "reinterpret" history in each generation, sociologists are continually modifying old concepts and offering new ones because of some dissatisfaction with the vocabulary as it stands. These dissatisfactions typically arise when someone discovers that the current definitions of standard concepts neglect or omit some range of fact which he regards as important. This concern with the reformulation of concepts suggests that there is some evidence for every set of concepts but as yet no agreed upon procedure by which consensus could be achieved.

An earlier version of this paper was published in *Koelner Zeitschrift fuer Sociologie.* We are indebted to Llewellyn Gross, Leo Lowenthal, Philip Selznick, and Milton Singer for critical comments on that version. R.B. and B.B.

I. DEFINITIONS OF "THE SOCIAL FACT"

One reason for this lack of agreement stems from the failure of many discussants to reflect on the sense of the "real" which lies behind their conflicting definitions of the "social fact." Attention to these different ideas of what is significant, or "real," in society may help to improve the chances for reaching agreement, where this is possible. And where it is not, such attention will at least clarify the reasons why the same divergent perspectives recur in ever new guises.

Simmel's work is illuminating for the present discussion because he, more than most theorists, was explicitly concerned with delimiting the subject matter of sociology. In his effort to establish sociology as an independent discipline, Simmel began by challenging the familiar assumption that only the individual was "real" while society was "merely" an abstraction. No concept, he argued, could be more "real" than any other, since every concept presupposed an abstracting operation which distorted the facts by simplification and exaggeration. For Simmel, the realm of the "social" was as worthy of study as the realm of the "individual," and he identified this social realm with the process of interaction between individuals. Yet, in making this case for sociology as an independent discipline, Simmel also suggested that the traditional concepts of social science, such as "state," "administration," "church," and others lacked "real" social content: only if the interactions between individuals were studied could the meaning of these "official social formations" be revealed.[1] Thus, Simmel argued against the common notion that certain concepts are more "real" than others; yet inadvertently he argued in favor of the concept "interaction" as the proper focus of sociological inquiry on the ground that this was a "realistic" approach to the study of society.

Simmel's dilemma on this point was not fortuitous. One cannot argue in favor of a concept on the ground that it is more realistic than another. All concepts are based on *some* evidence which the theorist arranges in order to facilitate understanding. But when Simmel argued in favor of sociology on the ground that its interaction approach, abstract though he knew it to be, was more realistic than the traditional concepts of social science, he revealed inadvertently that the definition of concepts is also a social act. Just as research cannot be initiated without some sense of the significant, so sociological theorizing cannot be developed without a strong sense of what is "real" in society. It is each theorist's sense of the "real" which is expressed in his definition of the "social fact." [2]

Simmel, as we have seen, was preoccupied with the process of *interaction* between individuals. On the other hand, Durkheim was especially concerned with the individual's group affiliations as a source of individual and collective morality. For Durkheim, the central social fact was the *coercive aspect* of the beliefs and practices which were imposed upon the individual from without and to which he had to conform if he were not to risk social ostracism. Max Weber, in turn, defined the central social fact as the *meaning* which individuals in society attach to their own actions and those of others. For the dominant impulse of his work was to account for the transvaluation of meaning in Western Civilization, exemplified by the disappearance of magic and the rise of rationalism in many spheres of life. Men like Simmel, Durkheim, and Weber tended to define the "social fact" in apparent accordance with the major impulse which informed their scholarly work. Unwittingly perhaps, they used their own intellectual orientations to substantive problems as the basis for formulating the fundamental categories of sociological theory. In doing this, they tended to foster pseudocontroversies, since the differences among various theories were often due to different *purposes* of cognition rather than to differences of cognition itself.[3] This tendency appears unsatisfactory, despite the eminent names associated with it, because it makes the basic categories of sociology dependent upon a purpose of cognition which is specific to the work of a given scholar.

To terminate this "war of schools," Professor Parsons undertook, in his *The Structure of Social Action,* to show that Pareto, Durkheim, Marshall, and Weber were in basic agreement on certain fundamental concepts concerning the actions of men in society. During more recent years he has continued this endeavor by seeking to find a common universe of theoretical discourse among outstanding representatives of anthropology, sociology, and psychology. This effort to formulate and make internally consistent the sum total of usable concepts about the actions of men in society has been linked with the attempt to develop an inclusive theory of society as a system of action. But it is noteworthy that this work of integration employs yet another vocabulary of concepts which is based on yet another selectively perceived "reality." In this case the "definition of the social fact" appears to derive from the belief that the concept "system" is indispensable if sociological theory is to become scientific.[4]

These approaches, however, do *not* exhaust the available alternatives. The major purpose of this paper is to outline another approach to sociological theory, which may transcend these disjunctions of perspective, but which appears to have been neglected *despite the fact that every major sociological theorist has been familiar with it.*

II. THE PERSPECTIVE OF DUAL TENDENCIES

The "sociological perspective" has come largely to mean the study of the ways in which group influences dictate the behavior of the individual. But the task of sociological theory should be to consider not only the social conditioning of the individual but also his capacity for independent action for which that conditioning is only the necessary basis. Dewey pointed out long ago that habits facilitate action as well as restrict it; and it hardly seems necessary to re-emphasize the fact that culture and society not only determine how others expect the individual to act, but also enable him to comply with, or to resist, these expectations. This simultaneous attention to the social and the individual aspect of behavior in society has a venerable intellectual ancestry. It involves an image of man and society (a definition of the "social fact") which views both, not as finite systems, but as capable of indefinite (though not infinite) elaboration. This insight has been variously expressed in terms of tendencies or forces which are linked and opposite at the same time. From Empedocles' view of the world divided by love and hate to Freud's theory of death and eros, from the medieval idea of a universal determinism coupled with individual freedom to Marx' view of men as partly free and partly involuntary political actors under given historical circumstances, from the Confucian concepts of Yin and Yang to Kant's idea of "unsocial sociability": the variations increase, but the theme remains.[5] At the end of his analysis of freedom and equality in American society, Alexis de Tocqueville formulated this theme as his own basic creed:

I am aware [he wrote] that many of my contemporaries maintain that nations are never their own masters here below, and that they necessarily obey some insurmountable and unintelligent power. . . . Such principles are false and cowardly. . . . Providence has not created mankind entirely dependent or entirely free. It is true that around every man a fatal circle is traced beyond which he cannot pass; but within the wide verge of that circle he is powerful and free; as it is with man, so with communities. The nations of our time cannot prevent the conditions of men from becoming equal, but it depends upon themselves whether the principle of equality is to lead them to servitude or freedom, to knowledge or barbarism, to prosperity or wretchedness.[6]

What Kant and Marx, Tocqueville and Freud expressed in philosophical, ethical, and psychological terms has also been reflected in sociological theory. In his discussion of group affiliations, Simmel emphasized the coexistence of socializing and individualizing effects.

Each new group with which [an individual] becomes affiliated circumscribes him more exactly and more unambiguously. . . . As the person becomes affiliated with a social group, he surrenders himself to it. . . . But the person also regains his individuality, because his pattern of participation is unique.[7]

The multiple group affiliations characteristic of modern society may have a double effect according to Simmel. Under certain conditions they may strengthen an individual personality and give it the capacity to sustain great internal tensions; but they may also, under other conditions, threaten the integration of the personality, far more than would be the case in a simpler society with little differentiation between groups. In carrying this idea of his teacher, Simmel, further, Robert Park combined it with the related concepts of Ferdinand Toennies. In his studies of the city, of newspapers, of the interaction between racial groups, and other topics, Park distinguished between interactions in terms of their individuating and socializing repercussions.

> Competition and communication, although they perform different and uncoordinated social functions, nevertheless in the actual life of society supplement and complete each other. . . . Competition seems to be the principle of individuation in the life of the person and of society. . . . Communication, on the other hand, operates primarily as an integrating and socializing principle.[8]

Another example of a somewhat different kind is contained in the social psychology of George H. Mead, who distinguished the organic actions and reactions of the individual (the "I") from the "generalized other" which the individual incorporates in his personality through his interactions with others in society (the "Me").

Again, Max Weber's work is characterized by a somewhat implicit recognition of the same perspective. In his definition of the social fact, Weber emphasized the subjective meaning which individuals in society attach to their actions.[9] This emphasis is reflected in his study of the Protestant Ethic, which eschewed all imputation of motives because "the people of that period [the Reformation] had after all very specific ideas of what awaited them in the life after death, of the means by which they could improve their chances in this respect, and they adjusted their conduct in accordance with these ideas." [10] Yet, Weber also analyzed the social structures which in part conditioned such ideas. He showed, for example, that the political and military autonomy of Occidental cities was an important precondition of bourgeois class consciousness and as such prepared the way for the ideas of the Puritan sects in particular.[11]

Apparently, this perspective is well-known in sociological theory. Yet, in important respects it runs counter to the "sociological determinism" characteristic of much contemporary sociological literature. Group membership and participation in the culture are used in the literature as explanatory principles which account for the conduct of individuals in society. Such terms as culture-pattern, subculture, social role, reciprocal role-expectations, social class, status group, mores and folk-ways, communication, human relations, and many, many others are em-ployed in such a way that individuals appear to act as group influences dictate. Unwittingly perhaps, this vocabulary has often had the cumula-tive effect of suggesting that the individual merely does what is expected of him—in the literal sense in which the actor on the medieval stage reads his text from the rolled script in his hands.[12] A case in point, ad-mittedly flagrant but conceivably symptomatic, is Ralph Linton's attempt to formulate the relation between the individual and his culture. After describing culture as "the way of life of any society" which consists of "the normal anticipated response of *any* of the society's members to a particular situation" and which provides these members with "an indis-pensable guide in all the affairs of life," Linton continues:

> I realize that in the foregoing discussion of society and culture emphasis has been laid mainly upon the passive role of the individual and upon the way in which he is shaped by culture and social factors. It is time now to present the other side of the picture. No matter how carefully the individual has been trained or how successful his conditioning has been, he remains a distinct organism with his own needs and with capacities for independent thought, feeling, and action. Moreover, he retains a considerable degree of individuality. His integration into society and culture goes no deeper than his learned responses, and although in the adult these include the greater part of what we call the personality, *there is still a good deal of the individual left over.*[13]

In this view, culture and society are used as explanatory principles, and what they fail to explain is left over as a residue, which is indeed a "good deal," since Linton himself emphasizes that no two individuals in a culture are exactly alike. The trouble with this approach is that it conceptualizes only part of the evidence, while the "remainder" is left unaccounted for. Unavoidable as this procedure is where we deal with the formulation of hypotheses in particular inquiries, it is not admissible with regard to the basic concepts of sociological theory.

III. PAIRED CONCEPTS OF INTERACTIONS AND INSTITUTIONS

The basic concepts of sociological theory should be applicable to all societies. With the aid of such concepts, we should be able to for-mulate propositions which are true of men by virtue of the fact that they have been members of social groups everywhere and at all times.[14] In order to achieve such comprehensiveness, these concepts should, at their appropriate level of abstraction, encompass the full range of human experience in society rather than single out some dominant feature of that experience and thereby leave some residue aside. Yet this objective cannot be achieved by the formulation of single concepts, since each of these necessarily excludes as well as includes; as Spinoza put it, "omnis determinatio est negatio." It may be possible, however, that the desired comprehensiveness can be achieved by the *paired concepts* which are familiar in sociological theory. Examples are: socialization and individualization, primary and secondary relations, status and contract, symbiosis and co-operation, Gemeinschaft and Gesellschaft, bureaucracy and patrimonialism, and so forth. Such paired concepts are attempts to conceptualize what we know about the range of variability of social phenomena so that we are enabled to deal abstractly with their known extremes, regardless of whether we focus on the level of interactions, of institutions, or of societies as wholes. We recognize that these paired concepts of sociological theory have been developed more or less *ad hoc,* but we also believe that their theoretical utility has not been given as much attention as seems warranted. One difficulty has been that these concepts appeared to invite a dichotomous classification: interactions are either "intimate" or "impersonal," organizations are either "formal" or "informal," societies are either "folk" or "urban." A given set of facts was, then, seen as approximating one or another of these concepts, and hypotheses were formulated in order to analyze the factors associated with this degree of approximation to (or deviation from) the type. The result of this procedure has frequently been that at the end of the investigation the concept appeared much less serviceable than at the beginning, for "urban" elements are found in folk societies, informal relations are present in formally rational bureaucracies, and so forth. Accordingly, the dichotomous classifications are actually misleading or inappropriate; and this may be one reason why a number of sociologists have tended to discard paired concepts altogether.

A second difficulty has been that the formulation of paired concepts has not been clearly distinguished from the formulation of testable hypotheses. As Redfield has shown, communities may be distinguished in terms of whether they are more or less isolated, more or less heterogeneous, more or less literate, and so forth. In using the terms "folk" and "urban" society, he sought to indicate that these traits *tend* to vary together, e.g., as isolation increases so does homogeneity. But it is clearly an empirical question whether or not and to what extent this tendency occurs in fact; and explanatory hypotheses concerning social and psychological processes are needed to explain this covariation or its absence.[15]

Finally, there is the difficulty that many of these paired concepts have not been fully analyzed. Instead, social theorists have frequently produced new paired concepts which in part overlap with, and in part differ from, analogous formulations of the past. The most familiar example is the similarity of Sir Henry Maine's distinction between societies of status and societies of contract to Durkheim's contrast between organic and mechanical solidarity, to Toennies' contrast between Gemeinschaft and Gesellschaft, to MacIver's contrast between culture and civilization, to Redfield's contrast between folk and urban societies, and still others.[16] Admittedly, these broad contrasts have had many drawbacks. But these should not be allowed to obscure their potential utility, for it might well be a good rule of thumb to search for the missing and, perhaps, hidden opposite when a single concept is proposed.[17]

The frequent formulation of paired concepts in sociology may be seen as an intellectual response to the "perspective of dual tendencies" mentioned above. We believe that the empirical foundation of this perspective lies in the fact that concrete human relationships are ambiguous, and that this ambiguity is manifest in social action and its consequences. This is another way of saying that mankind is neither entirely dependent nor entirely free, that social interaction is partly communicative and partly competitive, that *both* the I and the Me participate in every social transaction, and so forth. This insight, however, is often lost somewhere between the point at which concepts are formulated and the point at which testable hypotheses are developed.

Paired Concepts of Interactions

To say, for example, that primary relations are personal and intimate, that they "involve responses to whole persons rather than to segments," that in them "communication . . . is deep and extensive," and that "personal satisfactions are paramount" [18] is to formulate a concept. But to say that "the family" (defined independently of the quality of the relationships among its members) is the classical locus of primary relations is an empirical statement which is only partly true because it neglects such facts as formal arrangements for property settlements in a family, and the hard-headed attitude of families toward the marriages of its members—even though primary relations may remain dominant in the family. Secondary relations, on the other hand, are impersonal and instrumental by definition. Yet, people engaged in such relations tend to impart to them some personal and emotional qualities which contrast with the dominant character of the relationship. Accordingly, these two concepts may be formulated as a universal proposition: all relations between men in society are both intimate and impersonal.[19] Such a proposition has a double utility.[20]

First. It is based on generalized, inductive knowledge and points to a problem with which men in all societies deal, not to the solutions which they find for this problem. It is, therefore, a guide to relevant questions which may be asked of every society.[21] For example, one might expect a highly personalized relationship of two people genuinely in love to be entirely without impersonal elements. But our knowledge of the universality of these impersonal elements would lead us to expect that significant social and personal problems will arise in a primary relationship from which they are absent. Love relationships tend to be fragile unless formal arrangements also provide them with some buttress of impersonality. Similarly, the absence of accepted ritual creates special psychological burdens for the survivor of an exclusively primary relationship. Yet such a relationship also militates against accepting the relevance of impersonal considerations: a happily married couple is likely to regard a detailed legal settlement of their obligations to each other and their respective relatives as a lack of trust and/or an intolerable, i.e., impersonal, consideration of eventual death. Related questions arise when the intrusion of intimacy in secondary relationships is considered. Personal elements in secondary relations have been widely denounced as fraudulent; the term "pseudo-Gemeinschaft" has been coined in reference, for example, to the "folksy" approach of radio advertisers. Yet this critique overlooks the fact that intimacy in impersonal relations is many-sided. Although intimacy is often faked for personal advantage, say in the relation between salesman and customer, an appeal to the implicit obligations of intimacy can also be used as a stopgap against the exploitation of the relationship. Indeed, this use of intimacy for and against the exploitation of an impersonal relation points to a major problem of hierarchical organizations in the United States. Equalitarianism together with the human-relations approach has led to highly personalized work relationships. These tendencies have forfeited the advantages of personal and social distance without which the impersonal criteria of organizational efficiency can be applied only with considerable difficulty. If intimacy in secondary relations is maximized, the social problems and psychological burdens arising from this intrusion may be as great as if it were minimized, though the two conditions will produce very different dilemmas of action. These examples may suffice as illustrations of the way in which the paired concepts may guide us in the formulation of sociological problems.[22]

Second. Universal propositions direct our attention to the fact that the very concepts we use limit our ability to see beyond them. If we know that all relations among men in society are both intimate and impersonal, then we are prompted to examine a predominantly primary relationship for its frequently hidden, secondary attributes, and vice versa. The paired concepts of interactions may be conceived of, therefore, as two ends of a scale so that the relations, say, between some brothers and sisters could be ranked in terms of their relative intimacy and impersonality. But such rankings only enable us to classify the data as a first step toward analysis. For example, the ready contact or great isolation of a community with regard to the world outside can be defined in terms of the number of communications with that world, and communities can be ranked accordingly. Yet, to measure the frequency of communications is clearly not enough. Two communities with exactly the same number of communications may possess very different degrees of contact (or isolation).[23] Hence, an accurate measure of a community's isolation is not meaningful without an analysis of the contacts involved (and vice versa), just as a primary relation cannot be fully understood apart from its impersonal attributes.

The paired concepts of sociological theory, then, must always be considered *together* when one is engaged in developing testable hypotheses because both concepts are necessary for an analysis of those universal tendencies of social action which, while pointing in opposite directions, are at the same time inextricably linked. A classic example of such an analysis is contained in Max Weber's discussion of class and status.

> The term "class" refers to any group of people . . . [who have the same] typical chance for a supply of goods, external living conditions, and personal life experiences, in so far as this chance is determined by the amount and kind of power, or lack of such, to dispose of goods or skills for the sake of income in a given economic order. . . . "Class situation" is, in this sense, ultimately "market situation."
>
> In contrast to the purely economically determined "class situation" we wish to designate as "status-situation" every typical component of the life fate of men that is determined by a specific, positive or negative, social estimation of honor. . . . In content, status honor is normally expressed by the fact that above all else a specific style of life can be expected from all those who wish to belong to the circle. . . . Besides the specific status honor, which always rests upon distance and exclusiveness, we find all sorts of material monopolies. . . .[24]

Weber thought of these two conditions of collective action as antithetical. The market knows of no personal distinctions. For example, transactions on the stock exchange are reduced to a few standardized phrases or hand symbols. The only relevant distinctions among the brokers are factual and impersonal, depending upon their respective credit rating. In principle, economic actions are oriented entirely to "a rationally motivated adjustment of interests."[25] Exactly the reverse is true of the status order, in which men are grouped in terms of their prestige and style of life. To safeguard their status, such men will oppose vigorously any and

all suggestions that economic acquisition and power as such can constitute a valid claim to "status honor." Stratification based on the status
order would be undermined quickly if a wealthy man could claim more
"honor" than those who rest their claim upon family lineage and style
of life. Thus, economic interests militate against the dominance of status
distinctions, especially in periods of rapid economic change, while considerations of status "hinder the strict carrying through of the sheer market principle," especially in periods of relative economic stability.[26] But
these antithetical tendencies of the economic and the social order are
also linked. Actions based on economic interests frequently aim at the
preservation or acquisition of "honor": Weber pointed for example to
the voluntary and exclusive association among English stock brokers
who safeguarded fair dealing on the market by excluding "unreliable"
elements from membership in these associations. And status groups frequently use their social prestige in order to monopolize economic opportunities: thus the east German landowners (*Junkers*) used the privileges
of their aristocratic status in order to maximize their economic interests
as landowners. In order to understand both the linkages and the antith-
eses between these two orders it was necessary, according to Weber, to
define each unambiguously, i.e., *as if* they were mutually exclusive and
as if each was governed by a principle of internal consistency.[27]

Paired Concepts of Institutions

The preceding discussion of paired concepts has been concerned
with the categories appropriate for the analysis of some universal patterns of interaction (e.g., primary or secondary relationships, and mar-
ket-oriented or status-oriented collective actions). Many sociological
concepts are not concepts of action, however, but of more or less permanent institutions or institutional complexes like bureaucracy, types of
urban society, specific status groups and social movements, etc. The sociologist can only observe actions, but he is bound to develop many of his
concepts in terms of the social conditions and institutional complexes
underlying the actions he observes and in terms of the enduring results
which these actions help to produce and sustain. He makes the assumption that these conditions and results exist only in so far as individuals
can be observed to embody them in their actions. This assumption provides a useful roadblock against reification. But such a methodological
caution has not prevented sociologists from developing concepts of collectivities and institutions even though their use is exposed to the danger
of reification.[28] We believe that the above interpretation of paired concepts can be applied to this level of analysis as well.

A case in point is Max Weber's analysis of bureaucracy. The elements of Weber's definition are generally familiar and are repeated here in abbreviated form. A bureaucracy *tends* to be characterized by:

a) Defined rights and duties, which are prescribed in written regulations;

b) Authority relations between positions which are ordered systematically;

c) Appointment and promotion which are regulated and are based on contractual agreement;

d) Technical training or equivalent experience as a formal condition of employment;

e) Fixed monetary salaries;

f) A strict separation of office and incumbent in the sense that the employee does not own the "means of administration" and cannot appropriate the position;

g) Administrative work as a full-time occupation.[29]

These characteristics stand for conditions of employment which have been more or less successfully instituted in modern economic enterprises and governmental agencies in the course of recent developments of Western civilization. To understand the concept "bureaucracy" fully, it is necessary, therefore, to contrast these characteristics with the corresponding aspects of an administrative staff under traditional authority.

a) In place of a well-defined impersonal sphere of competence, there is a shifting series of tasks and powers commissioned and granted by a chief through his arbitrary decision of the moment.

b) The question who shall decide a matter—which of his officials or the chief himself— . . . is treated . . . [either] traditionally, on the basis of the authority of particular received legal norms or precedents, [or] entirely on the basis of the arbitrary decision of the chief.

c) As opposed to the bureaucratic system of free appointment, household officials and favourites are very often recruited on a purely patrimonial basis from among the slaves or serfs of the chief. If the recruitment has been extra-patrimonial, they have tended to be holders of benefices which he has granted as an act of grace without being bound by any formal rules.

d) Rational technical training as a basic qualification for office is scarcely to be found at all among household officials or the favourites of the chief.

e) In place of regular salaries, household officials and favourites are usually supported and equipped in the household of the chief and from his personal stores. Generally, their exclusion from the lord's own table means the creation of benefices. . . . It is easy for these to become traditionally stereotyped in amount and kind.[30]

This conceptualization of the administrative staff under bureaucratic and traditional authority refers to the external coercions and enduring results which are embodied in historically evolved institutional complexes. These concepts also refer to linked and opposite tendencies of action of which one or the other will be more or less dominant *under given historical conditions.*

The last phrase suggests a level of abstraction which differs from that considered so far. A concept such as "primary relations" refers to a universal tendency of action. But if we say that the rights and duties of an administrative staff are defined in accordance with written regulations rather than with a chief's arbitrary decisions of the moment, then we have the first part of a contrast-conception based on historical experience.[31] Similar contrasts can be observed under the other conditions enumerated above. Two caveats must be remembered, however. The conditions of bureaucratic or of traditional authority *need not actually occur together.* For example, the rights and duties of an administrative staff may be clearly defined in written regulations, while appointments and promotions are handled with personal arbitrariness, just as a chief might be arbitrary in assigning different tasks but highly rational and legalistic in his delegation of authority. Also, each of these institutional complexes is *relatively unstable.* For example, the written regulation of rights and duties may permit a great deal of alteration by personal influence, though the intent is to preclude such influence, while a chief's arbitrary assignment of tasks and of authority may permit the growth of independent power on the part of his officials and thus limit his arbitrariness, even though the intent is to preclude such a development. Yet despite this instability there is a secular tendency favoring the coincidence of the several conditions of bureaucratic and of traditional authority.

This statement of a historical tendency refers to the enduring results of collective actions and to the external coercions which are the partial causes and consequences of these actions. Hence, the statement is not primarily an "as if" proposition in the sense of the definitions cited earlier, as for example that the market knows no personal distinctions *if* the impersonal relations dictated entirely by economic considerations were allowed to work themselves out to their logical conclusion. The stipulation of rights and duties in accordance with written regulations or training and experience as formal conditions of employment are not definitions in that sense but descriptive statements. And the statement that these characteristics tend to develop together is likewise descriptive. (Indeed, these and related institutional arrangements are so widely accepted today that even the distribution of patronage positions by politicians involves some show of adherence to these characteristics of a bureaucracy.) Yet, the definitions of administrative staffs under legal, bureaucratic authority and under traditional authority also differ from mere descriptions in that they extrapolate the observed characteristics on the assumption that the actors themselves are completely consistent and successful. To say that the market knows no personal distinctions, *if* . . . involves logical considerations by the scholar. To say that bureaucracy is defined (in part) by training and experience as a condition of employment has reference to the more or less successful endeavor of the advocates of civil service reform. That is, the first conceptualizes actions in terms of the logical principles underlying them; the second conceptualizes actions in terms of the actual and the desired effects of social groups in the struggle for power.[32]

These examples suggest that concepts of institutional complexes also occur in "pairs" in the sense that they refer to manifold tendencies of action which are linked and opposite. It is necessary, therefore, to keep *both* concepts in mind for the purposes of any specific analysis, even though one *or* the other is primarily applicable to the given case. We saw, for example, that fixed monetary salaries of bureaucratic officials were contrasted with the dependence of traditional officials upon the household and/or the benefices of a chief. Although salary scales are readily fixed and administered, fringe benefits, promotion, and job classification are frequently subject to bargaining and personal influence. Conceivably, such bargaining and influence might go so far that they make a mere fiction out of the basic salary scale. Whether or not this will be the case depends in the first instance upon the conflicting efforts of those who seek to administer the scale and of those who use bargaining and influence to maximize their own advantages. If the latter were completely successful, they might re-establish a condition of traditional authority by making their remuneration primarily dependent upon the arbitrary decision of a chief. If the former were successful all the way, they would codify fringe benefits, promotions, and job classifications minutely so as to minimize the possibilities of bargaining and personal influence, and hence of arbitrary decisions. The same applies to the other contrasting characteristics of administrative staffs. Each of the concepts represents, therefore, an institutional pattern which has resulted from the successful activities of certain social groups under given historical conditions. And the relevant universal proposition tells us that such success is never complete or permanent and that it is necessary for the analyst to consider the actual and potential forces which tend to circumscribe that success and which under favorable conditions may impose contrasting conditions of their own.[33]

IV. CULTURE, SOCIETY, AND GROUP CONFLICT

The conditions of human existence are reflected in the fact that universal tendencies of action are linked and opposite at the same time. The problems of meaning posed by this fact lie in the province of the philosophers and theologians. However, the sociologist also becomes concerned with these problems when he considers the implications of paired concepts for an understanding of the culture and structure of whole societies. Contemporary social science tends to use the word "culture" to refer to the way of life of a people: their artifacts and their patterns of conduct, as well as their ideas and ideals. This use of the term tends to emphasize, as we noted earlier, that individuals in a culture "fit in" with that way of life, as a matter both of choice and of compulsion. And the term "subculture" has been used to conceptualize the fact that every known culture is internally differentiated. While this terminology emphasizes an important aspect of society, it also has peculiar disadvantages.[34] Each culture is made to appear as a whole which possesses different parts (subcultures) as well as an over-all unity (the way of life), but in which the actions of individuals and of groups are limited to pre-established patterns and tend to re-enforce the culture of which they are a part. If formal institutions like an administrative staff may be conceptualized as the "arena" of contending groups, then it may also be useful to look upon the culture of a society in a similar way.

In lieu of the word "culture" Max Weber used the term "ethos," partly because the German equivalent "Kultur" had ethical connotations which he sought to avoid, and partly also because he felt that terms like "culture" tended to be question begging.[35] The reasons for this choice of terms are of interest here. By using "ethos" as a general designation of different ways of life, Weber wanted to emphasize that each man's participation in his society involved a personal commitment to the behavior patterns, the ideas, and the interests of a particular status group. By virtue of their styles of life, such groups

are the specific bearers of all "conventions." In whatever way it may be manifest, all "stylization" of life either originates in status groups or is at least conserved by them.[36]

Such styles of life may become characteristics of a whole society. Thus, Weber was much concerned with the fact that the domineering and patriarchal manner of the *Junkers* had influenced many aspects of German society. Again, certain ideas of ascetic Protestantism had gained widespread influence in modern capitalism; they "prowl about in our lives like the ghost of dead religious beliefs." [37] Weber, in fact, summarized one aspect of his studies in the sociology of religion by designating the status group which was in each case the principal exponent of a world religion.[38] To be sure, religious beliefs as well as other ideas and behavior patterns frequently exert a far-reaching influence beyond the status group to which they are originally or primarily related. But by relating a given idea and its corresponding style of life to a particular group from which these had spread, Weber construed the culture of a nation as an outgrowth of group power and group conflict in their historical development. Accordingly, the analysis of historical legacies is an essential part of the interpretation of culture, because the group relations and styles of life which prevail in modern society can be understood only as more or less temporary end products of past conflicts among the ideas and behavior patterns of status groups.[39]

This formulation has the advantage of relating the concept "culture" to the phenomenon of power in society. If the "social roles" of individuals provide opportunities for action as well as limit the available alternatives, it follows that in many societies the individual is able to engage in more or less continual attempts to redefine his roles. We may think of culture as a way of life which is characterized by a more or less enduring pattern of interaction among dominant and subordinate status groups, each with a vested interest in the material and ideal aspects of its style of life. Hence, culture may be related to society and power by an analysis of the groups which struggle with, and against, other groups in their attempts to reformulate and institutionalize role definitions in their own interest. For example, the Negro in the United States occupies the status of a lower caste, and acts accordingly; or the government administrator occupies a well-defined position concerned with the execution of legislative policy. But the characterization of "status and role" in these terms obscures certain very relevant facts. Important Negro spokesmen in the United States today, for example, are using the nationalistic movements of colored peoples everywhere as a weapon in their own struggle for improving the "Negro's share" at home; they say, in effect: "If you want less trouble abroad, you must improve our position at home." Or the government administrator who asks his "clientele" for their wishes with regard to services from his agency may run head-on into an irate congressman who claims that it is *his,* and not the administrator's, job "to know what the public wants." These illustrations suggest that it is misleading to characterize the "status and role" of an individual or group in static terms because each is engaged in some strategy of argument and action designed to define their respective roles in a manner that appears advantageous to themselves.

It is necessary to combine this emphasis upon the more or less continual struggle **among** status groups and their partially **conflicting** styles of life with propositions that are true of an entire social structure. One way of doing so is suggested by the empirical observation that at any one time, and frequently for prolonged periods, a particular status group and its style of life are dominant in a society. Yet at best, this is only a partial answer. Any given pattern of interaction among dominant and subordinate groups is so unstable that it is still necessary to consider the changing particulars of that interaction in relation to the more enduring characteristics of the society as a whole. Max Weber's answer to this question was his familiar assertion that it was necessary to simplify and exaggerate selected historical facts. In his earliest statement of this view, he maintained that such exaggerations were justified, if the facts selected for this purpose were indeed typical.[40] But to ascertain what was typical depended in his view upon a wide-ranging use of the comparative method. A model illustration of such an analysis is contained in the work of Alexis de Tocqueville, and it is instructive for our purposes to examine how he accomplished his results.

In the first volume of his *Democracy in America* Tocqueville had dealt with the institutions of a democratic society, principally in a descriptive manner. But in the second volume he had used

the ideas derived from American and French democracy only as data, . . . [in order] to paint the general features of democratic societies, no complete specimen of which can yet be said to exist. This is what an ordinary reader fails to appreciate. Only those who are much accustomed to searching for abstract and speculative truths, care to follow me in such an inquiry.[41]

To know how men will act tomorrow and how they will deal with coming events, one must be in a position to see continually what they are doing and what they are thinking. But to judge what the men of a society are prepared to become one must take a bird's-eye view of affairs in order to understand the "sentiments, principles, and opinions, the moral and intellectual qualities" which are given by nature and by an education that has lasted for centuries.[42]

In his second volume on America, Tocqueville was concerned with this truth for the long run. He had set himself the task of reconciling the republican champions and the aristocratic opponents of democracy. The progressive development of democracy appeared to him inevitable. And though he favored it, he endeavored to show that it was not a brilliant and easily realized ideal, that such a government was not viable "without certain conditions of intelligence, of private morality, and of religious belief." [43] As a nation, France had not yet attained these conditions. Indeed, she provided Tocqueville with the image of a society in which the democratic revolution had gone astray, uncertainty alternating between despotism and anarchy with no signs at all as to when and how a stable social order might again be established. If he had children he would advise them to be prepared for everything and to rely on nothing that might be taken away.[44] And yet he wrote:

> You suppose my view of the prospects of democracy to be more gloomy than it is. . . . I have endeavored, it is true, to describe the natural tendency of opinions and institutions in a democratic society. I have pointed out the dangers to which it exposes men. But I have never said that these tendencies, if discovered in time, might not be resisted, and these dangers, if foreseen, averted. It struck me that the republicans saw neither the good nor the evil of the condition into which they wished to bring society. . . . I therefore undertook to bring out both as clearly and as strongly as I could, that we may look our enemies in the face and know against what we have to fight.[45]

Thus, the classic insights into the structure of American society arose for Tocqueville from an analysis of the dangers to a democratic society which had become manifest in France, but which were so far held in check in the United States.

> In my work on America . . . though I seldom mentioned France, I did not write a page without thinking of her, and placing her as it were before me. And what I specifically tried to draw out, and to explain in the United States, was not the whole condition of that foreign society, but the points in which it differs from our own, or resembles us. It is always by noticing likenesses or contrasts that I succeeded in giving an interesting and accurate description of the New World. . . . I believe that this perpetual silent reference to France was a principal cause of the book's success.[46]

Tocqueville's remarkable insight into the despotic possibilities inherent in even the most successful democratic society arose from this implicit extrapolation of American conditions in the light of how analogous conditions had developed in the course of 19th century French history. And French society in turn only provided him with a picture of the "sentiments, principles, and opinions, the moral and intellectual qualities," which might lead to a "species of oppression unlike anything that ever before existed in the world." [47]

Tocqueville's analysis of American society does not, then, contain statements about its "whole condition," but rather *comparisons* with analogous conditions in another society. And beyond that it contains "speculative truths" concerning future developments which *may* materialize if present tendencies are allowed to work themselves out to their logical conclusion. For Tocqueville this latter assumption was useful only as an analytical tool so that society can act "like a strong man who knows that [the] danger before him . . . must be met, and is alarmed only when he cannot see clearly what it is." [48] Yet, such knowledge of the dangers that threaten can never be more than a knowledge of the limits and possibilities of development.

I own, that this old world, beyond which we neither of us can see, appears to me to be almost worn out; the vast and venerable machine seems more out of gear every day; and though I cannot look forward, my faith in the continuance of the present is shaken. I learn from history that not one of the men who witnessed the downfall of the religious and social organizations that have passed away was able to guess or even to imagine what would ensue. Yet this did not prevent Christianity from succeeding to idolatry; servitude to slavery; the barbarians from taking the place of Roman civilization, and feudalism in turn ejecting the barbarians. Each of these changes occurred without having been anticipated by any of the writers in the times immediately preceding these total revolutions. Who, then, can affirm that any one social system is essential and that another is impossible? [49]

It is apparent that this was a reasoned conviction which held the balance between overconfidence and despair. Tocqueville did not think it possible to predict the future of society because in his view it depended upon men and nations whether their drift toward equality would lead to servitude or freedom. Yet, he also believed that the possible directions of social change were limited in number and that it was feasible to foresee them by means of "speculative truths" which extrapolated observed tendencies on the fictitious assumption that nothing would interfere with their ultimate realization. In our judgment, this approach fits in well with a view of culture and social structure which regards both as more or less enduring end products of past group conflicts.

V. SOME IMPLICATIONS

The paired concepts discussed above appear to reflect the dichotomies characteristic of much sociological theorizing in the past. These dichotomies may be regarded as a methodological safeguard against the bias inherent in every conceptualization. Twenty years ago Kenneth Burke called attention to this aspect with his phrase "perspective by incongruity."

Any performance is discussible either from the standpoint of what it *attains* or what it *misses*. Comprehensiveness can be discussed as superficiality, intensiveness as stricture, tolerance as uncertainty—and the poor *pedestrian* abilities of the fish are clearly explainable in terms of his excellence as a *swimmer*. A way of seeing is also a way of not seeing. . . .[50]

The paired concepts of sociological theory may, thus, be regarded as a methodological or linguistic device.

But these paired concepts also have theoretical implications, because they are especially well adapted to the reciprocity characteristic of social life. If it be true that social isolation, strictly speaking, does not exist, that every action in society evokes or provokes reactions, that every action must have, therefore, manifold consequences, intended and un-intended, valued and devalued, then it follows that sociological inquiry should search each social fact for what it hides as much as for what it reveals. This consideration has special relevance for all attempts to analyze the "function" or "dysfunction" of given social facts, i.e., their objective consequences which contribute to the successful adaptation or to the impairment of a society. The difficulties here are considerable. For example, frequent industrial strikes prevent maximum production. This statement of cause and effect is unsatisfactory, for the objective of socio-logical analysis is to arrive at generalizations. This objective would be achieved if it were possible to demonstrate a determinate relationship between given levels of strike activity and the degree of co-operation necessary for the successful adaptation of enterprises or of the society at large. To do that we would need a value-free criterion of "successful adaptation," which, since such a criterion is not available to the social scientist, is simply another term for the ideal of "social health." In its absence, he is frequently tempted to achieve the desired level of gen-eralization by categoric statements, e.g., frequent industrial strikes im-pair the level of co-operation or cohesion required for the adaptation of enterprises or of the society.[51] Yet the facts are that strikes may interfere with maximum production only in the short run. In the long run, they may help to accelerate capital investment and to increase over-all pro-ductivity. While these actions may be designed to forestall the hazard of strikes, their ultimate effect may be to increase co-operation as well as productivity. Apparently, societies have inherent sources of conflict and strain (e.g., political parties, civil rights, interest groups, etc.) *which help to maintain the social structure,* which are indeed an important element of its "successful adaptation." And if it be accepted that generally soci-eties are characterized by co-operation and conflict, conformity and devi-ance, socialization and individualization, etc., it appears probable that *every* social fact (minority status, crime, strikes, etc.) has some conse-quences *both* for the continued adaptation and for the impairment of the social structure.

The burden of this discussion is to suggest that we cannot specify the limits of what is possible in a society, even though such limits probably exist. We know that the actions of individuals in society fall within a range of tolerance, but we cannot identify the limits of this range because they are in a continual process of redefinition. The dilemma posed by this fact is best resolved, in our view, if we do not search for the attri-butes of society as a "system," such as a minimum of consensus or of satisfaction. In every society, efforts are repeatedly made to define the limits beyond which no member is permitted to go; yet individuals often fail to comply with what is expected of them. It is necessary that sociological theory comprehend both tendencies. And to do that attention must be focused on the boundary-extending as well as upon the boundary-maintaining activities of individuals, on the permissive aspects of culture and society which enable individuals *to experiment with what is possible* as well as upon the social controls which limit the range of tolerated behavior without defining that range clearly.[52]

The orientation to social theory presented in this paper is also based on an attitude toward the role of knowledge in society.[53] All social scientists desire to see the advance of their discipline and hope for the rational solution of pressing social problems. But it seems to us wise to adopt an attitude of hope *and* uncertainty concerning the constructive potentialities of knowledge. We do not know enough to be sure of what cannot be known, but we do not accept the tenet that man must only know enough in order to control society. It may be better to be more temperate than the pessimists who think sociology as a science impossible *and* the optimists who think that it is a science already.

The approach presented here is obviously tentative, requires considerable elaboration, and does not stand or fall on superseding all other approaches. We candidly regard it as experimental and would like to have it read in the same spirit. As stated at the beginning, it is related to an intellectual tradition which views men and society in terms of tendencies or forces which are linked and opposite at the same time. This tradition has special relevance for contemporary sociological theory. For in the wake of the conflict between conservatism and liberalism in the nineteenth century, sociological theories have generally sided with the former by emphasizing the integration of the individual with the group, while the nonintegrative aspects of the individual were relegated to the unexplained residues of "deviation" and creative effort. The approach presented in this paper may help to emancipate sociological theory from the limitations of this intellectual heritage. But the import of these concluding remarks is not to label given theories or thinkers as conservative, liberal, or anything else. It is to make plain, rather, that the definition of the "social fact" embodies each theorist's image of society and that this image is the source of each theory's utility and unique blindness.

NOTES

1. "To confine ourselves to the large social formations resembles the older science of anatomy with its limitation to the major, definitely circumscribed organs such as heart, liver, lungs, and stomach, and with its neglect of the innumerable, popularly unnamed or unknown tissues. Yet without these, the more obvious organs could never constitute a living organism. On the basis of the major social formations—the traditional subject of social

science—it would be similarly impossible to piece together the real life of society as we encounter it in our experience." K. Wolff, ed., *The Sociology of Georg Simmel* (Glencoe, Ill.: Free Press, 1950), p. 9. See also pp. 10-13 and 187-88.

2. By the phrase "sense of the 'real' " we refer not to formally stipulated assumptions but to the intuitive feeling for what is significant in society and basic for a scientific theory of society. The multiplicity of social theories is in part attributable to this psychological involvement of the social theorists. Yet, the assessment of theories should be independent of this consideration, for the criteria by which a theorist defines "the social fact" must be abstract themselves as well as explicit, so that they may be judged by others. This theoretical level must be maintained, else theorists would merely argue about why they make statements, rather than about what they say. Nonetheless, it is important to recognize this psychological precondition of our theorizing about society, because this recognition helps us to explain, and also to take into account, the peculiar perspectivism of social theories. However, the more developed a science is, the less important these considerations are likely to become.

3. It is partly for this reason that there is no "sociological theory" but only "sociological *theories*"; sociologists tend to choose their theoretical equipment in accord with how well it suits the kind of substantive problems which interest them, and these, in turn, are intimately connected with their "sense of the real." This tendency creates "schools of thought," whose controversies are usually due to the attempt to impose a theoretical perspective, developed on the basis of certain substantive interests, on *all* substantive interests. It is partly for this reason too, perhaps, that so much criticism of sociological theories has an undertone of emotionalism.

4. See Talcott Parsons, *The Social System* (Glencoe, Ill.: Free Press, 1951), vii, 3: "The title, *The Social System,* goes back, more than to any other source, to the insistence of the late Professor L. J. Henderson on the extreme importance of the concept of system in scientific theory. . . .

"The fundamental starting point is the concept of social systems of action. The *inter*action of individual actors, that is, takes place under such conditions that it is possible to treat such a process of interaction as a system in the scientific sense and subject it to the same order of theoretical analysis which has been successfully applied to other types of systems in other sciences."

5. Cf. the related discussion of the "principle of polarity" in Morris Cohen, *Reason and Nature* (Glencoe, Ill.: Free Press, 1953), *passim*.

6. Alexis de Tocqueville, *Democracy in America* (New York: Vintage Books, 1945), II, 352.

7. Georg Simmel, *Conflict and the Web of Group Affiliations* (Glencoe, Ill.: Free Press, 1955), pp. 140-41.

8. Robert E. Park, *Race and Culture* (Glencoe, Ill.: Free Press, 1950), p. 42. See also Robert E. Park, *Human Communities* (Glencoe, Ill.: Free Press, 1952), pp. 258-59 and *passim*.

9. Max Weber, *The Theory of Social and Economic Organization* (New York: Oxford University Press, 1947), p. 88.

10. Max Weber, "Kritische Bemerkungen zu den vorstehenden 'Kritischen Beiträgen," *Archiv für Sozialwissenschaft,* XXV (1907), p. 248.

11. Max Weber, *Wirtschaft und Gesellschaft* (Tübingen: J. C. B. Mohr, 1925), II, pp. 562 ff.

12. The term "role" was originally derived from this reference to the "roll" in the hands of the actor. Cf. David Bidney, *Theoretical Anthropology* (New York: Columbia University Press, 1953), for an illuminating exception to the foregoing characterization.

13. Ralph Linton, *The Cultural Background of Personality* (New York: D. Appleton-Century Co., 1945), pp. 19, 22, and *passim.* Our italics.

14. This is the formulation of the late Louis Wirth.

15. Within this conceptual framework it is quite feasible to handle the fact that a relatively isolated community is found which is individualistic, lacking in solidarity and secularized, for such a finding does not disprove the utility of the variables which are subsumed under the concept "folk-society." Cf. the questionable criticism of Redfield in Oscar Lewis, *Life in a Mexican Village* (Urbana: University of Illinois Press, 1951), pp. 427-40. Much the same criticism has been leveled at Weber's concept of "bureaucracy," because administrators were found to engage in actions which are out of keeping with the formally stipulated conditions of their work. Cf. Alvin Gouldner, "On Weber's Analysis of Bureaucratic Rules," in R. K. Merton, *et al.,* eds., *Reader in Bureaucracy* (Glencoe, Ill.: Free Press, 1952), pp. 48-51 and Peter Blau, *Bureaucracy in Modern Society* (New York: Random House, 1956), pp. 35-36. The trouble with these critiques is that they do not distinguish between concept formation and the formulation and testing of hypotheses. In cases where such critiques are justified, it would be necessary to replace the discarded with a new concept, which is more serviceable. As it is, a concept is sometimes criticized and then used anyway.

16. As Redfield has shown in his *Folkculture of Yucatan,* these comprehensive terms are in fact composites of many paired concepts. To subsume a number of these (like isolation, homogeneity, predominance of the sacred) under one ideal type like "folk society" may suggest a closer degree of association than is useful. But not to do that also raises problems, for a concept like "competition" has many usable opposites like "communication," "cooperation," "solidarity," and others, which are in fact interrelated. There is need for a further refinement of such paired concepts, and the choice among them depends, of course, upon the purpose of inquiry, for which one set of terms will be more useful than another.

17. An example may make this clearer. Recently, Robert Bierstedt noted that Weber's concepts of traditional and rational authority differ from his concept of charisma in the sense that the latter refers to leadership, not to authority. Implicitly, Weber appears to have acknowledged this point since he referred to charismatic leaders under conditions of traditional and of rational authority. But then the question may be asked what concept we should use for leadership which is noncharismatic, an eventuality for which Weber employed the phrase "routinization of charisma" though he did not explicitly formulate this idea as a contrast-conception. Cf. Robert Bierstedt, "The Problem of Authority," in Morroe Berger, Theodore Abel, and Charles

Page, eds., *Freedom and Control in Modern Society* (New York: Van Nostrand Co., Inc., 1954), pp. 67-81. It may be added that the absence of an opposite term is often due to the linguistic difficulty of finding an equally appropriate word for both concepts. "Routinization of charisma" is not as neat as "charisma."

18. Leonard Broom and Philip Selznick, *Sociology* (Evanston, Ill.: Row, Peterson and Company, 1958), pp. 124-26.

19. This formulation is identical with Redfield's statement: "In every primitive band or tribe there is civilization, in every city there is the folk-society." See Robert Redfield, "The Natural History of a Folk Society," *Social Forces,* XXXI (March, 1953), p. 225.

20. In addition, such universal propositions can also reveal the limitations of sociological analysis. That is, their claim to universality can be refuted, when instances are found in which, for example, no impersonal qualities enter into a primary relationship.

21. Functionalists would say here that societies must find some balance between intimacy and impersonality in human relationships, if man's basic needs are to be satisfied sufficiently for societies to survive. This formulation attributes the results of men's problem-solving activities to "the society" which is said to have properties of its own that are in some sense independent of these activities. And one of these properties is thought to consist of some given, but unknown degree of satisfaction which is indispensable for the survival of society. Thus, functional propositions will refer given attributes to "society," while propositions using paired concepts would refer such attributes to social actions with their anticipated and unanticipated consequences. Cf. also the discussion in section V. of this essay.

22. Cf. the related comments on the "dialectic of opposites" in Robert Redfield, *The Little Community* (Chicago: University of Chicago Press, 1955), Chapter IX.

23. Karl Deutsch has suggested such a measure in his calculation of "input-output" ratios of foreign mail, showing among other things that in 1928–38 Germany and the United Kingdom had a similar excess of foreign mail sent out over foreign mail received (0.65 for Germany and 0.70 for the U.K.). But the U.K. was the center of an Empire with no restrictions on international communications, while for half this period Germany was a dictatorship whose censorship isolated the country culturally and politically, even if the volume of foreign mail remained unaffected. Cf. Karl Deutsch, "Shifts in the Balance of Communication Flows," *Public Opinion Quarterly,* XX (1956), pp. 147-48. Some logical techniques for handling the problems of typology which are involved here are discussed in Paul F. Lazarsfeld and Allen H. Barton, "Qualitative Measurement in the Social Sciences: Classification, Typologies, and Indices," in Daniel Lerner, ed., *The Policy Sciences* (Stanford: Stanford University Press, 1951), pp. 155-92.

24. Max Weber, "Class, Status, Party," in H. H. Gerth and C. Wright Mills, eds., *From Max Weber: Essays in Sociology* (New York: Oxford University Press, 1946), pp. 181, 182, 186-87, 190-91.

25. *Ibid.,* p. 183.

26. *Ibid.,* pp. 185, 193-94.

27. In this connection, Parsons and Shils have stated that goal-directed actions must be analyzed by establishing "primacies among types of interests" so that "the . . . ambiguities intrinsic to the world of social objects" can be resolved. The authors accomplish this resolution of ambiguities by stipulating that the actions of the individual must be examined and classified when he makes his choice, on the knife-edge of the present as it were. The discussion of pattern-variables appears to be based on the assumption that all choices are dichotomous *in fact* if analyzed minutely enough, whereas for Weber the internal consistency of any action was a *logical* construction. See Talcott Parsons, E. A. Shils, *et al., Towards a General Theory of Action* (Cambridge: Harvard University Press, 1951), p. 91. Our view is that choices are provisional and interests ambivalent. Accordingly, Weber's "as if" construction appears to us less rationalistic than the assumption made by Parsons and Shils.

28. Swanson has pointed out that Parsons and Shils have failed to derive the classic concepts of collectivities from the "action frame of reference" which they have developed. See Guy E. Swanson, "The Approach to a General Theory of Action by Parsons and Shils," *American Sociological Review,* XVIII (1953), pp. 132-33.

29. Gerth and Mills, *op. cit.,* pp. 196-98.

30. Max Weber, *The Theory of Social and Economic Organization* (New York: Oxford University Press, 1947), pp. 343, 344, 345. In this passage, Weber did not explicitly contrast the last two conditions of employment. It may be added, however, that under traditional authority the chief's arbitrary decisions frequently identify an office with the household official or favorite who occupies it; and the holders of benefices frequently attempt and succeed in appropriating the position. The term "full-time occupation" is not applicable to an administrative staff under traditional authority, either. Cf. also Max Weber, *Religion of China* (Glencoe, Ill.: Free Press, 1951), pp. 33-104, for an analysis of patrimonial government which shows close approximations to this concept of traditional authority.

31. To define "primary relations," one assumes that complete intimacy prevails and all impersonal considerations are excluded. It would be possible to construct a model on this basis similar to that developed in economic theory, although the preceding emphasis on "paired concepts" suggests a reason why this has not been done in sociological theory. To define an administrative staff in terms of written regulations, on the other hand, is a statement of historical fact; either there are written regulations or there are not. An assumption or "as if" construction enters in only when these regulations are said to preclude arbitrary decisions. For a discussion of Weber's concept of "bureaucracy" in modern society, which parallels the above contrast between administration under rational and traditional authority, cf. Reinhard Bendix, *Work and Authority in Industry* (New York: John Wiley & Sons, Inc., 1956), pp. 244-51.

This discussion deliberately avoids the term "ideal type" because of the many meanings which are associated with it. The distinction between theoretical models and historical types in Weber's treatment of this problem was analyzed in Alexander von Schelting, "Die logische Theorie der historischen Kulturwissenschaft von Max Weber und insbesondere sein Begriff des Idealtypus," *Archiv für Sozialwissenschaft,* XLIX (1922), pp. 726-31.

32. The contrast is not absolute, therefore. Both theoretical models and historical types involve the extrapolation of given tendencies of action.

33. This perspective may be considered a corollary of Georg Simmel's emphasis upon the reciprocity of all social relations. But attention is focused here on collective actions and institutions rather than upon the interactions of individuals.

34. Cf. Robert Bierstedt, "The Limitations of Anthropological Methods in Sociology," *American Journal of Sociology*, LIV (July, 1948), pp. 22-30.

35. Cf. the remark that "the appeal to national character is generally a mere confession of ignorance" in Max Weber, *The Protestant Ethic and the Spirit of Capitalism* (New York: Charles Scribner's Sons, 1930), p. 88.

36. *From Max Weber . . .* , p. 191.

37. *Protestant Ethic*, p. 182.

38. Thus, Confucianism is the work of the world-ordering bureaucrat, Hinduism of the world-ordering magician, Buddhism of wandering mendicant monks, Islam of world-conquering warriors, Judaism of itinerant traders, Christianity of itinerant craftsmen. See Max Weber, *Wirtschaft und Gesellschaft* (Tübingen: J. C. B. Mohr, 1925), I, p. 293 and the detailed discussion of this theme on pp. 267-96. A brief summary is also contained in *From Max Weber . . .* , pp. 268-269.

39. See E. R. Leach, *Political Systems of Highland Burma* (Cambridge: Cambridge University Press, 1954) for an anthropological field study which illustrates the usefulness of this perspective. Professor Leach's theoretical position is quite similar to the one discussed in this paper (cf. pp. 1-17 of his work).

40. See Max Weber, "Die ländliche Arbeitsverfassung," *Gesammelte Aufsätze zur Sozial- und Wirtschaftsgeschichte* (Tübingen: J. C. B. Mohr, 1924), p. 446.

41. Letter to J. St. Mill of Dec. 18, 1840, in *Memoirs, Letters and Remains of Alexis de Tocqueville* (Boston: Ticknor & Fields, 1862), II, p. 68.

42. Cf. *ibid.*, II, pp. 230-31, 237, 272.

43. Letter to Stoffels, dated February 21, 1835, in *ibid.*, I, p. 376.

44. Letter to Stoffels, dated July 21, 1848, in *ibid.*, I, p. 400.

45. Letter to M. de Corcelle, dated April 12, 1835, in *ibid.*, II, pp. 13-14.

46. Letter to Louis de Kergorlay of October 19, 1843, in *ibid.*, I, p. 342.

47. Alexis de Tocqueville, *Democracy in America* (New York: Vintage Books, 1954), II, 336.

48. Letter to M. de Corcelle, April 12, 1835, in *ibid.*, II, 14.

49. Letter to Mrs. Grote, July 24, 1850, in *ibid.*, II, 104-5.

50. Kenneth Burke, *Permanence and Change* (New York: New Republic, 1936), p. 70.

51. Every social theorist recognizes the deficiencies of this procedure. The practice persists, nevertheless, presumably because sociologists are not satisfied with the unscientific character of political judgments. Yet, in the

absence of agreed-on criteria of "social health" it remains a political judgment whether or not a given number of strikes impairs the desired cooperation or cohesion in society. As Merton has stated, "Embedded in every functional analysis is some conception, tacit or expressed, of functional requirements of the system under observation. . . . This remains one of the cloudiest, and empirically most debatable concepts of functional theory." See R. K. Merton, *Social Theory and Social Structure* (Glencoe, Ill.: Free Press, 1949), p. 52.

52. This experimentation with what is possible can be identified in the boundary-extending activities of individuals, whether these consist of criminal activity and all other forms of deviance or of scientific research and all other forms of creative work. But this identification does not preclude the search for "hidden" results (say, the boundary-extending implications of boundary-maintaining actions, or vice versa), which our paired concepts suggest. Cf. Talcott Parsons, *The Social System* (Glencoe, Ill.: Free Press, 1952), for a different view of "boundary-maintenance" in a social system.

53. Cf. Reinhard Bendix, *Social Science and the Distrust of Reason* (Berkeley: University of California Press, 1951) for a discussion of this point.

III

SOCIAL ORDER

4

Nominal and Real Definitions in Sociological Theory

ROBERT BIERSTEDT

The City College of New York

Some years ago, at a session of the American Sociological Society devoted to sociological theory, an argument developed between two eminent practitioners of the discipline. The details of the argument are no longer remembered with precision, but the subject of it was definitions in sociology. One of the protagonists, George A. Lundberg, maintained that it is important and indeed necessary to have clear and carefully articulated definitions of our concepts before we begin our inquiries in order that we may always know what it is that we are talking about. For this purpose he advocated, of course, the adoption of "operational" definitions, an advocacy he supported on the ground that, among other advantages, the meaning of the concept defined would always be closely associated with the procedures employed in investigating the phenomenon in question, metaphysical controversies over "real" essences or meanings would be avoided, and the progress of science in sociology would thereby be enhanced.

The other protagonist, Herbert Blumer, maintained on the contrary that clear and accurate definitions of our concepts can neither be "given" nor "constructed" at the beginning of inquiry, that in scientific procedure it is not always desirable to have exact definitions (because they may put a cloture on research), and that, in any event, a definition emerges properly only as one of the results and consequences of inquiry. Mr. Blumer contended, in short, that definitions increase in accuracy as a result of successive approximations and empirical confirmations, that they become increasingly definite as research and inquiry proceed, and that it is unrealistic therefore to insist that they be clear and precise at the beginning of the process.

The argument, as fallible memory recalls,[1] waxed warm at times. In the absence of an umpire or referee, however, and in the absence too of a court of final appeal, the issue remained unsettled at the conclusion of the meeting.

If we leave Chicago, the scene of the logomachy just described, and turn to Athens in the fourth century B.C., we shall find two ancients arguing, like Blumer and Lundberg, about a similar problem. Their names are Hermogenes and Cratylus and they appear in the Dialogue of Plato that bears the name of Cratylus. At the beginning of the piece, Hermogenes is insisting that words are purely arbitrary and conventional affairs, that they have no necessary or inherent relationship with their referents, and that custom is the sole arbiter of language. Cratylus, on the other hand, has a feeling that words somehow necessarily mean what they say, that the connection between words and their referents is neither haphazard, nor incidental, nor merely conventional, and that, consequently, a study of words can contribute to our knowledge of the nature of things. Unable to come to an agreement, they seek out Socrates and beg him to tell them who has the better part of the argument. Socrates, after an appeal to the names of the Athenian deities and to a series of improbable and over-ingenious etymologies, casts his lot with Cratylus and suggests that words do have more than a chance or incidental connection with the things to which they refer.

Because of the hegemony that words exercise over our intellectual domains it is the fashion today to reject the Socratic solution to this problem and to hold with Hermogenes that words, however necessary, serve merely a utilitarian function in the acquisition of knowledge, that definitions of them, accordingly, are wholly arbitrary and conventional, and that definitions therefore can neither be true nor false. We go further. Because of the errors that arise through a failure to estimate correctly the relationship between words and things, especially errors of hypostasis or reification, we assert that words have little or nothing to do with things and that our refusal always to recognize this constitutes a prime source of confusion in scientific communication. Since the operations employed in defining concepts, like words themselves, can apparently be arbitrarily selected, and since there is no independent criterion for selecting one operation rather than another, it appears that Hermogenes would be on the side of Lundberg, though the issues are not in all respects identical, with Cratylus and Socrates in support of Blumer.

Before we accept the minority view, however, let us stop a moment in the London of 1851, and particularly in Hyde Park, the scene of the Great Exhibition. If we stray into Crystal Palace we may happen to see there Augustus De Morgan, logician, and professor of mathematics at University College. The professor is listening to the playing of an organ by a performer who seems especially anxious to exhibit one of his stops. The rest of the story, in De Morgan's words, goes as follows:

" 'What do you think of that stop?' I was asked.
" 'That depends on the name of it,' said I.
" 'Oh! what can the name have to do with the sound? "That which we call a rose," etc.'
" 'The name has everything to do with it: if it be a flute stop, I think it very harsh; but if it be a railway-whistle stop, I think it very sweet.' " [2]

It is unfortunate that cosmic matters are not so arranged that Lundberg and Blumer, Hermogenes and Cratylus, the organist and Professor De Morgan cannot get together to discuss this problem.

In any event, before we leave the realm of the imagination, however, and turn to the more sober concerns of logic and sociology, we should perhaps look in once, and hastily, on Adam and Eve in the Garden of Eden. The perennial human problems had their origin there, and the first pair did after all have a need to name the things they were the first to be privileged to see. Fortunately, we have Eve's diary, "translated from the original" by a latter day descendant named Mark Twain, and can learn how this initial issue was confronted and solved:

"During the last day or two I have taken all the work of naming things off his [Adam's] hands, and this has been a great relief to him, for he has no gift in that line and is evidently very grateful. He can't think of a rational name to save him, but I do not let him see that I am aware of his defect. Whenever a new creature comes along I name it before he has time to expose himself by an awkward silence. In this way I have saved him many embarrassments. I have no defect like his. The minute I set eyes on an animal I know what it is. I don't have to reflect a moment; the right name comes out instantly, just as if it were an inspiration, as no doubt it is, for I am sure it wasn't in me half a minute before. I seem to know just by the shape of the creature and the way it acts what animal it is." [3]

Now so long as Eve is only gaily inventing names and applying them to the new animals, we have no logical problem with her. When she remarks, however, that the name that pops out instantly is the "right" name and that she knows by the shape of the creature—and how it acts —what it is, then we are again plagued by our little puzzle.

Fortunately, there is a solution to the puzzle that all of these stories pose, a solution that has rigor, elegance, and power—a solution, furthermore, that is taught in an introductory course in traditional logic. The general issue, moreover, is one that has ramifications in contemporary sociology, and particularly in that part of sociology known as "theory."

It concerns what we shall call the vectors of inquiry. Before we examine the solution, however, let us attend to a situation in contemporary sociological theory.

A common and indeed facile observation in our field today concerns what everyone assumes to be the distressingly large gap between sociological theory and sociological research. Various writers, Merton for example, speak of a "codification" or "consolidation" of theory and research,[4] and followers of Parsons, as another example, tell us how useful his system of concepts is in helping them to see research problems, in directing their research, and in providing a conceptual frame in which to announce their conclusions. There is a feeling indeed that theoretical formulations need to justify themselves as useful in research and that unless the Parsonian architectonic, for example, is "usable" in research its justification disappears. Efforts to demonstrate utility thus increase in intensity out of respect for what must in the case of Parsons be regarded as an astonishing achievement of the human mind.

We have had occasion to remark before on this rather odd emphasis that would make theory subordinate to research.[5] Indeed, this same accent on utility then appears as a criterion in terms of which sociological theories in general are judged. In discussing the classical theories, for example, Parsons has remarked that "Generally speaking, as total systems they have not proved usable by the contemporary research social scientists, and those smaller elements of them which are useful have for the most part become incorporated into more recent work in more usable form than the original."[6] And Merton has supported this sentiment by saying, "The theories of a Comte or a Spencer, of a Hobhouse or a Ratzenhofer are chiefly of historical interest—little of what they wrote remains pertinent today. . . . They testify to the large merits of talented men, but they do not provide guidelines to the present analysis of sociological problems."[7] Utility is thus seen to be the bridge that will connect theory and research and make them more accessible to each other.

We want to contend in this paper that the issue as thus presented is misconstrued. The really distressing gap in sociology today is not that between theory and research—as serious as that may be—but between two different kinds of theory, to one of which the criterion of utility is relevant and to the other of which it is not. The important lacuna—to employ a less inelegant but more pedantic word—is that between metasociological theory on the one hand and sociological theory on the other or, stated differently, between methodological theory and substantive theory. Metasociological theory is now a highly developed discipline; sociological theory, on the contrary, is still a weak and pallid thing whose pursuit receives no special encouragement within the profession and whose major achievements frequently come not from academicians but from novelists, journalists, publicists, and those relatively few sociologists who are not afraid of epithets like "unscientific." One of the questions that concerns us is the distinction between metasociological theory and sociological theory. Indeed, we shall contend that the latter enterprise is vastly more significant for our discipline even when its conclusions fall short of the confirmation that is ordinarily required by the canons of scientific inquiry. Utility can of course serve as the criterion by which metasociological theory is judged, but of sociological theory cogency, not utility, is the measure.

The instrument we shall use in an effort to attack these problems is the instrument that solves the issues raised by the little stories with which we began. This instrument is the distinction between nominal and real definitions, a distinction accepted in contemporary logic but one relatively unknown in other disciplines. It is not the most powerful of our analytical and logical tools—it would do no good to overemphasize its merits—but it can remove some of the perplexities in the current sociological scene. It has a peculiarly apposite application to our puzzles.

The issue between Blumer and Lundberg, for example, is completely resolved by it. The most interesting aspect of their argument is not the enthusiasm with which they advanced their contrary views, but the fact that both were right—and both wrong. That is, Lundberg, who maintained that we ought to have our definitions clearly articulated at the beginning of our inquiries, was right if he was talking about nominal definitions. Blumer, who maintained that definitions can emerge only in the process of inquiry, was right if his subject was real definitions. There can be no question that, as Lundberg insisted, the adoption of precise nominal definitions is desirable at the beginning because they outline and delimit the ensuing research. As a matter of fact, loose and imprecise nominal definitions are to be countenanced at no stage of inquiry. On the other hand, as Blumer insisted, real definitions are not given at the outset of inquiry, either "operationally" or any other way, but result only from empirical investigation of the phenomenon in question. It is necessary to rely upon the investigation itself in order to determine whether or not the properties the definition ascribes to the concept actually do belong to it, whether, to put it bluntly, the *definiens* does in fact define the *definiendum,* whether, in short, the definition is "true." Attention here to an elementary distinction completely resolves an issue and ends an argument.[8]

In the same way we can referee the dispute between Hermogenes and Cratylus, this time without the help of Socrates. Hermogenes is right if he is talking about the nominal definitions of words, for these are wholly arbitrary and one has with respect to them a limitless range of choice. Cratylus, on the other hand, is right if he means that when a word once has a meaning, i.e., a connotation or an intension, it may not subsequently be applied in such a manner as to contradict that connotation. That way leads to madness, and to chaos in communication. And similarly for De Morgan and the organist. The organist can call his stop anything he desires, anything at all, but only, so to speak, if the word he chooses is not yet in the language. He is perfectly free to call it either a railway-whistle stop or a flute stop, as he likes. If these words are already in the language, however, the situation is somewhat different. If the sound is high and piping and somewhat aspiratory, he should not call it a railway-whistle stop; and if it is lonely, melancholy, and slightly disturbing in the distance, he should not call it a flute stop. In other words, once railway whistles and flutes have their characteristic sounds, and once, as words, they have their characteristic connotations, the organist has some obligation to call his new stop one or the other in accordance with his judgment of what it more nearly resembles. To do the reverse, though logically permissible, would add confusion rather than clarity to the language and to the processes of communication that it serves. And finally, Eve. She is at perfect liberty to call the new animal a dodo,[9] or anything else that springs to her mind. If, however, the word "dodo" is already in her vocabulary as carrying a connotation of stupidity and if the creature appears to be intelligent, then she would be careless or capricious to do so. In this event, Adam should assert his authority and name the animal himself; and the Serpent should persuade her to eat yet another apple from the tree of the knowledge of good and evil.

It is necessary now to examine the distinction between nominal and real definitions a little more closely and a little more systematically. In doing so, we shall follow the discussion of Ralph Eaton in his *General Logic,*[10] because the distinction is treated there with both brevity and rigor. We shall first define each of these kinds of definitions, then consider their properties, and finally treat their functions, or uses. At the conclusion of the discussion we shall attend to certain rules that apply to both kinds of definition.

A nominal definition (sometimes called a verbal definition) "is a declaration of intention to use a certain word or phrase as a substitute for another word or phrase." [11] The word or phrase with which we begin is called the *definiens;* the word or phrase we substitute is the *definiendum.* A nominal definition has three important properties: (1) the meaning of the *definiendum* is dependent upon that of the *definiens;* that is, the expression or concept defined has literally no other meaning than that given arbitrarily to it; (2) the definition has no truth claims; that is, it can neither be true nor false, it is not a proposition, and therefore (3) it cannot serve as a premise in inference.

It is necessary to insist upon the literal truth of these three characteristics of nominal definitions. With respect to the first of them, as Eaton says, a concept defined nominally has no other meaning than that given arbitrarily to it. It has the form commonly used in algebra when we say, Let x stand for the unknown quantity. Throughout the working of the problem x has no other meaning whatever. Similarly, when Stuart Dodd, for example, develops a tension theory of societal action, he uses the symbol *"E"* to mean "equilibration index" and in this theory *"E"* means only that—nothing else.[12] As a third example, W. A. Anderson once suggested, in a communication to the *American Sociological Review,*[13] that the word "hurelure" might be adopted as a substitute for "human relationship structures." Since this neologism has no independent meaning in the language, it follows that its meaning is wholly dependent upon its *definiens.*

Attending now to the second characteristic of nominal definitions, it obviously makes no sense to inquire whether an *"E"* really is an equilibration index, or whether a "hurelure" really is a human relationship structure, whether equilibration indexes and human relationship structures are now correctly labeled. That is, a nominal definition has no truth claims and it is therefore senseless to ask whether it is true or false. It is merely a resolution, a stipulation, a convention, an agreement, an expression of volition to use a word or other symbol in a particular way. Of course, as Cohen and Nagel point out,[14] the assertion that a writer has conformed to his own resolution and consistently used a word in the sense that he himself has stipulated may be true or false, but this has nothing to do with the nominal definition itself.

Finally, such definitions as these examples, like all nominal definitions, cannot serve as premises in inference. This follows as a simple corollary of the second characteristic. Only propositions can serve as premises in inference and a nominal definition, being neither true nor false, is not a proposition. As an *a fortiori* consequence, of course, no nominal definition can contribute one iota to our knowledge of fact. It indicates only how we intend to use the language.

A real definition differs from a nominal definition in that it operates not only on the symbolic or linguistic level but also on the referential level. It may be defined as follows: a real definition is a proposition announcing the conventional intension of a concept. In more technical language, a real definition is a proposition predicating a distributed intension of its subject term. A real definition also has three important properties, as follows: (1) a real definition states that two expressions, *each of which has an independent meaning,* are equivalent to each other;

(2) it has truth claims, i.e., it is a proposition; and (3) it can therefore serve as a premise in inference.[15]

It is convenient to illustrate these characteristics by means of an example that Eaton supplies, contrasting a real definition with a nominal definition. We can take the word "good," for example, and define it nominally as any object of desire; that is, we may submit the resolution, *Let the word "good" mean any object of desire*. It follows that "it would be vain—and meaningless—to question my statement that 'any object of desire is good,' for I am not asserting a truth about objects of desire or goods. All I am saying is that this is how to use the word 'good,' and one may use words in any way he chooses. However, I could not conclude from this definition that 'no objects of desire are evil.' The only legitimate process which the definition permits is verbal substitution; and all that this statement can mean is that 'no objects of desire are non-good, i.e., are not objects of desire.' " [16] On the other hand, quoting Eaton again, "If the term 'good,' for example, has a meaning of its own, the real definition—'the good is any object of desire'—might be false. We can ask, is it true that what is meant (independently) by 'good' is the same as what is meant by 'any object of desire'? And, if evil, as most religions maintain, can be desired, this definition cannot stand as 'a primary and indemonstrable truth.' " [17]

In other words, if it is true—and if it is a definition—that the good is any object of desire, it is also true that no object of desire is evil, a conclusion that can be inferred from a proposition but not from a resolution.

The logical danger here, and one we want to emphasize, is that when nominal definitions become familiar, as they tend of course to do, we sometimes forget they are nominal and begin to treat them as real. The word we have introduced by stipulation and to which we have arbitrarily given a meaning comes, through use and repetition, to be regarded as necessarily having that meaning. Once again we cannot refrain from quoting Eaton on this matter:

> Having introduced definitions as purely nominal, many writers tend later to treat them as if they were real—as if they conveyed some information about the concept defined, and so, analyzed this concept. Ethical philosophers who nominally define 'the good' as 'any object of desire' often end by arguing that this is the only meaning 'good' can have, since everything that is good is an object of desire, and there is no object of desire that is not good. Tacitly they assign an independent meaning to the term 'good'; and their erstwhile nominal definition becomes an important truth in their minds.[18]

One may suspect, of course, that this human tendency to transform nominal definitions into real ones is to be found not only among ethicists but also among those who construct systems of sociological theory. It seems hardly necessary to add that one does not in this fashion "create" new truths about society.[19]

Let us consider some additional examples. Suppose we are constructing a coinage system and that we have already decided to call ten cents a dime. We are now ready to introduce the next larger unit and want a word for the amount equal to ten dimes. We may choose any word we want for this purpose. Suppose we hit upon the word "dollar." We then say, in effect, let the amount represented by ten dimes be called a dollar. This is a nominal definition. It makes no sense, of course, to question its truth because we are not asserting anything. All we are doing is resolving to call the amount of money equal to ten dimes or one hundred cents a dollar. The definition is neither true nor false. If, however, we have already placed the word "dollar" in our system, defining it as an amount equal to one hundred cents—i.e., if it has an independent reference before we equate it with ten dimes—then the definition is real, and it is true. If we now say that a dollar is ten dimes we are asserting the equivalence of two expressions, each of which has an independent meaning. The definition is a proposition. The simple act of multiplication demonstrates its truth and now we may not, on pain of contradiction, define a dollar as nine dimes, eleven dimes, or any other number of dimes except ten.

Consider, on the contrary, the definition of man as a rational animal. Under no present circumstances may we consider this a nominal definition. When we define "man" as a "rational animal," we do not imply merely that we resolve to call a rational animal by the shorter expression "man" in any discussion in which we might be engaged. We imply that a man actually is a rational animal and that whatever "man" may mean, "rational animal" means the same, i.e., this time, that they have the same denotation. It makes sense, furthermore, to inquire whether or not man really is a rational animal and indeed there might be some dispute over the matter. Consider, finally, the purely nominal definition mentioned above—a hurelure is a human relationship structure. Here the word "hurelure" has no independent meaning. Mr. Anderson simply resolves to use it as an abbreviation for the longer expression, "human relationship structure." To inquire whether a hurelure really is a human relationship structure is not an intelligible question.

Nominal definitions have four important functions which are usually listed as follows:

1. Nominal definitions offer the only possible way of introducing new words into a language and, *pari passu*, new concepts into scientific terminologies.

2. Nominal definitions indicate the special importance of certain cor-

cepts in scientific schemata, implying, as they do, that the *definiens* is worthy of careful consideration—so worthy in fact that it has been given an equivalent expression.

3. Nominal definitions permit us to economize space, time, and attention, in the same way that abbreviations do.[20]

4. Nominal definitions permit us to substitute new concepts for the familiar words of ordinary speech that have emotional or other nonlogical connotations and thereby enhance the emotional neutrality of scientific discourse.

The functions of real definitions, as distinguished from nominal definitions, follow directly from their properties. Real definitions not only indicate the meaning of a word, as nominal definitions do, but they also assert something about the referent of the concept defined. They predicate, in propositional form, the conventional intension of the concept—that is, the essential or most important property of the concept to be associated with it in scientific communication. A real definition, furthermore, can serve as a premise in inference and, possibly more important, as an hypothesis concerning the nature of the phenomenon under investigation. It has all of the general functions of propositions and in addition the specific functions of a definition; it operates both on the referential level and on the symbolic level.

We judge nominal definitions, in short, by their utility; real definitions by their truth.

In what sense now is the intension announced in a real definition conventional?[21] It is conventional in the sense that it is a matter of agreement or resolution which of various properties comprising the objective intension of a concept we choose to use as the *definiens;* that is, which property we shall regard as central for the purpose at hand. This depends upon our interest in general and the criterion of classification in particular, and may be different in separate treatments of the same subject matter. Although the choice may in one sense be arbitrary—in the sense that we decide to focus our definition upon one rather than another of the properties—the question whether or not the referent of the concept actually has this property is neither a matter of choice nor of convention. It is still appropriate and necessary, therefore, to inquire into the truth of a real definition. Thus, it is possible to define a triangle either as a plane figure in Euclidean space bounded by three straight lines, or as a plane figure in Euclidean space containing three angles whose sum is 180°. Both definitions are real, and both are true. It is a matter of convention, relative to the purpose for which the concept "triangle" is employed, which of the two definitions is used, but both must be true. This is what is implied, and all that is implied, in the word "conventional" when we say that a real definition is a statement announcing the conventional intension of a concept.

The adjective "conventional," traditional in discussions of this subject in the logic texts, also helps us to understand what committees can and cannot accomplish in the direction of clarifying and standardizing concepts and conceptual usages. Some years ago, for example, a "Committee on Conceptual Integration" existed within the American Sociological Society, a committee devoted to the purpose indicated by its name. The distinction between nominal and real definitions helps us to understand what a committee of this kind can—and cannot—do. It can do much to encourage the adoption by sociologists of uniform *nominal* definitions of the concepts sociologists employ, to aid in the establishment of uniform practices in the use of words that have risen to the prominence of concepts, and even to assist in the organization, classification, and "integration" of concepts. All of these activities, if successfully pursued, could theoretically at least contribute to the linguistic facility and accuracy of sociological communication.

By no stretch of the imagination, however, can such co-operative endeavor succeed in establishing uniform *real* definitions of sociological concepts. In order to arrive at real definitions, as the discussion above suggests, it is necessary to leave the level of verbal equivalence and enter the field of sociological research. When we seek a real definition of any sociological concept we no longer want to know what the word stands for, in terms of other symbols, but what the referent of the concept actually is, and what its properties are—especially those properties that enable us to use *this* word, with its own independent meaning, as a terminological and logical equivalent. And this discovery cannot be the work of a committee but constitutes instead the task in which all sociologists are engaged as they pursue their separate labors.

Again, we may inquire into the efficacy of a dictionary of sociological terms, such as the one now in progress under the auspices of UNESCO. Those who were engaged in the preparation of preliminary documents for this project recognized quite clearly that there is room for improvement in the terminologies of the social sciences, that science advances as it is able to standardize these terminologies, and that regularity and consistency in conceptual usage is of vast assistance in hastening the maturity of a discipline. Their estimate of the current situation in these respects was not sanguine. They expressed the opinion that the terminology of the social sciences continues to be vague, that social scientists spend a great deal of their time in vocabulary construction, and that the net result is more words and fewer standardized concepts than before. It is for these reasons apparently that the dictionary project has been undertaken.

There is no doubt that these sentiments are correct. Sociologists who have been invited to participate in the project can contribute a great deal

to the discovery of the conventional intension of concepts now in use—
and this in itself is a meritorious and altogether praiseworthy enterprise.
Such discoveries, and the definitions associated with them, can help to
reduce the wholly subjective intensions frequently found in contemporary
vocabularies. But no finite number of contributors, however competent,
and no board of editors, however expert, can establish uniform real definitions of sociological concepts. The dictionary can select and support
one conventional intension over another, but it cannot determine the
truth or falsity of the real definition that contains and announces it. This
again is the job of all sociologists as they go about their professional
duties.

We want now to list the standard rules of definition and then to comment on one of them. They are usually given in some such manner as
the following:

1. A definition should be *per genus et differentiam,* wherever possible.
(This is still a useful rule when Aristotelian assumptions regarding fixed
essences are relinquished.)
2. A definition must be commensurate with that which is to be defined;
i.e., it must be applicable to everything included in the concept defined, and
to nothing else. In short, a definition must be convertible *simpliciter.*
3. A definition should not, directly or indirectly, define the subject in
terms of itself; i.e., it should not be circular.[22]
4. A definition should not be stated negatively when it can be stated
positively.
5. A definition should not be stated in obscure or figurative language.[23]

The second rule is the one most relevant to our present purpose, the
rule that requires that definitions be convertible *simpliciter.* We have
said that a real definition is a proposition. It is also a particular kind of
a proposition, namely, a universal affirmative proposition. Thus, when
we define man as a featherless biped we are asserting that all men are
featherless bipeds. Now, all students of logic know that a universal
affirmative proposition is not convertible *simpliciter* but convertible only
per accidens, or by limitation.[24] That is, from the truth of the proposition just expressed we can infer, by conversion, not that all featherless
bipeds are men but only that some are. The rule, however, states that a
definition must be convertible *simpliciter;* in other words, the relationship established by the copula is not one of class inclusion or of class
membership but of equivalence. In order to be a definition, it must also
be true that all featherless bipeds are men.

A nominal definition, of course, is convertible by fiat. We simply
resolve to use the *definiendum* as the equivalent of the *definiens.* The
situation with respect to real definitions, however, is a little more complicated. Since, in order to be a definition, the proposition must be convertible *simpliciter,* and since we cannot so convert it formally, it follows

that we must know *on other than formal grounds* that its converse is true. It is vital to recognize that these other grounds cannot be formal. They must be empirical.

The conclusion follows that no real definition of any concept in any field can be constructed without empirical knowledge of the phenomenon in question. Thus, if we want to define man as a featherless biped, and want our definition to have ontological and not merely symbolic implications—i.e., if we want it to be a real and not a nominal definition—we have to know not only that all men are featherless bipeds but also that all featherless bipeds are men. And if a plucked chicken is a featherless biped, as the ancient story has it, then some featherless bipeds are not men and we may not declare as a real definition that man is a featherless biped. Thus, in more general terms, all real definitions are propositions but not all propositions are real definitions. The universal affirmative proposition, *All men are mortal,* is true, but we may not define man as a mortal being because it does not conform to the rule requiring unlimited convertibility. Real definitions, in short, have ontological and not merely logical consequences; they have empirical and not merely rational implications; and it is these characteristics that give to the distinction itself a certain relevance to contemporary sociological theory.

We want to contend in what follows that the distinction we have been discussing can do more than solve the vexatious little puzzles with which we began this essay, and more too than articulate the logical limitations upon the enterprise of making dictionaries. It can be of major assistance in addition in helping us to evaluate systems of sociological theory and in determining what kind of theory these systems represent. That is, the more nearly a given sociological theory resembles a set of nominal definitions, the more easily can we recognize that it has no truth claims. The more nearly it resembles a collection of real definitions—i.e., the more real definitions it contains—the more easily can we recognize it as a contribution to sociological knowledge. To state the matter in a different way, the more we are tempted to judge a system of theory in terms of its utility, the more likely it is that it is a nominal system and has methodological or metasociological significance. The more we are tempted to judge it in terms of its truth, the more likely it is that it is a "real" system—in the sense of real definitions of course—and has substantive and sociological significance. Let us apply these criteria to two contemporary examples of sociological theory, the one constructed by Stuart Carter Dodd and the other by Talcott Parsons.

The *Dimensions of Society,*[25] of course, is a work of prodigious effort and of almost incredible ingenuity. Motivated by the wholly meritorious goal of introducing mathematical methods into sociology, Dodd has worked out in detail one of the most consistent and comprehensive systems of symbols in existence. It is apparent, however, almost upon immediate examination, that the "S-system" is not a collection of propositions about society but rather an ingenious set of nominal definitions. It makes no sense to inquire, for example, whether the symbol "S" "really is" a social situation, and the same for the symbols "T," "I," "L," and "P," whether they "really are" time, characteristics of people, space, and number of people. These are literally meaningless—and improper—questions. It is certainly the case that Dodd may express quantitatively recorded social situations in terms of a combination of four indicators, although it is not the case, as his front papers lead one to suggest, that this is a rigorous statement of the proposition that people and their characteristics change. In any event, most of the book is devoted to an elaboration, with multitudinous examples, of the way in which sociological data may be expressed in terms of these particular symbols which are, in turn, related to one another through a minimal set of "operators."

Needless to say, Dodd does not assert that his controlling equation is true, nor that it says anything about society. He inquires, rather, as we do, into its utility. The uses of "S-theory," or "S-system" as he later came to call it, are the subject of a separate paper. Among these uses are that it is (1) a contribution to the nomenclature of sociology, a nomenclature in some instances susceptible to mathematical manipulation; (2) a method for guiding "the inductive and deductive manipulations, the analysis and synthesis, in various operationally defined ways, of the recorded observations" of sociology, and (3) a system of second-order symbols "for making summaries and conclusions, for defining concepts and stating relations, for interpreting and predicting, in short for helping to convert recorded observations into laws." [26]

The interesting thing about these claims is that most of them are valid. There is no question that Dodd's S-system can do many of these things—and do them very well. The degree of *system* that characterizes the *Dimensions* is almost phenomenal. Everything has its place, and there is a place for everything. The S-system is comprised of versatile symbols and they can express many things. So, in the same sense, can any series of nominal definitions. No such series is a theory, however, and none is a "system" in any logical or scientific sense. To be a system in the latter sense means to be a system of propositions, including real definitions, each one related to another and each asserting something that can be inferred from other propositions in the system. And if real definitions are included, as they must be, evidence is needed in addition to inference—that is, evidence from the empirical world in order to validate the convertibility *simpliciter* of the definitions.

Although Dodd's formulae, like abbreviations, help to conserve time, space, and energy, and although they may greatly assist the processes of classification, they are not real definitions. In one of his passages, he recognizes this and indeed discusses the difference between what he calls descriptive equations on the one hand and calculative equations on the other—a distinction that appears to be identical to that between nominal and real definitions:

In a descriptive equation one member is observed and defines the other member which is set equal to it. Thus here, the left-hand member, S, is not directly observed independently of the right-hand member. In a calculative equation both members may be independently observable. If a term is unknown in the calculative equation, it can be solved for. As many unknowns can be solved for as there are independent simultaneous calculative equations. But in a descriptive equation the term defined is the unknown, and a second unknown in the same equation, taken alone, cannot be solved for. Defining concepts by descriptive equations based on objectively observable quantities is the first step, however, in manipulating them and discovering and testing relationships among the concepts.[27]

It is Dodd's hope, of course, that his system will be increasingly productive of calculative equations and that some day he will be able to solve them for "sociological unknowns." Surely there is no more respectable ambition than this. The goal, however, is not yet achieved. The basic difficulty with such an invention as Dodd's lies in inducing others to adopt it. Unfortunately, his colleagues in the sociological enterprise seem to prefer their own nominal definitions to the systematic set that he has supplied. In any case there is a danger here, as in any system of nominal definitions, that a growing familiarity with them, on the part of their author or anyone else, will in time encourage the misconception that they are real definitions.

To suggest the nominal character of the symbol structure contained in the *Dimensions of Society* in no way reduces the merit of Dodd's achievement in creating so consistent and comprehensive a scheme for the classification of quantified data in sociology. It needs only to be remembered, as outlined in great detail in the foregoing paragraphs, that nominal definitions are not real definitions and that the characteristics of the two types of definition are fundamentally dissimilar. To make the point almost platitudinous, one might simply say that it is forever impossible to get more out of a nominal definition than is put into it in the first place. And so with a symbol system, a system of notation, however ingeniously contrived. Whatever important and indeed necessary functions it may perform on the nominal level, it is sterile in itself. Whatever it contributes to the nomenclature of sociology, the S-system of Dodd is not a calculus. It cannot inseminate the data it embraces and it can play no intimate creative part in the ongoing processes of science. Like the mule, an amiable beast, it has no pride of ancestry, no hope of progeny.

Nevertheless, we may not conclude that nominal definitions are unimportant simply because they are not real definitions. Nominal definitions have their own important functions to perform. If, as some sociologists believe, the prime task of current methodology in sociology, and indeed in all the social sciences, is to adopt a common system of symbolic notation, the notation constructed so painstakingly in the *Dimensions of Society* may be regarded as an outstanding contender for that position. In terms of its precision, its parsimony, its consistency, and its comprehensiveness, the S-system possesses high qualifications, and one cannot help but admire the labor that Dodd has expended upon it and the zeal with which he has brought it to public attention.[28]

We turn now to Talcott Parsons in an effort to discover whether the distinction between nominal and real definitions has any relevance to the vast theoretical structures he has contributed to contemporary sociology. The enterprise on which Parsons has been engaged for upwards of twenty years has often seemed a puzzling one not only to those who have not had the benefit of personal participation in his seminars at Harvard but even to some of those who have enjoyed this privilege. Fortunately, Parsons, like Dodd, is a sophisticated methodologist, one who is thoroughly aware of what it is he is trying to do and who often stops to explain it to his readers. Although couched in different language from that employed in the present chapter, many of his observations are directly relevant. We shall not pursue these through the impressive corpus of his work, but confine our attention at the moment to certain statements that appear in *The Social System*.[29]

Parsons is quite clear, in fact, that the content of this book is sociological theory in a very special sense of the term. He does not intend to offer the book as a critique of the literature of sociological theory,[30] as a codification of empirical knowledge, or as a theory of any concrete phenomenon in society. It is, on the contrary, an essay in systematic theory, a logically articulated conceptual scheme, a frame of reference explicitly defined, an effort at theory construction.[31] The following comments are so suggestive that they require direct quotation:

> The book is thus an essay *in* systematic theory but the suggestion is quite explicitly repudiated that it attempts in one sense to present a system *of* theory, since it has been consistently maintained that in the present state of knowledge, such a system cannot be formulated. Put a little differently, it is a theory of systems rather than a system of theory.[32]

This engaging juxtaposition of the two words "theory" and "system" helps us enormously in understanding what it is that Parsons is "about" even though we may not share his optimism concerning the utility of a general theory of social action—nor his pessimism that a system of theory, as contrasted with a theory of systems, cannot now be formulated. It appears in particular that the distinction so neatly articulated here has more than a little in common with that treated in this chapter—namely, the distinction between nominal and real definitions—and, in addition, with the distinction between methodological (or metasociological) theory on the one hand and substantive (or sociological) theory on the other.

In this respect, it is interesting to observe and, we hope, not unfair to either author to note that the general methodological intent of Parsons' work is basically similar to Dodd's, however dissimilar the symbols in the two systems. To a very large degree both authors have supplied— and both with prodigious labor—a set of nominal definitions for sociological use. Both authors, curiously enough, in spite of their many obeisances to empiricism (in Dodd's case to "operationalism," a radical variant of empiricism; and in Parsons' to an especial fondness for the word "empirical"), have taken a highly formal and indeed taxonomic approach to sociology. Both authors have built their nominal definitions into elaborate conceptual schemes. Both authors contend, finally, that these conceptual schemes can embrace multifarious phenomena from other disciplines. Dodd, as we have seen, suggests that symbolic logic, the equations of mathematics, the formulae of statistics, and the categories of Aristotle and Kant can be translated into the S-system—a claim we have conceded. Parsons has recently maintained, for his part, that the body of economic theory is a special case of his general theory of social systems and of his general theory of action, a claim we have also conceded.[33] It remains only, perhaps, to translate the "pattern variables" and their companions into the S-system and Dodd into "Parsonian," and we have little doubt that both translations are possible.

In any event, there is a vector of inquiry involved here that Parsons and Dodd tend to share. Inquiry in general has two vectors; it proceeds, in short, in two directions, and these directions can be characterized by the differences between nominal and real definitions. Sometimes we begin with our observations of objects, phenomena, or properties that have something in common and we want to apply a name either to this common characteristic or to the class of objects in question. In this case, we move from *definiens* to *definiendum* and the result is a nominal definition. At other times, we begin with a concept and want to discover and to articulate the properties associated with its referent. In this case we move from *definiendum* to *definiens* and the result is a real definition. In the first case, that of a nominal definition, we have a conceptual scheme that may or may not be useful. In the second case, we have a real definition that may or may not be true.[34] In moving along one of these vectors we aim at a continuously improved conceptual scheme; in moving along the other we aim to contribute true propositions to the sum of sociological knowledge. Both vectors of inquiry are important. But they are different. In the one direction, we are constructing the instruments of inquiry and the categories of classification; in the other, we are building substantive sociological theory.

There is, of course, a certain artificiality in the first of these enterprises when carried on in independence of the second. It can lead to a system, or even a "theory of systems," that, however aesthetically satisfying and logically imposing, is sterile. The creator of a set of tools can admire their shine and their cutting edge, and can go on polishing and sharpening forever, without heed to Lotze's remark that "the constant whetting of an axe is apt to be a bit tedious if it isn't proposed to cut anything with it." The inventor of a generalized conceptual scheme can obviously be quite prolific in the multiplication of concepts (one cannot say that Parsons is altogether free of this tendency) and can spin out increasingly complex and elaborate series of nominal definitions. We shall ultimately have to require of such a system, however, that it produce progeny in the form of propositions.

As in the case of Dodd, we do not wish to imply that the corpus of Parsons' work is devoid of substantive theoretical propositions. Indeed, the latter are quite numerous, not only in his papers directed to special topics,[35] but also throughout *The Social System*. In the latter place, for example, we find illuminating discussions of kinship, of the socialization of the child, of the institutionalization of scientific investigation. of the role of the artist in society, of the problem of social change, and, most especially perhaps, of modern medical practice. Most of these discussions, however, appear largely as incidental suggestions (e.g., the penetrating observations on the use of family symbolism in fraternities and in the Catholic Church [36]) rather than as carefully worked out propositions, hypotheses, or theses. In view of the finely wrought systematic quality of his nominal definitions, it is somewhat surprising to see his real ones presented so haphazardly. The explanation is that they are introduced in fact not on their own account but as illustrations of the utility of the schema that is being constructed. They are, literally, "cases," and not conclusions.

As helpful as the distinction between nominal and real definitions is, it should not be supposed that it is powerful enough to solve all of our problems. It contains certain residual difficulties of its own, of which we shall mention two. There is a sense, in the first place, in which real definitions can appear in purely formal systems even though they have no contact whatever with an empirical content. Equivalences introduced by fiat can be related to other equivalences also introduced by fiat in such a way that *definiendum* and *definiens* could, in the process of construction of a system, acquire independent meanings. In these cases, the new definition would have a truth claim but no reality claim. The "truth" involved would be a purely formal matter and would depend upon two prior sets of nominal definitions. In other words, although nominal definitions do not appear as empirical propositions, formal systems can be co-ordinated with real definitions, as, for example, in applied mathematics.

Secondly, there is a sense in which it is impossible to give a nominal definition to a word or phrase that has a structure. Eaton, for example, holds that "where any phrase has a structure, it cannot be nominally defined by a phrase with a structure," and again:

> Only a single word (or symbol) could be given a nominal definition in the strict sense, for it has no structure. The existence of a structure in a propositional expression is already the existence of an independent framework of meaning; that which has an independent meaning can be analyzed, or shown to be equivalent to, some other independent meaning, but it cannot be nominally defined.[37]

On this reasoning, for example, it would be impossible to offer a nominal definition of a concept like "consciousness of kind." But single words too would fall under this proscription if they have prefixes or suffixes, especially the former, with independent connotations. It would thus be impossible to give a nominal definition of Dodd's "presuperdescript" because this word, prior to definition, has a structure that connotes a locus—namely, before and above—and one cannot therefore resolve to let it stand for an exponent, which would be a "postsuperdescript," without contradiction. The word "triangle," used in an earlier illustration, presents a similar case. The question arises whether the hyphen in such a concept as "pattern-variable" in Parsons gives the expression a structure that would prohibit its nominal definition. We should be inclined to answer in the negative; but the issue, as can be seen, is a difficult one.

Finally, we cannot use the distinction between nominal and real definitions as an infallible guide to, nor even as a criterion of, a "reality claim" on the part of the concept defined. There is no question but that at some point a real definition assumes not merely a logical but also an ontological significance. This problem cannot be treated in anything less than an essay in metaphysics, but we want to invite attention at least to Edel's paper in this volume and particularly to his discussion of "locus-candidates." He suggests that even though locus-candidates "may have been advanced as categories for an analytical framework structuring the whole field of study [as, one presumes, in Dodd and Parsons, for example—R.B.], they still must exhibit some empirical content and maintain a material status." Edel's paper in fact involves, as he says, "treating locus-candidates seriously as empirical or material categories descriptive of level qualities, rather than as abstract categories structuring the inquiry prior to beginning it."

Similarly, Gouldner, in an incisive paper on recent sociological theory, insists that key postulates have a substantial empirical base:

It is particularly necessary to raise questions concerning the empirical status of even key postulates in a theoretical system, and to treat this as an independent problem when the system is not a truly deductive one, as, for example, in the case of Parsons' theory.[38]

And again:

Even if one sets aside questions of the logical niceties of Parsons' analysis of 'social action,' there still remain important empirical issues. A specification of the elements of social action is no more attainable by formal definition alone than are the attributes of 'life,' which the biologist regards as the 'subject matter' of his discipline. Znaniecki, almost alone among the systematic theorists who have raised the question, has stressed that the characteristics of social action cannot be taken as *a priori* data but are also to be inductively sought and empirically validated.[39]

The distinction we have been discussing is not, unfortunately, powerful enough to guarantee the ontological status of locus-candidates, nor can it confirm the independent empirical presence of *definienda*. It may be, therefore, that we have overemphasized its importance to sociological theory. We find it, however, a suggestive and helpful device in the respects we have noted, and especially in exhibiting the two primary vectors of inquiry.

Mention of mathematics above in relation to formal systems induces us to include a brief comment on one methodological matter in which it appears that Parsons is almost certainly in error. In an early paper on sociological theory, a paper whose arguments he apparently still supports,[40] he disputes the views of the extreme empiricists that a science can be "purified of theoretical infection" and consist only of collections of heterogeneous and unrelated facts, although we should be surprised if anyone subscribes to this view. In his discussion he emphasizes the importance of mathematics in the natural sciences and insists that "mathematics in physics *is* theory." [41]

It seems doubtful, however, if this is a position that Parsons would want permanently to defend. He may have forgotten Bertrand Russell's witty and yet obviously correct remark that the mathematician never knows what he is talking about or whether what he is saying is true. It is possible to develop all kinds of mathematical systems, based upon postulates that have nothing to do with the actual world, as both Euclidean and non-Euclidean geometries testify. Nor is there any clear sense in which it can be maintained, for example, that the binomial theorem expresses a proposition about the physical world. Propositions in physical theory are quite another matter. The most fateful equation of our time— $E = mc^2$—is an apparently true statement about the universe and it is true in independence of the symbols used in order to give it expression. It may be doubted that this equation could ever have been discovered without mathematics, but the relationship it expresses has an ontological status in the world as we know it and is not something, like the binomial theorem, that is true only within a formal system. It is, in short, a proposition about the universe and not merely about some formal system in which the symbols *"E," "m,"* and *"c"* have been given meanings. And it is as true in English as it is in mathematical symbols.

John Stuart Mill was doubtless the last philosopher to hold seriously to the view that mathematics is an empirical science. Contemporary writers, whatever their philosophical orientation, take, on the contrary, the view just expressed. Furfey, for example, is quite explicit in saying that "The concepts of the mathematician are not limited by existing reality," and that the nature of mathematical entities "is determined by arbitrary decision, not by experience." [42] And von Mises writes, "One can construct in many ways tautological systems in which there exist, according to fixed rules, absolutely correct statements; but if one wants to state anything about relations between observable phenomena, e.g., in astronomy, then one is subject to control by future experiences. The application of mathematical methods can never guarantee the correctness of a nonmathematical proposition." [43] With respect to the use of mathematical models in sociology, a recent statement by Peter H. Rossi, too long to quote, is both accurate and comprehensive.[44] Models alone are not enough,[45] and mathematics itself is neither physical theory nor sociological theory. The analogy between mathematical models and nominal definitions, though not perfect, again illuminates the issue with which the present paper is principally concerned.

In conclusion, we may say again that, just as nominal definitions and real definitions are two different things, and illustrate different vectors of inquiry, so also are methodological theory and substantive theory in sociology. If utility is the test of the first, truth is the test of the second.[46] It is one thing—and an important thing—to develop a language, a schema, a system of symbols for use in sociology. It is quite another thing to develop a theory. A theory is a point of view and requires an assertion. A conceptual scheme is a language, and requires only a stipulation. A schema is sterile unless it can produce a theory. Substantive theory, in short, is propositional. Its propositions are assertions about society. Its concepts have referents in the empirical world. Its definitions are convertible *simpliciter*. Its conclusions have truth claims. And it is the ultimate goal of sociological inquiry.

NOTES

1. If the memory is too fallible, the writer begs the indulgence of both of the gentlemen mentioned, and offers apologies. For their views about this time, the reader is referred to Herbert Blumer, "The Problem of the Concept in Social Psychology," *American Journal of Sociology*, 45 (March, 1940), pp. 707-19; and George A. Lundberg, "Operational Definitions in the Social Sciences," *American Journal of Sociology*, 47 (March, 1942), pp. 727-43.

2. Augustus De Morgan, *A Budget of Paradoxes* (Chicago: The Open Court Publishing Company, 1915), II, 91.

3. "Eve's Diary," from *The $30,000 Bequest and Other Stories* (New York: Harper & Brothers, 1935).

4. See Robert K. Merton, *Social Theory and Social Structure*, revised edition (Glencoe, Ill.: Free Press, 1957). See also "Discussion" of "The Position of Sociological Theory," by Talcott Parsons, *American Sociological Review*, 13 (April, 1948), pp. 164-68.

5. Robert Bierstedt, "A Critique of Empiricism in Sociology," *American Sociological Review*, 14 (October, 1949), pp. 584-92.

6. Talcott Parsons, "The Position of Sociological Theory," *American Sociological Review*, 13 (April, 1948), p. 157, note 3.

7. Robert K. Merton, "Discussion," *op. cit.*, p. 165.

8. This paragraph, like some of the others in this chapter, is taken with modifications from the author's unpublished doctoral dissertation, *Logic, Language, and Sociology*.

9. "When the dodo came along he [Adam] thought it was a wildcat— I saw it in his eye. But I saved him. And I was careful not to do it in a way that could hurt his pride. I just spoke up in a quite natural way of pleased surprise, and not as if I was dreaming of conveying information, and said, 'Well, I do declare, if there isn't the dodo!' " Mark Twain, *op. cit.*

10. Ralph Eaton, *General Logic* (New York: Charles Scribner's Sons, 1931), pp. 294-305. See also Morris R. Cohen and Ernest Nagel, *An Introduction to Logic and Scientific Method* (New York: Harcourt, Brace and Company, 1934), pp. 224-41.

11. Eaton, *op. cit.*, p. 295.

12. Stuart Carter Dodd, *The Dimensions of Society* (New York: The Macmillan Company, 1942), pp. 265-71.

13. W. A. Anderson, "A Note on the Phenomena of Sociology," *American Sociological Review*, 6 (December, 1941), pp. 882-84.

14. Cohen and Nagel, *op. cit.*, p. 229.

15. Eaton, *op. cit.*, pp. 296-97.

16. *Ibid.*, pp. 295-96.

17. *Ibid.*, p. 297.

18. *Ibid.*, p. 299.

19. For that matter, logicians themselves sometimes succumb to this temptation. See Eaton's strictures on Whitehead and Russell, *ibid.*, pp. 299-300, and note.

20. Cohen and Nagel comment on this function as follows: "If we continued to use ordinary words and did not introduce such technical terms of higher mathematics and physics as 'differential coefficient,' 'entropy,' and the like, our expressions would become so long and involved that we could not readily grasp the complex relations indicated by these terms. Thus it is easier to read Newton's *Principia* translated into the technical language of the modern calculus than in the more familiar language of geometry in which Newton wrote." *Op. cit.*, p. 229.

21. On the intension of terms, and the distinction between subjective, objective, and conventional intension, see Eaton, pp. 235-72, or Cohen and Nagel, pp. 30-33.

22. All definitions, of course, are ultimately circular and for this reason there remain undefinable or primitive terms in any system. The circle need not be "vicious," however, unless it is too small.

23. It is not very helpful, for example, to define "network," as Dr. Johnson did, as "anything reticulated or decussated, with interstices between the intersections."

24. Without the existential assumption a universal affirmative proposition is not formally convertible at all; nor can we, without this assumption, infer the truth of a particular affirmative proposition from the truth of its superaltern universal affirmative.

25. *Op. cit.*

26. "Of What Use Is Dimensional Sociology?" *Social Forces*, 22 (December, 1943), pp. 169-82. See also the note to p. 179 where Dodd takes Talcott Parsons to task for failing in his review to grasp the essential nature of the enterprise. Parsons' review is in the *American Sociological Review*, 7 (October, 1942), pp. 709-14. Read Bain's "Communication," *American Sociological Review*, 8 (February, 1943), pp. 214-16, is also pertinent.

27. *Dimensions of Society, op. cit.*, p. 59.

28. Nothing in the above discussion implies that Dodd's sociological writings are limited to nomenclatural concerns. Among his many substantive contributions we should like to mention especially his work on message diffusion.

29. Glencoe, Ill.: Free Press, 1951.

30. Except for references to the unpublished dissertation of his own students and an occasional bow to Weber, the work in question makes almost no mention of the work of other sociological theorists.

31. All of these expressions are to be found on p. 536.

32. *Ibid.,* pp. 536-37.

33. See Talcott Parsons and Neil J. Smelser, *Economy and Society* (Glencoe, Ill.: Free Press, 1956) and the writer's review of this book in the *American Sociological Review,* 22 (June, 1957), p. 345.

34. And if it is false, of course, it can no longer be a definition.

35. See, for example, his *Essays in Sociological Theory,* revised edition (Glencoe, Ill.: Free Press, 1954) for a representative collection.

36. *The Social System, op. cit.,* pp. 406-07.

37. Eaton, *op. cit.,* p. 300, note.

38. Alvin W. Gouldner, "Some Observations on Systematic Theory, 1945–55," in *Sociology in the United States of America,* Hans L. Zetterberg, ed. (Paris: UNESCO, 1956), p. 35, note.

39. *Ibid.,* p. 37.

40. "The Present Position and Prospects of Systematic Theory in Sociology," reprinted in *Essays in Sociological Theory,* revised edition, *op. cit.,* pp. 212-37.

41. *Ibid.,* p. 224.

42. Paul Hanly Furfey, *The Scope and Method of Sociology* (New York: Harper & Brothers, 1953), pp. 113-14. This superior treatise, candidly metasociological, should be consulted on a number of matters relevant to the present discussion. See especially the treatment of formal and nonformal sciences, pp. 112-15; the inverse interpretation of formal systems, pp. 250-58; and the whole of Chapter 9, "The Logical Structure of Science," pp. 199-216.

43. Richard von Mises, *Positivism* (Cambridge: Harvard University Press, 1951), p. 6.

44. Peter H. Rossi, "Methods of Social Research, 1945–55," in *Sociology in the United States of America, op. cit.,* p. 24.

45. On some of the studies of Simon and Rashevsky, for example, Rossi comments that they are "of interest almost solely as examples of mathematical virtuosity; they do not specify how the variables used may be given empirical definition." *Ibid.*

46. "Truth" is so complex a problem in philosophy that "cogency," a word used earlier, would be the superior criterion in sociological theory. We touch here, however, an issue that can be developed only in a separate paper. The reason for this observation, however, may be briefly indicated. We regard Max Weber's thesis on capitalism and Protestantism as one of the most distinguished of all contributions to sociological theory, and yet we have no idea whether or not it is true. Its truth may forever elude us. Certainly it escapes the ordinary methods of confirmation used so successfully in the experimental sciences. Our judgment, in short, is based not upon its truth but upon its cogency.

5

Order, Causality, Conjuncture

N. S. TIMASHEFF

Fordham University

1. THE POSTULATE OF ORDER

Science is built up on three levels:

1) Singular propositions, or statements of the type: in place S, at time T, phenomenon P was observed.

2) General propositions, or empiric generalizations unifying, from diverse points of view, singular propositions, still with reference to concrete time and space; e.g., in contemporary America, the population is stratified in four (or, say, six) classes.

3) Theoretical propositions unifying, again from diverse points of view, empiric generalizations, without reference to concrete time and space. Let us use as instances two famous propositions: "If unchecked . . . population grows in geometrical ratio" (Malthus) . . . "in competitive society, market prices are determined by the correlation of supply and demand" (classic economists). The second instance shows that a theoretical proposition may be qualified by conditions described typologically ("in competitive society"). But the qualification cannot contain any reference to concrete time and space. We can say: the first instance is an explicitly universal proposition. The second is also universal, but implicitly: it covers phenomena obtaining at any time and place, provided that society is competitive; outside of competitive society, it is not invalid, but inapplicable. But the first proposition is also inapplicable

to populations which are checked, e.g., by food deficiency, high mortality, or birth control.

Logically, theoretical propositions depend on the postulate of order. Order exists if there are invariant relations between phenomena; with Montesquieu,[1] we could add "according to their nature." In actuality, no qualification is thereby introduced: the nature of X is tantamount to its "constant properties," and these constant properties are manifested in invariant relations to other phenomena.

The postulate of order is tantamount to the assertion that, in general, there are invariant relations between phenomena. It is the logical prerequisite of inductive reasoning but, itself, cannot be demonstrated by induction or deduction.

But the postulate of order is at least a tacit assumption of every purposive activity. Men act on its basis in everyday life. They assume that water will boil when sufficiently heated, that water will flow down from a higher to a lower reservoir, that game will be killed or wounded if an arrow or bullet pierces its body. They assume also that men will honor their formal obligations, that within an area of peace they will not be attacked by anybody, but also that men will reciprocate insults or injuries. In that regard, there is no difference between primitive and advanced society: the primitive man knows less about order around him than the civilized one; but, so far as he knows, he acts accordingly.

In advanced society, all the major differentiated and specialized activities are based on the tacit acceptance of the postulate of order. The highly complicated technological processes would have been unthinkable if there were doubts about the consequences of specified manipulations with matter and energy. The economic processes would have been unthinkable if there were doubts about the acceptance of the "rules of the game" by an overwhelming majority of the participants. The legal processes would have been impossible without stability in the adjudication of routine cases. The medical processes would have been meaningless if the effects of treatments were random.

So, when men of science proceed taking for granted the postulate of order, they do not separate themselves from the crowd of laymen. Some scholars, philosophically minded, are aware of the basic postulate of their activity; other ones, just as men-on-the-street, are not.

The postulate of order may be conceived in two manners. First, it may be ascribed universal validity; then, order covers all phenomena in all their aspects: in other words, all phenomena stand in invariant relations with each other. Such a conception dominated in the early nineteenth century and was given a famous expression by Laplace.[2]

Second, order may be conceived as a principle operative within certain limits. Then the postulate means only that, as far as order goes, there are invariant relations between phenomena. In physical science, the shift from the universal (absolute) to the limited (relative) conception of the postulate of order has begun with the formulation of Heisenberg's principle of indeterminacy. It is now in full swing because of recent developments in quantum mechanics and microphysics.[3] In the social sciences, there has always been a division of minds between the universal and the limited conception. Comte emphasized that social laws were more flexible than the physical, a proposition compatible with the limited conception only; but Spencer and his school insisted on a cosmic evolution plausible only in terms of a universal conception; so did the classics in political economy (e.g., Ricardo's iron law of wages). A belated adherence to the universal conception underlies the work of many neopositivists. Sorokin [4] and Gurvitch [5] offer cogent arguments in favor of the limited conception.

2. CAUSALITY

Order, be it universal or limited, may be predicated with respect to the coexistence (simultaneity) of phenomena—this is static order; or with respect to their sequence—this is dynamic order.

In physical science, Einstein's formula is a good instance of static order; according to it, the quantity of potential energy is a function of mass and light velocity. In the social sciences, Sorokin's theorems, "predicting" from the dominant epistemology of a culture its aesthetic, ethical, legal, economic, and other aspects, can serve as illustrations.[6] A large number of statements made by the functionalists could be converted into statements describing certain aspects of static order. In the same way, one could interpret the majority of the statements of T. Parsons and his school about the social system.

Invariant relations between phenomena succeeding in time are denoted as causality. The category of causality is applicable only if phenomena are contemplated in the time dimension. When one contemplates phenomena in the framework of static order, he must refrain from explanation in terms of causation. In the static perspective, causal propositions may be replaced by propositions about functional relationship, in the meaning given to it by modern functionalists.[7]

The statements above may seem outmoded. Today, it is fashionable to avoid the very term "cause," or at least to deny that causation implies sequence in time. The latter is replaced by "asymmetry," denoting cases when B depends on A but A does not depend on B. But, according to H. Simon, an adept of the new "metalanguage," it is surprising to find the term causation *"in common use* in scientific writing." [8] He himself often speaks of causal ordering, "causal relationship," or simply "cause," and has to refer to common-sense causality judgments to draw meaningful conclusions from the manipulation of concepts in the new style.[9]

The source of the tension between experimentalists and methodologists is conspicuous: for the experimental scientists, causation "means dependence of real things of nature on one another," and does not refer to concepts including the mathematical ones.[10] The elimination of causation from the number of the tools of scientific reasoning or the elimination, from causality, of the time dimension, is closely related to the ultramodernistic tendency to replace real phenomena by concepts. Some sixty years ago, with the appearance of K. Pearson's *Grammar of Science*, real phenomena started being replaced by "routine sense impressions"; now, sense impressions are being replaced by concepts. Conceptualism is, of course, one of the possible philosophical positions,[11] just as is moderate realism, which underlies the work of the vast majority of the experimental scientists, or as is the thought processes and actions of ordinary men. Since, between concepts, there can be no causal relations, the modern conceptualists must eliminate the concept of causality. For the students of real phenomena, of referents and not of symbols, there is no obligation to follow suit.

Consequently, when applying the category of causality, one legitimately distinguishes between the antecedent, cause, and the sequence, effect. In concrete cases, this relationship of cause and effect is irreversible, since time is irreversible. But when discussing invariant relations between phenomena *in abstracto,* cases show up when cause and effect seem to be interchangeable. From the (static) proposition that the volume of a gas is determined by pressure and temperature one can derive that (1) if the volume is decreased (cause), pressure increases (effect), and (2) if pressure is decreased (cause), volume increases (effect). In social phenomena, one meets situations when phenomenon N tangibly affects phenomenon $P,$ but P feeds back on N and causes change in it. For instance, such is the relationship between racial prejudice and the depressed economic and cultural state of the Negroes: racial prejudice is obviously one of the causes of the low economic and cultural state of the Negroes, but this low state feeds back on racial prejudice. Because of the existence of such cases, Sorokin prefers to apply the term function in place of cause and effect, or to speak of causal-functional relations.[12] The use of the term "function" would be confusing;[13] one could perhaps speak of "circular processes." But relative to each phase of a circular process the distinction between cause and effect can and must be made, on the basis of the time relationship between the phases (antecedent—subsequent). For example, analyzing a conversation or a quarrel, the investigator, remaining on the superficial level, may assert that all the phases appear to be so firmly concatenated that no distinction between causes and effects is possible. In actuality, verbal behavior a_1 of A (the originator of interaction) caused behavior b_1 of B, which caused behavior a_2 of A, which again caused behavior b_2 of B, and so on.

Causally relevant statements can be made both on the abstract and the concrete level. In the example above, concrete behavior a_1 was treated as the cause (or an element of the cause) of behavior b_1, and so on. In a similar way, we may assert that Hitler's invasion of Poland caused World War Two, or that in the fall of 1956 the interference of the United States and the Soviet Union caused the retreat of Great Britain and France from Egypt. Such statements correspond to singular propositions and empiric generalizations. Statements on the level of concrete causation mean that the phenomenon treated as effect (b) can be interpreted as depending on the phenomenon treated as cause (a). This is logically warranted if (a) and (b) may be shown to be specimens of classes of phenomena between which invariant relations (in the time dimension) are known to exist. Here, causation is treated on the abstract level. Of course, these are not two different types of causality, but two "ways of application." [14]

The concrete approach prevails in works of the historians, general or special (economic, political, legal, and so forth). They discuss what was the cause, or were the causes, of the American, French, or Russian revolution; of World War I or II; of the great depression; of the debunking of Stalin. As has already been stated, logically, statements on this level presuppose valid causal knowledge on the abstract level: one may assert that, at time T, a caused b, only if one knows that (1) if A is present, B follows; (2) a bears the essential traits of A and b the traits of B. In actuality, the historians, sometimes the social scientists also, either take causal propositions on the abstract level for granted, or formulate them *ad hoc;* the latter procedure is sometimes called inverse deduction. It is logically unwarranted, but may yield good results. Thus, for instance, on the basis of a number of case studies expressed in terms of singular propositions and empiric generalizations, the criminologists came to the conclusion that the broken home situation was a contributive factor of delinquency.[15]

Statements about causality on the abstract level are often called laws of nature or, in the social sciences, social laws. According to usage, however, only the more important from among such propositions are so called; but, since for the large residue, no commonly accepted term exists, let us call them laws also.[16]

3. CONJUNCTURE

Laws, or causal propositions on the abstract level, are often formulated in this manner: "If *A*, then *B* (follows)." This is, however, an
oversimplification obfuscating the real meaning of laws. *A*, by necessity,
is complex; it involves, at a minimum, a typologically defined situation
(consisting of a juxtaposition of traits) plus an "operator" or "precipitant," [17] something added to, or subtracted from, the situation. Let us
take for instance the outbreak of a contagious disease. Such a disease is
caused, say, by the inhalation of microorganisms by an animal possessing no special immunity against this particular disease. The sickness is
caused by the concomitance of a specified situation (an animal possessing no immunity) and an operator (inhalation of the microorganisms).
On the social level, the causation of delinquency, in terms of Sutherland's theory, may be formulated as follows: If a boy possessing no
special immunity against crime (in the form of strongly internalized
social norms and values) associates with bad companions, crime or delinquency results. More often than not, the situation is more complex.
The present author has tentatively formulated a hypothesis on war
causation which, in a simplified form, reads as follows: If, between two
nations, a serious tension (of specified types, not to be discussed here)
exists; if, in addition to this, the peaceful means of conflict solution have
failed or have been rejected by one of the parties; if, moreover, each of
the parties has reasons to believe in victory, then war is likely to break
out.[18] An incident takes place and plays the part of an operator. It seems
to cause war. In actuality, a complex situation identified above has been
relevant.

Therefore, much better is the formula: If conditions *N, P, R* are
present, effect *B* follows; in this formula, $N + P + R = A$ of the one
offered above. The cause is never simple; it is concomitance of two or
more conditions (factors). Taken separately, each factor, appearing in
a field or force, creates a "causal tendency," i.e., the objective possibility of the realization or the effect. If the chance of the realization of the
possibility is measurable, we call it probability.

In every situation, many causal tendencies are present. Depending
on what additional causal tendencies will appear, different effects will
follow. Therefore, one is entitled to assert that a given situation may
develop in two or more different ways; in other words, relative to a
given situation, two or more possibilities (eventually, probabilities) may
be asserted objectively to exist. Judgments in these terms are possible
not only on the level of anticipation (often in the form of choice between two or more courses of action), but also *a posteriori:* looking

as the intersection of two causal chains. The unfolding of every chain is, by definition, covered by the postulate of order; but their intersection is not. No theoretical proposition is possible according to which the intersection *had* to take place at *T* in *S*. This is self-evident: a theoretical proposition is characterized by absence of reference to concrete time and space; but an intersection of causally relevant developments takes place in concrete time and space. This copresence, or conjunction, of relatively independent causal developments producing the phenomenon under study is *conjuncture*.[19]

Let us illustrate these abstract statements by a few instances. An automobile accident has taken place. Experts can causally explain why automobile *A* followed the path it did; the explanation will be "multi-factorial," including objective factors (the make and state of the auto-mobile, the state of the road, visibility, the official and customary traffic rules, etc.) and subjective factors (the intentions, driving abilities, and hab-its of the driver, as well as his biophysic state). They can make the same explanation relative to the path of automobile *B*. In both cases, in princi-ple, the explanation can be given in terms of numerous causal proposi-tions referring to invariant relations between phenomena. But the fact that cars *A* and *B* met at *T* in *S* escapes such an explanation. The fact was not inherent in any aspect of order, while the results of the collision are again covered by the postulate. In this instance, the intersection of causal chains is physically observable, which is by no means always the case.

Let us choose another instance from history, which, incidentally, is a predominantly conjunctural science, because the historical process is conjunctural: what really happened has been caused by numerous meet-ings of relatively independent developments. Today, the historical process is marked by a sharp conflict between the American led West and the Russian led East. Until recently, the two developments, the American and the Russian, were almost independent; until the middle of the nineteenth century, American history could be well presented without reference to events in Russia, and Russian history without refer-ence to events in America. Then, the two developments started inter-secting, first in the area of the Behring Strait, then in the Far East, and finally throughout the world. This intersection, of the American and Russian developments, just at the time mentioned, is purely conjunctural, irreducible to theoretical statements about the development of human societies. Even now, *a posteriori,* no theoretical proposition can be formulated from which the intersection of American and Russian ways, then and now, could be "predicted" (or, more exactly, logically derived).

As a third instance, the becoming of the configuration of a culture may serve. A culture is what its life story made it to be. The bearers of the culture, an ethnic group, have been exposed to many challenges,

retrospectively at a past situation, one may reasonably assert
could have developed at variance with the actual course of events.
ern historians, in contradistinction from those of fifty years ago, c
longer share the necessitarian view; they do not assert that what
pened had to happen, and that it could not have been otherwise.
Russian revolution had not necessarily to end in the establishmen
the Communist dictatorship; the triumph of democracy, or the rise c
military dictatorship, or the restoration of monarchy (in a modif
form) were possible. The great American crisis of the early thirties h
not necessarily to end in the New Deal; it could also have ended in a f
reaching disintegration of the American social and economic systen
or perhaps in a technocratic revolution. This new look at historica
events corresponds to the shift from the universal to the limited conception of the principle of order (see above section 1).

As has been stated, the appearance of one of the factors (conditions)
forming the cause of a definite effect may be conceived as the rise of a
causal tendency pointing to the effect. If another factor shows up, the
possibility becomes more distinct (eventually the probability increases).
If and when all the factors have materialized, and inhibitive factors are
absent, the effect follows. One may interpret the causally relevant development as the gradual accumulation of factors.

Another image is, however, often used, that of the intersection of
causal chains. This image is applicable, if one takes one or two steps
back from the situation characterized by the accumulation of all the
necessary conditions. Each of these conditions can be eventually explained causally (provided that it is covered by the postulate of order).
The explanation can again be offered in terms of gradual accumulation
of factors or necessary conditions. Out of these conditions, the investigator often chooses one, not necessarily as being prepotent (perhaps,
there are no such conditions), but as the one offering the greatest insight, the best understandable explanation of the effect. This procedure
can be repeated. Logically, it can go *ad infinitum;* but no reasonable investigator cares to go too far back. Assume that the effect under study
(E) has been caused by the concomitance of two conditions, C_1 and C_2.
Both C_1 and C_2 may be regarded as the effects (E_1 and E_2) of two
further concomitances; but, of the two forming each pair, one chooses
one only, respectively C^1_1 and C^1_2. Then we have:

$$C^1_1 \rightarrow E_1 \ (= C_1) \searrow$$
$$ E$$
$$C^1_2 \rightarrow E_2 \ (= C_2) \nearrow$$

The development from C^1_1 to E and from C^1_2 to E may be called
causal chains. Then, the causation of the phenomenon may be perceived

both external and internal, and have found more or less satisfactory responses, often diverse in similar situations. Contemporary sociology is able to formulate a few "laws" about the development of culture; they are pertinent to inventions (technical, behavioral, ideological), to acceptance or rejection of inventions, and to diffusion, or imitation of culture by another culture with which it is in contact. Applying these laws to a concrete development, a sociologist or an historian can satisfactorily explain a culture configuration, e.g., the configuration of contemporary American culture. But, using these laws, he could not have "predicted" it; in addition to the knowledge of the laws, he needs knowledge about conjuncture, the time-space distribution of innumerable phenomena. There was no necessity (in the meaning or "invariant relations") that courageous emigrants from seventeenth century England and therefore bearers of her culture would have landed in a thinly inhabited area, with adequate climate, richly endowed with diverse natural resources and safe from strong and well armed neighbors. Each of these factors, and many more, have contributed to the making of American culture; the presence or appearance of every factor can be causally explained. But their copresence cannot; it is conjunctural.

4. CONJUNCTURE AND CAUSAL PROPOSITIONS

Order is limited to invariant relations. Invariant relations do not cover everything that is, was, or is becoming; in addition to order, there is conjuncture. There may be other limitations of order, but they are not being explored in this paper.

In the continuous stream of phenomena, order and conjuncture are so closely interwoven that one could not separate the phenomena into two classes, some causally determined and others conjunctural; in concrete phenomena (provided that they stand under the postulate of order) one may analytically distinguish a causally relevant and a conjunctural aspect.

To grasp this relationship, let us first contemplate the simplest possible case. Assume that a law denotes change in a closed (limited) system under the impact of one causal tendency (operator or precipitant). If the system passes from state S_0 to state S_1 then,

$$S_0 + P = S_1$$

In this formula, conjuncture is expressed by the sign $+$: the precipitant must be apposed to the system if the effect (change from S_0 to S_1) is to take place; the invariant relation (change from S_0 to S_1 under the impact of P) is expressed by the sign $=$. However, the formula does

not express one important condition, namely the absence of other causally relevant developments affecting S. If the system is under the impact
of two or more causal tendencies, the individual law is not invalidated,
but its effect is modified or checked by the other developments.

Therefore, the formula above should be modified and receive this
shape:

$$S_o + P \rightarrow S_1$$

where the sign $\rightarrow$ connotes a causal tendency.

Situations corresponding to the simplest modality of causation are
created by the experimentalist in his laboratory who almost never finds
them outside of the laboratory. In the laboratory situation, the research
man tries physically to keep constant all the relevant aspects of the
situation, except one, which, on the contrary, is added to, or subtracted
from, the total situation, or changed in magnitude. In the social sciences,
the research man sometimes tries to create quasi-laboratory situations,
by matching, to the limit of possibility, the experimental and the control
group of which the former is, and the latter is not, exposed to the
causal development under study (e.g., impact of additional years of
schooling, of rehousing, of one or another treatment devised by contemporary criminology).

One of the best instances of simple causation in the realm of the
social sciences is Malthus' population law: *"If unchecked,* population
increases in geometrical ratio."* The italicized words (which are commonly omitted in quotations) are highly important; they much better
express the logic behind such elementary laws than the usual formation
"other things equal," because they directly point to the absence of other
causal chains affecting the situation. The law may be read as expressing
the causal tendency of every population (S_o) to change in size (become
S_1) under the impact of the allegedly constant sexual urge (P).

In Sorokin's work, one finds the idea that a sociocultural system of
type X will develop through stages X_1, X_2, X_3. Of course, if its development is not affected by external factors, especially by developments in
other systems with which the one under observation is in contact; then,
but only then, the sociocultural system will develop immanently, by the
unfolding of its nature (sensate, idealistic, ideational) under the impact
of forces inherent in it.[20]

A vast number of "theories of the middle range" formulated by contemporary sociologists may be considered to be specimens of (tentative)
laws unveiling causal tendencies affecting specified (typologically described) social systems (often, mere aggregations of human beings)
which materialize if and when they are unchecked. In the formulation
of tentative laws of this type, one is commonly guided by knowledge

available as to the nature of social systems in general or of specified types of such systems.

Already on this level, order and conjuncture meet to give shape to the total social phenomenon. In the laboratory, the conjuncture is artificially created; outside the laboratory, it is more or less artfully singled out from the uninterrupted flow of phenomena.

One must, however, not commit the mistake of identifying conjuncture with the sumtotal of the conditions, or factors. If this identification is made, conjuncture becomes the cause of the effect under study. But conjuncture is not the sumtotal of conditions; it is intersection, in concrete time and space, of causal chains standing behind each factor, eliciting, in togetherness, the effect. There is a great difference between individual factors and conjuncture; the factors are phases in the unfolding of causal chains; they are under the postulate of order. But their intersection cannot be identified with any causal chain; it is outside the scope of order. One could say that each formula of the type "if $N, P, R,$ then B follows" includes a tacit element (common to all causal formulas), namely copresence of N, P, R in time and space. The conjuncture does not cause the effect just as time does not, although time, perhaps infinitesimal, is a necessary aspect of every becoming. Conjuncture transforms each causal tendency (corresponding to one of the necessary conditions) from a potential into an actual force; this takes place by the very fact that the other tendencies (conditions, factors) are also present. While each condition is necessary, their copresence in time and space makes their sumtotal sufficient. Whether this "sufficiency" is or is not given transcends, however, the scope of order and causality.

Causation is complex when invariable relations obtain not between two states of a relatively closed system under the impact of an operator, but determine the resultant of the composition of forces corresponding to intersecting causal chains. Such are, for instance, the laws of elementary mechanics. Similar laws abound in the social sciences. One may perhaps understand some parts of the "general theory of action," as presented by T. Parsons and his associates,[21] as a system of abstract causal propositions about the effect of various combinations of motivational and value orientations on action. Studies of conditions under which competition or co-operation prevail,[22] or under which racial conflicts are exacerbated, reduced or resolved,[23] are additional instances. The sociology of law has, among its major problems, to study the simultaneous impact on human conduct of legal, purely ethical, and purely political forces, in addition to the background of presocial or asocial drives.[24] Predictive tables with respect to recidivism, the outcome of marriage and so on, can be conceived as first approximations to causal statements of the type now considered. On the basis of accumulated knowledge, the criminologists ascribe criminogenic (i.e., causal) significance to many factors (such as culture conflict, family disorganization, growing up in a slum, bad companionship, or bad industrial habits). The predictive table is then an attempt to determine the resultant of the composition of forces corresponding to the causal tendencies present in a field of observation.

It is obvious that, in situations governed by laws about the composition of forces (causal tendencies), order and conjuncture are both present exactly as in the case of simple causation: conjuncture as to the intersection of causal chains in concrete time and space; order as to the consequences of intersection. The instance of an automobile collision offered above may again serve as a good illustration.

The interpretation given above to the relationship of order and conjuncture throws some light on the obscure problem of plural or multiple causation.[25] Plural causation connotes the fact that, in causal relations between phenomena, the antecedent (cause) is commonly complex, being the resultant of the intersection of several causal chains. Assume that the effect under consideration, X, is caused on the background of conjuncture $A + B + C$. Assume furthermore that in some cases some of the elements (say, A and B) are present, but not yet C; then C shows up, the conjuncture is completed, the effect follows. But in another case, A and C, and in still another case, B and C are present; then, respectively B or A shows up, the conjuncture is completed, and the effect follows. At first glance, it seems that the effect has been caused in three different ways. But it is not so. What distinguishes the cases from each other pertains to conjuncture, to the sequence in which the necessary and sufficient conditions appear. In principle, such sequences, as related to concrete time and space, are not governed by abstract causal propositions. When causally analyzing concrete phenomena, we narrate them: first, a appeared, then b, and then c, and the effect x followed. As has already been stated, this explanation is warranted, if there is reason to believe that the combination A, B, C (typologically described conditions) caused X (the typologically described effect).

The interpretation of the relationship between order and conjuncture solves also a problem or perhaps a pseudoproblem sometimes puzzling the social scientists when the list or catalogue approach to the causation of complex phenomena is used. Criminologists have often complained that there are many known antecedents of crime, but none is necessary, in the meaning that it must be present prior to the performance of a criminal action.[26] In the field of the sociology of war, L. L. Bernard [27] has listed a large number of antecedents and offered a multidimensional classification. The theoretical gain, however, is nil. Why? Because the nature of the interweaving of causality and conjuncture is ignored. The Ems dépêche played a part in the outbreak of the

Franco-Prussian War of 1870, but many wars broke out without insults of one government by another, and many insults of this kind did not elicit wars. In that case, the insult contributed to the outbreak of the war, but only because the system of relations between the two states was strained almost to the breaking point, so that an "incident" (which may have been not an insult, but something else, e.g., trespassing of the boundary by an armed detachment of the hostile state) was sufficient to elicit war. In any case, the particular elements of the antecedent must be sufficiently generalized and correlated with the relevant properties of the social systems involved (in case of war, of the State and of the community of nations). Then the long lists of antecedents of crime or war are replaced by propositions of the type exemplified by the present author's hypothesis on war causation (summarized above). In the etiology of crime, a similar generalizing hypothesis could be formulated, juxtaposing the malfunctioning of the agencies of socialization (the family, the neighborhood, the school, the Church, the social organizations exercising the functions of crime prevention and repression); specified deviations of the personality of the offender from the modal; opportunity and/or the emergence of a situation eliciting strong motivation oriented to crime. Each of the factors creates a criminogenic tendency; their accumulation (tantamount to conjuncture) activates these tendencies. Work done by modern criminologists furnishes, if not all, the majority of the elements necessary for the construction of a set of theoretical propositions about crime causation; what is lacking is the understanding of the mode of the integration of parts into a theoretically meaningful whole.

Laws about the composition of forces are statements about causality of higher complexity than laws about the impact of operators on closed systems. The highest level of complexity is reached in statistical laws.

Statistical laws are statements about invariant relations between two or more states of a "universe" or "population." Change in the state of a universe (tantamount to the difference between two successive states) is the product of the composition of forces (causal tendencies) inherent in the units forming the universe; the behaviors of these units are too numerous to be taken in account one by one, and numerous enough to warrant a calculable probability of the effect predicated by the law. In consequence, statistical laws are merely probability statements; but such are, after all, also the laws about simple or complex causation. More exactly: all types of laws point to invariant relations; but, in fact, even laws about simple causation yield knowledge about causal tendencies only, since, almost without exception, actual phenomena deviate from predictions on the basis of the laws. This happens because conjunctures are more complicated than assumed by the investigator, or because more

factors are involved than stated in the conditional clause of the law.
The mere probability (not certainty) character of the statements called
laws increases from simple to complex causation and from complex
causation to causation dealt with by statistical laws. Nevertheless, as
convincingly shown by F. C. S. Northrop,[28] the existence of a statistical
law in the meaning just described presupposes that there are invariant
relations between behaviors of the units forming the universe. What this
means can be best demonstrated by the example of the laws of heredity,
which permit the prediction of the biological composition of a later
generation, if one knows the biological composition of the preceding one
and the mode of selection of the mates (e.g., endogamy). This prediction is reliable because the conjunctions of the genes occur by chance
and are numerous enough to warrant the operation of the principle of
large numbers. But these conjunctions can yield the specified result only
because there are invariant relations between the characteristics of each
pair of genes passed from the parents to the progeny and the characteristics of the latter.

Nevertheless, prediction on the basis of Mendelian genetics may go
wrong if a mutation transmissible to the progeny takes place, or if an
extraneous operator affects the population, e.g., the human population
forming the object of prediction is conquered by another population and
interbreeding takes place. The failure of the prediction does not in-
validate the theoretical propositions forming its foundation. An unexpected conjuncture has appeared in the field, and the *emergence* of
conjunctures is not covered by theoretical propositions.

In the field studied by the social sciences, situations analogous to
those governed by the laws of heredity often obtain. There are recurring
mass phenomena observable in universes consisting of large numbers of
men. Sorokin offers a tentative catalogue of such phenomena, which include birth, death, marriage, divorce, suicide, morbidity, migration,
crime, demand and supply, solilarity, and antagonism.[29] These and
many other situations comply with the conditions warranting the formulation of statistical laws. Recent developments in statistics expand the
scope of such situations. There is, however, no theoretical reason for
assuming that, concerning any type of situations, statistical laws could
be formulated. This follows from the limited conception of the postulate
of order prevalent today. Moreover, statistical laws imply conjuncture
in the same meaning as laws of the types discussed above. A statistical
law can be formulated only about situations characterized by the juxtaposition of several factors. When the juxtaposition is given, the law
"works"; but whether it is given is not governed by the statistical law
in question. Of course, the presence of factors and/or the frequency
distribution of the components of the universe may be governed by

other laws, statistical or not. The intersection of causal tendencies thus elicited is, however, again conjunctural.

5. THE STUDY OF SOCIAL ORDER

Order, causality, and conjuncture are apparent in all phases of reality. But here we are interested in social reality and, consequently, in social order and social causation.

Social order is given if, in interpersonal relations, definite behavior patterns commonly prevail. The existence of such patterns is observable and often can be expressed statistically. But the patterns prevail only "commonly," that is, in the vast majority of cases; depending on the degree of prevalence, we can speak of more or less order. Never is there absolute order; irreducible conjunctural elements are always present. Most people most commonly behave lawfully. Nevertheless, criminal offenses are time and again committed, and their break through the legal phase of social order is legally foreseen. There are rules of penal law (= patterns of social behavior) imposing sanctions on eventual offenders.

An adequate study of social order presupposes knowledge of the mechanisms through which the uniformities of behavior corresponding to the order are formed. There are four basic mechanisms which may, however, merge into compound ones.[30]

First, there are "natural uniformities." They obtain whenever, among men, similar causes produce similar effects, without efforts tending to create and enforce a uniformity. For example, young people fall in love and marry. Merchants raise their prices when demand increases with no simultaneous increase of supply.

Second, there are imitative uniformities based on simultaneous choices, by many, of identical behavior patterns. Fashions and fads, not only in dress, but also in speech, eating and drinking patterns, artistic and even scientific activities, belong hereto. The uniformity is not imposed, but desired: the followers choose to look or act alike, which is not the case relative to "natural" uniformities. Since many imitate the same model of action (M), the action of each of the imitators may be expressed by the formulas $A_1 = M$, $A_2 = M$, $A_3 = M$. Since two magnitudes equal to a third are equal, $A_1 = A_2 = A_3$. Hence the uniformity.

Third, there are compulsory uniformities based on the imposition of specified patterns of behavior by coercion or threat of coercion. This happens when in fields not covered by the law general commands are issued by those in power and are followed by the addressees. In pure form, the phenomenon is observable in totalitarian societies and, to a

lesser extent, in despotisms and absolute monarchies. But even in societies where "the rule of law" dominates, discretionary power is often
ascribed (in definite limits) to specified bearers of authority, and the
exertion of this power gives rise to compulsory uniformities.

Fourth, there are ethical uniformities. They obtain if objective patterns of behavior are commonly re-enforced by the specific experience
that the patterned behavior ought or ought not to be. Innumerable customs and usages belong hereto, as well as rules of decency and politeness, or rules to be followed in the accomplishment of tasks of diverse
occupational groups.

Out of compound uniformities, the legal ones are of greatest importance. There are laws in which the compulsory element prevails and
other ones where the ethical one is paramount. Laws on taxation, on the
draft, on ceiling prices may be cited as specimens of the former type, and
laws protecting basic human values belong to the latter type. Between
the two, one may observe many transitions. But, in actuality, in law, the
two elements always merge: a legal norm is a statement about a behavior
which ought to be, but also about a behavior which eventually will be enforced by a social power.

Of course, not all human behavior can be distributed along the uniformities surveyed. There is spontaneous behavior of which invention
or innovation is the socioculturally most important specimen; but there
is also erratic, or quite unexpected, behavior. How often one says that he
never expected his friend or neighbor to do just that!

But the vast majority of human actions can be located in one or another of the uniformities surveyed. Their location is not random. Ethical
and legal behavior is predominantly group behavior. It could not be
otherwise, since ethical and legal norms are generated and enforced in
the framework of social groups. The study of social order thus obtaining
is tantamount to the study of conforming behavior according to the nature of the corresponding groups. Propositions about simple causation,
supplemented by causal propositions on the consequences of the conjunctural intersection of causal tendencies thus generated, are to be striven
for; among the latter, some must concern themselves with the resultants
of the composition of forces obtaining through the overlapping of groups
and on the background of intergroup conflicts. Such a study, begun by
men in time immemorial and refined in sociology, is based mainly on
participant observation, on everyone's immediate experience of group
membership and group pressure. On that background, theoretical propositions on the level of simple and complex causation can be formulated,
especially relative to primary groups, the structure and articulation of
which is given in immediate experience. On the assumption that the
mechanisms of interaction in secondary groups are derived from those

obtaining in primary groups, further inferences, again concerning simple and complex causation, may be made. Statistical devices may be helpful, but rather for the verification of hypotheses than for their construction.

Behavior forming natural and imitative uniformities is predominantly mass (or collective) behavior. It transcends group organization (though the performers are deeply affected by their group memberships) and may be adequately studied by statistical methods, since the uniformities concern themselves with the behavior of large numbers of individuals affected by similar causes (in natural uniformities), or more specifically by the attraction of a model (to imitative uniformities). Of course, statistical findings about such uniformities are predominantly on the descriptive level: they accurately describe what, in concrete time and space, has been the behavior of a universe under the impact of such and such causal tendencies. But it is sometimes possible to raise the findings onto the theoretical level and to formulate propositions not referring to concrete time and space. One of the conditions of scientific validity is, however, too often overlooked: [31] This is reference to a definite type of society, defined by the juxtaposition of a certain number of relevant traits. Neglect of this condition may result in scientific catastrophes. This happened, for instance, with the laws of classic economics which were erroneously formulated as universally valid propositions. On that basis, in the twenties, predictions about the necessary and rather imminent collapse of the economic order created by the communists were made—and failed. Nevertheless, the laws are not invalid, but limited to societies based on free enterprise and free competition. To ascertain what traits are relevant is a difficult task. Most commonly, it can be achieved only by painstaking comparison of different universes and by the finding of negative cases resulting in the narrowing down of the conditional clause of the theoretical proposition. Thus, for instance, the early American ecologists were inclined to generalize their findings about the genesis and location of slums. Comparison with other societies should compel them to restate their hypothesis approximately as follows: "In a rapidly advancing industrial society lacking knowledge about the detrimental consequences of rapid urbanization and/or willingness to combat them . . ."

Behavior belonging to compulsory uniformities occupies an intermediary position. In the rule, it is group behavior, since social power is a widely spread trait of group organization: one meets social power in political, economic, religious, educational, and domestic groups. To that extent, the study of compulsory uniformities must follow the same line as that of ethical and legal uniformities. But the influence of a power center may transcend the compass of existing groups; in *statu nascendi,* social power always presents this feature. Behaviors thus elicited cannot be theoretically derived from group properties. Here, as relative to natural and imitative uniformities, statistical treatment is warranted, provided that the number of units (persons) is sufficiently large.

6. SUMMARY

This exploration of the relationship of order and conjuncture, with special emphasis on social phenomena, may be summed up as follows:

1. Order, i.e., the presence of invariant relations, does not cover the whole field of scientific investigation. In addition to order which, by definition, defies reference to concrete time and space, there is conjuncture, or copresence of, or interaction between, phenomena in concrete time and space.

2. Causality is the dynamic aspect of order. Knowledge about dynamic order is couched in causal propositions which, if they attain a certain degree of generality, are commonly called laws.

3. Social order is observable in the form of behavioral uniformities, or in the recurrence of behaviors conforming with specified patterns. Depending on the mechanisms through which the uniformities are engendered and sustained, one may distinguish natural, imitative, compulsory, and ethical uniformities, with legal uniformities as one of the typical compounds. Ethical, legal, and partly compulsory uniformities are tantamount to group behavior, i.e., behavior elicited through order prevailing in the group. Relative to these aspects of social order, laws expressing simple causality or determining the resultants of the intersection of causal chains prevail and can be formulated as derivations from the basic properties of social groups in general and of groups of specified types. Natural, imitative, and partly compulsory uniformities manifest behavior within unorganized human masses; here statistical laws must prevail; but, to make these uniformities understandable, the explorer must penetrate into the underlying causal tendencies governing the behavior of the constituent units and the laws of the composition of such tendencies in typical situations.

NOTES

1. In the very sentence of *Esprit des lois* (1748). The phrase "according to nature" reappears in Robert M. MacIver, *Social Causation* (Boston: Ginn and Company, 1942), p. 28.

2. *Essai philosophique sur les probabilités* (the statement appears in Vol. II, p. 3, of the 1921 edition).

3. Among recent statements of P. W. Bridgman, "Science and the

Broad Point of View," *Proceedings of the National Academy of Science,* 42 (1956), pp. 315-25.

4. Pitirim A. Sorokin, *Social and Cultural Dynamics* (1937), Vol. I, pp. 10-13, 48, 161-73, where he distinguishes recurring and unique phenomena. In Bridgman, *op. cit.,* one reads: "There are situations . . . which cannot be made to repeat" (p. 319).

5. *Déterminismes sociaux et liberté humaine* (Paris: Presses universitaires de France, 1955).

6. The derivation of the various phases of culture from its central theme is explicitly treated in *Social and Cultural Dynamics* (New York: American Book Company, 1937), I, 72-101; but, to a certain extent, all the four volumes of the work may be considered as a substantiation of the basic thesis concerning that derivation; it has been summarized by Sorokin in *Fads and Foibles in Modern Sociology and the Related Sciences* (Chicago: Henry Regnery Company, 1956), pp. 273-74.

7. Cf. Nicholas S. Timasheff, *Sociological Theory: Its Nature and Growth* (New York: Doubleday & Company, Inc., 1955), p. 220.

8. Herbert A. Simon, *Models of Man, Social and Rational* (New York, John Wiley & Sons, Inc., 1957), p. 11. (Italics mine—N.T.)

9. *Ibid.,* pp. 39-41.

10. Max Born, *Natural Philosophy of Cause and Chance* (Oxford: Clarendon Press, 1949), p. 6.

11. In Sorokin, *op. cit.* (Vol. II, pp. 247-60), one may find a quantitative survey of the fluctuations of conceptualism in the history of Western philosophy.

12. *Sociocultural Causality, Space, Time* (Durham, N.C.: Duke University Press, 1943), p. 39; *Society, Culture and Personality* (New York: Harper & Brothers, 1947), p. 146.

13. Because of another connotation of the term in sociology and cultural anthropology; cf. Timasheff, *op. cit.,* pp. 219-20.

14. Born, *op. cit.,* pp. 7-8.

15. At the present time, the criminologists are inclined to consider the broken-home situation as a species of family disorganization which, as such, is criminogenic.

16. All abstract causal propositions are evidently theoretical propositions, e.g., propositions in the style of functionalism (what a smaller group does for a larger one) or propositions about the logicomeaningful integration of social phenomena (Sorokin).

17. MacIver, *op. cit.,* pp. 63 and 163.

18. Nicholas S. Timasheff, "War and Peace," *Thought,* September, 1950, pp. 394-98; the statements in text are abridged and simplified versions of propositions offered in that paper.

19. On conjuncture, cf. MacIver, *op. cit.,* pp. 29, 64-65, 119, 129, 313-21, 382-83, and Georges Gurvitch, *"Le concept de structure sociale,"* Cahiers Internationaux de Sociologie, 19 (1955), pp. 12-13.

20. *Social and Cultural Dynamics,* II, 54-206; IV, 590-92, 711-13. The validity of the proposition is not examined at this place.

21. Especially in *Towards a General Theory of Action* (Cambridge: Harvard University Press, 1951); but also in *The Social System* (Glencoe, Ill.: Free Press, 1951), pp. 180-200.

22. Margaret Mead, *Cooperation and Competition Among Primitive Peoples* (New York: McGraw-Hill Book Company, Inc., 1937).

23. Robin Williams, *The Reduction of Intergroup Tensions* (Social Sciences Research Council Bulletin No. 57, New York, 1947).

24. Timasheff, *Introduction to the Sociology of Law* (Cambridge: Harvard University Committee on Research in the Social Sciences, 1939), *passim.*

25. Sorokin, *Sociocultural Causality,* pp. 47-52 and 75; *Society, Culture and Personality,* pp. 504-06.

26. E.g., Walter C. Reckless, *Criminal Behavior* (New York: McGraw-Hill Book Company, Inc., 1940), pp. 177, 181, 239, 254-56, doubts the criminogenic significance of feeble-mindedness, community disorganization, and poverty because crime does not result in numerous cases in which these conditions are present. In actuality, the factors enumerated are causal tendencies which more often than not are checked by antagonistic behavior tendencies. Jerome Michael and Mortimer Adler, *Crime, Law and Social Science* (New York: Harcourt Brace & Company, Inc., 1933), called "absurd" attempts to draw etiological conclusions from the findings of criminology. In actuality, they are not, if one overcomes the somewhat primitive conception of causality obtaining when the "if unchecked" clause is omitted.

27. L. L. Bernard, *War and Its Causes* (New York: Henry Holt & Company, Inc., 1944).

28. According to F. C. S. Northrop, *The Logic of the Sciences and the Humanities* (New York: The Macmillan Company, 1947). "If there are certain laws in science which are statistical, then there must be also laws in that science which are not statistical" (p. 216). Otherwise, the statistical universe "will be in such a state of flux that no prediction could be made" (p. 215).

29. Sorokin, *Fads and Foibles,* p. 154.

30. The types of social uniformities have been discussed by Timasheff, *An Introduction to the Sociology of Law,* pp. 5-16. The types are, of course, "ideal," or "pure types," in the meaning ascribed to these terms by Max Weber.

31. Arnold M. Rose, *Theory and Method in the Social Sciences* (Minneapolis: University of Minnesota Press, 1954), pp. 256-68.

IV

SOCIAL CHANGE

6

The Concept of Levels in Social Theory

ABRAHAM EDEL

The City College of New York

I

The concept of levels, which was sharpened primarily in evolutionary philosophies, refers initially to the emergence of qualities in the process of historical development. In this familiar sense, the appearance of life in the world constituted a new integrative level, the appearance of consciousness another; and again, in human affairs, new steps (fire, farming, machine technology, etc.) brought in new stages by altering profoundly and pervasively the qualities of human life. Philosophically, the concept of levels involves the ideas of some continuity of the new with the old, a maturing causal process which constitutes the emerging, a field of novel or distinctive qualities with some order of its own (hence an element of discontinuity with the past), some degree of alteration in the total scene and its modes of operation because of the presence of the new. Methodologically, a new level requires new descriptive concepts and, many believe, new empirical laws, independent of those of the old level.

I should like to comment briefly on each of these several strands in the levels concept because it seems important in the work of the social scientist to distinguish them and to realize that they constitute to some degree independently applicable theses for a field of investigation. There has, of course, been considerable philosophical discussion of these ideas

in recent decades, in attempts to get the "mystery" out of the emergence
concept, in refining the notion of causality and determinism involved, in
seeking to remove the "epiphenomenalist" character of the new (its
supervening or helpless floating above, as it were, while the real "executive" work is being done on the lower order).[1] Much of this seems to
me to have been successful in breaking older philosophical stereotypes.
But it would carry us too far afield to discuss even the general philosophical issues that have been raised. Many of them, while interesting and
important as problems in the logic of science, do not directly affect the
actual work of the social scientist, at least in the present stages of the
social sciences. I shall therefore limit myself to the points indicated.

The concept of emergent levels involves a historical or developmen-
tal perspective, not merely a concern with the relations of qualitatively
distinct bands of coexistent phenomena in a static field. A quality is novel
not because it is distinctively different, but because nothing like it existed
at an earlier period, and it does exist and recur at a later period. However, the mere occurrence of a particular novel quality is not usually
greeted as a fresh "level." A new art style may be unique without affecting a revolution in art, let alone in human history. The concept of emergent levels thus contains additional ideas which may be of rather different orders of strength or scope. The minimal sense is probably simply
that the novel quality (or a family of them) reappears with sufficient
frequency so that it should be regarded as a regular inhabitant of the
world, worthy of separate systematic study. But most actual use of
the levels concept in biology and in the sciences of man involves also the
element of continuity, the additional thesis that there are causal conditions under which the novel phenomena came into existence and conditions which support their continued occurrence. These are statable as
historical descriptions and translevel laws. Thus, sensory color experiences came into existence with a certain development of animal eyes, and
are supported under definite optical-retinal-brain conditions. Similarly,
that the political state came into existence at a definite point is generally
agreed by social scientists, although it is not wholly established what
were the critical factors involved.

Wider concern with transitional periods prior to the definite emergence of the new phenomena increasingly calls attention to the variety of
intermediate forms, the piling up of variations, and the processes of consolidation and crystallization of the new levels. This is found, for example, in contemporary genetic studies of variational direction in mutation,
in chemical studies of the borderline of the living and nonliving, and in
discoveries of the probable transition in the animal world from the prehuman to the human type. Comparable study in the social sciences provides clues for generalizing about the conditions of the historical origin

of specific social institutions. There has not always been a careful enough distinction, however, between conditions of historical origin and conditions supporting continuation. These need not always coincide, but when they do not, one should always be sensitive to the possibility that there has been a qualitative transformation in the character of the phenomena themselves.

Most conceptions of integrative levels add to the discontinuity in the appearance of the novel qualities the further assertion that there are discoverable laws on the higher level in terms of that level—e.g., biological, psychological, social laws. There may, of course, be a parting of the ways in future prospects of reduction. Although there is general agreement that we have at present a set of sciences each of which is, so to speak, on its own, a reductive view sees this as a halfway house to a future unified science in which all the sciences are integrated. For example, chemistry is integrated within the framework of physics. A nonreductive view expects all sorts of intermediate fields (biochemistry, physiological psychology, etc.) but interprets these as literally relations of separate fields, not abolition of some on behalf of others. The levels concept is usually nonreductive in type; this involves at least the insistence that all translevel laws are genuine *empirical* laws, with terms descriptive of higher-level novel qualities as part of their statement.

A further addition is sometimes found in the assertion that the behavior of lower-level elements after the emergence of the higher-level phenomena may follow different laws from what it did when the higher-level phenomena had not yet existed, or from what it does in areas where they are not present. This may be loosely described as the interference of the higher-level entities in the lower level, or the assertion of higher level causality, or the denial that the higher level phenomena are epiphenomenal. Precisely how it is to be described depends on the analysis of these terms. Descriptively, in ordinary language, the point is familiar enough in the view that once man is on the globe, part of the explanation of what happens in the domain of the physical is in terms of what men want to do and actually do, whether it be in denuding or planting surface areas or creating new elements. Nor need this refer to man alone. For example, if the oxygen in our atmosphere is the result of photosynthesis, then important phenomena in our physical environment can only be explained by reference to the interaction of the higher-level phenomena of life.[2] And the same thing can be said concerning the effects of water, once it has emerged from earlier gases. How far the interference of higher-level phenomena may go in the lower level is of course a separate empirical question. A great part of the physical world goes on its way, even on our globe, impervious to the existence of life. But in the case of man, even as compared to the other animals, the cultural level permeates the individual fairly completely, so that man is often described as "bio-social." If there are distinguishable levels in society itself, one may completely replace another in which it grew up, as something like urban life may conceivably wholly replace rural life.

What can the methodology of social theory hope to gain from these distinctions, or the use of the concept of emergent levels as a whole? The past gains from the general concept have been clear enough. It has helped the social sciences resist the reductive tendencies to impose upon them the concepts and methods of the physical and biological sciences in *a priori* fashion. It has also, in the reverse direction, helped them oppose the attempts to isolate the study of man from the sciences, in the interests of non-naturalistic conceptions of man. Again, it has helped them avoid falling into the seductive metaphysical trap of seeing whatever order they discover in a partial segment of human history as the permanent nature or essence of man and society. For the levels concept brings, methodologically, a constant historical perspective to social description and explanation. It can become a sensitive alertness to the possible emergence of stable new forms, to their interaction, both in their rise and their maturity, with the milieu in which they emerge, to the conditions that make for continued stability or change, and to the way in which interaction at any given point may produce further incipient transitions.

It is also clear what as a methodological concept the levels concept cannot do. It cannot supply out of itself the specific hypotheses—in this case what are to be marked out as the major stages in the development of mankind, how varied and how globally interactive this development has been. It cannot specify in advance even which of the components within itself—the various possible theses we have seen as constituting the idea of levels—will be found applicable in the various domains of human phenomena. For example, when fresh areas of phenomena are staked out for systematic study, such as linguistic phenomena and value phenomena, it may be possible that one turns out to have a considerable internal "autonomy" on its own level and in its own terms (as language apparently does), while the other may not, and its phenomena may require constant explanation "from below." (We need not prejudge this question at the present stage of development of the value field.) Nor again, in applying each methodological strand, does the levels concept itself prejudge the specific content of that strand. For example, it insists on the search for continuity, for causal conditions under which novel phenomena come into existence. But whether such determination will come from a single preponderant source or a shifting source is not settled antecedently. To take a simplified illustration, Comte emphasizes mode of thought in explaining successive stages of human development,

Marx emphasizes changing mode of production, and Buckle appeals to geographic factors as crucial in earlier stages and intellectual factors in later stages. All these and many other important questions not here raised have to be settled as theses or hypotheses or investigatory principles in a *specific* levels theory in the social sciences. Such are the tasks involved in the growing current attempts to work out a social evolutionary understanding which will avoid the mistakes and simplifications of nineteenth century evolutionism, and will see the outlines of economic institutions, social structure, political institutions, and intellectual and emotional forms of expression in relation to the whole mode of life of the given stage of human development.

The distinction of the several strands, and the recognition that some may apply where others do not, liberalizes the levels concept considerably. It suggests that we have within the major integrative levels all sorts of processes going on which are not in character different from the "level-producing" processes on the broad evolutionary scene. The common generalized use of the term "levels" itself suggests as much. In physics, we find distinctions between macroscopic and microscopic levels, and there are levels of complexity or organization. There are qualitative changes of "state," as when a gas turns into a liquid form or a liquid into solid form. Biological evolution is constantly going on, issuing in new forms, if not constant consolidation of new species. When we pass from contrasting the inorganic level with the level of life, or the animal level with that of the human being capable of symbolic representation and wider purposive-planning activity, to the delineation of level stages in the historical development of mankind, we have already liberalized the use of the term. In social life, we see new levels frequently emerging in behavior, organization, and thought. Nations emerge, and some day we expect mankind to achieve an international level, not as mere organization but as altered quality of life. Social classes congeal to present a ladder-level structure. Thinking rises to a new level when systematic science emerges. We are so used to the historical comment that moral consciousness reached a new level that we may forget to take it literally. For there was a time, for example, when men in parts of the globe looked on men of other bands or tribes as food rather than as fellow men! Now much of this use of the term "level" may be metaphorical, but there is enough in common to suggest a general type of process. To cease to think of levels en bloc is in effect to try to apply to everyday processes and their description the same broad attitude and methodological approach that proves enlightening on the wider evolutionary scope. We shall suggest that it is possible to develop more specific senses of the levels concept, set within the basic *qualitative-emergence* sense, that prove useful for clearer social description and for the sharper formulation of research problems; and that the general methodological approach itself helps break up and restructure issues that have proved stumbling-blocks in social theory.

II

Within contemporary social theory, we find that many of the fundamental controversies about the nature of the field itself are cast in terms reminiscent of levels disputes. There are accusations of reduction of the social to the psychological, occasional insistence on the autonomy of the cultural and the reality of the superorganic, assertions about the distinctness of subject matter of group phenomena and social structure, and so on. These questions—usually precipitated in sociological works by the innocent preliminary inquiry, "What is society?"—are a tempting field for a philosophical investigation sharpened in terms of the levels concept. We shall first consider this question as a whole, then break it into several parts, attempting to show that its central sociological relevance is clarified by restructuring it as a special type of levels problem.

The question *"What is society?"* raises what we may call the *locus problem*—the selection of basic unit or object in terms of which social and cultural traits or properties are to be analyzed, or subjects to which they are to be referred. If we gather the answers in a comparative fashion, and range the elements out of which theorists have attempted to "construct" society or into which they have sought to "break it down" in an order from the smallest to the largest, we get a most impressive array. At one end are the states of consciousness, out of which the nineteenth century introspectionists wished to compound bodies, selves, economic processes, and social relations. The modern analogue is more behavioristic, consisting of behavioral acts, or compounds of attitudes as dispositions to acts. Next in line come individuals, for in some sense society "really and truly" consists of individuals. Some prefer this locus because only the individual has consciousness, others because the individual does the physical behaving, still others because the forces of cohesion which hold the group together are spotted within the individual's needs and psychological economy, as for example in Freud's view that love relationships or, more neutrally, emotional ties constitute the essence of group mind.[3]

One step beyond and the central focus becomes interpersonal relations. Social science is here called on to think in terms of bundles of relations, or interactions, or transactions with individuals as parties, but the individual himself is either denied meaning or shipped off to individual psychology.

Next come groups. As Logan Wilson says in a review article, "Regardless of the analytical framework used, the group factor is an important one." [4] And indeed it is. From Aristotle's definition of the *polis* as the union of families to achieve the good life to contemporary studies of all sorts of groups in society, all sorts of extensions have been invoked as basic—from the local community and the country to the whole of mankind.[5]

From the description of groups, especially in structural terms, one can slip quite readily into a view of social science as concerned with traits and patterns. This has been found especially in anthropological controversy. Individuals and even whole peoples can be seen as merely vehicles for the patterns whose career is being traced. People do not have social forms so much as "it is the cultures which possess the people who have been born into them." [6]

If the locus problem is pursued through different analyses of culture, the array of locus candidates is further increased. Many writers treat culture as a going concern, so that we have a kind of interactive whole of multifarious activity as the subject. Lowie takes the view that "There is only one natural unit for the ethnologist—the culture of all humanity at all periods and in all places." [7] On such a view, the subject of the whole story is mankind. If we go to the idealist philosophers of history, we can round out this end of the spectrum. At the extreme, there will be the Hegelian conception of the whole of history as exhibiting the growth in the self-consciousness of the Absolute; in such a sense, the ultimate subject is the Totality.

Our appreciation of the locus problem is enhanced by comparison of various specialized fields of social inquiry. The same range, for example, appears in ethical theory as the problem of the ultimate subject or locus of value. Is the subject to which the predicate "good" is to be attached ultimately the present momentary feeling or state of consciousness of a human being? Is it the total life of an individual self? Is it states of mutual relations or interaction, whether cast as meaningful shared experience or joint activity? Is the good really a property of a community living a kind of organized life, and the notion meaningless when referred to any fragment or abstraction? Or is the fit subject of good ultimately some ideal pattern to which striving is really directed, to be distinguished from its existential embodiment? Or again, is the ultimate good nothing less than the totality, so often cast in religious ethics as God?

In political theory, there is the familiar problem of loyalty or allegiance. Where is loyalty ultimately to be conceived as directed? To myself, in a Hobbesian vein, to my family ("my own"), my friends, to those beyond with whom I have "contracted," to my country? To the group Will, in Rousseauesque style? To ideals ultimately? To all mankind? To the historical totality, as in Burke's famous description of the state as a partnership between the living, the dead, and those who are to be born? To the religious object as over-all totality?

Recent psychological-anthropological study reveals a similar set of problems in the picture of the self. What is the actual feeling or picture that an individual has of himself, viewed as a phenomenological problem? Does he see himself as an isolated individual? As a continuous being over many lives, as in Hindu transmigration theory? As a multiplicity or bundle of roles? (Gabriel Marcel complains that modern man feels himself as a set of functions and is left with a hollow center.) As a cog in a machine or a branch of a social organism? As a fragment of a wider totality, whether in the ancient Stoic sense of a spark from the central fire or in the religious sense as part of God? As an instrument for an external or transcendent purpose? Hallowell's pioneering paper in which he examines such problems on a transcultural basis [8] has brought this subject within the scope of scientific treatment, extremely difficult though it be to penetrate to the phenomenal self picture of different cultures. (The recent rise of the self concept to a more central role in psychology can help this development immensely.) By examining the basic orientations provided by the culture and the ways in which the functioning of societies depends on the kind of self-awareness in its members, Hallowell seems to me to have shown in effect that theories about what the subject matter "really is" are not to be regarded merely as theories, but as describing patterns of effective or functioning "social reality," in short as qualitative emergents in the individual person. This is the sense, I take it, in which Kroeber and Kluckhohn in one of their formulations speak of culture as "the topmost phenomenal level yet recognized—or for that matter, now imaginable—in the realm of nature." [9]

The most abstract formulation of the locus problem is to be found in metaphysical theory. Is reality to be regarded as a flux of sense elements, a set of events, qualities, and relations? As substance? As pattern of universals? As process or goings-on? As absolute totality? And so on. These controversies provide the sharpest formulation of the general alternatives. Those who regard metaphysics as providing basic truth will be tempted to seek there a wholesale solution to the locus problem, and derive from it an application to social theory. Those who, like the present writer,[10] tend to regard metaphysics rather as the domain in which basic categories are compared, analyzed, and evaluated as alternative possible modes of organizing linguistic instruments, long-range factual lessons, and basic purposes, will look to a solution of the locus problem in a specific field like social theory by probing for the variety of underlying interests, hypotheses, and purposes which are to be found there.

In the locus problem in social theory, there are after all two separate questions involved. One is the claim for some type of "reality" for the

preferred candidate; the second is the claim that it has some basic character or role which qualifies it as the ultimate subject matter of the social
sciences. (Let us refer to these as the reality claim and the ultimacy
claim respectively.) We may restructure the first question as a levels
problem in the liberalized sense of the term indicated above. This means
that in the arena of human social life there are all sorts of forms crystal-
lized, with qualities of their own appearing in behavior, organization,
and consciousness—emerging, stabilized, breaking down, re-emerging,
almost comparable, if we allow an oversimplified analogy, to the way in
which some matter passes from liquid to solid, or liquid to gas, and back
again. In social theory, we may assume that such locus candidates as individuals, interactions, interpersonal relations, and various subgroup and
group levels in their claim for reality, correspond to definite qualitative
levels in the living activity of a definite span or spread of human beings.
Let us call this type of level *group-generalization level.* The different locus
candidates may then be construed as different types of possible group-
generalization levels. We do not here raise the question whether all actually occur among men, e.g., whether the sheer individual or the sheer
superorganic is more than a speculative possibility. Our interest is rather
in the methodological question of what they would have to show in order
to establish their reality.

Methodologically, the point may be made rather simply if we take
our clue from sociological practice rather than sociological speculation.
For in practice, terms specifying some qualitative organization over a
given span have always some explicit or implicit *empirical* interpretation.
When it is asked whether a particular assembly is a crowd, or a mob,
or a meeting, more or less identifiable criteria are involved, so that one
gathering can be identified as a mob, another as a meeting, another in
flux from one state to the other, and so on.[11] Or again, when detailed
investigation is carried out in a rural area of the form of the household
group, the dooryard group, the neighborhood group, the village group,
the county group, or the regional group,[12] each is identified in particular
terms. Then it is possible to ask under what conditions such groups can
exist, under what conditions they tend to break down, and what role the
existence of the several groups in this order plays in processes of transformation. Or again, when it is asked whether a particular getting together of definite people who proceed to inquire into and give their views
of a controversy is an informal gathering, a structured group having
opinion-forming influence but no coercive power, or a formal court,
there is no difficulty in establishing the answer in a particular case.

Similarly, in conceptual development oriented to actual descriptive
study of the span or spread of groups and the comparative incidence of
types of behavior among them, the mode of identifying levels is thor-

oughly empirical. For example, A. M. Lee [13] develops Sumner's concepts to distinguish the *individual* level with "a continuum of patterns
that ranges from practices to habits," the *group* level, with a continuum
"that extends from folkways to mores," and the *societal* level with a continuum "running from conventions to morals or moral principles." He is
thus able to diagram the divergence in levels and the deviations thus
found, and to employ such concepts as "immoretic morals" and "im-
moral mores." His primary interest is in the relation of society-wide cultural elements and subsocietal group elements. Similarly, concepts of
institutional variation and deviance might be analyzed by reference to
group levels; for example, when R. M. Williams says, "Many of the so-
called contradictions in a large, complex, heterogeneous society reflect
diverse levels of sociocultural regulation," [14] these regulation levels may
themselves admit of analysis in terms of specific group interactions. (An
obvious example would be the problem of legal rules on divorce vs.
actual practice.) Again, concepts of the local, national, and global level
provide a ready empirically identifiable framework for mapping certain
types of attitudes—e.g., how far in America assistance to other areas
of the world is seen as participation in a global community, how far as
means beyond national boundaries for national aims. And similar conceptual approaches are readily discernible in studies of the impact of
technical change on cultural patterns.

All this is commonplace enough both in sociological practice and in
the fashioning of middle-sized concepts. Extended to locus candidates
asserting a reality claim, it would mean that even though they may have
been advanced as categories for an analytical framework structuring the
whole field of study, they still must exhibit some empirical content and
maintain a material status. Thus, instead of asking whether our subject
matter pertains to individuals, interpersonal relations, or groups, once
we have the empirical criteria, we will be able to ask of a given population or part of a population, "How far are they operating on an individual level and in what respect, how far on an interpersonal relations
level, how far on a (more or less structured) group basis, and how far
on a consolidated symbolic superorganic basis?" For, in effect, if these
terms indicate different qualitative levels, then to describe a situation in
one way is to assert that it is in fact qualitatively different from what it
would be like if described in the other way. It should then be possible,
speculatively at least, to think of a society operating wholly on an individual basis (a Hobbesian state of nature with each on his own), or
wholly in terms of ties between individuals, or in terms of various sorts
of groups. The question of *whether* particular societies can so operate
or do so operate would then be an *empirical* matter. Other important
scientific questions, some requiring extensive research involving socio-

psychological collaboration, might be: Does the existence of the higher level always presuppose the existence of each lower level? Is higher-level behavior always instrumental (for example, as in groups over a wide area with unacquainted participants)? Does the individualistic pattern emerging from a group pattern always involve a sense of disintegration? (Cf. Merton on anomie; or compare Redfield's view of the shift from folk society to urban society as a kind of loss of firm scope in the moral order with Tawney seeing the shift from medieval to individualistic morality as a shift from one morality to another.[15]) Are certain types of qualitative levels grounded in psychological needs so that if they lose their character in one context they will re-emerge in another, as has been suggested by the way in which the breakdown of familial primary groups sometimes is followed by the assumption of primary group quality by other types of association?

If we generalize this procedure, we would have to ask whether a given population does in fact have a culture, or whether people there do have roles, or whether they constitute a social system. This may seem strange, but perhaps the strangeness may come from the fact that these are always to be found where populations have managed to survive. Certainly there is nothing strange in asking whether a population uses language (even though we can predict the answer invariably), or whether it constitutes a nation or just a tribe or a village. Similarly, it may seem strange to ask whether a man has a self; but I doubt whether the concept will really be clear until we can answer such a question and show under what conditions a human being would be without one and why, if it is the case, he would not survive. A further advantage of such an empirical interpretation of structural categories is that it makes possible a clear evaluative approach thereafter. We can ask whether it is desirable for a population to fall under a certain category, what are the advantages and disadvantages, and so forth.

Methodologically, therefore, the proposed reinterpretation involves treating locus candidates seriously as empirical or material categories descriptive of level qualities, rather than as abstract categories structuring the inquiry prior to beginning it. Two objections will occur at once. Some of the candidates, such as sensations, obviously cannot fit too comfortably into such a reinterpretation—for only in a dream or perhaps under the influence of drugs could social reality take the phenomenal form of isolated states of consciousness in associated bundles! The other objection is that an inquiry must be structured somehow, or else how can it get started? That is, it must be either a psychological or a culturological inquiry, or within a framework of some theory of action. Both these objections can be analyzed if we turn to the second question raised above, the ultimacy claim of the locus candidates.

At the more atomistic end of the range, which thinks in terms of states of consciousness and units of behavior, the reality claim is usually in the background, whereas the ultimacy claim is prominent. Here we find a dominant epistemological interest. This locus has appealed to investigators because verification of statements about social configurations does lie in observing items of behavior, though not, perhaps, going all the way to sensations as general verification termini. This trend was encouraged by the earlier positivist view that equated meaning with mode of verification. But a pendular swing has come in philosophy. The distinction between what the statement asserts and how it is verified is coming into its own again. Hence, the locus candidates at this end of the spectrum are robbed of their philosophic support and must stand on their own feet. And once they do this, it becomes clear that their ultimacy claim is relative to a concentration on what they regard as the most available units of observation. For example, Nadel says that "no legitimate isolate can be discovered more basic than that of a standardized pattern of behavior rendered unitary and relatively self-contained by its tasklike nature and its direction upon a single aim." [16] He gives as examples of such a "behavior cycle" a mother tending her child, farmers working on the land, and the performances of a sacrifice. But obviously this is geared to a particular state of anthropological observation. Why not, instead, a mother feeding her child, holding her child, washing her child, in the one direction, or in terms of the meaning of the act, a mother building up the family, or providing supports for her old age, or rearing a defender of the state, in the other direction? Instead of a conception of basic isolate we have really the proposed level on which observation may start, or the area of verifying observations, or something of that sort.

The objection that some categories are required for initial structuring of investigation need not mean that these have to have other than the empirical or material status we have described. The ultimacy claim can be taken here as equivalent to the confident prediction that inquiry guided by these material categories—i.e., exploration of this particular level of phenomena—will prove scientifically fruitful in terms of readier conceptualization and greater facility in the discovery of laws. For example, the culturological thesis says in effect that we should forget about the culture-bearers as other than—in extreme cases—space-time positions, just as in describing individual behavior we ignore the particular molecules in the body. And indeed this is not impossible in many fields. We could map the appearance, distribution, and extent pulsations of a disease or a language on the face of the globe, without asking how it spread, or who were the carriers. The central question of scientific significance is whether such a perspective will in fact put us in a position to advance systematic theoretical knowledge in the terms that it provides. And this cannot be settled *a priori*. But it is this, and not the desire that one's own scientific garden have a separate identity, which constitutes the legitimate core of the ultimacy claim.

I am not suggesting that all social categories have to be taken as descriptive. But I am suggesting that most of the locus candidates, other than those expressing a purely epistemological interest, can most fruitfully be treated as types of group-generalization levels. I do not underestimate the difficulties in making such wide sociological concepts subject to such limitations. For example, it may be that considerably more work will have to be done from a phenomenal or phenomenological type of approach, to understand how people see themselves and their relations. But there will be a tremendous gain in clarity, and perhaps also a vast increase in theoretical power.

III

Once the concept of levels has been liberalized beyond the original sense of *quality-emergence* levels to cover also *group-generalization* levels, it becomes possible to suggest further senses of a more specialized sort. The basic setting is, of course, still the process of social change in which group differentiation takes place. But as there occurs an increasingly complex division of labor among groups, areas of activity are sifted out which may be compared on a means-ends basis in some type of ascendance order within a total interactive organization. Let us speak of these as *instrumental-functional* levels. For example, in the economic life of a country, one may distinguish the levels of consumption, production of consumption articles, and production of instruments of production (tools, factories, etc.). In such a mapping, the higher levels constitute a kind of functional generalization. For example, a factory is set up to process a metal which will be used in a variety of ways in many other factories. Similarly, schools may teach skills of wide applicability instead of letting children learn particular applications at work, as in much of primitive learning. Or in another area, basic scientific research may become a specialized occupation, with results widely applicable in technology, and these again applicable in actual production. In this sense, many of our institutions—schools, banks and money, scientific research—may be thought of when they become socially established separately, as on a higher generalization level. On the other hand, it must never be forgotten that all these elements in a society function interactively on the primary level. Material processes and tool factories, as well as schools and banks and laboratories, all involve buildings on *terra firma,* with a corps of men and women who often have specialized interests. Thus to speak of higher generality in this sense is to point to an ordered variety of functioning relationships, but all in concrete contexts of human interaction.

Historically, economics has probably dealt with the relation of such levels and their interaction most concretely. Certainly, traditional economic theory is a storehouse of controversies concerning the relations of consumption, production, exchange, and all the various processes that enter into the economy and the functional groups that become separated out. Valuable general lessons might be learned from seeing economic questions in the light of a levels mapping in the present sense. For example, the way in which a particular material such as gold became a commodity and then a standard for exchange seems to be precisely an account of concrete generalization in social activity through instrumental-functional relationship. In this process, money became almost the universal social symbol of the means. (On the other hand, it may be that it has reached its limit, and that in the present stage of productive development some category more directly concerned with production—even physical energy itself—may come to play the role of generalized means.)

There are areas of human activity far removed from the economic, in which instrumental-functional levels may fruitfully be mapped. Many areas exhibit a socially differentiated structure in which there is a basic ground floor of social activity of some sort, a second story in which some *regulative* process occurs directed toward the ground floor, and a third story in which some kind of ordering takes place and is directed toward the second story. Technology in production, technological research, and basic scientific research constitute one example. Teaching, teaching teachers, and developing the theory of education are another. Law-abiding and law-violating activity, positive law, political and legal theorizing make up a third. And so on, in many distinct fields.

Whether or not a general theory of means-ends relations can stem from a levels differentiation along these lines, I do not know. General theories have to be approached with caution. But certainly there can be a discernment of common types of problems, and perhaps the development of some general criteria for the evaluation of means. For example, there are obvious analogous problems of the overweighting of the ground-floor level by the higher levels. When does the regulative mechanism use up so much of the resources as to begin to drain the basic activity area? Under what condition does the burden of heavy industry become so great as to bring consumption to the danger minimum? Or the activity of literary criticism so heavy as to threaten literary enjoyment? Or the weight of morality so great as to take the joy out of life? Obviously, there will be no uniform answer. The desirable level for courts and political controls is to have a minimum use; for scientific levels, the increase of the highest theoretical level has its own intrinsic values, and a desirable ground-floor situation might be one of a development in which less work on that level was required. Other general problems that have in one way or another been raised include: problems of distance among levels and difficulties of communication; problems of control and tendencies to iron laws of oligarchies and hierarchies; problems of standardization at higher levels and the degree to which they produce liberating or constricting effects at lower levels; and so on. Since many of these issues arise in different particular fields, they may perhaps most fruitfully be discussed there rather than in general terms. But the comparison of areas is likely to be highly suggestive.

In order to examine the utility of such levels analysis concretely, I shall take an extended example from a field in which such mapping is on the whole rather untried. Let us see how far such formulations would help clarify concepts and facilitate empirical research in ethics. We may begin by distinguishing a basic or ground-floor level of conduct, with its associated feelings and desires; a second story of moral codes or patterns, which involves some sort of regulative-selective function in relation to conduct; and a third story of ethical justification which involves reflective support for or criticism directed upon the second level. All three function interactively in the arena of human behavior. For moral reprimand of a violator is as much human behavior as the goal seeking in the violation of the code, and the justification is, like any other discourse, a part of human symbolic-manipulative behavior. The use of particular functional relations for initial identification does not, however, preclude the discovery of various other empirical relations between the levels. In fact, it helps open up numerous such problems for research.

For example, a clear distinction between the levels makes us sensitive to the different functions that the same content may have in different cultural patterns—how a particular goal or character trait or feeling or sanction may be nonmoral in one society, be profoundly moral in another, and be on a still higher level in a third. Happiness, for example, may be on the ground floor in an ascetic morality—it is simply something not to be overdone. In another, it may be one of the goods to be sought. In still another, it may be the ultimate justification of all goods. We also have to keep an eye out for change, or for the circulation of elements among the levels. Perhaps the best example on a large scale in Western civilization is the rise of egoism. Egoistic behavior or "selfishness" was for a long time regarded as conduct inimical to morality, therefore ground floor or perhaps subbasement! In the breakup of the medieval world outlook, it moved up the ladder to the moral rung and became acceptable partly as a means to the good life, and partly as the content of the "self-regarding" duties. In Hobbesian and later Benthamite ethics, it blossomed on the justification level as the inevitable principle of justification of all conduct.

One might feel tempted to look for "laws of motion" among the levels. Do high values in the second level tend to become ethical justification principles? Are they forced up by the "pressure" of values below? Love, for example, seems to have come from the moral pattern into the third level by a process of generalization and extension. Plato's *Symposium* is a good illustration of a moment of transition, in which its meaning is moving from a valued feeling into the idea of a unified quest of the self embodying all aspiration. On the other hand, reason seems to have followed the opposite path. If unreasonableness as a vice is to any extent now approximating a position in the moral level, it is only because the efficacy of reason as a mode of ethical justification has gradually become established. However, the attempt to find laws of such types is premature. A more careful study of crystallization processes and critical points on a wide comparative basis is first required, and then some integration of these studies within a theory relating our three levels to other phases of civilization or culture in action.[17]

A consequence of progress in such a study would be the possibility of wider historical and functional investigations of the relation of levels. What are the further relations that a moral pattern may have to the conduct pattern, apart from guidance and control? How may it be "geared" to serve varieties of social, economic, political, and cultural needs? Does a justification level merely provide "major premises" for a morality? Actually, a considerable variety of relations is possible. There may be justification that supports, as, for example, a hierarchical view of each soul aspiring only so far as its nature permits served to support a hierarchically ordered feudal morality of duties according to rank. Or again, the justification level may have a critical impact, as an individualistic conscience ethic challenged the feudal moral order. But if the third level can have opposite relations in this way, then it is to some extent an independently variable order. And so we find ourselves dealing not merely with logical relations, but with problems of historical interaction between all three levels.

Again, there can be no *a priori* assumptions about the comparative order and rates of change on the three levels. It is very likely that changes on the ground-floor level come first, but these may sometimes be advanced only far enough to raise problems, not to alter patterns of conduct. We cannot assume, however, that given social changes, the moral pattern must change first and the justification pattern change as a causal consequence. Sometimes the justification pattern cracks first, and serves as a lever for shifting the moral pattern. In our present world, for example, a globally oriented ethical justification system is increasingly taking hold, following the practical interconnections of the globe. Many elements in existing moralities require alteration as a consequence. In general, just as in the relations of ideas and practice, shifts in justification often reflect changing forces and prefigure changes that are to come in existing institutions and beliefs. That is why institutions of great scope and practical importance in human affairs have, in their maturity, tended to pay great attention to the principles upon which they are justified, and why theoretical disputes in religion, politics, and social theory have had such immense practical significance.

Another levels problem in the relation of the three stories takes us back to questions of emergence. Selective-discriminative behavior is clear in the prehuman animal world. But at what point does such behavior pass into organized aspiration? And where does the sense of obligation appear? Darwin thought it highly likely that any people having familial or close group relations would have a moral sense, and Freud speculated about a specific origin of guilt feeling. Julian Huxley illustrates a fuller type of historical approach when he offers the thesis that in preagricultural society moralities are largely concerned with propitiation and group solidarity. He suggests that in postagricultural early civilization moralities relate to class domination and group rivalry.[18] Huxley looks also for the psychological functions of morality and for its changing forms in contemporary life, then ends up with proposals for its orientation in the modern world. Similar detailed inquiry is possible for justification patterns. Some may have been implicit in the particular forms that morality took. But conscious ethical theorizing was a later product whose origins we can trace to some extent as part of the growth of what we call civilization. The answers to these questions are scientific-historical matters, not to be settled by postulation or sheer speculation, or even by present introspection into the state of consciousness at a particular stage in the development of mankind. Even where we do not have the answers, the recognition of the questions will keep us from uncritical approaches.

IV

The various senses of the levels concept we have so far considered together point to a way of looking at the work of the social sciences. On-going human activity is seen as crystallizing into structured forms on various historical levels. It involves group and subgroup differentiation and integration in virtue of interactive processes which embody instrumental functions. But where in all this does conceptualization as the activity of the social scientist itself fit? In the preceding section, theoretical activity was itself treated as one type of level in connection with other human activities. In the first section there was some suggestion that human consciousness was to be regarded as a level in the development of the natural world. Obviously, conceptualization is not to be construed as a purely contemplative outside-of-the-world act. This has far-reaching consequences.

The Cartesian notion of mind as a contemplator, a noninterfering spectator, has dominated the Western intellectual horizon. Its effect in social theory is still greater than we are likely to assume. Only such a conception—to take a current sociological example—can explain why such a theoretical fuss has been made over the "discovery" that predictions in the social field can affect the outcome of the subject matter they are purporting to predict. The self-fulfilling prophecy is simply the case in which the act of prophesying helps produce the result prophesied. A man bellows, "There is an avalanche coming any moment!" By the energy of his sound, he might produce the avalanche itself, if the physical balance was precarious and he was strategically located. In the usual social examples, the result is produced by effects on the understanding of others and their response in terms of their habits of reaction (to rush to sell shares if a noted economist predicts a depression, etc.). What does this show? Simply that the act of prophesying is part of the phenomena in some cases. Therefore, its effects have to be measured if it is public, or else the form of its expression entered into the description of initial-state conditions. In this respect, it is parallel to the use of energy in observation of minute physical phenomena, where the apparatus of observation as an act (e.g., use of light) may interfere in the phenomena to be observed. The problem is one of the careful formulation of the initial conditions so that we can tell what will have been proved by the results of the experiment. Or else it is one of ingenuity—as in the use of one-way transparent screens to observe what nursery children will do when the adults are absent! [19]

Yet, why should contemporary social science be surprised to find that mind or intellectual reflection is to be viewed as an event in nature, arising under determinate conditions, involving in itself an expenditure of energy, and having effects of varying range depending on conditions? In short, why be surprised that intellectual reflection itself, together with its products, constitutes a social phenomenon which may be rising to a new level or sublevel position? One might have thought that this point of the natural character and office of reflection upon which Dewey spent his major philosophical energies would have had effects in social science at least comparable to those that his analysis of human nature had in educational theory. (Why it did not is itself probably an interesting social-science research problem.) In any case, it follows from this point of view that the formulation of abstract concepts itself expresses the conditions and problems of men and in varying degree reformulates outlook, mode of thought, and mode of handling the processes of life.

This means that the growth of more and more general concepts in the social field is to be regarded as a complex process. We may speak of levels of abstraction, as the semanticists do—from the lowest "unspeakable" level of microscopic events to the highest rung of the abstraction ladder—but we must not regard it as a simple verbal matter or even as a stripping-off process in which more and more of the initial mass of properties are stripped away to leave more widely applicable ideas. Nor, on the other hand, is it to be understood purely as free intellectual construction which in the hands of genius provides organizing relations so that, lo and behold, where there was a great deal of scattered information, now there is science. The emergence of a high-level concept or category is a real event in the natural world, and so what is really happening requires not merely logical examination but a whole psychological, social, and historical picture. The descriptive inquiry maps the career of the concept. The causal-explanatory inquiry offers hypotheses about its rise and the reasons for its spread. The logical-evaluative inquiry is itself a creative development of the concept, in instances where it is not a mere orderly presentation of how the concept has been used; for such an inquiry shows what the meaning of the concept is. This inquiry can be in relation to different theoretical areas and possible applications.

All that goes into the development of an abstract concept is not always appreciated. Even on a rudimentary level, there is a selective-generalizing process. For example, to speak of one's "brother" already sets aside differences of age in the family, or the sex of the speaker; "sibling" is even more abstract. And the idea of "kinship" itself is a fairly high-level concept, inviting formal systematization, study of correlation with patterns of control, and modes of feeling and prescription. As a high-level concept, it is only one step removed from the abstract category of "social relation"; one may venture the speculative suspicion that had it not been held back by the definite content of the biological relationship involved, it might have climbed to the heights and competed for the very definition of sociology. For, after all, Aristotle discusses various business and social relations in his *Nicomachean Ethics* under the rubric of "friendship," and all that was needed was to reinterpret friendship as a kind of social brotherhood or kinship of interests! In the social sciences, while high-level categories seem to get giddy in their rarefied atmosphere, middle-sized terms are more often conscious of their roots.

Perhaps the best analyzed examples of high-level categories are to be found in relation to the physical sciences, where the development of concepts of force, matter, space, and time constitutes a fascinating chap-

ter in the history of thought. The evaluative determination of the conditions for their proper use in the light of contemporary scientific knowledge is a major occupation of the philosophy of science. It is not too
much to say that it took Western man two millennia to develop adequate
conceptions here, even though the pace of recent progress sometimes
makes it seem a question of only three hundred years!

Let us compare two contemporary general concepts in social science,
one of which has climbed to a position of categorial eminence on a high
level, the other of which remains simply a tag for a variety of specific
qualities. The two concepts are *power* and *skill*. Power has made a definite and not unsuccessful bid for domination in current political science.
It is often cast for a fundamental role in social science comparable to
that of *energy* in physics.[20] This implies that, in principle, laws of human
social behavior would be stated in terms of power seeking as a basic
variable. Meanwhile, other classifications are refashioned in terms of its
demands. Men are divided not into workers and capitalists, or city folk
and country folk, or occupational groupings, but into leaders and followers. Creeds, philosophies, and even social theories are examined as
sources of power. Human desires and needs are reckoned chiefly as
causal bases for maintaining or losing power. By contrast, there has
seemed little temptation to make skill a general category with a general
theory. Instead, the social scientist is impressed by the diversity of skills
and their heterogeneous quality. A single abstract concept embracing
the different skills of an orator, a scientist, and a baseball player would
seem to be nothing more than a creation out of an artificial analogy. And
yet are not the power of a priest in whom men have faith, the power of
a gangster pointing his gun, the power of a doctor explaining the X ray
to a patient, and the power of a statesman resting on a democratic
election quite different in type? Or for that matter, we might observe
the diversity of forms in which physical energy appears—as heat, light,
electricity, mechanical motion.

Why the power idea should have risen to a higher level and the skill
idea not is a problem of social and intellectual history not perhaps as yet
fully explored. Some points are suggestive. The central role of certain
problems in modern life which involve force and power—war, economic
conflicts, general insecurity—does tend to give a sharper focus on the
power concept. The existence of states as political mechanisms and the
possibilities of "taking over power" give an institutional basis for its
conceptual unification. The existence of political theory as a single science
gives it an intellectual head start in terms of a set of theoretical formulations which it may undertake to unify. On the other hand, for skill there
are only a few recent tendencies. Among these few are the need for a

great variety of skills involving special education, the need for encouraging youth to enter these fields, the development of testing to determine promise of skill, and the increased rapidity of social change in occupations calling for development of skills in such a way as to ensure transferability. As for theoretical fields in which skill might play a part, there is very little, except perhaps that branch of psychology which deals with the emotional conditions of effective functioning. The concept of *productivity,* as used by psychoanalytical writers like Erich Fromm, might fit into a science of skill. But, on the whole, the notion of skill does not stand a chance compared with power, at least for the present.

When we look to the evaluation of the concepts, power finds itself drawing considerably more on credit than it pays in cash value. Compare it with energy. Energy is defined clearly on a macroscopic level; power is vague, and leans on its denotation or exemplification in the police, the courts, the government, and the army. The scientific use of the energy concept is enhanced when it is related to the microscopic level in terms of precise measurement of what goes on within the atom; the individual's love of power is a concept wavering between the general desire to get something in particular on given occasions and the promise of an internal psychological mechanism that becomes visible when it goes astray in sadistic-masochistic phenomena. In the case of energy, the microscopic theory is complete enough to explain and control the large-scale release of energy. At its best, the psychological theory of power does little to explain large-scale social, even political, events. Our task here is not to evaluate fully the concept, but to illustrate the kind of promise that warrants extending credit to it. The gap between promise and payment seems so wide in the case of the power concept that I am tempted to look for its ideological role as a large component of its rise to prominence.

Forgoing any generalizations about causal conditions, we may note that our brief samples suggest at least three conditions that warrant the extension of credit to a general or abstract high-level category for structuring an area of social inquiry: (1) when there is a promise of the development of greater theoretical knowledge by its use, in reference to some specific set of theoretical problems already articulated; (2) when there are definite institutional forms or practices which it expresses, so that it has at least an anchored meaning whose extension is being proposed for a wider field; (3) when there is some set of unified purposes that the concept can help to articulate. These criteria add up to what may be called a contextual approach to categories.

This type of approach was involved in the evaluation of the locus problem in section two, and especially in the insistence that locus categories either be referred to specific epistemological problems or be treated themselves as embodying explicit descriptive content. I believe that the contextual approach should be extended to all top-level categories in social theory, that these categories have explicit or implicit relations in at least one of the three ways indicated to some context, and that they cannot be fully understood and evaluated without reference to the context. For example, the older conception of *superstructure,* as it appeared in historical materialism, was readily intelligible in terms of the theory that changes in the mode of production determine changes in a definite way in the realms of consciousness; the utility of the category stands or falls with the adequacy of the underlying theory. Or again, when MacIver drew a sharp distinction between *civilization* and *culture* —the former embracing material and social apparatus of living in man's endeavor to control the conditions of his life, the latter embracing ends (modes of living and thinking and expression)—it was evident that, in part, this rested on an underlying distinction between the material and the expression of spirit, and, in part, it also involved the explicit belief that cumulative evolution could be traced for the material products and social techniques, but not for the ever-varying and spontaneously recurring spiritual life. Recent presentation of categorial schemes does not always make clear the context from which they stem or to which they refer. For example, to set off culture as a separate symbolic system does make sense if we are thinking of the learning-in-growing-up context *from the point of view of the learner,* but not if we are thinking of the stable on-going social situation in which almost every property of action or every habit of action can be seen as broadly "cultural." In the latter context, we would feel much more inclined to use the traditional Tylor category of culture. It would be worth multiplying categorial sets even speculatively, to throw open more widely this whole area of inquiry. Some categories would stem from considering the diffusion situation; others from inquiry into uniformity of behavior and deviation, with an eye to controls that keep men in line; others from looking at a distance as a man may at an ant hill; others perhaps from looking at society through the eyes of a particular occupational group (as Holmes in the narrower field of law tried to see how the law looked from the bad man's point of view); and others from approaching the field with a particular interest, such as looking for patterns in psychological-personality terms. Kroeber and Kluckhohn's valuable review of the culture concept should provide an excellent starting point for testing the merits of a contextual approach in making sense of the extreme diversity of definitions.[21] And this would be a necessary preliminary, I believe, for an evaluation of the concept as it has emerged in recent scientific work. For it cannot be too often repeated that the mere use of a generic concept—as in our example of skill, if one were to write a "General Theory of Skill"—is no guarantee of a fruitful systematic unity whether for theoretical or practical purposes. The decision to develop the general concept, or the realization that it has been done, represents an accomplishment in moving up to a high or abstract conceptual level only if it corresponds to something more than arbitrary stipulation.

The problems just raised and the approach worked out can be illustrated more fully from the current usage of the terms "value" and "norm," both of which have broadened out to cover an extraordinarily wide range of content. Although the term "value" has become well-entrenched in ethical, psychological, and sociological writing, there have been divergent trends in its use. There has been a wider use equating value with interest generally, and a narrower use insisting on some element of appraisal or preference in the idea itself.

The wider use has, on the whole, prevailed among philosophers. A man's "values" means the totality of his attitudes *for or against* anything. R. B. Perry in his classic *General Theory of Value* set the preponderant mood by defining a value as any object of any interest. This covers everything that a man wants, enjoys, is awed by, or responds to aesthetically, as well as what he feels he ought to do or pursue as the good. It is interesting to note that Laird went even further in developing a principle of natural election to cover physical "attraction" and chemical "affinity" in the material world.[22] Departure from the broader notion is to be found chiefly in writers who, like Dewey, stress the role of appraisal in value judgment and contrast it with the immediacy of affective quality or prizing.[23]

In psychological and social or cultural descriptions of men's values, the usage of the term varies. Sometimes value is equated with object of any desire (e.g., Ellis Freeman [24]). Sometimes the stress falls on preference among motives or goals (e.g., Kimball Young [25]). Sometimes the term is used to denote affective quality in attitudes (e.g., Sherif and Cantril [26]). Often it becomes simply a synonym for affective-motor attitude. Sometimes, however, the value is seen as an entity which affects thought and behavior, in part by generating attitudes (e.g., Broom and Selznick speak in this way of personal identity as a deeply rooted value having such effects; to be a value is equated apparently with being prized [27]). Recently, however, some writers have been explicit in limiting the term. Kluckhohn says: "A value is a conception, explicit or implicit, distinctive of an individual or characteristic of a group, of the desirable which influences the selection from available modes, means and ends of action." [28] He adds that it is not just a preference but one felt or considered to be justified. Similarly, R. M. Williams, in formulating concepts for sociological description, says: "Values are not the con-

crete goals of action but rather the criteria by which goals are chosen." [29]
Kingsley Davis says: "A value is that which is considered desirable,
which is thought worthy of being pursued . . ." [30] Parsons distinguishes
sharply between the "cathectic" orientation and "evaluation" as a
process of ordered selection.[31] In general, the somewhat narrower and
critical conception of *value* is becoming predominant in scientific work.

The concept of *norm* provides an interesting contrast. Here the
tendencies are reversed. Among philosophers, "normative" generally,
perhaps even universally, connotes *ought*. It therefore embodies the
critical selective component which the broad use of the value concept
lacks.[32] Among psychological and social scientists, however, the term
has often been broadened in a way analogous to the extension of *value*
among philosophers. Every social custom or cultural element comes to
be seen as a *norm*. For example, Cantril calls standardized ways of a
society "social norms." [33] (It is interesting to note that such broad use
of "norms" forces a narrow use of "values"; Cantril calls prevailing
evaluations of norms "social values." [34]) Williams uses an extremely
broad concept of norms. He regards the concept of culture as a normative structure, pointing to "a continuous gradation from almost purely
technical or cognitive norms (how to boil an egg, the most efficient way
to manufacture TNT) to 'moral' norms (thou shalt not kill). At the
intermediate steps, one finds, among others, conventional norms ('custom,' 'etiquette,' etc.) and aesthetic norms (standards of taste, of beauty,
etc.)." [35] Davis similarly sees the whole social system as normative: "Its
integration rests upon the fact that its members carry in their heads, as
part of the culture heritage, the notion that they *ought* or *ought not* to
do certain things." [36] Although norms are said to represent "an imaginary construct" and to be "subjective," [37] they are central to understanding society. Bierstedt gives the concept of norms a central place,
and uses it to refer "not to ways of thinking but to ways of doing"; [38]
norms are the "grooves" in which conduct runs along, but they also
function as rules or standards, as societal expectations.[39] By presenting
a wide concept of norms which can accommodate all sorts of different
types, Bierstedt is able to dispense entirely with the term "values." On
the other hand, Broom and Selznick, who appeared to use a wider concept of values, appear to use a narrower concept of norms, regarding
them as "blueprints for behavior, setting limits within which individuals
may seek alternate ways to achieve their goals. Norms are based on
cultural values . . ." [40]

One may wonder why the concept of norms should be conceived so
broadly that every social custom or cultural element should come to be
seen as a norm. In line with our insistence that there has to be some
basis for the higher-level abstract concept, unless it is merely a tag word

for an area of possibly miscellaneous elements, we have to look for some theory promised, or some institution or practice given expression, or some purpose furthered. So far at least it is hard to see any theory advanced or promised; at most, there is an attempt to classify. And, from the point of view of theory, there is, in both the case of norm and value, a definite disadvantage which comes from the occasional tendency to reify, to regard the terms as designating existent forces or generative sources, as if to refer to the value or the norm were to explain the cause of an attitude or behavioral tendency. In this sense, the terms, intended as theoretical constructs by the methodologically self-conscious scientist, may function as a last refuge or surrogate for spirit, in the sense in which the older dualistic philosophies used it as a mode of explanation. On the other hand, if we look to general point of interest in the use of the norm concept, the context of use is overwhelmingly clear. It arises in a concentration on the process of socialization of the growing individual, in an interest in the mechanisms of transmission of existent forms and patterns to the next generation, also in the methods of control and regulation to maintain the pattern. From this perspective, the use of the general concept of norms makes sense at least at the beginning. I suspect that in the long run it will prove as strong as, but not stronger than, the theory of a general social psychology which it expresses, or perhaps implicitly promises.

And what about the basis for the general value concept, whether taken in its wider or in its narrower appraisal sense? I have suggested elsewhere [41] that the mere use of a generic value concept cannot settle the question of its utility. Stipulation alone, or the existence of a generic mark, is not enough. The unity sought has to be found either in some quality that is central in experience, or else in some central tendency in human desire, or else in some unifying psychological, cultural, or social pattern, or in some set of practical needs or converging historical demands. Thus, to argue that all life is the expression of a single quest,[42] or that every culture must have a patterned unity, can possibly become a base for fashioning and justifying a general or abstract concept of value. It is interesting to note that Bentham, who reduced all disparate qualities to the uniform search for pleasure, nevertheless used the concrete term "pleasure," not the term "value" in this context. For him, value literally refers to measurement, to finding the value of a given lot of pleasure by reckoning its intensity, duration, etc.[43] In this older and in many respects very appealing sense, one would not speak of *a value* in any other sense than one would speak of *a price* or *a weight*. Value was, so to speak, not a substantive but a question to be answered by reference to comparative standards of measurement. That there has been some distortion in generalizing what was essentially a process of comparative measurement seems fairly clear. But whether the distortion is in theory, or in the quality of the life which theory reflects—such as the measurement of aesthetic value by the price the work will bring—is another and very complicated social question.

I used to think sometimes that the psychological and social sciences would gain in concreteness and lose little theory if such terms as "value" and "norm" were demoted to a lower level! But, apart from its being too late, the question is not a purely verbal one, even though words can cause confusion. We are embarked in contemporary social science on the large-scale study of value phenomena—for example, in the Harvard Values Studies, to cite only one of the numerous approaches in the behavioral sciences. It is up to results to show whether the general value concept has a unified structure or whether it remains at best a tag. But methodologically what is here proposed is simply that, in fashioning a high-level abstract concept, we firmly maintain the lines of relevance to the promise of theoretical advance, to the institutional or practical forms or historical tendencies, or to any unified purposes involved.

The trend of our argument in this paper may be summarized briefly. The traditional concept of emergent levels requires a logical overhauling which, at the very least, disentangles its several theses. When liberalized, however, it helps provide a historically oriented methodological approach that can bear considerable fruit in social theory. Further senses of "levels," specialized with a view to mapping types and degrees of group-generalization and instrumental-functional relationships, can help clarify connections and formulate research problems within the framework provided by the basic sense of qualitative emergence. Intellectual production as participant in historical process admits of such treatment as well, and when this is done the development of categories acquires greater scope. Their evaluation is rooted in a fuller reference to their implicit operations and underlying tasks.

NOTES

1. For analysis of some of the problems in the concepts of emergence and novel qualities, see:

A. O. Lovejoy, "The Meanings of 'Emergence' and Its Modes," *Proceedings of the Sixth International Congress of Philosophy* (1926), pp. 20-33.

Gustav Bergmann, "Holism, Historicism and Emergence," *Philosophy of Science,* 11 (October, 1944), pp. 209-21.

Paul Henle, "The Status of Emergence," *Journal of Philosophy,* 39 (August 27, 1942), pp. 486-93.

Abraham Edel, *The Theory and Practice of Philosophy* (New York: Harcourt, Brace & Company, 1946), pp. 48-64.

Maurice Mandelbaum, "A Note on Emergence," in Baron, Nagel, and Pinson, eds., *Freedom and Reason* (Glencoe, Ill.: Free Press, 1951), pp. 175-83.

P. E. Meehl and Wilfrid Sellars, "The Concept of Emergence," in Herbert Feigl and Michael Scriven, eds., *The Foundations of Science and the Concepts of Psychology and Psychoanalysis* (Minnesota Studies in the Philosophy of Science, Minneapolis: University of Minnesota Press, 1956), pp. 239-52.

For integrative levels, in relation to different fields, see:

Alex B. Novikoff, "The Concept of Integrative Levels and Biology," *Science*, 101 (March 2, 1945), pp. 209-15.

R. W. Sellars, V. J. McGill, and Marvin Farber, eds., *Philosophy for the Future* (New York: The Macmillan Company, 1949); essays by J. B. S. Haldane, T. C. Schneirla, and B. J. Stern.

For related problems of whole and parts, see Ernest Nagel, "Wholes, Sums, and Organic Unities," *Philosophical Studies*, III (February, 1952), pp. 17-32.

2. J. B. S. Haldane, "Interaction of Physics, Chemistry, and Biology," in Sellars, McGill, Farber, eds., *op. cit.*, p. 215.

3. In *Group Psychology and the Analysis of the Ego* (New York: Liveright Publishing Corporation).

4. Logan Wilson, "Sociography of Groups," in Georges Gurvitch and Wilbert E. Moore, eds., *Twentieth Century Sociology* (New York: The Philosophical Library, 1945), p. 140. He is referring to Znaniecki's view that "the same basic facts about man in society can be subsumed under a systematic theory of social actions, of social relations, of social persons, and of social groups."

5. For a review of some of these aspects, Florian Znaniecki, "Social Organization and Institutions," in Gurvitch and Moore, eds., *op. cit.*, pp. 172-217. See also S. F. Nadel, *The Foundations of Social Anthropology* (Glencoe, Ill.: Free Press, 1953), chapters V and VII; and N. S. Timasheff, "The Basic Concepts of Sociology," *American Journal of Sociology*, LVIII (September, 1952), pp. 176-86.

6. Leslie A. White, *The Science of Culture* (New York: Farrar, Straus and Company, 1949), p. 126. Compare his assertion: "Culture thus becomes a continuum of extrasomatic elements. It moves in accordance with its own principles, its own laws; it is a thing *sui generis*. Its elements interact with one another, forming new combinations and syntheses. New elements are introduced into the stream from time to time, and old elements drop out." ("Ethnological Theory," in Sellars, McGill, Farber, eds., *op. cit.*, p. 374.)

7. Quoted in A. L. Kroeber and Clyde Kluckhohn, *Culture, A Critical Review of Concepts and Definitions* (Cambridge: Papers of the Peabody Museum of American Archaeology and Ethnology, Harvard University, Vol. XLVII, No. 1, 1952), p. 87.

8. A. Irving Hallowell, "The Self and Its Behavioral Environment," in his *Culture and Experience* (Philadelphia: University of Pennsylvania Press, 1955).

9. Kroeber and Kluckhohn, *op. cit.,* p. 148.

10. See my "Interpretation and the Selection of Categories," in *Meaning and Interpretation,* University of California Publications in Philosophy, Vol. 25 (Berkeley: University of California Press, 1950), pp. 57-95.

11. Cf. Hadley Cantril, *The Psychology of Social Movements* (New York: John Wiley & Sons, Inc., 1941), ch. 4.

12. Betty W. Starr, "Levels of Communal Relations," *American Journal of Sociology,* 60 (September, 1954), pp. 125-35.

13. A. M. Lee, "Levels of Culture as Levels of Social Generalization," *American Sociological Review,* X (August, 1945), pp. 485-95.

14. Robin M. Williams, Jr., *American Society* (New York: Alfred A. Knopf, Inc., 1955), p. 31; cf. ch. X.

15. Robert K. Merton, "Social Structure and Anomie," in his *Social Theory and Social Structure* (Glencoe, Ill.: Free Press, 1949); Robert Redfield, *The Primitive World and Its Transformations* (Ithaca, N.Y.: Cornell University Press, 1953); R. H. Tawney, *Religion and the Rise of Capitalism* (New York: Mentor Books, 1947).

16. Nadel, *op. cit.,* p. 76.

17. Such investigation needs a clearer mapping of the constituents of a morality. An attempt to do this on a comparative cultural basis will be found in a forthcoming collaborative book, *Anthropology and Ethics,* by the present writer and Dr. May Edel, to be published by the Charles C. Thomas Publishing Co. The questions of methodology and the three levels will be more fully discussed in the writer's *Method in Ethical Theory,* to be published by The Liberal Arts Press.

18. T. H. Huxley and Julian Huxley, *Touchstone for Ethics* (New York: Harper & Brothers, 1947), p. 127.

19. For a careful formulation, including some physical parallels to the self-fulfilling prophecy, see Adolf Grünbaum, "Historical Determinism, Social Activism, and Predictions in the Social Sciences," *The British Journal for the Philosophy of Science,* VII (November, 1956), pp. 236-40. Cf. also the treatment of this problem in Robert K. Merton, *op. cit.*

20. Bertrand Russell, *Power, A New Social Analysis* (New York: W. W. Norton & Co., Inc., 1938); H. D. Lasswell and Abraham Kaplan, *Power and Society, A Framework for Political Inquiry* (New Haven: Yale University Press, 1950).

21. Kroeber and Kluckhohn, *op. cit.* See my review of the book, *Journal of Philosophy,* LI (September 16, 1954), pp. 559-63.

22. John Laird, *The Idea of Value* (Cambridge: Cambridge University Press, 1929), ch. III.

23. John Dewey, "Theory of Valuation," *International Encyclopedia of Unified Science,* II, 4 (Chicago: University of Chicago Press, 1939).

24. *Social Psychology* (New York: Henry Holt & Company, 1937), p. 123.

25. *Social Psychology* (New York: F. S. Crofts and Company, 1945), p. 123.

26. *The Psychology of Ego-Involvements* (New York: John Wiley & Sons, Inc., 1947), p. 24.

27. *Sociology* (Evanston, Ill.: Row, Peterson and Company, 1958), p. 278.

28. Clyde Kluckhohn and others, "Values and Value-Orientations in the Theory of Action," in Talcott Parsons and Edward A. Shils, eds., *Toward a General Theory of Action* (Cambridge: Harvard University Press, 1951), p. 395.

29. Williams, *op. cit.*, p. 374.

30. *Human Society* (New York: The Macmillan Company, 1948 and 1949), p. 124.

31. *The Social System* (Glencoe, Ill.: Free Press, 1951), p. 7.

32. This does not mean that the theorists using the broad concept of value necessarily neglect the evaluative side. Perry couples his initial tolerance of any interest with elaboration of criteria for the integration of interests. Even his initial tolerance is given a justification explicitly in a general conception of love, which supports any interest whatever it may be, as a starting point in evaluation.

33. *The Psychology of Social Movements* (New York: John Wiley & Sons, Inc., 1941), p. 4.

34. *Ibid.*, p. 7.

35. *Op. cit.*, p. 25.

36. *Op. cit.*, pp. 10-11.

37. *Ibid.*, pp. 52-53.

38. *The Social Order* (New York: McGraw-Hill Book Company, Inc., 1957), p. 140.

39. *Ibid.*, p. 175. Cf. also pp. 149-50 on "ideologies."

40. *Op. cit.*, p. 64.

41. "Concept of Values in Contemporary Philosophical Value Theory," *Philosophy of Science*, 20 (July, 1953), pp. 198-207.

42. As in Plato or Freud. Cf. Kingsley Davis: "All human behavior can be interpreted as motivated by the need for unity. Particular motives are simply expressions of this main motive." (*Op. cit.*, p. 239.)

43. *An Introduction to the Principles of Morals and Legislation*, ch. IV.

7

Social Theory and Social Change

HORNELL HART

Duke University

METHODOLOGICAL POSTULATES

In the critical review which constitutes this chapter, it will be assumed, without supporting argument, that the following principles are basic to the development of sound social theory.

The Goals of Social Theory

It is postulated that every social theory may be evaluated (1) in terms of the practical aid which it promises to provide toward the solution of social problems, or (2) in terms of its value as an intellectual stimulus, and as a tool to aid abstract thinking, regardless of any immediate practical applications, or (3) in terms of both. The present analysis is primarily concerned with the possible practical values of theories of social change.

A social theory is most directly useful when it identifies a cause or causes, through which a problem variable may be controlled (as when biological theory identified the typhoid bacillus). Even when a problem variable cannot be controlled, social theory may be useful in predicting it—as when population theory makes it possible to predict the number of school rooms which will be needed five years from now. When neither

196

direct control nor prediction is presently feasible, social theory can still be practically useful to the extent that it promotes clearer understanding of specific problems.

Steps to Be Taken Toward Reaching Those Goals

It is postulated that the following steps are important in the development of social theory:

1. *Scholarly research is basic.* At any stage in social research, the theories and concepts developed by preceding investigators need to be analyzed comparatively. Taken by itself, scholarly research is certainly not sufficient as a basis for social theory. But it is indispensable to any social scientist who seeks to avoid the blunders of his predecessors, and who hopes to take advantage of their valid contributions.

2. *Verifiable definitions are required* for all crucial concepts and variables. This should state how the thing defined is to be identified or measured. Definitions are needed not merely in terms of synonyms (as is usually done in dictionaries), but also in terms of the repeatable operations and verifiable observations by means of which items can be reliably included under or excluded from the defined categories, or by means of which the designated variable may be measured. The descriptions of the specified operations and observations are required to be such that all competent users of the definition will agree, within reasonably close margins of error, as to how a given item is to be classified or measured.[1] This technique has been illustrated in a recent article in relation to the concept *operation*.[2]

The procedure specified above is to be distinguished clearly from behavioristic operationism. The latter attempts to exclude everything except sensory observations and motor operations. That would rule out all private experience, and hence would exclude all values and all meaning. The above procedure of verifiable definition is applicable to private experience, and to purposes, values, and meanings. It recognizes that mental as well as sensorimotor observations and operations are verifiable, and are indispensable in social science—and, indeed, in all science.

3. Intermediate between casual, common-sense generalizations and rigorously verified conclusions from controlled experiments, it is useful and necessary to employ *informal induction from instances.* One of the weaknesses of books and articles about social research has been their failure to describe adequately this intermediate method.

Even before rigorous definitions have been developed, informally described instances of such phenomena as invention, diffusion, cultural acceleration, cultural lag, social movements, and social planning can be

collected by common-sense methods. Many of the most useful contributions toward the achievement of scientific knowledge of social change
have been made by people who have attempted systematically to collect
instances more or less informally, to formulate hypotheses, to collect
further instances, to revise their hypotheses, and finally to come to a
point where rigorously quantitative research becomes feasible. One brilliant example of the method of informal generalization from instances
is Ogburn and Thomas' 1922 "List of Some Inventions and Discoveries
Made Independently by Two or More Persons." [3] Another example is
Lyford P. Edwards' *Natural History of Revolution* (1927).[4] Informal
collections of this kind can stimulate and guide the formulation of more
rigorous definitions and of tentative generalizations. These in turn can
stimulate and guide the collection of data by more systematic and rigorous methods.

Two essential features differentiate the method of instances from the
mere presentation of illustrations or examples: (1) The method must
be used inductively. Its purpose is to test hypotheses, not to prove preconceived theories. (2) The method requires that the instances be
collected impartially, and as comprehensively as feasible, with particular
attention to instances which fail to fit in readily with the investigator's
preliminary hypotheses. Previously collected groups of instances are
highly desirable raw materials, but as far as feasible, such collections
should have been made with diverse objectives and theories, so that the
user of the instances may avoid being misled by the biases of previous
collectors.

As distinguished from the case method, the method of instances
makes use of data collected originally for other purposes than the study
in hand, and the traits of the instances analyzed are not defined with
the rigor demanded by stringent case methods. As distinguished from
statistical procedures, the method of instances applies no mathematical
tests of significance, reliability, or validity. The major weakness of the
method of instances is its proneness to produce loose, vague, and inadequately verified generalizations.

4. Hypotheses derived by the use of the above methods need to be
verified, so far as possible by means of controlled experiments, and in
any case by the use of the best available statistical methods for determining the reliabilities of specific predictions. Wherever feasible, the
generalizations emerging from the inductive study of data need to be
reduced to mathematical descriptions, and suitable coefficients of association need to be calculated, with the application of appropriate measures of statistical reliability.

SOME PRELIMINARY DEFINITIONS

The methodological postulates summarized in the preceding section are to be employed in two different ways in this chapter. Their primary purpose is to provide criteria by means of which the present status of social theory in the field of social change may be appraised. But also these postulates outline procedures which need to be employed in our own study of social change. Critical comparative analysis of textbook materials, treatises, and articles on social change provides the foundation for this chapter. But, before undertaking that review, it is important to define some of the terms which are basic to the discussion.

Lack of space prevents developing experimental evidence as to the observational-operational quality of the following definitions, but they have been drafted with a view to facilitating such tests.

Social change has occurred in a stated area when the culture or the demographic conditions in that area are measurably or verifiably different, to a statistically significant extent, at one date as compared with another.

Culture includes all those patterned ways of thinking, feeling, and reacting acquired and transmitted by social learning, including their embodiments in artifacts, or in social processes or structures.[5]

Progress consists in social changes that enable human beings to fulfill their purposes more adequately.[6]

A purpose consists in any objective on which time, attention, and effort are expended.[7]

Specific progress has to do with the more adequate fulfillment of a stated purpose, without regard to the effects of that progress on the attainment of other purposes. For example, specific progress of a racketeering gang in obtaining a wider illicit sale for habit-forming drugs might negate progress in various other lines such as reduction of organized crime, and maintenance of industrial efficiency and of successful family life.

Progress in general would consist in a significantly positive total of all specific progresses with respect to all the purposes which are held by the individual or the group involved.

THREE TYPES OF SOCIAL-CHANGE THEORIES

During past centuries, on the basis of prophetic dreaming, armchair theorizing supported by illustrations, and loose generalization stemming from more or less systematic collections of instances, various theories have been current, of which three types may be distinguished.

1. *Consummational theories have prophesied a future golden age.* From 200 B.C. to A.D. 350 or thereabouts, Judaistic and early Christian

thinking was dominated by apocalyptic theories about the world ending in final judgment, with establishment of an eternal Messianic kingdom. The Christian version of this theory is still powerfully influential today among theologians.

Condorcet (1743–1794) divided man's history into nine epochs, the final one, ushered in by the French Revolution, to be characterized by the perfectability of man, in which aspirations for social justice and individual development were to be realized.

Karl Marx (1818–1883) interpreted all history in terms of class struggle, which was finally to be superseded by a classless society—a worker's paradise—introduced through dictatorship of the proletariat.

2. *Social evolution theories have stressed progress.* In 1857, Herbert Spencer published his essay on "Progress, Its Law and Cause." In 1859, Charles Darwin published his *Origin of Species.* Spencer popularized the idea that human progress is inevitable. A whole school of social thinkers developed Social Darwinism, and later other types of theories of social evolution were published.[8] Among anthropologists, Lewis Henry Morgan, in *Ancient Society* (1877), developed the theory that the culture of mankind everywhere must evolve through inevitable definite stages.

3. *Cyclical theories have emphasized trendless fluctuations.* For centuries past, the rise and decline of empires have been obvious to students of history, and have been a factor in stimulating cyclical theories of social change. Among such theories in recent times have been the following:

Sir W. M. Flinders Petrie's *The Revolutions of Civilization* (1912); [9]
Oswald Spengler's *Decline of the West* (1918); [10]
Arnold Toynbee's *Study of History* (1934–1939 and 1954); [11] and
Pitirim Sorokin's *Social and Cultural Dynamics* (1937–1941).[10]

Theories of all the above three types have been tendential. They have embodied theses which their proponents have attempted to prove by theoretical arguments and by examples selected to that end, rather than inductive findings emerging out of dispassionate study of adequate samples of data. Yet these theories did adumbrate hypotheses which the systematic, inductive study of data has developed into what are now two factually supported laws of social change.

CULTURAL ACCELERATION

After centuries of theorizing and dogmatizing about the end of the world, social progress, social evolution, cycles in human history, and the like, two laws of social change have become more and more clearly established. These may be stated here in a preliminary, categorical way, and the pertinent factual data can then be presented.

The Law of Cultural Acceleration: Over the long sweep of time, man's power to carry out his purposes, in the material, biological, psychological, and sociological realms, has tended to increase at an accelerating rate (though with recurrent stagnations and setbacks), and the rate of acceleration has itself tended to accelerate.[12]

The Law of Logistic Surges: Progress with respect to specific purposes, as expressed in individual inventions and in the growth of specific social organizations and culture complexes, has tended to take place in the form of surges, progressing slowly at first, then speeding up, and finally slowing down to a stop or a collapse. In scores of instances, the indexes of these surges can be fitted mathematically with logistic curves.

Can these justifiably be called "laws"?

One critic has objected to referring to "these rather general hypotheses as 'laws.'" This is a twofold criticism, one objection being implied in the word "general," while the other is implied in the word "hypotheses."

By "rather general" the critic presumably means *vague* rather than *comprehensive.* For certainly the Law of Gravitation and the Second Law of Thermodynamics are no less laws because they are universe-wide in scope. But as to whether laws can deal with tendencies, consider Gresham's Law, and the Law of Diminishing Returns (which may be regarded as a special application of the Law of Diminishing Productivity). Both of these deal with tendencies rather than with hard-and-fast, invariable phenomena-sequences.

The second phase of the criticism ignores the distinction between an hypothesis and a law. Hypotheses are provisional principles or tentative laws, formulated for the purpose of testing them in the light of experimental or spontaneous evidence. The two laws of social change, as stated above, have passed through successive hypothesis stages, and have been confirmed by extensive testing against data on the part of various social scientists in various disciplines.

A Rigorous Hypothesis of Loglog Cultural Acceleration

A dictionary definition of scientific law is:

A statement of an order or relation of phenomena which, so far as known, is invariable under the given conditions.

If the Law of Cultural Acceleration, as stated above, fails to conform fully with this rigorous definition, neither does Gresham's Law nor the

Law of Diminishing Returns. But a more rigorous formulation can be offered, in hypothetical form, subject to further factual testing:

When research opportunities and consumer choices are kept fully free, and when makers of cultural choices are provided with available information as to the probable effects of alternative choices upon their own valued ends, the fulfillment of those ends, as measured by the most reliable measurable indexes, will progress at accelerating rates of acceleration.

Some Illustrations of Accelerating Progress in Material Culture

Indexes of man's power to carry out his purposes with respect to the material environment are relatively easy to measure. Some outstanding examples are presented graphically in charts 1 *A* to 1 *D*. The data on which these charts are based are presented and discussed in *Technology and Social Change,* by Francis R. Allen and others.[13] Very briefly, the facts shown in the charts may be summarized as follows:

Man's technological competence in the cutting and shaping of materials has increased as much in the last 3,000 years as it did in the previous million years (Chart 1 *A*).

As to speed of travel, improvements in the locomotive added more in the years between 1829 and 1910 than had been achieved in all the previous million, while during the years since 1910, twenty times as much speed has been added as the locomotive contributed during its time of leadership (1 *B*).

As to diffusion—the spreading of new inventions and discoveries from their place of origin—it took 400 years for the use of pottery to spread 100 miles, when it first was developed in Egypt, about 16,000 B.C. But the use of insulin spread clear around the world within one year (1 *C*).

As to man's power to kill and to destroy, the most useful index for our purposes is the *killing area,* defined as meaning, for any given date, the maximum area within which lives and property may be destroyed by projectiles which travel through a nonstop flight from a single base. Leaving out the details, the basic facts can be summarized in the following table:

DATE	KILLING AREA IN SQUARE MILES
1400	1
1900	125
1954	197,000,000

The trend is shown in Chart 1 *D*.

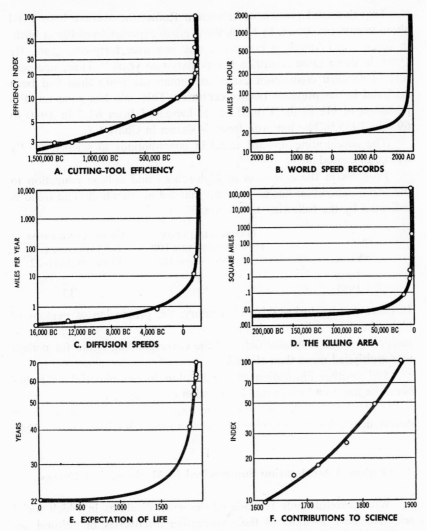

Chart 1. *Six examples of cultural acceleration, graphed on ratio grids.*

Accelerating Progress in Non-Material Culture

Man's accelerating conquest of death has been partly the result of technological progress which has made possible a rising standard of living. Far more, however, the progressive gains in expectation of life have resulted from progress in medical science and in the efficiency of political and health organizations.

Two thousand years ago, in ancient Rome, the average baby lived about twenty-two years. In 1840, the average expectation of life at birth, in seven Euro-American countries, was just over forty-one years. By 1940, in those same countries it was sixty-two years.[14] Thus, one century of modern civilization extended human life more than had been achieved in the previous twenty centuries. This gain has gone on. Expectation of life in the United States increased from 64.2 in 1940 to 69.6 in 1955.[15] The long-run trend is shown in Chart 1 *E*.

The accelerating upward trend in contributions to science (1 *F*) will be discussed later.

Progress in the extension of high-school and college education to the rising generation has also shown marked acceleration. The trend is indicated by the following tabulation: [16]

YEAR	GRADUATING FROM HIGH SCHOOL PER 100 PERSONS AGED 18	GRADUATING FROM COLLEGE PER 100 PERSONS AGED 22
1900	6	2
1955	58	13

In other words, during this half century, the proportion of persons of high-school age who were being given a full high-school education was multiplied more than ninefold, and the corresponding figure for college was multiplied more than sixfold.

Still another illustration of acceleration in non-material fields has been the more and more rapid expansion of the size of governing areas —the areas in which law and order have been maintained by single governments. A curve showing this trend appears in Chart 3 (page 224).

Cultural Acceleration Summarized in Mathematical Curves

When careful study is made of the generalizations in which social scientists have formulated their successive discoveries of cultural acceleration, two facts are notable:

First, the statements about the speed-up of social change have always (until very recent years) been in quite general, qualitative terms, supported merely by a few illustrations of man's more and more rapid progress. These early social explorers of the theory of social change were not progressing beyond the method of instances.

Second, there has cropped out in the writings of one social scientist after another the intimation that these changes really do conform to scientific law—not merely to a qualitative general principle, but actually to some sort of mathematical formula. Lewis H. Morgan, for instance, as early as 1877, spoke of human progress as "essentially geometrical." [17] Ogburn, in 1922, sought "some better insight into the nature of the growth of material culture" by "speculating as to its possible resemblance to the compound-interest curve." [18]

More specific factuality began to creep in when F. Stuart Chapin, in 1925, charted the growth of the number of governmental activities of the State of Minnesota and also of the City of Detroit. He commented: "The effect is almost that of an exponential curve." [19] It was not until 12 years later that Stuart Dodd confirmed this hypothesis by actually fitting an exponential curve to Chapin's data for Detroit.[20]

From Generalization to Formulas

Vague qualitative references to a mathematical ("exponential," or "compound-interest") law of cultural acceleration have continued to be made—in 1937,[21] in 1940,[22] and in 1956.[23]

These references to the "compound-interest curve" are based (in general) on the method of instances, without rigorous curve-fitting on the part of the authors of the statements, or on the part of sources which they cite. Just what does this "compound-interest curve" mean, as related to underlying laws of cultural evolution? Look back for a moment to Chart 1. Each of the six curves shown there is charted on a "ratio grid." No one of them can reasonably be represented by a straight line, such as a compound-interest curve would make on such a chart.

The Super-Acceleration of Human Speeds

Enough examples have been summarized in Chart 1 to raise serious doubts about the "Law of Cultural Growth" as stated in terms of the compound-interest curve (which Stuart Chase adopted from Ogburn and others). As far as evidence has been obtained, the rates of acceleration in at least six important areas of cultural change have curved upward more steeply than this simple exponential type of curve can describe. But the data supporting some of these examples involve considerable degrees of subjectivity. The results shown in the chart are suggestive rather than conclusive—until statistical tests of comparative goodness of fit can be applied to objectively measured data.

This more rigorous testing of the hypothesis of loglog acceleration in social change can be carried out in connection with speed records. When successive world records for speed, from 1800 to 1951, are

charted on a ratio grid, the results shown in Chart 2 are obtained. The
best-fitting compound-interest trend is shown by the straight line. But
that trend is too high for all the records between 1890 and 1928, and
too low for all the records before and after that period. Obviously, such
a straight-line trend is invalid; even on a ratio grid the rate of development of speed records has followed an accelerating curve. Indeed, statistical analysis shows that a trend formula based on logarithms of logarithms (i.e., a "loglog" curve) fits so much better that the difference
would occur by chance less than once in 170 such studies.

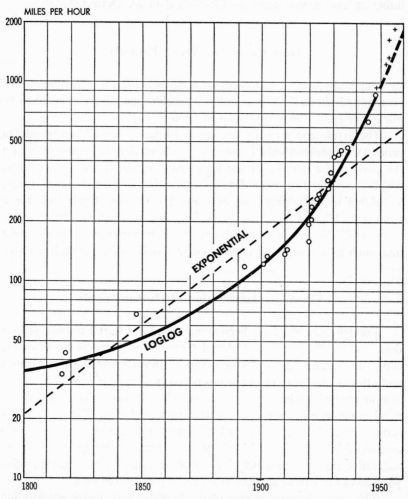

Chart 2. *Record-breaking human speeds, 1800 to 1956, fitted with exponential and loglog trends.* [Source: *American Sociological Review*, 11 (1946), p.
284; *Facts on File, passim.*]

Similar statistical checks can be applied to various other series representing indexes of specific progress. When such tests are applied we find two amendments emerging relative to earlier statements of the law of cultural acceleration:

1. Not only is social change accelerating, but (at least in such instances as those cited in Chart 1) the rate of acceleration has itself been accelerating. If, after the subtraction of a suitable constant in each case, the logarithms of successive items in such an index are charted on ratio grids, the resulting curves tend to approximate straight lines. In other words, we have here not merely an exponential (or logarithmic) rate of acceleration, but a loglog acceleration.

2. Instead of this tendency being confined to technological indexes, as has often been assumed by pioneer students of social change, the same tendency appears in indexes representing specific non-material progress.

To what extent may these curves be regarded as predictive? The mathematical fitting of curves is a valuable device for stating hypotheses accurately, and then measuring accurately the extent to which the actual data deviate from the specified trend. But once the mathematical regularity of such trends has been measured, the question of causation comes up with increased urgency.

A critic has raised this question:

Do these curves really apply to the future? Remember, United States population estimates made in the 1950's were considered to be valid to a degree beyond most predictions of social behavior. Yet they have all been discarded because of a change in the United States birth rate.

Any mathematical curve descriptive of past trends can be used predictively only on the hypothetical assumption that the causes which produced the described regularity will continue to operate in the future as they have in the past, without the intervention of new causal factors. For example, the orbit of a comet may be predicted by astronomers, on the basis of calculated mathematical curves. But such curves are predictive only on the assumption that no significant new heavenly body invades the gravitational field through which the predicted course of the comet is projected. The question of the predictive value of social-trend curves calls, therefore, for an examination of underlying causes.

THE CAUSES OF CULTURAL ACCELERATION

Various investigators have suggested accumulation *as the explanation for cultural acceleration.*

Behavioral scientists interested in social change have, to a considerable extent, applied the method of informal induction from instances in their search for hypotheses about causes. Thus, Morgan in 1877,[24] Ogburn in 1922,[25] and F. Stuart Chapin in 1928,[26] all referred to cultural accumulation. Most of the current textbooks use the fact of accumulation as if it were the adequate and complete explanation of cultural acceleration.

Even the method of instances, however, leads to recognition that the causes are more complex. In order to get at these causes, an analysis of the nature of invention is necessary.

Every invention is a new combination of old elements.

For example, an airplane is roughly an adaptation of a box-kite, a windmill, a gasoline engine, a pilot, and the atmosphere, each of these (except the atmosphere) being adapted by various modifications. Similarly, a telegraph is essentially an electromagnetic circuit, plus sending and receiving keys, plus two telegraphers, plus a Morse Code. The automobile is essentially a carriage, plus a gasoline engine, plus transmission and steering gears, plus a driver, plus a road, plus a filling station, plus a repair shop. In a narrower sense, the automobile mechanism itself is a combination of previous inventions. In 1928, Chapin published a chart entitled "Invention of the Automobile Showing the Integration of Six Known Culture Traits into a New Pattern," referring to the gas engine, differential gears, clutch, tires, etc.[27]

Mechanical inventions may seem at first to be merely combinations of physical and biological parts, such as raw or prefabricated materials, plus an environment, plus properly trained operators. However, even mechanical inventions always include also certain *ideas,* which enter into combinations with these other factors. In some kinds of inventions, the crucial part played by ideas becomes particularly obvious. For example, Galileo's telescope was not merely a combination of lenses and certain other physical parts, but also—and crucially—a combination of the laws of optics (as understood by Galileo) and the problem of seeing heavenly bodies more clearly. A slide rule is a combination of two rulers, the matched-lumber principle, a mathematician, and crucially the principle of logarithms.

Often the decisive factor in a new invention or discovery is the precedent created by a previous invention or discovery. For example, the discovery that certain molds in the earth secrete a chemical called penicillin, which kills off certain kinds of disease germs, provided a key idea which has led to the discovery of a whole series of antibiotics.

Scientific instruments and healing drugs, as well as machines, are invented by new combinations of old elements. This same principle holds true in the invention of social institutions.[28] When the Constitution of the United States was being drafted, the inventors of our form of democratic government were putting together a combination of various pre-existing institutions (such as courts of law, legislative bodies, and executive officers), with certain ideas and ideals (such as the ultimate sovereignty of the people, equality of voting rights, balance of power, and equality before the law). Chapin's chart, showing the elements out of which the commission form of government was invented in Galveston in 1900, illustrates the same fact on the municipal level.[29] All of these examples are seen thus to illustrate the one principle—that inventions consist of new combinations of previously existing elements.

When the elements combined in new inventions are sorted out, it appears that they can be classified into six categories, as follows:

1. Material factors, such as raw materials and previously invented material parts (cogwheels, lenses, and batteries, for example).

2. Biological factors, including the organisms of persons who are to operate or make use of the inventions, and sometimes other organisms such as domesticated animals, seeds, and even bacteria.

3. Psychocultural factors, such as ideas, technical terms, and mathematical symbols.

4. Sociocultural factors, such as organizations that manufacture, sell, and utilize the invention.

5. Population factors, such as the persons of given ages and other characteristics constituting potential customers, salesmen, or transmitters of the invention.

6. The needs, interests, and desires which the invention may fulfill. These are particularly important among the causal factors which enter into inventions. While they are primarily psychocultural, they may also be closely related to each of the other four categories. They may be biological in character, such as the need for food, water, and temperature adjustments. Or they may be psychocultural, such as the craving of the reading public for new mystery thrillers. Or they may be sociocultural, such as the desire for jewelry, for stylish clothing, or for Christmas presents, or the need of business establishments for better dictating machines.

The above analysis leads to the following definitions:

A culture trait consists in a single unit-part of an invention—such as the steering wheel of an automobile, the driver's hand, the directional road sign, or the school where automobile drivers are trained. Traits are of all of the above six types.

A culture complex consists in the interrelated inventions and social organizations which cluster about a central invention. An example is the automobile complex.

A discovery, under the above analysis, is merely a special kind of invention. It consists in the combination of (1) a significant fact in nature, (2) an observer capable of knowing and understanding that fact, and (3) consumers of some sort, capable and desirous of utilizing the fact thus made available to them.

Only a tiny fraction of the culture traits, inventions, and culture complexes employed by an individual have been invented by that individual. He has acquired all of the others by the process of *diffusion*. This may be defined as the transmission of culture complexes from one individual or one group to another. This transmission may have occurred through informal imitation, by systematic instruction, or by advertising, propaganda, and other forms of promotion.

An extreme exaggeration of the part played by diffusion was the Children of the Sun Theory. G. Elliott Smith and W. J. Perry, in 1922 and 1923, argued that all higher culture, both in the Old World and the New, was derived by diffusion from The Children of the Sun in ancient Egypt.[30]

The basic causes of cultural acceleration may be stated in terms of the factors defined above.

Since inventions consist of new combinations of previously existing elements, the opportunity for new inventions increases roughly as a function of the number of possible permutations and combinations of available elements. But, mathematically, the number of possible permutations and combinations increases as the factorial of the number of elements to be combined. And factorials increase with more than geometrical acceleration as the number of elements increases.

The speed of diffusion is increased acceleratingly as the means of communication are improved by the accelerating speed of invention.

The methods of research, whereby the psychocultural elements are developed and the inventions themselves are made, are improved with accelerating speed by the acceleration of invention. This produces a benign spiral, which further intensifies the acceleration.

The basic facts about the inventive process, as analyzed above, need to be stated in more detail. This can be done in terms of the following five factors, on which it will be seen that the speed of social change, in culture in general and in specific cultural complexes, depends:

1. *The first cause of cultural acceleration consists in the increasing number of culture elements from which new inventive combinations can be made.*

As to the number of culture elements from which new inventive combinations can be made, consider the situation of the cave-dwelling inventor, and the elements which he had available to combine into new inventions. He had, of course, his own body, with its hands, its sense organs, and its brain. He had also clay, water, branches of trees, and stones of various kinds. More than a million years ago, he had fire. Moreover, he was surrounded by various sorts of living plants and animals. On the psychological level, he had only the crudest number system, quite probably running only from one to five, and a primitive, unwritten language.

In contrast, consider the modern research team. Instead of a limited variety of sticks, stones, hides, and mud, the modern man has at his command practically all the chemical elements in purified form, and a nearly endless variety of chemical compounds, plastics, textiles, metal alloys, cutting tools, machines to control temperatures, sources of almost limitless energy, instruments for almost unlimited magnification of the sensory powers, and an immense and rapidly increasing variety of previous inventions to work on. Whereas cavemen had no written language, the modern inventor has access to hundreds of thousands of books and scientific articles, elaborately indexed, and quickly available through the aid of reference experts. Cultural accumulation, by adding continually to the number of elements available to be combined into new inventions, would obviously produce an accelerating number of potential permutations and combinations.

Yet this is not by any means the whole of the story. Certain inventions and discoveries are specially prolific in giving birth to other inventions. For example, fire became the means by which men cooked, heated their huts, smelted iron, made glass, and carried out various chemical reactions. Each of these inventions in turn became the ancestor of multitudinous progeny. Glass gave birth to costume jewelry, drinking goblets, window panes, lenses, Crookes tubes, X-ray tubes, electric light bulbs, photoelectric tubes, radio tubes, television tubes, and various other products. Lenses in turn gave birth to eyeglasses, simple magnifying glasses, telescopes, compound microscopes, cameras, range-finders, and searchlights.

Thus, certain inventions have become enabling factors in a geometrically increasing number of derivative inventions. Both through simple accumulation and geometrical multiplication, therefore, the number of elements available to combine into new inventions increases faster and faster.

While the availability of prerequisites tends to facilitate invention, the absence of prerequisites may prevent inventive achievements, even when the needs and the theoretical ideas are already present. As Broom and Selznick observe:

Leonardo da Vinci, for example, invented many machines which became practical in succeeding centuries, but in his day (fifteenth century) the base of technological skills and knowledge was not ready to translate most of his ideas into practical reality.[31]

2. *The units combined become more and more powerful.*

A second major factor in cultural acceleration is the fact that the units which the modern inventive engineer combines are each of them vastly more powerful than the units with which the primitive or even the early modern inventor had to work. Take, for example, the men who have pioneered for progress in travel. Those daring innovators who first had the courage to leap onto the backs of wild horses were able to add ten or fifteen miles per hour to the speed of travel. But a modern engineer has the energy of ten thousand horses tied up in one engine. Or take the first spectacle-maker, who by using a simple lens, added two or three diameters to the power of the human eye to see details. The modern engineer, using magnets to bend streams of electrons, multiplies the power of previous microscopes by thousands.

3. *Accelerated diffusion rates further accelerate cultural change.*

The third major factor contributing to acceleration in cultural change is faster and faster diffusion, due to the greater and greater ease and swiftness of communication. Today hundreds of millions of people speak the English language in areas covering a considerable fraction of the entire globe. Back in prehistoric times, these same areas were inhabited by hundreds of different tribes, using hundreds of mutually unintelligible languages. Every prehistoric invention had not only to struggle against rock-ribbed conservatism in the tribe in which it was born but, before it could be widely adopted, it had to traverse wall after wall of foreign language and of aversion to everything foreign. In addition to the abolition of such barriers, the acceleration of invention of devices for more and more swift and adequate communication has speeded diffusion.

The speed-up in the rate of culture transmission may be illustrated by three examples: [32]

DATE	INVENTION	DIFFUSION RATE IN MILES PER YEAR
16,000 B.C.	Pottery making	.25
1440 A.D.	Printing	12.5
1925 A.D.	Insulin	12,000

This table shows that pottery making, in the Early Neolithic Age in Europe, took 400 years for each 100 miles that it spread from community to community, while insulin, invented in Canada in 1925, spread throughout the world in less than a year. The trend is shown graphically in Chart I C.

4. *The invention of better methods of invention raises acceleration to a higher power.*

The fourth great reason why social change accelerates is that the methods of making inventions are themselves a part of the culture, and that, like the other parts, these methods tend to improve faster and faster. Back in prehistoric times the only inventive method was "fumble and succeed." Even as recently as 1830, Charles Goodyear invented vulcanization of rubber by a blundering process of trial and error. Edison took a major advance by systematically trying out all possible combinations. For example, when he was seeking the right combination of factors to produce a good storage battery, he tried more than 9,000 experiments.

When the factors to be combined are many, and when each factor varies through a long range, the number of combinations becomes so huge that exploring all of them is quite impossible. That is where scientific theory comes in. The modern chemist, for example, working on the synthesis of some drug which may save millions of lives, does not have to try all possible combinations blindly. Scientific knowledge of the structure of molecules enables these leaders of the laboratory to focus their efforts on the processes where results can be obtained relatively swiftly.

Science consists in systematization and increased efficiency in the process of truth-seeking. Underlying principles are discovered by means of which the number of useless combinations to be tested can be vastly reduced. Devices for measuring and calculating are developed, so that new combinations can be described accurately, and their results precisely determined. The methods of logic, statistics, and experiment are themselves systematically improved. Thus the acceleration of progress is raised to a still higher power.

5. *The relative intensity of inventive drives affects relative speeds of progress.*

The motivation of inventions provides a fifth factor affecting the speed of social change. Here, however, the chief significance is in determining the *relative* speeds in various fields. In particular, the excessive acceleration in the development of weapons of death and destruction has been due to the urgent necessity of self-defense, both by individuals and by groups, in the face of the powerfully motivated drive to attain power and wealth by conquest.

Is continuing loglog acceleration conceivable?

A critic has raised the following question:

If the rate of acceleration of social change is also accelerating, there will soon come a point when the rate of social change reaches infinity. Is it then asserted that an infinite rate of change is achievable? No matter how beautifully these curves fit the past, they may or may not fit the future.

Infinity is not something which can be "reached." To say that a quantity is infinite means simply that it is larger than any assignable quantity. Any quantity which increases continuously will (sooner or later) reach a value larger than any previously assigned quantity. A value which is increasing acceleratingly would exceed a specifically assigned quantity sooner than one that was increasing at a constant rate (assuming equal increases in the early stages). A quantity increasing at a rate of acceleration which was also accelerating would exceed the specified value even more rapidly. The fact of loglog acceleration, therefore, merely intensifies the problem which is presented by the general fact of continuous and persistent social trends.

It was pointed out earlier that any scientific law used for predictive purposes is subject to the assumption that the causal factors involved continue to operate as before, without the intervention of new causes. It is always appropriate that such laws, when formulated, be challenged by anyone who can show any reasonable probability that the previous causal factors will be altered or that new factors will be introduced.

That the causal factors which have produced loglog acceleration in cultural change are basic and fundamental, and that they have been operating over at least hundreds of thousands of years of culture history and prehistory, has been demonstrated in preceding sections of this chapter. But it is pertinent to pause at this point and raise two questions: (1) Would the continuation of the demonstrated loglog accelerations in various specific trends produce inconceivable and basically irrational conditions? (2) Are there new causal factors which may reasonably be expected to change these trends—or which have any plausible likelihood of changing them?

To be realistic, let us examine these probabilities in terms of the next decade or two, without attempting any estimate as to what may happen beyond the next twenty years. By that time, it is to be expected that social science will have advanced so far that any analysis which might be drawn up at the present date will have become quite obsolete.

With respect to the first of the above two questions, let us review (in a necessarily cursory way) the conceivable effects of further continuation of loglog accelerations in the six trends graphed in Chart 1:

Cutting-tool efficiency may be taken as a special aspect of the efficiency of mechanical tools in general. The current development of automation may be regarded as a contemporary aspect of the accelerating progress in the efficiency of tools. It does not seem to be inconceivable that the efficiency of tools—including the efficiency of tools designed to operate tools—should continue to accelerate at accelerating rates of speed over at least the next few decades.

As to world speed records, it must be recognized that various limiting factors have to be dealt with. Among these are the amount of acceleration to which the human organism can be subjected without intolerable damage, the traffic problems which arise from greater and greater speed of more and more vehicles traveling in more and more directions at the same time, and ultimately the factors related to speed of light as an absolute limit. A few years ago the "sound barrier" appeared to be a more or less impenetrable limit, but this has been transcended. The heat barrier is at present a major temporary limitation, but technologists are grappling with it.

As to diffusion, the trend may be easier to deal with speculatively if we use the reciprocal of the rates of diffusion speeds. In that case, it becomes evident that diffusion is more and more nearly approaching instantaneousness. With the swift development of radio, television, and international news services the technological obstacles against instantaneous diffusion appear to be dwindling. The psychological obstacles loom large, but it is worth remembering that in former centuries they were undoubtedly far greater.

As to expectation of life, it may again be helpful to take the reciprocal of this trend or, more precisely, to discuss the decline of the death rate toward zero. Nothing inherently inconceivable appears to be involved, though the practical and detailed obstacles will of course be obvious. Remember, however, that such obstacles have always been in evidence, and that past loglog trends have persisted in spite of them.

The increase of contributions to science appears less spectacular in Chart 1 than any of the other five curves of acceleration. Here, however, the likelihood of future acceleration seems even easier to conceive than in some of the other cases.

Steep loglog acceleration in the killing area represents only one arbitrarily isolated aspect of the accelerating acceleration in man's power to kill and destroy. To project such a trend into the future is probably one of the most disturbing forecasts which can emerge from the present chapter. From the sheer standpoint of technology, the likelihood of a continuation in the present trend seems extremely probable, unless some really fundamental limiting factor can be presented (and at present I am aware of no such factor). Yet, if the present trend is projected for even a few decades, we are pushed toward conceiving of a (presently incredible) state in which a master technologist might push a button, whereupon the entire universe would disappear. The lag in the development of techniques for social control stands out even more starkly than at present when we ask ourselves: "How might this master technician be restrained from pushing the button?"

One factor which must not be lost sight of is the way in which these mathematical curves oversimplify the actual process of cultural change.

The developments which are represented by smooth curves actually have involved revolutionary transitions from one mode of culture to another. One of the most striking examples is the shift from preatomic to atomic sources of energy, both for constructive and destructive purposes. The shift from land travel to air travel is another example. The transition from prehistoric illiteracy to the use of written language is a more ancient instance.

In view of these precedents, it seems highly probable that similar transitions lie before us in future cultural development. But one barrier prevents any really candid and searching exploration of such possibilities. The difficulty is that just before any such transition occurs no one except the tiny innovative minority regards the impending change as worthy of rational discussion. Those who catch predictive visions of it are derided and often persecuted. There may perhaps be in the world today a few dozen people who are sufficiently intelligent, with sufficiently broad and deep knowledge of science, philosophy, psychology, political science, science fiction, and other disciplines to be able to conceive what the next phases along certain lines might be. But if this elite group were to get together and were to thrash out the best agreement which they could reach relative to future probabilities, their conclusions would undoubtedly be contemptuously rejected by the sophisticated Philistines who assume that our cultural evolution has already brought us to the peak and the terminus of human history. And quite possibly even the members of such an elite group would be found later to have been grossly mistaken.

LOGISTIC SURGES ARE CHARACTERISTIC OF SOCIAL CHANGE

The preceding section of this chapter has been devoted to analyzing data related to the long-run accelerating trend of progress in various aspects of culture. The existence of such trends appears to be inescapable when the accumulated evidence is thoroughly and dispassionately examined.

Another basic type of social change is also unmistakably evident when the data about the development of specific inventions and the growth of specific social organizations and culture complexes are assembled—namely, upsurges which start slowly, gather momentum, reach a maximum rapidity of change, and then slow down, cease to progress, and either stagnate on a plateau or in some cases retrogress.

Political Logistic Trends

The first recognition of this fact took place not in the field of technology but rather in that of political integration. The studies of Petrie, Spengler, and Sorokin appear to have been stimulated by recognition of the rise and decline of empires. Chapin showed that similar trends are to be found in the development of municipal and state activities.[19] The work done by Park indicates that urban centers undergo cyclical phases that are predictable and accompanied by specific categories of social action.[33]

That the growth of empires, as measured in terms of the square miles of territory ruled by one central government, actually conforms to mathematical trends was first brought out in 1948 in an article entitled "The Logistic Growth of Political Areas." [34]

Other Types of Logistic Trends

Decades before that article appeared, however, logistic curves had been fitted to various series of data related to population, and to economic production. Gradually, this type of mathematical description was applied to various other social series. A bibliography of such studies was published in an article on "Logistic Social Trends" in March, 1945.[35] A supplementary article on "Depression, War, and Logistic Trends" presented additional examples in 1946, and reached the following conclusions: [36]

Some Broader Hypotheses

The present study, and other investigations which have previously been published, suggest the following general theoretical propositions, which are presented here, not as demonstrated, but rather as a stimulus to further research.

1. Human culture develops through a series of growth surges, in which the size of a given measurable variable at a given time tends to be a constant mathematical function (usually logistic; less often Gompertz) of the condition at the immediately preceding time.

2. Such surges are often inaugurated, disrupted, or terminated by crises, such as basic inventions (e.g., steam engine, steamship, gasoline engine, atomic bomb), discoveries (e.g., of Western Hemisphere), wars (e.g., American Revolutionary, and World Wars I and II), and major economic depressions (e.g., 1929–39).

3. Obsolete culture complexes (e.g., sailing ships, horse-drawn vehicles and farm machines, and lynching) often decline along logistic trends.

4. Both in prehistory, over the long sweep of history, and in modern times the slopes of logistic surges show a tendency to increase acceleratingly.

5. Minor logistic surges tend to compound into supersurges (e.g., individual empires into land-borne and sea-borne group trends; populations of cities, states, and nations into surges of larger units; speeds of various types of vehicles into a general speed curve, and the examples cited in the present article).

6. Mathematical formulas have been found useful in describing and interpreting phenomena on various levels of reality—atomic, molecular, crystalline, cellular, organic, species, and astronomic. All such formulas describe units as total configurations, in which the parts cannot be understood except in relation to wholes. The foregoing hypotheses sketch a mathematical theory, inductively arrived at, which does the same thing for certain sociological phenomena.

7. Just as artillery must adapt itself to mathematical trajectories and as mechanical engineering must adjust to formulas for pressures, acceleration, stresses, and the like, so also social engineering must adapt itself to logistic and Gompertz surges.

Acceleration and logistic surges are related to Ogburn's and Chapin's theories.

The two laws of social change, as developed in this and the preceding section, are recognizably similar to qualitative conclusions previously reached by two great pioneers in the field of scientific theory of social change—Ogburn and Chapin. The findings of these pioneers have been admirably summarized by Martindale and Monachesi.[37]

The type of trend has predictive consequences.

Earlier in this chapter, attention has been called to the widespread assumption that cultural acceleration has tended to follow exponential ("compound-interest") types of trend. Subsequent discussion has shown the frequency with which two other types of trend occur—namely, the loglog and the logistic. If it is assumed that the true trend is exponential when actually it is of a loglog character, the resulting predictions will tend to be underestimates, as is illustrated in the case of speed records since 1920, as graphed in Chart 2. But if the trend is assumed to be exponential, when actually it is logistic, the predictions are likely to be excessively high. This was the case in my own forecasts of aviation traffic, as published in February, 1949.[38]

How are the two types of trend related?

Logistic trends tend to characterize the development of a given invention (such as the seaplane) or movement (such as proliferation of birth-control clinics) or the growth of a given social organization (such as the British Empire). This seems to be due to the fact that a new invention or a new organizational surge can gain effectiveness by progressively assimilating elements in its cultural environment. This assimilation starts out by accelerating, but tends to slow down again as the available elements in the cultural environment become assimilated or used up. Loglog trends tend to characterize the long-time development of basic capacities (such as the use of power, speed in travel, expectation of life, and power of destruction). This seems to be due to the four causes of cultural acceleration discussed earlier in this chapter.

CULTURAL LAG—A CONTROVERSIAL CONCEPT

Stuart Chase popularized cultural lag in a simplified and easily understandable form which may be called *The Tandem Theory:* [39]

Inventions are usually accepted into culture in two stages. To begin with, people change their day-by-day behavior to accommodate the new device. . . . Then, considerably later on, people change their institutions and belief systems to allow for the invention, and arrange means for controlling its effects in the interest of society. The time between the first and the second stages is known as the cultural lag, a term invented by Ogburn.

The Tension Theory

The Tandem Theory focuses attention on the effect of a single invention, presenting it as a one-two-three kind of sequence. Actually the process is much more complex, as is indicated in Ogburn's Tension Theory. We might begin to get a more adequate idea by thinking of a wire hoop with rubber bands stretched across it in various directions, and with a network of crisscross bands knotted to these strands at many different points. Now let us suppose that one end of a new rubber band is fastened into the network at some point and then is pulled. This new band may be thought of as a new invention. If all the bands were perfectly elastic (though of different degrees of size and strength), the ways in which the whole network is stretched and twisted by the pull of the new band might be taken as a greatly simplified and idealized representation of the cultural adjustments called for by a new invention or discovery.

If the new rubber band is a small one and if, after it is tied in, it is pulled slowly and gently, and is tied to other strands which it crosses, we may think of the new invention as having been assimilated into the culture, with relatively minor adjustments. But suppose that a large and strong rubber band is tied into the network and then is jerked suddenly and powerfully. The old network will then be twisted and stretched in much more violent ways. This represents what happens whenever social change of a swift and powerful nature takes place. But the principle of cultural acceleration means that larger and larger changes occur faster and faster. In our world today, therefore, the network of cultural adjustments is being stretched and strained to a very high degree.

For purposes of simplification, we have thought of the strands of existing culture and of new inventions as being perfectly elastic. But this, obviously, would misrepresent the facts. Some strands are young and frail, whereas some others are old and rotten. They break down under the stresses of innovations. Other strands are strong and inelastic. Others are more like tigers' tails which, when jerked, produce powerful reactions. Still others are like lanyards on great guns which, when pulled, set off far-away explosions. And the transmission of the invention's pull takes time. The strands may be like new vines which have to grow and put forth leaves, or like the network of fire hoses which need to be connected up and brought to bear in a great conflagration. Complications like these involve cultural lags.

Six Agreements and Three Issues

In 1908, E. D. Roberty set forth the following *law of lagging:* That the philosophy or religion of a society lags behind its science, that its aesthetic thought lags behind its religion, and that applied thought lags behind all previous forms of thought.

In 1922, William F. Ogburn published his first formulation of the law of cultural lag. Between then and 1950, at least twenty additional outstandingly significant discussions of the subject appeared in scholarly periodicals and textbooks.[40] A systematic analysis of these discussions brings out the fact that sociologists who have given special attention to the subject are fairly well united as to six agreements, but that three major issues have emerged. The agreements may be epitomized as follows:

1. That culture involves both material and non-material aspects.

2. That material culture usually (though not always) changes faster than, or in advance of, related non-material culture.

3. That various aspects of culture are interdependent, so that a change in any one aspect calls for adaptive changes in other aspects.

4. That such changes take time.

5. That this time lapse or difference in speed involves lag, strain, disorganization, or other maladjustments adverse to values held by various people affected by it

6. That the above facts do not imply mechanistic determinism, since (*a*) technology involves and depends on science; (*b*) invention and diffusion take place largely through mental behavior; and (*c*) mental and social (as well as technological) inventions cause lags.

The three points on which major disagreements have emerged are as follows:

1. Is the division of culture into two parts—material and non-material an adequate analysis?

2. Can the value judgment implied in the term *lag* be reduced to objective and verifiable facts?

3. How can the differences in speed of innovation in various parts of the culture, and the time lag between inventions and subsequent adaptations to those inventions, be measured validly and reliably?

In the present chapter these issues can be dealt with only briefly, as follows:

Lag is three-dimensional.

Analysis of the culture fabric shows that the division into material and non-material culture traits is far from simple. Culture may be analyzed horizontally into six institutional slices: the economic, familial, educational, political, religious, and leisure time. Vertically, culture traits may be classified into four levels in relation to the sciences which have primary concern with them: namely, the material sciences (physics, chemistry, geology, and so forth), the biological (zoology, botany, anatomy, physiology, and medicine), the psychological (psychology, functional psychiatry, and education), and sociological (sociology, cultural anthropology, and political science). Cultural lag may relate to functional maladjustment between the culture complexes of the various institutional slices, and also between the traits on the various science levels.

Thus, both culture and cultural lag are three-dimensional. The wire hoop with the rubber bands stretched crisscross on it provides a two-dimensional diagram of cultural lag. But actually we need three dimensions. We must think of culture interlaced with tensions, up and down, side to side, and past to present to future. In view of the great variety of combinations of different types of lagging traits, no broad generalization is worthy of casual acceptance without detailed explorations in terms of actual instances, with due regard to the six institutional slices, the four science levels, and the time dimension.

The valuational aspects of the lag concept can be dealt with verifiably.

One of the most frequent objections raised against the concept is that it inherently involves valuation. The second of the three issues listed above is this: "Can the value judgment implied in the term *lag* be reduced to objective and verifiable facts?" In considering this issue it is essential to recognize that all cultural behavior is dynamic, that most if not all invention is goal-directed, and that valuational aspects therefore cannot be excluded. Social change results from the dynamics involved in valuational behavior. The process can be understood only when this valuational behavior is dispassionately and fully understood, and when the problems involved are worked out along appropriate dynamic lines.

Any legitimate objection to the valuational implications of the cultural-lag concept may be eliminated by stating, explicitly and objectively, the value-frame within which the lag to be investigated is conceived, and by developing verifiable and reliable indexes of the values involved. A comprehensive study of the attitudes of sociologists toward value judgments has led to the formulation of certain conclusions which seem to be practically universally accepted.

Among these is the proposition that it is entirely proper, scientifically, for applied sociology, having discovered what human purposes are most fundamental, or what ones are most widely accepted as ideal, to seek and disseminate knowledge as to how these purposes may be more adequately fulfilled.[41] For example, it is almost universally conceded that the killing and maiming of human beings through automobile accidents is undesirable. When technological progress increased the speed of automobiles, there was at first no concomitant increase in methods for preventing accidents. The resulting rise in traffic death rates may be regarded as an index of this particular form of cultural lag.

Cultural lag can be measured.

We have defined cultural lag in terms of a time interval. One of the criticisms of loose uses of the cultural-lag concept has been that quite frequently a quantitative variable was implied but never actually defined or measured. This is the essence of issue 3. Mueller has said: [42]

By far the most commonly employed type of lag refers to the hypothesis of the varying rates of change of two different culture categories. This differential rate is presumably the cause of maladjustment or friction which produces unrest and disorganization. Now, in order to establish a differential rate of change, either the rates of movement must be commensurable, or the gap between the two related categories must be measurable.

When neither of these conditions is fulfilled, Mueller regards the alleged lag as spurious.

The seriousness of this difficulty becomes increasingly evident when one attempts to reduce to actually quantitative terms some of the purportedly quantitative formulations of cultural lag. For example, how measure the time gap between the invention of the automobile and the development of the adaptive complexes for which that invention created a need? How measure the "strain which exists between two correlated parts of culture which change at unequal rates?" Yet this strain constitutes cultural lag as defined in Ogburn's Tension Theory.

Measuring lag as a gap between two indexes using the same units.
The first method of measuring cultural lag is suggested by Mueller's first alternative—". . . the rates of movement must be commensurable. . . ." For example, one phase of the recent biological phenomenon of a rising birth rate is the increase which is now going on in the number of children of school age. This biological aspect of the family complex calls for an expansion in the material level of the school complex. But there is a marked lag in such expansion. The lead development can be measured in terms of the number of children needing places in school buildings, and the lagging variable can be measured in terms of the number of places available in the appropriate schools. The resulting lag variable has two dimensions—time, and number of places lacking in schools.

Another example of this type of measurement will be found in Chart 3, where both military destructive power and preventive government power are represented by indexes in terms of geographical area, the lag being represented by the widening gap between the two.

A second method of measuring cultural lag is to find a quantitative index of the unprevented or potential damage resulting from the innovation for which adaptive measures are lagging. An example is the death rate from automobile accidents.

Defining Cultural Lag

In the light of the above analysis, *cultural lag* may be defined as consisting in a time interval between two phases in the development of a culture complex or of two different culture complexes, and where generally accepted social ends would be promoted if the length of the interval could be shortened. When specific examples are studied, it becomes evident that two extremes need to be distinguished. These may be labeled "trait lag" and "complex lag." *Trait lag* may be defined as the time interval between a specific invention and the achievement of a specific adjustment called for by that invention. An example would be the invention of the automobile and the invention of radar speed-timing. This is the sort of thing which Stuart Chase suggests in his Tandem Theory of

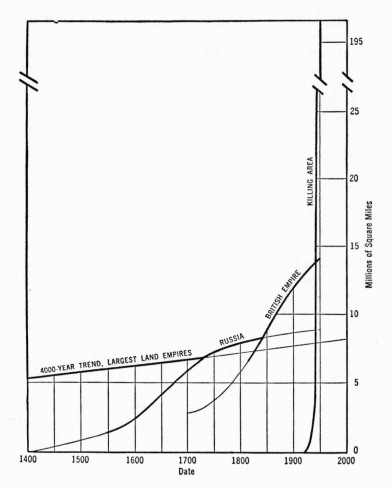

Chart 3. *The slow increase in governing areas, compared with the precipitate growth of killing areas.* [Source: Hornell Hart, "Atomic Cultural Lag: II. Its Measurement," *Sociology and Social Research,* Vol. 32 (March-May, 1948), p. 847.]

cultural lag. *Complex lag* is more closely related to the Tension Theory. It may be defined as the time interval between emergence of a stated social need (as the result of the development of a stated culture complex) and the meeting of that need by the development of adequate adaptive complexes. An example is the gap between the accelerating development of mass-destructive military technology and the lagging development of the international-law-and-order complex. A much more generalized example is the lag which has often been pointed out between technology and social science. As social science develops, it becomes increasingly possible to foresee impending or future cultural lags, to develop scientific generalizations about methods of solving them, and to come to grips with cultural lag itself as a basic phenomenon, capable of being analyzed and solved by the methods of science.

Once the contrast is stated, it becomes evident that trait lag and complex lag merge into each other. To regard the automobile as a single, specific invention is an obvious oversimplification. Traffic accidents are the result of the developing highway-speed complex, and of the lagging highway-safety complex. On the other hand, specific developments in the mass-destruction complex, such as the invention of the atomic bomb, have provided focal points of evident need for adaptive social inventions.

THE FUTILITARIAN VIEW OF SOCIAL CHANGE

The view that social scientists can do little or nothing to direct or control social change is epitomized in the title of William Graham Sumner's essay on "The Absurd Effort to Make the World Over." [43] He stressed the glacier-like development of the mores, with their massive resistance to social reform. Such arguments against the feasibility of social engineering appear to gain some weight from consideration of the various factors capable of control only with great difficulty and uncertainty, or to very limited degrees. A partial list of such factors is as follows.

Climatic changes, and other alterations of the physical environment not caused by human action have, to a minor extent, caused uncontrollable changes in social life. Theoretically, spontaneous biological mutations might cause social changes, but it is generally agreed that this has been of negligible importance during the course of recorded history.

Far more important have been the unintended cumulative effects of human action. Cutting down forests and plowing up prairie land have had important effects on climate and soil erosion. Significant, too, is the depletion of natural resources, by deforestation without replacement, by exhaustion of mines, and by stripping soil of its fertility. Differential fertility, reducing the reproduction of innately superior groups, has been depletional. Migrations and conquests have also introduced powerful and unforeseen factors in social change.

Lack of Control Over Inventions

Inventions are humanly produced causes of change. But Ogburn has raised the question whether inventions are inevitable.[44] He and Dorothy

Thomas listed 148 inventions and discoveries made independently by two or more persons.

That inventions produce unforeseen effects has often been pointed out. The effect of the steam engine in producing urban congestion and the effects of the automobile on various aspects of social life are well recognized examples.

Moreover, the socially disrupting effects of technological inventions are increasing at accelerating rates, while adaptive measures lag, along with the social science on which it might be hoped that such measures might be based.

Doubts as to the Possibility of Social Prediction

At the start of this chapter it was suggested that one way in which social science may be useful toward the solution of social problems consists in prediction. But the very possibility of such prediction has been the subject of an extended controversy, which has been reviewed in the recent text, *Technology and Social Change,* in a chapter entitled "Predicting Future Trends." [45] The conclusion of that chapter is as follows:

> The facts reviewed . . . seem sufficient to refute the defeatism of those social thinkers who have denied the possibility of social prediction. It must be recognized that the prediction of social phenomena is a difficult and hazardous process. However, instances cited in the present chapter show that a number of quite specific predictions have been fulfilled. Not only is all social scheduling based upon routine forecasts of human behavior, but specific and fairly complex events and trends can (in some cases) be predicted within reasonable margins of error. If sociology is to become a science worthy of the name, the energies of its practitioners might better be directed toward improving the techniques of prediction rather than toward demonstrations that prediction is impossible.

That controlled experiments can be used in some types of problems to obtain statistically reliable and valid predictions has been exemplified by the study on "Overcoming Resistance to Change," made by Lester Coch and John French in a pajama factory in Marion, Virginia, in 1947.[46] This study validated the prediction that when social changes affecting a given group are to be made, the greater the participation extended to the group in making the plans for change, the less will be the resistance to the change, and the faster will be the recovery rate.

The Ever-Widening-Gap Theory

The gap between the need for social science and the achievements of social science has grown wider and wider. Indeed, this chronic and increasing lag of social wisdom behind accelerating technology might be expressed in generalized terms somewhat as follows:

The *Ever-Widening-Gap Theory* regards technological progress as one aspect of social change, evolving with an ever-accelerating speed, while agencies of social control are regarded as a separate aspect, developing at much slower acceleration, the difference in rates being regarded as inherent and incurable.

One of the most important questions confronting social science today is whether the Ever-Widening-Gap Theory, as thus stated, is necessarily valid.

Technological acceleration creates greater and greater demands for economic planning and economic co-operation. The growth of economic and political units and the superacceleration in development of weapons of destruction bring about greater and greater demands for co-operation in creating and maintaining law and order. But the capacity for such co-operation has been lagging. Hence came the unprecedented economic depression of the 1930's and the unprecedented world wars of the twentieth century. All the developments customarily referred to as social disorganization are also pertinent in this connection.

Taking into account all the above factors, the task of exerting any intelligent control over social change might seem hopeless. But a series of opposing considerations needs to be recognized.

CONSTRUCTIVE POSSIBILITIES OF SOCIAL ENGINEERING

Various types of engineering (electrical, hydraulic, aerodynamic, and so forth) deal with particular forms of energy. Engineers are concerned with how to generate, accumulate, control, direct, and utilize energy. *Social engineering deals with social energy.*

Social life consists in energy flows. Within limits and under certain circumstances, social energy can be generated, accumulated, controlled, directed, and utilized. To work out and apply systematically the best methods for doing these things is the task of social engineering. If the futilitarians were right, that task might well seem to be hopeless. But let us examine the other side of the argument.

Inventions are not inevitable. Ogburn's brilliant use of the method of instances, in compiling his list of parallel inventions, should have been supplemented by another list of seemingly obvious inventions which were *not* made. A few candidates for such a list are as follows:

The phonetic alphabet was invented basically only once, although conditions appear to have been "ripe" for such an invention in many other places and times.[47]

The wheel, as an aid to transportation, was never invented in the pre-Columbian Western world. Potter's wheels and cartwheels were non-existent in ancient America, though they were in use in Egypt about 4,000 B.C. Toy four-wheeled carts have been found in pre-Columbian remains, but the principle was never given practical utility.[48]

The "inevitability" of the invention of the airplane, the typewriter, and the electric telegraph might give rise to the feeling that inventors are unimportant, and that no social policy need be developed to encourage innovation. Such an attitude would be rather obviously false even in the field of technology. Certainly our patent laws are supposed to be for the purpose of encouraging inventors to invent. But if creative inventors are needed in the field of technology, how much more are they needed in the fields of political, philanthropic, ethical, religious, and other intellectual forms of invention?

Social movements effect social changes. As analyzed by Rudolf Heberle, *a social movement* consists in a collective attempt to bring about fundamental changes in the patterns of human relations and social institutions, when the acting individuals have become aware of themselves as being united with each other for fulfillment of sentiments and goals which they are aware that they have in common.[49] One way to classify social movements is into the following four groups:

Social reform movements are at least ostensibly altruistic collective endeavors, within the framework of existing government, to eliminate social injustices or other causes damaging to some underprivileged, unfortunate, or exploited group. The crusade against child labor, the movement to reduce infant mortality, and the movement to prevent infantile paralysis are examples.

Social revolutions endeavor to overthrow the existing government, by methods not legal under that government, and to set up a new government whose power will be in the hands of the revolutionists. Certainly history has been altered in major ways by revolutions. The Bolshevik revolution in Russia is an example.

Pressure movements endeavor, within the framework of existing government, to advance the interests of the members of the movement as opposed to the interests of other groups. The farm, labor, and manufacturers' lobbies have certainly achieved major effects on legislation and thus on our social structure.

Nonpolitical movements include all social movements whose objectives do not require changes in existing law. Examples are artistic, theological, educational, and scientific movements.

Social planning applies social engineering systematically.[50]

Like social movements, social planning involves collective action to achieve shared objectives by means of social change. But social planning differs from reform and pressure movements in two specific ways:

(1) Social reform is ordinarily motivated by strong emotional revulsion against some form of cultural lag. Social planning on the other hand stresses much more dispassionate appraisal of the social needs involved, and much more systematic application of research and of established scientific knowledge to the development of techniques for meeting those needs.

(2) Social reform must usually acquire the power to act, by electing a slate of candidates or passing legislation, whereas social planning is usually based on authority already acquired, and is concerned with the wise utilization and application of that power.

Examples of Successful Social Engineering

Broadly speaking, social engineering may be taken to include both social reform and social planning. Interpreted in this broad sense, social engineering has been seeking remedies for three types of cultural lag, which may be distinguished roughly as the exploitive, the aggressive, and the accidental. In all of these three types, the basic causes of cultural lag (as described in previous sections of this chapter) are usually operating, and must be dealt with if the lag is to be corrected. But, in the exploitive type, the problem is complicated by the fact that the profit motive, or the will to power, are, to a greater or less extent, opposed to correcting the lag. In the aggressive type, the motives of hatred, antagonism, or belligerency tend to perpetuate the lag. The third type is "accidental" in the sense that while the usual causes of cultural lag are operative, these are not complicated by motives of exploitation or aggression, and hence the problem confronting the social engineer is to that degree simpler. It must be recognized that the line of demarcation between the three types may be hazy at times, and that opinions may differ as to motives which may be thought to complicate the problem. Indeed, one of the tasks of the social engineer is to arrive at a valid appraisal of the motivational social forces which may obstruct or aid the work of eliminating the lag which he is seeking to control.

Successful reduction of lags of each of the three types is illustrated in Chart 4. Air fatalities are, of course, only one of a number of illustrations of accidental cultural lag which might have been used. Accidents on highways, on railroads, in coal mines, and in other industries have shown similar (though less pronounced) downward trends. Deaths from disease also are included in our "accidental" category. Enteritis, colitis, and closely affiliated diagnoses once accounted for infant mortality rates up in the hundreds per 1,000 babies under one year old. Similar trends have been evident in death rates from such diseases as typhoid fever, tuberculosis, and many others.

The decline in child labor illustrates an achievement in social reform where the profit motive was strongly opposed to the enactment and enforcement of the legislation chiefly responsible for the improvement. The complexity of motivation in such matters is illustrated by the fact that many farmers sincerely opposed anti-child labor legislation on the grounds that it interfered with the normal and wholesome participation of farm children in the family enterprise, and by the fact that, in England, many opponents of legislation in this field were sincerely convinced that restrictions on child labor would bring national ruin.

The decline in the lynching rate illustrates a reform in which violence has gradually been reduced, by enlightenment and co-operation rather than by legislation.[51] The lynching illustration comes closest to providing an analogy for the war problem. War is an aggressive and exploitive form of cultural lag, with which social engineering has as yet been unable to deal successfully—except perhaps for the temporary success of the peace movement between 1650 and 1913.[52]

The four illustrations presented in Chart 4, and the innumerable other examples which might be cited, would certainly seem to indicate that the effort to make the world better (defining verifiably the values involved) is very far from being the absurdity which William Graham Sumner asserted it to be.

The Successive-Emergence Theory of Cultural Lag

Auguste Comte did his work a century before Ogburn coined the concept of cultural lag. Yet Comte stated some basic principles which foreshadowed the Successive-Emergence Theory. This differs from the Ever-Widening-Gap Theory by recognizing that human thought emerges into the scientific stage in successive sequence, bringing surges of progress in one aspect of culture after another. This conception would suggest at least the possibility that scientific methods of thinking, which have emerged successively in such fields as physics, chemistry, biology,

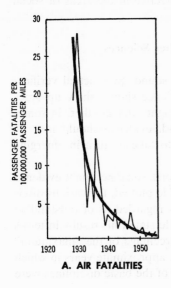

A. AIR FATALITIES

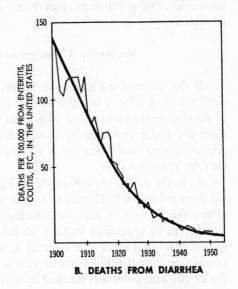

B. DEATHS FROM DIARRHEA

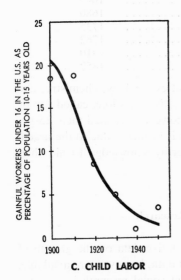

C. CHILD LABOR

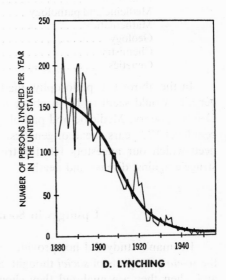

D. LYNCHING

Chart 4. *Four examples of successful social engineering.*

economics, and psychology, may become effective in the areas of social relations.

Successive Upsurges in Other Sciences

If the Successive-Emergence Theory is sound, two factual verifications should follow. First, the history of science should show upsurges of development in one phase of human thought after another, in something the order indicated by Comte. Second, evidence should now be appearing that social thought is beginning to take its turn in emerging into the scientific stage.

As to the first of these possible verifications, some pertinent evidence has been published by Harvey C. Lehman.[53] He plotted, for various disciplines, the number of creative contributions regarded as of outstanding importance by specialists within each field. He stated his results in terms of production for each time interval as a percentage of the "maximum" production rate. Reading from his charts, the approximate years in which the 25-per cent point was reached by certain of the basic disciplines were as follows:

Philosophy	1640
Medicine and pathology	1680
Mathematics	1735
Geology	1762
Chemistry	1810
Genetics	1852

In the above list, philosophy, mathematics, geology, chemistry, and genetics would seem to be in about the relative positions called for by Comte's theory. Medicine and pathology, however, reached their 25-per cent level 172 years ahead of genetics. This is probably due to the urgent need which our ancestors felt for trustworthy knowledge to aid their struggle against disease and death.

Upsurges in Social Research

Lehman's study did not provide quantitative data on the growth of the *scientific* aspects of *social* thought. Such data, however, are available, and when they are analyzed they show that social research in general, and experimental social psychology and business-cycle theory in particular, have had upsurge dates later than any of those in the above list —as the Successive-Emergence Theory has predicted. The demonstration of this fact has been published previously, and cannot be repeated here.[54] Suffice it to say that, from 1920 up to World War II, social-research methodology in general, social psychology in particular, and at least one phase of economic research developed upsurges. The central tendency of these upsurges seems clearly to have been logistic in character. When this development is compared with the upsurge of mechanical inventions which preceded the Industrial Revolution, it is clear that the recent flowering of social research has been much swifter than the growth of applied science which produced the technological upsurges of the past century. All of this is consistent with the Successive-Emergence Theory of cultural lag.

THE SCIENTIFIC STUDY OF SOCIAL SCIENCE

Acceleration in social change (as we have seen) depends in part upon the invention of new methods of invention. To invent a method of invention twice as good as previous methods might be thought of as raising the process to the second power. Actually, various inventions of new inventive techniques have certainly shifted the speed of progress into higher gears. Among such inventions, we might recall Francis Bacon's formulation of the scientific method, the development of controlled experiments, and the invention of the miscroscope, the standard deviation, the slide rule, and the radioisotope.

If social science is the most promising instrument for speeding up desirable social developments, is not a valid science of social-science methods the most promising instrument for promoting the needed upsurge? Science can be used as an instrument for improving science. All that we know of scientific method needs to be brought to bear upon our present stumbling and inadequate techniques of science, in order that we may build up intellectual capital. Our factories produce with almost incredible abundance because our captains of industry built machines for the purpose of building machines. Social science is urgently in need of such an investment of intelligence toward promoting intelligence.

A Project to Stimulate Conceptual Progress

Our review of the literature on social change shows clearly that social theory (at least in this field) suffers at present from a radically inadequate thoroughness in comparison of data, concepts, theories, and generalizations. What is needed now is the carrying forward of searching comparisons of the best work in this field, bringing out the agreements and the issues. A project (confined in this illustration to the field of social change) might be laid out along the following lines:

Half a dozen or so of the leading contemporary contributors in the field of social change, selected on the basis of objective ratings of their published researches, might be invited to co-operate. An appropriation from foundation funds might be made available, sufficient to allow the selected leaders to devote their major attention for a year or so to a really thoroughgoing analysis of the subject. The principal concepts, agreements, and issues in the field should then be reduced to observational-operational terms. Specific research projects should be designed, under ruthless reciprocal criticism by members of the team, and research programs should be set up to produce verifiable and reliable findings on these issues.

CONCLUSION

We all know that the requirements of science are arduous, and that the difficulties of fulfilling them in the areas of human behavior explain much of the halting backwardness which is so evident in our field. But the task is certainly not hopeless. Achievements of the past and the rapidly growing insights of recent years point to the possibility of major attainments in the near future. Let us then seek to become as expert as we may in the processes by which social change occurs and can be achieved. Let us then apply this knowledge to changing for the better the procedures and techniques of ourselves and others in social research.

NOTES

1. Stuart C. Dodd, "Operational Definitions Operationally Defined," *American Journal of Sociology,* 48 (January, 1943), pp. 482-91.

2. Hornell Hart and associates, "Toward an Operational Definition of the Term 'Operation,'" *American Sociological Review,* 18 (December, 1953), pp. 612-17.

3. William F. Ogburn and Dorothy Thomas, "Are Inventions Inevitable?" *Political Science Quarterly,* 37 (March, 1922), pp. 83-98; reprinted in Ogburn's *Social Change with Respect to Culture and Original Nature* (New York: The Viking Press, 1922 and 1950), pp. 90-102.

4. Lyford P. Edwards, *The Natural History of Revolutions* (Chicago: University of Chicago Press, 1927).

5. Cf. A. L. Kroeber and C. Kluckhohn, "The Concept of Culture: A Critical Review of Definitions," *Papers of the Peabody Museum* (Harvard University), 41 (1950); Arnold W. Green, *Sociology: An Analysis of Life in Modern Society* (New York: McGraw-Hill Book Company, Inc., 1952), p. 7; and Ronald Friedman *et al., Principles of Sociology* (New York: Henry Holt & Company, Inc., 1952), p. 35.

6. Cf. Arnold M. Rose, *Sociology: The Study of Human Relations* (New York: Alfred A. Knopf, Inc., 1956), p. 333.

7. Cf. Hornell Hart, "Value Judgments in Sociology," *American Sociological Review*, 3 (December, 1938), pp. 863-65.

8. Nicholas S. Timasheff, *Sociological Theory: Its Nature and Growth* (Garden City, N.Y.: Doubleday & Company, Inc., 1955), pp. 59-96. See also Don Martindale and Elio D. Monachesi, *Elements of Sociology* (New York: Harper & Brothers, 1951), pp. 560-68, 588-96.

9. W. M. Flinders Petrie, *The Revolutions of Civilization* (New York: Harper & Brothers, 1912).

10. For an excellent critical summary, see Howard Becker, "Historical Sociology," in *Contemporary Social Theory*, edited by Harry Elmer Barnes, Howard Becker, and Frances Bennett Becker (New York: D. Appleton-Century Company, 1940), pp. 533-39.

11. For a brief but comprehensive summary, see Timasheff, *op. cit.*, pp. 268-71.

12. Cf. Francis E. Merrill and H. Wentworth Eldredge, *Culture and Society: An Introduction to Sociology* (New York: Prentice-Hall, Inc., 1952), pp. 583-87.

13. Francis R. Allen, ed., *Technology and Social Change* (New York: Appleton-Century-Crofts, Inc., 1957), pp. 28-47.

14. Hornell Hart and Hilda Hertz, "Expectation of Life as an Index of Social Progress," *American Sociological Review*, 9 (December, 1944), p. 612

15. *Statistical Bulletin* of the Metropolitan Life Insurance Company, *passim*.

16. Based on data from U.S. Government's *Biennial Surveys of Education, passim*.

17. Lewis H. Morgan, *Ancient Society* (New York: Henry Holt & Company, Inc., 1877), p. 38.

18. William F. Ogburn, *Social Change* (New York: B. W. Huebsch, 1922), p. 106.

19. F. Stuart Chapin, "A Theory of Synchronous Culture Cycles," *Journal of Social Forces*, 3 (May, 1925), p. 598.

20. Stuart C. Dodd, *Systematic Social Science* (Ann Arbor, Michigan: Edwards Brothers, Inc., 1947), p. 135.

21. Robert L. Sutherland and Julian L. Woodward, *Introductory Sociology* (Philadelphia: J. B. Lippincott Company, 1940), p. 72.

22. William F. Ogburn and Meyer Nimkoff, *Sociology* (Boston: Houghton Mifflin Company, 1940), pp. 791-93.

23. Stuart Chase, *The Proper Study of Mankind* (New York: Harper & Brothers, 1956), pp. 130-31.

24. *Loc. cit.*: cf. Ronald Freedman, Amos H. Hawley, Werner E. Landecker, and Horace M. Miner, *Principles of Sociology* (New York: Henry Holt & Company, Inc., 1952), p. 321.

25. William F. Ogburn, *Social Change,* 1922, p. 105.

26. F. Stuart Chapin, *Cultural Change* (New York: Century Company, 1928), pp. 596-604.

27. *Id.,* pp. 335-36.

28. Cf. Freedman *et al., op. cit.,* p. 313.

29. *Loc. cit.*

30. For a brief résumé of the Children of the Sun Theory, see Hornell Hart, *The Technique of Social Progress* (New York: Henry Holt & Company, Inc., 1931), pp. 116-17. For an analysis of factors responsible for pre-Columbian cultural parallels between the Old World and the New, see *id.,* pp. 92-115.

31. Leonard Broom and Philip Selznick, *Sociology—A Text with Adapted Readings* (Evanston, Ill.: Row, Peterson and Company, 1958), p. 72.

32. Hornell Hart, *The Technique of Social Progress* (New York: Henry Holt & Company, Inc., 1931), p. 680.

33. Don Martindale and Elio D. Monachesi, *Elements of Sociology* (New York: Harper & Brothers, 1951), p. 574.

34. Hornell Hart, "The Logistic Growth of Political Areas," *Social Forces,* 26 (May, 1948), pp. 396-408.

35. Hornell Hart, "Logistic Social Trends," *American Journal of Sociology,* 50 (March, 1945), pp. 337-52.

36. Hornell Hart, "Depression, War, and Logistic Trends," *American Journal of Sociology,* 52 (September, 1946), pp. 112-22. Additional material on logistic trends will be found in Hornell Hart, "Technological Acceleration and the Atomic Bomb," *American Sociological Review,* 11 (June, 1946), pp. 283-86.

37. Martindale and Monachesi, *op. cit.,* pp. 578, 583-86.

38. Hornell Hart, "Predicting Passenger Miles Flown," in *Technology and Social Change,* pp. 459-62.

39. Stuart Chase, *The Proper Study of Mankind* (New York: Harper & Brothers, 1948), p. 115.

40. The various sources, preceded by their dates, are as follows:
1908 E. D. Roberty, *Sociologie de l'Action* (Paris), pp. 182 ff.
1922 William F. Ogburn, *Social Change (op. cit.),* pp. 202-03.
1924 Floyd H. Allport, "Social Change: An Analysis of Professor Ogburn's Culture Theory," *Social Forces,* 2 (September, 1924), pp. 671-76.
1928 Stuart Chapin, *Cultural Change* (New York: Appleton-Century-Crofts, Inc.), p. 210.
1928 Pitirim Sorokin, *Contemporary Sociological Theories* (New York: Harper & Brothers, 1928), pp. 742-64.
1933 William F. Ogburn and S. C. Gilfillan, "The Influence of Invention and Discovery," in *Recent Social Trends* (New York: McGraw-Hill Book Company, Inc., 1933), I, 162.
1934 Lewis Mumford, *Technics and Civilization* (New York: Harcourt, Brace & Company, Inc., 1934), pp. 316-20.

1934 James W. Woodard, "Critical Notes on the Culture Lag Concept," *Social Forces,* 12 (March, 1934), pp. 388-98.

1934 James H. S. Bossard, *Social Change and Social Problems* (New York: Harper & Brothers, revised ed., 1938), pp. 110-14.

1937 Abbott P. Herman, "Answer to Criticisms of the Lag Concept," *American Journal of Sociology,* 43 (November, 1937), pp. 440-51.

1937 R. M. MacIver, "The Hypothesis of 'Cultural Lag' " in his *Society* (New York: Farrar & Rinehart, Inc., 1937), pp. 272-73 and 469-70.

1937 William F. Ogburn, "Change, Social," *Encyclopaedia of the Social Sciences,* III, 332.

1938 John H. Mueller, "Present Status of the Cultural Lag Hypothesis," *American Sociological Review,* 3 (June, 1938), pp. 320-27.

1939 Constantine Panunzio, *Major Social Institutions* (New York: The Macmillan Company, 1939), p. 534.

1940 Robert L. Sutherland and Julian L. Woodward, *Introductory Sociology* (New York: J. B. Lippincott Company, revised, 1940), p. 735.

1941 Edward Byron Reuter, *Handbook of Sociology* (New York: Dryden Press, 1941), p. 105.

1944 Mirra Komarovsky, in Fairchild's *Dictionary of Sociology* (New York: Philosophical Library, 1944), p. 170.

1945 Joseph Schneider, "Cultural Lag—What Is It?" *American Sociological Review,* 10 (December, 1945), pp. 786-91.

1948 Hornell Hart, "Atomic Cultural Lag: I. The Value Frame," *Sociology and Social Research,* 32 (March-April, 1948), pp. 768-76.

1948 *Id.,* "II. Its Measurement," (May-June, 1948), pp. 845-55.

1949 Kimball Young, *Sociology* (New York: American Book Company, 1949), p. 616.

1950 William F. Ogburn, *Social Change* (New York: The Viking Press, 1950 edition with supplementary chapter).

41. Hornell Hart, "Value Judgments in Sociology," *American Journal of Sociology,* 3 (December, 1938), pp. 864-65.

42. John H. Mueller, *op. cit.* (1938), p. 320.

43. William Graham Sumner, *War and Other Essays* (New Haven: Yale University Press, 1919), pp. 208-10.

44. William F. Ogburn and Dorothy Thomas, "Are Inventions Inevitable? A Note on Social Evolution," *Political Science Quarterly,* 37 (March, 1922), pp. 83-98.

45. Hornell Hart, "Predicting Future Trends," in *Technology and Social Change* (cited above), Chapter 19.

46. Lester Coch and John R. P. French, Jr., "Overcoming Resistance to Change," *Human Relations,* 1 (August, 1948), pp. 512-32. Republished in modified form in Leonard Broom and Philip Selznick, *Sociology—A Text with Adapted Readings* (Evanston, Ill.: Row, Peterson and Company, 1958), pp. 537 ff.

47. Hornell Hart, *The Technique of Social Progress,* pp. 515-16; A. L. Kroeber, *Anthropology* (New York: Harcourt, Brace & Company, Inc., 1948), pp. 221, 514.

48. A. L. Kroeber, *op. cit.,* p. 357.

49. Rudolf Heberle, *Social Movements: An Introduction to Political Sociology* (New York: Appleton-Century-Crofts, Inc., 1951), pp. 6-7. On pp. 2-3, he has given a brief survey of sociological literature in this country on social movements. For case studies of the Buchman (Moral Rearmament) Movement and the Townsend Plan Movement, see Arnold W. Green, *Sociology: An Analysis of Life in Modern Society* (New York: McGraw-Hill Book Company, Inc., 1956), pp. 538-55.

50. For admirable discussions of social planning see Merrill and Eldredge, *op. cit.,* pp. 517-49, and Martindale and Monachesi, *op. cit.,* pp. 661-67.

51. For a more detailed discussion of these and related illustrations, see Hornell Hart, "Planning in the Atomic Crisis," Chapter 20 in *Technology and Social Change,* edited by F. R. Allen (New York: Appleton-Century-Crofts, Inc., 1957), pp. 474-95.

52. *Id.,* pp. 496-98.

53. Harvey C. Lehman, "The Exponential Increase of Man's Cultural Output," *Social Forces,* 25 (March, 1947), pp. 281-90; *Id.,* "National Differences in Creativity," *American Journal of Sociology,* 52 (May, 1947) pp. 475-88.

54. Hornell Hart, "The Pre-War Upsurge in Social Science," *American Sociological Review,* Vol. 14 (October, 1949), pp. 599-607.

V

FUNCTIONAL THEORY

8

Reciprocity and Autonomy in Functional Theory

ALVIN W. GOULDNER
University of Illinois

The intellectual fundament of functional theory in sociology is the concept of a "system." Functionalism is nothing if it is not the analysis of social patterns as parts of larger systems of behavior and belief. Ultimately, therefore, an understanding of functionalism in sociology requires an understanding of the resources of the concept of "system." Here, as in other embryo disciplines, the fundamental concepts are rich in ambiguity.

The recurrent use of organismic models by leading contributors to functionalism, such as Durkheim and Radcliffe-Brown, has its major intellectual justification in the fact that organisms are *examples* of systems. To the extent that the organismic model has proved fruitful in sociological analysis it has been so because the organism was a paradigmatic case of a system. It has been easier to unravel the implications of system-thinking by the direct inspection of a concrete case of a system, such as an organism or, for that matter, a machine, than it has been to analyze formally the implications of the concept of a system treated in full abstraction.

Yet the occasional vulgarities of those using organismic models clearly indicated the hazards of this procedure.[1] Indeed, we might say that the organismic model has been misleading in sociological analysis precisely insofar as it led to a focus on characteristics which were peculiar to the organism but not inherent in a generalized notion of a "system."

Thus the need to distinguish between the concrete case, namely the organism, and the thing it was a case of, namely a "system," became increasingly evident to functional theorists.

Yet in one sense the organismic theorists were correct. That is, if social behavior is to be understood by application of system models, a generalized concept of a system alone is insufficient. For there is always a question of the *kind* of system model that shall be employed in the understanding of social behavior. There are at least two ways of approaching this problem. One is the strategy of the organismic theorists, namely to take a concrete case of a system and use it as a guide. But even this is ambiguous because biological organisms vary enormously and there remains the difficult problem of stipulating *which* organism is to be used as a model. A second route, to be followed here, is to make explicit the most generalized dimensions in terms of which systems, formally construed, may vary and then to stipulate the conjunction of formal system dimensions which are to be applied to social behavior.

From a sociologist's standpoint, the two most important aspects of a "system" are the "interdependence" of a number of "parts" and the tendency of these to maintain an "equilibrium" in their relationships. Consequently, much of system analysis and functional theory resolves itself into questions about "interdependence" and "equilibrium." As shall be indicated later, equilibrium necessarily implies interdependence, but interdependence does not necessarily imply equilibrium. Agreeing with Parsons that "the most general and fundamental property of a system is the interdependence of parts or variables," this paper shall therefore focus on the concept of interdependence, leaving the equilibrium problem for later analysis.[2]

There is another problem to be considered here. It is implicit in the concept of system, and becomes manifest as soon as an effort is made to apply it to any given subject matter. This is the problem of identifying the interdependent parts. That is, what elements shall be held to constitute the system and on what grounds shall a decision be made to include certain elements in the system?

SYSTEM MODELS IN MERTON AND PARSONS

It has been suggested above that system analysis is central to sociological functionalism. This will be documented by examination of the two leading American contributors to functional theory in sociology, Robert K. Merton and Talcott Parsons. As shall be seen below, system concepts play a pivotal role in both their formulations of functional theory. It will also be noted, however, that the nature of their commitment to a system model differs, Parsons' being what may be called a total commitment, while Merton's can be regarded as a strategy of minimal commitment.

With characteristic cogency, Robert Merton has stated his conception of the "central orientation of functionalism." This he finds is "expressed in the practice of interpreting data by establishing their consequences for larger structures in which they are implicated. . . ."[3] It is instructive to contrast this with the more extended formulation by Talcott Parsons: "The most essential condition of successful dynamic analysis is continual and systematic reference of every problem to the state of the system as a whole. . . . Functional significance in this context is inherently teleological. A process or set of conditions either 'contributes' to the maintenance (or development) of the system or it is 'dysfunctional' in that it detracts from the integration and effectiveness of the system. It is thus the functional reference of all particular conditions and processes to the state of the total system as a going concern which provides the logical equivalent of simultaneous equations in a fully developed system of analytical theory."[4]

Without doubt, there is substantial convergence in these two statements concerning the fundamentals of functional analysis. Both Merton and Parsons agree that in accounting for any social or cultural pattern an effort must be made to relate this to the context in which it occurs, so that it may not be understood in isolation but must be analyzed in its relation to other patterns. In short, both postulate a system model in dealing with social and cultural phenomena.

There is, however, a notable difference in emphasis in Merton's and Parsons' formulations. This is expressed in Parsons' stress on the notion of a "system" while Merton persistently avoids explicit use of this concept. In fact, there is but one reference to it in the index to Merton's volume on *Social Theory and Social Structure*. More importantly, Merton's avoidance of the system concept is above all suggested by the architecture of his basic paradigm of functional analysis.[5] This does not begin with an analysis of "social systems," but, rather, with a directive to identify the "units" which are problematic in any given case. For Merton, the first step in functional analysis involves stipulation of "some standardized (i.e., patterned and repetitive) item, such as social roles, institutional patterns, social processes, cultural patterns, ..."[6] In brief, for Merton functional analysis is focused on some delimited unit of human behavior or belief, with a view to accounting either for its persistence or change by establishing its consequences for environing social or cultural structures.

System analysis could have entered into Merton's directives for functional analysis in at least two major ways: either by treating the structural context to which the unit is linked as a system, and/or by analyzing the unit itself as a subsystem composed of interdependent parts. Neither of these courses is explicitly stressed in Merton's formulations.

When Merton does take up the structural context in his paradigm, his comments are primarily devoted to a consideration of the ways in which this context generates constraints, limiting the range of variation in the problematic pattern with which the functional analyst is directed to begin. He does indicate that social structures are composed of inter-dependent elements, and to this extent acknowledges their systemic character, but this never becomes an object of formal analysis.

Furthermore, the problematic unit pattern with which Merton's paradigm of functional analysis begins is not itself explicitly identified as subject to system analysis. In the operational protocols which follow the paradigm, Merton states that the unit pattern on which the analysis focuses must be seen as implicated in the behavior of people who are differently located in the larger social structure. He indicates also that it is necessary to locate "these people in their inter-connected social statuses." The emphasis here, however, seems to involve a structural location of the component elements rather than a focus on the systemic character of the structure itself.

For example, Merton does not require that the problematic unit be related to any postulated "need" of the contextual structure *as a system*. Indeed, while Merton concedes that "in every functional analysis (there) is some conception of the functional requirements of the system under observation," he goes on to insist that the notion of functional require-ments or needs of the social system "remains one of the cloudiest and empirically most debatable concepts in functional theory." [7]

For Parsons the central theoretical and empirical problems are those which involve a social system as such, and which explain how it is main-tained as a going system. Empirically delimitable units become impor-tant for him primarily as they enter into the maintenance of the social system, in the satisfaction of its needs, or in their resolution of its prob-lems. In contrast to Merton, Parsons does not focus on the explanation of empirically delimited units of social behavior or belief, but instead centers attention directly on analysis of the contextual structure as a system.

THE SELECTION OF SYSTEM PARTS

Parsons' assumption is that it is impossible to understand adequately any single pattern except by referring it to some larger systemic whole. He therefore assumes that the *whole* system must be conceptually constituted prior to the investigation and analysis of specific patterns. In consequence, Parsons is led forthwith to the analysis of the *total* anatomy of social systems in an effort to identify their constituent elements and relationships. This presumably makes it possible to refer any given problematic pattern in a systematic manner to all the component structures constituting the system. The theoretical strategy here requires that all the constituents of the whole system be *immediately* constituted in an *ex cathedra* manner.

But whether or not a given structure in the social anatomy is in fact there, or whether it is useful to postulate it, is an important part resolvable only by empirical research. The specification of the component elements of social systems is, in principle, no more attainable by theoretical postulation alone than are the attributes of "living" systems, which the biologist regards as the systems with which his discipline deals. What seems to have been neglected is that the elements of social systems cannot be merely constituted *a priori,* but must also be inductively sought and empirically validated.

It is in large measure because of their differing orientations to the role of empirical operations not in science in general, but in theory construction in particular, that Parsons and Merton differ in this regard. That is, part of the problem here is how one identifies and provides a warrant for the elements held to be constitutive of a social system. In large measure, Merton differs from Parsons because he feels that *empirical* operations are necessarily involved in the very admission of elements as part of a social system. He does not regard this problem as solely resolvable by theoretical postulation. Although he has not committed himself on this specific point in any extended manner, Merton's emphasis on theories of the "middle range," which he counterposes to Parsons' stress on systematic, all-encompassing theories,[8] indicates that he takes much more empirical and heuristic approach to the process of consti-ing a social system.

Pursuing Merton's strategy of middle-range theories, no commitment would be made to any variable which could not pay its way empirically. The expectation is that cumulative research would, through successive approximations, sift out a battery of explanatory variables and establish their interrelations.[9] This is by no means a new species of empiricism, nor a new espousal of the prerogatives of research against those of theory. It is simply an insistence that theoretical considerations alone cannot provide scientifically legitimate grounds for the admission of elements to a social system.

Objection may be lodged against this approach on the grounds that, not having staked out in advance *all* the constituent elements of the social system, the problematic pattern cannot then be related to the system as a whole. The procedure can therefore yield only incomplete explanations of any particular pattern. This is quite true, but it is an objection just as applicable to Parsons' strategy. For although Parsons takes cognizance of the "total" social system, this is by no means a closed and complete system, but an open and partial one. Many of the things accounting for variance in particular patterns of social behavior will, also, fall outside of its jurisdiction and it, too, can account for no more than part of the variance.

The basic gain of the Mertonian strategy is that it prevents either premature commitment to, or premature exclusion of, any given structure as an element in the social system. The latter, the exclusion of structures from the social system, is as vital a decision as that of inclusion, and would seem no more susceptible to a purely theoretical resolution.

As Parsons formulates his conception of the social system, elements in the biological constitution and physiological functioning of man, as well as features of the physical and ecological environment, are excluded. So, too, seems to be the historically developing cultural complexes of material artifacts. To a Malinowski it might well seem that this is a form of academic monasticism in which men are cleansed of their baser passions for sex, food, and material possessions by theoretical purification.

Among other tendencies, Parsons' theory of the social system leads research attention away from *systematic* efforts to develop and validate generalized propositions concerning the manner in which ecological and other properties of the physical environment of groups structure patterns of social organization. In exiling these from the social system, Parsons at best derives a purely formal advantage, namely that of establishing a distinct class of systems which may form the object of an independent social science. But in doing this he fails to make a systematic place for numerous cogent researches which, if lacking in formal elegance in thi sense, do illuminate the important ways in which social behavior is str tured by ecological forces. To constitute the social system thusly well accomplish the objective of establishing a charter for an indepe social science. But it may be a Pyhrric victory bought at the cost o scientific ritualism, where logical elegance is substituted for empirical potency.

The systematic omission of such ecological forces from models whi seek to account for variance in social and cultural behavior would, mor over, seem to have varying degrees of appropriateness, depending on the society under study. Evans-Pritchard's [10] and Steward's [11] studies of primitive groups clearly demonstrate the potency of ecological forces in shaping social organization in folk societies. In societies with advanced technologies and urban centers, however, these forces are patently less powerful in structuring social behavior. Thus Parsons' model of a social system may have an *unequal* capacity to account for variance in social behavior in different social systems. It may, because of its exclusion of ecological elements, be a more powerful tool in dealing with industrially advanced urban societies than with "underdeveloped" primitive groups which have much less control over nature.

While it is for this reason tempting to think of Parsons' model as essentially one of an industrially developed social system, we cannot do so because no systematic provision is made for some of the very elements which characterize these. In particular, Parsons' model of the social system excludes all "material" elements, including tools and machines. This would seem dubious on several interlocking grounds: First, precisely because these are man's own unique and distinctive creations, the very products of his social interaction. Secondly, because they enter intimately as mediating instruments of communication and hence of symbolic social interaction. Thirdly, because they are also instruments of transportation, often making possible the very interchanges among social parts which enable them to establish interdependences. Fourth and last, because modern electronic and cybernetic devices have developed to the point where the distinction between human thinking and machine operation is no longer so radical as was assumed in the organismic tradition from which functionalism grew.[12]

The line between the interaction of man with man, on the one side, and the interaction of men with machines, on the other, has begun to grow wavery. Parsons holds that "a social system consists of a plurality of individual actors, interacting with each other in a situation . . . and whose relations . . . [are] defined and mediated in terms of a system of culturally structured and shared symbols." [13] If this is so, then it may well be that modern machinery qualifies, not simply as the environment in which social interaction occurs, but as a *party* to the interaction itself, as a member of the social system, as well as a cultural artifact which, like shared symbols, mediates communication.

Here again it is necessary to insist that the matter cannot be decided by *a priori* postulation alone. Whether we want to constitute a model of the social system as a man-made system or, instead, as a men-machine system, depends in important part on the empirical consequences stemming from the inclusion or exclusion of machines. Internal consistency and parsimony, such as they are in modern social theory, are necessary but not sufficient criteria of the postulate sets of an empirical sociology. One might well remember Ruskin's sarcasms about a fictitious science of gymnastics which postulated that men had no skeletons.

In one respect, Parsons' work manifests a fairly widespread tendency among sociologists, namely an inclination to rest content with a demonstration that some sociological variable "makes a difference." If a variable can be shown to control even the smallest proportion of variance in a problematic pattern it is all too readily regarded as a memorable contribution to sociology and all too ceremoniously ushered into its theoretical hall of fame. It is surely no treason to theory to suggest that, in the last analysis, not only empirical researches in general, but mathematical ones in particular, will have a voice in legitimating conceptual innovation. For unless sustained interest is manifested in the *degree* of variance which a variable controls, and, unless, further, we can identify sociological variables that certifiably control *substantial* proportions of variance in specified patterns of human behavior, sociology will remain scientifically immature and practically ineffectual.

THE PRINCIPLE OF FUNCTIONAL RECIPROCITY

It would seem clear from the foregoing that the ways in which Merton and Parsons seek to apply the notion of a "system" to sociological analysis differs and, particularly so, with reference to the manner in which constituents shall be identified and admitted to or excluded from the system. Yet it needs to be stressed that this involves no necessary difference in principle with respect to the strategic place of the concept of a system, especially as an *explanatory* tool.

This can be documented by reference to Merton's analysis of the latent functions of political machines in the United States.[14] He opens this by inquiring how it is that political machines manage to continue operating, despite the fact that they frequently run counter to both the mores and the law. In the more generalized terms of his paradigm of functional analysis, Merton begins by identifying a social pattern, the political machine, and seeks to explain its persistence by establishing its consequences for the larger social structures in which it is implicated. The *general* form of his explanation of the persistence of the political machine is to demonstrate that it performs "positive functions which are at the same time not adequately fulfilled by other existing patterns and structures." [15]

Among these are (1) the organization and centralization of power so that it can be mobilized to "satisfy the needs of diverse subgroups in the larger community. . . ," (2) including personalized forms of assistance —jobs, legal aid, foodbaskets, for deprived, lower class groups, (3) political privileges and aid to business groups, (4) channels of social mobility for disadvantaged groups in the society, and (5) "protection" for illicit rackets.

Now insofar as the objective of the above analysis was to provide an *explanation of the persistence* of the political machine, then the mere establishment of the consequences of the machine for the larger structures in which it is involved provides only a partial and one-sided answer. The explanation is incomplete insofar as the analyst has not explicitly traced the manner in which the groups or structures, whose needs have been satisfied, in turn "reciprocate" and repay the political machine for the gains it provides them. In this particular case, the patterns of reciprocity are so largely evident and well documented that it would be belaboring the obvious to dwell upon them, and were perhaps for this reason omitted. The reciprocities involved are all too clearly implied in the notion of the "corruption" of the machine.

Ordinarily, however, the formal adequacy of a functional *explanation* of the persistence of a social pattern would seem to require that the analyst demonstrate not merely the consequences of A for B, but, also, the reciprocal consequences of B for A. The only logically stable terminal point for a functional analysis is not the demonstration of a social pattern's function for others, but the demonstration of the latter's reciprocal functionality for the problematic social pattern.

In short, functional analysis premises the operation of a "principle of functional reciprocity," a principle variously employed by Marx,[16] by Mauss,[17] by Malinowski,[18] by Levi-Strauss,[19] and by Homans [20] in different empirical contexts. This underlying functionalist assumption might just as well be made explicit and could be stated in the following generalized form: (1) Any one structure is more likely to persist if it is engaged in reciprocally functional interchanges with some others; (1.1) the less reciprocal the functional interchange between structures, the less likely is either structure, or the patterned relation between them, to persist—(1.2) *unless compensatory mechanisms are present.*

Essentially, the principle of reciprocity implies a system of interdependent parts engaged in mutual interchanges. It is in this sense that the notion of a system is necessarily involved in Merton's analysis of the political machine as, we think, it must be in any functional analysis.

It needs to be stressed, however, that "mutual interchange" does not necessarily imply that the relations among parts of a social system are invariably those of symmetrical functional reciprocity. It does, however, imply either that such functional reciprocity exists, or that there has developed some compensatory mechanism for coping with the lack of or breakdown in it. It is, we suspect, precisely because Merton saw that the relations between parts were not invariably those of symmetrical functional reciprocity that he did not commit himself to a generalized principle of reciprocity. Nonetheless, it is implied by his analysis. It is only by chancing an explicit formulation of the assumption and laying it open to critical examination, that it can be tempered and refined, or invalidated and rejected.

There is something of a tactical dilemma here which needs to be resolved. It seems evident, on the one hand, that to cease analysis before attempting to *establish empirically* the reciprocal functionality of B for A, and to explain the persistence of A by demonstrating its functions for B, is to substitute postulation for research. On the other hand, there are substantial empirical grounds for rejecting an unqualified principle of reciprocity. For this would involve the dubious assumption that structures which derive gains from others are invariably "grateful" and that power-constrained services, with little or no reciprocity, are not merely unstable but totally impossible.

An unqualified principle of reciprocity diverts attention from the specific social or cultural mechanisms which may compensate for the lack of functional reciprocity. Among such compensatory mechanisms may be culturally shared prescriptions of unconstrained "generosity" such as the Christian notion of "turning the other cheek," the feudal concept of *noblesse oblige,* or the Roman notion of "clemency." [21] There may also be cultural prohibitions banning the examination of certain interchanges from the standpoint of their reciprocity, such as the sociologically wise cliché, "It's not the gift but the sentiment that counts." Again, power arrangements may serve to compel continuances of services for which there is little functional reciprocity. Although these may be expected, from the present standpoint, to be less stable than those where functional reciprocity motivates continued performances, they are certainly not for that reason sociologically unimportant.

Another arrangement which may serve to prevent or control failures in functional reciprocity is the mutual sharing of structures A and B, of some third structure C. To use Lévi-Strauss' terminology [22] in a broader sense, we would say that a situation of "generalized interchange"—where A supplies B's needs, B supplies C's, and C supplies A's needs—may be more stable than that of a "restricted interchange" between A and B alone. This case is relevant to Parsons' discussion of the basic equilibrium model of the social system. The minimal social system, comprised of two role players, Ego and Alter, is postulated by Parsons to be in equilibrium when each conforms to the other's expectation and is rewarded by him for such compliant behavior. It is clear, first, that this model implicitly utilizes the principle of reciprocity and may be regarded as a special case of it. More to the point here, however, note that Ego may in fact continue to comply with Alter's expectations, not because Alter reciprocates or rewards such compliances, but because Ego's compliances are expected and rewarded by a third role player. In short, the system may be maintained, and guarded against defaults in functional reciprocity, through the intervention of "third" structures which perform what may be termed a "policing" function.

It is impossible to do justice here to the question of whether this implies that the minimal model of a social system should be constituted of three rather than two role players. As a conservative inference from the foregoing, however, it would seem that an important focus of functional analysis couched in role terms should be centered on the stabilizing activities of such "third parties" as the witness, *amicus curiae,* police, friend of the family, arbitrators, or ritual adjudicators such as "old men of the earth." [23] In complex social systems it may be expected that such third party roles will be structurally specialized and differentiated from others; in simpler social systems it may be that such policing functions will be conjoined with others.

It is clear from all this, then, that in explaining any social pattern it cannot be merely assumed that functional reciprocity will operate in any given case, but it is necessary to establish empirically its occurrence. Failing in this, it is necessary to search out compensatory arrangements which provide a functional substitute for reciprocity.

There are important connections between the principle of functional reciprocity and the older anthropological concept of a vestigial "survival." A social pattern was commonly regarded as a "survival" if it could not be established that it made any contributions to the adaptation of a going system in which it was *presently* implicated. The polemical opposition of the earlier functionalists to this concept logically rested on the tacit assumption of an *unqualified* principle of reciprocity. That is, they premised that a structure which persisted was obviously securing satisfaction of its needs from others, and, if it continues to receive these, this can only be because this structure somehow reciprocally contributed to the others' adaptation. The anthropological functionalist was therefore enjoined to exercise his ingenuity to search out what were, in effect, hidden reciprocities.

The early functionalists' polemical opposition to the notion of a survival, however, tended to obscure the significance of varying *degrees* of functional reciprocity, and to neglect the mechanisms which might control the instabilities resulting from a breakdown in functional reciprocity. The early functionalist neglected the fact that a "survival" was simply a limiting case of a larger class of phenomena, much deserving of study, namely, relations between structures in which there is little functional reciprocity. Essentially, the early functionalists' opposition to the concept of a "survival" now has unwarranted survival in the neglect of the problem of asymmetrical patterns of functional reciprocity.

INTERDEPENDENCE AS PROBLEMATIC

It is one of the central implications of these comments that the notion of interdependence, so crucial to the concept of a system, needs to be taken as problematic rather than as given, if a system model adequate to the analysis of social behavior is to be developed. One of the reasons why this has not been systematically done in Parsons' analysis is related to the distinction which he makes between a "theoretical" and an "empirical" system. The former refers to a logically interrelated conceptual scheme or a set of propositions. An empirical system, on the other hand, "has to do with the criteria for coherence and harmony to be applied to some specific body of subject matter." [24]

There are, it would seem, two meanings which might be attributed to Parsons' use of the term "empirical system." One is that it unwittingly retains vestiges of eighteenth century usage, referring to a "natural" system which is somehow there "in itself" in a realistic sense, that is, apart from any particular conceptualization. Despite the fact that this would be radically at variance with Parsons' methodological position, which is predominantly constructionist, there are uneasy moments when a reader may feel that such an inference is not altogether outlandish. Insofar, however, as an "empirical system" is held to consist of "criteria" to be applied to some subject matter, it is clear that the empirical system cannot be the referent of the theory, but must instead be a set of assumptions in terms of which these referents are to be studied.

A second and by far the most acceptable interpretation, therefore, is that what Parsons means by an "empirical system" is, perversely enough, what philosophers of science commonly term a "formal system." Purely formal systems, as in mathematics and logic, are those devoid of any kind of empirical content, and this is much the way in which Parsons uses the notion of an empirical system. When a formal system is applied to a specific subject matter it is said to be "interpreted"; some formal systems have many interpretations, others have none. The nub of the issue here is the nature of the interpretation to be given to the formal and empty notion of a "system" when it is applied to human relations. In order for a formal system to be successfully applied, it would seem necessary that the interpretation to which it is subjected be explicitly examined.

The significant point, however, is that the notion of a theoretical system denotes what Parsons regards as analytically problematical, while the formal concept of an "empirical system," is largely unexplored or taken simply as setting the terms within which the theoretical system must develop. As a result of this, the notion of "empirical system" does not become systematically problematic for Parsons, and he fails to explore the alternative interpretations which are possible even within such a commitment.

We, on the contrary, would stress that even on a formal level of system analysis, there are different elements involved in the conception of an "empirical system" and, combined or interpreted differently, they may constitute different types of empirical systems.[25] It is therefore necessary to choose among competing formal models and to identify those that constitute a better "fit" for the known, relevant data.

As mentioned above, the two key elements involved in the concept of system are first, "interdependence," and secondly, "self-maintenance" or equilibrium. It makes a good deal of difference whether interdependence and equilibrium are treated as undifferentiated attributes, or whether they are viewed as dimensions capable of significant variation in degree.

Unless the latter procedure is followed and unless, further, it is clearly seen that interdependence and equilibrium are not synonymous terms but are independently variable, then there is a compelling tendency to by-pass the possibility that there are significantly different types of empirical systems even on the most formal level of analysis. Mere use of the concept of an empirical system is much as if a mathematical physicist were to commit himself only to the use of "geometry" in general, without stipulating the specific system of geometry he proposes to employ in solving his particular problems.

Viewed in Parsons' way,[26] the concept of an empirical system is essentially an "ideal type" and is subject to the liabilities inherent in all such concepts. That is, it obscures the underlying continua involved in its constituents, and focuses attention on particular, and especially extreme, values of the dimensions. To speak of systems as characterized by an interdependence of parts and their equilibrium tends to obscure the fact that these are things which can vary in degree. Moreover, it tends to create a presumption that they universally covary in the same direction.

One may find, however, a conjunction of low interdependence with high equilibrium, where the low interdependence permits a localized absorption of externally induced trauma, thus guarding the remainder of the system elements from ramifying damage. It is this kind of a conjunction which would seem to be implied in the notion of "insulation," which Parsons, along with other functionalists, regards as a "defense mechanism" of social systems. In brief, the lowering of the degree of interdependence may contribute to an increase in the degree of equilibrium, or in restoring it to a higher level.

Conversely, an instance of a conjunction of high interdependence and low equilibrium would seem to be implied in the notion of a "vicious cycle." Here, the very interdependence of elements enables negative feedback cycles to develop with cumulative impairment of the system's equilibrium. From these considerations it seems clear that equilibrium and interdependence may vary independently and, consequently, conjunctions of different values of these two variables may be postulated concerning the character of social systems.

FUNCTIONAL AUTONOMY AND DEGREES OF INTERDEPENDENCE

A crucial assumption of the analysis here is that there are *varying degrees* of interdependence which may be postulated to exist among the parts of a system. At one extreme, each element may be involved in a mutual interchange with all others; at the opposite extreme, each element may be involved in mutual interchanges with only one other.[27] The former may be regarded as defining maximal interdependence and "systemness," the latter as defining minimal interdependence or "systemness."

Still another way of viewing interdependence is from the standpoint of the parts' dependence upon the system. The parts may have varying amounts of their needs satisfied by, and thus varying degrees of dependence upon, other system elements. A number of parts which are engaged in mutual interchanges may, at one extreme, all be totally dependent on each other for the satisfaction of their needs. In this case the *system* they comprise can be said to be "highly" interdependent, while these *parts* can be said to possess "low" functional autonomy. Conversely, a system may be composed of parts all of which derive but little satisfaction of their needs from each other; here the system would be minimally interdependent and the parts would be high on functional autonomy. Operationally speaking, we might say that the functional autonomy of a system part is the probability that it can survive separation from the system.

A conceptualization of "systemness" in terms of functional autonomy has been suggested here because the notion of mutual interdependence commonly used in definitions of systems tends toward a focus primarily on the "whole" or on the relations between parts, and on their functionally reciprocated need for each other. "Functional autonomy," however, focuses on the *parts,* albeit in their relation to each other; it directs attention to the possibility that any part may have little, as well as great, need for another, and that the mutual need of parts need not be symmetrical. In short, it focuses attention on interchanges where functional reciprocity may not be symmetrical, and thus directs analysis to tension-producing relationships.

In these terms, the question becomes, "What can be predicated about the functional autonomy of the parts of social systems, and in what ways does the problem of the functional autonomy of the parts enter into the analysis of social systems?" In the following comments, which explore several of these implications, it will be emphasized that the problem of functional autonomy is of considerable significance for the analysis of tension within social systems, and thus for the analysis of social change.

FUNCTIONAL AUTONOMY AND SYSTEM TENSION

To the degree that parts possess some measure of functional autonomy, they must be expected to seek to maintain this. In short, the equilibrium assumptions, applied to a social system as a whole, would seem equally applicable in principle to its parts. Thus, the parts of a social system should be expected to "maintain their boundaries." It must then be assumed that parts with some degree of functional autonomy will resist full or complete integration into the larger system. Conversely, the system itself, straining toward integration, can be expected to seek submission of the parts to the requirements of the position they occupy. Consequently, there may be some tension between the part's tendency to maintain an existent degree of functional autonomy and the system's pressure to control the part.

It would seem that this or some similar model underlies various theories, such as the Freudian, which postulate an endemic conflict between the individual and the society or group. Essentially, these have been answered by formulations counterstressing the malleability of the individual organism, the potency of the socialization process, and the inability of the organism to become a full "human being" apart from society.

Actually, however, the very malleability of the organism which makes it susceptible to socialization by one social system also allows it to be resocialized by another; its malleability is thus actually a condition of its functional autonomy. Furthermore, the relevant question here is the ability of the already socialized individual to remain such after separation from any given social system, not merely to become such without involvement in some society.

More pointedly, it would seem that, once socialized, many individuals do have a capacity to generate an "escape velocity"; and that human beings are not invariably characterized by a total dependence upon any one social system.[28] *Socialized* individuals have some measure of mobility, vertical and horizontal, among the social systems within their society, moving with varying degrees of ease or stress from one to another. They may and do also migrate to, or sojourn in, societies different from those in which they were originally socialized. They have, in our terms, considerable, if varying, degrees of functional autonomy in relation to any given social system. Consequently, if we think of the "socialized individual" as in some sense a "part," and not merely as the raw material, of social systems, it would seem necessary to eschew models which overstress the interdependence of the parts and to select those which systematically include concern with their functional autonomy. To fit the data of social behavior, the system model required must be such as to facilitate not only the analysis of the interdependence of the system as a whole, but also the analysis of the functional autonomy of its parts, and the concrete strains which efforts to maintain this autonomy may induce.

Two lines of sociological analysis which have recently been developed are highly relevant to these assumptions about functional autonomy. One stems from the study of occupations made by E. C. Hughes and his students, in which the repeated observation of diverse occupations—both noble and profane—indicates that their occupants typically strive to maintain a degree of functional autonomy. As Hughes puts it, they seek to maintain a degree of social distance or freedom, not merely from all in the same social system in which they operate but, most particularly, "from those people most crucially concerned with [their] work." [29]

A second and more generalized direction from which the problem of functional autonomy has been approached in sociological terms is that developed by Erving Goffman. Utilizing materials from his study of a mental hospital, Goffman distinguishes between two types of deference behavior, that is, the expression of appreciation of one person to and for another. One type, "avoidance rituals," refers to those forms of deference stipulating what one may *not* do to another, and which leads actors to maintain social distance from each other. The second, "presentational rituals," specify what *is* to be done and involve expressions of positive appreciation and regard. Goffman sums up his analysis as follows:

> I have mentioned four very common forms of presentational deference: salutations, invitations, compliments, and minor services. Through all of these the recipient is told that he is not an island unto himself and that others are, or seek to be, involved with him and with his personal concerns . . . avoidance rituals, taking the form of proscriptions, interdictions, and taboos . . . imply acts the actor must refrain from lest he violate the right of the recipient to keep him at a distance. . . .
>
> In suggesting that there are things which must be said and done to a recipient, and things that must not be said and done, it should be plain that there is an inherent opposition and conflict between these two forms of deference. . . . There is an inescapable opposition between showing a desire to include an individual and showing respect for his privacy. As an implication of this dilemma, we must see that social intercourse involves a constant dialectic between presentational rituals and avoidance rituals. A peculiar tension must be maintained for these opposing requirements of conduct

must somehow be held apart from one another and yet realized together in the same interaction; the gestures which carry an actor to a recipient must also signify that things will not be carried too far.[30]

It would seem that a system model which focused solely on the "wholeness" of the system and neglected the functional autonomy of the parts would be unable to fit the kind of data obtained in either Hughes's or Goffman's researches. Nor, above all, would it systematically cue the analyst to the tensions which result in social systems by virtue of the parts' strain toward functional autonomy, or to the analysis of the ways in which they maintain their functional autonomy. From the standpoint of the kind of system model which Parsons favors, the emphasis on inter-dependence would conduce to a one-sided focus—in Goffman's terms—on the "presentational rituals." That is, it conduces to a preoccupation with the mechanisms of social integration, and to a neglect of the avoid-ance rituals which constitute proper ways in which socialized individuals are enabled to resist total inclusion in a social system and total loss of their functional autonomy.

In Parsons' system model, concern is largely focused on the needs of the system as a whole, and the stability of this system is viewed as dependent upon their satisfaction. The implication here, however, is that there is a sense in which the very striving of the system to satisfy its needs may generate tension for it, insofar as this impairs the functional autonomy of the parts. This means that a need of systems, which possess parts having degrees of functional autonomy, is to inhibit its own tend-encies to subordinate and fully specialize these parts. In short, it must inhibit its own tendencies toward "wholeness" or complete integration if it is to be stable. The system model thus indicated for the analysis of social behavior is not one in which the system is viewed as a "plunger" playing an all-or-none game, but as a mini-max player seeking to strike a federalizing balance between totalitarian and anarchist limits.[31]

It is commonly assumed that the "organization" of the system, that is, the particular arrangement of its parts, provides primarily for the ave-nues of integration among them. In our terms, however, "organization" not only serves to link, control, and interrelate parts but also functions to separate them and to maintain and protect their functional autonomy. Organization is seen then as shaped by a conflict, particularly by the tensions between centripetal and centrifugal pressures, as limiting control over parts as well as imposing it, as establishing a balance between their dependence and independence, and as separating as well as connecting the parts.[32]

Social organizations, insofar as they involve role systems, manifest the dualism indicated above. It is of the essence of social roles that they never demand total involvements by the actors, but only segmental and partial involvements. To say that a person is an actor in a social system and that he plays a role there implies, on the one side, that he is subject to some system controls and to the requirements of the role, and that he has obligations to the collectivity of which his role is a part. On the other side, however, it also implies that his obligations to that system are somehow limited. Even when the actor is involved in a primary social system, where the role obligations are diffuse and numerous, he is never exposed to unlimited obligations.

One of the most common ways in which consideration of the functional autonomy of parts has implicitly entered into current sociological analysis has been as an element in the generation of system tension. The drive of the subpart to maintain or to extend its functional autonomy has been frequently understood as a source of tensions for the system. In "organizational analysis," in the technical sociological sense, the tensions between the "field offices" and the "main office," between the various departments within an organization, as well as in the commonly noted oscillation between centralization and decentralization, all imply cognizance of the significance of functional autonomy. Similarly, concern with the development of "organized deviance" and its potentially disruptive impact on the system again token a tacit appreciation of the tension-provoking potential of functionally autonomous parts.

Because parts have or strive to maintain different degrees of functional autonomy, it cannot be assumed that all have an equal role in the generation of tensions for the system. It would seem reasonable to suppose that those parts in a social system with most functional autonomy can more readily become loci of organized deviance and of effective resistance to system controls.

If it is reasonable to assume that some system parts have a greater role as loci of system tension, it would also seem consistent to maintain that not all have an equally deep involvement in the resolution of the tensions of the system, or in the mobilization of defenses against these. That is, those parts with least functional autonomy, those which cannot survive separation from a social system, are more likely to be implicated in its conservation than those which can.

Contrariwise, those with most autonomy are most able to press for or to accept changes, when these are consistent with their own autonomy. For example, it is evident that the eighteenth century French nobility had a greater involvement in the maintenance of the *ancien régime* than did the French *bourgeoisie,* which could and did survive separation from the older social system and acted as a stimulant to its basic reorganization. It would seem, then, to put the matter differently, that not all parts of a system have an equal "vested interest" in its maintenance. The concept of the differential functional autonomy of parts directs attention to the need to distinguish between parts having a greater or lesser vested interest in system maintenance.

THE STRATEGIES OF PARTS AND SYSTEMS

Among other things, the functional autonomy of a part implies that it is not totally contingent upon the parasystem for the satisfaction of its own needs. There are at least three importantly different strategies with which this situation can be played, from the standpoint of the part. One is the strategy of withdrawal. The part can, so to speak, go into business for itself and resist such a high degree of specialization that it loses power to service its own minimal metabolic needs. A second strategy is to spread its risks, so that its needs may be normally satisfied by a number of systems in which it is involved.

Both of these strategies for the maintenance of the functional autonomy of a part present difficulties and sources of tension for the parasystem. The functional autonomy of a part, whichever strategy it employs, allows it a degree of refractoriness to the imposition of controls from the system. This may be exemplified by the case of bureaucratic resistance to higher-echelon policy decisions.

A special source of tension derives from the part's involvement in multiple systems. To the degree that two systems share a part then the laws of both will affect the behavior of the part. This means not only that such a functionally autonomous part will be refractory to system steering, but that it will tend to oscillate and initiate changes for either system.

For example, it is not simply that the socialized human being may be refractory to the controls of a social system because he is involved in a biological system and is consequently required to eat, sleep, or breathe. But being involved in a biological system, the human being is also subject to various mundane liabilities such as illness, injury, and death. These are far from entirely governed by the laws of any social system and thus their occurrence is random relative to the functioning of social systems. Although social systems may develop mechanisms for cushioning their effects, for example, through "understudies" or prescribed rules of succession,[33] these effects must always, in some measure, be actively disruptive to the social systems, even if only to the personalized relations within them.

While we have here stressed the sharing of a part between a social and a biological system, the point is much the same in the case of parts shared between two or more social systems. The shared parts are more likely to engage in oscillations disruptive to one or both systems. In

sociological analysis, this has been recognized in the concern with multiple role involvements in general, and "cross-pressure" situations in
particular.

There is a third strategy which a functionally autonomous part may
adopt, in addition to withdrawal and spreading the risk. That is, it may
undertake a reorganization of the entire system in which it finds itself,
so that it may secure fuller satisfaction of its distinctive needs and so
that these are now higher on the schedule of priorities to which the new
system orients itself. In short, functionally autonomous parts may have
a "vested interest" in changing the system. Here, again, is an important
source of tension for the system.

There is, from this standpoint, an inherent ambiguity in a conflict
between a part and its encompassing system. Such a tension may signify
one of two different things: either (1) that the part generating the tension has not yet been controlled by or excluded from the larger system,
but that it ultimately will, or (2) that the friction-generating part is the
harbinger of a new reorganization of the whole system.

There seem to be at least three empirically important strategies
which a system can adopt to cope with the potentialities of tensions thus
induced. One is to insulate itself and withdraw its parts from the environing system, excluding or "alienating" parts possessing significant
functional autonomy, admitting only those it can highly control, and
refusing to share parts with other systems. Demands for deep occupational involvement, separation between family and work life, and highly
selective programs of recruitment would be examples of such a strategy
as practiced by many modern businesses. A second strategy is that of
expansion, in which the system attempts to engulf others which share its
parts and thereby tighten control over them. This is also exemplified by
the tendency of certain modern industries to develop an interest in the
employee's personal life, to concern itself with the character of his wife,
and to influence and regulate his residential living.[34] A third strategy is
that of "selective risk." That is, the system will maximize its security by
delegating its basic metabolic needs to structures within it which have
minimal functional autonomy. This statement, however partial, of the
specific and diverse strategies by means of which systems may respond
to tensions is, it would seem, a formulation appreciatively more determinate than the mere assertion that systems attempt to "maintain their
boundaries."

On the level of social systems, these considerations imply that distinctions will be made between core functions and peripheral ones,[35] and
between "reliable" and "unreliable" or disloyal personnel,[36] the former
functions being allocated to the former personnel. One would also look
for tendencies of limited purpose organizations to transform themselves

into "total institutions," or for total institutions to be transformed into limited purpose organizations by functional differentiation, specialization, and insulation of parts. Finally, the above considerations of system strategy would imply that it is necessary for the sociologist to identify and examine the particular policy which a social system has adopted in its relations to environing systems. It is to be expected that all social systems, not merely governments, but families, schools, or factories, will also develop some kind of a "foreign policy," tacit or explicit, which regulates its relations with surrounding social systems.[37]

It may be noted in passing that the threats to which the system is seen here to be variously responding derive from the defenses of its functionally autonomous parts. In this connection what is a threat from the system's standpoint is a defensive maneuver from the part's standpoint. Conversely, the system's defenses against these are, in turn, threats to the part's defenses.[38] Consequently, it is to be expected that efforts to reduce the threatening behavior of either the part or the system will be resisted. In short, not only efforts to change the system, but also those directed at *maintaining* it are likely to entail conflict and resistance.

FUNCTIONAL AUTONOMY AND STRUCTURAL DEDIFFERENTIATION

Insofar as a system is composed of some parts which have a degree of functional autonomy, it possesses potentialities for certain types of changes, or responses to tensions, which would not exist if it had no functionally autonomous parts. A system with no functionally autonomous parts would have only one of two dodges when confronted with powerful disruptions. It could either dissolve and be completely destroyed or it would have to undergo radical structural reorganization.

However, given a system some of whose parts have a measure of functional autonomy, there is a third response available to an extremely disruptive stimulus, namely dedifferentiation. That is, the system can surrender higher levels of integration and permit its functionally autonomous parts to regroup on a lower level of complexity. Sociologically speaking, this means that when a complex social system's defensive mechanisms do not permit it to cope adaptively with threats, it may destructure itself into component primary groupings, surrendering its sovereignty to the parts.

Julian Steward's theory of "levels of sociocultural integration" is, in effect, a statement of this possibility. As he remarks, "In culture, simple forms such as those represented by the family or band, do not wholly disappear when a more complex stage of development is reached, nor do they merely survive fossil-like. . . . They gradually become specialized, dependent parts of new total configurations. . . ." [39] Steward holds that it is useful to look upon the larger, more complex, social systems, such as the nation state, as a distinctive level of organization but one which is, nonetheless, composed of parts—families and communities—which continue to retain a significant measure of functional autonomy. In the event that the larger more complex system is dissolved, they may survive separation from it.

Steward has analyzed several anthropologically interesting cases in which this happened, one of the best documented of which is that of Cuna-Cueva Indians of the Isthmus of Panama. The evidence indicates that at the time of the Hispanic conquest, this tribe had a fairly complex state structure, with a ruling class of nobles and priests. The conquest, however, destroyed these national and state institutions of the Cuna. Neither Spanish governance nor Catholic religion effectively substituted for these, as the Cuna moved back into regions to which the Spanish were unwilling to follow. There Cuna life reorganized itself on a simpler communal basis, with the village becoming the largest unit of political life. It is clear, however, that such dedifferentiations of social structure are not peculiar to primitive peoples and have not infrequently occurred in historical European societies, most notably following the fall of the Roman Empire.

The phenomenon of dedifferentiation indicates that the functional autonomy of system parts may not only be *conducive* to system tensions, but can also provide a basis for responding to them. Indeed, the functional autonomy of the parts of a *social* system, allowing as it does for structural dedifferentiation, may be functional to the maintenance of the integrity of the *cultural* system. For the cultural system, the historically accumulated heritage of beliefs and skills may be maintained at least in some part in the smaller units into which the larger one has been dedifferentiated. To make this possible, however, the part must always be invested with more of the culture than it requires for the performance of its distinctive system function. In short, the part must not be overly specialized. It can be thus seen from another perspective why the parts of social systems *must be allowed* measures of functional autonomy by the system. The functional autonomy of parts then is not an unmitigated source of difficulty for the system, but may provide a basis for a defensive strategy of last resort, structural dedifferentiation.

Sociologists have, of course, long been aware of processes of structural dedifferentiation. In thinking of this, however, they have tended to focus primarily on the level of the atomization of the anomic individual, and to regard this as a purely pathological phenomenon. The existence of masses of men who are anomically cut adrift from larger social systems does, of course, imply that these systems are experiencing serious difficulty in maintaining themselves.

But such anomic dedifferentiation can also be seen as a desperate expedient through which the system is striving to maintain itself. As Merton states, "some [unknown] degree of deviation from current norms is probably functional for the basic goals of all groups. A certain degree of 'innovation,' for example, may result in the formation of new institutionalized patterns of behavior which are more adaptive than the old in making for realization of the primary goals." [40]

Tensionful as it may be, the anomic dedifferentiation of a social system need not be a requiem of its total dissolution, but a necessary prelude to its reorganization. For anomic disorder may make possible a ferment of innovation which can rescue the system from destruction.[41] When a system has exhausted its routine solutions for an important problem and when these have failed, then, at that point, anomic randomness is more functional than the treadmill and orderly plying of the old structures. The anomic individual may not merely be an uncontrolled "social cancer," but a seed pod of culture which, if only through sheer chance, may fall upon fertile ground. In short, *limited* increases in randomness, by way of structural dedifferentiation, may be the ultimate defense of systems in the face of extremity.

It has been suggested that the discrimination of functionally autonomous parts within a social system is significant because these aid in identifying possible loci of strain within the system, as well as marking out the boundaries along which dedifferentiation may occur. In the role terms so central to social system analysis, then, it would seem that the identification of the most and least functionally autonomous roles within the system may be a valuable point of departure for the analysis of strains within the system. We may speak of roles which have relatively great functional autonomy as "cosmopolitans" while those having little can be termed "locals." I have, in another connection, attempted to develop the thesis that certain important strains in social systems can be analyzed as an outcome of tensions between cosmopolitans and locals.[42] Not merely roles, however, but other kinds of parts within social systems can be examined from the standpoint of their functional autonomy, and systematic consideration of these can aid in the analysis of system tension and change.

SYSTEM THEORIES VERSUS FACTOR THEORIES

In the analysis of system changes, a distinction is commonly made between endogenous and exogenous sources of change, that is, between forces internal and external to the system. Our emphasis here on *degrees* of functional autonomy and *degrees* of system interdependence may be linked up with this distinction between exogenous and endogenous forces, and seen in its further ramifications for the analysis of change.

In noting that the functional autonomy of parts and system interdependence are matters of degree we, in effect, state that exogenous and endogenous factors are not qualitatively but quantitatively different. That is, they are simply at opposite ends of the same continuum of interdependence and functional autonomy. Hence, specific system parts may be both *partly* exogenous and *partly* endogenous. Thus, if exogenous forces are peculiarly important to the understanding of system change, as they are commonly held to be in Parsons' and other system models, *any* element *in* the system may be important in understanding system change to the extent that it possesses a degree of exogenousness, though all need not be equally so.

In some measure this may be regarded as a partial resolution of the classical tension between two lines of sociological theory. One of these, the position stemming from Comte and passing through Durkheim to Parsons, stresses that system change has to be thought of as deriving from exogenous forces, the system *model* itself not being conceived of as possessing internal sources of disequilibrium. The other, deriving from the Marxian tradition, stresses that the system can change due to its "internal contradictions," that is, endogenous forces. Here the point stressed is that social systems may be looked upon as composed of parts having varying degrees of functional autonomy and interdependence; thus the difference between the external and internal, the "inside" and "outside" of the system, is not an absolute distinction, and the thickness or permeability of the system boundaries varies at different zones.

It is in this sense that some system parts can be thought of as having relatively greater *independence* than others, vis-à-vis the system under study, and may thus be of strategic importance in accounting for system changes. In *Structure of Social Action,* Parsons has stressed that independent parts are also interdependent, but he has tended to treat both independence and interdependence as "constants" rather than as variables.[43] We, on the contrary, have emphasized that they are variables. To say that two parts are interdependent is not to imply that they are *equally* so and thus, even within a system of interdependent parts, various parts can have *varying* degrees of independence or freedom.

Having gone this far, it is now evident that a stress on the "web of interdependence" within a system by no means relieves the analyst of the problem of factor weighting or loading. The analyst must still cope with the task of determining the differential contribution made by different system parts to the state of the system as a whole. In short, different system parts make different degrees of contribution to either the stability or the change of the system, and these need to be analytically and empirically distinguished.

As a matter of fact, this tends to be done, even by Parsons, with respect to the analysis of system stability when he utilizes the notion of "defense mechanisms." In effect, this constitutes an effort at the qualitative analysis of components of the system which play a particularly important role in enabling it to maintain its integrity. Logically, a parallel analysis of those system elements which make more important contributions to system *change* would seem to be equally desirable. It may be that the notion of the differential functional autonomy of system parts may provide an analytic tool for the qualitative discrimination of factors contributing importantly to system change.

It is one implication of these comments that the divergence between analytic models conceiving of social behavior in terms of social systems of interdependent parts—long a cardinal doctrine of functionalists—and models stressing the importance of certain "factors" is not so radical as is often assumed. Although there are general grounds for believing that there are "no one or two inherently primary sources of impetus to change in social systems," there are equally plausible grounds for asserting that not all elements in a social system contribute equally to its change. There is nothing inherently incompatible between an effort to develop a *generalized* theory of social change along these lines and one which stresses, as does Parsons, "the plurality of possible origins of change." [44]

Historically speaking, it seems that as a result of the empirical difficulties which older and methodologically unsophisticated factor theories encountered, functionalists polemically counterposed a stress on the system as such. In taking systemness as problematic, and focusing solely on the question of an unclarified "interdependence" of elements, they were led to neglect the problem of the *differential* significance which various parts of the system had in determining changes in the system.

Although the methodological position of earlier functionalists commonly affirmed an amorphous interdependence of parts within a social system, it does not follow that the specific empirical analyses in which they engaged actually utilized this principle. In particular, the classic contributors, from Comte to Parsons, have often gone out of their way to stress the significance of "shared value elements" in maintaining the equilibrium of social systems.[45]

Contrariwise, some of the early "factor" theories can be regarded not as having denied, but as having taken system interdependence as given, and as having focused their analysis on the problem of identifying and weighting the various parts within it.[46] If this view of the matter is correct, it may be that the distinction between social theories has not so much been between system and factor theories, but rather between overt and covert factor theories, or between implicit and explicit system theories.

Factor theories are intrinsically difficult to demonstrate rigorously without the use of mathematical tools. For they imply a quantitative difference between two or more elements in determining a given outcome. Insofar as system models simply make a vague affirmation of the "interdependence" of parts they are more readily given empirical application in a purely qualitative manner.

It may be, therefore, that earlier functionalists neglected the problem of weighting system parts, because they then lacked the mathematical tools requisite for a rigorous resolution of the problem. Today, however, mathematical and statistical developments may be on the verge of making this possible and have, therefore, demanded that this dormant issue be reopened.[47]

NOTES

1. Many of the early users of the organismic analogy were well aware of its difficulties and by no means deluded themselves into believing that society *was* an organism. Indeed, some of the classic organismic theorists were far more methodologically astute than some who reject the organismic analogy with the banal and irrelevant criticism that it does not seem intuitively fitting. For a methodologically wise use of the organismic analogy see A. R. Radcliffe-Brown, *Structure and Function in Primitive Society* (Glencoe, Ill.: Free Press, 1952), ch. IX.

2. For a tentative and partial statement of my views on the problematics of the equilibrium model see A. W. Gouldner, "Some Observations on Systematic Theory, 1945–1955," in H. L. Zetterberg, ed., *Sociology in the United States of America* (Paris: UNESCO, 1956), pp. 34-42.

3. R. K. Merton, *Social Theory and Social Structure* (Glencoe, Ill.: Free Press, rev. ed., 1957), pp. 46-47.

4. T. Parsons, *Essays in Sociological Theory Pure and Applied* (Glencoe, Ill.: Free Press, 1949), p. 21.

5. Merton, *ibid.*, p. 50 *et seq.*

6. Merton, *ibid.*, p. 50.

7. Merton, *ibid.*, p. 52.

8. Merton, *ibid.*, p. 4 *et seq.*

9. Cf. Merton's critical appreciation of the method of "successive approximations" in P. F. Lazarsfeld and R. K. Merton, "Friendship as Social Process," in M. Berger, T. Abel, and C. H. Page, eds., *Freedom and Control in Modern Society* (New York: D. Van Nostrand Company, Inc., 1954), pp. 60-62. Contrast this with Parsons' statement that, "In a system of inter-

dependent variables . . . the value of any one variable is not *completely* determined unless those of *all* the others are known." T. Parsons, *The Structure of Social Action* (New York: McGraw-Hill Book Company, Inc., 1937), p. 25. (Our emphases—A.W.G.)

10. E. E. Evans-Pritchard, *The Nuer* (Oxford: Clarendon Press, 1940).

11. J. H. Steward, *Theory of Culture Change* (Urbana: University of Illinois Press, 1955), especially chs. 6-10.

12. Among a spate of recent literature on this see W. R. Ashby, *Design for a Brain* (New York: John Wiley and Sons, Inc., 1952); N. Wiener, *Cybernetics* (New York: John Wiley and Sons, Inc., 1948); L. A. Jefress, ed., *Cerebral Mechanisms in Behavior* (New York: John Wiley and Sons, Inc., 1951); H. Von Foerster, ed., *Cybernetics, Transactions of the 6th, 7th, and 8th Conferences* (New York: Josiah Macy, Jr., Foundation, 1950, 1951, 1952); perhaps the most cogent popular account is that of W. Sluckin, *Minds and Machines* (London: Penguin Books, Inc., 1954).

13. T. Parsons, *The Social System* (Glencoe, Ill.: Free Press, 1951), pp. 5-6.

14. Merton, *ibid.,* p. 71 *et seq.*

15. Merton, *ibid.,* p. 73.

16. The principle of reciprocity enters Marx's theoretical analysis not in peripheral but in central ways; it is most importantly implicated in his concept of "exploitation"; this is rendered technically specific in the manner of nineteenth century political economy in his analysis of "surplus value." If one puts aside Marx's moral condemnations of exploitation and considers only its sociological substance, it is clear that it refers to a breakdown in reciprocal functionality. It is a basic implication of Marx's analysis that exploitation in class societies induces social instabilities. Characteristically, however, Marx is interested in the sources of instability and change and thus focuses on the contrary of functional reciprocity. Marx is also concerned to analyze the compensatory mechanisms in modern society which conceal the breakdown in functional reciprocity and, in this connection, his concept of "fetishism" is clearly relevant. See especially K. Marx, *Capital,* vol. I, tr. by Eden and Cedar Paul (New York: E. P. Dutton and Co., Inc., 1930), pp. 43-59.

17. See M. Mauss, *The Gift* (Glencoe, Ill.: Free Press, 1954). Mauss stresses that there is a universally recognized obligation to reciprocate gifts which have been accepted. In his last chapter, Mauss also seems to be verging on a concept of "exploitation" when he comments that people have "a strong desire to pursue the thing they have produced once they realize that they have given their labour without sharing in the profit." P. 64.

18. This comes out most clearly in Malinowski's discussion of Trobriand society concerning which he remarks that its whole structure is arranged into "well-balanced chains of reciprocal services." Discussing the exchanges between the coastal fisherman and the inland gardeners, of fish and vegetables, respectively, he notes that such *reciprocity is a mechanism which underlies and induces conformity with the obligations they have to each other.* B. Malinowski, *Crime and Custom* (London: Paul, Trench, Trubner, 1926), pp. 46, 23 *et seq.* There is no doubt that Radcliffe-Brown

also assumed a principle of reciprocity which he called "the principle of equivalent return." This he held was expressed in the *lex talionis,* in the principle of indemnification for injury, and in the principle that those who give benefits should receive equivalent benefits. From his Chicago University seminar, "The Nature of a Theoretical Natural Science of Society," 1937.

19. C. Lévi-Strauss, *Les Structures élémentaires de la parenté* (Paris: Presses Universitaires, 1949). In this volume, which owes so much to Mauss and Durkheim, Lévi-Strauss presents his now near-classic theory of the "exchange" of women.

20. G. C. Homans and D. M. Schneider, *Marriage, Authority, and Final Causes* (Glencoe, Ill.: Free Press, 1955). This represents a criticism of particulars of Lévi-Strauss's theory. Homans' forthcoming work on a systematic theory of "exchange" is also fundamentally based on the principle of reciprocity.

21. For a discussion of such a mechanism in a modern industrial setting, see the analysis of the "indulgency pattern" in A. W. Gouldner, *Wildcat Strike* (Yellow Springs, Ohio: Antioch Press, 1954), pp. 18-26.

22. Lévi-Strauss, *ibid.,* p. 548.

23. See the discussion in Max Gluckman, *Custom and Conflict in Africa* (Glencoe, Ill.: Free Press, 1955).

24. T. Parsons and E. A. Shils, eds., *Toward a General Theory of Action* (Cambridge: Harvard University Press, 1951), p. 49.

25. For systematic efforts pointing in this direction see J. Feibleman and J. W. Friend, "The Structure and Function of Organization," *Philosophical Review,* 54 (Jan., 1945), pp. 19-44, and A. Angyal, "The Structure of Wholes," *Philosophy of Science,* 6 (Jan., 1939), pp. 25-37.

26. Cf. Parsons and Shils, *ibid.,* p. 107. "The most general and fundamental property of a system is the interdependence of parts or variables. . . . This order must have a tendency to self-maintenance, which is very generally expressed in the concept of equilibrium. . . ."

27. For an excellent discussion of this by a sociologist see G. Shapiro, *The Formulation and Verification of a Theory of Primary Social Integration,* unpublished doctoral dissertation, Cornell University, 1954, especially ch. 2.

28. In this connection, the significance of Asch's experiments on the effects of group influence on perception would not only be that some 33 per cent of his subjects distorted their perception to conform with the pressures of others in their group, but also that 67 per cent of them did *not* do so. See S. E. Asch, *Social Psychology* (New York: Prentice-Hall, Inc., 1952), ch. 16.

29. E. C. Hughes, "Work and the Self," in J. H. Rohrer and M. Sherif, eds., *Social Psychology at the Crossroads* (New York: Harper and Brothers, 1951), p. 322.

30. E. Goffman, "The Nature of Deference and Demeanor," *American Anthropologist,* 58 (June, 1956), pp. 486-88.

31. The philosophic posture here parallels that developed in E. Cassirir, *An Essay on Man* (New Haven: Yale University Press, 1944).

32. For discussion of some of the problems here from a philosopher's viewpoint see R. B. Winn, "The Nature of Relations," *Philosophical Review*, 50 (Jan., 1941), pp. 20-35.

33. On the problem of succession in social systems see A. W. Gouldner, *Patterns of Industrial Bureaucracy* (Glencoe, Ill.: Free Press, 1954), pp. 59-104.

34. A stimulating if impressionistic account of this pattern is to be found in W. H. Whyte, *Is Anybody Listening?* (New York: Simon and Schuster, Inc., 1952).

35. For a case of this see the discussion in A. W. Gouldner, *Wildcat Strike, ibid.*, p. 24.

36. This is more extensively developed in A. W. Gouldner, "The Problem of Loyalty in Groups Under Tension," *Social Problems*, 2 (Oct., 1954), pp. 82-87.

37. Cf. K. Mannheim, *Man and Society in an Age of Reconstruction* (New York: Harcourt, Brace and Company, Inc., 1941), p. 245.

38. For fuller discussion see A. W. Gouldner, *ibid.*, ch. 10, and especially p. 171.

39. J. H. Steward, "Levels of Sociocultural Integration," *Southwestern Journal of Anthropology*, 7 (Winter, 1951), p. 379.

40. Merton, *ibid.*, p. 182.

41. Of similar import are Morris Ginsberg's comments in his essay on "Moral Progress": "There is no reason, it seems to me, for believing that the men of this age are suffering from a weakening of moral fibre." Again, some of modern man's bewilderment "is a sign not of moral decay but rather of moral ferment." M. Ginsberg, *Reason and Unreason in Society* (Cambridge: Harvard University Press, 1948), pp. 317-18.

42. A. W. Gouldner, "Cosmopolitans and Locals: Toward an Analysis of Latent Social Roles," *Administrative Science Quarterly*, 2 (Dec., 1957), pp. 281-306 and (March, 1958), pp. 444-80.

43. T. Parsons, *The Structure of Social Action, ibid.*

44. T. Parsons, *The Social System, ibid.*, p. 494.

45. See the cognate analysis of Parsons' theory in the excellent piece by David Lockwood, "Some Remarks on 'The Social System,'" *British Journal of Sociology*, 7 (June, 1956), pp. 134-45, where the nub of the criticism is the neglect of structured but nonnormative elements in Parsons' work.

46. One of the most interesting cases of this is, of course, that of Marxism, which is commonly interpreted as a factor theory. It is clear, however, if not from Marx himself then at least from Engels, that they were deeply concerned about system analysis. Among Engels' frequent references to the matter are the following: "Marx and I are ourselves partly to blame for the fact that younger writers sometimes lay more stress on the economic side than is due it. We had to emphasize this main principle in opposition to our adversaries, who denied it, and we had not always the time, the place, or the opportunity to allow the other elements involved in

the interaction to come into their rights." Again, "According to the materialist conception of history the determining element in history is *ultimately* the production and reproduction in real life. More than this neither Marx nor I have ever asserted." Finally, "In nature nothing happens alone. Everything has an effect on something else and vice versa. . . ." K. Marx and F. Engels (tr. by D. Torr), *Selected Correspondence, 1846–1895* (New York: International Publishers, 1942), pp. 477, 475, 114. N. Bukharin was one of the first of later Marxists to develop formally the use of system analysis on a sociological level. For example, a society "may be regarded as a whole consisting of parts (elements) related to each other; in other words, the whole may be regarded as a system." N. Bukharin, *Historical Materialism: a System of Sociology* (New York: International Publishers, 1925), p. 87.

47. For example, Paul Lazarsfeld is developing a statistical model which "provides a procedure for discovering which of the interacting elements preponderate. . . ." Lazarsfeld and Merton, *ibid.,* p. 59.

9

The Logic of Functional Analysis

CARL G. HEMPEL

Princeton University

Empirical science, in all its major branches, seeks not only to *describe* the phenomena in the world of our experience, but also to *explain* or *understand* their occurrence: it is concerned not just with the "what?", "when?", and "where?", but definitely, and often predominantly, with the "why?" of the phenomena it investigates.

That explanation and understanding constitute a common objective of the various scientific disciplines is widely recognized today. However, it is often held that there exist fundamental differences between the explanatory *methods* appropriate to the different fields of empirical science, and especially between those of the "exact" natural sciences and those required for an adequate understanding of the behavior of humans or other organisms, taken individually or in groups. In the exact natural sciences, according to this view, all explanation is achieved ultimately by reference to causal or correlational antecedents; whereas in psychology and the social and historical disciplines—and, according to some, even in biology—the establishment of causal or correlational connections, while desirable and important, is not sufficient. Proper understanding of the phenomena studied in these fields is held to require other types of explanation.

I am greatly indebted to the Council of the Humanities at Princeton University for the award of a Senior Fellowship for the academic year 1956–57, which offered me an opportunity to do research while on a substantially reduced teaching schedule. This essay is part of the work done under the auspices of the Council. C.G.H.

Perhaps the most important of the alternative methods that have been developed for this purpose is the method of functional analysis, which has found extensive use in biology, psychology, sociology, and anthropology. This procedure raises problems of considerable interest for the comparative methodology of empirical science. This essay is an attempt to clarify some of these problems; its object is to examine the logical structure of functional analysis and its explanatory and predictive significance by means of an explicit confrontation with the principal characteristics of the explanatory procedures used in the physical sciences. We begin by a brief examination of the latter.

1. NOMOLOGICAL EXPLANATION: DEDUCTIVE AND INDUCTIVE

In a beaker filled to the brim with water at room temperature, there floats a chunk of ice which partly extends above the surface. As the ice gradually melts, one might expect the water in the beaker to overflow. Actually, however, the water level remains unchanged. How is this to be explained? The key to an answer is provided by Archimedes' principle, according to which a solid body floating in a liquid displaces a volume of liquid which has the same weight as the body itself. Hence the chunk of ice has the same weight as the volume of water its submerged portion displaces. Now, since melting does not affect the weights involved, the water into which the ice turns has the same weight as the ice itself, and hence, the same weight as the water initially displaced by the submerged portion of the ice. Having the same weight, it also has the same volume as the displaced water; hence the melting ice yields a volume of water that suffices exactly to fill the space initially occupied by the submerged part of the ice. Therefore, the water level remains unchanged.

This account (which deliberately disregards certain effects of small magnitude) is an example of an argument intended to explain a certain event. Like any explanatory argument, it falls into two parts, which will be called the *explanans* and the *explanandum*.[1] The latter is the statement, or set of statements, describing the phenomenon to be explained; the former is the statement, or set of statements, adduced to provide an explanation. In our illustration, the explanandum states that at the end of the process, the beaker contains only water, with its surface at the same level as at the beginning. To explain this, the explanans adduces, first of all, certain laws of physics; among them, Archimedes' principle; laws to the effect that at temperatures above 0°C. and atmospheric pressure, a body of ice turns into a body of water having the same weight;

and the law that, at any fixed temperature and pressure, amounts of water that are equal in weight are also equal in volume.

In addition to these laws, the explanans contains a second group of statements; these describe certain particular circumstances which, in the experiment, precede the outcome to be explained; such as the facts that at the beginning, there is a chunk of ice floating in a beaker filled with water; that the water is at room temperature; and that the beaker is surrounded by air at the same temperature and remains undisturbed until the end of the experiment.

The explanatory import of the whole argument lies in showing that the outcome described in the explanandum was to be expected in view of the antecedent circumstances and the general laws listed in the explanans. More precisely, the explanation may be construed as an argument in which the explanandum is deduced from the explanans. Our example then illustrates what we will call explanation by deductive subsumption under general laws, or briefly, *deductive nomological explanation*. The general form of such an explanation is given by the following schema:

$$
\begin{array}{ll}
L_1, L_2, \ldots, L_m & \\
C_1, C_2, \ldots, C_n & \text{Explanans} \\
\hline
E & \text{Explanandum}
\end{array}
$$

(2.1)

Here, $L_1, L_2, \ldots, L_m$ are general laws and $C_1, C_2, \ldots, C_n$ are statements of particular fact; the horizontal line separating the conclusion E from the premises indicates that the former follows logically from the latter.

In our example, the phenomenon to be explained is a particular event that takes place at a certain place and time. But the method of deductive subsumption under general laws lends itself also to the explanation of what might be called "general facts" or uniformities, such as those expressed in laws of nature. For example, the question why Galileo's law holds for physical bodies falling freely near the earth's surface can be answered by showing that that law refers to a special case of accelerated motion under gravitational attraction, and that it can be deduced from the general laws for such motion (namely, Newton's laws of motion and of gravitation) by applying these to the special case where two bodies are involved, one of them the earth and the other the falling object, and where the distance between their centers of gravity equals the length of the earth's radius. Thus, an explanation of the regularities expressed by Galileo's law can be achieved by deducing the latter from the Newtonian laws and from statements specifying the mass and the radius of the earth; the latter two yield the value of the constant acceleration of free fall near the earth.

It might be helpful to mention one further illustration of the role of deductive nomological explanation in accounting for particular facts as well as for general uniformities or laws. The occurrence of a rainbow on a given occasion can be deductively explained by reference to (1) certain particular determining conditions, such as the presence of raindrops in the air, sunlight falling on these drops, the observer facing away from the sun, etc., and (2) certain general laws, especially those of optical reflection, refraction, and dispersion. The fact that these laws hold can be explained in turn by deduction from the more comprehensive principles of, say, the electromagnetic theory of light.

Thus, the method of deducti e nomological explanation accounts for a particular event by subsuming it under general laws in the manner represented by the schema (2.1); and it can similarly serve to explain the fact that a given law holds by showing that the latter is subsumable, in the same fashion, under more comprehensive laws or theoretical principles. In fact, one of the main objectives of a theory (such as, say, the electromagnetic theory of light) is precisely to provide a set of principles —often expressed in terms of "hypothetical," not directly observable, entities (such as electric and magnetic field vectors)—which will deductively account for a group of antecedently established "empirical generalizations" (such as the laws of rectilinear propagation, reflection, and refraction of light). Frequently, a theoretical explanation will show that the empirical generalizations hold only approximately. For example, the application of Newtonian theory to free fall near the earth yields a law that is like Galileo's except that the acceleration of the fall is seen not to be strictly constant, but to vary slightly with geographical location, altitude above sea level, and certain other factors.

The general laws or theoretical principles that serve to account for empirical generalizations may in turn be deductively subsumable under even more comprehensive principles; for example, Newton's theory of gravitation can be subsumed, as an approximation, under that of the general theory of relativity. Obviously, this explanatory hierarchy has to end at some point. Thus, at any time in the development of empirical science, there will be certain facts which, at that time, are not explainable; these include the most comprehensive general laws and theoretical principles then known and, of course, many empirical generalizations and particular facts for which no explanatory principles are available at the time. But this does not imply that certain facts are intrinsically unexplainable and thus must remain unexplained forever: any particular fact as yet unexplainable, and any general principle, however comprehensive, may subsequently be found to be explainable by subsumption under even more inclusive principles.

Causal explanation is a special type of deductive nomological explanation; for a certain event or set of events can be said to have caused a specified "effect" only if there are general laws connecting the former with the latter in such a way that, given a description of the antecedent events, the occurrence of the effect can be deduced with the help of the laws. For example, the explanation of the lengthening of a given iron bar as having been caused by an increase in its temperature amounts to an argument of the form (2.1) whose explanans includes (*a*) statements specifying the initial length of the bar and indicating that the bar is made of iron and that its temperature was raised, (*b*) a law to the effect that the length of any iron bar increases with the temperature.[2]

Not every deductive nomological explanation is a causal explanation, however. We cannot properly say, for example, that the regularities expressed by Newton's laws of motion and of gravitation *cause* the free fall of bodies near the earth's surface to satisfy Galileo's laws.

Now we must give at least brief consideration to another type of explanation, which again accounts for a given phenomenon by reference to general laws, but in a manner which does not fit the deductive pattern (2.1). For example, when little Henry catches the mumps, this might be explained by pointing out that he contracted the disease from a friend with whom he played for several hours just a day before the latter was confined with a severe case of mumps. The particular antecedent factors involved in this argument are Henry's exposure and, let us assume, the fact that Henry had not had the mumps before. But to connect these with the event to be explained, we cannot invoke a general law to the effect that under the conditions just mentioned, the exposed person invariably contracts the mumps: what can be asserted is only a high statistical probability that the disease will be transmitted. Again, when a neurotic trait in an adult is psychoanalytically explained by reference to critical childhood experiences, the argument explicitly or implicitly claims that the case at hand is but an exemplification of certain general laws governing the development of neuroses. But, surely, whatever specific laws of this kind might be adduced at present can purport, at the very best, to express probabilistic trends rather than deterministic uniformities: they may be construed as *laws of statistical form,* or briefly as *statistical laws,* to the effect that, given the childhood experiences in question—plus, presumably, certain particular environmental conditions in later life—there is such and such a statistical probability that a specified kind of neurosis will develop. Such statistical laws differ in form from strictly universal laws of the kind adduced in our earlier examples of explanatory arguments. In the simplest case, a *law of strictly universal form,* or briefly, a *universal law,* is a statement to the effect that in *all* cases satisfying certain antecedent conditions *A* (e.g., heating of a gas under constant pressure), an event of a specified kind *B* (e.g., an increase in the volume of the gas) will occur; whereas a law of statistical form asserts that the probability for conditions A to be accompanied by an event of kind B has some specific value p.

Explanatory arguments which, in the manner just illustrated, account for a phenomenon by reference to statistical laws are not of the strictly deductive type (2.1). For example, the explanans consisting of information about Henry's exposure to the mumps and of a statistical law about the transmission of this disease does not logically imply the conclusion that Henry catches the mumps; it does not make that conclusion necessary, but, as we might say, more or less probable, depending upon the probability specified by the statistical laws. An argument of this kind, then, accounts for a phenomenon by showing that its occurrence is highly probable in view of certain particular facts and statistical laws specified in the explanans. An account of this type will be called an *explanation by inductive subsumption under statistical laws,* or briefly, an *inductive explanation.* For the purposes of the present essay, this sketchy characterization of the explanatory use of statistical laws will suffice; a precise analysis of the method, which requires an inquiry into rather complex technical issues in inductive logic and the theory of statistical inference, reveals certain fundamental differences between deductive and inductive explanation.[3]

The two types of explanation we have distinguished will both be said to be forms of *nomological explanation;* for either of them accounts for a given phenomenon by "subsuming it under laws," i.e., by showing that its occurrence could have been inferred—either deductively or with a high probability—by applying certain laws of universal or of statistical form to specified antecedent circumstances. Thus, a nomological explanation shows that we might in fact have *predicted* the phenomenon at hand, either deductively or with a high probability, if, at an earlier time, we had taken cognizance of the facts stated in the explanans.

But the predictive power of a nomological explanation goes much farther than this: precisely because its explanans contains general laws, it permits predictions concerning occurrences other than that referred to in the explanandum. These predictions provide a means of testing the empirical soundness of the explanans. For example, the laws invoked in a deductive explanation of the form (2.1) imply that the kind of event described in E will recur whenever and wherever circumstances of the kind described by $C_1, C_2, \ldots, C_n$ are realized; e.g., when the experiment with ice floating in water is repeated, the outcome will be the same. In addition, the laws will yield predictions as to what is going to happen under certain specifiable conditions which differ from those mentioned in $C_1, C_2, \ldots, C_n$. For example, the laws invoked in our illustration also yield the prediction that if a chunk of ice were floating in a beaker filled to the brim with concentrated brine, which has a greater specific gravity than water, some of the liquid would overflow as the ice was melting. Again, the Newtonian laws of motion and of gravitation, which may be used to explain various aspects of planetary motion, have predictive consequences for a variety of totally different phenomena, such as free fall near the earth, the motion of a pendulum, the tides, and many others.

This kind of account of further phenomena which is made possible by a nomological explanation is not limited to future events, but may refer to the past as well. For example, given certain information about the present locations and velocities of the celestial bodies involved, the principles of Newtonian mechanics and of optics yield not only predictions about future solar and lunar eclipses, but also "postdictions," or "retrodictions," about past ones. Analogously, the statistical laws of radioactive decay, which can function in various kinds of predictions, also lend themselves to retrodictive use; for example, in the dating, by means of the radiocarbon method, of a bow or an ax handle found in an archeological site.

A proposed explanation is scientifically acceptable only if its explanans is capable of empirical test, i.e., roughly speaking, if it is possible to infer from it certain statements whose truth can be checked by means of suitable observational or experimental procedures. The predictive and postdictive implications of the laws invoked in a nomological explanation clearly afford an opportunity for empirical tests; the more extensive and varied the set of implications that have been borne out by empirical investigation, the better established will be the explanatory principles in question.

2. THE BASIC PATTERN OF FUNCTIONAL ANALYSIS

Historically speaking, functional analysis is a modification of teleological explanation, i.e., of explanation not by reference to causes which "bring about" the event in question, but by reference to ends which determine its course. Intuitively, it seems quite plausible that a teleological approach might be required for an adequate understanding of purposive and other goal-directed behavior; and teleological explanation has always had its advocates in this context. The trouble with the idea is that in its more traditional forms, it fails to meet the minimum scientific requirement of empirical testability. The neovitalistic idea of entelechy or of vital force is a case in point. It is meant to provide an explanation for various characteristically biological phenomena, such as regeneration and regulation, which according to neovitalism cannot be explained by physical and chemical laws alone. Entelechies are conceived

as goal-directed nonphysical agents which affect the course of physiological events in such a way as to restore an organism to a more or less
normal state after a disturbance has occurred. However, this conception
is stated in essentially metaphorical terms: no testable set of statements
is provided (i) to specify the kinds of circumstances in which an entelechy will supervene as an agent directing the course of events otherwise governed by physical and chemical laws, and (ii) to indicate precisely what observable effects the action of an entelechy will have in such
a case. And since neovitalism thus fails to state general laws as to when
and how entelechies act, it cannot explain any biological phenomena; it
can give us no grounds to expect a given phenomenon, no reasons to say:
"Now we see that the phenomenon had to occur." It yields neither predictions nor retrodictions: the attribution of a biological phenomenon to
the supervenience of an entelechy has no testable implications at all. This
theoretical defect can be thrown into relief by contrasting the idea of
entelechy with that of a magnetic field generated by an electric current,
which may be invoked to explain the deflection of a magnetic needle. A
magnetic field is not directly observable any more than an entelechy; but
the concept is governed by strictly specifiable laws concerning the strength
and direction, at any point, of the magnetic field produced by a current
flowing through a given wire, and by other laws determining the effect
of such a field upon a magnetic needle in the magnetic field on the earth.
And it is these laws which, by their predictive and retrodictive import,
confer explanatory power upon the concept of magnetic field. Teleological
accounts referring to entelechies are thus seen to be pseudoexplanations.
Functional analysis, as will be seen, though often worded in teleological
phraseology, need not appeal to such problematic entities and has a definitely empirical core.

The kind of phenomenon that a functional analysis [4] is invoked to
explain is typically some recurrent activity or some behavior pattern in
an individual or a group; it may be a physiological mechanism, a neurotic trait, a culture pattern, or a social institution, for example. And the
principal objective of the analysis is to exhibit the contribution which
the behavior pattern makes to the preservation or the development of the
individual or the group in which it occurs. Thus, functional analysis seeks
to understand a behavior pattern or a sociocultural institution in terms of
the role it plays in keeping the given system in proper working order and
thus maintaining it as a going concern.

By way of a simple and schematized illustration, consider first the
statement:

(3.1) The heartbeat in vertebrates has the function of circulating blood
through the organism.

Before asking whether and how this statement might be used for explanatory purposes, we have to consider the preliminary question: what does the statement *mean*? What is being asserted by this attribution of function? It might be held that all the information conveyed by a sentence such as (3.1) can be expressed just as well by substituting the word "effect" for the word "function." But this construal would oblige us to assent also to the statement:

(3.2) The heartbeat has the function of producing heart sounds; for the heartbeat has that effect.

Yet a proponent of functional analysis would refuse to assert (3.2), on the ground that heart sounds are an effect of the heartbeat which is of no importance to the functioning of the organism; whereas the circulation of the blood effects the transportation of nutriment to, and the removal of waste from, various parts of the organism—a process that is indispensable if the organism is to remain in proper working order, and indeed if it is to stay alive. Thus understood, the import of the functional statement (3.1) might be summarized as follows:

(3.3) The heartbeat has the effect of circulating the blood, and this ensures the satisfaction of certain conditions (supply of nutriment and removal of waste) which are necessary for the proper working of the organism.

We should notice next that the heart will perform the task here attributed to it only if certain conditions are met by the organism and by its environment. For example, circulation will fail if there is a rupture of the aorta; the blood can carry oxygen only if the environment affords an adequate supply of available oxygen and the lungs are in proper condition; it will remove certain kinds of waste only if the kidneys are reasonably healthy; and so forth. Most of the conditions that would have to be specified here are usually left unmentioned, partly no doubt because they are assumed to be satisfied as a matter of course in situations in which the organism normally finds itself. But, in part, the omission reflects lack of relevant knowledge, for an explicit specification of the conditions in question would require a theory in which (*a*) the possible states of organisms and of their environments could be characterized by the values of certain physicochemical or perhaps biological "variables of state," and in which (*b*) the fundamental theoretical principles would permit the determination of that range of internal and external conditions within which the pulsations of the heart would perform the function referred to above.[5] At present, a general theory of this kind, or even one that could deal in this fashion with some particular kind of organism, is unavailable, of course.

Also, a full restatement of (3.1) in the manner of (3.3) calls for criteria of what constitutes "proper working," "normal functioning," and the like, of the organism at hand; for the function of a given trait is here construed in terms of its causal relevance to the satisfaction of certain necessary conditions of proper working or survival of the organism. Here again, the requisite criteria are often left unspecified—an aspect of functional analysis whose serious implications will be considered later (in section 5).

The considerations here outlined suggest the following schematic characterization of a functional analysis:

(3.4) *Basic pattern of a functional analysis:* The object of the analysis is some "item" i, which is a relatively persistent trait or disposition (e.g., the beating of the heart) occurring in a system s (e.g., the body of a living vertebrate); and the analysis aims to show that s is in a state, or internal condition, c_i and in an environment presenting certain external conditions c_e such that under conditions c_i and c_e (jointly to be referred to as c) the trait i has effects which satisfy some "need" or "functional requirement" of s, i.e., a condition n which is necessary for the system's remaining in adequate, or effective, or proper, working order.

Let us briefly consider some examples of this type of analysis in psychology and in sociological and anthropological studies. In psychology, it is especially psychoanalysis which shows a strong functional orientation. One clear instance is Freud's functional characterization of the role of symptom formation. In *The Problem of Anxiety,* Freud expresses himself as favoring a conception according to which "all symptom formation would be brought about solely in order to avoid anxiety; the symptoms bind the psychic energy which otherwise would be discharged as anxiety." [6] In support of this view, Freud points out that if an agoraphobic who has usually been accompanied when going out is left alone in the street, he will suffer an attack of anxiety, as will the compulsion neurotic who, having touched something, is prevented from washing his hands. "It is clear, therefore, that the stipulation of being accompanied and the compulsion to wash has as their purpose, and also their result, the averting of an outbreak of anxiety." [7] In this account, which is put in strongly teleological terms, the system s is the individual under consideration; i his agoraphobic or compulsive behavior pattern; n the binding of anxiety, which is necessary to avert a serious psychological crisis that would make it impossible for the individual to function adequately.

In anthropology and sociology the object of functional analysis is, in Merton's words, "a standardized (i.e., patterned and repetitive) item, such as social roles, institutional patterns, social processes, cultural pattern, culturally patterned emotions, social norms, group organization, social structure, devices for social control, etc." [8] Here, as in psychology and biology, the function, i.e., the stabilizing or adjusting effect, of the item under study, may be one not consciously sought (and indeed, it might not even be consciously recognized) by the agents; in this case, Merton speaks of *latent* functions—in contradistinction to *manifest* functions, i.e., those stabilizing objective effects which are intended by participants in the system.[9] Thus, e.g., the rain-making ceremonials of the Hopi fail to achieve their manifest meteorological objective, but they "may fulfill the latent function of reinforcing the group identity by providing a periodic occasion on which the scattered members of a group assemble to engage in a common activity." [10]

Radcliffe-Brown's functional analysis of the totemic rites of certain Australian tribes illustrates the same point: "To discover the social function of the totemic rites we have to consider the whole body of cosmological ideas of which each rite is a partial expression. I believe that it is possible to show that the social structure of an Australian tribe is connected in a very special way with these cosmological ideas and that the maintenance of its continuity depends on keeping them alive, by their regular expression in myth and rite.

"Thus, any satisfactory study of the totemic rites of Australia must be based not simply on the consideration of their ostensible purpose . . . , but on the discovery of their meaning and of their social function." [11]

Malinowski attributes important latent functions to religion and to magic: he argues that religious faith establishes and enhances mental attitudes such as reverence for tradition, harmony with environment, and confidence and courage in critical situations and at the prospect of death —attitudes which, embodied and maintained by cult and ceremonial, have "an immense biological value." He points out that magic, by providing man with certain ready-made rituals, techniques, and beliefs, enables him "to maintain his poise and his mental integrity in fits of anger, in the throes of hate, of unrequited love, of despair and anxiety. The function of magic is to ritualize man's optimism, to enhance his faith in the victory of hope over fear." [12]

There will soon be occasion to add to the preceding examples from psychoanalysis and anthropology some instances of functional analysis in sociology. To illustrate the general character of the procedure, however, the cases mentioned so far will suffice: they all exhibit the basic pattern outlined in (3.4). We now turn from our examination of the form of functional analysis to a scrutiny of its significance as a mode of explanation.

3. THE EXPLANATORY IMPORT OF FUNCTIONAL
ANALYSIS

Functional analysis is widely considered as achieving an *explanation* of the "items" whose functions it studies. Malinowski, for example, says of the functional analysis of culture that it "aims at the explanation of anthropological facts at all levels of development by their function . . ." [13] and he adds, in the same context: "To explain any item of culture, material or moral, means to indicate its functional place within an institution, . . ." [14] At another place, Malinowski speaks of the "functional explanation of art, recreation, and public ceremonials." [15]

Radcliffe-Brown, too, considers functional analysis as an explanatory method, though not as the only one suited for the social sciences: "Similarly one 'explanation' of a social system will be its history, where we know it—the detailed account of how it came to be what it is and where it is. Another 'explanation' of the same system is obtained by showing (as the functionalists attempt to do) that it is a special exemplification of laws of social physiology or social functioning. The two kinds of explanation do not conflict, but supplement one another." [16]

Apart from illustrating the attribution of explanatory import to functional analysis, this passage raises two points which bear on the general question as to the nature of explanation in empirical science. We will therefore digress briefly to comment on these points.

First, as Radcliffe-Brown stresses, a functional analysis has to refer to general laws. This is shown also in our schematic characterization (3.4): the statements that i, in the specified setting c, has effects that satisfy n, and that n is a necessary condition for the proper functioning of the system, both involve general laws. For a statement of causal connection this is well known; and the assertion that a condition n constitutes a functional prerequisite for a state of some specified kind (such as proper functioning) is tantamount to the statement of a law to the effect that whenever condition n fails to be satisfied, the state in question fails to occur. Thus, explanation by functional analysis requires reference to laws.[17]

The second point relates to a concept invoked by Radcliffe-Brown, of a historic-genetic explanation, which accounts for an item such as a social system or institution by tracing its origins. Clearly, the mere listing of a series of events preceding the given item cannot qualify as an explanation; temporal precedence does not in itself make an event relevant to the genesis of the item under consideration. Thus, a criterion of relevance is needed for the characterization of a sound historic-genetic explanation. As brief reflection shows, relevance here consists in causal or probabilistic determination. A historic-genetic explanation will normally proceed in stages, beginning with some initial set of circumstances which are said to have "brought about," or "led to," certain events at a later time; of these it is next argued that by virtue of, or in conjunction with, certain further conditions prevailing at that later time, they led to a specified further set of events in the historical development; these are in turn combined with additional factors then prevailing and lead to a still later stage, and so forth, until the final explanandum is reached. In a genetic account of this kind, the assertion that a given set of circumstances brought about certain specified subsequent conditions clearly has to be construed as claiming a nomological connection of causal, or more likely, of probabilistic, character. Thus, there is tacit reference to general laws of strictly universal or of statistical form; and a historic-genetic explanation can be construed schematically as a sequence of steps each of which has the character of a nomological explanation. However, while in each step but the first, some of the particular facts mentioned in the explanans will have been accounted for by preceding explanatory steps, the other particular facts invoked will be brought in simply by way of supplementary information. Thus, even in a highly schematic construal, a historic-genetic explanation cannot be viewed as proceeding from information about circumstances at some initial time, *via* certain statistical or causal laws alone, to the final explanandum: it is essential that, as the argument goes on, additional information is fed into it, concerning certain events which supervene "from the outside," as it were, at various stages of the process under study. Let us note that exactly the same procedure would be required in the case of the melting ice if, during the period of time under consideration, the system were subject to certain outside influences, such as someone's pushing the beaker and spilling some of the water, or salt being added to the water. Basically, then, historic-genetic explanation is nomological explanation.

Returning now to the main issue of the present section, we have to ask what explanatory import may properly be attributed to functional analysis. Suppose, then, that we are interested in explaining the occurrence of a trait i in a system s (at a certain time t), and that the following functional analysis is offered:

(4.1)

(a) At t, s functions adequately in a setting of kind c (characterized by specific internal and external conditions)

(b) s functions adequately in a setting of kind c only if a certain necessary condition, n, is satisfied

(c) If trait i were present in s then, as an effect, condition n would be satisfied

___

(d) (Hence,) at t, trait i is present in s

For the moment, we will leave aside the question as to what precisely is meant by statements of the types (a) and (b), and especially by the phrase "s functions adequately"; these matters will be examined in section 5. Right now, we will concern ourselves only with the *logic* of the argument; i.e., we will ask whether (d) formally follows from (a), (b), (c), just as in a deductive nomological explanation the explanandum follows from the explanans. The answer is obviously in the negative, for, to put it pedantically, the argument (4.1) involves the fallacy of affirming the consequent in regard to premise (c). More explicitly, the statement (d) could be validly inferred if (c) asserted that *only* the presence of trait i could effect satisfaction of condition n. As it is, we can infer merely that condition n must be satisfied in some way or other at time t; for otherwise, by reason of (b), the system s could not be functioning adequately in its setting, in contradiction to what (a) asserts. But it might well be that the occurrence of any one of a number of alternative items would suffice no less than the occurrence of i to satisfy requirement n, in which case the account provided by the premises of (4.1) simply fails to explain why the trait i rather than one of its alternatives is present in s at t.

As has just been noted, this objection would not apply if premise (c) could be replaced by the statement that requirement n can be met *only* by the presence of trait i. And indeed, some instances of functional analysis seem to involve the claim that the specific item under analysis is, in this sense, functionally indispensable for the satisfaction of n. For example, Malinowski makes this claim for magic when he asserts that "magic fulfills an indispensable function within culture. It satisfies a definite need which cannot be satisfied by any other factors of primitive civilization," [18] and again when he says about magic that "without its power and guidance early man could not have mastered his practical difficulties as he has done, nor could man have advanced to the higher stages of culture. Hence the universal occurrence of magic in primitive societies and its enormous sway. Hence we do find magic an invariable adjunct of all important activities." [19]

However, the assumption of functional indispensability for a given item is highly questionable on empirical grounds: in all concrete cases of application, there do seem to exist alternatives. For example, the binding of anxiety in a given subject might be effected by an alternative symptom, as the experience of psychiatrists seems to confirm. Similarly, the function of the rain dance might be subserved by some other group ceremonial. And interestingly, Malinowski himself, in another context, invokes "the principle of limited possibilities, first laid down by Goldenweiser. Given a definite cultural need, the means of its satisfaction are small in number, and therefore the cultural arrangement which comes into being in response to the need is determined within narrow limits." [20] This principle obviously involves at least a moderate liberalization of the conception that every cultural item is functionally indispensable. But even so, it may still be too restrictive. At any rate, sociologists such as Parsons and Merton have assumed the existence of "functional equivalents" for certain cultural items; and Merton, in his general analysis of functionalism, has insisted that the conception of the functional indispensability of cultural items be replaced quite explicitly by the assumption of "functional alternatives, or functional equivalents, or functional substitutes." [21] This idea, incidentally, has an interesting parallel in the "principle of multiple solutions" for adaptational problems in evolution. This principle, which has been emphasized by functionally oriented biologists, states that for a given functional problem (such as that of perception of light) there are usually a variety of possible solutions, and many of these are actually used by different—and often closely related—groups of organisms.[22]

It should be noted here that, in any case of functional analysis, the question whether there are functional equivalents to a given item i has a definite meaning only if the internal and external conditions c in (4.1) are clearly specified. Otherwise, any proposed alternative to i, say i', could be denied the status of a functional equivalent on the ground that, being different from i, the item i' would have certain effects on the internal state and the environment of s which would not be brought about by i; and that therefore, if i' rather than i were realized, s would not be functioning in the same internal and external situation.

Suppose, for example, that the system of magic of a given primitive group were replaced by an extension of its rational technology plus some modification of its religion, and that the group were to continue as a going concern. Would this establish the existence of a functional equivalent to the original system of magic? A negative answer might be defended on the grounds that as a result of adopting the modified pattern the group had changed so strongly in regard to some of its basic characteristics (i.e., its internal state, as characterized by c_i, had been so strongly modified) that it was not the original kind of primitive group any more; and that there simply was no functional equivalent to magic which would leave all the "essential" features of the group unimpaired. Consistent use of this type of argument would safeguard the postulate of the functional indispensability of every cultural item against any conceivable empirical disconfirmation, by turning it into a covert tautology.

Let I be the class of those items, $i, i', i'', \ldots$, any one of which, if present in s under conditions c, would effect satisfaction of condition n. Then those items are functional equivalents in Merton's sense, and what the premises of (4.1) entitle us to infer is only:

(4.2) Some one of the items in class I is present in *s* at *t*. But the premises give us no grounds to expect *i* rather than one of its functional alternatives.

So far, we have viewed functional analysis only as a presumptive deductive explanation. Might it not be construed instead as an inductive argument which shows that the occurrence of *i* is highly probable in the circumstances described by the premises? Might it not be possible, for example, to add to the premises of (4.1) a further statement to the effect that the functional prerequisite *n* can be met only by *i* and by a few specifiable functional alternatives? And might not these premises make the presence of *i* highly probable? This course is hardly promising, for in most, if not all, concrete cases it would be impossible to specify with any precision the range of alternative behavior patterns, institutions, customs, or the like that would suffice to meet a given functional prerequisite or need. And even if that range could be characterized, there is no satisfactory method in sight for dividing it into some finite number of cases and assigning a probability to each of these.

Assume, for example, that Malinowski's general view of the function of magic is correct: how are we to determine, when trying to explain the system of magic of a given group, all the different systems of magic and alternative cultural patterns any one of which would satisfy the same functional requirements for the group as does the actually existing system of magic? And how are we to ascribe probabilities of occurrence to each of these potential functional equivalents? Clearly, there is no satisfactory way of answering these questions, and practitioners of functional analysis do not claim to achieve their explanation in this extremely problematic fashion.

Nor is it any help to construe the general laws implicit in the statements (*b*) and (*c*) in (4.1) as statistical rather than strictly universal in form, i.e., as expressing connections that are very probable, but do not hold universally; for the premises thus obtained would still allow for functional alternatives of *i* (each of which would make satisfaction of *n* highly probable), and thus the basic difficulty would remain: the premises taken jointly could still not be said to make the presence just of *i* highly probable.

In sum then, the information typically provided by a functional analysis of an item *i* affords neither deductively nor inductively adequate grounds for expecting *i* rather than one of its alternatives. The impression that a functional analysis does provide such grounds, and thus explains the occurrence of *i,* is no doubt at least partly due to the benefit of hindsight: when we seek to explain an item *i,* we presumably know already that *i* has occurred.

But, as was briefly noted earlier, a functional analysis provides, in principle, the basis for an explanation with a weaker explanandum; for the premises (a) and (b) of (4.1) imply the consequence that the necessary condition n must be fulfilled in some way or other. This much more modest kind of functional explanation may be schematized as follows:

(a) At time t, system s functions adequately in a setting of kind c
(4.3) (b) s functions adequately in a setting of kind c only if condition n is satisfied

(e) Some one of the items in class I is present in s at t

This kind of inference, while sound, is rather trivial, however, except in cases where we have additional knowledge about the items contained in class I. Suppose, for example, that at time t, a certain dog (system s) is in good health in a "normal" kind of setting c which precludes the use of such devices as artificial hearts, lungs, and kidneys. Suppose further that in a setting of kind c, the dog can be in good health only if his blood circulates properly (condition n). Then schema (4.3) leads only to the conclusion that in some way or other, the blood must be kept circulating properly in the dog at t—hardly a very illuminating result. If, however, we have additional knowledge of the ways in which the blood may be kept circulating under the circumstances and if we know, for example, that the only feature that would ensure proper circulation (the only item in class I) is a properly working heart, then we may draw the much more specific conclusion that at t the dog has a properly working heart. But if we make explicit the additional knowledge here used by expressing it as a third premise, then our argument assumes a form considered earlier, namely that of a functional analysis which is of the type (4.1), except that premise (c) has been replaced by the statement that i is the *only* trait by which n can be satisfied in setting c; and, as was pointed out above, the conclusion (d) of (4.1) does follow in this case; in our case, (d) is the sentence stating that the dog has a properly working heart at t.

In general, however, additional knowledge of the kind here referred to is not available, and the explanatory import of functional analysis is then limited to the precarious role schematized in (4.3).

4. THE PREDICTIVE IMPORT OF FUNCTIONAL ANALYSIS

We noted earlier the predictive significance of nomological explanation; now we will ask whether functional analysis can be put to predictive use.

First of all, the preceding discussion shows that the information which is typically provided by a functional analysis yields at best premises of the forms (a), (b), (c) in (4.1); and these afford no adequate basis for the deductive or inductive prediction of a sentence of the form (d) in (4.1). Thus, functional analysis no more enables us to predict than it enables us to explain the occurrence of a particular one of the items by which a given functional requirement can be met.

Second, even the much less ambitious explanatory schema (4.3) cannot readily be put to predictive use; for the derivation of the weak conclusion (e) relies on the premise (a); and if we wish to infer (e) with respect to some future time t, that premise is not available, for we do not know whether s will or will not be functioning adequately at that future time. For example, consider a person developing increasingly severe anxieties, and suppose that a necessary condition for his adequate functioning is that his anxiety be bound by neurotic symptoms, or be overcome by other means. Can we predict that some one of the modes of "adjustment" in the class I thus roughly characterized will actually come to pass? Clearly not, for we do not know whether the person in question will in fact continue to function adequately or will suffer some more or less serious breakdown, perhaps to the point of self-destruction.

It is of interest to note here that a somewhat similar limitation exists also for the predictive use of nomological explanations, even in the most advanced branches of science. For example, if we are to predict, by means of the laws of classical mechanics, the state in which a given mechanical system will be at a specified future time t, it does not suffice to know the state of the system at some earlier time t_o, say the present; we also need information about the boundary conditions during the time interval from t_o to t, i.e., about the external influences affecting the system during that time. Similarly, the "prediction," in our first example, that the water level in the beaker will remain unchanged as the ice melts assumes that the temperature of the surrounding air will remain constant, let us say, and that there will be no disturbing influences such as an earthquake or a person upsetting the beaker. Again when we predict for an object dropped from the top of the Empire State Building that it will strike the ground about eight seconds later, we assume that during the period of its fall, the object is acted upon by no forces other than the gravitational attraction of the earth. In a full and explicit formulation then, nomological predictions such as these would have to include among their premises statements specifying the boundary conditions obtaining from t_o up to the time t to which the prediction refers. This shows that even the laws and theories of the physical sciences do not actually enable us to predict certain aspects of the future exclusively on the basis of certain aspects of the present: the prediction also requires certain assumptions about the future. But, in many cases of nomological prediction, there are good inductive grounds, available at t_o, for the assumption that during the time interval in question, the system under study will be practically "closed," i.e., not subject to significant outside interference (this case is illustrated, for example, by the prediction of eclipses) or that the boundary conditions will be of a certain specified kind—a situation illustrated by predictions of events occurring under experimentally controlled conditions.

Now, the predictive use of (4.3) likewise requires a premise concerning the future, namely (*a*); but there is often considerable uncertainty as to whether (*a*) will in fact hold true at the future time *t*. Furthermore, if in a particular instance there should be good inductive grounds for considering (*a*) as true, the forecast yielded by (4.3) is still rather weak; for the argument then leads from the inductively warranted assumption that the system will be properly functioning at *t* to the "prediction" that a certain condition *n*, which is necessary for such functioning, will be satisfied at *t* in some way or other.

The need to include assumptions about the future among the premises of predictive arguments can be avoided, in nomological predictions as well as in those based on functional analysis, if we are satisfied with predictive conclusions which are not categorical, but only conditional, or hypothetical, in character. For example, (4.3) may be replaced by the following argument, in which premise (*a*) is avoided at the price of conditionalizing the conclusion:

(5.1) (*b*) System *s* functions adequately in a setting of kind *c* only if condition *n* is satisfied

---

(*f*) If *s* functions adequately in a setting of kind *c* at time *t*, then some one of the items in class I is present in *s* at *t*.

This possibility deserves mention because it seems that at least some of the claims made by advocates of functional analysis may be construed as asserting no more than that functional analysis permits conditional predictions of the kind schematically represented by (5.1). This might be the intent, for example, of Malinowski's claim: "If such [a functional] analysis discloses to us that, taking an individual culture as a coherent whole, we can state a number of general determinants to which it has to conform, we shall be able to produce a number of predictive statements as guides for field-research, as yardsticks for comparative treatment, and as common measures in the process of cultural adaptation and change." [23] The statements specifying the determinants in question would presumably take the form of premises of type (*b*); and the "predictive statements" would then be of a hypothetical character.

Many of the predictions and generalizations made in the context of functional analysis, however, eschew the cautious conditional form just considered. They proceed from a statement of a functional prerequisite or need to the categorical assertion of the occurrence of some trait, institution, or other item suited to meet the requirement in question. Consider, for example, Sait's functional explanation of the emergence of the political boss: "Leadership is necessary; and *since* it does not develop readily within the constitutional framework, the boss provides it in a crude and irresponsible form from the outside"; [24] or take Merton's characterization of one function of the political machine: Referring to various specific ways in which the political machine can serve the interests of business, he concludes, "These 'needs' of business, as presently constituted, are not adequately provided for by conventional and culturally approved social structures; *consequently,* the extra-legal but more-or-less efficient organization of the political machine comes to provide these services." [25] Each of these arguments, which are rather typical of the functionalist approach, is an inference from the existence of a certain functional prerequisite to the categorical assertion that the prerequisite will be satisfied in some way. What is the basis of these inferences, which are marked by the words, 'since' and 'consequently' in the passages just quoted? When we say that *since* the ice cube was put in warm water it melted; or that the current was turned on, and *consequently,* the ammeter in the circuit responded, these inferences can be explicated and justified by reference to certain general laws of which the particular cases at hand are simply special instances; and the logic of the inferences can be exhibited by putting them into the form of the schema (2.1). Similarly, each of the two functionalist arguments under consideration clearly seems to presuppose a general law to the effect that, within certain limits of tolerance or adaptability, a system of the kind under analysis will—either invariably or with high probability—satisfy, by developing appropriate traits, the various functional requirements (necessary conditions for its continued adequate operation) that may arise from changes in its internal state or in its environment. Any assertion of this kind, no matter whether of strictly universal or of statistical form, will be called a (*general*) *hypothesis of self-regulation.*

Unless functional analyses of the kind just illustrated are construed as implicitly proposing or invoking suitable hypotheses of self-regulation, it remains quite unclear what connections the expressions 'since,' 'consequently,' and others of the same character are meant to indicate, and how the existence of those connections in a given case is to be objectively established.

Conversely, if a precise hypothesis of self-regulation for systems of a specified kind is set forth, then it becomes possible to explain, and to predict categorically, the satisfaction of certain functional requirements simply on the basis of information concerning antecedent needs; and the hypothesis can then be objectively tested by an empirical check of its predictions. Take, for example, the statement that if a hydra is cut into several pieces, most of these will grow into complete hydras again. This statement may be considered as a hypothesis concerning a specific kind of self-regulation in a particular kind of biological system. It can clearly be used for explanatory and predictive purposes, and indeed the success of the predictions it yields confirms it to a high degree.

We see, then, that wherever functional analysis is to serve as a basis for categorical prediction or for generalizations of the type illustrated by the passages from Sait and from Merton, it is of crucial importance to establish appropriate hypotheses of self-regulation in an objectively testable form.

The functionalist literature does contain some explicitly formulated generalizations of the kind here referred to. Merton, for example, after citing the passage from Sait quoted above, comments thus: "Put in more generalized terms, *the functional deficiencies of the official structure generate an alternative (unofficial) structure to fulfill existing needs somewhat more effectively.*" [26] This statement seems clearly intended to make explicit a hypothesis of self-regulation that might be said to underlie Sait's specific analysis and to provide the rationale for his 'since.' Another hypothesis of this kind is suggested by Radcliffe-Brown: "it may be that we should say that . . . a society that is thrown into a condition of functional disunity or inconsistency . . . will not die, except in such comparatively rare instances as an Australian tribe overwhelmed by the white man's destructive force, but will continue to struggle toward . . . some kind of social health. . . ." [27]

But, as was briefly suggested above, a formulation proposed as a hypothesis of self-regulation can serve as a basis for explanation or prediction only if it is a reasonably definite statement that permits of objective empirical test. And indeed many of the leading representatives of functional analysis have expressed very clearly their concern to develop hypotheses and theories which meet this requirement. Malinowski, for example, in his essay significantly entitled "A scientific theory of culture," insists that "each scientific theory must start from and lead to observation. It must be inductive and it must be verifiable by experience. In other words, it must refer to human experiences which can be defined, which are public, that is, accessible to any and every observer, and which are recurrent, hence fraught with inductive generalizations, that is, predictive." [28] Similarly, Murray and Kluckhohn have this to say about the basic objective of their functionally oriented theory, and indeed about any scientific "formulation," of personality: "the general purposes of formulation are three: (1) to *explain* past and present events; (2) to *predict* future events (the conditions being specified); and (3) to serve, if required, as a basis for the selection of effective measures of *control*." [29]

Unfortunately, however, the formulations offered in the context of concrete functional analyses quite often fall short of these general standards. Among the various ways in which those conditions may be violated, two call for special consideration because of their pervasiveness and central importance in functional analysis. They will be referred to as (i) *inadequate specification of scope,* and (ii) *nonempirical use of functionalist key terms* (such as "need," "functional requirement," "adaptation," and others). We will consider these two defects in turn: the former in the balance of the present section, the latter in the next.

Inadequate specification of scope consists in failure to indicate clearly the kind of system to which the hypothesis refers, or the range of situations (the limits of tolerance) within which those systems are claimed to develop traits that will satisfy their functional requirements. Merton's formulation, for example, does not specify the class of social systems and of situations to which the proposed generalization is meant to apply; as it stands, therefore, it cannot be put to an empirical test or to any predictive use.

The generalization tentatively set forth by Radcliffe-Brown has a similar shortcoming: Ostensibly, it refers to any society whatever, but the conditions under which social survival is claimed to occur are qualified by a highly indefinite "except" clause, which precludes the possibility of any reasonably clear-cut test. The clause might even be used to protect the proposed generalization against any conceivable disconfirmation: If a particular social group should "die," this very fact might be held to show that the disruptive forces were as overwhelming as in the case of the Australian tribe mentioned by Radcliffe-Brown. Systematic use of this methodological strategy would, of course, turn the hypothesis into a covert tautology. This would ensure its truth, but at the price of depriving it of empirical content: thus construed, the hypothesis can yield no explanation or prediction whatever.

A similar comment is applicable to the following pronouncement by Malinowski, in which we italicize the dubious qualifying clause: "When we consider any culture *which is not on the point of breaking down or completely disrupted, but which is a normal going concern,* we find that need and response are directly related and tuned up to each other." [30]

To be sure, Radcliffe-Brown's and Malinowski's formulations do not *have to* be construed as covert tautologies, and their authors no doubt intended them as empirical assertions; but, in this case, the vagueness of the qualifying clauses still deprives them of the status of definite empirical hypotheses that might be used for explanation or prediction.

5. THE EMPIRICAL IMPORT OF FUNCTIONALIST TERMS AND HYPOTHESES

In the preceding section, we mentioned a second flaw that may vitiate the scientific role of a proposed hypothesis of self-regulation. It consists in using key terms of functional analysis, such as 'need' and 'adequate (proper) functioning' [31] in a nonempirical manner, i.e., without giving them a clear "operational definition," or more generally, without specifying objective criteria of application for them.[32] If functionalist terms are used in this manner, then the sentences containing them have no clear empirical meaning; they lead to no specific predictions and thus cannot be put to an objective test; nor, of course, can they be used for explanatory purposes.

A consideration of this point is all the more important here because the functionalist key terms occur not only in hypotheses of self-regulation, but also in functionalist sentences of various other kinds, such as those of the types (a), (b), and (f) in our schematizations (4.1), (4.3), and (5.1) of functionalist explanation and prediction. Nonempirical use of functionalist key terms may, therefore, bar sentences of these various kinds from the status of scientific hypotheses. We turn now to some examples.

Consider first the terms 'functional prerequisite' and 'need,' which are used as more or less synonymous in the functionalist literature, and which serve to define the term 'function' itself. "Embedded in every functional analysis is some conception, tacit or expressed, of the functional requirements of the system under observation"; [33] and indeed, "a definition [of function] is provided by showing that human institutions, as well as partial activities within these, are related to primary, that is, biological, or derived, that is, cultural needs. Function means, therefore, always the satisfaction of a need. . . ." [34]

How is this concept of need defined? Malinowski gives a very explicit answer: "By need, then, I understand the system of conditions in the human organism, in the cultural setting, and in the relation of both to the natural environment, which are sufficient and necessary for the survival of group and organism." [35] This definition sounds clear and straightforward; yet it is not even quite in accord with Malinowski's own use of the concept of need. For he distinguishes, very plausibly, a considerable number of different needs, which fall into two major groups: primary biological needs and derivative cultural ones; the latter include "technological, economic, legal, and even magical, religious, or ethical" [36] needs. But if every single one of these needs did actually represent not only a necessary condition of survival but also a sufficient one, then clearly the satisfaction of just one need would suffice to ensure survival, and the other needs could not constitute necessary conditions of survival at all. It seems reasonable to assume, therefore, that what Malinowski intended was to construe the needs of a group as a set of conditions which are individually necessary and jointly sufficient for its survival.[37]

However, this correction of a minor logical flaw does not remedy a more serious defect of Malinowski's definition, which lies in the deceptive appearance of clarity of the phrase "survival of group and organism." In reference to a biological organism, the term 'survival' has a fairly clear meaning, though even here, there is need for further clarification. For when we speak of biological needs or requirements—e.g., the minimum daily requirements, for human adults, of various vitamins and minerals—we construe these, not as conditions of just the barest survival but as conditions of persistence in, or return to, a "normal," or "healthy" state, or to a state in which the system is a "properly functioning whole." For the sake of objective testability of functionalist hypotheses, it is essential, therefore, that definitions of needs or functional prerequisites be supplemented by reasonably clear and objectively applicable criteria of what is to be considered a healthy state or a normal working order of the systems under consideration; and that the vague and sweeping notion of survival then be construed in the relativized sense of survival in a healthy state as specified. Otherwise, there is definite danger that different investigators will use the concept of functional prerequisite—and hence also that of function—in different ways, and with valuational overtones corresponding to their diverse conceptions of what are the most "essential" characteristics of "genuine" survival for a system of the kind under consideration.

Functional analyses in psychology, sociology, and anthropology are even more urgently in need of objective empirical criteria of the kind here referred to; for the characterization of needs as necessary conditions of psychological or emotional survival for an individual, or of survival of a group is so vague as to permit, and indeed invite, quite diverse subjective interpretations.

Some authors characterize the concept of functional prerequisite or the concept of function without making use of the term 'survival' with its misleading appearance of clarity. Merton, for example, states: "*Functions* are those observed consequences which make for the adaptation or adjustment of a given system; and *dysfunctions,* those observed consequences which lessen the adaptation or adjustment of the system." [38] And Radcliffe-Brown characterizes the function of an item as its contribution to the maintenance of a certain kind of unity of a social system, "which we may speak of as a functional unity. We may define it as a condition in which all parts of the social system work together with a sufficient degree of harmony or internal consistency, i.e., without producing persistent conflicts which can neither be resolved nor regulated." [39] But like the definitions in terms of survival, these alternative characterizations, though suggestive, are far from giving clear empirical meanings to the key terms of functional analysis. The concepts of adjustment and adaptation, for example, require specification of some standard; otherwise, they have no definite meaning and are in danger of being used tautologically or else subjectively, with valuational overtones.

Tautological use could be based on construing *any* response of a given system as an adjustment, in which case it becomes a trivial truth that any system will adjust itself to any set of circumstances. Some instances of functional analysis seem to come dangerously close to this procedure, as is illustrated by the following assertion: "Thus we are provided with an explanation of suicide and of numerous other apparently antibiological effects as so many forms of relief from intolerable suffering. Suicide does not have *adaptive* (survival) value but it does have *adjustive* value for the organism. Suicide is *functional* because it abolishes painful tension." [40]

Or consider Merton's formulation of one of the assumptions of functional analysis: ". . . when *the net balance of the aggregate of consequences* of an existing social structure is clearly dysfunctional, there develops a strong and insistent pressure for change." [41] In the absence of clear empirical criteria of adaptation and thus of dysfunction, it is possible to treat this formulation as a covert tautology and thus to render it immune to empirical disconfirmation. Merton is quite aware of such danger: in another context he remarks that the notion of functional requirements of a given system "remains one of the cloudiest and empirically most debatable concepts in functional theory. As utilized by sociologists, the concept of functional requirement tends to be tautological or *ex post facto*." [42] Similar warnings against tautological use and against *ad hoc* generalizations about functional prerequisites have been voiced by other writers, such as Malinowski [43] and Parsons. [44]

On the other hand, in the absence of empirical criteria of adjustment or adaptation, there is also the danger of each investigator's projecting into those concepts (and thus also into the concept of function) his own ethical standards of what would constitute a "proper" or "good" adjustment of a given system—a danger which has been pointed out very clearly by Levy. [45] This procedure would obviously deprive functionalist hypotheses of the status of precise objectively testable scientific assertions. And, as Merton notes, "If theory is to be productive, it must be sufficiently *precise* to be *determinate*. Precision is an integral element of the criterion of *testability*." [46]

It is essential, then, for functional analysis as a scientific procedure that its key concepts be explicitly construed as relative to some standard of survival or adjustment. This standard has to be specified for each functional analysis, and it will usually vary from case to case. In the functional study of a given system s, the standard would be indicated by specifying a certain class or range R of possible states of s, with the understanding that s was to be considered as "surviving in proper working order," or as "adjusting properly under changing conditions" just in case s remained in, or upon disturbance returned to, some state within the range R. A need, or functional requirement, of system s relative to R is then a necessary condition for the system's remaining in, or returning to, a state in R; and the function, relative to R, of an item i in s consists in i's effecting the satisfaction of some such functional requirement.

In the field of biology, Sommerhoff's analysis of adaptation, appropriateness, and related concepts, is an excellent illustration of a formal study in which the relativization of the central functionalist concepts is entirely explicit.[47] The need of such relativization is made clear also by Nagel, who points out that "the claim that a given change is functional or dysfunctional must be understood as being relative to a specified G (or sets of G's)" [48] where the G's are traits whose preservation serves as the defining standard of adjustment or survival for the system under study. In sociology, Levy's analysis of the structure of society [49] clearly construes the functionalist key concepts as relative in the sense just outlined.

Only if the key concepts of functional analysis are thus relativized can hypotheses involving them have the status of determinate and objectively testable assumptions or assertions; only then can those hypotheses enter significantly into arguments such as those schematized in (4.1), (4.3), and (5.1).

But, although such relativization may give definite empirical content to the functionalist hypotheses that serve as premises or conclusions in those arguments, it leaves the explanatory and predictive import of the latter as limited as we found it in sections 4 and 5; for our verdict on the logical force of those arguments depended solely on their formal structure and not on the meanings of their premises and conclusions.

It remains true, therefore, even for a properly relativized version of functional analysis, that its explanatory force is rather limited; in particular, it does not provide an explanation of why a particular item i rather than some functional equivalent of it occurs in system s. And the predictive significance of functional analysis is practically nil—except in those cases where suitable hypotheses of self-regulation can be established. Such a hypothesis would be to the effect that within a specified range C of circumstances, a given system s (or: any system of a certain kind S, of which s is an instance) is self-regulating relative to a specified range R of states; i.e., after a disturbance which moves s into a state outside R, but which does not shift the internal and external circumstances of s out of the specified range C, the system s will return to a state in R. A system satisfying a hypothesis of this kind might be called *self-regulating with respect to R*.

Biological systems offer many illustrations of such self-regulation. For example, we mentioned earlier the regenerative ability of a hydra. Consider the case, then, where a more or less large segment of the animal is removed and the rest grows into a complete hydra again. The class R here consists of those states in which the hydra is complete; the characterization of range C would have to include (i) a specification of the temperature and the chemical composition of the water in which a hydra will perform its regenerative feat (clearly, this will not be just one unique composition, but a class of different ones: the concentrations of various salts, for example, will each be allowed to take some value within a specified, and perhaps narrow, range; the same will hold of the temperature of the water); and (ii) a statement as to the kind and size of segment that may be removed without preventing regeneration.

It will no doubt be one of the most important tasks of functional analysis in psychology and the social sciences to ascertain to what extent such phenomena of self-regulation can be found, and clearly represented by laws of self-regulation, in these fields.

6. FUNCTIONAL ANALYSIS AND TELEOLOGY

Whatever specific laws might be discovered by research along these lines, the kind of explanation and prediction made possible by them does not differ in its logical character from that of the physical sciences.

It is quite true that hypotheses of self-regulation, which would be characteristic results of successful functionalist research, seem to have a teleological character, asserting, as they do, that within specified conditions systems of some particular kind will tend toward a state within the class R, which thus assumes the appearance of a final cause determining the behavior of the system.

But, first of all, it would be simply untenable to say of a system s which is self-regulating with respect to R that the future event of its return to (a state in) R is a "final cause" which determines its present behavior. For even if s is self-regulating with respect to R and if it has been shifted into a state outside R, the future event of its return to R may never come about: in the process of its return toward R, s may be exposed to further disturbances, which may fall outside the permissible range C and lead to the destruction of s. For example, in a hydra that has just had a tentacle removed, certain regenerative processes will promptly set in; but these cannot be explained teleologically by reference to a final cause consisting in the future event of the hydra being complete again. For that event may never actually come about since in the process of regeneration, and before its completion, the hydra may suffer new, and irreparably severe, damage, and may die. Thus, what accounts for the present changes of a self-regulating system *s* is not the "future event" of *s* being in *R,* but rather the *present disposition* of *s* to return to *R;* and it is this disposition that is expressed by the hypothesis of self-regulation governing the system *s.*

Whatever teleological character may be attributed to a functionalist explanation or prediction invoking (properly relativized) hypotheses of self-regulation lies merely in the circumstance that such hypotheses assert a tendency of certain systems to maintain, or return to, a certain kind of state. But such laws attributing, as it were, a characteristic goal-directed behavior to systems of specified kinds are by no means alien to physics and chemistry. On the contrary, it is these latter fields which provide the most adequately understood instances of self-regulating systems and corresponding laws. For example, a liquid in a vessel will return to a state of equilibrium, with its surface horizontal, after a mechanical disturbance; an elastic band, after being stretched (within certain limits), will return to its original shape when it is released. Various systems controlled by negative feedback devices, such as a steam engine whose speed is regulated by a governor, or a homing torpedo, or a plane guided by an automatic pilot, show, within specifiable limits, self-regulation with respect to some particular class of states.

In all of these cases, the laws of self-regulation exhibited by the systems in question are capable of explanation by subsumption under general laws of a more obviously causal form. But this is not even essential, for the laws of self-regulation themselves are causal in the broad sense of asserting, essentially, that for systems of a specified kind, any one of a class of different "initial states" (any one of the permissible states of disturbance) will lead to the same kind of final state. Indeed, as our earlier formulations show, functionalist hypotheses, including those of self-regulation, can be expressed without the use of any teleological phraseology at all.[50]

There are, then, no systematic grounds for attributing to functional analysis a character *sui generis* not found in the hypotheses and theories of the natural sciences and in the explanations and predictions based on them. Yet, psychologically, the idea of function often remains closely associated with that of purpose, and some functionalist writing has no doubt encouraged this association, by using a phraseology which attributes to the self-regulatory behavior of a given system practically the character of a purposeful action. For example, Freud, in stating his theory of the relation of neurotic symptoms to anxiety, uses strongly teleological language, as when he says that "the symptoms are created in order to remove or rescue the ego from the situation of danger"; [51] the quotations given in section 2 provide further illustrations. Some instructive examples of sociological and anthropological writings which confound the concepts of function and purpose are listed by Merton, who is very explicit and emphatic in rejecting this practice.[52]

It seems likely that precisely this psychological association of the concept of function with that of purpose, though systematically unwarranted, accounts to a large extent for the appeal and the apparent plausibility of functional analysis as a mode of explanation; for it seems to enable us to "understand" self-regulatory phenomena of all kinds in terms of purposes or motives, in much the same way in which we "understand" our own purposive behavior and that of others. Now, explanation by reference to motives, objectives, or the like may be perfectly legitimate in the case of purposive behavior and its effects. An explanation of this kind would be causal in character, listing among the causal antecedents of the given action, or of its outcome, certain purposes or motives on the part of the agent, as well as his beliefs as to the best means available to him for attaining his objectives. This kind of information about purposes and beliefs might even serve as a starting point in explaining a self-regulatory feature in a human artifact. For example, in an attempt to account for the presence of the governor in a steam engine, it may be quite reasonable to refer to the purpose its inventor intended it to serve, to his beliefs concerning matters of physics, and to the technological facilities available to him. Such an account, it should be noted, might conceivably give a probabilistic explanation for the presence of the governor, but it would not explain why it functioned as a speed-regulating safety device: to explain this latter fact, we would have to refer to the construction of the machine and to the laws of physics, not to the intentions and beliefs of the designer. (An explanation by reference to motives and beliefs can be given as well for certain items which do not, in fact, function as intended; e.g., some superstitious practices, unsuccessful flying machines, or ineffective economic policies, etc.). Furthermore—and this is the crucial point in our context—for most of the self-regulatory phenomena that come within the purview of functional analysis, the attribution of purposes is an illegitimate transfer of the concept of purpose from its domain of significant applicability to a much wider domain, where it is devoid of objective empirical import. In the context of purposive behavior of individuals or groups, there are various methods of testing whether the assumed motives or purposes are indeed present in a given situation; interviewing the agent in question might be one rather direct way, and there are various alternative "operational" procedures of a more indirect character. Hence, explanatory hypotheses in terms of purposes are here capable of reasonably objective test. But such empirical criteria for purposes and motives are lacking in other cases of self-regulating systems, and the attribution of purposes to them has therefore no scientific meaning. Yet, it tends to encourage the illusion that a profound type of understanding is achieved, that we gain an insight into the nature of these processes by likening them to a type of behavior with which we are thoroughly familiar from daily experience. Consider, for example, the law of "adaptation to an obvious end" set forth by the sociologist L. Gumplowicz with the claim that it holds both in the natural and the social domains. For the latter, it asserts that "every social growth, every social entity, serves a definite end, however much its worth and morality may be questioned. For the universal law of adaptation signifies simply that no expenditure of effort, no change of condition, is purposeless on any domain of phenomena. Hence, the inherent reasonableness of all social facts and conditions must be conceded." [53] The suggestion is rather strong here that the alleged law enables us to understand social dynamics in close analogy to purposive behavior aimed at the achievement of some end. Yet the purported law is completely devoid of empirical meaning since no empirical interpretation has been given to such key terms as 'end,' 'purposeless,' and 'inherent reasonableness' for the contexts to which it is applied. The "law" asserts nothing whatever, therefore, and cannot possibly explain any social—or other—phenomena.

Gumplowicz's book antedates the writings of Malinowski and other leading functionalists by several decades, and certainly these more recent writers have been more cautious and sophisticated in stating their ideas. Yet, there are certain quite central assertions in the newer functionalist literature which are definitely reminiscent of Gumplowicz's formulation in that they suggest an understanding of functional phenomena in the image of deliberate purposive behavior or of systems working in accordance with a preconceived design. The following statements might illustrate this point: "[Culture] is a system of objects, activities, and attitudes in which every part exists as a means to an end," [54] and "The functional view of culture insists therefore upon the principle that in every type of civilization, every custom, material object, idea and belief fulfills some vital function, has some task to accomplish, represents an indispensable part within a working whole." [55] These statements express what Merton, in a critical discussion, calls the postulate of universal functionalism.[56] Merton qualifies this postulate as premature; [57] the discussion presented in the previous section shows that, in the absence of a clear empirical interpretation of the functionalist key terms, it is even less than that, namely, empirically vacuous. Yet, formulations of this kind may evoke

a sense of insight and understanding by likening sociocultural developments to purposive behavior and in this sense reducing them to phenomena with which we feel thoroughly familiar. But scientific explanation
and understanding are not simply a reduction to the familiar: otherwise, science would not seek to explain familiar phenomena at all; besides, the most significant advances in our scientific understanding of the
world are often achieved by means of new theories which, like quantum
theory, assume some quite unfamiliar kinds of objects or processes which
cannot be directly observed, and which sometimes are endowed with
strange and even seemingly paradoxical characteristics. A class of phenomena has been scientifically understood to the extent that they can be
fitted into a testable, and adequately confirmed, theory or a system of
laws; and the merits of functional analysis will eventually have to be
judged by its ability to lead to this kind of understanding.

7. THE HEURISTIC ROLE OF FUNCTIONAL ANALYSIS

The preceding considerations suggest that what is often called "functionalism" is best viewed, not as a body of doctrine or theory advancing
tremendously general principles such as the principle of universal functionalism, but rather as a program for research guided by certain heuristic
maxims or "working hypotheses." The idea of universal functionalism,
for example, which becomes untenable when formulated as a sweeping
empirical law or theoretical principle, might more profitably be construed as expressing a directive for research, namely to search for specific
self-regulatory aspects of social and other systems and to examine the
ways in which various traits of a system might contribute to its particular
mode of self-regulation. (A similar construal as heuristic maxims for
empirical research might be put upon all the "general axioms of functionalism" suggested by Malinowski, and considered by him as demonstrated by all the pertinent empirical evidence.[58])

In biology, for example, the contribution of the functionalist approach does not consist in the sweeping assertion that all traits of any
organism satisfy some need and thus serve some function; in this generality, the claim is apt to be either meaningless or covertly tautologous
or empirically false (depending on whether the concept of need is given
no clear empirical interpretation at all, or is handled in a tautologizing
fashion, or is given one definitive empirical interpretation). Instead,
functional studies in biology have been aimed at showing, for example,
how in different species, specific homeostatic and regenerative processes
contribute to the maintenance and development of the living organism;
and they have gone on (i) to examine more and more precisely the

nature and limits of those processes (this amounts basically to establishing various specific empirical hypotheses or laws of self-regulation), and (ii) to explore the underlying physiological or physicochemical mechanisms, and the laws governing them, in an effort to achieve a more thorough theoretical understanding of the phenomena at hand.[59] Similar trends exist in the study of functional aspects of psychological processes, including, for example, symptom formation in neurosis.[60]

Functional analysis in psychology and in the social sciences no less than in biology may thus be conceived, at least ideally, as a program of inquiry aimed at determining the respects and the degrees in which various systems are self-regulating in the sense here indicated. This conception clearly underlies, for example, Nagel's essay, "A Formalization of Functionalism," [61] a study which develops an analytic scheme inspired by, and similar to, Sommerhoff's formal analysis of self-regulation in biology [62] and uses it to exhibit and clarify the structure of functional analysis, especially in sociology and anthropology.

The functionalist mode of approach has proved highly illuminating, suggestive, and fruitful in many contexts. If the advantages it has to offer are to be reaped in full, it seems desirable and indeed necessary to pursue the investigation of specific functional relationships to the point where they can be expressed in terms of reasonably precise and objectively testable hypotheses. At least initially, these hypotheses will likely be of quite limited scope. But this would simply parallel the present situation in biology, where the kinds of self-regulation, and the uniformities they exhibit, vary from species to species. Eventually, such "empirical generalizations" of limited scope might provide a basis for a more general theory of self-regulating systems. To what extent these objectives can be reached cannot be decided in *a priori* fashion by logical analysis or philosophical reflection: the answer has to be found by intensive and rigorous scientific research.

NOTES

1. These terms are given preference over the more familiar words 'explicans' and 'explicandum,' in order to reserve the latter for use in the context of philosophical explication in the technical sense proposed by R. Carnap; see, for example, his *Logical Foundations of Probability* (Chicago: University of Chicago Press, 1950), secs. 1-3. The terms 'explanans' and 'explanandum' were introduced, for this reason, in an earlier article: Carl G. Hempel and P. Oppenheim, "Studies in the Logic of Explanation," *Philosophy of Science*, 15 (1948), pp. 135-75. Reprinted in part in H. Feigl and M. Brodbeck, eds., *Readings in the Philosophy of Science* (New York: Appleton-Century-Crofts, Inc., 1953). While that

article does not deal explicitly with inductive explanation, its first four sections contain various further considerations on deductive explanation that are relevant to the present study. For a careful critical examination of some points of detail discussed in the earlier article, such as especially the relation between explanation and prediction, see the essay by I. Scheffler, "Explanation, Prediction, and Abstraction," *The British Journal for the Philosophy of Science*, 7 (1957), pp. 293-309, which also contains some interesting comments bearing on functional analysis.

2. An explanation by means of laws which are causal in the technical sense of theoretical physics also has the form (2.1) of a deductive nomological explanation. In this case, the laws invoked must meet certain conditions as to mathematical form, and C_1, C_2, . . . , C_n express so-called boundary conditions. For a fuller account of the concepts of causal law and of causality as understood in theoretical physics, see, for example, H. Margenau, *The Nature of Physical Reality* (New York: McGraw-Hill Book Company, Inc., 1950), ch. 19; or Ph. Frank, *Philosophy of Science* (Englewood Cliffs, N.J.: Prentice-Hall, Inc., 1957), chs. 11, 12.

3. Some brief but lucid and stimulating comments on explanation by means of statistical laws will be found in S. E. Gluck, "Do Statistical Laws Have Explanatory Efficacy?" *Philosophy of Science,* 22 (1955), pp. 34-38. For a much fuller analysis of the logic of statistical inference, see R. B. Braithwaite, *Scientific Explanation* (Cambridge: Cambridge University Press, 1953), chs. V, VI, VII. For a study of the logic of inductive inference in general, Carnap's *Logical Foundations of Probability, op. cit.,* is of great importance.

4. In developing the characterization of functional analysis presented in this section, I have obtained much stimulation and information from the illuminating and richly documented essay "Manifest and Latent Functions" in R. K. Merton's book, *Social Theory and Social Structure* (Glencoe, Ill.: Free Press; revised and enlarged edition, 1957), pp. 19-84. Each of the passages from this work which is referred to in the present essay may also be found in the first edition (1949), on a page with approximately the same number.

5. For a fuller statement and further development of this point, see part I of the essay "A Formalization of Functionalism" in E. Nagel, *Logic Without Metaphysics* (Glencoe, Ill.: Free Press, 1957), pp. 247-83. Part I of this essay is a detailed analytical study of Merton's essay mentioned in Note 4, and thus is of special significance for the methodology of the social sciences.

6. S. Freud, *The Problem of Anxiety* (Transl. by H. A. Bunker. New York: Psychoanalytic Quarterly Press, and W. W. Norton & Company, Inc., 1936), p. 111.

7. *Ibid.,* p. 112.

8. Merton, *op. cit.,* p. 50.

9. *Ibid.,* p. 51. Merton defines manifest functions as those which are both intended and recognized, and latent functions as those which are neither intended nor recognized. But this characterization allows for functions which are neither manifest nor latent; e.g., those which are recognized

though not intended. It would seem to be more in keeping with Merton's intentions, therefore, to base the distinction simply on whether or not the stabilizing effect of the given item was deliberately sought.

10. *Ibid.,* pp. 64-65.

11. A. R. Radcliffe-Brown, *Structure and Function in Primitive Society* (London: Cohen and West Ltd., 1952), p. 145.

12. B. Malinowski, *Magic, Science and Religion, and Other Essays* (Garden City, N.Y.: Doubleday Anchor Books, 1954), p. 90. For an illuminating comparison of Malinowski's views on the functions of magic and religion with those advanced by Radcliffe-Brown, see G. C. Homans, *The Human Group* (New York: Harcourt, Brace & Company, Inc., 1950), pp. 321 ff. (Note also Homan's general comments on "the functional theory," *ibid.,* pp. 268-72.) This issue and other aspects of functional analysis in anthropology are critically examined in the following article, which confronts some specific applications of the method with programmatic declarations by its proponents: Leon J. Goldstein, "The Logic of Explanation in Malinowskian Anthropology," *Philosophy of Science,* 24 (1957), pp. 156-66.

13. B. Malinowski, "Anthropology," *Encyclopaedia Britannica,* First Supplementary volume (London and New York: The Encyclopaedia Britannica, Inc., 1926), p. 132.

14. *Ibid.,* p. 139.

15. B. Malinowski, *A Scientific Theory of Culture, and Other Essays* (Chapel Hill: University of North Carolina Press, 1944), p. 174.

16. Radcliffe-Brown, *op. cit.,* p. 186.

17. Malinowski, at one place in his writings, endorses a pronouncement which might appear to be at variance with this conclusion: "Description cannot be separated from explanation, since in the words of a great physicist, 'explanation is nothing but condensed description.'" (Malinowski, "Anthropology," *op. cit.,* p. 132.) He seems to be referring here to the views of Ernst Mach or of Pierre Duhem, who took a similar position on this point. Mach conceived the basic objective of science as the brief and economic description of recurrent phenomena and considered laws as a highly efficient way of compressing, as it were, the description of an infinitude of potential particular occurrences into a simple and compact formula. But, thus understood, the statement approvingly quoted by Malinowski is, of course, entirely compatible with our point about the relevance of laws for functional explanation.

Besides, a law can be called a description only in a Pickwickian sense. For even so simple a generalization as "All vertebrates have hearts" does not describe any particular individual, such as Rin-Tin-Tin, as being a vertebrate and having a heart; rather, it asserts of Rin-Tin-Tin—and of any other object, whether vertebrate or not—that *if* it is a vertebrate *then* it has a heart. Thus, the generalization has the import of an indefinite set of conditional statements about particular objects. In addition, a law might be said to imply statements about "potential events" which never actually take place. The gas law, for example, implies that if a given body of gas were to be heated under constant pressure at time *t,* its volume would increase. But if in fact the gas is not heated at *t* this statement can hardly be said to be a description of any particular event.

18. Malinowski, "Anthropology," *op. cit.*, p. 136.

19. Malinowski, *Magic, Science and Religion, and Other Essays, op. cit.*, p. 90. (Note the explanatory claim implicit in the use of the word "hence.")

20. B. Malinowski, "Culture," *Encyclopedia of the Social Sciences,* IV (New York: The Macmillan Company, 1931), p. 626.

21. Merton, *op. cit.*, p. 34. Cf. also T. Parsons, *Essays in Sociological Theory, Pure and Applied* (Glencoe, Ill.: Free Press, 1949), p. 58. For an interesting recent attempt to establish the existence of functional alternatives in a specific case, see R. D. Schwartz, "Functional alternatives to inequality," *American Sociological Review,* 20 (1955), pp. 424-30.

22. See G. G. Simpson, *The Meaning of Evolution* (New Haven: Yale University Press, 1949), pp. 164 ff., 190, 342-43; and G. G. Simpson, C. S. Pittendrigh, L. H. Tiffany, *Life* (New York: Harcourt, Brace & Company, Inc., 1957), p. 437.

23. Malinowski, *A Scientific Theory of Culture, and Other Essays, op. cit.*, p. 38.

24. E. M. Sait, "Machine, Political," *Encyclopedia of the Social Sciences,* IX (New York: The Macmillan Company, 1933), p. 659. (Italics supplied.)

25. Merton, *op. cit.*, p. 76. (Italics supplied.)

26. Merton, *op. cit.*, p. 73. (Italics the author's.)

27. Radcliffe-Brown, *op. cit.*, p. 183.

28. Malinowski, *A Scientific Theory of Culture, and Other Essays, op. cit.*, p. 67.

29. Henry A. Murray and Clyde Kluckhohn, "Outline of a Conception of Personality," in Clyde Kluckhohn and Henry A. Murray, eds., *Personality in Nature, Society, and Culture* (New York: Knopf, 1950), pp. 3-32; quotation from p. 7; italics the authors'.

30. Malinowski, *A Scientific Theory of Culture, and Other Essays, op. cit.*, p. 94.

31. In accordance with a practice followed widely in contemporary logic, we will understand by terms certain kinds of words or other linguistic expressions, and we will say that a term expresses or signifies a concept. For example, we will say that the term 'need' signifies the concept of need. As this illustration shows, we refer to, or mention, a linguistic expression by using a name for it which is formed by simply enclosing the expression in single quotes.

32. A general discussion of the nature and significance of "operational" criteria of application for the terms used in empirical science, and references to further literature on the subject, may be found in C. G. Hempel, *Fundamentals of Concept Formation in Empirical Science* (University of Chicago Press, 1952), secs. 5-8; and in the symposium papers on the present state of operationalism by G. Bergmann, P. W. Bridgman, A. Grunbaum, C. G. Hempel, R. B. Lindsay, H. Margenau, and R. J. Seeger, which form

ch. II of Philipp G. Frank, ed., *The Validation of Scientific Theories* (Boston: The Beacon Press, 1956).

33. Merton, *op. cit.*, p. 52.

34. Malinowski, *A Scientific Theory of Culture, and Other Essays, op. cit.*, p. 159.

35. Malinowski, *ibid.*, p. 90.

36. Malinowski, *ibid.*, p. 172; see also *ibid.*, pp. 91 ff.

37. In some of his statements Malinowski discards, by implication, even the notion of function as satisfaction of a condition that is at least *necessary* for the survival of group or organism. For example, in the same essay containing the two passages just quoted in the text, Malinowski comments as follows on the function of some complex cultural achievements: "Take the airplane, the submarine, or the steam engine. Obviously, man does not need to fly, nor yet to keep company with fishes, and move about within a medium for which he is neither anatomically adjusted nor physiologically prepared. In defining, therefore, the function of any of those contrivances, we can not predicate the true course of their appearance in any terms of metaphysical necessity." (*Ibid.*, pp. 118-19.)

38. Merton, *op. cit.*, p. 51. (Italics the author's.)

39. Radcliffe-Brown, *op. cit.*, p. 181.

40. Murray and Kluckhohn, *op. cit.*, p. 15. (Italics the authors'.)

41. Merton, *op. cit.*, p. 40.

42. Merton, *op. cit.*, p. 52.

43. See, for example, Malinowski, *A Scientific Theory of Culture, and Other Essays, op. cit.*, pp. 169-70; but also compare this with pp. 118-19 of the same work.

44. See, for example, T. Parsons, *The Social System* (Glencoe, Ill.: Free Press, 1951), p. 29, fn. 4.

45. Marion J. Levy, Jr., *The Structure of Society* (Princeton: Princeton University Press, 1952), pp. 76 ff.

46. R. K. Merton, "The Bearing of Sociological Theory on Empirical Research" in Merton, *Social Theory and Social Structure, op. cit.*, pp. 85-101; quotation from p. 98. (Italics the author's.)

47. See G. Sommerhoff, *Analytical Biology* (New York: Oxford University Press, 1950).

48. Nagel, "A Formalization of Functionalism," *op. cit.*, p. 269. See also the concluding paragraph of the same essay (pp. 282-83).

49. Levy speaks of eufunction and dysfunction of a unit (i.e., a system) and characterizes these concepts as relative to "the unit as defined." He points out that this relativization is necessary "because it is to the definition of the unit that one must turn to determine whether or not 'adaptation or adjustment' making for the persistence or lack of persistence of the unit is taking place." (Levy, *ibid.*, pp. 77-78.)

50. For illuminating discussions of further issues concerning "teleological explanation," especially with respect to self-regulating systems, see R. B. Braithwaite, *Scientific Explanation* (Cambridge: Cambridge University Press, 1953), ch. X; and E. Nagel, "Teleological Explanation and Teleological Systems" in S. Ratner, ed., *Vision and Action: Essays in Honor of Horace Kallen on His Seventieth Birthday* (New Brunswick, N.J.: Rutgers University Press, 1953); reprinted in H. Feigl and M. Brodbeck, eds., *Readings in the Philosophy of Science* (New York: Appleton-Century-Crofts, Inc., 1953).

51. Freud, *op. cit.*, p. 112.

52. Merton, "Manifest and Latent Functions," *op. cit.*, pp. 23-25, 60 ff.

53. L. Gumplowicz, *The Outlines of Sociology;* translated by F. W. Moore (Philadelphia: American Academy of Political and Social Science, 1899), pp. 79-80.

54. Malinowski, *A Scientific Theory of Culture, and Other Essays, op. cit.*, p. 150.

55. Malinowski, "Anthropology," *op. cit.*, p. 133.

56. Merton, "Manifest and Latent Functions," *op. cit.*, pp. 30 ff.

57. *Ibid.*, p. 31.

58. Malinowski, *A Scientific Theory of Culture, and Other Essays, op. cit.*, p. 150.

59. An illuminating general account of this kind of approach to homeostatic processes in the human body will be found in Walter B. Cannon, *The Wisdom of the Body* (New York: W. W. Norton & Company, Inc.; revised edition 1939).

60. See, for example, J. Dollard and N. E. Miller, *Personality and Psychotherapy* (New York: McGraw-Hill Book Company, Inc., 1950), ch. XI, "How symptoms are learned," and note particularly pp. 165-66.

61. Nagel, "A Formalization of Functionalism," *op. cit.* See also the more general discussion of functional analysis included in Nagel's paper, "Concept and Theory Formation in the Social Sciences," in *Science, Language, and Human Rights;* American Philosophical Association, Eastern Division, Volume 1 (Philadelphia: University of Pennsylvania Press, 1952), pp. 43-64. Reprinted in J. L. Jarrett and S. M. McMurrin, eds., *Contemporary Philosophy* (New York: Henry Holt & Co., Inc., 1954).

62. Sommerhoff, *op. cit.*

VI

MODELS IN
SOCIAL SCIENCE

10

Models and Theories in Social Psychology

F. H. GEORGE
Bristol University

1. SOCIAL PSYCHOLOGY

This article will outline some methods which might be applied in the future by social psychologists, sociologists, and all other people working on social problems from a scientific point of view.

It will be assumed that the social sciences in general are only partially scientific as yet, and that the explicit development of scientific methods on their behalf is a necessity—even an urgent necessity. There will be no explicit discussion of the present state of social psychology, but we shall say a few introductory words about it.

The first question we might ask is whether or not we can say that the problems of social psychology are essentially the same as those of general psychology, and whether an understanding of the individual is a prior necessity to an understanding of a social group. Are there different laws for the group and for the individual? The answer is that we shall conceive of the group as a collection of individuals who interact with each other in specifiable ways. This implies that prediction of the individual's behavior means prediction of his behavior *in any group*. The group itself can of course always be given a statistical specification and we can thus talk of group characteristics. We shall here only consider individuals and their interaction with respect to each other.

Nothing will be attempted, in this article, that bears on the problem

311

of carrying out measurements or observations on either individuals or groups. This matter, although quite vital, would take us too far from our general purpose, which is to outline some scientific models and theories, as well as methods, that should be of general use to the social psychologist.

The mode of discussion will be to summarize in outline a whole set of interrelated methods of approach without discussing any one in minute detail. This is because many of the methods have already been described elsewhere, and it is their general relation to each other and their application that seem to be the most important things to emphasize.

2. PSYCHOLOGICAL THEORY

The psychologist is in a position of having to construct theories of behavior—learning, perception, etc.—that satisfy some logical standards, and of having to incorporate our existing knowledge of behavior, neurology, and what is intuitively acceptable in those theories. Indeed the whole process of producing a theory of behavior requires the production of effective procedures for determining the application of the theory at a variety of different descriptive levels.

An essential point that needs to be mentioned is that any particular scientist must go through the well-known processes of making observations, generalizing upon those observations, and thus producing theories. Now it is of no special consequence whether what is being described, constructed, or reconstructed is mathematics, a science such as psychology, or a language. Whatever is under discussion or investigation at any particular time is what we will call the object language, and we must discuss it in some *other language*—a metalanguage. This metalanguage may be itself an object language for some other investigation, but this is of no importance to the investigator at the time. Of course, we are also concerned with the construction of object languages, and these can be represented as models of whatever the nonlinguistic entities are that need to be modeled.

Such scientists are forced to start from assumptions, which represent their prior agreements with themselves, or others, for the sake of a particular investigation. The assumptions are represented by only partially analyzed statements. The notion of partially analyzed terms is secondary to this, and will represent an internal analysis of sentences into their parts. Language, for that is what a scientific theory is part of, has the sentence as its natural unit. The use of models is the use of relational structures, such as the syntax of the propositional calculus or any systematic set of marks on paper. Indeed any structure such as a lattice, blueprint, or map is capable of being used as a model for a scientific theory, but here we make the essential distinction, also made by Braithwaite [1] and others, between a model for a theory and the theory itself. The model, it should be noticed, will be *explained* in the theory; to speak metaphorically, a model is a skeleton and the theory is the complete organism, including the flesh. The theory is to be couched in the natural or symbolic *language* that is used for descriptive purposes by the particular investigators, and we shall call this the 'theory language.'

It may be thought necessary to add other pragmatic devices to any scientific explanation in the form of ostensive rules or definitions, operational definitions, and the like. These may serve to sharpen the meaning of the language used for the theory, or the metatheory. For even here we soon find that very few and very limited investigations only can be restricted to one clear-cut theory language. We must therefore be prepared to think in interconnected chains of such theory languages, which will repeat different facts of nature (however this phrase is interpreted) on different levels of description and in different ways. It is in a sense the particular investigation that is the scientist's working unit. Thus, it is that the whole of science or any of its divisions can be reconstructed in any number of ways.

For the psychologist, working beyond the confines of a narrow Watsonian Behaviorism and yet determined to avoid that which cannot be treated on a strictly public and observable basis, the problem is to find more and more models, more and more interpretations and theory languages for the coherent description of his vast collection of empirical facts. When he has found them, he must, of course, know how to use them and be aware of their limitations and difficulties of application.

The uncertainty about the correct progress of theory and explanation in science has sometimes led to *models* being used *descriptively,* whereas in fact what needs to be developed is a model *with* a theory that has a controlled vagueness—that of the surplus meaning of the theoretical terms. This lack of specificity, this possibility of many interpretations of the same model, is necessary to the fruitfulness of science.

The psychologist will be concerned with the following procedures, listed roughly in the order they occur:

1. Reading the existing information as stated in textbooks and journals on a branch of the subject that we will call A. The journals must be tested for consistency (internally and externally). Some may be found wanting in certain respects either in generality or consistency.

2. The stating of simple observational facts collectively with inductive generalizations originally called A, now A^1 (if different from A). This requires a language, the foundations of which are to be agreed upon—not necessarily the same as used in 1, but necessarily capable of being interpretable at some level in the same language as 1, or, alternatively, 1 being interpretable in 2.

3. The generalizations are to be based inductively on a certain number of instances and always subject to revision.

4. A model for *A*, essentially deductive, which is utilized in terms of the inductive parts of the theory. It may be pictorial, symbolic, or anything at all as long as it is capable of interpretation in terms of the language of either 1 or 2.

5. If we merely use a descriptive language for the generalizations, we must be prepared to show the nature of the underlying structural model, since a description of empirical facts is really a description of complex structural relations (a model). This process of showing the structure of the model is called the *formalizing* of the theory.

6. This whole process will be sufficient both for general *and* social psychology, although of course social studies may demand the acquisition of indices and coefficients not always needed for the individual.

7. This process goes on without end, and with continual checking, criticism, and analysis, which may take any part or the whole of science as the object of its investigation. The process is essentially, to use Kantor's [2] term, 'interbehavioral.'

So much then for the initial complications, wherein theories are particular (or particularized) languages, or parts of independently formulated languages, ultimately capable of interpretation in natural language (or a slightly more rigorous equivalent). Thus, if we use the word 'language' for the interpretation of a system of marks, we are already committed to a certain theoretical structure. This is why a scientific theory and a language are interdependent and *may* be one.

3. MODELS

We are mainly concerned in this article with logic, and its equivalents, called logical nets, as models of behavior. We do not here intend to describe in any detail what the possible range of models that can be used in the processes of scientific theory construction is. The most obvious ones that have already been used are those of the syntax of the propositional calculus, the functional calculus, and the various existing calculi whose variables are intended to be given an interpretation as propositions and functions, and have thus been widely used by philosophers and mathematicians. These are open to use in science and will, if the logistic foundation of mathematics can be believed, lead to the whole of mathematics. Mathematical structures—lattices, abstract algebras, and so on—may also serve as such models. From the viewpoint of cybernetics, physical systems may also be constructed as models; any symbolic model can be regarded as a physical system and produced in hardware.

The first model that we shall outline is the principal one that we shall be discussing in this paper, although it will be seen to be closely related to other models and theories that we shall mention. The model we have in mind is that of a Finite Automaton, which for practical purposes is an idealized organism.

Pitts and McCulloch [3] suggested the basis of what they themselves called neural nets, and showed that systems of nets very like the nervous system could be described with complete accuracy in logical terms. Our aim here will not be neurological, but rather will be to seek, using the same model as can be used for neurology, to develop a theory that has social usefulness, indeed usefulness, precision, and the possibility of predictability at every level. First, though, we shall turn to a brief description of the nets.

The logical nets which we wish to describe are isomorphic with a part of logic, that part called the propositional calculus coupled with a part of the lower functional calculus, all suffixed for time. This means that there is a relationship between the nets that can be drawn and the formulas that can be written which is closely analogous to the relationship between, say, geometry and algebra. We shall try and indicate very briefly how both these forms of description operate and then allow ourselves the liberty of talking in general terms about these nets, leaving the translation into diagrammatic or logical form to those who actually need the precise details. There are straightforward rules for the translations.

A logical net is composed of elements, drawn as circles, and there are three kinds of elements that may occur. The three types of element have loose input fibres, loose output fibres, or neither loose input nor output fibres, where by 'loose,' we mean 'unconnected' to another element. These elements are called *sensory, motor,* and *inner* elements, respectively.

The fibres carry pulses from element to element. These pulses will, subject to certain conditions, fire the elements when they travel down an element's input. The element itself has a real number associated with it, called a threshold. This threshold number gives the excess of excitatory over inhibitory inputs that needs to be active at any instant in order to *fire* the element, where by 'firing the element' we mean the transmission of an impulse on the output of that element.

The above statement makes clear that there are both inhibitory and excitatory fibres, or rather fibres with excitatory and inhibitory endings on elements. These are represented in our diagrams by closed-in trangles and open circles respectively.

Let us consider the simple case of an element with two excitatory input fibres and the usual single output fibre, with threshold number 2.

Time, we should note, is assumed to be in equal intervals and all elements take a single instant to fire. Then the condition for the output c
to fire is that there should be impulses simultaneously in inputs a and b.

$$c_t \equiv a_{t-1} \cdot b_{t-1} \qquad\qquad (1)$$

This is pictured in Figure 1.

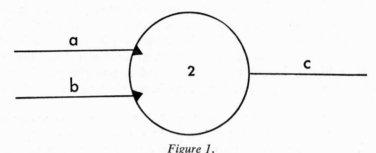

Figure 1.

Shows one element of threshold 2, two excitatory input fibres a and b, and
one output fibre c. c fires if, and only if, a and b fire together.

If the threshold number in Figure 1 had been 1 instead of 2, then
the condition for firing would have been

$$c_t \equiv a_{t-1} \vee b_{t-1} \qquad\qquad (2)$$

and it should be noted that these two simple nets of one element represent the logical operations of 'and' and 'or.'

Since the system depends on formal logic, before developing it
further we shall outline the logical systems to which it is related. There
is an obvious sense in which the propositional calculus and the functional
calculus are models of this net.

The Propositional Calculus

The propositional calculus is said to formalize the connectives *and,
or, not,* and *if . . . then.* There are many different systems and various
notations for the propositional calculus. The formulation (called P) which
we shall give is one of those used by Church.[4]

Thus P is composed of:

1. *Primitive Symbols:* [,], $\supset$, $\sim$., and an infinite list of propositional
variables for which the letters p, q, r, s, u, v, w (with or without numerical
subscripts) may be used.

2. *Formation Rules:*

A). Any variable alone is well-formed (w.f.).

B). If A and B are well-formed, so are $\sim A$ and $A \supset B$, where A and B are syntactical variables (variables in the syntax language) which designate formulas of the calculus (in this case $\overline{P}$).

3. *Rules of Inference:*

A). From A and $A \supset B$ to infer B (modus ponens).

B). From A to infer $S\,{}^{A'}_{B'}\,A\Big|$ where $S\,{}^{A'}_{B'}\,A\Big|$ means the result of substituting B' for A' in all its occurrences in A.

4. *Axioms:*

A). $p \supset [q \supset r] \supset \cdot p \supset q \supset \cdot p \supset r$

B). $p \supset \cdot q \supset p$

C). $\sim p \supset \sim q \supset \cdot q \supset p$

As a result of these axioms and the rules of inference we can define a theorem. A theorem is a w.f. formula (wff) which is obtainable from the axioms by a finite number of applications of the rules of inference. We could, it should be noted, reduce the list of rules of inference to only one by the omission of substitution and the use of an infinite list of axioms.

We are not, of course, concerned in this article with what might be called the technicalities of logic, so we shall not discuss the deduction theorem, regular formulas, completeness, duality, and independence. However, it is worth mentioning that the decision problem (an effective method for discovering whether any wff is a theorem) has been solved for the propositional calculus, and it says that every tautology is a theorem and every theorem is a tautology.[5] The decision-problem for the lower functional calculus, and therefore all higher functional calculi, has been shown to be unsolvable.[6] In the network model we shall generally use '$\equiv$' rather than '$\supset$,' where '$\equiv$' means 'if and only if' rather than the one-way relation 'if—then—.'

The Functional Calculi

To go from $\overline{P}$ to F^1 (the functional calculus of the first order) we need to add individual variables: $x, y, z, x_1, y_1, z_1, \ldots$ and functional variables $F^1, G^1, H^1, F^1_1, G^1_1, H^1_1, \ldots \ldots \ldots \ldots F^2, G^2, H^2, F^2_1,$ $G^2_1, H^2_1, \ldots F^n, G^n, H^n, F^n_1, G^n_1, \ldots \ldots$ there being singulary, binary, $\ldots$ n-ary functional variables.

The functional calculi permit the analysis of predicates and functions, and we shall wish to make assertions such as "for all $x, F^1(x)$" and "there exists at least one x, such that $F^1(x)$," and we shall thus need to add the Universal and Existential quantifiers respectively to our notation; they are (x) and $(\exists x)$ respectively which makes the above two sentences:

$$(x) \; F^1 \; (x) \; \text{and} \; (\exists x) \; F^1 \; (x) \; \textit{respectively.}$$

We shall need to construct new formation rules, rules of inference and axioms to meet the needs of our new primitive symbols, which will include as part of it the whole propositional calculus.

We can generalize further to the functional calculus of order 2 (F^2) (there are many different kinds of such functional calculi) and so on up to F^w.

We should now add a brief word on truth tables. We cannot discuss the Matrix method in detail but it is sufficient, for a two-valued interpretation where t and f are used (these may be thought of as 'truth' and 'falsehood' or 'firing' and 'not-firing' in the logical networks) if we ascribe t and f exhaustively to all the variables in our formulas. Thus to take a simple formula of $\overline{P}$ such as $\sim p$, its truth table is simply

p	$\sim p$
t	f
f	t

and $p \lor q$ (where $\lor$ may be read as "inclusive or," i.e., p or q or both) has truth table:

p	q	$p \lor q$
t	t	t
t	f	t
f	t	t
f	f	f

and then $p \supset q$ which can be translated as $\sim p \lor q$ has truth tables by combining the above two truth tables as follows:

p	q	$p \supset q$
t	t	t
t	f	f
f	t	t
f	f	t

For the functional calculus the truth conditions on the existential and universal operator demand that one or all values of X satisfy the respectively given formulas:

$$(\exists x) \; F^1 \; (x) \; \text{and} \; (x) \; F^1 \; (x).$$

It is easy to see how it may be possible to extend the notion of truth tables to 1, 2, ... , n truth-values. Thus a truth table for ∨ in a three-valued logic could be:

p	q	$p \lor q$
1	1	1
2	1	1
3	1	1
1	2	1
2	2	2
3	2	2
1	3	1
2	3	2
3	3	3

The network organs which can be developed from these brief beginnings are infinite in possibility. We are concerned here only with the development of simple organs which allow an interpretation for a molar theory of behavior.

Let us now extend our discussion of the relation of logic to logical nets. In the first place, the propositional calculus is an interpretation of the formal system stated above, where each of the variables is to be understood to represent a proposition and the ordinary intuitive meanings of *not, and, or,* and *material implication* are intended for the connectives. But, true to our earlier statement, this model may be given any consistent interpretation whatever and we are now in logical nets placing a different interpretation on the formal model; we are representing it in pictorial form and saying that these nets can be produced in hardware. Furthermore, we believe such nets can ultimately be interpreted as a nervous system and in any case have value as a model for the organism with interpretations at much cruder levels.

The same argument applies exactly to the lower functional calculus, although this is far less important to our purpose. The existential operator is used merely to describe the state of an element that has been fired at some previous time; a universal operator could express the fact that an element had been fired at all previous times in the life span of the automaton. Thus we could say for the existential operator that:

$$(\exists t)\, f\,(t)$$

says 'there exists a time t such that the element fired at t,' and usually we shall want to add the restriction 'and has not been stopped firing since.'

The relation between the existential and universal operator is given by:

$$(\exists t) \; f \; (t) = \; \sim \; (t) \; \sim f \; (t)$$

and merely describes the existence of some value satisfying a function; here the notation is simply the abstract notation of the formal model.

We should bear constantly in mind that we are constructing a model —one capable of being reconstructed in hardware—of an individual organism. To do this, we want to use no more than two-way switches, and we can use logical means to describe it completely. We shall not forget that our ultimate aim though is its use for social research, and not primarily for the description of individual behavior, although the two are assumed to be wholly interdependent.

We must now show a little more of the sort of Finite Automaton [7, 8, 9, 10] which we shall need for our predictive purposes.

First, we must add a loop element to the system already described. This is simply an element whose output fires into itself as an input and thus causes, or is capable of causing, a pulse to be retained in the element for as long as we need it; this is the basis of 'memory' in the automaton. Although we shall generally think of its store, or 'memory,' as in two parts—the temporary or high-speed part, and the permanent or slower and longer variety—this distinction is not perhaps necessary as far as the model is concerned.

We can conveniently divide the automaton into a control system (this has been referred to as a cognitive system or C-system for short) and a motivational system (M-system). We may also include an emotional system (E-system) which is closely related to motivation, apart from the permanent memory store referred to above. The classification of inputs and outputs involving perception and organized responses to stimulation will be regarded as being a part of the control system, as will be the high-speed memory store.

We shall start by describing the most important part: the C-system. There will be some obvious point in saying that the C-system is the name of that section of the model which will subsequently be interpreted as the control or cognitive system in the automaton.

The C-system includes the input classification system,[11, 12, 13] so we should start by summarizing this system.

Let the observable world be divided up into sets of sets, or properties, which represent the ultimate subdivisions of sensory discrimination. We shall think of these ultimate divisions as representing the colors, such as blue and red, and shapes, such as round and square. The divisions, of course, range over all perceivable properties. We shall not here worry about the fact that one can make one's description of the external world infinitely precise; we shall assume that a finite language is used for its description, thus implying a finite set of sets as the potential input. If we simply think of the different properties of the input ('primitive inputs' as we shall call them) as $a, b, \ldots n$ where n can be chosen as large as we please, then we shall want to be able to classify every possible combination of these primitive inputs $2, 3, \ldots n$ at a time. The vital thing is that we should be able to count all the possible combinations. Clearly for n primitive inputs there will be $2^n - 1$ combinations of them, if we exclude the null case where none of the inputs fires.

The use of the word 'fire' implies that we can now think of the n primitive inputs as sensory elements in a logical net. Figure 2 shows the principle on which the counting of the combinations is effected. It is shown there for the counting of a single combination $a \cdot b$ and it also counts the events $a \cdot \sim b$ and $\sim a \cdot b$ and does not count $\sim a \cdot \sim b$, although this could easily be done if it were thought necessary.

The simple example in Figure 2 also shows the counting procedure, where the length of the temporary memory, as exhibited by the loop elements, is a mere three occurrences of the conjunction of a and b and three for the disjunction of a and b, where the information retained does not distinguish between $a \cdot \sim b$ and $\sim a \cdot b$, although this distinction could be made if it were necessary, at the cost of extra loop elements.

Elsewhere, the counting mechanism has been written up in detailed and rigorous fashion,[8, 10] and it is easy to show the generality of the plan. Any number of inputs in any possible combination can be discriminated and counted by this system, without regard for economy[14] in the use of elements.

Clearly, if we restrict ourselves to the temporary memory of the loop elements, then we should have to face the fact that the number of loop elements available directly affects the nature of the probability that the net will work on.[9] Before we make this point a little clearer let us show the importance of the conditional probability on which the automaton will operate.

Let us suppose that a particular 'physical object,' using that term in the broadest sense that philosophers of perception would use it, is represented by a combination of primitive inputs, such as *abcdef*. We shall call this set A for short. Let us suppose that some number of physical objects $B, C, \ldots, N$ follow each other in that order. Then there are relations of an important kind that connect these physical objects.

The first important sort of relation that our system has to consider is the perceptual one, and this means, in the main, the problem of recognition. Given some properties $a, b, \ldots$ what is the probability of them belonging to some particular set A, say? This implies the use, by counting as above, of probabilities which suggest the appropriate set, of which

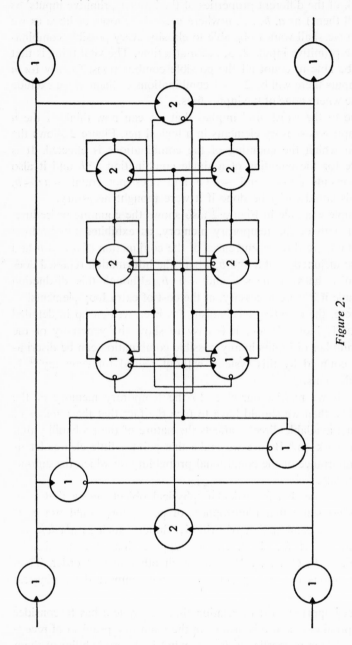

Figure 2.

Shows two input elements on the extreme left, three output fibres on the extreme right, and nine inner elements in between. The filled-in triangles within the circle of the elements imply excitatory fibre endings, and the open circles imply inhibitory fibre endings. The heavy dots indicate the contact of fibres. Where no heavy dot is shown, fibres do not have contact even when drawn as crossing each other.

what is sensed at any instant is a subset, possibly of course an improper subset.

We shall think of the operation of perceiving as a definite process of analyzing and classifying the environment, and as being spread over a finite time. It is an ordering process in which the probabilities vary as the information about the members of the set increases, wherever that is possible. The tachistoscope on one hand and the close analysis with ruler and calipers on the other represent the two extremes in this regard. Ideally, however, the process of perceiving—the word 'sensing' will be regarded by some as more appropriate for this seried operation [15]— will proceed in a series of probabilities

$$p_1, p_2, \ldots, p_n$$

tending to 1 in the limit: where ultimately each and every property of the finite set is identified. In practice, of course, this practically never happens, and we recognize objects (to think now of our interpretation) by small parts of them or at a glance, in a manner familiar to those who are acquainted with Gestalt theory. Roughly speaking, the more familiar the object, the more quickly we recognize it, and this is simply because a certain subset of properties *abcd,* say, is nearly always the subset of *A.*

Now the basis of this mechanism is clearly supplied by the counting and classification system described—the model of the cognitive system. In practice, however, recognition will also depend on *context.* Clearly, extra information will change the 'set' of the cognitive system, i.e., the probabilities accumulated on the basis of counting from the sensory classification system alone will have to be weighted by other relevant information. One will, of course, ask what 'relevant' means here and we must answer that the behavior of any organism at any instant depends on two factors: (1) the current state of the environment, both internal and external, and (2) the whole past of the organism, as stored in the memory store. Thus, we shall conceive of the counting as leading to responses on the basis of a count that is purely classificatory. They do *not* cause overt response, although naturally overt responses occur as a result of these classificatory responses *after* classification (perception) is complete.

4. THEORY OF PERCEPTION

The theory for the above model for perception is, strictly speaking, the interpretation placed on the model. In fact, the theory was formulated first and the model provided after.[15, 16] The theory of perception here stated is molar (psychological or in terms of the organism as a whole) and is itself subject to reinterpretation on the molecular (physiological) level. The theory of perception that the writer has proposed will now be briefly described. It will be seen that this is adequate as an interpretation of the net model, and is believed to be consistent with the observable and intuitively known facts of perception. We should again say that this model and theory are intentionally general and are not here discussed in detail, for lack of space, and because we are mainly concerned with illustrating method.

Perception is regarded as being the process of interpreting the messages that arise from the various sensory sources. This implies that we should regard the operations of sensing, perceiving, and believing, as on a sort of continuum in which the individual is not necessarily able to distinguish various points or intervals. There are difficulties over terminology that have themselves caused both philosophical and scientific puzzles, and these we shall not discuss here.[15]

The act of perceiving is represented as an organic process of selection and interpretation. The selection is partly due to the limits of application of the various senses and partly due to the 'set' of the individual, which means that the information in the store (representing his previous experience) will operate in conjunction with what is momentarily perceived.

Perceiving is thus the process of elaboration of sensory input, where there is a selection of all the potential stimuli in the environment and where there is a counter system (store) for each of the items perceived. The counting, it might be mentioned, may well be approximate, and certainly recoding of the store and other artifacts mainly concerned with the economy of storing information will also arise. The responses for this system are classificatory and are themselves stimuli to the overt response system. We have chosen to describe this in the terminology of *beliefs*. We say that perceptual beliefs are aroused as a result of the categorizing process that perception serves. These are ordinary beliefs, although distinguished from beliefs-in-general insofar as they are directly concerned with what is perceived, whereas other beliefs may be derived by other cognitive operations from what is already stored.

The word 'belief' is used here as a theoretical term from the behavioristic point of view, and it is hoped that it will be ultimately capable of being interpreted as the 'belief' that we refer to in ordinary language. This in itself raises philosophical problems that we shall not discuss here. To avoid confusion, let us think of *belief* [16] as a purely technical term which is closely related to a *hypothesis* [17] or an *expectancy*.[18, 19] We shall in fact use the word expectancy for an activated belief. Thus we shall want to say that there are various beliefs stored at various levels of generality and that at any instant an activating stimulus will arouse some of them, and those aroused are called *expectancies*. The arousal of beliefs, as well as the strengthening of beliefs by confirmation will depend on the motivational system as well as the perceptual and storage system.

5. MOTIVATION

Before completing our discussion of the control system, it would be convenient to summarize the role of motivation. The M-system at the model level, as exemplified by the logical network, is fairly simple.

The need for a motivational system in the model is clear if we want the system to be selective. Since our model is to be interpreted ultimately as an organism, it is certainly necessary that it should be selective. In the first place, selection must be on the basis of survival. Those activities which are bad for survival are omitted, and those which are good are included. Connected with this basic idea of two sets on which we are to map all our stimulus-response connections are many other basic motivators, such as food, drink, and sex. In the model these are built in, as they represent activities that are instinctive or innate, and thus passed from generation to generation by genetic means and are elicited by stimulation which will occur in the appropriate environment.

We shall think of the model as therefore having two sets of motivation chains, made up of elements with loops, so that any response which is followed by a reinforcing or non-reinforcing stimulus will in effect map that response onto either one or the other of the two sets. This will mean that the C-system will not operate its counting except in conjunction with the motivational effect of the response. Figure 3 shows a sample M-system and Figure 4 shows the C-system and M-system combined and thus how the activity of the C-system, now modified, is dependent on the outcome of the response.

In ordinary terms this means that the model must be capable of ensuring 'painful' things not occurring and 'pleasant' things occurring whenever they are needed or are possible.

At the level of the molar theory, we shall say that stimuli will not be effective in eliciting a response unless they are satisfying a need. Clearly, this is not true of the perceptual system which cannot tell whether a need is likely to be satisfied until recognition is carried through. However, here there is some reason to suppose that the classifying system of perception is influenced by the motivational state.

Behavior may be initiated in some obvious sense by motivational needs, or it may be initiated by external stimuli which have the effect of creating a need. This implies a complication that our model does not as yet cater for.

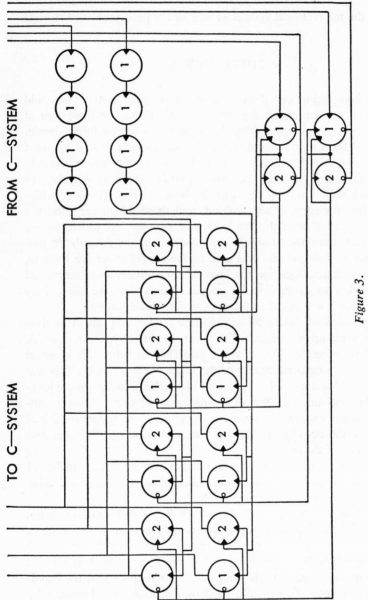

Figure 3.

THE M-SYSTEM

Shows twenty-eight inner elements. The group of eight on the upper right are merely delay elements. The four lower elements retain information about changes in motivation, and the group on the left selects the change of motivation (increase or decrease) to fire the information back to the appropriate elements in the C-system.

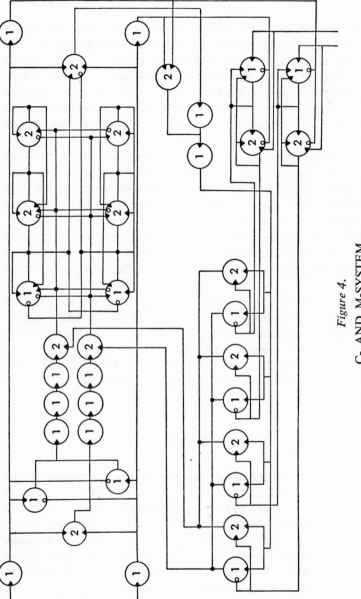

Figure 4.

C- AND M-SYSTEM

Shows a C-system and an M-system combined. The numbers in the elements indicate the threshold of that element. The closed-in triangles are excitatory fibre endings, and the open circles are inhibitory fibre endings. The heavy dots show fibres that have connections with each other.

6. EMOTION

Briefly, we can say about the E-system that it is concerned closely with the M-system insofar as it is a signal of different degrees of satisfaction being experienced by the organism. It has the job of facilitating the purely organic aspects that make it of importance as index of feelings, etc., which are part of what we are aware of. The whole problem of consciousness could perhaps be introduced into the system and regarded as an extra stimulus-response activity,[14] but we shall not attempt this here.

Machines in general do not have either motivational or emotional systems, simply because they are not normally *purposive*. However, there are certain purposive and selective systems in being, and for them the E-system and the M-system are vital, if they are to be in any sense autonomous and are to survive.

As far as the human being is concerned, there are various theories about the effect of emotion on his activities. It seems certain that they have both a disruptive and a facilitating effect. The main problem is to decide when the effect is disruptive and when it is helpful.

There is no purpose in drawing up a network for our E-system, as it could easily be constructed in a manner similar to the M-system, where its role would be to exhibit a set of specified signals as the appropriate states arise. Clearly, emotion is a factor that will have to be considered in any model (and therefore theory) of the individual, but we shall not attempt to take our argument further at the level of our logical network.

7. MEMORY

We should say something of memory in the theory and in the model. There will be at least two different stores, roughly comparable to those in a digital computer: (1) a high-speed counting store which will be associated with perception and recognition, and (2) the more permanent store, where as much as possible of everything that ever happens to the organism will be recorded in coded form. We should like here to add that we tend to think of the cognitive operations such as 'thinking' as being the processes of transfer for to and from the stores.

Let us briefly discuss the possible forms for memory devices. In the first place, our molar theories of behavior tell us that in recall there are simplifications and distortions of memory that make the remembering process almost one of reconstruction rather than reproduction. Bartlett [20] and others have shown these characteristics in operation and they can be seen to be connected with *set, attention,* and *perception.* The storage can be organized in a variety of different ways, and from the point of view of human organization, the only correct method can be arrived at by experimentation, presumably at the neurological level. Our purely molar behavioral account is only limited and heuristic.

We shall now say a little about the possible range of models. Culbertson [14] has listed some of the network devices that could be used, and we shall simply say that a system such as that in Figure 5 would obviously have the capacity to accept information and release that information on stimulation.

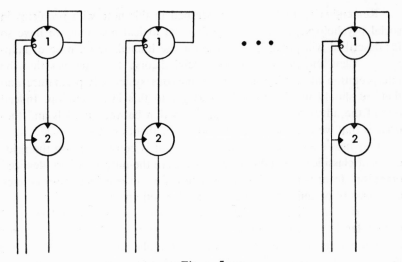

Figure 5.

Shows any number of storage elements of threshold one, each with an associated element of threshold two. For any one of the elements, an excitation along the left fibre sets off the storage element, which then continues to fire itself. If subsequently we wish to know whether the storage element is 'live' or 'dead,' we fire second fibre, which fires the associated element. The associated element is now 'live' if, and only if, the storage element is 'live,' thus giving off an impulse from this element. If the storage element is 'dead,' the associated element will not fire.

It could, of course, also be arranged to circulate the information released so that it returned to the store again if necessary. Such a net is a simple equivalent of a delay-line storage system in computer design. Instead of handling words as impulses in mercury tubes, the words are handled by sets of elements and the number of elements in the set dictates the length of the word handled. It is an open question whether what is remembered is coded as an instruction connecting sets of input elements, where the actual inputs referred to are localized by the anatomical location of the store. These sorts of matters are settled by neurological experiment.

It is in fact clear that there are a variety of ways we could store information in a logical net; even without loop elements we could arrange for chains of elements to circulate information indefinitely, and this would again be similar to the delay-line form of memory store.

8. MOLAR NETS

Remembering that we are concerned in this note with problems in social psychology, it seems likely that the logical nets that we have so far described will prove inadequate for the immediate purpose of helping the rigor and predictability of social theory. This suggests that the interpretation of the logical nets as nervous systems is premature and that we should not be committed as yet to this interpretation. Indeed one of the advantages of our clear distinction between models and theories is that we can use the same model for theories at various levels.

Our next step is to assert that a net that is constructed on the principles of classification and counting can serve the purpose of an idealized organism, from which point of departure we can consider the problems of groups of organisms and their collective activity.

Bearing in mind that a *belief* was the central theoretical term of our molar behavioral theory, we can interpret the belief as the unit which connects some set of inputs through a classification system. Using $A, B, \ldots, N$ as our basic units and ignoring the means by which these molar sets are arrived at, we can use the same nets as in Figures 1 and 2 as foundations for our molar net. We may assume that the full range of cognitive operations is possible for such a net and involves the derivation of information (further beliefs) from those beliefs that are already stored, as well as through the acquisition of new perceptual beliefs, as we have agreed to call them.

An alternative method of describing our logical nets should now be remarked upon. They can be represented by what we have called empirical calculi. The idea here is that we should map the classical calculi, such as the propositional and functional calculi, as well as the calculus of relations, onto the calculus of probability. This is because, at the level of empirical description, the classical calculi are too watertight to allow realistic description, and this can be remedied by making the class membership properties $p,$ instead of being absolute. p is to be interpreted as a probability. We would also designate as *p* the functions and relations between classes.

The actual process of carrying out the mapping in detail will not concern us here and in any case it can be done in a variety of different ways. Let us briefly illustrate what is involved. We shall take the calculus of relations as our example, but it will be easily seen that the methods can be extended to other calculi.

The Calculus of Empirical Relations

We need elements $x, y, \ldots$ and relations $R, S, \ldots$ with the usual relations of logic such as negation, class inclusion, and so on, which we now want to be able to interpret in terms of degree, where the degree is a probability. Suppose now that Rxy is the ordered relation between x and y. Then we shall not say that x and y have the relation R. That is, we shall not say that '*x* is the father of *y*,' for example, but rather $Rxyp$, which will mean x and y have the relation R *to the extent p*. Consider the example of 'is the father of' as a relation. It may seem odd to say this can be a matter of degree, but, of course, we may not know what relation exists between two people, when we shall subdivide the total relation into a set of statements that are part of what is required by the total relation and base a probability on these subrelations. This can be done in *a priori* fashion or by empirical statistical methods, and anyway will be relative to a partitioning of the complete relation into subrelations. This may be possible in any number of ways, and is also capable of being weighted in different ways.

The usual development of the calculus of relations will then be possible in terms of the ascribed probabilities. For example:

$$\sim R = df. \sim Rxyp$$
$$R \cdot S = df. min. \ (Rxyp, Sxyq)$$
$$R \vee S = df. max. \ (Rxyp, Sxyq)$$

and so on, where the interpretation placed on these relations of relations is both obvious and yet not the only possible one.

In similar fashion, the other calculi [21] can be mapped onto the calculus of probability, giving languages powerful enough for empirical descriptions. We can thus generate a set of languages that will bear a close relation with other such empirical languages, including mathematics. We shall not pursue this matter further here.

We should point out two things about these theories of an interlocked and many-leveled character that are of interest. In the first place, while we use a logical description for the finite automaton or logical net we start with, the process of logic must also arise within the system, and we will just indicate how this occurs. Consider a particular finite automaton or logical net N_1. Then it will be subject to certain input conditions that will result in the operations of classification and counting, taking place in such a manner that certain relations will be passed into the permanent store. This could be $A \to B$, where $\to$ will be interpreted as 'leads to.' Then later say $A \to C$ which implies that $A \to B \cdot C$ and this relation can be contingent or necessary for N_1 as a result of its stored experience. We shall say, in the social situation, that $A \to B \cdot C$ is contingent or necessary in terms of all the experience of the nets N_1, $N_2, \ldots, N_r$.

Realistically, this above argument merely allows for the deduction of certain consequences from relations that are inductively arrived at.

Our second point, which we shall merely mention, is that general purpose digital computers can, of course, be programed with the details of a finite automaton, provided there are no storage difficulties, and that the response states for different stimulus states under different control systems can be studied.

It is obvious, even from this brief description of the organization of nets in an environment, that they are essentially Markov processes which are inhabiting an environment that has a roughly ergodic source. Indeed, variations from the ergodic in any net's environment will probably be an important condition for different sorts of social behavior. This is merely another way of saying that homogeneity of environment is probably a necessary condition for a well-integrated net, or in the interpretation, a well-integrated organism.

This last statement could be regarded as obvious or irrelevant in isolation, but will nevertheless serve to indicate the use to which we should wish to put the present family of theories.

There is a coherence in the methods which allow us to slip from one interpretation to another without too much difficulty. This raises what seems to be an important point. While it is true to say that each and every part of theory construction should be carefully analyzed much more deeply than has been done here, there is also some value in showing the relation between different models, as their interrelated use is of the first importance, especially to the integration of scientific knowledge.

With respect to what has been said above about statistical methods, especially stochastic processes and Markov nets, we can see that the whole of our discussion of logical nets is closely related to information theory and is capable of translation into information-theoretic terms. This also implies, for our logical nets, that the sort of relations that the net will be interested in are relations that we have called *beliefs*. These relate different aspects of the environment through the individual's experience. We shall later generalize this to the individual in the group, by methods that are essentially the same. Meanwhile, we shall return to our description of our logical net model.

9. GENERAL

The model we have been outlining from the general point of view can be manufactured in a variety of different ways, but the interesting thing about logical nets is the fact that all the essential features of an organism seem to be capable of being reconstructed in them in terms of simple two-way switches. These two-way switches are obviously the beginnings of models that would be easy to interpret as neurons. Hence, there is a distinct resemblance between the structure of such a switching system and the nervous system. This is the way models should be constructed, with the theory and the intended interpretation in mind. It is this property that makes logical nets the most important of the list of models of behavior theories that have so far been created.

In a very short space of time, we have outlined a model of the human organism in a form that is still idealized and contrary to fact in many ways, but which can gradually be brought more into line with the empirical facts as these facts are yielded by experiment. We have briefly discussed an interpretation of the logical net model in the form of a molar theory of behavior, and this was derived independently as a direct result of molar behavioral experiments. In constructing the molar theory, however, we had philosophical as well as genuinely human problems in mind. We want to advance by slow, but careful, and accurate degrees towards a model that could be interpreted as a human organism. The model and the theory needed the sort of flexibility that allowed expansion both in detail and on other levels of description. No attempt will be made to illustrate even briefly how the same model of human behavior could be given an interpretation on the neurophysiological or biochemical level, but this could and should clearly be done.

A further point about the many-leveled methods employed is that the theory (or theories) itself could, of course, be formalized. We think of theories and models being connected in a definite way, and the process of formalization would be the process of showing the precise logical structure of the theory. It is certain that all theories should be capable of formalization, but theories can be formalized to different extents, and this is where we investigate the coherence, precision, and logical consistency of a scientific theory. The logical net is a ready formalization in logical terms of a behavior theory, although many other formalizations—all logically equivalent—are possible. In a sense, they may not even be logically equivalent since the use of theoretical terms in the theory or theory language are vague enough to allow a variety of possible interpretations.

We may now summarize the methods briefly. A theory in science—certainly in the behavioral sciences—may occur at many different levels of language which represent different sorts of levels of investigation. Behavior can be described introspectively, in molar observable terms, or in molecular terms. This roughly means in terms of private experience, or the behavior of the organism as a whole, or in terms of the physiological and biochemical internal states. A complete theory will plumb all these levels and thus allow the integration of science and allow workers dealing with all aspects of human behavior to draw on all the available information. These theories are all capable of having their logical structure and consistency analyzed and are all subject to confirmation. With the possible exception of introspective language, this means empirical confirmation by public test.

In discussing these methods of theory construction, we have introduced a few empirical statements, usually of a fairly general character, and we have not tried to show very much in the way of the detailed predictions and applications that follow from these empirical statements. Space forbids this. Hence, we have given no more than a skeleton theory of behavior, which would for any particular application need to be greatly expanded in detail, and of course be supplied with the individual constants or boundary conditions that may be applicable.

The idea behind these methods has been that we should have a flexible framework which would serve as a scientific tool for research to encompass the experimental work in progress, and be precise enough to avoid the pitfalls of ordinary language; and yet again be capable of being used as approximate models for theories to answer questions of varying generality at any time. Since we cannot wait for all the evidence to accumulate to use our idealized organism in the social situation, and since indeed the social situation itself puts much of the flesh on the semi-skeleton, we can only say that it can be used at any time in the social context and we can but hope that the predictions that follow will be sufficiently accurate. There is no alternative, except of course to go on using the relatively crude statistical methods of handling groups, attitudes, etc., and it is precisely these sorts of methods that need to be made more particular and more precise. Let us now consider some further problems that face the constructer of theories.

10. THE EVOLUTION OF SCIENTIFIC THEORIES

The next stage of our discussion is to enlarge on the methods of the last section at the most general level, and consider the possible modes of development of scientific theories. Let us explicitly consider the case of psychology. The existing state of psychology is perhaps at the transition from the "taxonomic" (collecting data) stage to the theoretical stage. The second stage of a theory is marked by the fact of having a theory language that allows the role of the experiment to become primarily that of a test for theoretical predictions. This clearly expresses the need for theory. Also it re-emphasizes the need for carefully considered experiment. So much of psychological theory is limited by the fact that most writers in the field use imprecise discursive methods and so many experimenters carry out experiments that are ill-conceived. It is surely obvious—certainly it must be so to anyone who has held advanced discussion groups or conducted classes in the design of experiments—that, while not all the questions involved in scientific theory construction are merely linguistic, a great many are, and even those which are not, are colored by linguistic considerations. What is needed in psychology, apart from rare skill in experimental techniques, is some of the linguistic skill of the analytic philosopher and the logician. These are not—for psychology—an end in themselves but an essential means to the more obviously psychological ends.

We will turn now to consider more explicitly the recent work of Braithwaite [1] in which the relation of models to theories has been analyzed. His view is that there is a sort of parallel between the development of scientific theories from observation statements on one hand and the reconstruction of empirical data from a model on the other. These are two parallel zip fasteners as it were, the theoretical zipper being tied to observations at the bottom, and the model zipper being tied to observations at the top. In this article we have discussed some of the problems of, and structure of, the formal languages and the cybernetic models which start from sets of marks on paper and proceed by rules to generate further sets of marks or strings. These sets of marks are models and are then open to interpretation as languages which may be used for any purpose whatsoever that is consistent with the interpretation placed on the marks. It is rather as if, to speak metaphorically, the collection of marks, called calculi, have certain structural properties like maps of anywhere at all, and the problem is to select a map that fits the country the scientist is interested in at any time.

It is certainly generally accepted that we can proceed from a set of statements of direct observation to generalizations, by inductive inference, and from the generalizations back to the testable particulars by deduction. This is the theory; the model is in essence the skeletal logical structure of this theory. There is thus clearly the closest relation between theory and model.

Before proceeding to pass any further comment on this view of Braithwaite's, it is important for theoretical psychologists to note that he has also given considerable support to a view held by F. P. Ramsey [22] that the theoretical terms that occur in scientific theories are not merely logical constructs, i.e., the theoretical terms cannot merely be defined in terms of observed entities if we wish our theory to be capable of expansion to incorporate new information as it arises, and this of course we surely do ultimately need.

Let us now consider the broader nature of *psychological* theories in particular. We shall start with natural language and its use as descriptive of particular occurrences and generalized hypotheses, and try and refine its statements by setting up glossary (or lexical [23, 24]) definitions for our principal logical constructions and observable variables. This involves the necessity of adding refining contextual definitions to all except the explicitly primitive terms of the system. We could, on a more precise level, do the same thing by using either reduction sentences or by reformulating from time to time our sets of explicit (eliminable) definitions. Rules of inference are not usually explicitly formulated at the natural language end of our continuum, but are so formulated, of course, as (and when) we proceed to the use of formalized languages. Indeed we regard the important sense of the word 'formalization' as that of 'making rigorous' and making the rules of use for a set of symbols explicit. We should proceed from the observables on the *molar* levels of observation and by use of theoretical terms (inferred entities, logical constructs, or intervening variables are points on a continuum of a Realist-Nominalist kind) build a psychological *qua* psychological theory. From this as our datum, the process of levels of language allows us to expand the system in many different (as it were) dimensions. The most obvious extension that seems to be necessary is to descriptions of a neurological kind. Thus the constructions on the 'molar' level should be capable of redefinition in the language of neurology. Indeed there is an important sense in which this procedure of redefinition on any level of description has been confused with a different thesis known as 'reductionism.' What is intended here is only the ability to translate from the language of one level of description to the language of another level. Indeed such translation should be possible between different linguistic frameworks on the same level of description. There is no obvious way, on a purely molar level, of granting priority to one linguistic system, with a certain choice of terms and categorizations, rather than another, except by the tests of a pragmatic kind that can be carried out at all levels of description. Thus any particular molar theory must be *tested* by seeing whether it uniquely defines, in certain test cases, such as under classical or instrumental conditioning, a definite operator, such as those that have been suggested by Estes [25] or Bush and Mosteller.[26] Molar theories may be further tested, of course, by the logical nets that may be derived from them. Two theories that are so vague that any mathematical operators or logical nets can be derived from them are insufficiently precise and can only be tested on molar-pragmatic grounds as to alternative interpretations of the same (and different) precise operations. Thus the psychological theorist is under obligation to show the breadth of utility of his theory and its plasticity in allowing precise rules to be derived from it whenever the need arises.

The above rather brief statement says that a theory must at least satisfy the following conditions. It must have certain molar explanatory properties that place it in advance of any existing theory and thus must have even crude explanatory powers in a language that has been made sufficiently precise for its use. It will be realized parenthetically that the precision of the questions to be answered will decide the precision of the theory to be used. Then the molar theory must be flexible enough to allow implicit redefinition of its primitives and theoretical terms at any other level of description (either more or less molar than the datum-language). We should thus be able to translate it into a molecular language that permits of being made precise at any moment and from which logical nets and mathematical models are capable of being derived. It is extremely important that a theory be tested in this ramified way since at the purely molar level it turns out that we cannot always adequately distinguish the predictive value of the different theories offered. It may, of course, be that there is an important sense in which the purely molar theories are little more than scaffolding for the presentation of the important questions which are concerned with (say) the relations of logical nets to each other, or the more general problem of producing a blueprint for the relation of the internal parts (variables) of the human machine.

We should notice the difficulty that the work of Braithwaite has made for the view that logical constructs are definable in terms of observable entities. This becomes more acute as we approach a more formalized level of language. However, Braithwaite's own suggestion that such theoretical terms should be reserved for the high-level statements and can only be implicitly defined is certainly acceptable. The writer has drawn attention to the use of logical constructs in psychological theory before [6] and has pointed out that it is precisely the vagueness attendant on the surplus meaning of such logical constructs that gives them both their power and their vagueness. The difficulties of theoretical terms in more formal languages still demands some further research. This problem appears already to have reared its head with the attempts that have been made to apply mathematics to psychology.

There are two further matters that now demand comment. The first is a sort of criticism of Braithwaite. It is that there is something of a gap between the way science actually works and the cut and dried systems he suggests. It is as if he were giving a prescription for the ideal state of an ideal science and we have tried to talk realistically in terms of the actual situation with which the social psychologist is faced. Thus, he starts with a great mass of data based mostly on observation, upon which generalization is to be made. The nature of the generalization will depend upon intuitive and anecdotal notions. Thus, although one may start in principle from a model and give interpretations of that model, one may also formalize a theory, i.e., may proceed from a set of scientific generalizations to the logical core of those generalizations. In fact, the original generalizations will be partially confused with a model as often as not, and the explicit stages of Braithwaite's view only arise after much work has been done on the confused mass of empirical data that represents the normal growth of a science.

Our next point takes us outside the theory construction to the directives and foundation principles upon which the theory is to be built. Here the cleavage is along the lines of behaviorism and introspectionism. There is a dispute characterized at some level by the 'Mind-Body problem.' At the working level of the scientist there are still problems of what behaviorism implies, i.e., how broadly or how narrowly the behavioristic notion is to be employed, and if taken too narrowly, how much of a science of psychology is lost, if anything.

The answers to these last questions can be given only briefly. Some form of behaviorism, involving at least the study of that which is obviously public, is quite vital. A science of behavior so based should include all the data that the introspectionist deals with, but will not use the same language. Indeed self-observation is essentially part of the subject matter of behavioristic psychology, but necessarily approached in a public manner. Thus self-observation statements are involved in a behavioral science, and such statements are continuous with (ordinary) observation statements. There should be no confusion here at the level of the absolute behavioristic science. In fact, confusion does sometimes arise since we do not always see where the observer enters into the apparently public scientific system. For psychology, we have in practice to combine, for many purposes, information from introspective and behavioristic sources, and we are forced into a degree of eclecticism. It is to the behavioristic approach that our processes of formalization, the applications of logic, and all the matters discussed in this paper are applied. Failure to recognize the nature of the complicated problems of constructing scientific theories has vitiated a great deal of the work of psychologists; recognition should improve his scientific standards, especially in the social sphere.

One last clarifying word should be said on the matter of behaviorism. What it is hoped to avoid in modern psychology is on one hand the narrowness of early behaviorism, which simply ignored problems that did not fit into its oversimplified notions. On the other hand, it is equally vital not to become embroiled in a morass of ontological and epistemological disputes. We are concerned with the systematic construction of scientific theories, metatheories, and criticisms of both. And we are concerned with the nature of the actual assumptions, the interbehavioral interpretation that is both possible and desirable for psychology and indeed for the whole of science.

11. EXPLANATION

We have seen that explanations may take more than one form. The reduction-sentence methods of Carnap are made necessary by the notion of 'dispositional properties.' The notion of *causal consequence* certainly presents a difficulty for logic, i.e., in the logical model, but for science it is not a genuine problem. We simply act in accordance with what we believe would happen if some action were performed. This is in fact induction at work, and no scientist is worried by the fact that he cannot be *certain* of what would have happened if he had done something that he didn't do. Thus, the general form of the Hempel-Oppenheim [27] theory looks near to what is needed as an explanatory system. The conditions they demand are in fact too strong, but the general form comes near to representing what scientists actually do.

However, what is needed by the psychologist is a systematic method for translating statements of observation into generalized laws or hypotheses, without hopeless vagueness. This demands that the metalanguage assumed and the language refined for the actual statement in the theory are sufficiently clear. For this, *definition* is perhaps vital; there is certainly no point in introducing false rigor, but for the more rigorous part of psychology, where disputes are mostly about terminology, the calculus of empirical classes and relations, already mentioned, is perhaps ideal. Here the terms and their relations are relative to the context of inquiry and do not insist on rigid class membership, but permit a degree of vagueness that heralds the use of probabilities. Here, as in all formalized systems, the theory and the model are closely and explicitly related. Such a formal, yet elastic, language also goes a long way to avoid the hazards of talking of "things having properties," etc.

The use of natural languages and scientific theories has one further complication. A precise descriptive language (including an explicit or implicit model) is a scientific theory. The marks on paper (or sounds in the air) which have no meaning (interpretation) are not, of course, a language. The point is that our precise descriptive language should be capable of interpretation in natural language, but that the precise relations cannot necessarily be precisely produced themselves in the natural language other than by analogy. To believe that natural language (a theory of the world on a crude level) is sufficient for science simply because the final interpretations of precise language have to be in natural language is merely to show confusion.

Very briefly, what it is vital for the psychologist to notice is that logic (all systematic languages) have two different roles to perform for them: (1) in clarifying their existing statements and theories, and (2) as precise descriptive languages themselves. Both roles are vital and it is vital to distinguish between them.

12. MODELS OF SOCIAL BEHAVIOR

We have already mentioned mathematical models in a variety of contexts, but it is clear that in social behavior we shall particularly need the sort of approximations that are suggested by the development of particular mathematical operators. The stochastic methods suggested by Bush and Mosteller [28] are just these sorts of approximations. They are models of molar behavior theory and take no account of molecular facts. This will often be desirable or even necessary, but we shall want to use models within which we can develop these molecular facts. The need for mathematical operators and molar mathematical models is due simply to the huge size of the human organism and the vast array of variables which make the development of molecular nets a long and tedious process. This same argument makes the use of computers as analogues of human behavior or as means of studying human behavior through other computers in the form of finite automata a great difficulty. If we couple these facts with the further complications that arise over the social interaction of organisms, then one may guess that from the point of view of sociological and social psychological theory the immediate theories will be interpretations of molar models. The most important particular models will be molar logical nets whether described in empirical logics, information theory, or natural language, although there will also be mathematical models available at an even more molar level.

These last considerations seem to lead naturally to the theory of games.[29] In the theory of games, we see developed a theory of certain aspects of social behavior. Along these same lines of development, we see also work on decision processes [30] and subjective probability, uncertain inference, and the like. These are all mathematical models, of a highly molar kind, of individual and especially social behavior.

Obviously, the theory of games, as such, needs no emphasis from the present writer, except insofar as it may be related to the rest of the many leveled models and theories that have been outlined.

The main point about the social situation is that, for any individual or net N_1, all the other individuals or nets are part of his environment. He will have special relations, characterized by his individual constants and variables with certain subsets of other individuals, and these in turn will influence his behavior. Group properties, social characteristics, and mores that represent different groups will enter to some extent into the individual characteristics of all those whom he meets in education, home life, and all aspects of his development. These are going to be special factors that will influence the nature of the prejudices and insights that he is likely to acquire, over and above what he will acquire as a result of being in transaction with almost any sort of civilized environment.

It is clear that logical nets suitably interpreted would be capable of being the individuals involved in playing 2-, 3-, or n-person games, so we can now arrive at specifications with respect to the individuals that do not leave their responses to particular Game situations—taken in the widest sense—as being based solely on the objective characteristics of the situation, or even the generalized subjective characteristics. We can design a theory that shows the various possible relations that may exist between r nets $N_1, N_2, \ldots N_r,$ and this surely is a mathematical or mathematico-logical program that could be carried through in terms of the empirical logics that we have mentioned. The formula

$$RN_1N_2p$$

suggests the form of relation between two nets, but we shall want to be capable of saying that this relation will not necessarily remain the same when a third net enters the situation thus:

$$RN_1N_2qN_3$$

Here we mean that the relation R exists between N_1 and N_2 to the extent q in the presence of N_3, and, of course, the same relation R may exist to some extent between N_1 and N_3 and N_2 and N_3. Other relations $S, T, \ldots$ may also exist between any number of nets (organisms) and relations may also exist between the relations.

This method of simple and precise description merely draws attention to the interaction of beliefs and expectancies in any group, and should occur in a description of any one of the N's as individuals. In common language, when we say 'Joe is shy' we should be meaning precisely something like

$$(N) \; RN_1 \, Np$$

'for all N, N_1 has the relation R with N to extent p' and R is relation of 'shyness with other people.' N_1 is Joe, and (N) is 'all other people,' and where p approaches 1. This index can clearly be ascertained at least in principle for any individual.

The scheme of things can be summarized briefly. We are now placing an interpretation of a molar kind on a set of interacting nets. They have the expandable form that allows us to derive the molecular details in terms of other scientific investigations, as well as the social ones themselves. This means that we can use the molar nets even though they are in a sense dependent on details of the individual's behavior, at the molar level and at the molecular level, which may be incompletely described.

We must define all the characteristics or properties of the individual in terms of time co-ordinates since they will not all be regarded as unchanging and invariant with time, and then for a particular time-slice the individual's characteristics and his relations with other individuals can be described in probabilistic terms as given by the empirical calculi already described. These can of course be replaced by statements in natural language or mathematics according to the needs (levels of approximation, etc.) of the user of the theory. At the same time, as we are thus 'building back' as it were from our carefully described social situation with a precise model that will continually be extended and modified, so we shall be 'building forward' with the physiological evidence and its relation to the molecular model. The prime object is to ensure that advances in *all* the sciences of behavior speak the same language, by using precisely the same model.

It should be emphasized that we are not attempting to provide ways and means for systematically carrying out the observations that would allow us to fill in the missing information or supply the comprehensive basis for the probabilities. This comes beyond the scope of theory construction as such.

The form here suggested is reminiscent of a model within a model within a model, etc. For mathematicians, it is rather like a matrix that has matrices for its elements which in turn have matrices for their elements, and we can pull off layer after layer of description without necessarily spoiling the description at any other layer. We can also suit our answers to the level of complexity of our questions.

13. POSSIBLE SOCIOLOGICAL APPLICATIONS

We will now try to outline briefly some of the various possible uses to which our model, or set of models, can be put. This especially means that we want to indicate more practical sociological uses of the calculus of empirical relations, as we have called it.

The calculus itself is simply a mapping of all of the classical calculi onto the calculus of probability. The idea is now actually to use these empirical logics as descriptions of, or models for, certain aspects of the empirical world. Briefly, we may think of the calculus as being made up of operators and variables to be operated upon, where the operators may be interpreted as connectives, relations, quantifiers, etc., and the variables as classes, individuals, and so on. A suitable interpretation can be given to any particular string of symbols according to the context of their application. One way in which this descriptive method has been used is in the situation where attempts have been made to associate certain physiological measures with molar behavioral states. Suppose, for example, we record the psychogalvanic skin response, heart rate, inspiration-expiration ratio, and any other measures of physiological change that we can handle. Now we can regard these measures as variables $x_1, x_2, \ldots, x_n$, where the variable, which is the measurement on some graduated scale, cannot necessarily be regarded as being independent of another variable, or even the whole set of such variables, and where it is the relation between the variables that is the most significant measure of the system.

We are in a position to consider the relations between the x's, taking them one, two, $\ldots$, n at a time. We can denote a particular relation between any x_i and any x_j, where $i \neq j$, by x_i/x_j. The general question of suitable scaling and suitable measures of the relation cannot be briefly discussed. However, let us consider the simplest sort of numerical measure, where one number is simply divided by the other. The ratio of any three variables can be written:

$$x_i/x_j/x_k$$

where the suffixes will always follow alphabetical (numerical) order. More generally we can write a function of (the ratio of in the special case considered) n variables in form:

$$x_i/x_j/ \ldots /x_n$$

where we shall assume a convention by association to the left, which means that the above formula becomes

$$(\ldots((x_i/x_j)/x_k) \ldots /x_n)$$

We shall now say that the complete set of all the variables in any situation taken *one, two, . . . , n* at a time, is the *profile* of the individual. We can talk of *state profiles,* which are standard states for different individuals, or *type profiles,* which earmark characteristic profile patterns for different types of people. This model will of course serve as well for groups—with group profiles—as for individuals.

Now to list briefly some of the uses for this sort of model, restricting ourselves to the physiological case:

1. We can find out which subrelations (making up a *subprofile*) are a sufficient measure of certain behavioral states, either temporary or more permanent. A statistical comparison between the full profile and any subprofile will elicit the extent to which the subprofile measures the profile. This allows us to say that, with a few s:mple measurements, we may be able to allocate a person to a type with a fairly high probability.

2. We can compare any individual's profile with his own state profile, or a type profile, with the idea of classifying him, at least probabilistically.

3. The arguments of 1 and 2 can of course be taken to apply to groups and their social norms. But to consider our example a little more informally, we can try and find out what critical states or measures, such as sensory thresholds, go with other physiological states, and all together with what sort of anticipated behavior. This could be a basis for the classification and prediction of types of social behavior. Specifically, if we find that a certain type of brain wave goes with a certain type of skin response, and both are the necessary and sufficient condition for a certain type of social behavior, we can use this information in selecting a person for a particular job.

Our logical nets are themselves capable of being defined within the calculus of empirical relations, especially their behavior, which in the main takes the statistical form of a Markoff net. A Markoff net is simply a sequence of events connected by probabilities, and thus involves the relation of 'immediately followed by' and an associated probability. We will remember that all relations contain relations, which contain relations, and so on indefinitely. It is the hierarchical model that we have already suggested we need, and is really a generalized model, of some possible precision, and capable of being used to model anything whatever.

To put the matter very broadly the probabilities can be either *a priori,* or frequencies, which are the result of a statistical sampling of the environment that is to be generalized upon. The logical nets are the internal structures of the profiles taken as individuals in the group situation, so that they themselves can be modified inside as a result of experimental evidence, and where the internal structure will itself be utilized in making predictions.

Lastly, we can mention some practical social problems that might gain from this straightforward, systematic, and fairly precise treatment;

a treatment which amounts (to use an alternative formulation) to setting up an expandable analogue of the system we want to make predictions about. The precise description of a system, however lengthy, can easily be handled by the use of a digital computer, and one thing that is already being worked out is the simple programming of a digital computer in terms of the models this paper has described. Take the organization of a group of people (defined as finite automata or logical nets) with as many indices as possible available for them, and as much in the way of background statistical information as possible. Suppose we choose a factory site, a product, even a factory, and then an organization to produce the output, which is to be maximized, like the productivity of a group of people. Now our model can be involved with the idea of selecting the most suitable type of person for the type of job, and then the individual for the particular job, and so on. Again, consider a social problem such as the effect of social class on certain age groups and their occupations. By setting up our analogue in the same manner, sampling the population, and discovering the appropriate relations that may be used as indices, we can compare our results with those obtained from other groups, in the same country or other countries, and so on.

It appears that any social problem can be rephrased in terms of the system we have outlined. In this way, we can seek sociological generalizations that can be applied readily to more and more social problems. In particular, we hope that our model will supply a series of tables of indices (profiles) for different social situations, and in terms of which validated tests may be used. This means that the statistical methods normally used in a deductive scientific argument can also be used descriptively in the theory itself, and this is certainly what we are suggesting. At the proper occasions, we have to consider the individuals that make up our groups as initially idealized and little more than elements in a matrix (theory of games), and then as mathematical operators (stochastic methods in psychology), and then as an expanding framework which allows us to put more and more individual detail into them (logical nets). At the same time, we are seeking the laws that govern the interaction of these idealized individuals, so that our theory can go from the group description to individual description and back again, encouraging the idea that our sociological knowledge and our knowledge of individual psychology can and should develop together. Ultimately, we may have a sufficient description of all the characteristic social situations and their causal implications. This is a huge plan which is just beginning, but some such large-scale attack on sociological problems seems very necessary.

In summary, what we are doing is supplying a highly precise generalizable and flexible system constructed in such a manner that we can *cumulatively* build up both our knowledge and our predictions of the individual and the group together. There is no guarantee that any individual problems can be solved by these means, since we depend upon experiment and precise observation as much as ever. All we are suggesting is the way we should try and systematically collate our results to construct a model and thus a theory of social behavior.

NOTES

1. R. B. Braithwaite, *Scientific Explanation* (Cambridge: Cambridge University Press, 1953).

2. J. R. Kantor, *Psychology and Logic*, I, II (Bloomington, Ind.: Principia Press, 1945); J. R. Kantor, *The Logic of Modern Science* (Bloomington, Ind.: Principia Press, 1953).

3. W. S. McCulloch and W. Pitts, "A Logical Calculus of the Ideas Immanent in Nervous Activity," *Bulletin of Mathematical Biophysics*, 5 (1943), pp. 115-33.

4. A. Church, *Introduction to Mathematical Logic* (Princeton: Princeton University Press, 1944).

5. E. L. Post, "Introduction to a General Theory of Elementary Propositions," *American Journal of Mathematics*, 43 (1921), pp. 163-85.

6. A. Church, "An Unsolvable Problem of Elementary Number Theory," *American Journal of Mathematics*, 58 (1936), pp. 345-63.

7. *Automata Studies* (Princeton: Princeton University Press, 1956).

8. F. H. George, "Logical Networks and Behavior," *Bulletin of Mathematical Biophysics*, 19 (1957).

9. ———— "Logical Networks and Probability," *Bulletin of Mathematical Biophysics*, 19 (1957).

10. ———— "A General Theory of Logical Nets" (to be published).

11. A. M. Uttley, "The Classification of Signals in the Central Nervous System," *E. E. G. Clinical Neurophysiology*, 6 (1954), pp. 479-94.

12. ———— "The Conditional Probability of Signals in the Nervous System," *RRE-Memorandum*, No. 1109 (1955).

13. F. H. George, "Mechanisms for Perception," *E. E. G. Clinical Neurophysiology* (to be published).

14. J. T. Culberton, *Consciousness and Behavior* (Dubuque, Iowa: Wm. C. Brown Company, 1950).

15. F. H. George and J. H. Handlon, "A Language for Perceptual Analysis," *Psychological Review*, 64 (1957), pp. 25-44.

16. F. H. George and J. H. Handlon, "Towards a General Theory of Behavior," *Methodos*, 7 (1955), pp. 25-44.

17. I. Krechevsky, "'Hypotheses' in Rats," *Psychological Review,* 39 (1932), pp. 516-32.

18. E. C. Tolman, "Cognitive Maps in Rats and Men," *Psychological Review,* 55 (1948), pp. 189-208.

19. K. MacCorquodale and P. E. Meehl, "Edward C. Tolman," in *Modern Learning Theory,* with the editorial assistance of A. T. Poffenberger (New York: Appleton-Century-Crofts, Inc., 1954).

20. F. C. Bartlett, *Remembering* (Cambridge: Cambridge University Press, 1933).

21. A. Kaplan and H. F. Schott, "A Calculus for Empirical Classes," *Methodos,* 3 (1951), pp. 165-90.

22. F. P. Ramsey, *The Foundations of Mathematics* (London: Kegan Paul, 1931).

23. F. H. George, "Logical Constructs and Psychological Theory," *Psychological Review,* 60 (1953), pp. 1-6.

24. ———— "Formalization of Language Systems for Behavior Theory," *Psychological Review,* 60 (1953), pp. 232-40.

25. W. K. Estes, "Toward a Statistical Theory of Learning," *Psychological Review,* 57 (1950), pp. 94-107.

26. R. R. Bush and F. Mosteller, "A Mathematical Model for Simple Learning," *Psychological Review,* 58 (1951), pp. 313-23, and "A Model for Stimulus Generalization and Discrimination," *Psychological Review,* 58 (1951), pp. 413-23.

27. C. G. Hempel and P. Oppenheim, "The Logic of Explanation," in *Readings in the Philosophy of Science,* Feigl and Brodbeck, eds. (New York: Appleton-Century-Crofts, Inc., 1953).

28. R. R. Bush and F. Mosteller, *Stochastic Models for Learning* (New York: John Wiley & Sons, Inc., 1955).

29. J. Von Neumann and O. Morgenstern, *Theory of Games and Economic Behavior* (Princeton: Princeton University Press, 1944).

30. R. M. Thrall, C. H. Coombs, and R. L. Davis, *Decision Processes* (New York: John Wiley & Sons, Inc., 1956).

11

Uses and Limitations of Mathematical Models in Social Science

ANATOL RAPOPORT

University of Michigan

Collaboration or at least attempts at collaboration between social scientists and mathematicians have become all but commonplace. As experience accumulates in this area of endeavor, problems of communication arise: people of different backgrounds speak virtually different languages, not only in the sense of different vocabularies but also in the sense that their concepts have roots in different soils. For the social scientist, the term "theory," for example, often means something quite different from what it means to a mathematician.

The mathematician or the physical scientist who turns to the construction of a social theory always has to face this problem of communication, specifically the problem of explaining to the social scientist the relevance of his theoretical construction to social science as the social scientist understands it.

The reverse situation does not arise. Hardly anyone untrained in mathematics will attempt to construct a mathematical theory dealing with the content of his investigations. An incompetently constructed mathematical "theory" can be immediately shown to be incompetently constructed. However, it is not easy to demonstrate, for reasons that will appear below, that a mathematical theory, consistent in itself, is irrelevant or useless from the point of view of social science. Objective criteria for evaluating the pertinence or the importance of a sociomathematical theory are lacking, because the ordinary criteria of "predictive power," standards for evaluating mathematicophysical theories, are not entirely applicable. This lack of unambiguous criteria of evaluation is, I believe, a major source of difficulty in communication between mathematicians or physical scientists and social scientists.

In this essay, I propose to examine the "tone" of present day interdisciplinary efforts which bring mathematicians (or, more generally physical scientists) and social scientists together; to examine more closely the causes underlying the difficulty of communication among them; to describe some examples of mathematicosocial theory construction; and to point out the value as well as the limitations of such constructions.

THE MATHEMATICIAN'S AND THE SOCIAL SCIENTIST'S CONCEPTION OF THEORY

Interdisciplinary conferences and committees, multiple-author publications, problem-oriented research—all of these have fallen, at least in the United States, into a pattern: a group of representatives from various academic disciplines is asked to exchange views, to merge methodologies, and to come up with a joint product—the solution of a problem involving several fields of knowledge, or even a "unified theory of human behavior." Among the cast of characters of such groups a mathematician is frequently present and sometimes a physicist or an engineer.

These representatives of physical science differ from other representatives (psychologists, sociologists, anthropologists) in one important respect. In their own work, "unification" is an accomplished fact. The whole body of mathematics, for example, is of one piece. True, there are specialized branches, such as algebra, topology, and analysis, but these branches are all firmly welded together. No one questions the pertinence of algebraic discoveries to geometry, once this pertinence has been shown by established rules of deduction. There is also a firm connection between mathematics and physics—the deductive reasoning used in physical theory *is* the process of mathematical deduction. There is a connection between physics and engineering—the systems studied by the engineer are clearly physical systems which obey physical laws. And there is a connection between physics and chemistry—the events on the molecular, atomic, and subatomic levels form the connecting bridge.

In principle, therefore, all of physical science is unified; it treats events involving matter and energy and describes these events in the language of mathematics. Thus, there is comparatively little methodological discussion and still less methodological polemic among the physical scientists. One suspects that this success in developing a unified science over the past three hundred years is the principal component in the prestige enjoyed by the physical scientist, particularly by the mathematician, and his participation in methodological discussions and in collective problem-oriented efforts of social scientists is solicited in the hope that he can impart the "secret of success" of physical science to others.

All too often, although by no means always, the mathematician assumes one of two attitudes in such situations. One attitude is a quixotic one—the belief that the methods of mathematical physics are directly translatable so as to apply to the content of social science. The other attitude is a passive one—an implied invitation to the social scientist to hand to the mathematician a ready-made list of definitions, relations, axioms, and postulates, so that the mathematician can begin to grind out theorems and conclusions.

Neither attitude seems particularly helpful; yet both have served a purpose. The "naive" mathematician, by constructing numerous "models" of society and social behavior, largely in the language of classical mathematics, has demonstrated that it is possible to create at least a semblance of a quantitative social science. Even if his models turned out to be useless, at least it was possible to say *why* they were useless and so to pose the problem of designing more useful models. No such definitive evaluation could ever be applied to the traditional (Continental) "literary" approach to social phenomena. The passive mathematician, on the other hand, who declined to say anything until the social scientist could tell him just what relations he was assuming among what entities, has been instrumental in spurring the social scientist on to seek out such entities and relations. Very rarely, the mathematician, turning to the problems of social science, succeeds in penetrating to the very core of the matter and holds up to the social scientist the really essential problems. Still more rarely the social scientist is able to recognize in these crystal-clear but "lifeless" abstractions the essential elements of his field of inquiry.

For a genuinely co-operative effort to begin, it is necessary that both the mathematician and the social scientist learn a great deal of each other's languages, methods, and problems.

Let us take a glimpse at the applied mathematician's traditional activity in order to understand his bias. Traditionally, the applied mathematician worked on problems in physics. Now physics is a science in which from the very beginning a few fundamental measurable quantities were singled out for study. In mechanics, for example, these quantities are length, time, and mass. Their unambiguous "measurability" was intuitively self-evident and, until the advent of modern positivist critique, there was no question that these quantities were objectively real. This framework of thought sufficed and was constantly reinforced by the success of celestial and terrestrial mechanics in describing and predicting events with remarkable accuracy.

When mathematical physics was extended to other classes of events, involving, for example, heat, electricity, and magnetism, it became necessary to isolate other measurables, such as temperature, electric charge, and magnetic field. But the list of these physical quantities is still small, and physics, by definition, deals with those events which can be described *entirely* in terms of these few fundamental quantities and their combinations.

Now the social scientist has no such list. In fairness to the social scientist, it must be admitted that he does try to invent one. The trouble is that whereas a Newton could begin with intuitively evident quantities (length as measured by sticks, time as measured by clocks, force as felt in the muscles), the social scientist cannot make such a beginning. The stuff from which human relations and social structure are made is not evident intuitively. It must somehow be distilled, or abstracted from innumerable "events," and the selection of these events depends to a great extent on one's experiences, cultural background, and biases.

Nevertheless, the social scientist does try to select the fundamental entities of his field of interest. This process of selection, however, is so laborious and involved that it often constitutes the bulk of the social scientist's effort, and so he hardly ever gets around to stating "postulates." He must first relate his terms to referents. These referents cannot be simply exhibited; they must themselves be abstracted from a rich variety of events, generalizations, and relations. By the time a number of these referents have been so abstracted and christened, one already has a bulky "system" before the work of seeking out "laws" has ever begun. Such "system," particularly in sociology, is sometimes taken to be "theories."

Here, then, is the first source of misunderstanding between the social scientist and the mathematician (who is primarily oriented toward physical science). For the mathematician, as for the physical scientist, a "theory" is a collection of theorems, that is, statements in the form of implications, which, if applied to the physical world, become predictions as to what will be observed if certain conditions obtain. For a social scientist, a "theory" is often (in effect) a system of reference, that is, a multitude of definitions which, if the social scientist is operationally oriented, are connections between terms and referents abstracted from observed events, and if the social scientist is not operationally oriented, he simply appeals to the reader to understand the terms as the writer understands them. That is to say, the theoretician of social science invites the reader to categorize his observations in a certain way, for example, to lump certain aspects of human behavior together and call them "role," or to lump certain individuals in a population and call them "class," or certain patterns of individual behavior and call them "personality," or certain rules governing the exchange of commodities and call them

"value." Obviously, there are many ways of categorizing. Social groupings alone can be described in terms of classes, castes, status, cultural
background, and in many other ways, not to speak of the obvious distinctions of sex, age, and geographic location. The nonobvious distinctions are often also ambiguous, and considerable effort is required to
make them clear and derivable from objective criteria. This effort constitutes a considerable part of the social scientist's preoccupation with
"theory."

The physical scientist often fails to understand the importance of
this preoccupation with definitions, and this leads to the first obstacle to
communication between him and the social scientist. To the physicist,
concepts come as natural by-products of observing certain regularities
inherent in relations among measurable quantities. It is found, for example, that when one surface is dragged over another, the force necessary
to drag it is proportional to the force pressing the surfaces together. Thus,
the ratio of these forces is observed to be a constant. This constant is
given a name—the "coefficient of friction," and so a concept is born. Or
it is found that the amount of electric current in a wire is proportional to
the potential difference impressed. Again the constant of proportionality
is given a name—the coefficient of resistance. We may, following our
obsolete semantic habits, reify these constants and speak of "friction"
and "resistance" as if they were real "entities," but the physicist never
forgets that behind these categories are only ratios or other mathematical
combinations of results of measurement.

It seems, then, to the physical scientist, who always deals with concepts stemming directly or indirectly from measurements (that is, operations) that the social scientist should also construct his concepts this
way. Actually, it may be pointed out, the social scientist also tries to
construct his concepts from operations; but his operations are not always,
not even frequently, measurements. They are certain kinds of "recognition," certain abstractions from observation. The physicist's concepts
make sense only if everyone gets the same results from measurements
under identical conditions. Similarly, the social scientist's concepts make
sense if everyone recognizes the same situations as identical and makes
the same abstractions from similar observations. Because it is harder to
learn to observe in a certain way or to abstract in a certain way than to
get consistent results from measurement, the social scientist's concepts
are harder to come by than the physical scientist's.

To restate the physical scientist's bias, he is predominantly occupied
with uncovering objectively identifiable and consistent regularities; in
old-fashioned terms, with associating identical "effects" with identical
"causes"; in modern quantitative language, with discovering equations
connecting variables, whose referents are results of measurement, and

with determining the values of the constants which enter those equations.

The question is to what extent are such equations discoverable and the constants identifiable in the subject matter of social science? Things that are of interest to the social scientist are not typically quantities but events. About the only way most events can be quantified is by being counted. To be counted they must be recognized. We have already seen how grave difficulties are involved in the recognition and classification of such events. More difficulties are involved in trying to make the counting of events mean something. Quantitative definitions of social concepts are proposed by the score, but it is not easy to make them stick in the face of objections. If, for example, someone decides that the "power" of *A* over *B* is measurable by the fraction of times that *B* does what *A* tells him to do in a circumscribed situation, someone is sure to point out that although the definition is fairly operational, it has hardly anything to do with "power" as it is understood in common-sense terms. *B* may do *A*'s bidding 100 per cent of the time, but only because *A* knows exactly when *B* will do so and restricts his requests or commands only to those instances. How is it possible by counting alone to discover what *A* "knows" or to distinguish this situation from one where *B* will do anything that *A* commands?

Even if satisfactory definitions could be given in terms of counting events, the job of recording all the pertinent events in any situation is easier proposed than done. However, the most serious objection to this sort of search for regularities is this: even if all pertinent data could be collected, even if the definitions satisfy everyone, even if regularities reveal themselves abundantly, a catalogue of resulting equations is no more a mathematical science than a collection of bricks is a house. A mathematical science must hang together. There must be few underlying assumptions and many conclusions. The more unrelated these conclusions seem at first sight, the more powerful is the science that is able to derive them from a few principles.

Difficult as the construction of such a science is in the absence of a toe hold (such as was provided for the physical scientist by the regularities in the notions of heavenly bodies), attempts in that direction have been made. The method of constructing a mathematicized social science is embodied in the concept of the so-called mathematical model.[1]

A word is in order on the way the mathematician uses the term "model," since this usage departs from that prevalent in other disciplines. Outside of mathematicized sciences, the term "model" often refers to an analogical explanation. To take an example, Marxist sociological theory explains revolutions as instances of quantitative changes suddenly becoming "qualitative" and cites as an analogue of such phenomena the change of state of water to steam upon being heated. With even greater vividness, a revolution may be likened to an explosion. Explosion is supposed to be a "model" for a revolution. Psychoanalysts postulate principles of "conservation of psychic energy" embodied in the construction of the so-called "hydraulic model" of psychodynamics, in which "forces" are supposed to be exerted by the various parts of the "psyche" upon the "border of consciousness." These are analogical or metaphorical models. Their explanatory value, if any, is in the appeal to see in a seeming similarity of two phenomena the explanation of the unfamiliar one in terms of supposed understanding of the familiar one.

With such constructs, mathematical models have only one thing in common—the property of "as-if-ness." Mathematical models also rest on fictions, on appeals to look at events *as if* the underlying "causes" had a certain structural analogy to the model proposed. But there the similarity ends. The mathematical model invariably leads to *specific* relations among *specific* variables. In principle, these relationships are verifiable by experiment or observation. If they are so verified, the assumptions underlying the model are *to a certain extent* corroborated.

The test of the mathematical model, then, is in the specific predictions, and *the simpler* the underlying assumptions, the more valuable the model. The Newtonian Law of Gravitation is a superb example of a mathematical model. In spite of its far-reaching predictive power, the system remains a model, because it retains its "as-if-ness." No one has ever measured directly the actual "pull" which heavenly bodies exert on each other. All we can say is that if we assume the simple mathematical form for the magnitude of mutual attraction, as given by Newton's Law of Gravitation, the motions of heavenly bodies can be predicted with great accuracy. It is *as if* they attracted each other with the force inversely proportional to the square of the distance between them; that is all.

Long before anyone had seen a chromosome, Gregor Mendel proposed a mathematical theory of the segregation and recombination of distinct inheritable traits. In effect, he said it was *as if* the character traits were attached to independent carriers transmitted intact from generation to generation. The force of the model was not in its "explanatory" value, nor in the reality of the carriers (which remained unknown until quite recently) but in its predictive power—it led to predictions of quantitative (statistical) relations involving frequencies with which certain characters were observed in successive generations of plants bred under certain conditions.

This, then, is the spirit in which the mathematician tries to construct his sociotheoretical mathematical models. He frequently cares little about the "reality" of the underlying assumptions, not even about the referents of his terms. They are all "as-if" terms and "as-if" assumptions. His object is to deduce from these postulates relations among quantities which can be in principle verified. If he discovers relations which seem surprising in the sense that they would not have been ordinarily suspected but are nevertheless verified, he feels doubly rewarded. Often, not even the predictive power of the model is important. The model can have "heuristic" value only. This aspect of mathematical models will be discussed later.

EXAMPLES OF MATHEMATICAL MODELS IN SOCIAL SCIENCE

1. A Theory of Mass Behavior

It is commonly observed that people imitate each other. Often, such imitative behavior results in more or less sudden outbursts of specific behavior patterns. In mild form they are fashions and fads; in more severe form instances of mass hysteria, mob action, and panic. The "causes" of such events fall, of course, within the scope of the social scientist's interest. The mathematician, however, is not concerned with "causal" explanations. "Cause," as it is understood in common terms, has long ago lost its value as a concept in physical science. "Explanations" of physical events are represented as equations. They "hang together" by the interdependence of the variables in the equations. In principle, any of the variables can be assigned the role of "cause," the others then automatically taking the role of "effects." In any mathematicized formulation, causes and effects are freely interchangeable.

The mathematician, therefore, approaching the phenomenon of social imitation, wishes to describe it in the language of equations. These will be derived from the relations he assumes among some postulated variables.

He may suppose, for example, as N. Rashevsky did,[2] that every individual in a population has a certain tendency to perform each of two mutually exclusive acts, which in a special case may be to do or not to do something. Some kinds of acts can be performed only once, at least in a given time interval, for example buying a home, getting married, or committing suicide. Other acts may be performed with a certain frequency, such as going to the movies or to church or spanking children or smoking. There are mathematical theories of mass behavior dealing with both kinds of acts. Rashevsky was mainly concerned with the latter type (repetitive acts).

The tendency to perform an act may be measured by the frequency of its performance. This tendency is assumed to be characteristic of

each individual (his natural preference for the act). In addition, however, there is added to this base line preference another source of this
tendency—the frequency with which an individual sees (or is otherwise
aware of) the act performed by others. If there are two mutually exclusive acts, the relative "densities" in the vicinity of the individual in
question of others performing each of the acts will contribute differen-
tially to the opposite tendencies to perform one act or another. The
dynamics of social imitation is then described by equations reflecting
how the rate of change of the tendency to perform each of the acts due
to imitation depends on the numbers of individuals performing each of
the acts at a given time. How "explosive" effects are achieved on the
basis of this model cannot be rigorously demonstrated without a mathematical argument, but an idea can be given as to how these effects can
come about.

Characteristically, equations which relate rates of change of some
quantities to the quantities themselves lead to the deduction of certain
equilibrium states. Such are the equations describing rates of chemical
reactions and sometimes ecological relations among populations of different species. Indeed the equations of social interaction postulated in
the theories of mass behavior are of a similar nature. They are assumed
to apply to any mass phenomena where quantities and their rates of
change are related in a particularly simple manner. Technically, these
relations are called differential equations of the first order. They are
chosen not so much because they can always be expected to be "correct"
but because they are the simplest equations relating quantities to their
rates of change. They form a natural *starting point* for any theory of
mass action where such relations can be reasonably assumed to operate.

Now if these differential equations are of a certain form, it can be
shown that there are regions of relative stability and of relative instability of equilibrium conditions. That is, once equilibrium is reached
and the two forms of behavior are distributed with certain frequencies
in the population, if the equilibrium is stable, accidental departures from
this equilibrium set "forces" in motion which restore the equilibrium.
(These forces are, of course, not physical forces but tendencies of
variables to change in a given direction as postulated in the differential
equations.) If, however, the equilibrium is unstable, a sufficiently large
departure from equilibrium (perhaps due to an accidental fluctuation,
perhaps to proselytizing efforts of zealots) tends to persist in the *same*
direction, snowballing, as it were, until another equilibrium state is
reached, or leading to an "explosion," an unbounded increase in the frequency of one of the acts.

Such effects—namely, the existence of equilibrium conditions, their
stability or instability, sudden shifts of equilibrium, and "explosions"—

are observed in a great many situations where mass behavior is involved. It does not particularly matter what the populations are. In chemistry, they are atoms and molecules; in zoology, animals and plants in their struggle for existence; in economics, buyers and sellers (recall financial panics and inflations). The mathematical model of imitative behavior resembles in its mathematical form many other models attempting to describe "similar" instances of mass behavior where changes of state occur when particles or individuals interact with one another.

Another type of theory of mass behavior concerns acts which can be performed only once, some of which we have mentioned above.[3] The individuals in the population are then considered to pass from the state of not having performed the act to the state of having performed it and once in that state, they stay there.

The most obvious single irreversible act performed by a person is dying. The fraction of dead recruited from a given population is therefore always increasing and tends to unity. Such curves are well known to actuarial statisticians. Mortality curves are of interest to behavior theory, because they probably are typical of cumulative curves of *non-imitative* acts (dying is seldom an act of imitation). Therefore, they may be taken as a base line with which to compare curves regarded as representing imitative behavior. From such comparisons, a fairly comprehensive theory of cumulative irreversible acts based on imitative interaction may possibly be constructed.

We have mentioned the "base line" tendency of an individual to perform an act. Although this tendency can be defined operationally through some index (e.g., in the case of a repeatable act on the basis of frequency of performance), the actual measurement of such indices is beset with great practical difficulties. Frequency is easier defined than actually measured, because of statistical fluctuations and secular trends. Moreover, if imitative factors are present in all actual situations, how are we to get at the "basic" tendency? It must be admitted, therefore, that the parameters assumed in mathematical theories of mass behavior, such as the ones mentioned, are operationally definable only in principle. In practice, they are not likely to be obtained with any accuracy which could justify the exact mathematical treatment implicit in differential equations. These parameters, therefore, must, for the time being, serve as merely theoretical constructs, "idea fixers," pegs on which to hang mathematical arguments in order to see where these mathematical arguments will lead us. They are tools of mental experimentation.

What pertains to individual parameters certainly pertains to their assumed distributions in the populations. These distributions are not directly ascertainable in any practical way (although "in principle" one can design any number of methods by which one could measure them).

Yet the distributions play an important part in the theory, and so without some practical procedure of ascertaining them, the theory must remain virtually without verifiable content.

The difficulties of imparting real content to theories of mass behavior are not confined to the measurements of the parameters involved in the differential equations. Even if all of these could be determined, the theory would remain one dealing with a completely structureless population, that is, only the properties of the individuals comprising the population would have been taken into account, but not the relations *among* the individuals. In the next example, we will examine another mathematical model attempting to deal with some aspects of population structure, but first we must dispel the possible impression that the "impracticality" of a theory necessarily detracts from its scientific value.

The value of theories such as the one just described is largely in the creation of a language in which to speak of certain features of mass behavior in quantitative terms. Sometimes from a thorough quantitative analysis some tentative qualitative conclusions may emerge, perhaps not about specific populations but about types of populations; for example, conclusions related to observable symptoms indicative of probable instability of behavior patterns.

One might point out that such symptoms are known in a purely intuitive way to certain experienced individuals sensitive to mass behavior to a degree surpassing the amount of knowledge to be gained from the theory in its present form. Again it must be admitted that in the present state mathematical theories of mass behavior can hardly lay claim to "practical" value. It may very well be that a canny politician knows more about mass behavior than can be concluded at this time from even the most sophisticated mathematical theory. But really intuitive and analytic knowledge should not be compared in terms of their relative usefulness at a given time. Often the immediate usefulness of intuitive knowledge far surpasses that of analytic knowledge. Intuitive knowledge, however, has two crucial limitations. There is no straightforward way of making it accessible to others, and it usually does not grow in breadth or depth beyond certain limits. In this way intuitive knowledge is like the "instinctual" knowledge of animals. It may be admirably adapted to a particular situation, but it does not contain potentialities for generalization and thus for growth. This is why attempts at constructing rational theories (particularly mathematical theories) must not be judged only on the basis of their immediate contribution to the actual understanding (in the sense of the ability to predict) of real events. In terms of such knowledge, a rational formal theory may be much behind the intuitive knowledge of the expert; but the rational theory has potentialities for growth and development which the specialized knowledge of the expert often lacks.

2. A Statistical Theory of Social Structure [4]

The social structure examined in this approach is not that ordinarily studied by sociologists (classes, social ecology, the anatomy of institutions, etc.) but that primarily of interest to the sociometrist and to some social psychologists.

The object of study is a population which is not too large, so that certain relations between all pairs of individuals in it can be examined, but not too small, so that certain statistical findings about its structure can be verified by actual frequency counts. Examples of such populations are a school, a professional organization, a middle sized firm of, say, a few hundred employees, or a very small town.

Some observable or inferable relation is chosen for study, which may or may not exist between an arbitrarily chosen pair of members. To fix ideas, let the relation be "best friend" and let its operational definition be a simple-minded one: B is A's best friend if, upon being asked, "Who is your best friend?" A answers *"B,"* or else if upon being asked to name his friends in the order of intimacy, B appears first on A's list.

It should be stressed that questions concerning the "validity" or the "consistency" of this definition are irrelevant at this stage. Of course, A may not have a "best friend," or A may name someone whom he would *like* to be his best friend, or he may not be consistent in his answer from Sunday to Monday. All these difficulties are ignored for the time being. It is assumed that everyone has a "best friend" and that his identity can be ascertained by a simple question.

When every member of the population has thus named some other member as "best friend," a chart or a "sociogram" can be constructed in which the individuals are points, from each of which issues an arrow leading to the corresponding "best friend."

The resulting structure is called by mathematicians a linear directed graph. Now there is a branch of mathematics which treats of the properties of such structures (much as geometry treats of the properties of figures, curves, and surfaces). The theory of graphs is considerably involved and becomes progressively more so as the number of points of the graph becomes large. It is impossible, of course, simply to enumerate all the different ways in which a given number of points can be connected: they are too many. To get an idea of the prodigious size of their number, consider that there are $N(N-1)$ ordered pairs of N points.

Between each pair an arrow may or may not exist (two possibilities). Therefore, there are $2^{N(N-1)}$ different ways to connect N points. Such a number staggers the imagination if N is anything but very small. For example, if N is 5, there are over a million ways to connect the points. If N is 20, the number of ways exceeds the estimated number of atoms in the universe.

In our sociometric example where only one arrow issues from each point, the number of possible graphs is not nearly so prodigious but still very large. If $N = 11$, there are one hundred billion possible sociograms.

A mathematical theory gets around the difficulty of handling such a prodigious number of objects by developing methods for classifying them. Then the very much smaller number of classes can be examined. An exact classification should specify explicitly the properties which put a graph in a given class. But even this approach soon becomes altogether unwieldy as the number of points in the graph becomes large. Therefore, another kind of classification must be devised—a statistical one, where the basis of classification is not an exact description of graph structure but some set of numbers which represent the characteristics of the graph as certain averages. This sort of simplification is familiar to everyone who deals with statistical descriptions of populations. Where it is impractical to list the age of every member of a population, the *average* age still gives some information; the variance of the age distribution gives more information, etc.

Let us see how averages can be used to gain some information about the sociometric structure of a population. Suppose that when each individual was asked to name a "best friend," he chose him with perfect indifference, as if by pulling a name out of a hat. The resulting graph would then be called a "random net." Now, certain rather definite things can be said about random nets, even though we are in total ignorance about the individual connections in them. It can be asserted, for example, with considerable confidence (the greater, the greater the population) that although everyone names exactly one person (and therefore everyone on the average is chosen once), there will be certain definite proportions among those who happened not to have been named at all, those who happened to have been named twice, three times, etc. In fact, if the naming is random, about 37 per cent of the population will be expected not to have been named at all, also 37 per cent to have been named just once, about 18 per cent twice, 6 per cent three times, 1½ per cent four times, etc.

Suppose now a sociometrist examines the sociogram of a town of about 2,000 population where everyone has been asked to name one best friend. On the basis of *completely* random choices, it is expected that fully 740 individuals will not be named at all. Thus, no conclusion whatsoever is warranted that the several hundred such individuals are in any way "less popular" or less attractive as friends: their being left out is what is expected on the basis of chance alone. Nor is any conclusion warranted about the few individuals that are named "best friend" as many as five times, instead of the expected average of one time. Such is the chance expectation. If, however, the distribution departs radically from the expected, hypotheses are in order about possible underlying reasons. We have here an illustration of the "null hypothesis" approach, which begins with the question, "What would happen if no influences were operating in the choice of 'best friend'?" This gives us a base line, something with which to compare actual observations. If the comparison reveals discrepancies, we can make further guesses about the possible underlying influences in the choice of friends.

Making such guesses systematic, precise, and verifiable is the object of a mathematical theory.

It is a far cry, of course, from the barest outlines of a statistical theory of social structure to a full-fledged mathematical science, but a beginning must be made somewhere. Having established a base line for a very simple aspect of social structure, such as the "best friend" relation, an attempt to develop the mathematical theory further leads us first to a classification of the kinds of biases which may be operating in making observed statistical features depart from those expected on the basis of the null hypothesis. One would naturally start with common-sense notions. One might consider some of the following:

1. *The bias of reciprocity.* Although it is by no means certain that if *A* names *B* as "best friend," *B* will name *A*, it may certainly be supposed that the probability of this happening is greater than chance.

2. *The bias of transitivity.* If *A* names *B*, and *B* names *C*, the probability that *C* will name *A* may be greater than chance.

3. *Clique bias.* The population may consist of certain well-defined subclasses (sex, age, education, political groupings) so that the chances that the best friend is within the same subclass is much greater than outside.

4. *Personality biases.* The chance of being named best friend may depend on certain personal characteristics, different in different individuals, etc.

A mathematical model demands a quantitative assumption for each of these hypotheses, that is, a tentative statement in mathematical language about just how each of these biases influences the probabilities of the connections. On the bases of these assumptions, which in themselves may be difficult or impossible to verify *directly*, the mathematician deduces (by mathematical techniques) certain conclusions which are observable; for example, the expected distribution of the best friend choices described above. This deduced distribution may then be compared with the actual. If there is agreement, the particular assumption made is cor-roborated (not proved). If not, other or modified assumptions may be made. Of course, all the biases mentioned may operate at once. A mathe-matical theory provides an opportunity for comparing their relative effects.

Sometimes a bias may be measured directly. For example, the reci-procity bias may be so measured by counting the frequency of mutual naming as best friends. Without a mathematical model, the determina-tion of this bias is only an isolated fact about a population. However, if the theoretical effect of the bias actually calculated is compared with the effect actually observed, we may find out whether the theoretical bias assumed accounts completely for the structure or whether, even after its effect has been taken into consideration, some bias still remains to be accounted for.

Moreover, the framework of thought underlying the model may even give rise to sociopsychological hypotheses, which might otherwise not have occurred. Suppose, for example, we fix our attention on the indi-viduals who are most frequently named as best friend, with frequency far exceeding chance. Their "popularity" may be attributed to two dif-ferent causes—personal attractiveness or to some status or prestige fac-tor. One might then ask whether these two effects can be separated. Suppose that associated with the "prestige" of an individual is a tend-ency of other individuals to include in their list of friends the friends of the "high status" individuals (a "reflected glory" effect) which may be observed in the naming of "second best friends." Suppose further that this transitivity effect (my second best friend is my best friend's best friend) is not associated with those individuals who are named best friend for purely personal reasons. Then, by observing the extent of the transitivity effect, the individuals enjoying popularity for prestige reasons and those enjoying popularity for personal reasons may be dis-tinguished by examining the sociogram of "second best friend" choices.

We have mentioned only one kind of graph which can be con-structed for a given population. There are, of course, many others: tracings through friends of different orders of intimacy, tracings through the *least* liked; tracings through several friends at once, etc. There are also many different statistical quantities to be observed in these tracings. Besides the ones mentioned, distributions of interest may be lengths of chains (how long until a tracing closes in on itself), the number of and sizes of cliques (portions of the population not connected by a naming or being named with any other portion), numbers of new contacts reached at each step of a tracing through several friends at once (how many "friends of friends," friends of third order, etc., does an indi-vidual in the population have on the average?), etc. Without a mathematical theory, all these innumerable statistics are isolated facts. A mathematical theory, on the other hand, no matter how crude, provides a means of unifying all such observations, of creating an underlying framework, from which the observations in all their rich variety are consequences.

3. New Approaches to Economic Behavior

Of all the social sciences, economics seems the easiest to mathematicize, because so many of the economist's working concepts can be expressed as quantities. Prices, production, consumption, rates of interest, wages, profits, budgetary allotments—all of these can be represented as numbers. Theoretical economics seeks to establish relations among these quantities. As in other such situations, the economist could proceed purely empirically, that is, by gathering data and by trying to deduce relations from examining the data. However, as we have pointed out above, this is seldom a fruitful procedure where many variables are involved. The mathematical economist, therefore, like other mathematical social scientists, seeks a model from which relations among the variables might be *deduced*. And he faces the same difficulties as other mathematical social scientists: most models are too simple to fit into the exceedingly involved interplay of variables associated with human behavior; opportunities for controlled experiment are extremely rare; parameters are difficult to estimate independently of each other. Nevertheless, general models of economic behavior exist.[5]

Most of these models are inspired by the methods of mathematical physics and chemistry. The variables are supposed to be connected by means of algebraic or, more characteristically, differential equations. The systems of equations are then examined for solutions of equilibrium, stability of equilibria, etc., so that the equations of mathematical economics often look exactly like those of mathematical physics and chemistry, as also do the equations of mass behavior examined above.

A crucial feature of such equations is their determinism. Given a set of initial conditions and a set of such equations, the entire course of the system they are supposed to represent is usually strictly determined. Of course, philosophical questions arise in the minds of many people as to what extent human behavior is "determined." There is no satisfactory philosophical answer to such a question. The only meaningful answer is a pragmatic one: to the extent that deterministic equations can describe human behavior (and it is not unlikely that mass behavior can be so described to a degree), we must admit that human behavior is subject to deterministic law.

More serious questions arise concerning the specific *assumptions* which underlie the equations of mathematical economics. Most commonly some sort of "maximizing" behavior is assumed; for example, that the individual firm tends to regulate its activities so as to maximize profit. Now the questions raised in connection with maximizing behavior concern not so much the accuracy of the assumptions (whether indeed, for example, firms tend to maximize profit) as the possibility of defining operationally that which is maximized. In the case of profit, there is no difficulty. But the consumer, in distributing his expenditures, is also supposed to maximize something. It certainly is not profit. What, then, is it that the consumer maximizes? To answer this question, a theoretical construct was invented: the consumer maximizes his "utility," vaguely felt to be some sort of satisfaction derived from the consumption of commodities. It is, of course, hopeless to measure this satisfaction directly, especially if one has to compare satisfactions derived from eating, keeping warm, and being entertained. The only hope is to infer the comparative satisfactions from actual preferences, but then it can be shown that only an *ordering* of satisfactions can be so determined, not differences among the degrees of satisfaction. Recently, it has been shown that if the consumer exhibits consistent preferences in situations involving choice of satisfactions under conditions of risk, a more definitive "utility function" can be established. A considerable amount of work both theoretical and experimental has been done recently on this psychological aspect of economic behavior.[6]

A radically different approach to economics appears in the recent development of a branch of mathematics known as the theory of games.[7] The name is superficially deceptive, giving the impression that the theory is applicable mainly to the area of recreation or amusement. To a certain extent the theory of games does deal with games but not in the way that would occur to someone whose conception of a game derives from the *content* of a game. Actually, a most thorough knowledge of the theory of games would not make anyone a better chess or bridge player. The theory of games penetrates to the very "soul" of the process in which people match wits and take chances, completely abstracting from the way this process occurs in a specific setting. The impact of the theory upon the conception of economic behavior and on social science in general will be examined in the course of our discussion.

There is a historical analogue to the development of the theory of games in the development of the theory of probability. It is well known that the theory of probability also started as a theory of games, namely, games of pure chance, that is, those which require no skill of playing but only skill of betting. Take the simplest of such games, such as *Rouge et Noire* or guessing heads or tails. The essential feature of both these games is that a bet is made on the outcome in a situation with two presumably equally possible outcomes. The "content," of course, is immaterial. Whether one guesses "heads or tails," "right hand or left hand," "even or odd" does not matter. The game is completely described by the probabilities of the two outcomes. Multiply the number of outcomes (as in dice or roulette), combine the outcomes into conjunctive or disjunctive sets, and you can describe all possible games of pure chance. The theory of such games is confined to the computation of outcome probabilities on which presumably betting policy will depend. The theory of probability provides a method for such computation. Of course, its method is not confined to gambling policies. The theory of probability applies to a great variety of situations where, because of the complexity of events under consideration, uncertainty prevails. The theory is applied in economics, in biology, and even in physics (as in statistical mechanics). Gambling situations merely provide a conveniently familiar and amusing setting in which to talk of the logic of uncertain events.

The more recent theory of games has a similar significance. It too begins with game situations to which, however, the element of "conflict" is added. This element is not present in the pure game of chance. In a game of pure chance, there is a single player against an impersonal "house." For example, when a man operates a slot machine, he is not in conflict with the machine (no matter what his feelings in the matter may be), because the machine is not trying to win. The theory of games, on the contrary, even in its simplest form, deals with two or more *intelligent* opponents.

Let us examine the simplest game of this kind, called a two-person zero-sum game. "Zero sum" means that what one player wins, the other loses.

Suppose each player, independently of the other, chooses one of two numbers, 1 or 2. There are then four possible outcomes corresponding to the four pairs of choices (1, 1), (1, 2), (2, 1), and (2, 2). With each outcome is associated a pay off, or that which player B pays player A (which, of course, may be negative, if actually A pays B). This game can now be completely described by a square array of the pay offs.

	1	2
1	+ 4	− 3
2	+ 2	+ 1

Player A is to choose a row, and player B a column. If A chooses row 1 and B column 1, B pays A \$4; if A chooses row 1, and B column 2, A pays B \$3, etc.

Let us see what will happen if both *A* and *B* play wisely. *A* would like, of course, to win $4, the maximum. But if he chooses row 1, he risks losing $3 (if *B* should choose column 2), and he knows this, and he knows that *B* knows this. Therefore, *A* will be wise to choose row 2, where he can be *sure* of winning at least $1. *B,* on the other hand can make sure that *A* wins *no more* than $1 by choosing column 2.

The $1 win for *A* is *determined* by the rational choices of both players. *A* can be sure of winning at least $1, and *B* can prevent him from winning any more. *B* can be sure of losing no more than $1, and *A* can force him to lose it. This game, therefore, will always be played the same way by rational players and hence need not be played at all. The game is actually no more than a directive for *B* to pay $1 to *A*.

This seems like an absurd conclusion but only because other values than pay offs are involved in actual games and because most adult games are too complicated to be played completely rationally. The conclusion does, however, have some pertinence to reality. The reason adults do not play ticktacktoe is because the game is dull for rational players. The outcome will always be a draw. This is because each player is guaranteed at least a draw, and each player can see to it that his opponent gets no more than a draw.

If we designate a won game by 1 and a lost game by -1, then ticktacktoe appears as a two-person zero-sum game. It is also a game of "complete information," that is, all the moves leading to the situation in which the players find themselves are known to both players. One of the principal results in the theory of games is that all two-person zero-sum games with complete information possess an unambiguous "solution," the prescribed wisest strategies for both players. What is at first sight surprising is that extremely involved games like chess also fall into this category. If chess were played by two completely rational players, it would be sufficient for each to choose a "strategy" at the start of the game. A strategy is a complete "program," in which *all possible* answers of the opponent to each of one's moves are taken into account, and one's own reply to each of these answers is indicated. The choice of strategies by each of the players determines the outcome, and, because of the determinacy of the solution of two-person zero-sum games with complete information, the outcome will always be the same, either always a win for White or always a win for Black or a draw. The either-or stands not for the uncertainty of what will happen in a given game but for our ignorance of what the certain outcome is. But the outcome *is* certain according to the theory of the zero-sum game with complete information. If ever this outcome is established and the corresponding strategies found, chess will be as dull as ticktacktoe.

It is still not clear at this point where the intrinsic interest of game theory lies and why it is important to social science. Let us therefore pursue the subject a little further. The two-person zero-sum game with complete information is, from the point of view of game theory, the game with the simplest structure. The most important achievement of game theory is its discovery of the logical structure of games completely abstracted from their content. Chess is enormously more complex than ticktacktoe; yet it is a game of the same "species," represented by the simplest prototype in our example of the two-row-two-column array. Each player chooses a "strategy"; the choices determine the outcome. There is a best way for choosing both strategies if both players play rationally.

However, the two-person zero-sum game with complete information is only one "species." Other kinds of games have different structures and are thus governed by different logical considerations. As an example, take "button, button." One player hides a button in one of his hands; the other tries to guess in which hand. Here it seems no rule can be established for hiding or for guessing so as to get the best results. Nevertheless, there is a rule. One way *not* to play is to hide or to guess with any regularity. For if this regularity is discovered by the opponent, he can turn it to his advantage. So much is clear. But one might think one could be very clever by establishing some pattern of hiding the coin as a "bait" to make the opponent fall into the pattern in his guesses and then suddenly change the pattern. The theory of the two-person zero-sum games extended to games without complete information deflates this hope. No strategy, according to that theory, can do for either opponent (in the long run) as well as the so-called "mixed" strategy of completely randomized guesses or hands. In that case each player can expect to win half of the time. Neither can do better by trying any patterned strategy. If he tries (and the other is rational), he can do only worse for himself.

It turns out, therefore, that "button, button," is a game of another species than chess. In chess, the player could select *one* strategy and ensure for himself the best that he could do. "Button, button" requires a *mixture* of strategies in just the right proportions. Thus, the theory of games places ticktacktoe and chess in one class and "button, button" in another, quite contrary to the general impression that the last two, being children's games, belong together, while chess, being an adult game of vast complexity, is not comparable to either. Nevertheless, the game-theoretical classification is the more significant one. The situation is somewhat analogous to that in biological science where a mouse and a whale are shown to be more closely related than a mouse and a frog, because of much deeper considerations than appearances.

Having provided a simplified framework for large classes of games (reducing the process to choices of strategies), the game theoretician proceeds to examine games of different species. Rather dramatic results begin to appear as soon as he begins to examine non-zero-sum games. Here one player's winnings are not always equal to the other player's losses. Therefore, both pay offs must be entered into the matrix for each pair of strategy choices. Consider the following game, nicknamed in the literature as "The Prisoner's Dilemma."

	1	2
1	9, 9	−10, 10
2	10, −10	−9, −9

Here if A chooses row 1, and B column 1, both win $9. If A chooses row 1 and B column 2, A loses $10 and B wins $10, etc. The first number of each entry represents A's gain, and the second B's gain. Suppose now A tries to reason, as in the zero-sum game, something as follows: "Whatever B does, it is to my advantage to choose row 2, since if B chooses column 1, I prefer $10 to $9; if he chooses column 2, I prefer to lose $9 to losing $10. Therefore, I must choose row 2." B reasons in the same way and is also driven to the conclusion that he must choose column 2. As a result, both players lose $9, whereas by choosing row 1, column 1 they could have each *won* $9. One is somewhat reminded of the reasoning behind armament races and mutual tariff restrictions. Each side seems to act in its own interest by trying to be stronger than the other or to achieve a favorable trade balance. As a result, both sides increase expenditures or costs of goods without necessarily increasing security or obtaining a favorable balance.

A non-zero-sum game appears as a drama of human co-operation and conflict of interest in miniature. Both players can combine against the house, provided each is confident that the other will not double cross him. Collective interest does not necessarily form a "summation of individual interests." For example, the risk of contracting smallpox in the United States today is so small that the risk associated with vaccination (though also extremely small) is actually greater. Thus, it would seem to the individual's (slight) advantage not to submit to vaccination. However, if each individual acted to his individual "advantage" in this case, the collective result would be disastrous.

The Prisoner's Dilemma [8] game illustrates the power of a coalition which resides essentially in the agreement of the coalition members to plan their strategy together. Whenever there are three or more players, the coalitions can be formed in various ways. It is evidently of advantage to the players who have been left out of a coalition to form a coalition of their own. A simple calculation shows that N players can be split into two coalitions in 2^N different ways. If this happens, the N-person game becomes a two-person game and can be treated accordingly. But, depending on how this split is made, the predetermined outcome of the game (if such exists) or the average outcome over many plays under conditions of rational play by both sides may be different for each split. Therefore, different coalitions "command" different final pay offs. It would be tempting to conclude that the coalition commanding the greatest pay off will be automatically formed, but the situation is much more complicated. Several coalitions may command the same pay off. At any rate, it often becomes necessary to induce players to join coalitions, and this raises the question of what inducements can be offered and by whom to whom.

Again we see how the situations which naturally arise in the purely formal (logical) theory of games strikingly resemble real-life situations where partially conflicting and partially coincident interests are interlaced. It cannot be emphasized too strongly that the theory of games is a *formal* theory. It does not purport to describe how people behave in real-life situations or even in games, but only to discover the inherent *logic* of certain situations common both to games and to real life. It does say how people would behave (1) if they were guided entirely by unambiguous interests (that is, they could always decide in each situation involving both alternative outcomes and risks which outcome they would prefer at which risk); and (2) if they were able to utilize all the information available to them and calculate the actual outcomes in determinate situations and expected outcomes in situations involving risks; and (3) if the rules governing the sequence and the range of permissible acts were explicit and fixed.

In a very simple game like ticktacktoe, all three conditions are satisfied. In more complicated games only the first and last of these conditions are usually satisfied. The practical impossibility of deciding once for all on the best strategy for all concerned is what makes games interesting. In real life, however, none of the conditions holds. People do not exactly know what they want; possible outcomes of action are too numerous even to be listed, let alone calculated; rules are usually ambiguous and change with time. What, then, is the scientific value of game theory? I believe its value is in the toe hold it affords to us in our efforts to understand behavior. By abstracting a highly simplified model of certain aspects of social behavior, the theory makes it possible to *stake out* an area of theoretical research in rational behavior.

One is reminded of the birth of physical science. Archimedes, in his mathematical formulation of statics (study of mechanical equilibrium) and Galileo in his mathematical description of motion also staked out areas, beachheads from which to launch further conquests. They too assumed highly idealized conditions: perfectly uniform rigid bodies, perfect vacuum, frictionless surfaces, etc. These conditions are nowhere met, and so no real bodies behave as Archimedes' statics and Galilean (later Newtonian) dynamics say they do. Yet without these beginnings there would be no physical science.

There is one important difference between the abstractions of mathematical physics and those of the theory of games. There are many actually observable phenomena which are good approximations to the models of mathematical physics, particularly astronomical events, and electromagnetic phenomena. No such richness of approximate realization is likely to be found in connection with the theory of games. But this is only repeating the observation familiar to all that human behavior is much more involved than the behavior of inert bodies. The journey to knowledge of Man is longer and harder than the journey to knowledge of inert matter, but it must be somehow begun.

CONCLUSION

Understanding among social and physical scientists (particularly mathematicians) can be achieved on the basis of mutual tolerance. The mathematician must realize that the social scientist *does* deal with events which really have no analogue in the realm of physical science. Coincident and conflicting interests (the area treated in the theory of games) is an outstanding example of the kind of situation completely absent in physical science. Here not only events but *estimation* of events and decisions made on the basis of expected decisions of others come into play and introduce an entirely new dimension into mathematical analysis. There may be other areas where the logic of the theory of games also fails, so that other intellectual schemes must be devised. The mathematician, therefore, must muster his creative powers to explore *new* deductive techniques. He must become less bound by the methods of deterministic mathematical analysis (which has been superlatively successful in physics) and by ordinary statistical and probabilistic methods (which have been successful in situations dominated by blind chance). So far, the theory of games stands almost alone as an entirely new mathematical approach to human behavior, taking into account the salient features of rationality.

It should not be forgotten, however, that the theory of games, in spite of its strong social-science flavor, is a product of mathematicians' minds. The social scientist, therefore, if he wishes the mathematician to continue such explorations, must also be patient and tolerant of the mathematician, who, preoccupied almost exclusively with the tools of his deductive method tends always to simplify situations beyond recognition. The mathematician must simplify, because only then can he begin working. The social scientist should not demand realism from the mathematician's models but only pertinence. It is sufficient if the model contains the essentials, no matter how crudely simplified, of some social process. The social scientist must therefore muster his intuitive powers to distinguish the salient features of the social process from the trivial.

It does not matter if the few salient features alone do not constitute a model which accurately describes or predicts. If the fundamentals have been captured, the work has started and can go on. Variables can be added, relations modified, and results interpreted in other contexts. The way to understanding is through doing, and the way to truth is through error. A most valuable contribution of mathematics to all approaches to reliable knowledge is that mathematics makes possible an accurate estimate of the errors made in the pursuit of knowledge. It enables the scientist to appraise the magnitude, the importance, and often the causes of errors. Moreover, it possibly suggests ways of correcting them. Mathematics is the only language we have which is uncontaminated by bias derived from content. Being contentless and independent of specific experience, mathematics is the only "cosmopolitan" language possessed by man. It makes possible the linking of theories of widely different content but with similar logical structures. It is therefore superbly suited to serve as the language of all science.

NOTES

1. Kenneth J. Arrow, "Mathematical Models in the Social Sciences," *The Policy Sciences,* D. Lerner and H. D. Lasswell, eds. (Stanford: Stanford University Press, 1951), ch. VIII.

2. N. Rashevsky, *Mathematical Biology of Social Behavior* (Chicago: The University of Chicago Press, 1951), Part III.

3. A. Rapoport, "Contribution to the Mathematical Theory of Mass Behavior: I. The Propagation of Single Acts," *Bulletin of Mathematical Biophysics,* 14 (1952), pp. 159-69.

4. A. Rapoport, "Diffusion Problems in Mass Behavior," *General Systems,* 1 (1956), pp. 48-55.

5. Wassily Leontieff, "Mathematics in Economics," *Bulletin of the American Mathematical Society,* 60 (May, 1954), pp. 215-33.

6. See, for example, R. M. Thrall, C. H. Coombs, and R. L. Davis, eds., *Decision Processes* (New York: John Wiley & Sons, Inc., 1954).

7. J. C. C. McKinsey, *Introduction to the Theory of Games* (New York: McGraw-Hill Book Company, Inc., 1952).

8. The name derives from the original formulation where each of two prisoners interrogated separately wonders whether the other has sold out. If each trusts the other, neither confesses, and the state has no case; but if neither trusts the other, both confess, hoping for lighter punishment, and both are convicted.

12

Models, Meaning, and Theories

MAY BRODBECK

University of Minnesota

The term "model" appears with increasing frequency in recent social-science literature. We encounter models of learning, of rational choice, of communication, of political behavior, of group-interaction, and so on, and so on. The term has moreover a decided halo effect. Models are Good Things. And if models are good, "mathematical models," needless to say, are even better. Yet, what exactly is a model and what purposes does it serve? I venture to suggest that ten model builders will give at least five different or, at least, apparently different answers to this question. What is the difference between a model and a theory? How can two theories have the same model, and what does it signify if they do? Are there any logical differences between models in physical science and those in the behavioral sciences? I shall attempt to answer these and similar questions.

Model ships appear frequently in bottles; model boys in heaven only. Model ships are copies of real ones. Asked to describe a ship, we could point to its model. A model boy, on the other hand, having no earthly counterpart, is everything a boy *ought* to be. A model ship, then, is a

---

A draft of this paper was written during the tenure of a Faculty Research Fellowship from the Social Science Research Council. It was revised during the author's participation in the Behavioral Science Conference at the University of New Mexico in the summer of 1957, under Project AF 49(638)-33 sponsored by the Behavioral Sciences Division, Air Force Office of Scientific Research, ARDC. I am indebted to these agencies for the time granted me. M.B.

three-dimensional replica. A model boy is a *norm*. They illustrate the two most common nontechnical uses of "model." The normative use is at most incidental in science and I shall not recur to it. I shall first of all explain those characteristics of three-dimensional models by virtue of which they are models. Then, after some preliminary clarifications, I shall turn to an analysis of the various uses of "model" for verbal or symbolic systems.

ISOMORPHISM

A miniature train is a model not by virtue of being diminutive, but because it imitates a real train. Not only does the model have its own chimney stacks and windows but these duplicate the relative proportions of the real thing. The model is constructed to scale. What purpose does it serve? Apart from being a toy, it is, like an architect's model of a building, a "nonverbal description" of the thing. Since it is, except for size and possibly materials, an exact imitation, we must know what the thing itself is like or, as in the architect's case, what it is going to be like before we can build the model. Though it may help some people to see the thing in detail, the details were already known, at least to the builder. A replica thus gives no new knowledge, not even of a simple descriptive kind. Replicas are therefore not, as such, scientifically interesting. Nevertheless, they have some features which will help us to understand more useful models.

The technical term for the similarity between a thing and a model of it is *isomorphism*. Isomorphism requires two conditions. First, there must be a one-to-one correspondence between the elements of the model and the elements of the thing of which it is the model. For every chimney stack, there is a miniature chimney stack. Every window has its replica, and conversely. Second, certain relations are preserved. For instance, if a door is to the left of a window in the original, their replicas are similarly situated; also, the model is constructed to scale. Among the relations which the model may or may not preserve, one kind is of special interest. The model may or may not "work" on the same principle as the original. If it does, I shall call the isomorphism *complete*. If, for instance, a model of a steam engine is also steam propelled, then the isomorphism is complete. The similarity or isomorphism of a planetarium with the heavenly bodies is not complete. All the planets with their moons and the sun, together with their spatial relations to each other, are duplicated. But the motions of these bodies across the hemispherical ceiling are not caused by gravitational attraction, as are, of course, the motions of the real planets in the heavens. Since the laws according to which the model works are different from those of the real thing, the isomorphism is incomplete. As far as three-dimensional models go, even a complete one, like the steam-propelled model steam engine, has only an incidental scientific value. Since the model is easy to manipulate, this may help discovery of the principles by which it works, if these are not already known. Diagrams and pictorial devices, in the nature of the case, cannot be complete. These models are at best suggestive to the visual-minded and, at worst, like all incomplete models, misleading if taken literally. Although social scientists occasionally resort to such pictorial devices, the term "model" is more frequently applied to various kinds of verbal or symbolic systems. In order to clarify the ambiguities in these uses, certain preliminary distinctions are needed.

CONTENT AND FORM: DESCRIPTIVE AND LOGICAL WORDS

The language of science, devoid of greetings, exclamations, questions, and commands, consists wholly of declarative sentences. By means of them, the scientist talks about the world. These sentences may be as simple and qualitative as the statement that ice is cold or as complicated and quantitative as the Newtonian law of attraction. In either case, all such sentences consist of certain arrangements of two kinds of words. Some of the words in a sentence are names for characteristics or attributes of individual things or events and for relations among these. They are called *descriptive* terms or concepts. They may name characteristics of inanimate physical things, of organisms, or of societies. Thus, green is an attribute of some physical objects, notably grass. Hunger at some time or other belongs to the state of an organism, while totalitarian is an attribute of some societies. A relation is any attribute requiring two or more individuals for its exemplification, like older, between, more populous, or smarter. Many terms, such as "married" or "mother," appear grammatically to be attributes of single individuals, but, like "south," are actually relational, requiring, when defined, reference to two or more individuals. These names for characteristics of things, whether relational or nonrelational, distinguish one area from another, psychology, say, from physics. The subject matter, or content, of an area is thus indicated by its descriptive terms.

Descriptive terms are connected with each other to form statements of fact, like "John is blond." Sentences, in turn, are connected with each other to form compound sentences, like "John is blond and Jim is redheaded." These compound sentences express connections among facts. The words that do this connecting, like "and," "or," and "if . . . then," are called *logical* words. They do not themselves denote anything. Logical words give language its form or structure by connecting terms that do denote. They are common to all sciences. For example, the sentences "He is a scholar *and* he is an athlete" and "He is a scholar *or* he is an athlete" are alike in that they have the same subject matter. But their *form* is different. On the other hand, "He is a scholar *or* he is an athlete" is like "The judge is elected *or* he is appointed" in that they share a common form. Their subject matter differs but both statements are disjunctions. The descriptive words of a sentence give it its meaning. If we know what they refer to, then we know what a sentence of a certain form is about and can determine whether it is true or false. A sentence may be stripped of its meaning, yet retain its form, by replacing all its descriptive words or component statements by letters. Thus *"X or Y," "X and Y,"* and *"If X, then Y"* are the form of a disjunction, conjunction, and conditional, respectively. As they stand, there is no way to distinguish *"X or Y"* from *"U or Z."* If, however, each letter-variable is replaced by a sentence containing different descriptive words, then the statements say different things while they have the same form. This notion of *having the same form* is essential to one important use of "model."

LOGICAL AND EMPIRICAL TRUTH

Words, then, are either logical or descriptive. Sentences are also of two kinds. For one kind, from the form alone, truth or falsity cannot be determined. In, for instance, "If *X* then *Y*," we must know what the letters refer to or mean before we can tell whether the sentence is true or false. Compare, however, "If *X* then *Y*" with "If *X* then *X*." Both statements have the same form, as expressed by the logical phrase "if . . . then"; they are both conditionals. But assuming that the same letters are always replaced by the same sets of descriptive words, the two statements differ notably. In "If *X* then *X*" we do not have to replace the letters by sentences about descriptive properties in order to tell whether it is true or false. It is true no matter what is put for *X*. If *X* stands for the statement that a judge is elected, then the whole sentence says "If a judge is elected, then a judge is elected," which is something less than controversial. A statement of this form is true no matter what its components are about. Another such statement is "Either *X* or not-*X*." Sentences true by virtue of their form alone are called *logical truths* or, also, tautological or analytic. In "If *X* then *Y*," on the other hand, we must know what descriptive words replace *"X"* and *"Y"* before we can tell whether the statement is true or false. Sentences whose truth depends upon their descriptive words as well as on their form are called *empirical* statements or, also, contingent or synthetic. One important subclass of logical or analytic truths are those of arithmetic. I use this latter term quite generally to cover everything from elementary arithmetic through calculus and higher mathematics, in order to avoid the confusing ambiguities which, as we shall presently see, beset the term "mathematical." All arithmetical concepts, like numbers and operations upon them such as addition, are ultimately definable in terms of logical words alone. The definition is cumbrous and need not concern us here. But, once carried through, it turns out that statements such as $5 + 7 = 12$, as well as those of more abstruse mathematics, are all true by virtue of their form alone. They contain no symbols referring to descriptive properties and relations and these are irrelevant to the truths of arithmetic. Like "If X then X," they say nothing about the world, so are neither confirmed nor refuted by it. Saying "nothing," they are, as we shall see, yet remarkably useful.

LAWS AND THEORIES

A concept, a statement of fact, a law, and a theory are all different things. A concept is a term referring to a descriptive property or relation. A "fact" is a particular thing, characteristic, event, or kind of event, like Johnny's I. Q. or the proportion of home owners, or the size of the Republican vote. To state a fact, then, is to state that a concept has an instance or a number of instances. Facts are significant insofar as they are connected with other facts to form generalizations or laws. To find such connections is the purpose of counting and measuring, whether one is counting heads or electrons. A law states that whenever there is an instance of one kind of fact, then there is also an instance of another. Laws, therefore, are always empirical generalizations, like, for instance, "Whenever there is a rise in wages, then prices increase." If we can state exactly how much prices increase with given increases in wages, then we have a quantitative law. Quantified generalizations or laws are expressed by equations. These equations state how the value of some concepts or "variables" change with the value of others. Thus, Galileo's law of falling bodies states that the distance a released body falls varies directly with the square of its time, that is, $d = 16t^2$.

Like all other sentences, quantified laws have a certain form. Many other physical properties besides distance vary as the square of some other characteristic. The so-called linear equation, $y = ax + b$, represents still another quantified form taken by some laws. The variables might stand for many different things, like weight and height or supply and demand, while the form remains the same. But a quantified empirical law such as $d = 16t^2$ differs from an arithmetic statement like $9 = 3^2$.

In the empirical law, the letter variables d and t must be given meaning as distance and time before its truth or falsity can be established. No descriptive terms occur in the arithmetic truths. When letters do occur in arithmetic statements, as in $x + y = y + x$, then it is understood that the letters are to be replaced by numbers. It is a logical truth about numbers that the order of addition does not make a difference. As we shall see later, if the letters do not stand for numbers, then the statement may well be false. Quantified empirical laws, like $d = 16t^2$, are often called "mathematical." It is obvious now why this term is confusing. A quantified law of empirical science is an empirical or synthetic assertion, whose truth or falsity depends upon its descriptive terms. Distance varies as the square of time, but demand probably does not. A statement of mathematics, on the other hand, is analytic. In order to stress the distinction between empirical laws and the tautologies of mathematics, I shall continue to use the term "arithmetic" for the latter.

A theory is a deductively connected set of laws. Some of these laws, the axioms or postulates of the theory, logically imply others, the theorems. The axioms are such only by virtue of their place in the theory. Neither "self-evident" nor otherwise privileged, they are empirical laws whose truth is, temporarily at least, taken for granted in order to see what other empirical assertions, the theorems, must be true if they are. Since empirical laws are inductive generalizations, they are also called "hypotheses." "Hypothetico-deductive" system is thus another name for such empirical axiom systems or theories. Laws, whether quantified or not, have a certain form, as expressed either by the verbal "if . . . then . . ." or by an equation. Theories differ from each other either in their descriptive terms, in which case they are about different things, or in the form of their laws, or both. For instance, theories within physics and those within sociology presumably differ from each other not only in their descriptive terms but also in the form of the statements connecting these concepts. "Time" and "distance," for example, are descriptive terms or "variables" of physical theory. The parabola $y = ax^2$, or a differential equation of a certain sort, gives the form of the law connecting these terms. Within sociology, the descriptive terms might be, say, "religious preference" and "political attitude." A law connecting these attributes might have the form of a nonquantified conditional, like "If anyone is a Catholic, then he is also a conservative." Or it might take the form of a quantified linear equation expressing a statistical correlation between the variables.

MODELS: ISOMORPHIC THEORIES

A model train, we saw, is similar to a real one in being isomorphic with it. The isomorphism is complete if both work on the same principles. Extending this notion to theories, we can formulate a precise meaning of "model." Two theories whose laws have the same form are isomorphic or *structurally similar* to each other. If the laws of one theory have the same form as the laws of another theory, then one may be said to be a *model* for the other. This definition of "model" in terms of an isomorphism between theories at least provides one unambiguous meaning for that term. That it is not consistently used in this way by scientists is, of course, one reason why the notion requires clarification. How do we discover whether two theories, or parts of them, are isomorphic to each other? Suppose that one area, as indicated by a set of descriptive concepts, for which a relatively well-developed theory is at hand is said to be a model for another area, about which little is as yet known. The descriptive terms in the theory of the better-known area are put into one-to-one correspondence with those of the "new" area. By means of this one-to-one correspondence, the laws of one area are "translated" into laws of the other area.[1] The concepts of the better-known theory are replaced in the laws by the concepts of the new area. This replacement results in a set of laws or hypotheses about the variables of the new area. If observation shows these hypotheses to be true, then the laws of both areas have the same form. The lawful connections are preserved and the two theories are completely isomorphic to each other. For example, suppose it is wondered whether rumors spread like diseases. That is, can the laws of epidemiology, about which quite a bit is known, be a model for a theory of rumor transmission? Or, to say the same thing differently, do the laws about rumors have the same form as the laws about diseases? The descriptive concepts in the laws of epidemiology are first of all replaced by letter variables. This reveals the form of the laws. The concepts referring to diseases are put into one-to-one correspondence with those referring to rumors. The letter variables in the epidemiological laws are replaced by the descriptive terms referring to rumors. This results in a set of hypotheses about rumors, which may or may not be confirmed. If, optimistically, these laws are confirmed, then the two theories have the same form.

The notion of "model" as isomorphism of laws is obviously symmetrical. However, when an area about which we already know a good deal is used to suggest laws for an area about which little is known, then the familiar area providing the form of the laws may be called a model for the new area. But once it is found that the laws of both areas do indeed share a common structure, then of course either is a model for the other. This definition of "model" is also the only clear sense in which one scientific area can be called an "analogy" for another. Two areas are structurally or formally analogous to each other if their laws have the same form. However, since nothing is to be gained by substituting one ambiguous term for another, I shall not persist with this use of "analogy."

Where knowledge is scarce, speculation abounds. Social science, not surprisingly, witnesses a plethora of speculative "models" or guesses about isomorphisms. A few illustrations will suffice. The notion of society as an organism, though repeatedly discredited, has a way of cropping up in one form or another. In its Spenglerian form, society is likened to a plant, complete with a seasonal life cycle. Like plants, a society has its vernal and autumnal phases. Or, again, society is compared to the growth and physiology of man, having like man its own states of development, its organic interrelatedness of parts, and its homeostatic controls. Evolutionary theory is another favorite model. Whole societies may be seen as engaged in a struggle for survival subject to natural selection. Within a society, the various institutions and codes of behavior are viewed in the light of their contribution to adaptation and adjustment. Or, again, individual learning is compared with the process of selective survival among random variations. The human brain is compared to an electronic computer. Servomechanisms, like the automatic pilot or thermostat, are now frequently evoked models for learning and purposive behavior. How does one go about testing these suggested models?

First, it must be possible to state clearly what is in one-to-one correspondence with what. Organisms grow; they increase in size and weight. What is *social* "growth"? What is the autumnal phase of society corresponding to the autumn of a plant? Relatively precise meaning can be given to adaptive and nonadaptive characteristics of organisms within evolutionary theory. Can we give correspondingly precise meanings to these notions for human institutions? What in learning, fitted to the evolutionary model, corresponds to the role of mutations? Second, once clearly defined empirical concepts in one area are made to correspond to the terms of the model, then formal similarities, if any, are sought. Nutrition is connected with growth in biology. Are the social concepts corresponding to nutrition and to growth similarly connected? In other words, not only must the terms of the two areas correspond, but the connections among these concepts must also be preserved, if the model is to be of any use. An area, either part or all of it, can be a fruitful model for another only if corresponding concepts can be found and if at least some of the laws connecting the concepts of the model also can be shown to connect their corresponding concepts. This implies that the model is from an area better developed than that for which it is used. If very little is known about either field, then to speak of a "model" is hardly more than loose and pointless talk.

UNNECESSARY USES OF "MODEL"

Isomorphism of the laws of one theory with those of another unequivocally defines the term "model." Unfortunately, the word has other uses. Two other meanings are especially prevalent. One of these has nothing at all to do with the notion of isomorphism. The other is connected with this notion, but in a manner different from that just discussed. The same term applied to at least three different kinds of things is of course confusing. Moreover, the resulting ambiguity is quite unnecessary, since other terms are at hand which adequately characterize these further uses. "One thing, one word" is still a good idea.

The first unnecessary use of "model" is as a synonym for "theory." In particular, the term is used for theories which have some or all of four different characteristics. (1) Any as yet untested or even untestable theory may be dubbed a "model." Speculative theories, like those about the neurophysiological correlates of behavior or the doctrines of psychoanalysis, for which empirical evidence is scarce, are sometimes called models, apparently because of a reluctance to honor them as full-fledged theories. But there is nothing in the notion of a theory, as a set of hypotheses about an area, which says that it must be true or is known to be so. (2) Constructing a theory entails abstraction. "Abstraction," like "model," is equivocal. In one context, it refers to that selection always necessary to describe the world. All theories, whether of human or nonhuman behavior, omit some variables simply because they are not relevant to the phenomena to be explained or predicted by the theory. Self-consciousness, not to say embarrassment, about such perfectly legitimate omissions seems to be peculiar to social science. It is suggested by phrases like "economic man" or "ideal type." The quite unnecessary diffidence about neglecting variables is sometimes reflected by calling these theories "models." Economic man, on one formulation, always chooses to maximize his utility. But this is part of a theory asserting in effect that, statistically at least, other motives can be neglected when predicting, say, the behavior of a firm. Similarly, ideal types of society implicitly assert that the effect of unmentioned variables is negligible. But this is true of any theory. The better the theory, the more knowledge we have about the conditions under which the neglected variables do or do not make a difference. If there are no economic men or if the ideal type of capitalism does not exist, then certain suggested theories are false. Calling them "models" will not make them truer. (3) In another context, "abstraction" refers to things like the perfect or ideal gas, absolutely rigid bodies, perfectly straight lines, frictionless bodies, and instantaneous velocities. These entities are all physically impossible. The infinitesimal is an artifact of our mathematical machinery, enabling us to compute changes of one variable with respect to another. Theories making use of this and other "ideal" entities are also called models. What is ideal about them? A perfect or ideal gas is not, like our model boy, everything a good gas ought to be. Yet, they are alike in that both of them characteristically deviate from anything actual. There conceivably could be perfect boys but probably there are none. In the nature of the case, there cannot be any frictionless bodies or dimensionless points. A frictionless engine is one whose coefficient of friction is zero; a dimensionless point has zero diameter. The scientist uses these imaginary "zero" notions when theorizing in order to predict how *other* properties of such entities, the engine or the gas, are connected, assuming the given one is absent. Only ideal gases, defined as those whose molecules have zero volume, exactly obey certain laws connecting the volume, pressure, and temperature of gases. Deviations from these laws, as under high pressures, may then be explained in terms of deviation from the ideal. These of course are independently confirmable by more general laws of which the "almost-zero" condition is a special case. The laws of theories making use of such entities are "ideal" because they hold rigorously only for the limiting case of zero value for certain specified variables. These laws are not false, but are an extrapolation from actual conditions to the physically unapproachable limit. Moreover, they state, implicitly or explicitly, the range of actual conditions for which they hold. These theories which extrapolate or idealize their laws for the zero value of specified variables are not the same as those theories which deliberately neglect variables, like that of economic man or ideal types. A detailed discussion involves another story for another time. But consider that it is not disturbing to say that there are no perfect gases or dimensionless points. Nobody ever thought there were. But to say that economic man or the ideal type of capitalism does not exist is to say that certain theories are false, either because they neglect unspecified but relevant variables or because the laws among those specified do not hold. (4) When numbers can be attached to the concepts of a theory, so that we can say how much of the property is present or how much it changes under certain conditions, then the theory is quantified. Social scientists now valiantly try to quantify their terms. Quantified theories may be constructed either directly from observed facts or, rather more frequently, from guesses about the facts. Quantified theories are after all just theories. Only in a very special case, to be discussed later, having no counterpart in social science, do physicists call theories "models." A physicist speaks of the Newtonian theory, not of the Newtonian model.

Yet, within social science, quantified theories are now frequently called "models," and, particularly, "mathematical models." The term "mathematical," I have already shown, is radically and harmfully ambiguous. The phrase "mathematical model" compounds the ambiguity. I shall recur to this point in a moment. In any case, uncertainty, selection, idealization, and quantification are characteristic to a greater or lesser degree of most worth-while theories. What then is gained, except unnecessary confusion, by calling theories which share in some or all of these characteristics "models"?

MODELS: ARITHMETICAL REPRESENTATIONS

A third prevalent use of "model" also has something to do with isomorphism, but not with that between the laws of empirical theories. "Mathematical model," as I just said, may simply mean any quantified theory. On the other hand, it may and frequently does mean any arithmetical structure of a kind I must now explain. We saw before that replacing all the descriptive terms or concepts in the theory of one area by those of a different area results in another theory with the same form but different content from the original. The isomorphic sets of laws, those of the model and of its "translation," are both empirical theories whose truth or falsity depends upon the facts. It is possible, and often highly desirable, to establish another kind of isomorphism, in which the result is not two empirical theories sharing a common structure. Instead, the laws, or some of them, of an empirical theory may have the same form as a set of purely arithmetical truths. If this is the case, then the latter is called an *arithmetical representation* of the empirical theory. This notion is best explained by means of illustrations. I shall briefly discuss four: analytical geometry, probability theory, measurement, and the theory of games.

ARITHMETICAL REPRESENTATION: ANALYTICAL GEOMETRY

Euclidean geometry is a physical theory. Its axioms and theorems are empirical laws about the properties of rigid bodies in space. Its axioms state certain connections among the entities, including relations, referred to by its undefined or basic descriptive terms, like "point," "line," "lies on," and "between." Its theorems, derived from the axioms and definitions, state connections among defined entities such as triangles and circles and relations like parallel and perpendicular. As in any empirical theory, only the connection between the axioms and theorems is logically necessary. Both axioms and theorems themselves are empirical hypotheses like all others, except that for ordinary magnitudes they are particularly well-confirmed. As we now know, in the realm of the very large, they do not hold. (Clarification of the empirical nature of geometry was one important by-product of the theory of relativity.) *Analytical* geometry is constructed from physical geometry by putting all the undefined descriptive terms of the latter into one-to-one correspondence with a set of defined arithmetical terms. (Alternative ways to speak of constructing a one-to-one correspondence are to say that one set of terms is "co-ordinated" to or "mapped" on to another set.) For example, the descriptive entity "point" is co-ordinated to an ordered pair of numbers, that is, the point corresponding to the pair of numbers $(0,5)$ is different from the point corresponding to the pair of numbers $(5,0)$. All of the geometrical figures correspond to equations or sets of equations. A straight line, for instance, corresponds to, say, $y = 5$ or $y = x + 3$; a circle to still a different equation like $x^2 + y^2 = 25$. More generally, the notion of, for instance, a straight line will correspond to the set of all number-pairs satisfying a certain form of equation. The descriptive relation "lying on," as of a point lying on a line, corresponds to the arithmetical notion of a pair of numbers satisfying a given equation. In this way, an isomorphism is constructed between the statements of physical geometry and a set of arithmetical statements. All the geometrical axioms and, of course, the theorems, will be "mirrored" by a set of purely arithmetical statements about numbers, equations, and sets of equations. This mirror-image or model is an arithmetical representation of the physical theory. In the representation, though the same words may be used, the geometrical terms, like "line" and "parallel," refer not to physical and spatial properties, but to purely arithmetic notions. Accordingly, though it has the same formal structure as the physical geometric theory, the arithmetical representation has one radically different characteristic. All of its axioms and theorems are tautologies, like all statements of arithmetic. The physical theory of geometry is a set of synthetic, empirical truths about space; the arithmetical structure isomorphic with it is a set of analytic or logical truths about numbers.

ARITHMETICAL REPRESENTATION: PROBABILITY THEORY

An arithmetical representation of analytical geometry was made by proceeding from the empirical theory to the arithmetical one. When applying the mathematical theory of probability we work in the reverse direction, that is, from an arithmetical representation or model to an empirical theory. We construct an empirical theory that is isomorphic to the mathematical theory of probability. The mathematical theory of probability may be formulated or axiomatized in many different ways.[2] These are all the same theory in the sense that, for example, in all of them the usual rules for the addition and multiplication of probabilities, Bayes' theorem, and so on, all hold. Since they permit the calculation of further probabilities from given probabilities, such theories, like other arithmetical systems, are also called "calculi." No matter how it is axiomatized, the calculus of probability is, in the first instance, a set of purely arithmetical, hence tautological or logically true, statements about numbers, in this case certain fractions called "probabilities." In the "frequency-theory" formulation of the probability calculus, the probability of an event is arithmetically defined as the limit of the relative frequency of that event in an infinite reference class. Packed into the notion of a "reference class" are certain arithmetically defined characteristics, notably random or irregular distribution and the convergence of relative frequencies to a constant number. Certain other concepts like "independence" are also arithmetically defined. Before the probability theory can be applied, these arithmetical notions must all be made to correspond to descriptive or empirical concepts. For instance, *arithmetical* "independence" of two events A and B is defined to mean that their joint probability in a given reference class is the arithmetical product of their separate probabilities. Co-ordinated to this is a *descriptive* concept of "independence." Two observed events A and B are empirically independent if the occurrence of one does not in any way influence the occurrence of the other. More precisely, two observations A and B are empirically independent if the probability of A is not changed by either the occurrence or nonoccurrence of B. The *arithmetical* notion of probability as the limit of a frequency in an infinite class is co-ordinated to the *descriptive* notion of a relative frequency in a finite class, for only the latter is actually observed. In this way, a one-to-one correspondence is set up between the arithmetical concepts of the calculus and descriptive terms. This is true no matter what arithmetical formulation of probability theory is used as a model, whether it be the frequency theory or the mathematically more abstract formulation in terms of sets of "points" (numbers [3]).

When the co-ordinated descriptive terms are substituted for the arithmetical ones in the axioms of the probability calculus, the resulting "translation" is now a set of empirical laws about the referents of these terms. It is, for instance, an empirical law that if two events are (empirically) independent, then their joint (empirical) probability is the arithmetical product of their separate probabilities. Different empirical theories have the same arithmetical representation or model when their descriptive terms are co-ordinated to the same arithmetical ones. Consider that instead of having the arithmetical probability, p, correspond to observed frequencies in a sample, alternative co-ordinations are possible. For example, let p stand for "degree of belief." Assign numbers between 0 and 1 to p in a manner that establishes an order, so that if p_1 is more intense than p_2, the number assigned to p_1 is greater than the number assigned to p_2. The axioms about p are now statements, not of the actual proportions in which things are distributed, but of people's feelings about or estimate of such proportions. The arithmetical representation, the mathematical theory of probability, requires, for instance, that if an individual estimates the probability of A as $\frac{1}{2}$ and that of B as $\frac{3}{4}$, then he should also estimate the probability of A and B together as $\frac{3}{8}$. Whether, under this "subjective" co-ordination, the axioms are satisfied may be tested in various ways, by asking people, or by observing their betting behavior, and so on. This illustration shows clearly how, by co-ordinating different sets of descriptive terms (people's beliefs, on the one hand, and objective observed relative frequencies, on the other), one arrives at two different empirical theories with the same arithmetical representation.

If the empirical laws isomorphic to the tautological axioms of the arithmetical representation turn out to be true, then all of the theorems of the latter may be used to compute further probabilities. Since the theorems in the arithmetical representation follow from axioms about infinite series, they cannot in general be derived directly from the descriptive or empirical laws about finite series of observations. The auxiliary use of the arithmetical calculus is therefore indispensable. The question of whether or not the theorems of this calculus can be applied to observed finite series of events is a matter of empirical fact. It is a matter of fact that, if given classes contain sufficiently large number of elements and the usual objective definition of probability in terms of relative frequencies, the axioms, then, are satisfied, under proper sampling procedures. The world, happily, is this way. It could be different, so that the model was not satisfied. This would be too bad for scientists, particularly social scientists. It would not, of course, affect either the validity of the connection between the axioms and theorems or the logical truth of the mathematical theory of probability.

ARITHMETICAL REPRESENTATION: MEASUREMENT

The process of *measurement* in empirical science also requires the use of an arithmetical representation. The elementary laws of arithmetic may themselves serve as such a model. Indeed, only when this is possible can arithmetic be used in empirical science. When laws are quantified, then arithmetical tautologies may be used for deducing other laws and facts from them. This is the most important use of such tautologies within science. If, in Galileo's law, $d = 16t^2$, distance is expressed in feet and time in seconds, then from that law in conjunction with the fact that the time of fall was three seconds, we may deduce that the distance was 144 feet. The additional factual premise about the time of fall permits the deduction from the law that the distance is equal to 16 times 3^2. Using the arithmetical tautology $3 \times 3 = 9$ as an additional premise, we deduce that the distance is 16×9. The tautology $16 \times 9 = 144$ permits the final deduction that the distance fallen was 144 feet. Since the arithmetical statements are tautologies, they may be added as premises without adding any more factual content than is given by the initial empirical premises about distance and time. In such simple calculations or deductions, the arithmetical premises are usually not stated explicitly, but are nevertheless being used. Arithmetic is a subtle and strong logic permitting deductions which, without it, might be quite impossible. What conditions must empirical properties meet before arithmetic can be applied to them?

Consider, first of all, the following three logical truths about numbers. The symbols ">" and "=" have their customary arithmetic meaning.

    1. For any three numbers, if $N_1 > N_2$ and $N_2 > N_3$, then $N_1 > N_3$.
    2. For any two numbers, at most one of $N_1 > N_2$, $N_1 = N_2$, $N_2 > N_1$ holds.
    3. For any two numbers, at least one of $N_1 > N_2$, $N_1 = N_2$, $N_2 > N_1$ holds.

For this set of axioms to be a representation of an empirical theory, a set of descriptive terms must be co-ordinated to the arithmetic entities and relations. Let the numbers correspond to individual people, the relation ">" to the descriptive relation "higher-in-status" and "=" to "same status." After this co-ordination, the statements are probably again true, but, if so, they are now empirical truths about the descriptive relation "higher-in-status." Other descriptive terms can easily be found for which the axioms fail. Let ">" be co-ordinated to "sibling" and "=" to "same person as." In this case, the second axiom is false. For, of course, if John is Peter's sibling, then Peter is John's sibling and the axiom states that not both of these can hold. The axioms are an arithmetic representation of those descriptive properties which can be ordered. Many other such properties also satisfy the axioms: men and the relationship taller than, physical bodies and heavier than, the relative hardness of stones, and students' scores on tests are a few more candidates for true correspondence with the structure of integers and the relation "greater than." All true representations of these axioms share a common structure. The theorems implied by the axioms exhibit still further structure, for instance, irreflexivity and asymmetry. "Irreflexivity" means that an individual cannot have the relation to himself. A person may love himself but he cannot be taller than himself. "Loves" doesn't satisfy the axioms, so the theorems need not be true of it. "Taller than" does, so it must also be asymmetric and irreflexive.

The axioms and theorems together tell us more than appears at first glance about the structure of whatever satisfies the axioms. Whether or not a descriptive property has this structure is a matter of observable fact. Some things do and, as we have seen, some things don't. Those that do have the structure of what is called a "complete ordering." The possibility of establishing an order of succession among attributes is not an unimportant characteristic, particularly in social science. This possibility is expressed by a set of empirical laws of which these axioms are an arithmetical representation. These empirical laws make ranking possible. There are many descriptive properties which satisfy the first two axioms of order, but not the third. Thus, when the properties of incomparable things are being considered, like food and plays or musicians and painters, then the relation, of say, "better than" does not satisfy the third axiom. Nor can we order all the people in the world by the relation "ancestor," since, given any two different individuals, one need not be the ancestor of the other. The first two axioms alone therefore express a "partial ordering." Only all three axioms express a completely ordered domain. Insofar as the descriptive concepts of different theories are true representations of some or all of the axioms of order, they share a common structure or form. By virtue of this shared structure, ranking is possible.

For measurement in the strict sense also to be possible, the descriptive properties must share certain other structural features of arithmetic. In particular, they must also have the same form as axioms like the following three:

4. For any two positive numbers, N_1 and N_2, there is exactly one other, N_3, such that $N_1 + N_2 = N_3$.
5. For any two positive numbers, $N_1 + N_2 = N_2 + N_1$.
6. For any three positive numbers, $(N_1 + N_2) + N_3 = N_1 + (N_2 + N_3)$.

Axiom 4 states that for any two numbers, there is uniquely a third which is their sum. Axiom 5 states that the sum of any two numbers is independent of their order; axiom 6, that when any three numbers are added, the result is independent of how they are grouped. These axioms state part of the structure of addition. Addition is a binary operation on the elements or members of the set of positive integers, that is, a way of combining two elements of the set to get a third. Note that while these axioms are logical truths about the addition of positive numbers, they are all false of subtraction on only the same elements. If we extend the system of elements to include both positive and negative numbers, then axioms five and six do not hold for the operation of subtraction. The kind of elements specified and the kind of operations performed on them determines whether the resulting statements will be logically true or false or, in the case of descriptive entities, empirically true or false.

For these arithmetical truths to be a representation of anything, the number elements and the arithmetical operations performed on them must be co-ordinated to descriptive entities and to operations on these descriptive entities. Just as the arithmetical relation "greater than" can be made to correspond to natural or physical relations like "heavier than," "prefers," "loves," or "higher-in-status," so there must be a natural or physical operation corresponding to addition. As numbers can be added, so things can be put into the same container, glued together, or, even, be simultaneously responded to. Suppose that our elements are lumps of sugar, each having a specified weight. Though numbers are assigned to the elements, indicating how much of the property it has, the corresponding operation is performed not on these numbers, but on the elements themselves. Only in the arithmetical representation are the elements themselves numbers. Weight is a measurable property of lumps of sugar because given two lumps of specified weight, the weight resulting from putting them both on the same side of a balance is the arithmetical sum of their individual weights. In other words, the operation of weighing two lumps of sugar has the same structure as the laws of arithmetic.

The sweetness of sugar, on the other hand, is not measurable. For measurable descriptive properties are those having the same form as the addition of numbers. Grinding together two lumps of sugar of equal sweetness, as indicated by some index of sweetness, would not give something twice as sweet. Or the order in which two things are mixed together might make a difference. Not only must a corresponding physical operation be found, but it must satisfy the axioms. If no corresponding physical or natural operation can be found or if it does not satisfy the axioms of addition, then the property cannot be measured. It may be ranked, however, if it satisfies the axioms of order. The measurability of descriptive properties is expressed by a set of empirical laws which are isomorphic to the laws of arithmetic. By virtue of this isomorphism, numbers may be assigned to the properties of things, resulting in quantified empirical laws. All the laws of arithmetic may then be applied to these numbers to derive new empirical laws and facts.[4]

ARITHMETICAL REPRESENTATION: THEORY OF GAMES

In what sense of the ambiguous phrase "mathematical model" is the theory of games a "model"? In a game, an individual has to take actions in the face of uncertainty, either the uncertainty of his opponent's moves or uncertainty about the distribution of events, like the cards of a hand, or both. Each player wants to win as much or lose as little as possible. How will he behave? If the theory of games answers this question, then it must be an empirical theory of human behavior. Actually, however, the connection between the theory of games and a theory of behavior is exactly the same as the connection between the axioms of arithmetic and the empirical laws which permit ranking and measurement or between analytical and physical geometry. That is, the theory of games is an arithmetical representation, given an appropriate correspondence with descriptive terms, of an empirical theory of behavior in "game" situations. The notation is set theoretic.[5] In addition to ordinary arithmetic and the probability calculus, the axioms contain terms referring to sets. The members of some of these sets are negative and positive numbers, ordered by the relation "greater than." These are put into one-to-one correspondence with the descriptive concept of all possible outcomes of the play of a game. The numbers these "outcomes" have in the representation correspond in the empirical theory to the value or utility they have for each player. These utilities are ordered by the relation of "preference," corresponding to the arithmetical "greater than." Some outcomes are preferred to others. Other sets consist of probabilities. These correspond to the chance events occurring in the course of a game. The probabilities and the utilities of outcomes are combined in all possible ways, to give the "mathematical expectation" of each play. Thus, if an event with a probability of ½ is worth $10 to a player, its mathematical expectation is $5. The arithmetical problem is a combinatorial one, namely, how to combine utilities and probabilities so as to maximize simultaneously a whole set of such expectations. These correspond to the amount each player can win. A solution to this mathematical problem becomes, in the corresponding empirical theory, a set of statements about how a "rational" player would behave. A "rational" player is defined as one who desires to maximize his utility. A solution is a set of rules for each player to follow in any conceivable situation, no matter what his partner does or what turns up on the cards. For certain kinds of two- and three-person games such a solution has been found. It consists in a strategy which, if followed by a player, will keep his losses at a minimum. As an arithmetical system, the theory of games is a mathematical computation of a set of simultaneous and conflicting maxima problems. Mapped into the empirical concepts, it predicts how people will behave, if they are rational in the sense defined. The theory may also be viewed as a normative statement of how people ought to behave, if they want to keep their losses to a minimum in games or in the many social, competitive situations which can be fitted to the game theory representation. Again, the theory of games is itself an arithmetical system of purely logical truths about, essentially, combinations of probabilities under complicated conditions of maximization. The trick for the mathematician, and it is no inconsiderable one, is to solve these maxima problems. The trick for the social scientist, and it is no less considerable, is to find appropriate descriptive terms which when co-ordinated to the arithmetical ones result in true empirical laws of human behavior. Theories of behavior in political, economic, and military situations, as well as in ordinary parlor games, may be constructed so as to be isomorphic with the arithmetical theory of games. Whether people actually do or do not behave in the way predicted by these theories is, of course, a matter for empirical test.

MODELS: FORMALIZATIONS

It is sometimes desirable to consider a theory "formally," that is, to lay bare the form of its axioms, by replacing all the descriptive terms by letters. For instance, $y = ax + b$ is a formalization of a linear relation; $y = ax^2$ is a formalization of a parabolic relation between the variables y and x. Laws may be thus considered formally in order to facilitate deductions or to check deductions already made. Or, if one is looking for isomorphisms, this may be done in order to compare the formal structures of two sets of laws about different phenomena. Any theory, quantified or nonquantified, may be formalized in this way. The result is called a *formalization* of the theory.[6] These expressions exhibit form but no content, since the letter variables have not been given descriptive meaning. They are therefore neither true nor false, since they are not complete sentences, but only the form of sentences. They become true or false only when either descriptive or arithmetical concepts replace the letter-variables. Such formalizations of theories are also sometimes called "mathematical models."

THREE MEANINGS OF "MATHEMATICAL MODEL"

It is time to sum up the ambiguities in the phrase "mathematical model." It may, first of all, mean any *quantified empirical theory,* that is, any theory whose descriptive terms have numbers attached to them. In this case, a "mathematical model" is a set of empirical laws. The phrase may, secondly, refer to any *arithmetical representation* of an empirical theory. In this case, the "mathematical model" is a set of analytic or tautological truths about numbers. Thirdly, the phrase may refer to the kind of *formalization* just discussed. "Mathematical model" therefore may refer to systems of either empirical, tautological, or indeterminate expressions.[7] Such systems are all very different things. A term that obscures important distinctions is worse than useless. The term "mathematical theory" shares in the confusion. Does it mean a quantified empirical theory or a tautological theory of pure mathematics? This ambiguity of "mathematical" led me to reserve the term "arithmetical" for the latter. Greater accuracy and less confusion would result if "mathematical" were used only for statements of pure mathematics. But the verbal habit of ambiguously using the term is probably by now beyond extinction. There is, however, no need to reinforce the relatively recent indiscriminate use of "mathematical model." In the basic sense of "model" as a set of statements isomorphic to another set, an arithmetical representation is of course also a model. The mathematically customary term "arithmetical representation" would, however, help distinguish this notion from that of empirical theories which are used as structural models for other empirical theories. Both arithmetical and empirical models are used as a source of hypotheses about the form of the laws taken by the descriptive terms co-ordinated to the terms of the model. But it makes a difference which kind of theory, arithmetical or empirical, is used as a model. When, for example, the empirical theory of servomechanisms is used as a model for purposive behavior, if the structure of some of the laws of the model doesn't fit the data, we can change these laws so that they will fit. When, on the other hand, we use an arithmetical representation, changes cannot be made at will. We cannot make two and two equal five because it would fit the data better. We can only lament the fact that our data are not measurable. These are not unimportant differences.

SIGNIFICANCE OF ISOMORPHISMS

It is all too easy to overestimate the significance of structural isomorphisms. The fact that all or some of the laws of one area have the same form as those of another need not signify anything whatsoever about any connection between the two areas. To be convinced of this, just think of all the different kinds of things which can be ranked and measured. All have the same structure as arithmetical addition and, to this extent, the same structure as each other. Only the isomorphism *with arithmetic* is in itself significant, because this permits us to apply all the laws about numbers to quantified descriptive concepts. But this implies no connection among all those things that are isomorphic to arithmetic, any more than there need be any connection among all the different kinds of things which satisfy the same form of empirical linear equation. I shall point out in a moment the very special and stringent conditions that have to be met before the existence of structural isomorphisms can be said to signify a more intimate connection between two areas.

To appreciate the significance or lack of it, as the case may be, of an isomorphism between two *empirical* theories, consider three further types of connection that sometimes lead one theory to be called a model for another. I refer to (1) that connection among two theories about apparently different phenomena that leads to the *identification* of one area with another. The classical illustration, which I shall use, is the identification of optics with electromagnetism. (2) That connection between two theories, by means of empirical *cross-connection laws,* by virtue of which one area is said to be reduced to the other. I shall illustrate this case by the relationship of psychology to physiology. (3) That connection between two theories, by means of *definition,* by virtue of which one area may be reduced to another. My illustration is the relationship of sociology to psychology. The analysis will show, I believe, that there really is no intelligible meaning of "model" in these contexts. It will also clarify the difference between a model of a theory and an explanation of it.

(1) The existence of a structural isomorphism, as I just pointed out, *need* not signify any connection between two areas. On the other hand, if the laws of one area have the same form as those of another, this *may* be a cue to some connection between them. If what appear to be two different areas are really one and the same, then, of course, their laws will have the same form. But the converse does not hold. What else, therefore, is required to justify the assertion that the concepts of one area not only obey laws of the same structure as those of another but also actually refer to the same kind of phenomena? Like the familiar linear equation, the so-called Wave Equation is a quantified expression of a certain form, only a bit more complicated than a linear equation. Descriptive concepts referring to many different kinds of phenomena, like water waves, the ripples in a vibrating string, sound, and light, all may be substituted for the variables in the wave equation, to give true empirical laws. Maxwell showed that the concepts referring to electromagnetic phenomena also satisfy the wave equation. But we do not say that sound and light are the same just because their laws have the same form, any more than we identify the relations of being taller and being

smarter just because they are both transitive. Yet, Maxwell's greatest achievement was to show that light and electricity are the same kind of thing. Two conditions, in addition to structural isomorphism, had to be met before this identification could be justified. Any constants in the laws of the two theories must be the same; and the same descriptive terms must be applicable to the phenomena described by each theory. The wave equation contains a constant representing the phase velocity of the propagation of waves. If light and electricity are the same thing, then their waves should have the same velocity. This constant turned out to be the same in both cases. Though having the same constant is one necessary condition for identity, it is not conclusive evidence. It might be merely "by chance" that both constants have the same value. But Maxwell claimed that waves of light *are* electromagnetic disturbances of a certain range of wave length. Optical concepts, like reflection and diffraction, are measured by means of light sources, lenses, slits, and mirrors. Instances of electrical concepts, like resistance and conduction, are observed by means of wires, coils, batteries, magnets, and such things. If Maxwell was right, then the operationally defined concepts of one area should permit the prediction of phenomena in the other area. After all, if two areas are the same, they should be describable in the same terms. For two concepts to be the "same" does not of course merely mean that the same words are used, as when "thought" is sometimes applied both to humans and machines, but rather that these terms refer to the same observable things measured in the same way. It should be possible, for instance, to find electromagnetic waves behaving just like light waves, in the sense that the same "optical" concepts describe their behavior. These were found. Hertz discovered electromagnetic waves exhibiting the *same behavior* when measured with the *same equipment,* though on a larger scale because of larger wave lengths, as that used for light waves. "Reflection," for instance, has the same descriptive or referential meaning when applied to electromagnetic waves as when applied to light waves and, of course, the same laws apply. The identification of one set of phenomena with another thus rests on three things: first, their laws have the same form; second, the same value for the constants in these laws, and, finally, the interchangeability of the empirical concepts. By condition one, two areas are merely shown to be structurally isomorphic. Only by conditions two and three can they meaningfully be said to be the same phenomena. If two theories are thus identified, there is clearly no sense in which one is a model for the other. They are merely two different ways of talking about the same things.

(2) There is considerable speculation about a possible isomorphism between mind and brain. It is at least conceivable that the laws of psychology and those of neurophysiology have the same form. If we have

or invent a neurophysiological theory believed to be structurally similar to behavior, two different theories result after the appropriate co-ordination of concepts is made. One of these theories is behavioral, the other physiological. Rashevsky, for instance, has tried this sort of thing, using a speculative neurological theory as a structural model for group behavior. Suppose an isomorphism is shown to hold between the laws of neurophysiology and those of psychology. Would this mean that mind and brain are identical? Or that behavioral and neurophysiological language are merely two different ways of talking about the same thing? It would not, because only one of the three conditions required for such identity would have been met. Even if the constants occurring in both sets of laws turned out to be the same, the third and most crucial condition could not be met. The basic terms of the theory of psychology refer to observed behavior of organisms. These are not interchangeable with terms referring to the physical-chemical behavior of the neurones and cells of the nervous system. The discharge of neurones may well be a concomitant of, say, a fear response, but neurones don't, for example, grow pale and faint. The behavior which defines "fear" is exhibited by organisms and not by their constituent parts. The joint occurrence of a psychological and physiological event is expressed by a psychophysiological law. Such laws, stating an observable connection at the same time between two different kinds of events, are called cross-connection laws. By means of them, as I shall now briefly indicate, psychology may, in principle, be "reduced" to physiology. But reduction, it will become clear, has nothing to do with similarity of structure. The use of the term "model" in such contexts therefore serves no good purpose.

MODELS, EXPLANATION, AND REDUCTION

Explanation *within* a theory is different from explanation *of* a theory. Scientific explanation and prediction always involve deduction, no matter how covertly. To cite a cause as an explanation of an event after its occurrence is, implicitly at least, to cite an instance of a law, as, say, when a rise in profits is cited as a cause of increased production. Deductions of this sort always require at least one generalization among their premises. In this case, the increase in production is explained by deriving it from the law connecting the rate of profit with changes in production, in conjunction with the fact that profits did indeed increase. Before the event, it could have been predicted from the same law and fact, assuming they are true. In the previous example of Galileo's law in physics, the distance fallen of 144 feet is predictable by deduction before it occurs. Conversely, it is explained, in the same manner, after its occurrence. To explain a law, we derive it from other laws or generalizations. Galileo's law is derived from and explained by the Newtonian law of attraction. The law about profits and production would be derivable from other laws about the behavior of firms under conditions of increased revenue or costs. Within a theory, the theorems are explained by deriving them from other laws, the axioms of the theory. The axioms themselves are not explained by the theory, but are the statements which do the explaining. This indeed is what is meant by calling them "axioms." If the axioms of one theory are derivable from the laws of a second theory, then we have an explanation *of* the first theory rather than within it. But if we have two different theories, one containing only behavioral (psychological or sociological) concepts, the other only physiological concepts, then there can be no deductive connection between their laws. The same is true of any two systems with different concepts, whether or not their laws have a common structure. The use of one theory as a structural model for another does not, therefore, explain one in terms of the other. On the other hand, one area, say chemistry, is reducible to another, say, physics, when its laws are derivable from the laws of the latter. The reduction of one theory to another therefore explains the former in terms of the latter. For this to be possible, a logical bridge between the two theories must be constructed which connects the referents of the concepts of the two areas. This connection, in the case of the reduction of psychology to physiology, would be made by the cross-connection psychophysiological empirical laws. That such "cross-connections" exist between behavioral and physiological events is doubtless the case. If we knew them, then from them in conjunction with the laws of the physiological theory, the behavioral laws could be deduced. Moreover, from laws about the neurophysiological system together with the laws connecting behavioral and neurophysiological events, we might even be able to derive as yet unknown behavioral laws. The cross-connection laws permit the reduction of psychology to physiology. Unlike mere structural isomorphism, reduction of course provides explanation. The behavioral axioms themselves would be deducible from, or explainable by, the physiological theory in conjunction with the cross-connection laws. In this case, the theory itself is explained by another theory. But now the laws of the theory which does the explaining are those of an enlarged "mixed" theory and not those of either behavior or physiology alone. Reduction explains one area by means of another. To explain is not to identify. There are still two different areas, so long as the bridge between them is formed, as it must be in the case of psychology and physiology, by empirical cross-connection laws.[8]

(3) The reduction of sociology or, more generally, any social science dealing with group behavior, to psychology, or the science of individual behavior, also has nothing to do with structural isomorphism or

of one area being a "model" for another. A social group consists of a congeries of individuals standing in certain descriptive relations to each other, like being friends, belonging to the same family, or working together. These patterns of observable individual behavior are the referents of the group concepts. The latter are therefore definable in terms of the behavior of individuals, including, of course, their relations to each other. These definitions alone, however, do not permit the explanation of group behavior by means of the behavior of individuals. Or, to say the same thing differently, definition alone is not sufficient for the reduction of sociology to psychology. In addition, there must be laws within psychological theory stating how the individuals *in* the group interact with each other to give the resultant behavior *of* the group. Such laws about the connections among the elements of a complex situation are called composition laws.[9] If these psychological composition laws exist, then the laws of group behavior are derivable from the definitions of the group concepts and the laws about the behavior of individuals in groups. *Definitions* of group concepts in terms of the behavior of individuals in the group *form the logical bridge,* permitting the deduction, between the sociological and the psychological theories. Since the two areas are connected by definitions alone, they may be said to be the same area. However, the situation is not the same as that in which optics are identified with electromagnetism. The difference requires some explanation.

The axioms or basic hypotheses of every theory contain terms, like distance, mass, and time in Newtonian theory, that are the basic or undefined terms of the theory. Although they must of course have referential or, in the case of quantified variables, operational meaning, these terms are not defined within the theory. They are the concepts in terms of which all other concepts of the theory, like velocity and acceleration, are defined. In the case of optics and electromagnetism, the *basic* terms of each theory were shown to be interchangeable. Connections among optical concepts gave true axioms of electromagnetism and conversely. In a sociological theory, the basic terms refer to complex patterns called groups, like families, trade unions, and the like. In a psychological theory, the basic terms refer to the elements of these complexes, that is, to the behavior of the individual members of the group. The sociological theory is about the behavior of the complex itself; the psychological theory is about the behavior of the elements of the complex.[10] The *basic* terms referring to complexes and those referring to members are not interchangeable. The composition laws of psychology are about how the "elements" or members interact with each other. The sociological laws are about the resultant behavior of groups. These two kinds of laws need not and in general will not have the same form. However, the basic group terms of sociology would be defined terms in a psychological theory. If psychological composition laws about the elements exist, then the sociological laws are derivable as theorems from the composition laws and the definitions of the group concepts. For example, laws about, say, the behavior of families as groups would be derivable from (*a*) the definition within a psychological theory of the sociologically basic concept "family" in terms of its members *and* (*b*) the composition laws of psychology about how these people interact with each other. In sum, when two theories are *identified,* then the basic terms of each theory are interchangeable. When one theory is *definitionally reduced* to another, then the basic terms of the reduced theory become defined terms of the theory from which it is derived. To put it differently, optics and electromagnetism are literally identical, while sociology is a deductive consequence of psychology, if reduction is possible. The practical meaning of this difference is as follows. Once it is realized that the basic terms of two theories refer to the same thing, then *ipso facto* we cannot have knowledge of one area without at the same time having knowledge of the other. If, however, one theory is a deductive consequence of another, that is, related to it as theorems to axioms, then clearly one can independently study the subject matter of the theorems. This will be done when, as at present, we do not know the appropriate axioms, that is, the composition laws of psychology, from which the theorems may be derived. If, however, there are such laws and we find them, then, of course, the group laws would deductively follow from them.

MODELS IN PHYSICS

Finally, something should be said about a use of the term "model" which is unique to atomic physical science. I shall only try to sketch here how the model itself and the way it is connected to the theory for which it is a model each differ from models and theories of nonphysical or, even more generally, nonatomic sciences. In the kinetic theory of heat, the science of mechanics serves as a "model" for thermodynamics. But the laws of these two sciences do not have the same form. What, then, is the meaning of "model" in this context? Classical Newtonian mechanics and thermodynamics are both macroscopic theories, that is, their variables refer to observable characteristics of things not further analyzed into molecules or atoms. The laws of mechanics are about mass and spatial, temporal properties; those of thermodynamics are about temperature, pressure, volume, and the like. The kinetic theory of heat forms the bridge between these two sets of concepts which permits the reduction of thermodynamics to mechanics. It achieves this by a double-barreled assumption. It assumes, first of all, that wherever there appears to be a continuous media like a gas, there are "really" millions of invisible particles. It is further assumed that these particles all bounce back and forth according to the laws of motion as stated in the theory of mechanics. The "mechanical model" for thermodynamics consists of these two assumptions. In this model, when mechanical properties, like mass and velocity, are attributed to the particles, they do not have the same meaning as when these properties are attributed to, say, billiard balls. The velocity of a billiard ball is measured, by the usual physical operations. The "velocity" of an atom is a number assigned to it on the basis of a special kind of connection between the atomic concepts and the concepts referring to the measurable thermodynamic properties of gases. Only the latter, like temperature, pressure, and volume, are descriptive concepts. An empirical law states a connection between empirical, descriptive concepts. The connection between the atomic concepts of the mechanical model and those of thermodynamics cannot therefore be that of an empirical cross-connection law. The bridge between the two areas is therefore not the same as that connecting psychology to physiology. Is the connection then definitional, like that of sociology to psychology? Not quite. Rather, it is definitional, but the "definitions" are of a kind peculiar to this type of model.

This model differs from any nonatomic science by the nature of its assumption about invisible entities. It further differs by the unique nature of the connection between the "model" and the theory which it is devised to explain. When definitions connect the concepts of two areas, these may be conceived as rules for co-ordinating these concepts. If the connection between the model and the macroscopic theory of heat were definitional, then each term of the model would be co-ordinated to a descriptive concept of thermodynamics. This is not the way it works. Some of the terms of the model are not individually co-ordinated to the concepts of the empirical theory. In particular, concepts referring to individual particles and their properties are not connected to the measurable properties of gases. Instead, certain statistical functions of two or more of these terms are thus connected. Average kinetic energy, for instance, a function of mass and velocity, is co-ordinated to the descriptive concept "pressure," but neither the mass nor the velocity of individual particles is separately co-ordinated. Thus, the connection is not strictly definitional, since not each term of the mechanical model is replaceable by a descriptive thermodynamic term. This unique type of connection is called "partial co-ordination," since not all the terms of the model are co-ordinated to descriptive terms. Accordingly, if the model and its theory are collapsed into one deductive system, with the co-ordination rules formulated as explicit definitions, the basic, unco-ordinated terms cannot be eliminated from this system.[11]

This ineliminability, due to the partial nature of the co-ordination, has fascinated some social scientists. Why, it has been asked, can we not similarly introduce concepts without tying them to something observable? A few comments are in order.[12] The candidates offered for such "unco-ordinated" terms of social science do not have the characteristics of these atomic physical concepts. Generally, such candidates are one of two kinds. First, they may be clinical or group concepts whose meanings are more or less vague because the list of defining symptoms cannot yet be completely itemized. When enough is known about which clusters of behavior permit predictions to other behavior, then the observable meaning of such concepts, like "schizophrenia" or "group-morale," can be completely specified. Or, secondly, they are speculative, neurophysiologi-cal notions whose referents have merely not yet been observed. Unlike particles, however, they could in principle be observed and one day may be so. Sometimes terms referring to "mental states" are offered as can-didates for basic, ineliminable concepts of psychological theory. To jus-tify introducing these unconfirmable characteristics of other people's minds, we should have available a theory of "mind" comparable to the theory of mechanics which, after at least partial co-ordination with be-havioral terms, would tell us more about behavior than we can learn from observing behavior itself. Why, for example, instead of supposing that there were invisible particles, wasn't it assumed that there were thou-sands of little gremlins pounding on the walls of the container? The reason is obvious. No adequate theory of gremlin behavior was available to permit, after proper co-ordinations, the derivations to the behavior of gases. The assumptions of the mechanical model transfer the laws of an already independently confirmed theory to the behavior of invisible enti-ties. By the unique method of partial co-ordination, some of these char-acteristics are connected with experimentally observed variables. If the "right" terms of the model are co-ordinated to the "right" descriptive terms of the theory, then not only may already known empirical laws be derived, but even new ones. If the model falls down on this job, as in fact it did, then we can change our assumptions about how the particles behave. These assumptions are not, after all, bound to observation as ordinary empirical laws are. So the model changes from year to year, and particles of all kinds proliferate tropically with the need to explain new observations. Like partial co-ordination, this radical discontinuity between the various "theories" or atomic models constructed to explain observations has no counterpart in sciences dealing with macroscopic, observable variables, whether these be social or physical sciences.

Nor is the statistical feature of recent physics comparable to that of social science. In the earlier mechanical model, nothing could be said about individual particles. In the extended model of quantum mechanics, though not individual values, probability distributions can now be assigned to statements about individual particles. This possibility is entirely due to the nature of the assumptions in the computational model and the way its terms are partially co-ordinated to what can be observed. It has nothing to do with the limits of measurement, which is a matter of empirical operations on the observable referents of descriptive concepts and not on the subatomic elements of the model. The concepts of social science refer to observed behavior, either of individuals or of groups. If it can only make statistical predictions, this is because it simply does not know enough to make predictions about the individual. This incompleteness and consequent statistical character of our knowledge is a practical limitation, not one of principle or logic. In physics, the statistical character of statements about subatomic particles is built into the model that permits the physicist to speak at all about such entities. It cannot be overcome without radically changing the model.

The terms of classical Newtonian theory are, like those of social science, all concepts referring to what can be observed. The relatively simple structure of such a powerful theory has, to put it moderately, not yet been deployed to its fullest advantage by social scientists. Why then should they hunger after the complexity of the invisible? In any case, it is yet to be claimed that the phenomena of social science are of atomic or subatomic dimensions. The notion of "model" appropriate to such entities has therefore no intelligible meaning in social science.

NOTES

1. This "translation" of the laws of one area into those of another by establishing a one-to-one correspondence between the concepts of both areas is sometimes called an "interpretation" of one theory by means of the concepts of another. But the term "interpretation" has so many overtones of meaning that I prefer to avoid using it.

2. For a more detailed discussion of axiomatization, see "Axiomatic Systems, Formalization, and Scientific Theories," by Hochberg in this volume.

3. Since the use of so-called "set-theoretic model" plays a large role in recent social-science theorizing, a few comments may be in order. The theory of sets is a branch of pure mathematics dealing with classes or sets of entities of any kind whatsoever. Everything and anything can be classified, that is, considered as a member of a certain class or set. This includes responses of various kinds, individuals who behave as predicted and those who do not, and various experimental situations, as well as the

classical shoes, ships, and sealing wax. The axioms of set theory merely state what else must be logically true, given that one set is included in another. Set theory thus offers a language for formulating statements about observations or predictions and, after being thus formulated, a group of tautologies for making deductions from these statements to other empirical hypotheses about combinations of sets. Since the axioms and theorems of set theory are tautologically true of all sets, they will also be true of the observed ones. When it is said that a set theoretic "model" is being used, all that is meant is that observations are described in the language or notation of sets and that tautologies about sets are used to make deductions from empirical hypotheses formulated in the language of sets.

4. This paper is on models, not measurement. For details, see G. Bergmann, "The Logic of Measurement," in *Proceedings of the Sixth Hydraulics Conference,* State University of Iowa, 1956; G. Bergmann and K. W. Spence, "The Logic of Psychophysical Measurement," in *Readings in the Philosophy of Science,* H. Feigl and M. Brodbeck, eds. (New York: Appleton-Century-Crofts, Inc., 1953); and section III of C. G. Hempel, "Fundamentals of Concept Formation in Empirical Science," *International Encyclopedia of Unified Science,* Vol. I, No. 6 (Chicago: University of Chicago Press, 1952).

5. See note 3 for remarks on set-theoretic models.

6. See the paper by H. Hochberg in this volume for a further discussion of formalization.

7. In the volume *Mathematical Thinking in the Social Sciences,* edited by P. F. Lazarsfeld (Glencoe, Ill.: Free Press, 1954), Anderson, Marschak and Simon (chapters 1, 4, and 8) use the term "model" to mean a quantified theory; in the papers by Rashevsky and Coleman (chapters 2 and 3) a "model" is an isomorphic empirical theory; the models discussed by Guttman and Lazarsfeld (chapters 5, 6, and 7) are arithmetical representations and formalizations. Learning theorists in psychology and theoretical economists usually use the term "model" as a synonym for quantified hypotheses and theories. For instances, see W. K. Estes and C. J. Burke, *Psychological Review,* 60, 1953, R. R. Bush and F. Mosteller, *Stochastic Models for Learning* (New York: John Wiley & Sons, Inc., 1955), K. W. Spence, *Behavior Theory and Conditioning* (New Haven: Yale University Press, 1956); the paper by the economist J. Marschak mentioned above and *Statistical Inference in Dynamic Economic Models,* edited by T. C. Koopmans (New York: John Wiley & Sons, Inc., 1950). In his *Models of Man: Social and Rational* (New York: John Wiley & Sons, Inc., 1957), H. A. Simon uses the term both for quantified empirical theories and formalizations.

8. The connection between psychology and physiology is also discussed in M. Brodbeck, "On the Philosophy of the Social Sciences," *Philosophy of Science,* 21, 1954.

9. For a thorough discussion of composition laws and their relation to explanation and reduction, see G. Bergmann, *Philosophy of Science* (Madison: University of Wisconsin Press, 1957).

10. A more complete analysis of the problems raised by group concepts and of the reduction of sociology to psychology is presented in M. Brodbeck, "Methodological Individualisms: Definition and Reduction," *Philosophy of Science,* 25, January, 1958.

11. For a more detailed discussion of "partial co-ordination" and of the nature of atomic models, see G. Bergmann, *op. cit.*

12. The advocacy of partial co-ordination or "implicit definition" specifically within social science is further analyzed and criticized in M. Brodbeck, "The Philosophy of Science and Educational Research," *Review of Educational Research*, 27, December, 1957.

VII

FORMALIZATION OF THEORY

13

Axiomatic Systems, Formalization, and Scientific Theories

Northwestern University

The task of this paper is to explicate the concepts "axiomatization" and "formalization" and their relation to theory construction in empirical science. In attempting such an explication one engages not in science itself but in the philosophy of science or, as some seem to prefer, the methodology of science. This latter discipline, unlike the various sciences, does not seek to discover laws or theories about nature. Rather, the philosopher of science concerns himself with questions like, "What is a scientific law?," "What are theories?," and, as here, "What is an axiomatic system?" The philosopher of science thus seeks not only to examine some questions raised about science, but also to explicate and analyze the concepts of the scientist. The scientist, on the other hand, asks questions about, so to speak, how the world lies. In making their analyses, some philosophers find that thinking in terms of a clarified language is helpful, if not indispensable. Since I shall make use of the idea of a clarified language as a tool of analysis, I will first explain what is involved in such a notion.[1]

I. ORDINARY LANGUAGES AND IMPROVED LANGUAGES

Consider the two sentences (1) 'Truman is not tall' and (2) 'Pegasus is not real.' They embody the same grammatical form. In (1), the proper

407

name 'Truman' designates a certain individual and the sentence states
that that individual does not have the property of being tall. If, led by
English grammar, we think of the second sentence as being like the first,
we may then consider the term 'Pegasus' to be a proper name.[2] With
'Pegasus' as a proper name, we may then wonder about two things. First,
what does 'Pegasus' name? Second, in (2), are we asserting that something does not have the property of being real as we assert in (1) that
something does not have the property of being tall? We thus find ourselves in a highly perplexing situation. We may then be led to reflect
about sentences which speak "about" Pegasus and other nonexistent
"objects." Historically, some philosophers were led to think of Pegasus
as possibly an "ideal object," perhaps an "essence" without existence, or
a possible but not actual object. All this was done in order to be able to
say what it was that we were talking "about" when we denied the reality
of Pegasus. For, if we were to say we were talking (and hence thinking)
about nothing, it did not seem that we could be saying anything significant at all. In order for (2) to be significant, it had to be about something: since the sentence had a grammatical subject, it seemed to require
a nongrammatical "subject." Just as (1) would not make sense if there
were not something named 'Truman,' (2) could not be meaningful if
there were not something named 'Pegasus' (which did not exist). Consequently, philosophers were led to postulate various types of entities other
than existents. A distinction was made between "being" and "existence."
Pegasus had being, though he did not exist, and hence we could talk
about "him" and even truly deny that he existed. To put it somewhat
paradoxically, classical philosophers seemed to think that in order to talk
about what did not exist they had to endow *the* nonexistent with being.
Questions, and systems, could then be raised about the relations and
nature of existence, being, and essence.

   Instead of following such metaphysical speculations and proceeding
to crowd our world with all kinds of (nonexistent) entities, one might
suggest that such speculation and creation were based upon a misconception concerning sentences like (2). For the perplexities we become involved in are due to the misleading character of English grammar which
dictates that 'Pegasus' is a proper name and that (1) and (2) have the
same grammatical form. Hence we are mistaken if, taking our cues from
our ordinary language, we seek an object for 'Pegasus' to name and do
not clearly distinguish (1) from (2). Thus, we might begin to suspect
that while classical philosophers thought they were uncovering new aspects
of "reality" by considering 'Pegasus' as a name, they were, in fact, being
led into a maze of problems due to the inadequacies of our ordinary language. The idea might then occur, as it did, that a language which did
not have such inadequacies—an improved or ideal language—would not

involve us in such perplexities. Thus, the point was made that philosophical puzzles are due, not to quirks in reality, but rather to certain linguistic inadequacies. In an improved language, for example, we would require that all grammatically proper names did in fact name. Consequently, we would neither have 'Pegasus' as a proper name nor the problems to which this problematic English term gives rise. Furthermore, the sentences in an improved language which would correspond to (1) and (2) would not share the same grammatical form. This of course is not all that must be said: to explicate and solve such problems adequately, one would have to show (*a*) how terms like 'Pegasus' are handled in such a language, (*b*) how they differ from proper names, and (*c*) how the sentences in which they occur differ from sentences in which genuine proper names occur. This task was accomplished by Russell with his celebrated theory of descriptions.[3] Here, however, I am not concerned with providing a detailed account of the solution to such puzzles. I simply wish to illustrate in what way the notion of an improved or ideal language arises in the context of philosophical analysis and how such an analytical tool is employed. The point to grasp is that an effective way of explicating philosophical problems is to think about what an improved language would be like. A few more examples may anchor the idea more firmly.

Consider the three sentences 'George is tall,' 'Mark Twain is Samuel Clemens,' and 'There is a mountain taller than Mt. Everest.' All three contain the term 'is.' In the first sentence, we encounter the 'is' of predication; in the second the 'is' of identity; in the third 'is' is used in the sense of 'exists.' Consequently, in an improved language there would be three different signs. Thinking in terms of such an improved language would not tempt us to become involved in problems that can stem from a mixing of these various senses of 'is.' Moreover, certain problems which arise from the way in which the term 'exists' is used in ordinary language may be dissolved. For example, the two sentences 'Rats exist' and 'There are rats' say exactly the same thing. In the first sentence 'exist' functions grammatically like 'run' does in 'Rats run.' Hence, we may be led to think of existence as a property (or perhaps an activity) referred to by the verb 'exist.' In the second sentence, the grammatical similarity to 'Rats run' is lacking. Thinking of existence as a property, we might then think (as some philosophers did and as some still do) in terms of things having or not having the property, of things that necessarily have it, and of things that possibly have it. Once again a misleading grammatical similarity may lead us to make claims about the population of the universe. Taking its cue from 'There are rats' rather than from 'Rats exist,' an analysis of the concept of 'existence' in terms of an improved language reveals that what corresponds to 'exist' in such a language is a term in a different grammatical category from terms like 'run.' Hence such a language would not tempt us to think of existence as a property. We may, in the course of such an analysis, also discover other reasons why it should not be considered as one. Consequently, the many problems that confront one who thinks of existence as a property would be dissolved.

For our last example, I will take the paradoxical statement 'This sentence is false.' It is, by the rules of English usage, a grammatically correct sentence. Yet, it leads to a paradox. Similarly, our ordinary language gives rise to many logical paradoxes. An ideal language would be constructed so as not to give rise to such paradoxes. Not only would such paradoxical statements be grammatically incorrect in an improved language, but by comparing such a language with our ordinary language, we would be able also to see why these paradoxes arose in the latter. In the solving of such problems we would also face the task of developing explicit criteria for a sentence's being meaningful. Since our ordinary language is notoriously inadequate in this respect, we can readily see that to raise a question as to what sentences (and terms) are meaningful is in effect to ask what would be an acceptable sentence (or term) in an improved language. Thus, when a philosopher of science attempts to analyze certain scientific concepts or certain questions about science, he may fruitfully think of them in terms of an idealized language of the scientist. The use of the idea of an improved language as a tool of analysis not only enables one to make clarifications not otherwise attainable but also to avoid pseudoproblems that stem from the vagueness and looseness of ordinary language. This does not mean that our ordinary language is not suitable for our ordinary purposes and even for the scientist's purposes (though the latter will of course enrich it by the introduction of technical terms). Nor must we think of an ideal language as a candidate to replace our ordinary language for everyday or even scientific pursuits. Such languages are "ideal" not only in the sense of being "improved" but also in the sense of being idealizations that are languages in principle only. An ideal language is really only a schema or outline of a language. One does not construct such a schema for purposes of communication or writing poetry; rather, one considers in analyzing specific problems what certain features of an ideal schema would be like. For the purposes of such analysis, a schema is sufficient. Thus, when I said that an improved language would not involve us in the problems which stem from "names" that do not name, I indicated a feature of an ideal schema without literally constructing a language. Likewise a schema suffices to show how such problematic terms like 'Pegasus' would be handled. At this point, an analogy may be helpful. A blueprint is detailed enough to enable a builder to construct a house. An architect's drawing is not. Yet, the latter suffices to let us see what the house will be like and to locate its general features. An ideal language is like an architect's drawing. The reason it suffices for purposes of philosophical analysis is that the philosophical puzzles often stem from certain general features of languages (names that do not name, for example). Their solution in turn requires our consideration of only such general features. Of course, for some problems we will have to be more specific, just as the architect will have to draw in certain details of the house and leave others out. But the point to be made is that an ideal schema is not a language in the sense in which English is a language. It will have none of the vagueness, ambiguity, and misleading grammar of an ordinary language. On the other hand, it will not have the richness and expressive possibilities of English. But, then, this is to be expected, since, as I said, such schema are not constructed to be used in place of an ordinary language. This point is important; for, as we shall note later, some loose talk about "formal languages" and formalizing science (in the social sciences and elsewhere) has been the result of some scientists uncritically taking such ideal languages for what they are not. In this misconstruction, they have been sometimes aided by philosophers writing about these ideal languages as if they were candidates for replacing ordinary languages. But more of this later; there are still a few more ideas to be explained before we turn to the questions of "axiomatization" and "formalization."

II. LOGICAL WORDS AND DESCRIPTIVE WORDS

The words 'or,' 'and,' 'all,' 'not,' and 'there is' seem to differ from other words such as 'George,' 'heavy,' 'red,' and 'rat.' The members of the second group may be thought of as referring to things or properties of things or kinds of things. The members of the first group do not refer to things at all. (There are rats but not ands—though, of course, there may be instances of the word 'and' just as there are instances of the word 'rat.') This is the basis for calling the members of the second group descriptive or referential terms. The members of the first group, having no such descriptive function, have a different role in language. As we shall see, they are essential for the analysis of logical inference and accordingly are called logical terms.

Let us look a bit more closely at the descriptive terms. Speaking of them as terms referring to or naming things (or kinds of things) is not unproblematic. For example, there seems to be a difference between terms like 'George' and terms like 'rat.' This difference is indicated by saying that 'George' names a physical object but 'rat' names a kind of physical object. One can point to the former but not, in the same sense, to the latter. For with respect to the latter, we can only point to instances of it; i.e., physical objects that are rats. Some philosophers would question whether or not words such as 'rat' and 'red' can be considered as names at all. This raises a crucial question in philosophy, but it is not one that I can take up here; from time to time we will come across many issues which we will not be able to deal with in this paper. To deal with them adequately would be to write not a paper on axiomatization but a book (or perhaps several books) presenting a philosophical system. Philosophical issues are interrelated; thus in taking up one of them a philosopher runs across others. This is why a philosopher and a philosophical position must be systematic. But then not every paper one writes can say everything about all that is involved. So I here offer a general apology for not taking up certain issues where questions may be raised. I will not stop to apologize again, though I will indicate those places where more might be said. Hence, I will consider terms such as 'George,' 'rat,' and 'red' as all being descriptive or referential terms. However, we may distinguish among them by referring to terms like 'George' as proper names and terms like 'rat' and 'red' as property or character words. Another question arises when we consider terms like 'unicorn.' If we are to classify, in an improved language, all terms as either descriptive or logical, it would certainly seem that 'unicorn' belongs with 'rat' and 'George' rather than with 'and' and 'or.' Yet, we might be puzzled by the question of what 'unicorn' refers to, since there are no unicorns. But we should recall that we cannot point at red or rat any more than we can at unicorn. Though, since there are red things and rats, we can point to them—to instances of red and rat. Since there are no unicorns, we cannot point to any unicorns. This certainly accounts for part of the difference between 'unicorn' and 'rat.' But a problem still remains. Its solution requires some further distinctions.

If one were asked what terms such as 'red,' 'blue,' and 'hot' mean, the simplest thing to do would be to present the inquirer with instances of these properties; i.e., red things, blue things, and hot things. If the inquirer were a man born blind, there is an obvious sense in which we cannot make him understand what 'red' means. This holds irrespective of the fact that we could present him with a machine which would click twice whenever a red object was placed in front of it. He could then tell us what objects were red, but he would no more know what 'red' means than a deaf lip reader would "hear" someone speak to him. To know the meaning of *some* property words, we must be directly acquainted with instances of that property. This does not hold for all property words. Take for example the property of being a ram. If one already knows the meaning of the words 'male' and 'sheep,' then one knows, if 'ram' is defined by the phrase 'male sheep,' the meaning of 'ram.' Thus, we can know the meaning of some property words if we know the meanings of the terms which are used in their definitions. Definition is thus one way of learning the meaning of (or giving meaning to) words. Not all terms can be defined, however. We saw that in our case of the blind man with the color red. We can see the point again if we consider a dictionary. Dictionaries provide definitions of terms. But, in order to understand the defined term, we must understand the terms that occur in the definition. Otherwise, we shall also have to look up the definitions of those terms. Anyone who has used a dictionary knows that if this process is kept up long enough, sooner or later we will come across the terms we were originally looking up. In short, dictionaries are circular. Their use presupposes that we know the meanings of some words independently of the dictionary. An Etruscan dictionary would be completely useless to someone who did not know a single word of Etruscan. Hence, in constructing an improved language, we could not define all its terms. Some terms would have to be undefined or primitive terms. For an undefined property term to have meaning, there would have to be a property to which it refers and with some instances of which we are directly acquainted. This need not be the case with defined property terms. For these latter are defined in terms of words that already have meaning. Hence they, so to speak, receive their meaning from the words combined in their definitions. This may lead one to say that defined property words do not name in the same sense in which undefined ones do—irrespective of whether the defined property word does or does not have instances. Thus, terms such as 'unicorn' cause no trouble. All meaningful property words that do not have instances will be defined terms in an improved language. All primitive or undefined property terms of such a language will be required to have instances. Our direct acquaintance with such instances provides the meaning for such primitive terms. This distinction between defined and undefined terms does not conflict with our distinction between descriptive and logical terms. What one would do, proceeding carefully, would be first to make the distinction between logical and descriptive words in terms of the undefined terms of the language. This distinction can then be extended to the defined terms. Any defined term that contains at least one descriptive term in its definition is also a descriptive term. Thus 'unicorn' would be a descriptive term. Recalling that in an improved language we would also require all proper names to name, we see that all undefined descriptive terms (both property words and proper names) of such a language would name. There is then no problem about the meaning of undefined terms. Since the other terms introduced into an improved language would be explicitly defined, there is no problem about their meaning either. That is, all defined terms will be introduced as abbreviations for combinations of meaningful terms. Thus, the typical pattern for a definition will be

'————' for '. . . . . .'

where the 'for' indicates that the introduced term (or sequence of terms) is stipulated to have the same meaning as the sequence of terms that constitute its definition. If we refer to the set of undefined terms of our improved language as first-level terms, we may then consider terms defined solely in terms of first-level terms to be second-level terms; terms whose definiens [4] contained at least one second-level term would be third-level terms and so on. We can thus picture an improved language as consisting of ascending levels of terms. The higher the level of a term, the further it is from the undefined terms. At this point, we can see one explicit meaning of the vague phrase 'abstract term.' One term is more abstract than another if it is of a higher level. This, of course, is not the only sense of 'abstract.' All property terms, as opposed to proper names, are sometimes called 'abstract.' There are still other senses of that term, one of which we shall encounter later. Notice, however, that no matter at what level a term is, it is connected by a definitional chain to the primitive terms of the language. Consequently, it can, in principle, always be replaced by its definition in terms of primitive terms alone. (If it could not, in what sense would it be defined?) This reveals that the key to the logic of definitions is the eliminability of the defined term.

It was mentioned above that, unlike the descriptive words, the logical terms do not refer but perform a different linguistic function. We will now look at these terms and their special linguistic role by examining the logical words 'and' and 'not.' From the two sentences (*a*) 'George is bright' and (*b*) 'Grace is bright,' we can, by the use of 'and,' make a new compound sentence (*c*) 'George is bright and Grace is bright.' This new sentence bears an interesting relation to the two original ones. If we know whether our two original sentences are true or false, we then know the truth value of our compound sentence (*c*). (*c*) is true if and only if both (*a*) and (*b*) are true. The same sort of relation holds for 'not.' A statement, (*a*) for example, is true if and only if its denial is false. We can represent this situation by a table. Let '*P*' and '*Q*' stand for any two sentences, '*T*' and '*F*' for 'true' and 'false,' and 'not-*P*' for the denial of '*P*.' We then have

P	*Q*	*P* and *Q*	not-*P*
T	*T*	*T*	*F*
F	*T*	*F*	*T*
T	*F*	*F*	
F	*F*	*F*	
1	2	3	4

The column for 'P and Q' (3) gives a truth value for all possible combinations of values for the separate statements 'P' and 'Q.' The column for 'not' gives a value for 'not-P' for all possible values of 'P.' Thus, we call signs such as 'and' and 'not' truth functional connectives. What goes for them also goes for 'or,' 'if . . . then . . . ,' and 'neither . . . nor.' Truth tables which standardize their behavior can be given for all these terms. Or, to put it another way, the truth tables provide rules that show us how these terms function. However, the essential point involved is that if we know the truth values of the sentences connected by the logical connectives,[5] we know the truth values of the compound sentences in which they occur. Thus, the use of these logical terms adds nothing to the descriptive content of the statements we make. In both (a) and (b) we assert (and describe) a state of affairs. (c), however, is used not to assert a new state of affairs but to assert simultaneously the facts stated in (a) and (b).

We must not be misled by the fact that these logical words are called 'connectives.' They are not used to state connections between the facts asserted by the sentences they combine into compound statements. Compare (c) with (d) 'The Greeks won the battle of Thermopylae and the moon is made of Swiss cheese.' (d) is a most extraordinary sentence. Our first and-statement (conjunction) was quite ordinary in that it combined two sentences that went together quite naturally. Our new sentence is a combination of two quite unconnected statements. What is puzzling about it is that we do not usually mention together what does not go together. Yet 'and' functions logically in (d) exactly as in (c)—asserting that two facts are the case. Thus, (d) is false since it is not true that the moon is made of Swiss cheese. We must not be misled by the fact that in our ordinary language 'and' is used in senses other than its truth-functional one. Sometimes it is used to express, as in (c), that the speaker believes that there is some connection between the two facts which the sentence asserts. Sometimes, however, we use 'and' to express a temporal relation between facts. ('He put on his parachute and jumped out of the airplane.') Some other times we use 'and' to state relations between things. For example, if we say 'Grace is bright and beautiful,' this is merely a stylistic variant for 'Grace is bright and Grace is beautiful.' But if we say 'Grace and Dolores are sisters,' this is not a stylistic variant of 'Grace is a sister and Dolores is a sister'; rather, it is a variant of 'Grace is a sister of Dolores.' It is used to state that the relation of being sisters holds between Grace and Dolores. These latter uses of 'and' differ radically from the truth-functional use considered above. The fact that our ordinary language uses the same word in such different ways can even lead us to blur the distinction between logical words and descriptive words.

We can see this quite clearly with a term such as 'but' in the statement 'Lillian is the brightest student in the class but she didn't pass the test.' In this example, 'but' is used to enable the speaker to express something without literally saying it. 'Lillian is the brightest student in the class and she didn't pass the test and that is unusual' could be what is understood in this case. Perhaps even more, or something different, is being expressed. The context of the statement is usually sufficient to enable us to understand what is expressed but not stated. In any case, what is usually understood by the listener, but not said by the speaker, can be stated in an additional clause. This additional clause is a descriptive statement of fact. If we take the trouble to add the additional clause, we can replace 'but' by 'and.' For 'but' serves the same logical function as 'and,' though this is disguised by the brevity, subtlety, and contextual use of ordinary language. We pay for such subtlety and brevity in ordinary language by ambiguity, the reliance on context, and the consequent blurring of such distinctions as that between logical and descriptive words. In an improved language, 'but' would be excluded. Moreover, the logical term standing for the truth-functional use of 'and' would not be employed for other linguistic tasks. We would thus achieve a clear distinction between logical and descriptive terms which, as we shall see, is essential for the analysis of logical inference (deduction). Before proceeding to consider the nature of deduction, it should be understood that all the logical words can be clearly distinguished from descriptive terms. What goes for 'and' goes for them all. However, not all logical words are connectives. The terms 'there is' and 'all' are not. In the literature, they are called 'quantifiers.' Yet, there is ample justification for considering them, together with the connectives, as logical terms. But this point cannot be elaborated here.[6]

III. LOGICAL TRUTH AND LOGICAL INFERENCE

The two sentences 'The sun is shining' and 'All bodies fall with a constant acceleration' will be characterized as true or false depending upon what the facts are. In the first case, we need only look and see; in the second, we must go through a more elaborate procedure. In a sense, the gathering of evidence relevant to the truth or falsity of statements of lawfulness is never completed. In this case, for example, the law is about all bodies, past, present, and future; hence, there is always the possibility of discovering the statement to be false. Yet, though we may go through different procedures to determine whether or not the statements are true or false, both statements share the following characteristic: factual evidence is relevant to their truth or falsity. By contrast, consider the statement (*a*) 'It is not the case that the sun is shining and not shining.' [7] This sentence, unlike the others, is true no matter what the facts are. Just as the statement (*b*) 'The sun is shining and not shining' is false irrespective of whether or not the sun happens to be shining. We can see this quite clearly and simply by recalling the truth tables for 'and' and 'not.' First, let us rewrite the statements in somewhat less colloquial form. In (*b*) we are asserting both a sentence and its negation. Letting '*P*' stand for the sentence 'The sun is shining' and 'not-*P*' for its negation, (*b*) is a sentence of the form '*P*' and 'not-*P*.' In (*a*) it is precisely this conjunction which we are denying. Hence, (*a*) may be represented by 'not-(*P* and not-*P*).' Our truth table would then be as follows:

P	not-*P*	*P* and not-*P*	not-(*P* and not-*P*)
T	*F*	*F*	*T*
F	*T*	*F*	*T*

Here we see that where '*P*' is true, 'not-*P*' is false, and hence the conjunction of '*P*' and 'not-*P*' is false. Since this conjunction is also false when '*P*' is false, it is false no matter what value '*P*' has—no matter what state of affairs is the case. On the other hand, (*a*), which denies this conjunction, is true—no matter what value '*P*' has. Hence, (*a*) is true no matter what the facts are. Since (*a*) is true and (*b*) is false independently of the facts, neither statement tells us anything factual at all. The difference between such statements and one like 'The sun is shining' is clear. Sentences like (*a*) and (*b*) are called analytic. Sentences that are factually informative are called synthetic. If an analytic statement is true, it is a tautology or logical truth. If an analytic statement is false, it is a contradiction. Since logical truths are true for all possibilities (no matter what the facts are), they are sometimes called 'necessary truths.' If we consider the tautology (*a*), we note that its truth depends only upon the logical words which occur in it, their order, and the identity and order of the component sentences. The truth of (*a*) does not at all depend upon what the component sentences state or whether they are true or false—'*P*' can be any sentence, true or false, without changing the truth value of (*a*). Since '*P*' can stand for any sentence we note that any descriptive terms that occur in any such sentence are not relevant to the truth of (*a*). To put it concisely, descriptive terms occur vacuously in tautologies. We can see this, perhaps more clearly, by considering the tautology 'If Peter is a taxpayer and all taxpayers are citizens, then Peter is a citizen.' Let us replace 'Peter' by the letter *a*; and the property words 'taxpayer' and 'citizen' by the letters '*T*' and '*C*' respectively. Our statement then reads 'If *a* is *T* and all *T* are *C* then *a* is *C*.' Note that aside from letter symbols our new statement contains only logical words. Note also that if each occurrence of *a* is replaced by a proper name and each occurrence of '*C*' and '*T*' is replaced by property words, the resulting sentence is true. Hence the truth of such statements does not at all depend on the descriptive words that occur in them, but only on the logical words and the order and arrangement of the terms. Hence, logical truths are sometimes called formal truths or linguistic truths, as opposed to factual or descriptive truths.

The explication of 'logical truth' presented above depended on the idea of 'logical word.' We shall now see how the phrase 'logical inference' may be explicated in terms of 'logical truth.' A logical argument is a sequence of propositions; one or more are the premises of the argument, another is the conclusion. The conclusion follows logically from the premises (is deduced from them, is implied by them, is entailed by them). An example of a valid argument is

$$(A) \qquad (p_1) \qquad \text{All taxpayers are citizens.}$$
$$\qquad\qquad (p_2) \qquad \underline{\text{Peter is a taxpayer.}}$$
$$\qquad\qquad (c) \qquad \text{Peter is a citizen.}$$

(p_1) and (p_2) are the premises and (c) is the conclusion. The question that we must answer is, "What makes (A) a valid argument?" Or, to put it another way, "What is logical inference?"

First we note that the validity of (A) does not depend on the truth or falsity of the statements that compose it. $((A)$ is a valid argument whether or not it is true that all taxpayers are citizens.) The validity of an argument depends on the *form* of the argument. We became acquainted with 'form' above when we spoke casually of 'formal truth.' The form of a statement is the skeleton that remains when all the descriptive words or, in some cases, complete sentences are replaced by letter symbols ('*P* or not-*P*' and 'If *a* is *T* and all *T* are *C* then *a* is *C*' are statement forms). Just as tautologies are so by virtue of their form alone, valid arguments are so by virtue of their form alone. Thus (A) is valid because

$$(A') \qquad \text{All } T \text{ are } C.$$
$$\qquad\qquad \underline{a \text{ is } T.}$$
$$\qquad\qquad a \text{ is } C.$$

(A') is a valid argument form. The validity of the argument depends on a *connection* between the premises and the conclusion. This connection is expressed by the idea that an argument is valid when: *if* the premises are true, then so is its conclusion. Or, as some may put it, if the premises are true, then the conclusion is *necessarily* true. Here 'necessarily' is used in the same sense as when we say a logical truth is necessarily true since there is no possibility that makes it false. This similarity between a valid argument and a logical truth provides the key to the explication of 'logical inference.' To say that when the premises of a valid argument are true, then, necessarily, so is the conclusion is to say that there is no possibility of the premises all being true and the conclusion being false. In other words where

$$
(B) \quad \begin{array}{c} p_1 \\ p_2 \\ \cdot \\ \cdot \\ \cdot \\ p_n \\ \hline c \end{array}
$$

is an argument, it is valid if and only if there is no possibility that makes 'p_1 and p_2 and . . . and p_n' true and 'c' false. Thus, to say that (B) is valid is to deny that 'p_1 and p_2 and . . . and p_n and not-c' *can be* true. But to deny that a statement can be true is to assert that its negation is necessarily true and hence that it is a tautology. Thus (B) is valid if, and only if, the statement 'not-$(p_1$ and p_2 and . . . and p_n and not-$c)$' is a tautology.[8] Since whether or not a statement is a tautology depends only on the form of the statement, we need only consider the form of an argument to determine its validity. A statement is logically inferred from other statements if an argument with the first statement as the conclusion and the other statements as premises is valid. This is the explication of 'logical inference.' Due to the tautological nature of logical inference, we often say that the conclusion of a valid argument contains nothing that is not already stated in the premises. It simply serves to make explicit what is already implicitly there. As some have picturesquely put it, if our minds were such that we could see all that is contained in our premises we would not need to make deductions. Not having such mental powers, we find deduction, tautological though it be, indispensable in our pursuit of knowledge.

IV. EUCLIDEAN GEOMETRY AND THE ORIGINS OF AXIOMATIZATION

Euclidean geometry is historically the first axiomatic system. It is also an excellent example for expository purposes. Historians inform us that from Thales on geometricians were putting forth "proofs" for certain geometrical truths. We may then think of various Greek geometricians proving "theorems" in specific areas of geometry; about angles, triangles, rectangles, circles, etc. In proving their theorems, they took various propositions for granted and specified certain definitions for terms they introduced. They used these propositions and definitions as a "basis" upon which their proofs depended. Statements once proved were, in turn, used in proving further theorems. The Greek achievement in geometry was thus to specify a set of statements and a list of definitions and, on this basis, to prove a great number of propositions embodying the geometrical knowledge of the time. They thus made the foundations of geometry explicit. In doing this they showed what depended logically on what and unified the various areas of geometry by making them part of one comprehensive "theory." In short, they axiomatized geometry. So far we have come across terms like 'prove,' 'theorem,' 'basis,' and 'theory.' Part of our task in explicating 'axiomatic system' and 'formalization' will consist in analyzing these terms. But there are some other notions that we have to add to our list. We may discover these by following the history of geometry a little further.

Suppose one were to ask why a certain theorem of geometry was true. A possible reply to the question would be to furnish the proof of that particular theorem; i.e., showing how it "followed" from the axioms and definitions. Definitions, being linguistic abbreviations, are a variety of analytic truths. But the axioms of Euclid's geometry are not analytic truths; and, unlike the theorems, we cannot justify the axioms of a theory by deriving them from other statements of the theory. For, if we did, then these other statements would constitute our theoretical basis—not the statements we derived. The Greeks took the axioms of geometry to be self-evidently true. They thus felt this science to have a firm foundation. But they were bothered by one of the statements of Euclid's basis—the so-called "parallel postulate." [9] This postulate, whose truth they did not doubt, nevertheless did not seem so self-evident as the other "axioms" and "postulates." They, and subsequent mathematicians, thus felt that it ought to be derivable as a theorem, since theorems need not be self-evident. All attempts to "derive" the parallel postulate from the other axioms and postulates failed. Finally, an Italian mathematician (Saccheri, 1667–1733) attempted to prove the parallel postulate by a *reductio ad absurdum* proof. That is, he attempted to derive a contradiction from Euclid's other axioms and postulates taken together with assumptions that were contrary to the parallel postulate. Though he obtained some theorems that seemed absurd to him and to his contemporaries, he did not obtain a contradiction (in the sense that I explained above). The "weird" results of these investigations ultimately led to the construction of the non-Euclidean geometries. Moreover, the new non-Euclidean systems no longer confined differences from Euclid's geometry to the parallel postulate. With the development of such axiomatic systems, the question about the truth of the axioms received a critical impetus. For if the axioms of Euclidean geometry were self-evidently true, those axioms of the non-Euclidean geometries that were incompatible with them were self-evidently false. A new metaphysics, Kantian critical-idealism, incorporated what amounted to the view that the statements of Euclidean geometry were self-evident truths. The prevailing influence of this metaphysical position thus lent its support to the deriders of the non-Euclidean systems. As these problematic and hopelessly vague philosophical terms are used, 'self-evidently true' is opposed to 'self-evidently false.' This latter phrase also has been used as a synonym for 'contradiction,' a term that we saw can be given an explicit and precise meaning. The opponents of the non-Euclidean geometries thus expected those systems to contain contradictions. Though they had not been proven inconsistent, this did not mean that their inconsistency might not subsequently be demonstrated. These hopes were destroyed when, in the nineteenth century, it was proved that if certain non-Euclidean geometries were inconsistent then so was Euclidean geometry. With such a proof, the non-Euclidean geometries were put on a respectable footing. They in turn contributed to the removal of "self-evidence" as a relevant criterion for questions of truth and consistency. Yet the question as to the truth of the competing axioms was still to be settled.

The Greeks had left another problem in the wake of their geometrical genius. What do the terms of Euclidean geometry mean? To be sure, the defined terms of the theory can be given meaning by their definitions. But, as we noted earlier, definition cannot proceed indefinitely. Some terms of the theory must be taken as primitive; e.g., 'length' is among Euclid's undefined terms. And, if the meaning of these undefined terms remains unspecified, then of course so does the meaning of the defined terms. Another problem along a similar vein was posed in the question, "What is Euclidean geometry about?" Are the lines and points spoken of in the theory physical lines and points? The Greeks did not think so; rather, they thought of physical lines and figures as approximations of geometrical lines and figures. The objects of geometry were held to be certain ideal objects or entities. Every physical line, for example, had some breadth, but geometrical lines did not. Hence, since geometry had to be about something (else their statements would be about nothing and hence meaningless), some Greek geometrician-philosophers created entities for geometry to be about. Here we see, once again, how the question of meaning and the illusion that all terms must be "about" something led to the hypostatization of ideal entities.

The questions that our brief historical account has led to, and the notions introduced in it, are the core of the explication of 'axiomatization.' To this task we may now proceed.

V. AXIOMATIZATION AND FORMALIZATION

We may begin our discussion of axiomatic systems by considering a simple miniature system, $(S\text{-}1)$. It contains the four propositions:

A-1: Every line has at least two points as members.
A-2: There are at least two lines.
A-3: Two lines do not have two points in common.
A-4: For any two points there is a line that they are both members of.

in its basis. The only undefined descriptive term of $(S\text{-}1)$ is 'point.' It has one defined term, 'line.' The definition is:

D-1: 'line' for 'class of points.'

All the terms besides 'point' and 'line' that occur in $(A\text{-}1)$ through $(A\text{-}4)$ are logical terms. Consider now the following sequence of statements:

Step 1: There are two lines—call them A and B.   By $(A\text{-}2)$
Step 2: A has two points, a_1 and a_2; B has two points, b_1 and b_2.   By $(A\text{-}1)$ and Step 1
Step 3: At most one point of A can be identical with one point of B. Hence there are three points.   By $(A\text{-}3)$ and Step 2

In view of this sequence, we may then add the following proposition to our system:

T-1: There are at least three points.

We may also construct another sequence of statements as follows:

Step 1: There are three points, a, b, and c.   By $(T\text{-}1)$
Step 2: There is a line, A, that contains a and b as members.
There is a line, B, that contains b and c as members.
There is a line, C, that contains a and c as members.   By $(A\text{-}4)$ and Step 1
Step 3: A, B, and C are distinct.   By Step 2 and the definition of 'line'

We may then assert another proposition in our system:

T-2: There are at least three lines.

(*S*-1) is an axiomatic system. Its axioms are (*A*-1) through (*A*-4). (*D*-1) is its only definition. Together the axioms and (*D*-1) constitute the basis of (*S*-1). (*T*-1) and (*T*-2) are two theorems of the system. The theorems were "proved" by constructing sequences of statements (the steps), each one of which is an axiom or previously proved theorem of the theory or follows logically from the definitions, axioms, theorems, and previous steps; the last statement of the sequence is the statement that has been proved. Any statement for which there is a proof from the axioms and definitions of the theory is a theorem of the system. An axiomatic system consists of a set of axioms, definitions, and the theorems that follow from them. The relation between the axioms and definitions, on the one hand, and the theorems on the other, is thus one of premise to conclusion. Note then that in view of what was said about logical deduction, this relationship has nothing to do with the truth or falsity of the axioms. But, if we know the axioms of such a system to be true, then we also know that the theorems are true. Knowing the theorems to be true does not, however, guarantee the truth of the axioms.

In the above proofs, certain principles of logic were taken for granted without being made explicit. For example, in the proof of (*T*-2), the logical truth that two collections are identical only if their members are was not explicitly stated or cited. This is characteristic of deductions made in empirical science as well as in mathematics. Formal logic is the discipline which attempts to make explicit the principles of logical inference while other disciplines use such principles implicitly. How and why this is so we shall discuss below.

We may construct a system which differs from (*S*-1) only with respect to (*A*-2). In this new system, (*S*-2), let the second axiom read as follows:

There are at least three lines.

The second axiom of (*S*-2) is simply the second theorem of (*S*-1). One can then immediately prove the statement 'There are at least two lines.' We may then realize two things. First, being an axiom is always relative to some axiomatic system. What is an axiom in one system may be a theorem in another. *Statements by themselves are neither axioms nor theorems.* Second, since we can prove the second axiom of (*S*-1) as a theorem in (*S*-2), (*S*-2) contains as an axiom or theorem every statement that is an axiom or theorem of (*S*-1). Likewise, everything that can be proved in (*S*-2) can be proved in (*S*-1). Thus, a set of propositions may be made into an axiomatic system in more than one way.

Though we have indicated what an axiomatic system is, we have not yet analyzed the puzzles about them that we raised earlier. In our analysis, we will make use of an idealization of the scientist's language. All undefined descriptive terms of such a language, we recall, refer to individual objects that we are directly acquainted with or to properties with whose instances we are so acquainted. Other descriptive terms are introduced by explicit definition. Let us call such a linguistic system L. All meaningful descriptive terms of L are then located somewhere in the hierarchy of defined and undefined terms. Suppose we construct (S-1) in L—that is, we state the axioms and theorems in the language L. For the axioms to be meaningful, the terms must be. Thus every term used must be either a descriptive term of L or a logical word. 'Point' must be then one of the defined or undefined descriptive terms of L, if the axioms containing that term are to be meaningful propositions. Notice that I said 'point' may be either defined or undefined in L. The fact that it is an undefined term in (S-1) does not mean that it is an undefined term of the language in which the axioms of (S-1) are stated. Its being undefined relative to (S-1), or *in* (S-1), simply means that there is no definition of that term among the definitions in the basis of (S-1). It may be also an undefined term of L, but it need not be. Thus 'point' may be defined in L in terms of the intersection of two fine hairs or even in terms of the intersection of two light rays. In any case, if 'point' is a term of L, we know what it means and, consequently, what (S-1) is "about." We may then wonder how what we have just said bears on (1) the complaint that no physical point (or circle, triangle, etc.) adequately represents the geometrician's terms, and (2) the special geometrical entities hypostatized to remedy the supposed difficulties. In order to make the connection and dissolve the puzzles, we will momentarily return to Euclid's geometry. Some of Euclid's "proofs" of theorems are spurious—they are not proofs at all. For a theorem to be proved in an axiomatic system, it must follow logically from the axioms and definitions alone. Euclid, in some of his "proofs," relied on diagrams (to provide geometrical "intuition") and on other assumptions not explicitly stated in the basis of his system. In short, he brought extraneous material into his proofs. Consequently the Euclidean axiomatization of geometry is not adequate.[10] One may guard against this kind of error by dispensing with a major source of the trouble. Instead of using familiar terms such as 'point,' 'line,' 'figure,' 'circle,' 'superimpose,' etc., about which we may be led to make certain assumptions based on experience, intuition, etc., we can substitute for these terms letter symbols that do not have such "associations" for us. Using such "marks" we would be less likely to make assumptions not explicitly stated in the basis of the system. For example, in (S-1), instead of using 'point' and 'line,' we might use the Greek letters 'Σ' and 'Λ.' Our definition would then read:

F Def. 'Λ' for 'class of Σ'

and our axioms:

FA-1: Every Λ has at least two Σ as members.
FA-2: There are at least two Λ.
FA-3: Two Λ do not have two Σ in common.
FA-4: For any two Σ there is a Λ that they are both members of.

We can now proceed to deduce theorems from these axioms. As we saw, deduction is carried out independently of the descriptive terms in the statements involved. Our replacing the descriptive words by letter symbols is thus essentially a precautionary measure to guard against our overlooking something in a proof and taking an illicit step. Suppose one now asked what do 'Σ' and 'Λ' mean? The question might well puzzle us, for we introduced the letter symbols in order to have signs without any meaning. They are simply marks on paper. Hence the axioms of this system, (*FS*-1), are not meaningful sentences of *L*! In fact, they are not statements at all but skeletons or schemata of statements. Yet, we can readily see how one can employ a system like (*FS*-1) to obtain an axiomatic system whose axioms are all meaningful sentences of *L*. One need merely "interpret" the letter symbols 'Σ' and 'Λ' by words of *L*. Actually, we need only interpret the undefined symbol(s) of (*FS*-1): for, upon the interpretation of the undefined signs, all defined signs are automatically interpreted. Upon interpretation all the axioms and theorems of (*FS*-1) correspond to statements in *L*. We then have an axiomatic system in *L* whose axioms are interpretations of the axioms of (*FS*-1). In our example (*S*-1) would be the axiomatic system obtained. (*FS*-1) is a "formalization" of (*S*-1). This is our first encounter with 'formalization' (though not with 'formal'). We will speak more about formalization shortly. Systems like (*FS*-1) are also called 'uninterpreted axiomatic systems' and 'abstract axiomatic systems.' [11]

It sometimes happens, upon the interpretation of an abstract axiomatic system, that the statements obtained are only approximations of empirical truths. For scientific purposes, such approximations may be adequate: the interpretations of geometries considered as uninterpreted axiomatic systems are adequate. But we can see how such approximations could be responsible for the idea that the interpretation does not furnish entities for the uninterpreted system to be "about." This, as we saw, led some to invent ideal entities for the purpose. If one understands the difference between an uninterpreted and an interpreted axiomatic system, this illusion of "aboutness" is dispelled—along with such problematic entities. The undefined signs of an uninterpreted axiomatic system are merely marks. They neither mean anything nor are about anything. The axioms of such a system are sentence schemata and not sentences; hence, they are neither true nor false. We can thus only speak of truth or falsity with respect to an interpreted axiomatic system. The distinction between interpreted and uninterpreted axiomatic systems enables us to arrive at a solution to the puzzles that bothered the Greek geometrician-philosophers without having to resort to either the creation of mysterious entities or the vacuity of self-evident truth.

Perhaps the following will further clarify the distinction. Instead of interpreting (FS-1) by means of L so that we arrive at (S-1), we may interpret 'Σ' by 'positive integer' (which we will assume is a term of L). Λ would then be interpreted by 'I-class,' which, let us imagine, is an abbreviation for 'class of positive integers' in L. Consequently, the axioms of (FS-1) would be interpreted as follows:

A'-1: Every I-class has at least two members.
A'-2: There are at least two I-classes.
A'-3: Two I-classes do not have two positive integers in common.
A'-4: For any two positive integers there is an I-class that they are both members of.

We thus have another axiomatic system stated in L; this one is about positive integers and classes of such (though it contains obviously false statements), instead of about points and classes of points. Hence, we see that an abstract axiomatic system can be interpreted in many ways to obtain different interpreted axiomatic systems. This pointedly illustrates that the letter symbols 'Σ' and 'Λ' are just marks without meaning. We can interpret them, however we wish, by means of terms of L.[12] However, some would contend that we should only speak of an interpretation of an abstract axiomatic system when the sentences made to correspond to the axioms of the abstract system turn out to be true. There is no point in arguing about how to use the term 'interpretation.' We can simply distinguish two senses of 'interpretation'; a broader and a narrower one. For all "interpretations" of abstract systems in the narrower sense will be interpretations in the sense I have been using, but the reverse is not the case. Unfortunately some misleading comments sometimes accompany this narrower sense of 'interpretation' when those who adopt it speak of the undefined signs of abstract systems as being "implicitly defined" by the axioms in which they occur. Strictly speaking, these terms are not defined at all, for they are not eliminable abbreviations in such systems. All that is reasonably meant by saying that they are implicitly defined is that, since we are usually concerned with interpretations of the terms of a system that make its axioms correspond to true statements, the set of axioms limits our choice of interpretations. But it is misleading to speak of a term being defined, when there are numerous, in some cases infinite, possible interpretations (even in the narrower sense). *Implicit definition* is a vastly different sort of thing from *explicit definition*. Since verbal similarities which conceal nonverbal differences often provide starting points for confused semiphilosophical excursions, the phrase has little to recommend it.

When we have attained a certain stage in the development of an area of a science, having accumulated a number of laws and significant concepts,[13] it may be fruitful to arrange this material into an axiomatic system. To do so is to construct a "theory." A theory is a set of laws and definitions deductively interrelated—in short, a theory is an axiomatic system. This is not to say that we would want to call all axiomatic systems theories. For we would expect the laws of any theory worthy of the name to have a certain range of application. What is meant by this can be illustrated by comparing Kepler's theory of planetary motion to Newton's theory of gravitation. The latter, applying to planetary motions and freely falling bodies (as well as other things) has a wider range of application. Just where one would draw the line concerning what is to be called a theory is a question bordering on a pseudo-issue. Usually what is involved is the prestige of a certain area of a science or, even, a science itself. (Do the social sciences have any *real* theories?) Since such disputes are often fruitless (sometimes nonsensical) and since one does not, after all, increase the scope of a set of laws by calling it a theory, the attempt to formulate precise criteria to distinguish theories seems as pointless as converting a flame thrower into a cigarette lighter. One must, especially in the social sciences, be wary of being sidetracked by such issues. This is pointedly illustrated by another term that has achieved some status in contemporary social science. I refer to 'formalization.' As I mentioned above, we have already been introduced, quite painlessly, to this term. An axiomatic system is formalized when we replace its descriptive signs by mere marks. As we saw above, formalization helps to prevent us from overlooking anything in deducing theorems from axioms. Formalization, as such, is thus not a method of discovering significant laws or concepts. One may wonder why, if formalization involves such a simple idea, some have taken it to be more than it is. This requires some additional remarks.

We may speak of having obtained (*FS*-1) by formalizing (*S*-1).[14] But we did not replace all the words used in (*S*-1) by mere marks— only the descriptive ones. We could, however, go further and replace all terms, logical and descriptive, by such marks. If we did, we would be doing what the logician does when he studies the nature of logical inference and logistic systems. We noted earlier the relation between logical inference and logical truth. The logician, to investigate both of these, constructs systems of logical truths by specifying certain tautologies as axioms and setting down explicit rules for the generation of other tautologies as theorems.[15] In order not to overlook anything, he replaces even the logical words by letter symbols. If one is attracted by such words, he might say that the axiomatic systems logicians study are "completely" formalized. But note that the logician deals with such formal systems because he is studying the nature of logical inference and hence cannot take even the logical words for granted. Once the logician does this, the empirical scientist, and even the mathematician, may and does take such logical systems for granted in making deductions. Thus, scientists who call for the complete formalization of scientific theories ask, at best, for a needless repetition of what the logician has already accomplished. Such inappropriate requests may have several motives. First, in this century modern logic has developed rapidly. To a certain degree, formalization was the key to this growth. Some social scientists eager for a royal road to scientific knowledge may think that what goes for logic goes for social science.[16] Second, partially due to the successful development of formal logic, partially for other reasons, systems of symbols have acquired an awe-inspiring quality for many people. Here, we must remember that we are often in awe of what we do not understand. Third, there is a great emphasis on quantification in science. Mathematical and logistic systems seem similar to many. After all, books in both fields contain many symbols interspersed with English commentary. Also, it is now generally known that Russell and Whitehead "reduced" arithmetic and analysis to logic. Consequently, some may absurdly think that if they formalize certain statements of a scientist they are introducing quantification into a science.

So far we have talked about 'formalization' in connection with axiomatic systems. One also speaks of formal languages. What is involved can be easily illustrated. Consider the following sign shapes:

$$\bigcirc, \quad \square, \quad \square, \quad \mathrm{D}, \quad \triangle.$$

Let us call them 'elements.' We may then introduce another notion, 'formula,' as follows:

    a)   A circle followed by a parallelogram is a formula.
    b)   A square followed by a semicircle is a formula.
    c)   A formula preceded by a triangle is a formula.
    d)   No other sequences of elements are formulas.

By the use of (*a*)—(*d*), given any sequence of elements, we can determine whether or not it is a formula. For instance

$$\triangle \quad \bigcirc \quad \square$$

is a formula since by (*a*)

○ ◻

is a formula, and by (c) a formula preceded by a triangle is a formula. Suppose now that by 'formula' we understand 'sentence' and by 'element' we mean 'word.' What I have done is specify the words of a sign system and what constitutes a sentence of such a system by referring only to sign shapes and their arrangement. No reference has been made to the meaning of the signs. If I now interpreted the signs of this system in terms, say, of English so that the sentences of the language corresponded to English sentences, I would have a miniature "language." For example, interpret the circle as 'Grace,' the square as 'George,' the parallelogram as 'is beautiful,' the semicircle as 'is tall,' and the triangle as 'not.' In such a "language," we could then say 'Grace is beautiful,' 'George is tall,' 'not (George is tall),' etc. But notice that what are elements and formulas of such a language are specified independently of the interpretation, though one might have a specific interpretation in mind. Languages constructed in such a fashion are called formal languages. We also speak of them as having been constructed syntactically. Here, as in our discussion of formalized axiomatic systems, the key to the phrase 'formal system' is the use of signs as mere shapes without meaning.[17]

I mentioned earlier that some of the problems concerning 'formalization' stem from the fact that some people take ideal languages for what they are not. Now I can explain. Some philosophers, as we saw, construct ideal languages as tools of analysis. In order not to prejudge certain issues and build unexamined assumptions into the language, they construct these languages syntactically. Just as, in order to avoid overlooking certain things, we may formalize an axiomatic system. Impressed by the philosophical clarity that may be gained by speaking in terms of an ideal language, one may think that scientific discoveries may be accomplished by such formalization. If one also thinks of an ideal language as something for the scientist actually to start using and speaking, he may then begin to advocate the formalization of the language of science—whatever that might mean. This "line of thought" may be a further source of the enthusiasm for formalization in the social sciences. There is still another source, to which we shall shortly come.

Given two theories, *M* and *N,* it may be the case, first, that both are interpretations of an abstract axiomatic system *O* and, second, *M* and *O* are well-developed systems in which we have proved a large number of theorems while *N* is not. We can then state a large number of theorems of *N* without bothering to construct proofs for them. They will be the statements in *N* which correspond (on the basis of the interpretation) to the theorems of *M* or of *O*. Discovering such a relation between N and another axiomatic system is thus one way of getting "wholesale," so to speak, a number of theorems. If O, for example, is an uninterpreted geometry and the axioms of N are laws of physics then, upon discovering that N is an interpretation of O, we have discovered a number of "new" laws. All the theorems of O, upon such interpretation, become physical laws. Understanding this, one can also see through some hopelessly misguided attempts to interpret abstract axiomatic systems in order to get such empirical laws "wholesale." Gestalt psychologists have sometimes talked of using topology for axiomatizing a psychological theory. This would mean that they hope to interpret an axiom set from a certain branch of mathematics so as to arrive at psychological laws. When one realizes what topology is, the absurdity of the program manifests itself. This case also pointedly illustrates the futility of introducing axiomatization uncritically and prematurely. Taking advantage of what I called the "wholesale" acquisition of laws depends on a certain level of development of a theory and a science.

Our illustration with M, N, and O reveals another point. I believe what is meant will be clear when I say that M and N have the same form. In the case of developed empirical sciences, this might well mean that the two theories will have equations of the same form, though the constants of the equations will differ. Thus, we establish a mathematical "identity" between the two theories. This is essentially what was discovered and put forth in the electromagnetic theory of light. Such an achievement may lead one to speak of a theoretical "unification" of different areas of a science.

There is another sense of 'unification' that our discussion encompasses. Let M_1 and N_1 designate two theories. The following three conditions may then hold. (1) To each undefined term of N_1 is co-ordinated a term (defined or undefined) of M_1. (2) This co-ordination puts every axiom of N_1 in correspondence with a theorem of M_1. (3) There is no such co-ordination that will put every axiom of M_1 in correspondence with a theorem of N_1. Let us call the set of statements establishing the correspondence the 'co-ordination rules.' Then, given the co-ordination rules and M_1, we can dispense with N_1 in making predictions. For, a prediction is made, using N_1, from (a) a law of N_1 which asserts that if certain initial conditions are fulfilled then a certain state of affairs follows,[18] and (b) the assertion that the initial conditions have been fulfilled. Given a description of such initial conditions in the terms of N_1, we first find the statement of M_1 that corresponds to it. We then, by the relevant law of M_1, predict the consequent conditions. Finally, we find the description in N_1 that corresponds to the description of the consequent conditions in M_1. Thus, any prediction made, using N_1, can now be made without that theory. In a certain sense N_1 is no longer needed. We may then say that N_1 has been *reduced* to M_1.[19]

In speaking of 'reduction'[20] we have come across a highly controversial notion in the behavior sciences. Perhaps part of the controversy may be "seen through" by reflecting on some of the things reduction involves. First, what is reduced is a theory (to another theory), not a science. Though, one could, I suppose, mean by the "reduction" of one science to another the reduction of all theories of the first to theories of the second. Second, we speak of reduction in terms of theories, in the sense of axiomatic systems. Consequently, the question of reduction can only be raised, sensibly, in areas of science that have achieved a certain level of development. Third, it is essential that no term of M_1 be co-ordinated to two terms of N_1 so that a description (of a state of affairs) expressible in M_1 corresponds to two descriptions in N_1. For we would then no longer be able to dispense with N_1. Let I_{n_1}, I_{n_2}, C_{n_1}, and C_{n_2} be abbreviations for statements of N_1, and I_{m_1}, I_{m_2}, C_{m_1}, and C_{m_2} abbreviate statements of M_1. Also let 'If I_{n_1} then C_{n_1}' and 'If I_{n_2} then C_{n_2}' be two laws of N_1. If I_{m_1} is co-ordinated with both I_{n_1} and I_{n_2} and C_{m_1} with both C_{n_1} and C_{n_2}, then we could no longer use the law of M_1, 'If I_{m_1} then C_{m_1},' and the co-ordination rules to predict C_{n_1} from I_{n_1}. In trying to follow the procedure outlined above, we could not carry out the third step, since C_{m_1} corresponds to both C_{n_1} and C_{n_2}. We could only predict that C_{n_1} or C_{n_2} would be the case without being able to specify which one. In such cases one may nevertheless not wish to relinquish the idea of reduction, since we can predict that one of the two will be the case without using N_1. Hence, one might, in such cases, speak of "incomplete" or "statistical reduction." Fourth, one may have a one-many correspondence between the terms of N_1 and M_1 (but not, as we saw, between those of M_1 and N_1) and still have "complete" reduction. Suppose, first, that I_{m_1} and I_{m_2} are both co-ordinated with I_{n_1}, and C_{m_1} and C_{m_2} with C_{n_1}; and, second, that M_1 contains the two laws 'If I_{m_1} then C_{m_1}' and 'If I_{m_2} then C_{m_2}.' We could still, from M_1 and the co-ordination rules alone, predict C_{n_1} from I_{n_1}. Thus, one state of the reduced theory may correspond to many states of the reducing theory. Fifth, since not all of the terms and laws of M_1 correspond to terms and laws of N_1, it is possible that this additional material will enable us to make predictions about states of N_1, using M_1, that we could not make from N_1. Suppose in N_1 we cannot predict C_{n_2} from I_{n_1}, but we can, in M_1, predict C_{m_2} from I_{m_1} (these being the co-ordinates of the two states of N_1). We can then, using M_1 and the co-ordination rules, predict C_{n_2} from I_{n_1}. I will call such predictions 'two-theory predictions.' If this prediction is not borne out, then we would not feel that N_1 has been reduced to M_1. Consequently, this imposes a further condition on reduction. On the other hand, if such predictions are borne out by the facts, this would be considered evidence for the reduction of N_1 to M_1. Sixth, I used throughout the discussion of reduction, the term 'co-ordination' and not 'interpretation.' This reflects the fact that we were speaking of two interpreted axiomatic systems. *Formally,* there is no difference between 'co-ordination,' as I used it above, and 'interpretation.' If we consider the descriptive words of N_1 to be mere marks, what we have is an interpretation of N_1 in terms of part of M_1. But 'co-ordination' in terms of two interpreted theories can cover two different situations. In one case, the co-ordination rules may be empirical laws. Thus if M_1 is a physiological theory and N_1 is a psychological theory, then the co-ordination rules are really laws asserting that certain physiological states accompany (correspond to) certain behavioral states. Laws of this type, connecting two theories, are called 'cross-sectional laws.' To reduce a behavior theory to a physiological theory, one must then discover such cross-sectional laws. Moreover, aside from other evidence for the existence of certain cross-sectional laws, the success of the two-theory predictions following from them, and the physiological theory, would constitute additional evidence.

Instead of cross-sectional laws, the co-ordination rules may consist of definitions of the terms of N_1. Such co-ordination rules would then simply be a set of definitions of L. Here, the laws of N_1 would follow from those of M_1 and the analytically true definitions. In our other case, the laws of N_1 follow from those of M_1 and further *laws*—the cross-sectional ones. A different case seems to arise when we propose *new* definitions of the terms of N_1 in order to achieve the reduction of that theory to M_1. But one may then wonder if, with new definitions, and hence laws that say different things, we are reducing N_1, or a new theory, to M_1. The puzzle arises because, in speaking of 'new definitions,' we may be mixing reduction by definition with reduction by means of cross-sectional laws. Thus if one said, for example, that a behavior state was defined in terms of a physiological state (if reduction had been achieved) he would be ignoring the fact that we discovered a law to hold between the two states and not, absurdly, a definition. One does not discover definitions; one makes them, so to speak. Though, of course, one may discover that with certain definitions one can establish a reducing connection. If the terms of N_1 are defined, in L, independently of the terms of M_1, then to reduce N_1 to M_1 we must employ cross-sectional laws. To speak of providing new definitions for the terms of N_1 would be either to confuse laws with definitions or to construct a new theory in place of N_1. All this depends on the concepts of N_1 having been properly introduced into L in the first place. If they are not terms of L, and thus not empirically meaningful, then to define them by means of the terms of M_1 is really to introduce them into L.

The dispute about the reduction of sociological theories to psychological ones centers about the proposal to define all sociological concepts in terms of psychological ones. Part of the dispute may stem from a confusion between definitional reduction and reduction by means of cross-sectional laws; another part may be due to the vagueness of the concepts of the "theories" involved. (When I speak of a 'dispute' here, I mean a dispute about reduction "in principle," since neither area, at present, contains theories of a stature sufficient to enable us to speak realistically of reduction.) But a major aspect of the dispute is about a methodological (philosophical) issue. This issue concerns the nature of "group terms" —terms like 'average height' and 'degree of segregation.' Some would hold that the only way to provide any group term with unproblematic meaning is to define it in psychological terms, i.e., in terms of items of individual behavior. Others deny this. Thus, the dispute is about how group terms may be properly introduced into L. Here again I must be content with merely indicating an issue without discussing it.

One more thread will complete our pattern. Again we require two axiomatic systems, say N_1 and A. In this case, however, A is an abstract system. Suppose, instead of interpreting A, we co-ordinate to *only some* of the terms of A terms of N_1. Thus, only some of the statements of A correspond to statements of N_1, while other statements of A would not correspond to empirically meaningful statements (and, of course, some terms of A would not have empirically meaningful correlates). If N_1 and A fulfil the conditions for reduction, N_1 would then be reduced to an abstract system. An abstract system like A is a *partially interpreted calculus*. Yet such a calculus enables us to obtain (1) two-theory predictions of states of N_1 and (2) if another theory, say M_1, is also reducible to A, we attain a kind of theoretical unification. Classical atomic theory is such a partially interpreted calculus. We are not familiar with the basic entities of such a calculus—i.e., we are not acquainted with any referents of its undefined terms.

Such calculus, employed in physics, furnishes us with two further points. (*a*) Some terms may be introduced into a science, not by being defined in L, but by partial interpretation of a calculus.[21] (*b*) Partial interpretation of a calculus furnishes us with a third sense of 'co-ordination.' Here we deal neither with definitions nor with discovered laws. The correspondence is *made* in the sense that we manipulate either the co-ordination or the calculus until we get what we want (successful two-theory predictions).

We saw earlier some motives that could be responsible for the current ideological concern with formalization in the behavior sciences. The particle models of physics indirectly furnish another. We are all familiar with the prestige of contemporary physics. On the other hand, the status of the behavior sciences is a disputed question. Hence, some behavior scientists may unconsciously believe that the construction of such calculi is the key to the development of their field. Furthermore, behavior scientists frequently are accused of employing empirically meaningless terms. Yet, they see that the basic terms of partially interpreted calculi are methodologically sound even though such terms are not empirical constructs. Thus, some might think that they establish the respectability of questionable terms, without specifying their meaning, by claiming that these terms belong to a partially interpreted calculus (or, perhaps more accurately, to a caricature of one). The incoherence of such claims is probably the only plausible explanation for their being seriously considered. What is forgotten or, perhaps, not understood is the level of development of physics, where such calculi are employed, and that the key to the use of the particle models was the application of the laws of mechanics to the particles. The situation becomes even more complicated and incoherent when some are led by the use of the same term, 'formal,' to confuse partially interpreted calculi with formal systems that we encountered earlier—those constructed to minimize the making of logical errors. Consequently, some may foolishly believe that by *formalizing* theories in the social sciences, they are doing what the physicist does when he constructs particle models.

NOTES

1. For a detailed explanation of the nature and use of a clarified language, see G. Bergmann, *Philosophy of Science* (Madison: The University of Wisconsin Press, 1957).

2. The single quotes (semantical quotes) are used when speaking about a sign or sequence of signs.

3. B. Russell, "On Denoting," reprinted in *Logic and Knowledge,* edited by R. C. Marsh (London: George Allen and Unwin Ltd., 1956), pp. 41-56.

4. The *definiens* is a meaningful expression of a language used in a definition to provide the meaning for an introduced expression, the *definiendum.* For a more detailed discussion of definition see C. Hempel, *Fundamentals of Concept Formation in Empirical Science* (Chicago: The University of Chicago Press, 1952), pp. 2-6.

5. Though 'not' combines with one sentence to form a compound sentence, it is also classified as a connective.

6. For such an elaboration see G. Bergmann, *Philosophy of Science,* pp. 41-48, and "Logical Positivism, Language, and the Reconstruction of Metaphysics," reprinted in *The Metaphysics of Logical Positivism* (New York: Longmans, Green and Co., 1954), pp. 30-77.

7. When we sometimes say that the sun is shining and isn't or that Jones is tall and isn't, it appears as if we are asserting that a sentence is both true and false. Actually this is not what we do. Such cases are due to the vagueness of reference of our descriptive terms, rather than to our belief that a sentence is both true and false.

8. With the customary truth table for 'If . . . then . . . ,' this statement is logically equivalent to the tautology 'If p_1 and p_2 and . . . and p_n then c.'

9. The parallel postulate may be stated as follows: If a straight line (AB) intersects two other straight lines (CD), (EF), then if the sum of the interior angles on one side of (AB) is less than two right angles, then (CD) and (EF) will meet on that side of (AB).

For the Greeks, axioms were supposed to be more general than postulates. Thus, axioms were truths not confined to geometry like 'The whole is equal to the sum of its parts.' Also, some apparently thought only axioms need be self-evident. Thus some propositions of Euclid's basis were axioms while others were postulates. Today, the distinction is found neither clear nor necessary.

10. An axiomatization of Euclidean geometry not open to such objections was first constructed by Hilbert in 1899.

11. Definitions need only be considered as part of the basis of abstract axiomatic systems. For interpreted axiomatic systems, being stated in L, will make use of the terms, and hence definitions, of L. Thus, to say that a defined term of L is an undefined term in some axiomatic system is simply to say (1) that it is used in the system but (2) not all the terms employed in its definition (in L) are so used.

This is not to say that in the course of developing an interpreted axiomatic system one may not define, as is often fruitfully done, new terms. For what we would actually be doing would be to introduce, by definition, new terms into L which are used in the system. States of affairs describable by the terms used in an axiomatic system are sometimes called 'states of the system.'

12. I spoke, above, of interpreting $(FS\text{-}1)$ in terms of L. We should note that while $(FS\text{-}1)$ is an axiomatic system, L is a language in which various axiomatic systems (interpreted ones) may be stated. L itself is not an axiomatic system: it makes no sense to ask for the axioms of a language.

13. 'Significance' is not to be confused with 'meaningfulness.' For an analysis of the former, see G. Bergmann, *Philosophy of Science,* pp. 50-52, and C. Hempel, *op. cit.,* pp. 39-50.

14. Sometimes I speak of getting $(S\text{-}1)$ from $(FS\text{-}1)$ by interpreting the latter. Some other times I speak of getting $(FS\text{-}1)$ from $(S\text{-}1)$ by formalizing $(S\text{-}1)$. One may then be puzzled as to which comes first. Actually, there is no problem. Which we develop *first,* in a temporal sense, is irrelevant. If one system is a formalization of another, then the second is an interpretation of the first.

15. Since an argument is valid if, and only if, a certain statement is a tautology, we can see the relevance of systems of tautologies for the study of logical inference.

16. This is perhaps a contemporary variant of the classical rationalist confusion between *logical inference* and *causal sequence,* and hence between matters of logic and matters of empirical lawfulness. One who recalls the tautological nature of logical inference is not likely to confuse the two.

17. I have here employed obvious shapes to illustrate the point of the discussion. But letter symbols too may be considered merely as geometrical shapes in the construction of a "language."

18. I have here considered only one form a law may take (if . . . then . . .) for reasons of simplicity since the discussion holds for other forms as well (equations, for example).

19. But see below for a further condition for reduction.

20. For a discussion of reduction and the use of models in scientific theories see M. Brodbeck, "Models, Meaning, and Theories" in this volume.

21. Terms defined in L are called 'empirical constructs'; the undefined terms of a partially interpreted calculus are sometimes called 'theoretical constructs.'

BIBLIOGRAPHY

BERGMANN, G. *Philosophy of Science.* Madison: University of Wisconsin Press, 1957.

———. "The Logic of Psychological Concepts." *Philosophy of Science,* 18 (1951), 93-110.

———. *The Metaphysics of Logical Positivism.* New York: Longmans, Green & Co., Inc., 1954.

———. "Reduction." *Current Trends in Psychology and the Behavioral Sciences.* Pittsburgh: University of Pittsburgh Press, 1955.

BRODBECK, M. "Methodological Individualisms: Definition and Reduction." *Philosophy of Science,* Vol. 25, No. 1, pp. 1-22.

———. "The Philosophy of Science and Educational Research," *Review of Educational Research,* Vol. XXVII, No. 5, pp. 427-40.

FEIGL, H. and BRODBECK, M. *Readings in the Philosophy of Science.* New York: Appleton-Century-Crofts, Inc., 1953.

HEMPEL, C. "Geometry and Empirical Science," reprinted in *Readings in Philosophical Analysis,* H. Feigl and W. Sellars, eds. New York: Appleton-Century-Crofts, Inc., 1949.

———. *Fundamentals of Concept Formation in Empirical Sciences.* Chicago: University of Chicago Press, 1952.

WILDER, R. L. *The Foundations of Mathematics.* New York: John Wiley and Sons, Inc., 1952.

14

An Axiomatization of the Phonologic Aspect of Language

JOSEPH H. GREENBERG

Columbia University

The axiomatic method may be briefly characterized as the most explicit possible application of a logico-mathematical model to a specific subject matter. Most of the essentials of this method can be understood from a brief consideration of what was historically its first application, the geometry of the Greeks as elaborated and codified in Euclid's *Elements*. The basic rules are: 1. In proving a theorem we cannot adduce any proposition which has not itself already been proved (i.e., is a theorem). 2. We cannot introduce a new term without defining it by means of terms already defined. This potentially infinite regress from theorem to theorem and from definition to definition must find its stopping place somewhere in a set of terms undefined in the system and propositions not proved in the system. The former are usually designated as the undefined or primitive terms of the system, the latter as its axioms, postulates, or primitive propositions.

The Greeks themselves and their successors until the invention of the non-Euclidean geometries of the nineteenth century viewed these ultimate and unproved propositions as self-evident truths about the physical world. The axiomatic method of step-by-step deduction from explicitly stated, initially self-evident assumptions was during this period regarded as the model for all investigations which might yield indubitable results.

The invention of non-Euclidean geometries in the nineteenth century, all internally self-consistent, yet all contradicting each other in regard to the parallel axiom, made the traditional interpretation of axioms as self-evident truths no longer tenable. Henceforth, the axioms were treated as premises from which the theorems were deduced. What was asserted was that the theorems indeed followed without logical flaw from the axioms as premises. The questions of truth that might be discussed then were purely logical. For example, they involved such considerations as the independence and consistency of the axioms and the noncircularity of the definitions. However, if a subject matter could be found such that, when the primitive terms of the system are identified with specific objects or events of this subject matter, the axioms are true, it will follow that all of the theorems validly deduced will likewise be true on the same interpretation.

Therefore, when a system is given a particular factual interpretation, two distinct sets of truth problems arise, the logical one of the internal consistency of the system itself and the empirical observational truth of the axioms when applied to the subject matter. For the truth of our ultimate conclusions, both are equally necessary. The latter must be guaranteed by co-ordinating definitions which specify the meanings to be given the abstract terms of the calculus by means of clearly specified and practicable operations (operational definitions). It seems necessary to point this out since the expressions "undefined terms" and "postulates" have sometimes led to the notion that one may assume anything one cares to. It should be clear that what is meant in this context is undefined *within the system*.

The other basic contribution of the nineteenth century was, in a sense, purely technical, but of considerable significance for the development of axiomatic method, the invention of symbolic logic. Dissatisfaction with the scope and precision of traditional Aristotelian syllogistic reasoning led to the development of a symbolic notation with formalized rules of manipulation analogous to those of an algebra. These two streams of the traditional axiomatics in its newer interpretation as a calculus and the formal methods of symbolic logic meet in the *Principia Mathematica* of Whitehead and Russell. In this work, from one primitive relation between propositions and a small number of axioms, all the basic concepts of logic and mathematics are derived by the axiomatic method and within a purely symbolic language.

The axiomatic method has since been applied in a number of nonmathematical fields, e.g., biology (Woodger), switching circuits (Shannon), and learning theory (Hull), and others.[1] Such axiomatizations, including the one presented here, contain two classes of terms, those with subject-matter interpretations (descriptive terms) and those with logico-mathematical interpretations (logical terms). Moreover, purely logico-mathematical theorems may be applied wherever required without being proved in the system. Were this not so, the same generally valid logical propositions would have to be deduced again from logical primitives in each case.[2]

The reputation for methodological rigor and clarity of results enjoyed by linguistics among those sciences dealing with human sociocultural behavior suggests that it is in a stage ripe for axiomatization. However, it is precisely one of the values of such an attempt that it demonstrates wherein the gaps and weaknesses in theory and empirical data of a particular subject matter lie. The following considerations will show that linguistics does not at present have a general theory as this term is employed, e.g., in physics. What can be axiomatized is rather the descriptive methodology of the science. The subsequent discussion will seek to show that this more modest goal may be of distinct value in the ultimate development of higher-level explanatory theory.

By a theory of a science, we mean, first, that there exists a set of empirical generalizations of universal scope; that is, a set of implications with universal quantification. For example, the statement that lead melts at 327.7°C. is a universal empirical generalization and may be cast in the universally quantified symbolic form (x) $Fx \supset Gx$, for all values of x, if x has the property F it has the property G. In the present instance, if anything has the defining properties of lead it has the property of melting at 327.7°C. We expect, moreover, that such generalizations will not stand isolated but that numbers of them will be deducible from general statements called laws. The measure of progress of a science is the extent to which its empirical generalizations and lower-level laws are mutually connected in a single deductive structure and its fruitfulness in producing novel generalizations deducible from such laws.

Measured by such standards, linguistics offers but few empirical generalizations and no genuine deductive structure of scientific laws. The term "law" has been traditionally employed in certain instances within the historical-comparative branch of the science. Thus, the statements first made by Jakob Grimm concerning certain changes in the sound system of Proto-Germanic in the course of its development from Proto-Indo-European often go under the name of Grimm's law.[3] A schematic statement of these changes is as follows, the earlier sound being placed on the left and the later sound on the right in each formula and arranged according to the point of articulation (rows) and manner of articulation (columns):

$$b^h > b \qquad b > p \qquad p > f$$
$$d^h > d \qquad d > t \qquad t > \not{b}$$
$$g^h > g \qquad g > k \qquad k > x$$

The symbol þ indicates the initial sound of English *three* and *x* the final sound of German *Dach,* "roof." Now such statements, however impressive in appearance, are not even empirical generalizations of universal scope, for we do not know under what conditions changes similar to those stated in the above formulas would recur in other languages at different times and places.

The application of axiomatic method undertaken here, therefore, does not have as its subject matter a general theory of language comparable to that of physics in the physical world, since such a theory, as has been seen, does not exist. Linguistics shares with other social-cultural sciences the peculiarity that its data are provided in terms of a universe of subsystems, individual languages, cultures, and societies, and its lowest-level generalizations are not of universal scope but refer to the existence of certain phenomena within such particular subsystems. The basis for the widely held opinion concerning the methodological superiority of linguistics among the social sciences appears to rest mainly on its success in establishing rigorous descriptive methods for such subsystems in terms of units of universal occurrence such as the phoneme and the morpheme. This does mean that there is comparability between statements about different linguistic subsystems (i.e., languages) and that the way lies open to statements of universal scope referring to all languages.

However, an examination of the actual practice of linguists as well as the extensive theoretical literature of phonology and grammatical analysis will show that such terms are applied by different writers in somewhat different ways. In other words, different linguists, or even the same linguist when operating with different languages, employ different, usually unstated definitions of basic units.[4] No harm is done when only the practical or aesthetic exigencies connected with a single language are concerned. However, the recently revived interest in typological (i.e., nonhistorical comparison) raises the question of comparability in acute form. How, for example, can we arrive at generalizations concerning the relative frequency of phoneme combinations in languages in general when for the same language different analytic procedures might yield drastically different numbers of phonemes?[5]

It is not intended here, even if it were possible, to legislate some single method for stating the results of descriptive phonological analysis. The purpose is rather theoretical clarification so that the researcher interested in deriving generalizations of universal scope can, if necessary, reformulate through a uniform procedure the raw data of phonetic fact where necessary and so attain interlinguistic comparability.

The part of linguistic theory chosen here for axiomatization is descriptive. This will explain the prominence of definitions and the absence of theorems, most of which would be trivial and of little interest. Within descriptive theory, phonology, the analysis of sound systems, has been chosen as necessarily preceding the main body of grammatical analysis and as being basic to it. The present treatment of phonology is not quite complete. Attention is concentrated on the ultimate definition of the most important unit, the phoneme. A second unit, juncture, or significant boundary, is defined as an incidental result. The third, constructive features, are not defined but the lines along which such an operation might be carried out is indicated. An example of constructive feature is the pattern of intonation in English which distinguishes a question from a statement.

In what follows, an attempt is made to indicate more systematically the areas of linguistic theory within which axiomatization seems possible and the place occupied by that portion, namely, descriptive phonology, chosen for the present attempt.

The three basic aspects of any system of significant symbols are: 1. The physical specifications of the elements which are to function as the symbol vehicles; 2. The rules of permitted combination of these elements; 3. The interpretation in extrasystemic terms of the expressions of the system. In terms of natural spoken language these are phonology, grammar, and semantics respectively. We make the by now common distinction between object language (O), the language described, and metalanguage (M), the language of the description itself. In the present context by M will be meant more particularly the uninterpreted calculus of an axiomatized metalanguage. Hence, for each of the three, phonology, grammar, and semantics, we may speak of languages O and M.

It would be generally granted that the methods of semantics are not yet sufficiently advanced for axiomatization. Of grammar and phonology, it is agreed that on the whole phonology has logical priority. Thus, virtually all grammars begin with a discussion of the sound system of the language as being basic to the grammatical description that follows. The present results tend to confirm this by showing that practically all of the primitive notions adequate to both grammar and phonology are phonetic and that it seems far more natural to move directly from these to the development of phonology as a whole rather than to develop grammatical analysis first and then phonology, assuming that this is feasible.

Along a further axis we may distinguish comparative treatments of all kinds, whether those of dialect geography, genetic-historical linguistics (classical comparative linguistics), or typological (nonhistorical) comparison. In all such cases prior description is necessary since languages cannot be compared until they have been described. In this sense also, the subject matter of the present axiomatization, being descriptive, has methodological priority.

To axiomatize phonology or any other aspect of linguistic theory in general is different from axiomatizing the description of some particular language. A language in which the former is carried out will be called here a *universal metalanguage,* and those of the latter category *particular metalanguages.* The present treatment belongs to the former, or universal, class. There are certain salient logical characteristics which distinguish these two types. The universal language does not assert the existence of anything. When definitions are set up within such a language, conditions for its application are stated, but it is not implied that such conditions are necessarily fulfilled anywhere. On the other hand, particular metalanguages assert that certain classes of terms have actually existing members and that certain relations among them actually hold.

This may be illustrated as follows. In the axiomatization presented here it would be possible to construct a definition of geminate clusters, that is, sequences of two like sounds as in Italian *fatto,* "done," as follows:

Def. *gmcl* $= \hat{\alpha} \{\alpha \, \epsilon \, Sequ. \, Nc^{\prime} \, \alpha \, \epsilon^2 \cdot (x) \, (y) \, x \neq y \cdot x, y \, \epsilon \, \alpha \supset x \, Phsm \, y\}$

This is to be read: Geminate clusters are those classes the members of which are in sequence, whose cardinal number is two and such that if any two distinct entities belong to it, they are phonetically similar to each other.

In the axiomatization of some particular language in which such sequences are found instead of a definition one would find an existence assertion:

$\exists$! *gmcl*

This is to be read: The class of geminate clusters has members. Note also that in such a particular metalanguage the definition of *gmcl* as given in a universal metalanguage may be taken for granted. Although neither universal nor particular formal axiomatizations have as yet been carried out in linguistics, this is the tacit assumption of all grammars of particular languages, namely, that there is a universal set of definitions and analytical procedures with which we approach any particular language so that terms such as geminate cluster are normally introduced without definition.

The question may be raised regarding the status of the axioms of a universal metalanguage. Some of them might be looked upon as partial definitions of language. So it would be possible to say that Axiom 1 of the present system which states the logical characteristics of the relation "preceding in time" of sound segments is a partial definition of language, for if we examined any structure and no relation with this logical structure appeared we would not call it a language. On the other hand, the fact that any structure to qualify as a language must have a relation which satisfies this axiom does not, in itself, constitute a definition of language. It is a necessary but not sufficient condition since there may well be other classes of phenomena exhibiting a relation with the same logical structure. To sum up, certain axioms are definitions, but only in conjunction with co-ordinating definitions specifying objects and operations outside of the system.

The other axioms all have to do with phonetics. With the interpretations given here, all of these are necessarily true, since they might be deduced presystematically from the physical impossibility of one thing being in two or more places at the same time. Thus, let's consider Axiom 2, which states that the laryngeal features of closed glottis, whispering, voicing, unvoicing, and murmur are mutually exclusive. If this axiom were false, according to the interpretation of the symbols employed, it would mean that, for example, the glottis might be closed and open for voicing at the same time. The proposition that the same thing cannot be in two or more places at the same time is probably to be considered analytically true (tautological).

Thus, the axioms of the universal phonological metalanguage presented here and with the interpretations specified are all analytically true either as constituting definitions of language or as being deducible on the above view from the analytic principle that more than one thing cannot be in the same place at the same time.

In any system provided with an interpretation, the interpretations themselves must be expressed in some symbol system. In distinction to M, the metalanguage itself, we may define another language C, the language of co-ordinating definitions. The question widely discussed among linguists—whether the approach to phonetic data should be articulatory, acoustic (that is, refer to the physical nature of the sound wave), or perceptual—belongs here. The nature of the interpretation suggested here is indicated by the choice of symbols in the metalanguage, most of which refer to articulations (e.g., *rnal*, "rounded lips"), while a few refer to sound perception (e.g., *Ihrp*, "initially higher or equal in pitch"). Since, however, no formal version of the C corresponding to M is given here, this is not meant to exclude other operational procedures. It is generally assumed that the results of the analysis must be equivalent at any rate as regards articulation and perception. In general, to every kinesthetically and visually distinguishable articulation type there corresponds an auditory perceptual sound type. However, the relation in general between articulation and perception is not one-one but many-one. Clearly, one could not consistently produce two separate classes of perceptual sounds by means of the same articulations. On the other hand, it is possible by two or more distinct articulations to produce the same perceptual impression. For example, a lateral consonant (e.g., *l* in English) can be produced unilaterally, that is, with absence of contact with the hard palate on one side of the tongue. Whether the absence of contact is on the right or left appears to produce no consistent difference in the perceptual effect. Since these two articulations cannot be distinguished, they cannot be employed as functionally distinct elements in the structure of the language. They will be in free variation as defined below, since to every expression with a right-side lateral there will always correspond a possible expression with a left-side lateral in the corresponding position. The distinction will therefore be eliminated as irrelevant to the linguistic code. But it will be eliminated at a later stage of the analysis than if we had started with an interpretation of our primitive terms of *M* on the basis of sound perception. This was what was meant above by the statement that the end results of these two types of interpretation must be equivalent.

The difference between interpretations in terms of either articulation or sound perception on the one hand and acoustic-physical phenomena on the other is far more drastic. Such an acoustic approach presumably would use instrumental techniques such as that of the sound spectrograph. It is to be noted that even in this case we ultimately rely on human perception, since someone must perceive and interpret the visual records made by the machine. The machine does not, and obviously cannot, reproduce this wave free of distortion and loss, although it gives in most respects a far more sensitive rendition of the actual sound waves than does the human ear. The machine therefore has its capabilities just as does the human ear. In a few instances, sound distinction can be perceived more reliably by the human ear than by the machine.

But the question does not concern whether the machine or human ear has the finer perceptive discrimination. Were the machine a thousand-fold more sensitive than the human ear, we should still choose perceptual and articulatory procedures for our co-ordinating definitions. We are concerned with what the human ear can reliably report because only such differences can be utilized in speech communication. Sounds are considered phonetically similar in the present interpretation only if they are perceptually distinguishable. No doubt the sound of initial *s* in particular utterances such as *sit* and *sick* can be shown by instrumental means to be physically different. But, for our purposes, this difference is of no significance. Even a repetition of *sick* on two separate occasions would show differences on the machine.

This is not to deny either the very great contributions which instrumental research can make to psychoacoustic problems, or the possibility that resort to instrumental techniques might be profitable under certain circumstances. It is assumed that a qualified phonetician can always distinguish sounds which the speakers of the language investigated can distinguish. However, where there is evidence from the report of the speakers themselves of a difference not detectable by the phonetician or where he finds difficulty in distinguishing certain sounds in certain sound environments, instrumental aids can often be of great value. However, no one has ever described a language by instrumental means alone without listening to it, nor does such a description appear feasible; on the other hand, many satisfactory descriptions exist in which instrumental methods were never employed.

A similar problem arises in regard to segmentation, that is, the division of the stream of speech into a definite finite number of parts. No doubt, as acoustic research demonstrates, the sounds, in Hockett's striking figure, are like a set of battered eggs on a conveyor belt.[6] However, the problem is not to assign each bit of yolk to its egg but to know how many eggs of different kinds have passed, and this, it appears, can always be done. To sum up, the language of C in the opinion of this writer is basically, in current philosophical terminology, phenomenological rather than physicalistic.

Another aspect of linguistic activity is the formulation of representation rules by means of which, based on a prior analysis of O in M and with an interpretation in C, the expressions of O can be formulated in a more stable, usually visual, medium. We distinguish expressions in the transcription itself, T, from the language in which the representation rules of the transcription are stated. This latter we call R. As before, there will be universal R and particular R. For example, the definition of phonemic, syllabic, and ideographic writing will be stated in universal R, a language without existence assertions, while the rule that a particular visual shape p represents a particular sound unit /p/ as defined in the particular M belongs in a particular R. The general theory of R is often called graphemics.

The clear distinction between M and R and indeed different kinds of R, which will not be discussed here, is one of the great merits of Chao's treatment and its neglect leads to certain difficulties.[7] A general principle of relativity holds among the languages thus far characterized. By this, we mean that the same linguistic facts in O can sometimes be accounted for in alternate ways by placing it in one language rather than another, with resulting differences of the statements in both. This may be illustrated from M and R as follows. If in a language with two significant pitch levels, high and low for every vowel, there are likewise three vowel qualities a, i, u with every possible combination of pitch and quality occurring, these facts can be accounted for in at least two ways. In the first, the M and associated C of phonology defines high-pitched a, low-pitched *a*, high-pitched *i*, low-pitched *i*, etc., as six distinct phonemes and the rules of representation *R* states that each will be represented by a distinct symbol as follows: *á, à, í, ì, ú,* and *ù.* In the second we define in *M* three phonemes of quality and two of pitch, five in all, therefore, rather than six, and specify a relation of simultaneity between the qualities and the pitches. In *R* we assign the symbols *a, i, u, ',* and *`* respectively to the five defined units and represent simultaneity between pitch and quality by "written above." In either case the facts of *O* are accounted for and the transcription in *T* appears exactly the same.

The relativity of *C* and *M* is particularly important. The difference between those who take a "realistic" as opposed to a "nominalistic" view of the phoneme can be stated in terms of this relativity. The realists would presumably construct a phonologic metalanguage in which the phonemes would be the primitive ideas. The sound variations within the same phonemic unit would be accounted for by complex rules of interpretation within *C,* the language of co-ordinating definitions. Thus, if within a particular language the phoneme /k/ had a fronted variant *ǩ* before front vowels, a central variant *k* before *a* and a retracted variant before back vowels, it would be stated that unit /k/ as specified in *M* was to be interpreted as *ḳ, k,* and *ḵ* under the conditions as stated above. The expression "realized as" with Platonic overtones is often used here.[8]

On the nominalist view, the particular sound qualities actually heard are the primitive ideas of *M* whose interpretation in *C* is simple in that to every such primitive in *M* there is only a single interpretation. On the other hand, phonemes must be defined within *M* from the actual sounds by a complex procedure of logical analysis. Therefore the realist has a simple *M* and a complex *C,* the nominalistic a simple *C* and a complex *M.*

The nominalist view seems here more plausible in that the phonemes in fact can only be reached by certain logically complex procedures from the phonetic data actually given in experience. The realist, as it were, tacitly assumes this analysis, which can be reconstructed from his co-ordinating rules in *C.* But, in a sense, these rules stand in need of justification, or at least exposition by a kind of meta-*C* which might in many instances be logically equivalent to the *M* of the nominalist, when we consider that the end results of phonemic analysis are generally very similar regardless of the presumed theoretical orientation of the analyst.[9]

To define the phoneme is essentially to describe the analytic process by which, starting from the sounds of speech as presented to human physical perception, we arrive at the kinds of units employed in alphabetic writing. To the nonlinguist, it may well seem surprising that approximately twenty axioms and more than one hundred definitions are required to carry out this operation. The operation, if he has ever given thought to it, must seem a simple one by which there is made to correspond to each distinct physical sound a single symbol. Unless he has considered the matter closely and has, moreover, some acquaintance with phonetics, a speaker, no matter how great his sophistication in other matters, is not aware of the many perceptually distinct sounds which he considers to be examples of the same "sound." Thus, the sound represented by *p* in *s p i n,* which is unaspirated, is quite different from the *p* in *p i t,* which is aspirated. Nor will it do to say that they are so similar that no elaborate analysis is necessary to decide that they belong to the same unit. In Chinese, this very distinction between aspirated and nonaspirated is sufficient to distinguish words with quite different meanings and therefore these same sounds would be indicated by different symbols in an alphabetic writing of Chinese. Since we cannot tell *a priori* which particular sound distinctions are significant in each language, some general procedure becomes necessary.

It might perhaps be thought on the basis of the above example that recourse to the potential of distinguishing meanings would provide a simple solution, but this is not true either. In English, the unreleased final *t* of *pit* is phonetically different from the initial aspirated *t* of *tell.* The difference between the two, it is true, could never function to distinguish separate words. But this is likewise true of the final unreleased *p* of ca*p* and the initial *t* of *tell,* since the former only occurs in syllabic final and the former in syllabic initial position. Hence, a more precise notion of phonetic similarity, combined with considerations of distribution, is required. That is, we need observations concerning the positions and combinations in which elements can occur. The solution may in all of these cases seem intuitively self-evident, particularly to a native speaker. But professional linguists whose first language is English differ on such matters as whether the sound rendered by *ch-* in *cheese* is a single unit or a sequence of two units *t-š* (i.e., *t-sh*) and whether the diphthong represented by *-a-* in *mate* is a sequence of *e* followed by *y* or is to be considered an individual unit.

We might, indeed, simplify our language *M* drastically by defining a phoneme as a class of sounds perceptually indistinguishable from some given sound. (This is the α-phone as defined below.) We would then require only two primitive ideas, a relation interpreted as preceding in time and another relation of sound similarity. However, this would leave us with several hundred such units in any language. Moreover, if we define grammar, in the manner described earlier, as the statement of rules of combinations of the signs, then—and this is another instance of linguistic relativity—we have simplified our phonology by complicating our grammar. For all of the peculiarities of distribution which are usually accounted for as subphonemic must be stated now as rules of combinations of our phonemes. Moreover, this complicates the grammatical description at the level of the combination of meaningful units. For example, if we now describe in our grammar of English the formation of an agent noun *beater* from *beat* we cannot treat it as the simple addition of *-er* to an unchanged stem. Since the phonetically different *t* of *beater* and *beat* must now be different phonological units, we have in this and innumerable other cases created grammatical irregularities.

In fact, the phoneme has shown itself to be a highly useful, virtually indispensable unit for descriptive phonology as indicated by actual practice of linguists. Through it, we reduce greatly the number of distinct sound units in the language, provide the basis for simple and practical orthographies for texts and dictionaries, and vastly simplify the task of grammatical description. However, all this is not accomplished without a price, as will be evident from the subsequent portion of this paper, namely, the complexity of phonemic theory itself.

The notation employed here is that of the *Principia Mathematica* (hereinafter referred to as *P.M.*), with minor exceptions, where noted. Parentheses instead of dots are used as separators. Subject-matter terms are indicated by sequences of three or four letters. Relations are distinguished from classes by initial capitals. Where several related concepts of differing logical type are required, those of higher types are indicated by using capitals entirely. It is not possible within the scope of this article to give an explanation of the logical symbols. For a fuller understanding, therefore, a knowledge of symbolic logic is required for which the standard textbooks and in particular the *Principia* should be consulted. However, it is hoped that the paraphrases in nonsymbolic language and the illustrative examples will help the reader ignorant of symbolic logic to follow the main features of the exposition.

I. TEMPORAL SEQUENCE OF SOUND SEGMENTS

Primitive relation: *Prcd* (precedes in time)

Def. 1. $Fllw = Cnv^{\prime} Prcd$

Fllw (follows in time) is the converse of precede.

Def. 2. $prps = \vec{B} {}^{\prime}Prcd$

prps (prepause) is the class of those elements which begin the relation precede.

Def. 3. $pstp = \vec{B} {}^{\prime}Fllw$

pstp (postpause) is the class of those elements which begin the relation follow.

Def. 4. $sgmn = C^{\iota} \, Prcd - (prps \cup pstp)$

The class *sgmn* (segment) is the field of precede minus the sum of prepause and postpause.

The segments are the individual sounds.

Axiom 1. $Prcd \in 1 \to 1 \cap as \cdot (x) \; x \in C^{\iota} \, Prcd \supset (\overrightarrow{Prcd_*^{\iota}} \, x \cap prps$
$\in 1 \cdot \overleftarrow{Prcd_*^{\iota}} \, x \cap pstp \in 1$

Precede is a one-one asymmetrical relation and, for all *x*, if *x* is a member of the field of precede, then the intersection of the class of those elements which are in the relation precede-ancestral to *x* and the class of prepausal elements is a class with one member, and the intersection of the class of those elements to which *x* is in the relation precede-ancestral and the class of postpausal elements is a unit class.

By this is meant that the relation precede always holds between a sound segment and the one which immediately precedes, and that, upon taking any elements, we reach a member of postpause if we go forward, and a member of prepause if we go backwards. Such a portion of the relation precede is an utterance and is defined immediately below.

Def. 5. $uttr = \hat{R} \, \{(\exists x) \; R = Prcd \restriction \overleftrightarrow{Prcd_*^{\iota}} \, x$

uttr (utterance) is the class of those relations, *R*, for which there is some *x* such that *R* is the relation precede with its field limited to the precede-family of *x* (that is, those terms to which *x* is in the relation precede-ancestral and those which have this relation to *x*).

The notions of precede, follow, and utterance will sometimes be required to be confined to segments, that is, without prepauses or postpause. They are defined as follows:

Def. 6. $Prcs = Prcd \restriction sgmn$

Prcs (precede limited to segments) is the relation precede with its field limited to the class of segments.

Def. 7. $Flls = Cnv^{\iota} \, Prcs$

Flls (follow limited to segments) is the converse of precede limited to segments.

Def. 8. $utts = \hat{R} \, \{(\exists x) \; R = Prcs \restriction \overleftrightarrow{Prcs_*^{\iota}} \, x$

utts (utterances confined to segments) is the class of relations, *R*, for which there is some *x* such that *R* is the relation precede confined to segments with its field limited to the family of *x*.

The relation precede holds within each utterance but not among utterances, which, moreover, in the absence of limitation, are taken to be infinite in number. Two instances of the "same" utterance are later defined as having phonetic similarity among their members and being arranged in the same order.

The separation of an utterance into segments is not yet operationally defined, but when the sound features have been treated (sections II-X) it will be possible to say that we have passed from one segment to the next when at least one feature has changed.

II. LARYNGEAL FEATURES

Primitive classes: *vocd* (voiced), *uvcd* (unvoiced), *mrmr* (murmur), *whsp* (whisper)

Def. 9. *clgl* $=$ *sgmn* $-$ (*vocd* $\cup$ *uvcd* $\cup$ *mrmr* $\cup$ *whsp*)

The class *clgl* (sounds with closed glottis) is the class of segments minus the sum of the classes of voiced, unvoiced, murmured, and whispered sounds.

All the features defined here and later are taken extensionally as the class of those sound segments which have the feature.

Def. 10. $LRFT = \hat{\alpha} \{\alpha = clgl \lor \alpha = vocd \lor \alpha = uvcd \lor \alpha = mrmr$
$\lor \alpha = whsp\}$

The class of classes *LRFT* (laryngeal features) consists of those classes which are identical with closed glottis, voiced, unvoiced, murmur, or whisper.

Axiom 2. *LRFT* ϵ *Cls²* *excl*

The laryngeal features are a class of mutually exclusive classes. The choice of *clgl* as a defined term rather than, for example, *vocd* is, of course, arbitrary. In this and subsequent sections articulations are treated beginning with the larynx and proceeding upward and forward through the vocal tract.

III. PITCH

Primitive relation: *Ihqp* (initially higher or equal in pitch)

Def. 11. *Ilqp* $=$ *Cnv' Ihqp*

Ilqp (initially lower or equal in pitch) is the converse of initially higher or equal in pitch.

Def. 12. *Ieqp* $=$ *Ihqp* $\cap$ *Ilqp*

Ieqp (initially equal in pitch) is the intersection of initially higher or equal in pitch and initially lower or equal in pitch.

Def. 13. *Ihrp* $=$ *Ihqp* $-$ *Ieqp*

Ihrp (initially higher in pitch) is the relation initially higher or equal in pitch minus initially equal in pitch.

Def. 14. $Ilrp = Ilqp - Ieqp$

Ilrp (initially lower in pitch) is the relation initially lower or equal in pitch minus initially equal in pitch.

Def. 15. $IPLV = \hat{\alpha} \{(x) \ \alpha = \overrightarrow{Ieqp^{\iota}} \ x\}$

IPLV (the initial pitch levels) is the class of those classes α for which there is some x such that α is the class of those elements which are initially equal in pitch to x.

Primitive relation: *Fhqp* (finally higher or equal in pitch)

Def. 16 $Flqp = Cnv^{\iota} \ Fhqp$

Def. 17. $Feqp = Fhqp \cap Flqp$

Def. 18. $Fhrp = Fhqp - Feqp$

Def. 19. $Flrp = Flqp - Feqp$

Def. 20. $FPLV = \hat{\alpha} \{(_{\exists}x) \ \alpha = \overrightarrow{Feqp^{\iota}} \ x\}$

No paraphrase is furnished for definitions 16-20 since they are precisely parallel to definitions 11-15. The defined terms are as follows: *Flqp* (finally lower or equal in pitch); *Feqp* (finally equal in pitch); *Fhrp* (finally higher in pitch); *Flrp* (finally lower in pitch); *FPLV* (final pitch levels).

Primitive relation: *Ifhq* (the initial pitch of x is higher than or equal to the final pitch of y)

Def. 21. $Iflq = Cnv^{\iota} \ Ifhq$

Def. 22. $Ifeq = Iflq \cap Ifhq$

Def. 23. $Ifhr = Ifhq - Ifeq$

Def. 24. $Iflr = Iflq - Ifeq$

These definitions which connect the initial pitches of segments with the final pitches of segments are parallel to 11-14 and 16-19. The interpretations of the defined terms are as follows: *Iflq* (initial pitch is lower than or equal to final pitch); *Ifeq* (initial pitch is equal to final pitch); *Ifhr* (initial pitch is higher than final pitch); *Iflr* (initial pitch is lower than final pitch).

Def. 25. $lvlp = \hat{x} \{x \ Ifeq \ x\}$

lvlp (level pitched segments) is the class of those elements whose initial pitch is equal to their final pitch.

Def. 26. $flpc = \hat{x} \{x \ Ifhr \ x\}$

flpc (falling pitched segments) is the class of those elements whose initial pitch is higher than their final pitch.

Def. 27. $rspc = \hat{x} \{x \; Iflr \; x\}$

rspc (rising pitched segments) is the class of those elements whose initial pitch is lower than their final pitch.

Def. 28. $CNTR = \hat{\alpha} \; (_{\exists}x) \; \alpha = \overrightarrow{Ieqp'} \; x \cap \overrightarrow{Feqp'} \; x$

CNTR (tonal contours) is the class of those classes α, for which there is some x such that α is the intersection of the class of those elements which are initially equal in pitch to x and those which are finally equal in pitch to x.

Segments belonging to the same class of contours have the same initial and final pitches.

Axiom 3. *Ihqp, Fhqp* ϵ trans $\cap$ refl $\cap$ connex

Initially higher or equal in pitch and finally higher or equal in pitch are transitive, reflexive, connected relations. From the transitivity of those relations it follows that initial and final pitches can be ordered, e.g., from lowest to highest.

Axiom 4. $C' \; Ihqp = C' \; Fhqp = C' \; Ifhq = vocd \cup mrmr$

The field of initially higher or equal in pitch is equal to the field of finally higher or equal in pitch is equal to the field of initial pitch is higher than or equal to final pitch is equal to the sum of the class of voiced and murmured segments.

This axiom connects pitch with the laryngeal features of the previous section. All voiced and murmured segments and only voiced and murmured segments have pitch.

The initial pitch of a segment is to be interpreted as its beginning pitch and final as its end pitch. In languages with only level pitches $Ihqp = Fhqp$ would hold and only one primitive, higher or equal in pitch, would be needed. On the other hand, in a very few cases the existence of a third medial pitch point would require additional primitives. This case is not considered here.

IV. ORALITY AND NASALITY

Primitive class: *oral* (the class of oral sounds)

Def. 29. $nasl = sgmn - oral$

nasl (the class of nasals) is the class of segments minus the class of orals. From this definition in conjunction with Axiom 19 and Def. 66 it is possible to derive as a theorem that all segments are either oral or nasal but never both.

V. CONTACT ARTICULATIONS BY MOBILE ORGANS

Primitive four-place relation: *Cnar* (contact articulation). $(\alpha\beta\gamma x)$ *Cnar* is to be interpreted: segment x is articulated by mobile organ α at point β in manner γ. The necessity of a four-place relation is explained below.

Def. 30. $MBGN = D_1{}^\iota\, Cnar$

MBGN (the mobile organs) is the first domain of the four-place relation of contact articulation. Since the *P.M.* does not deal with relations of more than two places, the notations D_1, D_2, etc., are introduced for the classes of terms occupying the first, second, etc., place of the relation. The members of *MBGN* are specified as classes in Axiom 8 below so that *MBGN* is a class of classes.

Def. 31. $PLAR = D_2{}^\iota\, Cnar$

PLAR (the places of articulation) is the second domain of the four-place relation of contact articulation.

Def. 32. $MNAR = D_3{}^\iota\, Cnar$

MNAR (the manners of articulation) is the third domain of the four-place relation of contact articulation.

Def. 33. $CNAF = MBGN \cup PLAR \cup MNAR$

CNAF (the contact articulation features) is the sum of mobile organ articulations, place of articulations, and manners of articulation.

Axiom 5. *labl, tapx, tbld, tbck, uvul* ϵ *MBGN*

The classes of labial, tongue apex, tongue blade, tongue back, and uvula articulations are members of the class of classes of mobile organ articulations. All of these members of *MBGN* are primitive classes.

Axiom 6. *lips, dent, alvl, fplt, mplt, bplt, uvul, phrx* ϵ *PLAR*

The classes of articulations against the lips, teeth, alveolar ridge, front palate, mid palate, back palate, uvula, and pharynx are members of the class of classes of places of articulation. All the members of *PLAR* are likewise primitive classes.

Axiom 7. *stop, slit, rill, shbl, ltrl, snnt, trll, flap* ϵ *MNAR*

The classes of stop, slit fricative, rill fricative, shibilant (broad aperture fricatives like š), laterals, sonants, trills, and flaps are members of the class of classes of manners of articulation. All the members of *MNAR* are primitive classes.

Axiom 8. $(\alpha\beta\gamma x)\, Cnar \supset x\, \epsilon\, sgmn\, \cap\, \alpha\, \cap\, \beta\, \cap\, \gamma$

If the four-place relation *Cnar* holds among α, β, γ, and x, then x

belongs to the intersection of the class of segments and the classes α, β, and γ.

If x occupies the fourth place in this relation it is a segment and belongs to the classes α (by Def. 30 a member of *MBGN*), β (by Def. 31 a member of *PLAR*), and γ (by Def. 32 a member of *MNAR*).

The necessity of a four-place relation arises from the fact that if an articulation involves two mobile organs simultaneously, for example a tongue tip fricative and a velar (tongue-back) stop, it is not sufficient to state that segment belongs to the tongue tip, velar, fricative, and stop classes of articulations simultaneously, since it will not be possible to determine whether the fricative contact is by the tongue-tip or tongue-back and similarly for the stop contact. Hence, it is necessary to order the organ, place, and manner of contact by a relation.

VI. NONCONTACT ARTICULATIONS BY MOBILE ORGANS

Primitive relation: *Hrqt* (higher or equal in tongue height)

Def. 34. $Lrqt = Cnv^{\prime} \, Hrqt$

Def. 35. $Eqth = Hrqt \, \cap \, Lrqt$

Def. 36. $Hrth = Hrqt - Eqth$

Def. 37. $Lrth = Lrqt - Eqth$

Def. 38. $TNGH = \hat{\alpha} \, \{ (_{\exists}x) \, \alpha = \overrightarrow{Eqth^{\prime}} \, x \}$

Once again the development is parallel to that of definitions 11-15 and 16-20. The interpretation of the defined terms is as follows: *Lrqt* (lower or equal in tongue height); *Eqth* (equal in tongue height); *Hrth* (higher in tongue height); *Lrth* (lower in tongue height); *TNGH* (the class of classes of tongue heights).

Axiom 9. *Hrqt* ϵ *trans* $\cap$ *refl* $\cap$ *connex*

High or equal in tongue height is a transitive, reflexive, connected relation.

Primitive relation: *Feqt* (forward or equal in the tongue back-forward dimension)

Def. 39. $Beqt = Cnv^{\prime} \, Feqt$

Def. 40. $Eqbf = Beqt \, \cap \, Feqt$

Def. 41. $Frtp = Feqt - Eqbf$

Def. 42. $Bktp = Beqt - Eqbf$

Def. 43. $BKFT = \hat{\alpha} \, \{ (_{\exists}x) \, \alpha = \overrightarrow{Eqbf^{\prime}} \, x \}$

The treatment is analogous to definitions 34-38. The meanings of the defined terms are: *Beqt* (backward or equal in tongue position); *Eqbf* (equal in tongue position); *Frtp* (farther forward in tongue position); *Bktp* (farther back in tongue position); *BKFT* (positions of the tongue in the back-forward dimension).

Axiom 10. *Feqt ϵ trans $\cap$ refl $\cap$ connex*

The relation forward or equal in tongue position is a transitive, reflexive, connected relation.

Axiom 11. *C' Hrqt = C' Feqt. C' Hrqt $\subset$ vocd $\cup$ mrmr $\cup$ uvcd $\cup$ whsp*

The field of the relation higher or equal in tonque height is equal to the field of the relation forward or equal in tongue position, and the field of higher or equal in tongue position is included in the sum of the classes of voiced, murmured, unvoiced, and whispered sounds.

The ordinary voiced vowels can be defined as the intersection of the field of higher and equal in tongue position and the class of voiced sounds.

Primitive classes: *rndl* (sounds produced with rounded lips); *sprl* (sounds produced with spread lips)

Def. 44. *ntrl = sgmn — (rndl $\cup$ sprl)*

ntrl (the class of sounds produced with neutral lips) is the class of segments minus the sum of the class of rounded lip and spread lip articulations.

Def. 45. *LPPS = $\hat{\alpha}$ {α = rndl $\vee$ α = sprl $\vee$ α = ntrl}*

LPPS (the lip-positions) is the class of those classes α such that α is equal either to the class of rounded lip, spread lip, or neutral lip articulations.

Axiom 12. *LPPS ϵ cls^2 excl*

The class of classes of lip-positions is a class of mutually exclusive classes.

VII. SYLLABIFICATION

Primitive relation: *Slst* (syllabic satellite)

Def. 46. *peak = $\hat{x}$ {(y) $\sim$ x Slst y}*

peak (the syllabic peaks) is the class of those x's such that for all y, x is not a syllabic satellite of y.

The peaks are the segments which are syllabically subordinate to no other segment. They are usually, though not always, voiced vowels.

Def. 47. *icnc = $\hat{x}$ {($_{\exists}y$) x Slst y $\cdot$ y Slst x $\cdot$ x Prcd y $\cdot$ (u) (v) (x Slst u $\equiv$ u = y) $\cdot$ (v Slst y $\equiv$ v = x)}* *icnc* (initial member of complex nucleus) is the class of those x's for which there is some y, such that x is a syllabic satellite of y and y is a syllabic satellite of x and x precedes y and for all u and all v, x is a syllabic satellite of u if, and only if, u is identical with y, and v is a satellite of y if, and only if, v is identical with x.

A complex nucleus is a succession of two syllabics in the same syllable without dominance by either number.

Def. 48. $fcnc = \hat{x} \ \{(\exists y) \ y \ \epsilon \ icnc \cdot x \ Fllw \ y\}$

fcnc (final member of complex nucleus) is the class of those x's such that there is some y such that y is an initial member of a complex nucleus and x follows y.

Def. 49. $slbc = peak \ \cup \ icnc \ \cup \ fcnc$

slbc (syllabic) is the sum of the classes of peaks, initial and final members of complex nuclei. It is possible to prove as a theorem that these are mutually exclusive classes.

Def. 50. $prst = \hat{x} \ \{(\exists y) \ x \ Slst \ y \cdot y = min \ (Prcd_{po} \ \overrightarrow{\wr Fllw_{po}} \ x) \ 'slbc$
$\cdot \ (z) \ x \ Slst \ z \equiv z = y \cdot ((u) \ u \ \epsilon \ Prcd \ (x—y) \ \supset \ (u \ Slst \ y \cdot$
$(v) \ u \ Slst \ v \equiv v = y))\}$

prst (presatellite) is the class of those x's for which there is some y such that x is a syllabic satellite of y and y is the minimum with respect to the proper ancestral of precede with its field limited to the class of elements in the relation of proper ancestral of follow to x of the class of syllabics and for all z, x is a syllabic satellite of z if, and only if, z is identical with y, and, for all u, if u is a member of the exclusive interval between x and y, then for all v, u is a satellite to v if, and only if, v is identical with y.

The class of presatellite is the class of segments dependent on a following syllabic, e.g., the m of *man*.

Def. 51. $ptst = x \ \{(\exists y) \ x \ Slst \ y \cdot y = max \ (Prcd_{po} \ \overrightarrow{\wr Prcd_{po}} \ x)$
$'slbc \cdot (z) \ x \ Slst \ z \equiv y = z \cdot ((u) \ u \ \epsilon \ Prcd \ (y—x) \ \supset \ (u$
$Slst \ y \cdot (v) \ u \ Slst \ v \equiv v = y))\}$

The definition of *ptst* (post satellite) is analogous to that of presatellite with the appropriate substitutions. The n of *man* is a post satellite.

Def. 52. $intl = \hat{x} \ \{(\exists y) \ (\exists z) \ x \ Slst \ y \cdot x \ Slst \ z \cdot y = min \ (Prcd_{po}$
$\overrightarrow{\wr Fllw_{po}} \ x) \ 'slbc \cdot z = max \ (Prcd_{po} \ \wr Prcd_{po} \ x) \ 'slbc \cdot (u)$
$x \ Slst \ u \cdot u \ Fllw_{po} \ x \equiv u = y \cdot ((v) \ x \ Slst \ v \cdot v \ Prcd_{po}$
$x \equiv v = z \cdot) \ ((s) \ s \ \epsilon \ Prcd \ (z—x) \ \supset \ (s \ Slst \ z \cdot (t) \ s \ Slst$
$t \equiv t = z)) \cdot ((q) \ q \ \epsilon \ Prcd \ (x—y) \ \supset \ (q \ Slst \ y \cdot (r) \ q$
$Slst \ r \equiv r = y \cdot))\}$

The definition of *intl* (interlude) combines the conditions of definitions 50 and 51. Interludes are segments within which a syllabic boundary falls so that they are satellites both to some syllabic that follows and some that precedes. An example is the *r* of *hurry*.

Def. 53. $SLTP = \hat{\alpha} \{\alpha = slbc \lor \alpha = prst \lor \alpha = ptst \lor \alpha = intl\}$
SLTP (*syllabic types*) is the classes of those classes α, such that α is equal to the class of syllabics, presatellites, post satellites or interludes.

Axiom 13. *s 'SLTP = sgmn*
The sum of the class of classes of syllabic types is equal to the class of segments. It can be proven from this axiom, together with the definitions of the various syllabic types, that *SLTP* is a class of mutually exclusive classes. According to this axiom, every sound segment belongs to one of the four syllabic types.

VIII. STRESS

Primitive relation: *Hrqs* (heavier or equal stress)

Def. 54. $Ltqs = Cnv' \, Hvqs$

Def. 55. $Eqst = Hvqs \cap Ltqs$

Def. 56. $Hvst = Hvqs - Eqst$

Def. 57. $Ltst = Ltqs - Eqst$

Def. 58. $STLV = \hat{\alpha} \{(\exists x) \, \alpha = \overrightarrow{Eqst'} \, x\}$
This set of definitions is again parallel to 11-15. The defined terms are: *Ltqs* (lighter or equal in stress); *Eqst* (equal in stress); *Hvst* (heavier in stress); *Ltst* (lighter in stress); *STLV* (the class of classes of stress levels).

Axiom 14. *Hvqs ∈ trans ∩ refl ∩ connex*
Heavier or equal in stress is a transitive, reflexive, connected relation.

Axiom 15. $C' \, Hvqs = slbc$
The field of the relation heavier or equal in stress is the class of syllabics. All syllabics have stress and only syllabics have stress.

Axiom 16. $(x) \, (y) \, (x \in icnc \cdot y \in fcnc \cdot x \, Prcd \, y) \supset x \, Eqst \, y$
For all x and all y, if x is an initial of a complex nucleus and y is the final of a complex nucleus, then x has equal stress with y.

IX. IMPLOSIVES AND EJECTIVES

Primitive classes: *impl* (implosive sounds); *ejct* (ejective sounds)

Def. 59. *IMEJ* = $\hat{\alpha}$ {$\alpha = impl$ V $\alpha = ejct$}

The class of classes *IMEJ* (implosives and ejectives) is the class of those classes α such that α is equal to the class of implosives or is equal to the class of ejectives.

Axiom 17. *impl* ∩ *ejct* = Λ

The intersection of the class of implosives and ejectives is the null class.

Implosives and ejectives are produced by rarefaction or compression of air above the lungs, e.g., by lowering or raising the closed glottis or sliding the back of the tongue backward or forward against the velum. The point at which this is done can be inferred from the contact articulation and laryngeal features.

X. DURATION

Primitive relation: *Lrqd* (longer or equal in duration)

Def. 60. *Srqd* = *Cnv' Lrqd*

Def. 61. *Eqdr* = *Srqd* ∩ *Lrqd*

Def. 62. *Lgdr* = *Lrqd* — *Eqdr*

Def. 63. *Shdr* = *Srqd* — *Eqdr*

Def. 64. *DGRL* = $\hat{\alpha}$ {$(_{\exists}x)$ $\alpha = \overrightarrow{Eqdr'}\, x$}

Once more the exposition is parallel to 11-15. The defined terms are: *Srqd* (shorter or equal in duration); *Eqdr* (equal in duration); *Lgdr* (longer in duration); *Shdr* (shorter in duration); *DGRL* (the class of classes of degrees of length).

Axiom 18. *Lrqd* ∈ *trans* ∩ *refl* ∩ *connex*. *C' Lrqd* = *sgmn*

Longer or equal in duration is a transitive, reflexive, connected relation and its field is equal to the class of segments.

By this axiom all segments have duration and are comparable in duration.

XI. FEATURES

Def. 65. *FEAT* = $\hat{\alpha}$ {$\alpha \in LRFT$ V $\alpha \in IPLV$ V $\alpha \in FPLV$ V $\alpha = oral$
V $\alpha = nasl$ V $\alpha \in CNAF$ V $\alpha \in TNGH$ V $\alpha \in BFKT$ V $\alpha \in$
LPPS V $\alpha \in STLV$ V $\alpha \in IMEJ$ V $\alpha \in DGRL$}

The class of classes *FEAT* (features) is the class of those classes α, such that α is a member of the classes of classes of laryngeal features, initial pitch levels, or final pitch levels, or is equal to the class of orals or to the class of nasals, or is a member of the class of classes of contact articulation features or tongue heights or tongue forward-backward positions or lip positions or stress levels or implosives-ejectives or degrees of length.

Axiom 19. $s\,'FEAT = sgmn$

The sum of the features is equal to the segments.

According to this axiom, only the members of the class of segments belong to any feature and every member of the class of segments belongs to at least one feature.

XII. PHONETIC SIMILARITY AND α-PHONES

From this point, no further primitive ideas or axioms are needed. The following operations are all logistical and lead to the concept of the phoneme in terms of the primitive ideas and definitions of sections I-XI. Our axiomatization of phonetics is not quite complete. Certain other axioms might have been added, referring to certain special restrictions on the possible combinations of features to which the same segment can belong. Two further primitive ideas might have been used. One refers to muscular tension, tense versus lax. However, it always seems to be accompanied by other differences and its status is somewhat doubtful. Pauses within the utterances should perhaps also have been included as a primitive. However, relatively little is known about them, and it seems possible, for reasons not discussed here, to exclude them without affecting the description. At any rate, grammars have up to now been written without taking them seriously into account.

Since we start from qualities, the features, and define each individual sound type, the α-phone of this section, by a unique membership in a number of such quality classes, our language is, in the terminology of Goodman, realistic rather than particularistic.[9] If we had started with each particular sound type as a primitive idea, we would have then defined individual qualities as that which is common to certain particular sound types. This would have led to certain technical difficulties connected with the abstraction of qualities and would also have required a much larger number of primitive ideas.

Def. 66. $Phsm = \hat{x}\,\hat{y}\{((\alpha)\,\alpha\,\epsilon\,FEAT - CNAF) \supset (x\,\epsilon\,\alpha \equiv y\,\epsilon\,\alpha)$
$\cdot (\overrightarrow{Cnar'}\,x = \overrightarrow{Cnar'}\,y)\}$

The relation *Phsm* (phonetic similarity) holds between x and y, if for all α, where α is a class belonging to the class of classes of features minus the class of class of contact articulation features, then x belongs to α if, and only if, y belongs to α, and the class of those ordered triples which are in the four-place relation of contact articulation to x is equal to the class of ordered triples which are in the four-place relation of contact articulation to y.

The necessity of a separate treatment of *Cnar* is explained earlier. By this definition, two segments which have all their features in common are phonetically similar.

Def. 67. α-phone $= \hat{\alpha}\ \{(\exists x)\ \alpha = \overrightarrow{Phsm^{\iota}\ x}\}$

The class of classes of α-phones is the class of those classes α for which there is some x such that α is the class of those elements which are in the relation of phonetic similarity to x.

The α-phones are therefore the different perceptually distinguishable sound types. The distinction between α-phones and β-phones as defined in the next section is partly analogous to that of Hockett, from whom the terminology derives.[10]

XIII. β-PHONES

In this section, the $\hat{\beta}$-phone, a unit of higher type than the α-phone, is defined.

Def. 68. $PHSM = \hat{R}\hat{S}\ \{\overline{Phsm}\ \restriction C^{\iota}\ S\ \epsilon\ Rsmor\ S\}$

The relation *PHSM* (phonetic similarity) holds between the relations R and S if *Phsm* (phonetic similarity between segments) is an ordinal correlator of R and S.

This relation, for example, would hold between two different instances of the "same" utterance.

Def. 69. $Seqr = \hat{R}\ \{(\exists x)\ (\exists y)\ R = Prcd\ \restriction Prcd\ (x\text{—}y)\ \cup\ I\ \restriction C^{\iota}$
    $Prcd\}$

Seqr (the class of sequential relations) is the class of relations R for which there is some x and some y such that R is the relation precede with its field limited to the inclusive interval between x and y and identity limited to the field of precede.

This relation holds between any member of a continuous sequence and the following member. The latter part of the definition allows us to treat single segments as limiting cases of sequences.

Def. 70. $Seqs = \hat{R}\ \{(\exists x)\ (\exists y)\ R = Prcs\ \restriction Prcs\ (x\text{—}y)\ \cup\ I\ \restriction C^{\iota}$
    $Prcs\}$

This is precisely analogous to the preceding definition but excludes those sequences with prepause or postpause as members.

Def. 71. $SEQU = \hat{\alpha} \{(_{\scriptscriptstyle{H}}S) \ S \ \epsilon \ Seqr \cdot \alpha = D \ 'S \cap \mathsf{C} \ 'S\}$

The class of classes *SEQU* (the members of sequential relations) consists of those classes α for which there is some sequential relation S such that α is the intersection of the domain and counterdomain of S. If, for example, in English we have *Seqr* holding from prepause through the form "h'it" ("hit") and followed by postpause, then *Seqr* has as members the relation of prepause to *h,* of *h* to '*i,* etc. The corresponding member of *SEQU* is the class *h,* '*i, t.*

Def. 72. $Smsq = \hat{\alpha} \ \hat{\beta} \ \{\alpha, \ \beta \ \epsilon \ SEQU \cdot \alpha \ sm \ \beta \cdot (x) \ x \ \epsilon \ \alpha \ \supset \ ((_{\scriptscriptstyle{H}}y)$
$y \ \epsilon \ \beta \cdot x \ Phsm \ y \cdot (x \ Seqr \ | \ Phsm \ | \ Cnv^{\prime} \ Seqr \ y \vee y \ Seqr \ |$
$Phsm \ | \ Cnv^{\prime} \ Seqr \ x))\}$

Smsq (similarity of classes which are members of sequential relations) holds between α and β if they are members of sequential relations, are cardinally similar (i.e., have the same number of members), and if for all x, if x belongs to α, there is some y which is a member of β, which is phonetically similar to y and such that either x is in a sequential relation to a segment which is phonetically similar to a segment which sequentially follows y, or y is in a sequential relation to a segment which is phonetically similar to a segment which sequentially follows x.

This relation holds between sequences of one or more members if they are phonetically similar and in the same order.

Def. 73. $SMSQ = \hat{\kappa} \ \{(_{\scriptscriptstyle{H}}\alpha) \ \kappa = \overrightarrow{Smsq^{\prime}} \ \alpha\}$

SMSQ (the classes of similar sequences) is the class of class of those classes κ for which there is some α, such that κ is equal to the class of those classes which are sequences similar to α.

This is the corresponding set of abstractive classes. In the above instance $h_1, \ i_1, \ t_1, \ h_2, \ i_2, \ t_2 \ldots$ would be a member of *SMSQ*.

Def. 74. $DTSM = \hat{\kappa} \ \{\kappa \ \epsilon \ SMSQ \cdot (\alpha) \ (x) \ (y) \ \alpha \ \epsilon \ \kappa, \ x, \ y \ \epsilon \ \alpha \cdot x$
$Prcd_* \ y \ ((R) \ R \ \epsilon \ \overrightarrow{Potid^{\prime}} \ Prcd \ \supset \ ((u) \ (v) \ u \ \epsilon \ Phsm^{\prime} \ y \equiv$
$R^{\prime} \cup Phsm \ x \vee v \ \epsilon \ Phsm^{\prime} \ x \equiv (Cnv^{\prime} \ R)^{\prime} \ v \ Phsm \ y))\}$

DTSM (determined segments) is a class of those classes of classes κ such that κ is a class of similar sequences and for all α, x and y, if α is a member of κ and x and y are members of α and x is in the relation precede-ancestral to y, then if R is any power of precede then for all u and v, either u is a member of the class of those segments which are phonetically similar to y if, and only if, the R of u is phonetically similar to x, or v is a member of the class of those segments which are phonetically similar to x if, and only if, the segment which is in the converse of the relation R to v is phonetically similar to y.

The class *DTSM* contains all the sequences of length one as a limiting case where *Potid* '*R* is the zero power, that is, identity in the field of the relation precede. The other members are longer sequences, in practice almost always with two members. Either the first members are always followed by second members which are phonetically similar to each other, or the second is always preceded by first members with the same property, or both conditions hold. For example, in Spanish, the segment, or rather class of segments š, are always preceded by a member of the segment (α-phone) *t,* but *t* is not necessarily followed by š. The sequence class *tš* (*ch* in Spanish orthography) is therefore a member of *DTSM.* A further example is *qu* in written English. The definition is generalized to sequences longer than two where similar dependencies exist.

Def. 75. β-phone $= \hat{\alpha}$ $\{(_{\exists}\beta)$ β ϵ $DTSM \cdot \alpha = \beta - \hat{\gamma}$ $(_{\exists}\delta)$ δ ϵ
$DTSM \cdot s^{\prime} \gamma \subset s^{\prime} \delta\}$

β-phones is a class of class of classes for which there is some class of classes β which is a determined segment and α is equal to β minus the class γ such that there is some δ which is a determined segment and the sum of γ is included in the sum of δ.

Where nothing satisfies the condition beginning $\hat{\gamma}$, $\alpha = \beta$ and β-phone coincides with determined segment. The above-cited condition applies, for example, in regard to the Spanish *t.* Since š is always preceded by *t* but *t* is not always followed by š, the class of sequences *tš* is one β-phone, but for *t* we must subtract those cases in which *t* is followed by š since it belongs to the β-phone *tš,* while all the other instances of *t* belong to another β-phone. Hence, in some cases, members of the same α-phone are not members of the same β-phone.

XIV. β-FUNCTIONS

Since the operations of this and the following sections employ β-phones rather than α-phones, it will be necessary to define certain terms analogous to those already defined but utilizing β-phones. Since the β-phones are a class of class of classes whereas the α-phones are a class of classes these will always be of a higher logical type. These terms are defined without comment. Note that *β-sml* corresponds to *Phsm.*

Def. 76. $\beta\text{-}Prcd = \hat{\alpha}\,\hat{\beta}\,\{\alpha, \beta \,\epsilon\, s^{\prime}\,\beta\text{-phone} \cdot (((_{\exists}x)\ (_{\exists}y)\ x\,\epsilon\,\alpha \cdot y\,\epsilon$
$\beta \cdot x\ Prcd\ y) \vee ((_{\exists}x)\ x\ \epsilon\ prps \cdot \alpha = \iota^{\prime}\ x \cdot (_{\exists}y)\ y\ \epsilon\ \beta$
$\cdot x\ Prcd\ y) \vee ((_{\exists}y)\ y\ \epsilon\ pstp \cdot \alpha = \iota^{\prime}\ y \cdot (_{\exists}x)\ x\ \epsilon\ \alpha \cdot x$
$Prcd\ y))\}$

Def. 77. $\beta\text{-}sml = \hat{\alpha}\,\hat{\beta}\,\{(_{\exists}\kappa)\ \kappa\ \epsilon\ \beta\text{-phone} \cdot \alpha, \beta\ \epsilon\ \kappa\}$

Def. 78. $\beta\text{-}Seqr = \hat{R}\,\{(_{\exists}\alpha)\ (_{\exists}\beta)\ R = \beta\text{-}Prcd\ \dot{\iota}\beta\text{-}Prcd\ (\alpha - \beta)\ \cup$
$I\,\dot{\iota}C^{\prime}\,\beta\text{-}Prcd\}$

Def. 79. $\beta\text{-}SEQU = \hat{\alpha} \{(_{\exists}S)\ S \in \beta\text{-}Seqr \cdot \alpha = D'\ S \cap \mathbb{C}'\ S\}$

Def. 80. $\beta\text{-}Smsq = \hat{\alpha}\ \hat{\beta}\ \{\alpha,\ \beta \in \beta\text{-}SEQU \cdot \alpha\ sm\ \beta\ (x)\ x \in \alpha \supset$
$((_{\exists}y)\ y \in \beta \cdot (x\ \beta\text{-}sml\ y \cdot (x\ \beta\text{-}Seqr \mid \beta\text{-}sml \mid Cnv'\ \beta\text{-}Seqr$
$y \lor y\ \beta\text{-}Seqr \mid \beta\text{-}sml \mid Cnv'\ \overrightarrow{\beta\text{-}Seqr\ x})))\}$

Def. 81. $\beta\text{-}SMSQ = \hat{\kappa} \{(_{\exists}\alpha)\ \kappa = \beta\text{-}\overrightarrow{Smsq'}\ \alpha\}$

XV. γ-PHONES

In this section, the relation of free variation is defined. β-phones or, in some cases, subclasses of β-phones which freely substitute for each other, form the next higher unit called γ-phones, in terms of which all subsequent operations are carried out and by means of which the phoneme is ultimately defined.

Def. 82. $Envr = \hat{R}\hat{S} \{S \in Seqr \cdot (_{\exists}U)\ U \in uttr \cdot R = U - S\}$

Envr (environmental relation) is a relation between relations R and S, such that S is a sequential relation and there is some utterance U, such that R is U minus S.

If we take an utterance and remove a sequence from it, then the remainder is its environment.

Def. 83. $Envs = \hat{R}\ \hat{\alpha} \{(_{\exists}S)\ S \in Seqr \cdot R\ Envr\ S \cdot \alpha = D'\ S \cap \mathbb{C}'\ S\}$

The relation *Envs* (environment of a sequential class) is the relation of a relation R to a class α where there is some S to which R is in the environmental relation and α is equal to the intersection of the domain and counterdomain of S.

Def. 84. $Frvr = \hat{\alpha}\ \hat{\beta} \{\alpha,\ \beta \in \beta\text{-}SMSQ \cdot (R)\ R \in Envs''\ s''\ \alpha \supset (_{\exists}S)$
$S \in Envs''\ S''\ \beta \cdot R\ PHSM\ S\}$

Frvr (free variation) holds between α and β if they are both β-similar sequences and if for all R, if R is one of the class of environments of the sums of the members of α, then there is some S such that S is one of the class of environments of the sums of the members of β and R is phonetically similar to S.

If, for example, in some language p may always be substituted for f and vice versa, then for every environment of p there is some phonetically similar environment of f and vice versa, so that $p\ Frvr\ f$ and $f\ Frvr\ p$. If, however, every environment of p has some phonetically similar environment of f but not vice versa, then $p\ Frvr\ f$, but not $f\ Frvr\ p$. This happens in the case of so-called conditioned free variation if, e.g., p and f vary freely before vowels but only f occurs elsewhere. Every member of $\beta\text{-}SMSQ$, including those with a single member, is likewise by this definition in free variation with itself.

Def. 85. $FRVR = \hat{\alpha}\ \{(_{\exists}\beta)\ (_{\exists}\gamma)\ \beta\ Frvr\ \gamma \cdot \alpha = \beta \cup (\gamma \cap \hat{\delta}\ \{\delta$
$\subset \gamma\}) \cdot ((R)\ (R\ \epsilon\ Envs''\ s''\ \beta \supset ((_{\exists}S)\ S\ \epsilon\ Envs''\ S''\ \delta \cdot$
$R\ PHSM\ S)) \cdot ((T)\ T\ \epsilon\ Envs''\ s''\ \delta \supset ((_{\exists}U)\ U\ \epsilon\ Envs''\ s''$
$\beta \cdot T\ PHSM\ U))\}$

FRVR (the free-variants) is the class of those classes α for which
there is some β and some γ such that β is in free variation with γ, and α
is equal to the sum of β and the intersection of γ with δ such that δ is included in γ, and for all R, such that R is a member of the class of environments of the sum of the members of β, there is some S which is a member
of the class of environments of the sums of the members of δ, and R is
phonetically similar to S; and for all T, if T is a member of the class of
environments of the sums of the members of δ there is some U which is a
member of the class of environments of the sums of the members of β,
and T is phonetically similar to U.

FRVR is a class each of whose members is a set of sequences in free
variation with each other. Just as α-phones are sometimes members of
different β-phones, so members of the same β-similar sequence may belong to different members of *FRVR*. Thus if, as in the above example, p
is in free variation with f before vowels but only f appears elsewhere,
those f's which are in free variation with p will belong to the same subclass of *FRVR*, while the other f's will form a separate subclass.

Def. 86. $\gamma\text{-phone} = s''\ \hat{\kappa}\ \{\kappa\ \epsilon\ FRVR \cdot\ (_{\exists}\alpha)\ \alpha\ \epsilon\ \kappa \cdot Nc'\ \alpha\ \epsilon\ 1\}$

γ-phone is the class of the sums of the members of κ such that κ is a
free variant and there is some α which is a member of κ the cardinal number of whose members is one.

FRVR contains sequences of any length. Since such sequences are
always in free variation with themselves, we need a definition of γ-phones
which limits this to members of *FRVR* which have at least some members
which are single β-phones. The employment of s is to reduce the type.
The γ-phones are a class of class of classes. Each member, then, is a class
of classes.

XVI. γ-FUNCTIONS

Since the remaining operations will usually employ γ-phones as units,
it will be necessary to redefine certain terms, utilizing γ-phones in place
of α- or β-phones. These definitions, as in the case of β-Functions, are
presented without comment.

Def. 87. $\gamma\text{-}sml = \hat{\alpha}\ \hat{\beta}\ \{(_{\exists}\kappa)\ \kappa\ \epsilon\ \gamma\text{-phone} \cdot \alpha,\ \beta\ \epsilon\ \kappa\}$

Def. 88. $\gamma\text{-}Prcd = \hat{\alpha}\ \hat{\beta}\ \{\alpha,\ \beta\ \epsilon\ s'\ \gamma\text{-phone} \cdot (((_{\exists}x)\ (_{\exists}y)\ x\ \epsilon\ \alpha \cdot$
$y\ \epsilon\ \beta \cdot x\ Prcd\ y) \vee ((_{\exists}x)\ x\ \epsilon\ prps \cdot \alpha = \iota'\ x \cdot (_{\exists}y)\ y\ \epsilon\ \beta \cdot$

$$x \ Prcd \ y) \lor ((\exists y) \ y \ \epsilon \ pstp \cdot \alpha = \iota^{\prime} \ y \cdot (\exists x) \ x \ \epsilon \ \alpha \cdot x$$
$$Prcd \ y)))\}$$

Def. 89. $\gamma\text{-}Prcs = \hat{\alpha} \ \hat{\beta} \ \{\alpha, \ \beta \ \epsilon \ s^{\prime} \ \gamma\text{-phone} \cdot (\exists x) \ (\exists y) \ x \ \epsilon \ \alpha \cdot y \ \epsilon \ \beta$
$\cdot \ x \ Prcs \ y\}$

Def. 90. $\gamma\text{-}Seqs = \hat{R} \ \{(\exists \alpha) \ (\exists \beta) \ R = \gamma\text{-}Prcs \ \overleftrightarrow{\ \gamma\text{-}Prcs \ } (\alpha \text{---} \beta)\}$

Def. 91. $\gamma\text{-}utts = \hat{R} \ \{(\exists \alpha) \ \alpha \ \epsilon \ \gamma\text{-phone} \cdot R = \gamma\text{-}Prcs \ \overline{\ \gamma\text{-}Prcs_{*}^{\prime} \ } \alpha\}$

Def. 92. $\gamma\text{-}PHSM = \hat{R} \ \hat{S} \ \{R, \ S \ \epsilon \ \gamma\text{-}Seqs \cdot \gamma\text{-}sml \ \epsilon \ R \ smor \ S\}$

XVII. COMPLEMENTARY VARIATION

Def. 93. $Cmvr = \hat{\alpha} \ \hat{\beta} \ \{\alpha, \ \beta \ \epsilon \ \gamma\text{-phone} \cdot (R) \ (S) \ R \ \epsilon \ s^{\prime\prime} \ Envs^{\prime\prime} \ \alpha \cdot$
$S \ \epsilon \ s^{\prime\prime} \ Envs^{\prime\prime} \ \beta \supset R \sim \gamma\text{-}PHSM \ S\}$

Cmvr (complementary variation) is the relation between two classes of classes α and β such that α and β are γ-phones, and for all R and all S, if R is a member of the sums of the environments of members of α and S is a member of the sums of the environments of the members of β, then R is not phonetically similar to S.

XVIII. JUNCTURE

Def. 94. $PREJ = \hat{\alpha} \ \{\alpha \ \epsilon \ \gamma\text{-phone} \cdot s^{\prime} \ \alpha \ \cap \ Prcd^{\prime\prime} \ pstp \neq \Lambda\}$

PREJ (the class of prejunctural γ-phones) is the class of those classes of classes which are γ-phones and the intersection of whose sum with class of those segments which precede postpause is not null.

PREJ is the class of γ-phones, some of whose members appear in utterance final position.

Def. 95. $PSTJ = \hat{\alpha} \ \{\alpha \ \epsilon \ \gamma\text{-phone} \cdot s^{\prime} \ \alpha \ \cap \ Fllw^{\prime\prime} \ prps \neq \Lambda\}$

PSTJ (the class of postjunctural γ-phones) is the class of γ-phones of which some members occur in utterance initial position.

Def. 96. $Jndv = \hat{\alpha} \ \hat{\beta} \ \{ \sim (\alpha \ \epsilon \ PREJ \cdot \beta \ \epsilon \ PREJ) \cdot \sim (\alpha \ \epsilon \ PSTJ \cdot$
$\beta \ \epsilon \ PSTJ)\}$

Jndv (juncturally diverse) is a relation which holds between α and β if it is not true that both are prejunctural and it is not true that both are postjunctural.

Def. 97. $Jnvr = \hat{\alpha} \ \hat{\beta} \ \{\alpha \ Jndv \ \beta \cdot \sim \alpha \ Cmvr \ \beta\}$

Jnvr (junctural variation) is a relation which holds between α and β if they are juncturally diverse and not in complementary variation.

Junctural variation refers to boundary differences. When γ-phones are not in complementary variation, but the variations concern γ-phones which have different peculiarities in regard to initial and final occurrence, the variation is considered junctural and is later eliminated as nonphonemic. The place of the internal boundary is itself, however, significant and is usually indicated in texts by a hyphen or space. Such a boundary is called a juncture. It may be defined as follows:

Def. 98. $Jnct = \hat{x}\,\hat{y}\,\{(_\exists\alpha)\ (_\exists\beta)\ \alpha \in PREJ \cdot \beta \in PSTJ \cdot x \in s'\ \alpha \cdot y$
$\in s'\ \beta \cdot x\ Prcd\ y \cdot ((_\exists\gamma)\ \gamma\ Jndv\ \alpha \lor (_\exists\delta)\ \delta\ Jndv\ \beta\}$

The relation $Jnct$ (juncture) holds between two segments where there is some α and some β such that α is prejunctural and β is postjunctural and x is a member of the sum of α and y is a member of the sum of β and there is either some γ which is juncturally diverse from α or there is some δ which is juncturally diverse from β.

Definitions 93-97 may be illustrated by the following example. In English the difference between *an aim* and *a name* may be stated in terms of boundary characteristics. The n_1 of *an aim* is syllabically post-satellite and of greater duration than the n_2 of *a name* which is pre-satellite and shorter in duration. They are members of different γ-phones. The n_1 of *an aim* is prejunctural because it may occur in utterance final whereas n_2 is not prejunctural because it never occurs in this position. Similarly, n_2 is postjunctural and n_1 is not. Hence they are juncturally diverse. Since their environments in this example are similar, they are not in complementary distribution. Therefore, they are in junctural variation. The n_1 of *an aim* is in junctural relation with the following vowel, while the n_2 of *a name* is in junctural relation with the preceding vowel.

XIX. STYLISTIC VARIATION

A further instance in which direct contrast is not evaluated as phonemic concerns differences which are usually evaluated as part of a pattern of constructive features distributed over a "sentence" (phonologic phrase as defined below). For example, in English the falling pitch of *ran* in "You ran." as opposed to the rising pitch of *ran* in "You ran?" is attributed to a different pattern of constructive features rather than to a phonemic difference between *ran* with rising and with falling pitch.

Def. 99. $Part = \hat{Q}\hat{R}\,\{Q \subset \gamma\text{-}Seqs \cdot R \in \gamma\text{-}Seqs \cdot C''\ Q \in cls^2\ excl$
$\cdot s'\ C''\ Q = C'\ R\}$

Q is a partition of R if Q is a class of sequences included in the γ-sequences, and R is a γ-sequence; and the fields of the members of Q are a class of mutually exclusive classes; and the sum of the fields of the members of Q equals the field of R.

Def. 100. $PHNP = \hat{R} \{ (_{\exists}Q)\ Q \in \gamma\text{-}utts \cdot R \in \overrightarrow{Part^{\prime}}\ Q \cdot (S)\ S \in R \supset$

$(_{\exists}T)\ T \in \gamma\text{-}utts \cdot T\ \gamma\text{-}PHSM\ S \cdot (U)\ U \in \overrightarrow{Part^{\prime}}\ S \supset \sim$

$((V)\ V \in U \supset (_{\exists}W)\ (W \in \gamma\text{-}utts \cdot W\ \gamma\text{-}PHSM\ V)) \}$

PHNP (the phonological phrases) is the class of those classes of relations R for which there is some Q which is a γ-utterance; and R is a partition of Q; and, for all S, if S is a member of R, there is some T which is a γ-utterance and is phonetically similar to S; and for all U, if U is a partition of S; then it is not true for every V which is a member of V that there is some γ-utterance W which is phonetically similar to V.

Phonologic phrases are partitions of utterances such that each part is phonetically similar to some whole utterance and such that it cannot be further divided into parts all of which are phonetically similar to whole utterances.

Def. 101. $Ufms = \hat{R}\hat{S} \{ R,\ S \in PHNP \cdot R \sim PHSM\ S \cdot {_{\exists}}!\kappa\ (\kappa \subset$

$\gamma\text{-phone} \cdot (\alpha)\ \alpha \in \kappa \supset \alpha \cap C^{\prime}\ R = \Lambda \cdot {_{\exists}}!\lambda\ (\lambda \subset$

$\gamma\text{-phone} \cdot (\beta)\ \beta \in \lambda \supset \beta \cap C^{\prime}\ S = \Lambda \cdot \kappa \cap \lambda = \Lambda \cdot (_{\exists}T)$

$T\ {\restriction}C^{\prime}\ S \in R\ smor\ S \cdot\ (x)\ (y)\ x \in D^{\prime}\ T \cdot y = T^{\prime}\ x \supset$

$(Cnv^{\prime}\ T)^{\prime\prime}\ (\overrightarrow{\gamma\text{-}sml^{\prime}}\ x \cap Œ^{\prime}\ T) \subset \overrightarrow{\gamma\text{-}sml^{\prime}}\ y \cdot (X)\ X \in PHNP$

$\cdot \kappa \cap C^{\prime}\ X = \Lambda \supset (_{\exists}Y)\ T\ {\restriction}C^{\prime}\ Y \in X\ smor\ Y \}$

Ufms (uniform stylistic variation) is a relation between the relations R and S when R and S are phonological phrases; and R is not phonetically similar to S; and there is a non-null class of γ-phones κ, such that the intersection of each of its members with the field of R is null and there is an non-null class of γ-phones λ, such that the intersection of each of its members with the field of S is null and the intersection of κ and λ is null; and there is a relation T with its counterdomain limited to the field of S which is an ordinal correlator of R and S and for all x and all y, if x belongs to the domain of T and y is the T of x, then all those terms which are in the relation T converse to the members of the class formed by the intersection of the domain of T and the terms which are γ-similar to x are included in the γ-similars of y and for all X if X is a phonological phrase and the intersection of κ and the field of X is null, then there is some Y such that T with its counterdomain limited to the field of Y is an ordinal correlator of Y.

An example would be the relation between any nonwhispered and whispered form of the same sentence. The class of γ-phones whispered a, whispered e, etc. would correspond to κ of the above definition. The absence of these in a nonwhispered utterance may be called the mark of the style. Similarly, the voiced vowels absent in the whispered form correspond to λ. The part of the definition beginning with $(x)(y)$ states that there must be a rule of correspondence for each member of R such that all γ-similar members of R have some class of γ-similars in S as their correspondents. In this case, all the consonants in R have similar consonants in S and to each nonwhispered vowel there corresponds a particular whispered vowel. The last portion beginning with (X) sets up the requirement that for every phonological phrase which has this mark (e.g., nonwhispered vowels) there must be a corresponding phrase according to the same rule that holds between R and S. This prevents the setting up of trivial, sporadic classes which would not normally be considered stylistic.

The following two definitions are required in order to define the more complex type of stylistic variation of Def. 104.

Def. 102. $\gamma\text{-}Feat = \hat{\gamma}\,\hat{\alpha}\,\{\alpha \,\epsilon\, \gamma\text{-phone} \cdot (_{\mathfrak{A}}\beta)\,\beta \,\epsilon\, Phsm^{\prime\prime}\,s^{\prime}\,\alpha \cdot \gamma \,\epsilon\, FEAT \cdot \beta \subset \gamma\}$

The relation $\gamma\text{-}Feat$ (γ-Features) holds between two classes of classes γ and α where α is a γ-phone; and there is some β, which is one of the classes of those segments phonetically similar to some member of the sum of α, and γ is a feature in which β is included.

The γ-Features of a γ-phone is then the class of those classes of features to which any member of the γ-phone belongs.

Def. 103. $Ftpr = \hat{\lambda}\,\hat{\mu}\,\{\mu \subset \gamma\text{-phone} \cdot \lambda = \hat{\nu}\,\{s\ \nu = \lambda \cdot (\alpha)\ (\beta)$
$\alpha, \beta \,\epsilon\, \nu \supset (p^{\prime}\,\gamma\text{-}Feat^{\prime\prime}\,\alpha - p^{\prime}\,\gamma\text{-}Feat^{\prime\prime}\,\mu) \cap (p^{\prime}\,\gamma\text{-}Feat^{\prime\prime}$
$\beta - p^{\prime}\,\gamma\text{-}Feat^{\prime\prime}\,\mu) = \Lambda\}$

Ftpr (feature partition) is the relation between λ and μ where μ is included in the class of γ-phones; and λ is the class of those classes ν such that the sum of ν is λ; and for all α and all β, if they are members of ν, then the intersection of the product of the γ-features of the members of α, minus the product of the γ-features of the members of μ, and the product of the γ-features of the members of β, minus the γ-features of the members of μ, is null.

If, for example, we take the class of all γ-phones in a language which are vowels, then a class of classes such that one of these classes contains the high-pitched vowels while another contains the low-pitched vowels is a feature partition of the class of vowels.

Def. 104. $Prds = \hat{R}\hat{S}\,\{R, S \,\epsilon\, PHNP \cdot R \sim \gamma\text{-}PHSM\ S \cdot (_{\mathfrak{A}}T)\ T\ \text{\textbar}C^{\prime}$

$S \,\epsilon\, R\ smor\ S \cdot (_{\mathfrak{A}}\mu)\ \mu \subset \gamma\text{-phone} \cdot (_{\mathfrak{A}}\lambda)\ \lambda\ Ftpr\ \mu \cdot (\delta)$
$\delta \,\epsilon\, gen^{\prime}\,(\gamma\text{-}Prcd_{*}\,\text{\textbar}s^{\prime}\,\mu)_{1} \cdot (x)\ (y)\ x \,\epsilon\, \delta\, \cap\, C^{\prime}\,R \cdot x\,T\,y \supset$
$(_{\mathfrak{A}}\eta)\,(_{\mathfrak{A}}\theta)\,\eta, \beta \subset \zeta \cdot \gamma\text{-}sml^{\prime}\,x \,\epsilon\, \eta \cdot \gamma\text{-}sml^{\prime}\,y \,\epsilon\, \theta \cdot \gamma\text{-}Feat^{\prime}$
$\gamma\text{-}sml^{\prime}\,x - p^{\prime}\,\gamma\text{-}Feat^{\prime\prime}\,\eta = \gamma\text{-}Feat^{\prime}\,\gamma\text{-}sml^{\prime}\,y - p^{\prime}\,\gamma\text{-}Feat^{\prime\prime}$
$\theta \cdot \sim (w)\ w \,\epsilon\, C^{\prime}\,R\, \cap\, s^{\prime}s^{\prime}\,\mu \supset T^{\prime}\,w\ \gamma\text{-}sml\ w \cdot (u)\,(v)\ u \,\epsilon\,$

The relation of alternation will hold between any two γ-phones which are in any of these three types of variation.

Def. 108. $ALTR = \hat{\kappa} \{(\alpha) \, (\beta) \, \alpha, \beta \, \epsilon \, \kappa \cdot \alpha \neq \beta \supset \alpha \, Altr \, \beta\}$

$ALTR$ (the classes of alternating γ-phones) is the class of those classes such that for all α and all β, if α and β are distinct members of κ, α is in alternation with β.

Every member of $ALTR$ is, then, a class of γ-phones such that each member alternates with every other member of the class. As a limiting case, $ALTR$ will contain, for each γ-phone, the class whose only member is the γ-phone itself.

Def. 109. $GRDF = \hat{\alpha} \, \{\alpha \, \epsilon \, FEAT \cdot (_{\mathfrak{A}}R) \, R \, \epsilon \, trans \, \cap \, connex \, \cap$
$\quad - sym \cdot \alpha \, \epsilon \, D^{\prime} \, sg^{\prime} \, (R \, \cap \, Cnv^{\prime} R)\}$

$GRDF$ (gradual features) is the class of those classes α, such that α is a feature and there is some relation, R, which is transitive, connected and not symmetrical, and α is the domain of the sagittal of the intersection of R and its converse.

Gradual features are those such as the pitch levels, degrees of duration, and tongue heights, derived by abstraction from a primitive relation, such as initially higher or equal in pitch, which satisfies the conditions of the definition.

Def. 110. $DSCF = FEAT - GRDF$

$DSCF$ (discrete features) are the features minus the gradual features.

Def. 111. $Grdf = \hat{\kappa} \, \hat{\alpha} \, \{\kappa = \gamma\text{-}Feat^{\prime} \, \alpha \, \cap \, GRDF\}$

$Grdf$ (gradual features of a γ-phone) is the relation between κ and α such that κ is the intersection of the γ-features of α and the gradual features.

Def. 112. $Dscf = \hat{\kappa} \, \hat{\alpha} \, \{\kappa = \gamma\text{-}Feat^{\prime} \, \alpha \cap DSCF\}$

$Dscf$ (discrete features of a γ-phone) is the relation between κ and α such that κ is the intersection of the γ-features of α and the discrete features.

Def. 113. $Grfr = \hat{\alpha} \, \hat{R} \, \{\alpha \, \epsilon \, GRDF \cdot R \, \epsilon \, Ser \cdot \alpha \subset C^{\prime} \, R\}$

$Grfr$ (the relation of a gradual feature to its generating relation) is the relation between α and R such that α is a gradual feature and R is a serial relation and α is included in the field of R.

For the definition of allophone we need the relation of a gradual feature to some derived serial relation, e.g., higher in initial pitch, rather than the primitive relation, e.g., higher or equal in pitch.

Def. 114. $GRRL = \mathbb{C}^{\prime} \, Grfr$

$GRRL$ (the class of gradual relations) is the counterdomain of the relation $Grfr$.

Of the classes of γ-phones, *ALTR*, defined in 108, some contain members which share unique common features sufficient to define a phoneme but, in general, some which do not. For example, a syllable-initial *t*- and syllable-final -*k* might well be each in complementary distribution with each other and therefore form a class belonging to *ALTR*. Likewise, all of the γ-phones containing alveolar, stop, and unvoiced features might form another class of *ALTR*. We wish to pick out classes of this latter type by their possession of a common set of features not found as the common features of any other class of *ALTR*. However, the gradual features do not allow of this procedure and must be handled separately. Suppose, for example, that vowels of *e*-quality and of four pitches numbered 1, 2, 3, 4 from high to low exist in a language and that e_1 and e_2 belong to one subclass of *ALTR* and e_3 and e_4 to another. We wish to consider the first class as containing a common feature of high pitch as opposed to the low pitch of the second. But since each pitch level is a separate feature, the class containing e_1 and e_2 will only have the features of *e* outside of pitch as common features, and the second class will have the same common features as the first. Hence, gradual features are treated here in terms of their serial relations, and by common features is meant the section of the series bounded by the extreme members belonging to the same member of *ALTR*.

Def. 115. $ALLP = \hat{\alpha} \{ \alpha \, \epsilon \, ALTR \cdot \sim [(_{\exists} \, \gamma) \, \gamma \, \epsilon \, ALTR \cdot \gamma \sim \subset \alpha$
$\cdot (p^\zeta \, Dscf^{\zeta\zeta} \, \alpha \subset p^\zeta \, Dscf^{\zeta\zeta} \, \gamma \lor p^\zeta \, Dscf^{\zeta\zeta} \, \gamma \subset p^\zeta \, Dscf^{\zeta\zeta} \, \alpha) \cdot$
$(R) \, R \, \epsilon \, GRRL \supset (min \, (R)^\zeta \, s^\zeta \, (Grdf^{\zeta\zeta} \, \gamma \cap \overrightarrow{Grfr^\zeta \, R}) \, R$
$max \, (R)^\zeta \, s^\zeta \, (Grdf^{\zeta\zeta} \, \alpha \cap \overrightarrow{Grfr^\zeta \, R})) \lor (min \, (R)^\zeta \, s^\zeta$
$(\overrightarrow{Grdf^{\zeta\zeta} \, \alpha \cap Grfr^\zeta \, R}) \, R \, max \, (R)^\zeta \, s^\zeta \, (\overrightarrow{Grdf^{\zeta\zeta} \, \gamma \cap Grfr^\zeta}$
$R))]\}$

ALLP (allophones) is the class of those classes α such that α is a class of alternating γ-phones and there is no γ, such that γ is a class of alternating γ-phones which is not included in α, and such that either the product of the discrete features of the members of α is included in the product of the discrete features of the members of γ or the product of the discrete features of the members of γ is included in the product of the discrete features of the members of α; and for all *R*, if *R* is a gradual feature, then the minimum with respect to the relation *R* of the sum of the intersection of the gradual features of members of γ and the gradual features generated by *R* is in the relation *R* to the maximum with respect to *R* of the sum of the intersection of the gradual features of members of α and the gradual features generated by *R* or the minimum with respect to *R* of the sum of the intersection of the gradual features of the members of α and the gradual features generated by *R* is in the relation R to the maximum with respect to R of the sum of the intersection of the gradual features of the members of γ and the gradual features generated by R.

The allophones are classes of alternating γ-phones which share a unique set of discrete features. The gradual features, if any, cover a unique continuous range such that no other class of alternating γ-phones overlaps it.

In actual practice, the allophones will usually turn out to be mutually exclusive and exhaustive, in the sense that every γ-phone belongs to some allophone. However, it is logically possible, and occasionally true in fact, that these conditions are not met. The following definitions are required to deal with these cases.

Def. 116. $NEAL = \hat{\alpha} \ \{(_{\exists}\beta) \ \beta \ \epsilon \ ALLP \cdot \alpha \neq \beta \cdot \alpha \cap \beta \neq \Lambda\}$

NEAL (neutralized allophones) is the class of those classes α, such that there is some β which is an allophone and α is not identical with β and the intersection of α and β is not null.

NEAL is the class of allophones which share some members with other allophones. The situation from which this arises is generally called neutralization. If, for example, in some language p is in alternation with b and p is likewise in alternation with f but p and b are not themselves in alternation, then both $\{p, b\}$ and $\{p, f\}$ are allophones, with the former having a common feature of bilabial articulation not found in any other member of *ALTR* not contained in it and the latter having unique features of lower lip articulation and lack of voicing.

Def. 117. $NEUT = \hat{\alpha} \ \{(_{\exists}\beta) \ (_{\exists}\gamma) \ \beta, \ \gamma \ \epsilon \ NEAL \cdot \beta \cap \gamma \neq \Lambda \cdot$
$\alpha = \hat{\delta} \ \{\delta = \beta \cap \gamma \lor \delta = \beta - \gamma\}\}$

NEUT (neutriphone) is the class of those classes α, such that there is some β and some γ which are neutralized allophones and whose intersection is not null, and α is the class of those classes δ such that δ is either equal to the intersection of β and γ or is equal to β minus γ.

In the example given under Definition 116, $\{p\}$ would be a neutriphone, since it is the intersection of $\{p, b\}$ and $\{p, f\}$ while $\{b\}$ and $\{f\}$ would be neutriphones also since $\{b\}$ is $\{p, b\}$ minus $\{p, f\}$ and $\{f\}$ is $\{p, f\}$ minus $\{p, b\}$.

Def. 118. $UNPH = \hat{\alpha} \ \{\alpha \ \epsilon \ \gamma\text{-phone} \cdot \sim ((_{\exists}\beta) \ \beta \ \epsilon \ ALLP \cdot \alpha \ \epsilon \ \beta)\}$

UNPH (uniphones) is the class of those classes α, such that α is a γ-phone and there is no β such that β is an allophone of which α is a member.

The uniphones are the γ-phones which do not belong to any allophones. This is a theoretical possibility which might arise as follows. Suppose that, in some language, p and β, a bilabial unvoiced stop and bilabial voiced fricative respectively are in free variation so that they belong to the same γ-phone. Suppose also that there is another γ-phone consisting of the free variants ϕ and b, an unvoiced bilabial fricative and a voiced bilabial stop. If these two γ-phones are not in alternation with each other, they will both have the same common features, which will therefore not be unique. I know of no actual example.

Def. 119. $PHNM = (ALLP - NEAL) \cup NEUT \cup UNPH$

PHNM (phoneme) is the sum of the classes allophone minus neutralized allophones, neutriphone, and uniphone.

Each phoneme except the rare and probably only theoretical uniphone can be defined by a unique set of features. Logically, the phoneme is a class each of whose members is a class of γ-phones, while each γ-phone in turn is a class of classes. Hence, the class *PHNM* is a class of class of class of classes.

As explained in the introductory section, certain procedures more complex than those outlined here are sometimes employed in particular language descriptions in order to reduce the number of phonemes. Their legitimacy for this purpose is not in question here. Some of these procedures, however, are arbitrary in that there seems to be no general principle which can justify them. For example, the common practice of abstracting pitch in tonal languages as a separate phoneme of tone simultaneous with another phoneme contained in the remaining features would require an arbitrary choice of just this feature for abstraction. It is probable that the special treatment accorded this feature derives from the fact that traditional orthographies do not provide separate symbols for each combination of vowel quality and pitch. There are some instances, however, where such a treatment does simplify the grammatical treatment. This practice can be most conveniently considered a device in *T*, the language of transcription in accordance with the principle of linguistic relativity mentioned earlier.

Other more complex procedures sometimes depend on idiosyncratic facts concerning the grammatical structure of a particular language. One instance is a practice that might be called distention, in that a γ-phone with one member is divided into a sequence of two phonemes each of which belongs to different mutually exclusive features. The order of the phonemes is based on convenience for grammatical description or the general pattern of the remaining phoneme sequences of the language.

It would be an interesting investigation to show the conditions under which it is possible, without logical contradiction, to proceed from an initial simple phonemicization, such as that of the present article, to a grammatical analysis followed by the utilization of these data for a more complex phonemicization.

INDEX OF LOGICAL SYMBOLS

α *mnct* β: minimal contrast based on opposition of α and β: relation between classes of relations between classes: D. 105, 106.

α-phone: alpha phone: class of classes: D. 67.

β-phone: beta phone: class of class of classes: D. 75, 76, 77.

β-*Prcd:* beta precede: relation between classes: D. 76, 78.

β-*Seqr:* beta sequential relation: class of relation between classes: D. 78, 79, 80.

β-*SEQU:* members of beta sequential relations: class of class of classes: D. 79, 80.

β-*sml:* beta similar: relation between classes: D. 77, 80.

β-*Smsq:* similarity of classes which are members of beta sequential relations: relation between classes of classes: D. 80, 81.

β-*SMSQ:* beta similar sequences: class of class of class of classes: D. 81, 84.

γ-*Feat:* gamma feature: relation between classes of classes: D. 102, 103, 104, 111, 112.

γ-phone: gamma phone: class of class of classes: D. 86, 87, 88, 89, 91, 93, 94, 95, 101, 102, 103, 104, 105, 118.

γ-*PHSM:* gamma phonetic similarity between relations: relation between relation between classes: D. 92, 93, 100, 101, 104, 105.

γ-*Prcd:* gamma precede: relation between classes: D. 88, 104, 105.

γ-*Prcs:* gamma precede limited to segments: relation between classes: D. 89, 90, 91.

γ-*Seqs:* gamma sequential relations limited to segments: class of relations between classes: D. 90, 92, 99 .

γ-*sml:* gamma similar: relation between classes: D. 87, 92, 101, 104.

γ-*utts:* gamma utterance confined to segments: class of relations between classes: D. 91, 100.

ALLP: allophone: class of class of class of classes: D. 115, 116, 118, 119.

Altr: alternation: relation between classes of classes: D. 107, 108.

ALTR: classes of alternating gamma phone: class of class of class of classes: D. 108, 115.

alvl: alveolar: class: P. I.: Ax. 6.

Beqt: backward or equal in tongue position: relation: D. 39, 40, 42.

BKFT: tongue positions in back-forward dimension: class of classes: D. 43, 65.

Bktp: farther back in tongue position: relation: D. 42.

bplt: back palate: class: P. I.: Ax. 6.

clgl: closed glottis: class: D. 9, 10.

cmvr: complementary variation: relation between classes of classes: D. 93, 97, 107.

CNAF: contact articulation feature: class of classes: D. 33, 65, 66.

Cnar: contact articulation: four-place relation: P. I.: D. 30, 31, 32, 66. Ax. 8.

CNTR: tonal contour: class of classes: D. 28.

dent: dental: class: P. I.: Ax. 6.

DGRL: degree of length: class of classes: D. 64, 65.

Dscf: discrete features of a γ-phone: relation between class of classes and class of classes: D. 112, 115.

DSCF: discrete features: class of classes: D. 110, 112.

DTSM: determined segment: class of class of classes: D. 74, 75.

ejct: ejective: class: P. I.: D. 59. Ax. 17.

Envr: environmental relation: relation between relations: D. 82, 83.

Envs: environment of a sequential class: relation of relation to class: D. 83, 84, 85, 93.

Eqbf: equal in tongue position: relation: D. 40, 41, 42, 43.

Eqdr: equal in duration: relation: D. 61, 62, 63, 64.

Eqst: equal in stress: relation: D. 55, 56, 57, 58. Ax. 16.

Eqth: equal in tongue height: relation: D. 35, 36, 37, 38.

fcnc: final of complex nucleus: class: D. 48, 49. Ax. 16.

FEAT: features: class of classes: D. 65, 66, 102, 109, 110. Ax. 19.

Feqp: finally equal in pitch: relation: D. 17, 18, 19, 20, 28.

Feqt: forward or equal in tongue position: relation: P. I.: D. 39, 40, 41, Ax. 10, 11.

Fhqp: finally higher or equal in pitch: relation: P. I.: D. 16, 17, 18. Ax. 3, 4.

Fhrp: finally higher in pitch: relation: D. 18.

flap: flap: class: P. I.: Ax. 7.

Flls: follow limited to segments: relation: D. 7.

Fllw: follow in time: relation: D. 1, 3, 48, 50, 52, 95.

flpc: falling pitched segments: class: D. 26.

Flqp: finally lower or equal in pitch: relation: D. 16, 17, 19.

Flrp: finally lower in pitch: relation: D. 19.

fplt: front palate: class: P. I.: Ax. 6.

FPLV: final pitch level: class of classes: D. 20, 65.

Frtp: farther forward in tongue position: relation: D. 41.

Frvr: free variation: relation between class of class of classes: D. 84, 85.

FRVR: free variants: class of class of class of classes: D. 85, 86.

Ftpr: feature partition: relation between class of class of class of classes and class of class of classes: D. 103, 104.

Grdf: gradual features of a γ-phone: relation between class of classes and class of classes: D. 111, 115.

GRDF: gradual features: class of classes: D. 109, 110, 111, 113.

Grfr: relation of a gradual feature to its generating relation: relation of a class to a relation: D. 113, 114, 115.

GRRL: gradual relation: class of relations: D. 114, 115.

Hrqt: higher or equal in tongue height: relative: P. I.: D. 34, 35, 36. Ax. 9, 11.

Hrth: higher in tongue height: relation: D. 36.

Hvqs: heavier or equal in stress: relation: P. I.: D. 54, 55, 56. Ax. 14.

Hvst: heavier in stress: relation: D. 56.

icnc: initial of complex nucleus: class: D. 47, 48, 49. Ax. 16.

Ieqp: initially equal in pitch: relation: D. 12, 13, 14, 15, 28.

Ifeq: initial pitch of x is equal to final pitch of y: relation: D. 22, 23, 24, 25.

Ifhq: initial pitch of x is higher than or equal to final pitch of y: relation: P. I.: D. 21, 22, 23. Ax. 4.

Ifhr: initial pitch of x is higher than final pitch of y: relation: D. 23, 26.

Iflq: initial pitch of x is lower than or equal in pitch to final pitch of y: relation: D. 21, 22, 24.

Iflr: initial pitch of x is lower than final pitch of y: relation: D. 24, 27.

Ihqp: initially higher or equal in pitch: relation: P. I.: D. 11, 12, 13. Ax. 3, 4.

Ihrp: initially higher in pitch: relation: D. 13.

Ilqp: initially lower or equal in pitch: relation: D. 11, 12, 14.

Ilrp: initially lower in pitch: relation: D. 14.

IMEJ: implosives and ejectives: class of classes: D. 59, 65.

impl: implosive: class: P. I.: D. 59. Ax. 17.

intl: interlude: class: D. 52, 53.

IPLV: initial pitch level: class of classes: D. 15, 65.

Jnct: juncture: relation: D. 98.

Jndv: juncturally diverse: relation between classes of classes: D. 96, 97, 98.

Jnvr: junctural variation: relation between classes of classes: D. 97, 107.

labl: labial: class: P. I.: Ax. 5.

Lgdr: longer in duration: relation: D. 62.

lips: lips: class: P. I.: Ax. 6.

LPPS: lip-position: class of classes: D. 45, 65. Ax. 12.

LRFT: laryngeal features: class of classes: D. 10, 65. Ax. 2.

Lrqd: longer or equal in duration: relation: P. I.: D. 60, 61, 62. Ax. 18.

Lrqt: lower or equal in height: relation: D. 34, 35, 37.

Lrth: lower in tongue height: relation: D. 37.

Ltqs: lighter or equal in stress: relation: D. 54, 55, 57.

ltrl: lateral: class: P. I.: Ax. 7.

Ltst: lighter in stress: relation: D. 57.

lvlp: level pitched segments: class: D. 25.

MBGN: mobile organ: class of classes: D. 30, 33. Ax. 5.

MNAR: manner of articulation: class of classes: D. 32, 33. Ax. 7.

mplt: mid palate: class: P. I.: Ax. 6.

mrmr: murmur: P. I.: D. 9, 10. Ax. 4, 11.

nasl: nasal: class: D. 29, 65.

NEAL: neutralized allophone: class of class of class of classes: D. 116, 117, 119.

NEUT: neutriphone: class of class of class of classes: D. 117, 119.

ntrl: neutral lips: class: D. 44, 45.

oral: oral: class: P. I.: D. 29, 65.

Part: partition: relation between class of relations between classes and relation between classes: D. 99, 100.

peak: syllabic peak: class: D. 46, 49.

PHNM: phoneme: class of class of class of classes: D. 119.

PHNP: phonological phrase: class of relations between classes: D. 100, 101, 104, 105.

phrx: pharynx: class: P. I.: Ax. 6.

Phsm: phonetic similarity: relation: D. 66, 67, 68, 72, 74, 102.

PHSM: phonetic similarity between relations: relation between relations: D. 68, 84, 85.

PLAR: place of articulation: class of classes: D. 31, 33. Ax. 6.

Prcd: precede in time: relation: P. I.: D. 1, 2, 5, 6, 47, 50, 51, 52, 69, 74, 76, 88, 94, 98. Ax. 1, 16.

Prcs: precede limited to segments: class: D. 6, 7, 8, 70, 89.

Prds: prosodic stylistic variation: relation between relation between classes: D. 104, 106.

PREJ: prejunctural γ-phone: class of class of classes: D. 94, 96, 98.

prps: prepause: class: D. 2, 4, 76, 88, 95. Ax. 1.

prst: presatellite: class: D. 50, 53.

PSTJ: post-junctural γ-phone: class of class of classes: D. 95, 96, 98.

pstp: postpause: class: D. 3, 4, 76, 88, 94. Ax. 1.

ptst: postsatellite: class: D. 51, 53.

rill: rill fricative: class: P. I.: Ax. 7.

rndl: rounded lips: class: P. I.: D. 44, 45.

rspc: rising pitched segments: class: D. 27.

Seqr: sequential relations: class of relations: D. 69, 71, 72, 82, 83.

Seqs: sequential relations limited to segments: class of relations: D. 70.

SEQU: members of sequential relations: class of classes: D. 71, 72.

sgmn: segment: class: D. 4, 6, 9, 29, 44. Ax. 8, 13, 18, 19.

shbl: shibilant: class: P. I.: Ax. 7.

Shdr: shorter in duration: relation: D. 63.

slbc: syllabic: class: D. 49, 50, 51, 52, 53. Ax. 15.

slit: slit fricative: class: P.I.: Ax. 7.

Slst: syllabic satellite: relation: P. I.: D. 46, 47, 50, 51, 52.

SLTP: syllabic type: class of classes: D. 53. Ax. 13.

Smsq: similarity of classes which are members of sequential relations: relation between classes: D. 72, 73.

SMSQ: similar sequences: class of class of classes: D. 73, 74.

snnt: sonant: class: P. I.: Ax. 7.

Sprl: spread lips: class: P. I.: D. 44, 45.

Srqd: shorter or equal in duration: relation: D. 60, 61, 63.

STLV: stress level: class of classes: D. 58, 65.

stop: stop: class: P. I.: Ax. 7.

Stvr: stylistic variation: relation between classes of classes: D. 106, 107.

tapx: tongue apex: class: P. I.: Ax. 5.

tbck: tongue back: class: P. I.: Ax. 5.

tbld: tongue blade: class: P. I.: Ax. 5.

TNGH: tongue height: class of classes: D. 38, 65.

trll: trill: class: P. I.: Ax. 7.

ufms: uniform stylistic variation: relation between relations between classes: D. 101, 106.

UNPH: uniphone: class of class of class of classes: D. 118, 119.

uttr: utterance: class of relations: D. 5.

utts: utterance confined to segment: class of relations: D. 8.

uvcd: unvoiced: class: P. I.: D. 9, 10. Ax. 11.

uvul: uvula: class: P. I.: Ax. 5, 6.

vocd: voiced: class: P. I.: D. 9, 10. Ax. 4, 11.

whsp: whisper: class: P. I.: D. 9, 10. Ax. 11.

NOTES

1. J. H. Woodger, *The Axiomatic Method in Biology* (London: Cambridge University Press, 1937); C. E. Shannon, "A Symbolic Analysis of Relay and Switching Circuits," *Transactions, American Institute of Electric Engineering,* 57 (1938), 713-23; C. L. Hull, *A Mathematico-Deductive Theory of Rote Learning* (New Haven: Yale University Press, 1940). A number of examples, both mathematical and nonmathematical, may be found in R. Carnap, *Einfuehrung in die symbolische Logic* (Wien, Springer-Verlag, 1954).

There have been two pioneer attempts in linguistics: Leonard Bloomfield, "A Set of Postulates for the Science of Language," *Language,* 1 (1925), pp. 37-51; and Bernard Bloch, "A Set of Postulates for Phonemics Analysis," *Language,* 24 (1948), pp. 3-46. I have benefited greatly from these, particularly the latter, which deals with phonology, the subject of this paper. Neither is, however, a formalized treatment.

2. For a clear exposition of the relation between logical and subject-matter calculi, see J. H. Woodger, "The Technique of Theory Construction," *Encyclopedia of Unified Science,* Vol. 2, No. 5 (Chicago: University of Chicago Press, 1939), particularly pp. 69-71.

3. First enunciated systematically by Jacob Grimm in 1822.

4. In one instance, at least, the same linguist has consciously published two differing phonemecizations of the same language based on the same data. See Bernard Bloch, "Studies in Colloquial Japanese IV Phonemics," *Language,* 26 (1950), 86-125.

5. Cf. Sol Saporta, "Methodological Considerations Regarding a Statistical Approach to Typologies," *International Journal of American Linguistics,* 23 (1957), pp. 109-13, where this difficulty is discussed.

6. C. F. Hockett, *A Manual of Phonology* (Baltimore: The Waverly Press, 1955), p. 210.

7. Chao Yuen-ren, "The Non-Uniqueness of the Phonemic Solutions of Phonetic Systems," *Bulletin of the Institute of History and Philology, Academia Sinica* (1934), Vol. IV, part 4, pp. 363-97.

8. The present remarks are not intended to be understood in the sense that there exist nominalist and realist "schools" in linguistics, but rather that these terms represent general tendencies to which the terms nominalist and realist can be conveniently applied.

9. N. Goodman, *The Structure of Appearance* (Cambridge: Harvard University Press, 1951), particularly pp. 107-09.

10. C. F. Hockett, "A System of Descriptive Phonology," *Language,* 18 (1942), pp. 3-21.

VIII

VALUES AND THEORY CONSTRUCTION

15

Theory Construction and the Problem of Objectivity

W. H. WERKMEISTER
University of Southern California

The problem with which I am here concerned arises from the inter-relation of three facts which, separately and in combination, are relevant to any discussion of the social sciences as sciences. The first and most obvious fact is that, in one way or another, social scientists aspire to be scientific. The second fact, often acknowledged but more often simply assumed by social scientists, is that, because of their success in interpreting and explaining the events in nature, the exact natural sciences serve as the model for any and all sciences and therefore for the social sciences as well. The third fact is that, for better or for worse, the social sciences are concerned with valuing subjects and valuational behavior. Since, traditionally, the natural sciences which serve as the model of scientific enterprise insist upon the principle of "value neutrality," the question arises, Can the social sciences be scientific and value neutral? Can they give us interpretations and explanations of social phenomena in terms of theories whose objective significance is not despoiled by subjective biases and valuations? Can they be objective in the sense of a value-neutral science?

In the pages which follow, I shall attempt to give constructive answers to these questions. In order to do so, however, I shall have to discuss at some length (1) the procedures and the ideal of the exact sciences; (2) the problem of value in the social sciences; and (3) the problem of objectivity.

I

When one acknowledges that the exact natural sciences provide the model for all sciences, one may mean either that their procedures and methods should be emulated or that their ideal of an integrated theory should be accepted. The methods and procedures are but means and techniques for gaining operational control over the events in nature; the ideal is a formalized rationalization of reality which makes possible a conceptual understanding of the facts in the case. In the end, however, methods and ideal are truly inseparable; for what science aims at is the interpretation and explanation of the facts of observation.

In order to understand what this means, we must distinguish between a *description* of reality and an *explanation* of the described facts. When such a distinction is not made, the resultant confusion infects the whole business of science.

By *description* is meant a simple enumerative account of the observable features or qualities of individual things, acts, or events. Thus, when a geographer tells us that such and such mountain ranges separate a given coast line from its hinterland, that the mountain streams on the west slopes form part of a vast river system which drains fertile plains of such and such an extent, that these plains stretch westward to another mountain range of such and such character, whose streams on the eastern slopes contribute to the very same river system—when he tells us all this, and much more, about the mountains and the plains, then he gives us a description of a vast region. Again, when an archeologist gives us an account of the distinctive features of the ruins of some ancient burial place or temple which he has discovered; or when a cultural anthropologist gives us a word picture of the customs and dances and rites of a certain primitive culture—then, they, too, give us descriptions. Descriptions, in other words, are but answers to the question, What is the case? What are the particular and observable facts?

An *explanation,* on the other hand, is an attempt to account for the facts, to show why they are what they are. Thus, when an astronomer tells us how an eclipse of the sun is caused when the moon moves between the sun and earth, preventing the light coming from the sun from reaching us, he gives us an explanation of the eclipse. Similarly, when the physicist tells us that the planets circling the sun are held in their orbits by gravitational forces which exactly balance the centrifugal forces generated by the forward motions of the planets, then he, too, gives us an explanation of the observed facts. Explanations are thus answers to the question, How do things and events come about? What causes them? What are the laws which determine their occurrence?

Ultimately, all scientific explanation involves some law or laws which provide the "principle of explanation"; and science, in so far as it aims at the formulation of laws, also aims at explanation rather than at mere description. We shall here be chiefly concerned with the problems of scientific explanation. We must note, however, that although the ultimate aim of science is the formulation of explanatory laws, the first step in scientific research is the collection and description of facts, the precise statement of what is the case. In the exact sciences, such descriptions are given in quantitative terms—in terms of distances, time intervals, masses, charges, boiling points, pressures, etc. Accurate measurements must here at all times augment, correct, or replace unaided observations. Scientific accuracy demands that we record not merely that an object *A* moves faster or is heavier or warmer than an object *B,* but that it moves *so and so much* faster, is *so and so much* heavier or *so and so much* warmer. The social scientists, for the most part, have learned this lesson well. However, because of the nature of their subject matter, their quantitative descriptions of facts are usually restricted to statistical records and surveys. Indeed, so prominent is the rôle of statistics in the social sciences today that at times one gets the impression that statistical surveys and analyses are the sole aim of the scientific enterprise in this field of study. It is well known, however, that the mere collection of data, even when the data are statistically treated, is insufficient and often misleading. Interpolations and interpretations are necessary if the statistical data are to disclose significant facts; and such interpolations and interpretations carry us back ultimately to causal interrelations and, thus, to explanatory laws.

At this point, the natural sciences have an advantage which the social sciences do not have: they can and do resort to experimentation. The rigid controls under laboratory conditions, so essential to modern physics and chemistry, are not feasible when we deal with the intricacies of human behavior in normally functioning social groups. To the extent at least to which experimentation is an essential part of the procedures and techniques of the natural sciences, the methods of the social sciences must be developed independently and in close conformity with the requirements of the specific subject matter with which social scientists are concerned.

Quantitative descriptions and experimentation, however, are but two aspects of scientific method. The formation of interdependent concepts and theory construction are other and equally important aspects. And, if in the social sciences, experimentation is impossible and quantitative analysis is restricted to statistical surveys and their interpretations, the formation of interdependent concepts is all the more essential.

In ordinary speech, the meaning of a concept depends in large measure upon the context within which it is used, and no meaning is ever rigidly fixed and final. This is true the more so because emotional attitudes of the speaker or writer often color the meaning of the terms he employs. The scientist, however, must insist upon reducing to a minimum the vagueness and the shifts in meaning of his concepts; otherwise the clarity and the exactitude of thought necessary in science cannot be achieved. Hence, whenever a new concept is introduced into a field of science, it is at once related to all other concepts in that field, and its meaning is defined so that, together with the concepts already accepted, it forms a system of interrelated meanings. Ideally, therefore, every science aims at a system of meanings which is self-contained and complete. So far, however, only the mathematician has actually attained this goal. His system of numbers, for example, is precise in every respect and contains nothing which does not essentially belong to the system. The individual numbers have no existence, and the number concepts have no meaning, except as members of the system itself.

On the face of it, it seems impossible to duplicate this achievement of mathematics in the empirical sciences, for the latter deal with given facts of experience rather than with ideally constructed entities. The concepts of the physical sciences, for instance, have a referential significance with respect to things and events which the concepts of pure mathematics do not possess. Still, even the natural sciences cannot deal with perceptual facts directly but must translate them into concepts. When the physicist, for example, deals with data of observation, he at once projects them into a new dimension of comprehension. He supplements or replaces the qualitative descriptions with quantitative representations. He assigns numbers to the measurable properties of our sense data and translates their qualitative characteristics into quantitative indices. He defines things not in terms of sense qualities but in terms of scales of measurement. He speaks of "atomic weight," of "specific gravity," of "electrical conductivity," of "tensile strength," of "boiling points," of "thermal conductivities," and so on; and in terms of these measurable properties, which are specifically constant for each substance, he defines the thing with which he deals. The interrelations of these properties he tries to express in his general laws.

A simple example—that of a physical body in motion—may illustrate in what sense the various terms of a physical science are interrelated. In its measurable aspects a "body" is something possessing simultaneous extension in the three dimensions of space. It is in "motion" when it changes its position in space during a given time interval. The time rate of motion in a specific direction is called "velocity." Velocities may change either in "speed" or in "direction." The time rate of such change is called "acceleration" and is defined by the equation $a = \dfrac{v_t - v_o}{t}$. If the acceleration of a body is reduced to zero, the body is either in "rectilinear uniform motion" or it is "at rest," depending on whether it does or does not change its position in space. A body which offers resistance to any change in its state of rest or motion is said to be "physical." The power of resistance is the body's "inertia." The measure of inertia is "mass." All changes in the state of rest or motion of a body must be produced by conditions not inherent in that body. These conditions are called "forces." The measure of such forces—and this measure alone is significant for physics—is given by the equation $F = kMa$, where k is a "constant," M is the mass and a the acceleration of the body. Other terms—such as "momentum" (mv), "work" (Fs), and "kinetic energy" ($\frac{1}{2}mv^2$)—can now also be defined; but it is unnecessary to go on. From what has been said it is clear that a number of closely interrelated concepts, concisely and quantitatively defined, have become integral parts of a "closed system"—in this case the system of classical mechanics. The unity of a science is, thus, first of all a unity of interdependent concepts. Whether or not such a unity can be attained in the social sciences is a different question. So far there has been little advancement beyond rudimentary beginnings in this respect. To what extent more can be done remains to be seen.

Now, concept formation in the sense just illustrated is an integral part of theory construction; and theory construction is indispensable to the development of science. In fact, the history of our most advanced natural sciences shows that theory construction has been at the very core of scientific achievement; for it is theory that leads to comprehension, and it is theory that provides an explanation of experimental findings and that inspires new experiments.

A theory, reduced to its bare essentials, consists of a set of definitions and postulates from which certain theorems or laws descriptive of observed facts can be logically derived. Schematically we have:

Set A		Set B
I. Definitions		Theorems
1........		1........
2........		2........
3........		3........
4........	Logic	4........
II. Postulates	$\longrightarrow$	5........
1........	(Transforma-	....
2........	tion Rules)	....
3........		....
4........		
5........		

Pure geometry—in its Euclidean and non-Euclidean forms—exemplifies this schematism. The one indispensable condition requisite to the construction of such a system—and therefore of a theory—is that the Set A of definitions and postulates be not self-contradictory. The system is "integrated" when there is no theorem in Set B which is not derivable from Set $A;$ it is "closed" when no problem can arise within the system that cannot also be solved by means of the system.

When we turn to the natural sciences, however, one further condition pertaining to the system must be fulfilled—the condition, namely, that at least one of the derivable theorems must apply to the facts of observation. As a rule, of course, the facts of observation are available first, for the theory is constructed for the specific purpose of explaining the facts. Nevertheless, operational means must be provided in connection with the system itself which definitely relate the conceptual framework to the facts of observation. A concrete example from the field of physics may make the relationship clear.

In 1885, Balmer discovered that a series of spectral lines occurring in an electric discharge through hydrogen—the observed facts—can be represented by a formula

$$\nu = cR \left(\frac{1}{2^2} - \frac{1}{n^2} \right),$$

where ν is the frequency, c the velocity of light, R a constant, and where $n = 3, 4, 5, \ldots$. Lyman and Paschen later discovered similar series, describable by

$$\nu = cR \left(\frac{1}{1^2} - \frac{1}{n^2} \right) \qquad n = 2, 3, 4,$$

and

$$\nu = cR \left(\frac{1}{3^2} - \frac{1}{n^2} \right) \qquad n = 4, 5, 6, \ldots,$$

respectively. Each formula is a partial but concise description of observed facts. But the three formulas can be generalized into

$$\nu = cR \left(\frac{1}{n_1^2} - \frac{1}{n_2^2} \right)$$

which, when appropriate substitutions are made for n_1 and n_2, describes all the facts.[1] But the generalized description, which may be called the "law of spectral lines," is itself without explanation so long as we do not construct a theory which contains it as a theorem derivable from the definitions and postulates of an initial Set A. Niels Bohr, making use of Rutherford's conception of nuclear atoms and of Planck's discovery of the energy quantum $h\nu$, succeeded in developing the required theory.

Among the postulates of his Set A were (a) the assumption of quantized circular orbits for the moving electrons, and (b) the stipulation that the emission of energy occurs only in the form of quanta of value $h\nu$. From his Set A Bohr could then derive as a theorem the equation

$$\nu = \frac{2\pi^2\mu Z^2\epsilon^4}{h^3}\left(\frac{1}{n_1^2} - \frac{1}{n_2^2}\right),$$

which has the form of the generalized description of the spectrum given above and is quantitatively identical with it.[2] The "Bohr theory" thus provides an explanation of the experimentally obtained data.

When, later, it was found that under certain conditions the number of lines is doubled, Sommerfeld could show that by adding to Bohr's Set A the further stipulations (a) that electrons may move in elliptical as well as in circular orbits, and (b) that the principles of Einstein's theory of relativity apply to the electrons, the doubling effect could also be explained. And when it was discovered that under still different conditions the number of spectral lines was again doubled, Uhlenbeck and Goudsmit could show that by adding to the Set A of the Bohr-Sommerfeld theory the further postulate of "spinning electrons," the theory again could account for the facts.

Certain facts pertaining to the problem of theory construction in physics are now clear. First, the investigator starts with certain quantitatively determinable facts at the common-sense level of things—in this case, with spectral lines and their measurable interrelations. He then tries to obtain a generalized description which embodies all the facts. He finally constructs a theory which incorporates the descriptive formula as a theorem and which thus explains the formula and, ultimately, the facts in terms of the definitions and postulates of the theory. Throughout the process of theory construction the conception of an integrated and closed system is and remains the guiding ideal.

Secondly, any modification of a theory necessitated by new facts is accomplished, within limits, by modifying or adding to the original set of definitions and postulates. But care must be taken that the modified Set A remains free from internal contradictions. If, in view of new facts, modifications of Set A are required which make the set self-contradictory, the theory as a whole must be abandoned in favor of another theory which avoids all contradictions. The new theory will be acceptable, however, only if it also accomplishes everything the old theory accomplished. In fact, the new theory will generally be so constructed as to include the valid theorems of the old theory as "limiting" or "boundary" cases. Einstein's theory of relativity thus "contains" Newton's law of gravitation as valid for those special cases in which the motions of the bodies concerned can be neglected; and modern quantum physics contains the equivalent of the valid Bohr equations for hydrogenic atoms. The history of science thus strongly reveals again the ideal of an integrated and closed system as a dynamic force in the development of science.

The same ideal is implied by still other considerations. After all, it is a fundamental principle of logic that of two contradictory statements at least one *must* be false (although both *may* be false). The most effective way to avoid accepting mutually contradictory statements is to develop a logically consistent system within which all laws required for the interpretation of the given facts can be derived from an initial set of a few broad definitions and postulates. The system of interrelated concepts, referred to earlier, points in the same direction. The trend toward the integrated and closed system, best exemplified in mathematics and physics, is thus not only discernible in the development of our most advanced sciences, but is also an ultimate requirement of logical thought itself.

I have dwelt at such length upon the problems of theory construction in the physical sciences because, as I stated at the beginning of this chapter, the physical sciences have been widely accepted as the model after which to pattern all sciences; and because the nature of theory construction, best exemplified in our most advanced sciences, is the same everywhere. If the social scientist wants to emulate the physicist, then the pattern is now clear. At the same time, however, we must realize that the complexities of human relations and the ever-changing dynamics of cultural interactions may create problems for the social scientist that should caution us against a too hasty emulation of the natural sciences.

The difficulties encountered in the social sciences arise not only because of the immense complexity of the social phenomena but also and, I believe, primarily because human actions are conscious and deliberate and, therefore, subject to modification on the basis of insights and comprehensions. Ideas are not only weapons, they are also dynamic forces capable of transforming whole cultures; and prediction in the social sciences finds its inevitable limitation in the fact that, knowing the predicted course of events, man can alter that course, thereby nullifying the prediction itself. The conscious and deliberate actions of man thus create special problems for the social scientist—problems not encountered in the realms of physics and chemistry, or even in biology.

The truth of the matter is that, confronted with the problems just referred to, the social scientists themselves are sharply divided into two groups. On the one side are those investigators who, despairing of ever finding laws which govern social events in the same sense in which the laws of physics and chemistry govern the events in nature, tend to look upon social phenomena as essentially unique historical events which must be studied in their uniqueness, and who, for this reason, tend to reduce the social sciences to historical studies of "what is the case," to studies, that is, which permit little or no generalization. On the other side are those social scientists who, despite all historical uniqueness of the social events, still have faith that, in the end, laws of general validity can be discovered; that there are uniformities of development and of interactions of sufficient stability to warrant a logico-formal statement of laws and the integration of such laws into explanatory theories. They point out that, strictly speaking, even the processes and events with which physicists and chemists are concerned are unique, each in its own time and in its own context; and that the natural sciences are possible only because this historical uniqueness of the events is neglected in favor of what is common to all of them. They argue that, on this point, the difference between the natural and the social sciences is one of degree only; that in the social sciences an abstraction from historical context is feasible and that, difficult as it may be, it ought to be attempted.

The facts in the case, it seems to me, are such that both of these positions contain a kernel of truth but are untenable in their extreme orientations. The concrete subject matter of the social sciences is inseparable from the historico-cultural context within which the events take place and can therefore not be described adequately in abstraction; but neither is it possible to overlook the structural and functional uniformities which are characteristic of all similar social events. It is perfectly true, for instance, that the French Revolution and the October Revolution in Russia are, each in itself, concretely unique historical events which, in their uniqueness, can be understood adequately only within the broad historico-cultural context of the whole of Europe. But it is also true that, as revolutions, they have common aspects and features which may warrant the formulation of a set of generalized "laws" descriptive of all revolutions, and such laws may become integral parts of explanatory theories.

In the social sciences more than in any other field of investigation it is important to keep in mind that the individual event, situation, or process occurs only within a much wider context; that there exists a reciprocal relation between the context and any event included therein; that neither the context nor the event can be understood in itself, and that an adequate interpretation of either must always involve an interpretation of its functional correlation with the other. In such an interpretation, the opposition between the individual or the unique and the general or the recurrent can be overcome, and the subsumption of particular events under generalized laws is at least not impossible.

With respect to the nature of such laws, however, the social scientists are again sharply divided. There are those who hold to the essentially naturalistic thesis that the laws governing social events must be patterned after the laws of the natural sciences; that, in fact, social events can be subsumed under law only if they are interpreted "downwards" in terms of behavioral psychology, biology, ecology, and other "natural" sciences. The argument is that only through such reductionistic naturalism can the unity of science, and therefore the spirit and nature of science itself, be preserved. But there are also those social scientists who repudiate all reductionism and, while maintaining that laws governing social events can indeed be discovered, firmly hold that such laws must be appropriate to the nature of the social events and, therefore, must be laws *sui generis*. Their argument is that any description, any attempt at explanation, in order to be meaningful and significant, must be adequate to its subject matter; that no other considerations can be decisive; and that a reductionism, either up or down, is essentially a falsification of the facts.

In this controversy, the arguments of the second group seem to me to be cogent. No explanation really explains if it is not adequate to the facts to be explained; and since man stands committed to values and consciously and deliberately pursues even ideational goals, a reductionism which neglects these aspects of human behavior in favor of a value-free and nonpurposive "natural" explanation is in effect a falsification of the social events. Social events are *sui generis,* and so are the laws governing them. The principle of the unity of science is unaffected by this fact.

The task of science is the discovery of laws which govern the different levels of reality, to integrate these laws in explanatory theories and, ultimately, to provide a unified interpretation without falsifying the facts. This task, however, does not imply the reduction of one science to another. On the contrary, it merely means that any adequate interpretation of the more complex or higher levels cannot contradict the facts of the less complex or lower levels but must allow for them or "contain" them as "limiting" cases when the factors which are specific to the higher levels cancel out or are set aside. The Galileo transformation equations of Newtonian mechanics (e.g., $t' = t$)[3] have thus been superseded by the much more complex equations of Einstein's theory of relativity, such as:

$$t' = \frac{t - \dfrac{v}{c^2}}{\sqrt{1 - \dfrac{v^2}{c^2}}}.$$ But the former are, nevertheless, preserved within the

latter and remain valid for all "limiting" cases in which the velocity of the observer, $v,$ is so small in comparison with the velocity of light, $c,$ that $\dfrac{v}{c^2}$ and $\dfrac{v^2}{c^2}$ can be neglected. Similarly, as far as elementary particles are concerned, the simple laws of molar mechanics have been superseded by the much more intricate laws of quantum physics; yet the former remain valid and are derivable from the latter whenever we deal with things consisting of many particles. More recently, the old causal pattern of a unilinear cause-effect sequence has become a "limiting" case in a broader conception of causation which is essential to the understanding of "equilibrating" systems, such as the living organism. But here again the simple pattern of cause and effect is retained as valid for those "limiting" conditions when life ceases or when we neglect it in the study of isolated processes. In more technical terms, the idea of an "open" system has superseded the idea of a "closed" system—at least in the biological sciences, although the physicists are also aware of it; and the laws of an "open" system not keyed to the principle of entropy, when fully formulated, will replace but also retain as "limiting" cases the laws of the "closed" systems. In this way the uniqueness of the various levels of reality and the principle of the unity of science will both be preserved. The inclusion of still higher types of laws—i.e., of laws pertaining to social phenomena—in the integrative unity of science would in this sense be only a further advance in the development of the scientific ideal without sacrificing the distinctive character of the phenomena in question. The laws governing social events would then be appropriately modified extensions of laws governing other levels of reality and would not entail a reduction of the higher levels to the lower, or vice versa. The laws of the lower levels would remain valid for all "limiting" cases when the events under investigation cease to be social events or can be treated as nonsocial.

To be sure, the phenomena which are the subject matter of the social sciences are so complex that as yet it is not possible to obtain that degree of precision in description and the formulation of laws which is requisite to the ultimate integration. In fact, the descriptive phase of scientific inquiry will predominate in the social sciences for a long time to come. Without theory construction, however, the social sciences will never reach full scientific maturity. Even statistically disclosed uniformities are at best only descriptive of "what is the case." As in any other science, their explanation depends upon their being derivable as theorems or laws from a Set A of definitions and postulates.

The task ahead is a difficult one; no one knows this better than the social scientist himself. But it is by no means an impossible one. Steps in the right direction have already been taken. It is essential, however, that the completely historical orientation, the concentration on the uniqueness of social events, be abandoned. All sciences must formalize the phenomena with which they deal in order to obtain relatively typical and recurrent events. In the natural sciences, notably in physics and chemistry, a very high degree of formalization is possible because of the simplicity of the events under study. In these sciences, functional invariants and basic constants can be found which facilitate the formulation of general but precise laws. In the social sciences, only relatively stable conditions and factors can be found. Nevertheless, the social scientist must and does proceed on the assumption that there are typical and recurrent situations and patterns at the social level which are the result of typical and recurrent processes or functional interdependencies. His concern is and must be the discovery of laws governing what is typical and recurrent —even under the complex conditions of an "open" system—and, through general laws, to apprehend reality.

Laws, however, involve concepts; and concepts, if they are to connect the laws with reality, must have referential significance. Directly or indirectly they must refer to the facts of observation. In the physical sciences, this referential significance is established—at least for key concepts—through various operations of "measuring." In the field of the social sciences, however, such operations may not be altogether adequate. Care must be taken that the means of connecting the concepts with the observed facts do not in themselves imply a commitment to a physicalistic reductionism which would falsify the facts before a description is even attempted. Neither, of course, is it sufficient to define the key concepts in terms of subjective intensions alone. Ways and means must be found to transcend purely verbal constructions and to enable all investigators in the field clearly and objectively to discern the intended meaning. At all times, we must keep in mind that the goal is an analysis and comprehension of reality, not an analysis of concepts per se.

We have seen, however, in the case of Newtonian mechanics at least that it is not sufficient to define our concepts as concisely as possible and to relate them operationally to the facts in the case; the concepts themselves must be interrelated in such a way as to form a systematic whole; for their interrelations constitute the first great step forward in any attempt at theory construction. The history of the natural sciences shows clearly that the critical revision and integration of concepts has at all times been indispensable to the advancement of science. It was so at the time of Galileo and Newton, of Torricelli and Boyle, of Dalton and Faraday; and it is so in our own time. The development of relativity theory and quantum physics is but proof of the fact. The social sciences have currently reached a phase in their development when this critical and integrative revision of key concepts as an indispensable step toward theory construction can no longer be postponed.

One important point must be noted, however; namely, that not all concepts needed in theory construction need have direct reference to some facts of observation. On the contrary, the more of the concretely defined concepts with referential meaning included among the definitions of Set *A*, the more restricted in scope is the theory. Conversely, the more abstract those initial concepts are, the wider in its range of application and the more fertile in its consequences is the theory. Concreteness per se is no advantage in theory construction. What is necessary is merely that the derived laws have operationally determinable applications. In this respect, the lessons to be learned from quantum physics are unmistakable.

II

If experimentation is regarded as essential to a science, then, obviously, our social studies will never become truly scientific. It has been our thesis, however, that, in the physical sciences, theory construction is as important as experimentation; that, in its results, science is a body of logically integrated knowledge—a body of laws which are descriptive of the facts of observation but which are also derivable from the definitions and postulates of an explanatory theory. This interpretation of science is broad enough, I believe, to include the social sciences and to preserve their uniqueness in the scale of the sciences. I now wish to discuss this uniqueness more fully.

It is evident from the pioneering work of Roger Bacon, Leonardo, Galileo, and Kepler in developing our physical sciences, re-enforced as this work is by the labors of Newton, that experience was to be the basis of science, but that measured data alone were to be regarded as "real," and that whatsoever could not be measured was to be excluded from the subject matter of science. Our contemporary physicists and chemists pursue this same ideal. They are all concerned with facts and the quantitative interrelations of facts. In no case are values or valuations part of the data which the physical scientist tries to interpret. No values or valuations are integral parts of the systems of laws and the theories which are based upon, or which can be confirmed by, the value-free data which alone concern the physicist or the chemist. And, indeed, no values or valuations can be deduced from value-free premises—not even when science itself gives us the premises.

The social scientist, however, by the very nature of things, is concerned with a subject matter of which values and valuations are essential ingredients, and, being part of the social context which is subject matter for his science, is himself deeply involved in the intricacies of valuations and value relations—a fact which makes his task doubly difficult and which confronts us with the problem of value and the social sciences.

This problem, frequently discussed by social scientists themselves, has at least three distinct aspects. Concerning these aspects much confusion prevails even in scholarly journals in the field. It is essential, however, that the aspects be clearly separated before an attempt is made to consider the particular problems of value and theory construction, and of objectivity. We shall here speak of (*a*) value *of* the social sciences, (*b*) values *in* the social sciences, and (*c*) values *for* the social sciences.

a) The question of the value *of* the social sciences constitutes no particular problem. In so far as any knowledge in whatever field of inquiry is of value to us, the knowledge obtained in the social sciences is, of course, also of value—and it is so in a twofold sense. On the one hand, knowledge is valued simply for its own sake, as satisfying man's innate curiosity. To deny the significance of this aspect of the value of knowledge would be to disregard the primary motive in basic research. It is and remains a fact, as Aristotle already knew, that men simply want to know; that to them knowledge is an end in itself and is valued as such. On the other hand, however, it is also a fact that knowledge is of crucial importance as the basis for rational decisions and reasonable actions, that it has practical or pragmatic value in the service of man's aspirations, intentions, and hopes—including his aspiration to understand himself and to control his environment.

It must be especially noted, however, that the significance of scientific knowledge for man's decisions and actions is purely "instrumental," and that scientific knowledge as such does not take the place of the decisions and actions themselves. The physicists, for example, have given us the knowledge requisite to the control over the vast amounts of energy locked up in the atom. They can tell us that under such and such conditions the energy will be released in a terrific explosion; that under such and such other conditions the energy may become fuel for various power plants; and that under still different conditions radioactive particles will be available for medical research and therapy. But whether we manufacture bombs or power plants or use the fissionable materials for other purposes is not a problem of physics. It is not a problem even for social scientists as scientists. It is true, of course, that, whatever knowledge we have concerning the facts relevant to the case, the time at which we make the decision will be of value to us; for that decision, if it is to be a rational and reasonable one, must take into account the total world situation, including all foreseeable consequences of the decision itself and the value commitments of a civilized humanity. But a decision is an act of the will, not an aspect of knowledge; and the responsibility for the decision is not the responsibility of a scientist as scientist—although it may be his in his rôle as a citizen. In a similar way, the knowledge obtained in the social sciences may well be essential to any and all "social engineering." But the policy decisions requisite to social engineering involve value judgments which are not themselves part of the scientific knowledge basic to the decision. Science can determine the appropriateness of the means for attaining a given end. It may enable us to estimate the probability of achieving that end and to determine the cost of achieving it in terms of a predictable loss of other values. In fact, the knowledge made available to us in the sciences may well lead to a reconsideration and revision of the desired end itself. Nevertheless, science as such does not define the norms and ideals which constitute the value framework within which the facts of science are themselves appraised relative to man's hopes and aspirations and in the light of his value commitments.

b) Although we must be clear as to the specific rôle which science plays in our pursuit of human ends, the value *of* science for the pursuit of these ends is beyond dispute. But what about the quite different question of value *in* science?

This question, it seems to me, is ambiguous. In an obvious and superficial sense it is true, of course, that the data with which social scientists are concerned include value judgments and valuations on the part of individuals comprising any social group, whereas the data of the natural sciences do not include values in this sense. It is therefore an incontrovertible fact that the social sciences, but not the natural sciences, must be concerned with values and valuations. In a much more profound sense, however, the question means: Is a reference to value as an explanatory category essential to the scientific enterprise?

In order to understand the significance of this question let us take a brief glance at the history of ideas and concepts which has culminated in the development of modern science.

Modern science arose in opposition to the Aristotelian tradition—a tradition which dominated the Middle Ages and was keenly felt even centuries later. This tradition, it may be remembered, was technological in orientation and was dominated by value concepts. Heavenly bodies are spherical, so the argument was, because the sphere is the most perfect form. Each element has its "natural" place in the universe and strives to attain it, so it was said, just as each entity has its own inherent end or purpose which it tends to realize. If nature abhors a vacuum, so the reasoning was, it does so only because it is better to be than not to be. In the Aristotelian scheme of things, value terms were thus indispensable as explanatory categories. To understand things and events meant to understand them in terms of the values which they embody or which they tend to realize.

During the fourteenth century, beginning with Roger Bacon and Albertus Magnus, this point of view was challenged repeatedly. But even Copernicus's thought, in the sixteenth century, was still value charged. In arguing for his heliocentric view of the universe, he maintained that it is better to have the stars at rest rather than the earth, for they are nobler and more divine than the latter. The universe is spherical, he contended, because the sphere is the most perfect form; and since, of all motions, circular motion is the best, the motions of heavenly bodies must be circular.

To be sure, Aristotle himself had maintained that "science is knowledge of a cause"; but he had distinguished between (1) material cause (or the indeterminate "matter" which is the basis of all that is), (2) formal cause (or the specific nature of any existing thing), (3) efficient cause (or the actual thing or event which brings about any change), and (4) the final cause or purpose for the sake of which the change is effected. In his metaphysics, the material cause and the formal cause are most important; but in his science the efficient cause and the final cause predominate. The efficient cause, however, is but a means in and through which the final cause, the purpose in question, finds realization. Although efficient causes are indispensable to our understanding of nature, only the final causes determine the direction of all processes and events, and only a thorough grasp of the final cause gives us in each instance a complete understanding of what transpires in nature. A stone dropped from a high place will fall toward the center of the earth because that center is the "natural" place for all heavy objects.

It was not until Galileo and Newton had done their work and Torricelli had determined the magnitude of air pressure that this Aristotelian point of view faded out of the picture as far as the basic natural sciences were concerned. But from the time of Newton on, interpretations of the mechanistic processes in nature were given in terms of efficient causes only. Terrestrial and celestial motions were now found to conform to the same laws, and value categories receded into the background. Deism, interpreting the world as a vast machine, put purpose and value into a transcendent realm untouched by science. In the exact natural sciences, the principle first enunciated by Galileo now generally prevailed—the principle, namely, that in science nothing is to be admitted as real which is not quantity or reducible to quantity. The ideal of a value-free science had emerged.

It must not be presumed, however, that the liberation of science from value categories was now complete. In the biological sciences, for example, this was definitely not yet the case. Teleological categories were still in use in the interpretation of evolution and of the functionally integrative development of the organism. The mechanism-vitalism issue merely pointed up the problem. Although Kant had refused to accept purpose as an explanatory category, it was Darwin's theory which reduced evolution to efficient causation only, and it is our modern conception of "open systems" and the "feedback" principle which finally eliminates value terms from our theories of ontogenetic development and homeostatic "equilibration." In the natural sciences, therefore, a value-free approach is thus at last a reality.

In the social sciences, however, the situation is by no means so simple. Here values and valuations are essentially unavoidable. In fact, they enter the social sciences in two ways: (1) as factual matter for analysis, and (2) as valuational premises within factual analysis. After all, human beings are end-pursuing creatures. The ends pursued are evaluated, individually and socially, and these evaluations are part and parcel of the facts of social living—the very subject matter which the social scientist studies and interprets.

The conditions under which values arise, the specific values accepted by particular groups, the ways in which values become modified, the effects of valuations on human behavior—all these matters belong to the legitimate domain of facts with which the social scientists are concerned. Social studies may center around cultural value patterns or may be concerned with the relation of values and valuations to biological drives or psychological needs. They may involve attempts to determine what value judgments are actually made by a particular group or how the value commitments of one group differ from similar commitments of some other group. Ruth Benedict's study, *Patterns of Culture,* illustrates the point. Values and valuations in the sense here referred to are, after all, but part of the factual data to be interpreted and analyzed. They constitute no serious problem for the scientist.

It is otherwise with the second way in which values and valuations enter the social sciences. In fact, this second way is crucial to the very nature of the social sciences themselves. Nothing less is involved here than the question of value as an explanatory category; and this problem arises irrespective of any commitment or noncommitment to Aristotelian presuppositions. It arises simply because, consciously and deliberately, human beings pursue ends which they value. If this fact is not taken into account, human behavior, in so far as it is purposive, remains inexplicable and social science cannot advance beyond the stage of mere description. To put it otherwise: in social matters, explanation and prediction are impossible without reference to the basic value commitments of the agents involved. A change in those commitments may alter the whole series of events with which the social scientist is concerned. But once basic value commitments are understood, many otherwise inexplicable phenomena fall into a coherent pattern and find their explanation in their relation to those commitments.

It may now be argued, of course, that even in the area of social studies the employment of value categories should be avoided; that unless this is done, social studies cannot attain the status of a science. The so-called mathematical school of economics presumably points the way, formulating laws governing the exchange of goods without reference to conceptions of utility or to valuations which spur men into action. Closer inspection reveals, however, that even this most scientific branch of a social science rests upon two assumptions which entail valuations and value commitments: the assumption (*a*) that all goods to be exchanged involve some factor of production; that, if no effort were required to produce the goods, the buyer would not be willing to pay for them; and the assumption (*b*) that every producer of goods seeks to maximize his profits and that he acts rationally toward that end. A corollary of these assumptions is the principle of marginal utility to the consumer and of marginal return to the producer—a corollary which also involves an obvious reference to valuations. It would seem, then, that mathematical economics points the way, not to a value-free social science, but to social studies which can be scientific despite the fact that explanations are ultimately given in value terms. What is required for the construction of an integrated and closed system of laws in the social sciences is not that all values be neglected or eliminated (to do this would result in a distortion of facts), but that the key valuations be included in the Set *A* of definitions and postulates from which the Set *B* of laws governing the phenomena can be derived.

One obvious limitation to theory construction in the social sciences is, of course, the requirement that the value premises of a proposed theory express not the personal predilections and biases of the investigator but the basic value commitments inherent in the phenomena to be explained. That is to say, the value premises should state what *has been* or *is being* valued in the social group under investigation, not what *should be* valued in the opinion of the investigator. The explanatory value categories, in other words, must be indigenous to the subject matter itself.

c) It is true, of course, that the investigator also makes certain value commitments—and that he makes them both as a person and as a scientist. His commitments as a person belong to the general subject matter of the social sciences; his commitments as a scientist, however, play a particular role in the enterprise which is science, for they define the general value framework within which scientists operate. We shall speak here of values *for* science rather than of values *in* science.

Included in the general value framework within which scientists operate are the over-all value commitments and valuations of any given culture or period in history. Surely it is evident that the over-all valuations in contemporary America are much more favorable to the sciences than were the value commitments of medieval Europe. But even in our own time we are witnessing shifts in value commitments—induced, no doubt, by military and industrial requirements—which increasingly tend to emphasize science rather than the humanities. Even so, however, the value pattern of our culture delimits the extent to which social experiments may be attempted, and our over-all value commitments are important in the selection of problems for inquiry.

In addition, the individual scientist has his own value commitments which influence not only his choice of a field of research but his interest in specific problems and the tenacity with which he pursues his goals as well. To say that all this has no bearing upon the enterprise we call science would be to distort the facts and to delude ourselves into thinking that science is somehow carried on in a vacuum—which it is not. It is true, of course, that the over-all value commitments and valuations here referred to are not in themselves ingredients of scientific research. They are neither constituent elements of the methods of science nor are they essential parts of explanatory hypotheses or theories. They simply are part of that nonscientific framework within which science exists and develops as an aspect of our culture and our human enterprise.

There are, however, value commitments which, although not constituting values *in* science, are much more intimately bound up with science than are the general valuations just mentioned; for the moment we accept scientific rather than nonscientific procedures of investigation, and we are caught up in that pattern of valuations summarized in the term "standards of research." Exactitude and meticulous care in the compilation of data, integrity and intellectual honesty, sound reasoning, objectivity in the evaluation of facts, imagination to see alternative possibilities of interpretation, courage to follow an argument to its logical conclusion, and a willingness to abandon cherished ideas in the light of new evidence—these are but some of the qualifications and valuations indispensable to the enterprise of science as such. Indeed, the determination of scientific truth itself presupposes value judgments. As scientists, therefore, we are irrevocably committed to a specific value pattern which alone makes science the significant endeavor that it is. Because we appreciate the value *of* science, we are inescapably committed to values *for* science. But only value as explanatory category is of crucial significance as value *in* science.

III

In discussing values *for* science, I spoke of a value framework within which scientists operate and construct their theories. I shall now attempt to show briefly that, in connection with this value framework, problems arise which are crucial to science but which must be solved, if they are to be solved at all, in the realm of philosophy rather than that of science. I shall center my discussions around the problem of objectivity.

The dictionaries speak of "objectivity" as (*a*) "objective reality," and (*b*) "the quality or character of being objective." The problem of objectivity in the first sense, basic and difficult though it is, rightfully belongs to the problems of epistemology and does not pertain to the value framework of science. We can therefore neglect it here. The problem of objectivity in the second sense, however, requires special attention.

To define 'objectivity' in the relevant sense here intended as "the quality or character of being objective" means very little, however, unless we know what is meant by 'being objective.' When we consult the dictionaries, we find that 'objective' means "treating a subject so as to exhibit the actual facts, not colored by the feelings or opinions of the speaker or writer," "being detached, impersonal, unprejudiced." We must realize, however, that "being objective" even in this apparently well defined sense involves two distinct aspects. One is essentially the popular meaning of 'unprejudiced.' In this sense the problem of objectivity is humanly important but theoretically trivial. It need not concern us here unduly. The second aspect, although related to the first, is more technical and more profound in its implications.

In the more popular sense, the problem of objectivity arises when we stubbornly and blindly adhere to certain beliefs and valuations—and do so in the face of factual or logical disproof—merely because we give way to emotions and desires rather than to reason, or because we prejudge a case or person or situation; we make up our minds before we know or understand all the facts and relevant circumstances. Here the requirement of objectivity seems to be clear. As usually stated, the requirement is that we always be guided by the facts and by logically sound inferences from these facts. But the matter is not as simple as such an admonition seems to imply, for the so-called facts do not always exist definitively determined and in clean-cut isolation. A fact, actually, is but a more or less isolated segment of a highly complex totality of intricately interrelated events. The selection and demarcation of a fact are therefore determined by basic assumptions which define a problem and delimit its scope, and by valuations which guide the investigator at every step. Galileo's principle that in physics nothing is to be regarded as real except quantity and that which can be reduced to quantity is such a principle of selection. But the social scientist, in particular, is enmeshed in valuations which define his facts. He is himself an integral part of the culture in which he lives and can free himself only with difficulty from the dominant preconceptions and biases prevalent in his environment. The normative ideas characteristic of his culture pattern (e.g., human rights, private property, public welfare) and his own value orientations (be they conservative or liberal, static, dynamic, or anything else) affect his research, and may affect it at all stages, from its inception to its conclusion. They may affect the selection and formulation of the problem, the approach, the collecting of relevant data, the recording of observations, the interpretation of the "facts," and the manner in which the results are finally presented. As a rule, the investigator himself is not even aware of the influence which these valuations have upon his work.

Various safeguards against bias may, of course, be employed. Observations may and, in many cases, ought to be repeated and checked, preferably by different observers. If the selection of the data is suspect, alternative hypotheses should be employed in rechecking them. The conclusions reached in any investigation should be clearly related to the premises upon which they depend. If they cannot be logically derived from the premises which have been explicitly stated, some hidden bias of the investigator may be involved. Once this is known, there is a chance that the bias can be eliminated. Personal biases of an individual investigator may be eliminated, if the specific problem with which he is concerned is interrelated with broader aspects of the economic, social, judicial, and cultural life of the group under investigation. But even such broadening of the problem is no absolute guarantee of objectivity because of the basic valuations which permeate each culture—valuations which may differ radically (as between the United States and Soviet Russia) or may vary significantly in some respects (as between the United States and Great Britain). Objectivity is achieved not by denying these valuations but by acknowledging them and stating them explicitly as integral parts of the projected research. If this is done, then the value premises themselves may be evaluated in the light of criteria which increase the chances of achieving objectivity.

A basic requirement for objectivity in research is that the full statement of a problem include the delimitation of its scope, the guiding hypothesis, the principles for the selection of data, the definitions of all terms, and a clear and concise formulation of the value premises. These premises must themselves be submitted as hypotheses, subject to future revision, and not as self-evident truths which are absolute and final. They should, however, be significant in the sense that they represent valuations of major groups within a society, if not of society as a whole. If relevant valuations are mutually incompatible, they should be stated as alternative hypotheses. It may then be possible to use one set of compatible valuations in all preliminary investigations and another set (or sets) as a check on those investigations. Different sets may also be used to interpret the findings in terms of alternative valuations.

It may be argued, of course, that the social scientist should attempt simply to serve the ends sanctioned by the traditions of the society in which he lives; that he should accept unquestioningly the value framework which that society provides. But such an argument completely misses the point. It may be acceptable doctrine to say that, since the ideal of the equality of all men is an integral part of our American creed, the sociologist ought to devote himself to the discovery of ways and means of realizing that ideal more fully, and that in so doing he can achieve objectivity. But time cannot yet have erased from our memories the nazi ideal of the supremacy of the "Aryan race" and Hitler's demand that German social scientists discover ways and means to its full realization. A concern for means only is obviously not sufficient to entail more than a spurious objectivity. Some ultimate standard must be established.

But at this point the situation is aggravated by the fact that ultimate presuppositions cannot be proved either factually or logically. Their very nature as ultimate presuppositions places them beyond definitive proof. The best we can hope for is a fairly general acceptance of our basic premises. The question is, "How is such consensus to be achieved?" Since no proof is possible, we must have recourse to some form of persuasion. Traditionally, this recourse has been an appeal to supporting facts and to the general reasonableness of a proposed interpretation. In recent years, however, and in the wake of logical positivism, the thesis has been advanced that value statements have no cognitive meaning and that therefore our ultimate recourse can be only an attempt at emotive persuasion. It seems to me, however, that agreement on an issue can be reached either way. But there is this difference: An appeal to supporting facts and to the reasonableness of a proposed interpretation, no matter how inadequate it may be in any given situation, implies in principle an appeal to factors which can be confirmed or disconfirmed and which thus assure an element of objectivity. An attempt at emotive persuasion by the use of words or statements which, though emotionally loaded, have no cognitive significance, makes all confirmation or disconfirmation impossible and therefore destroys in principle the last vestiges of objectivity; for mere consensus, no matter how general, is not sufficient to assure objectivity. The crucial question is, "How was the agreement achieved?" Emotive persuasion is in all cases an appeal to favorable or unfavorable prejudices, to love, fear, pride, aspiration, to desires, aversions, and instinctive drives. Hitler demonstrated only too effectively what can be achieved by emotive persuasion on a large scale, and he demonstrated also that, in the last analysis, emotive persuasion is always an appeal to force. The rationale of science, however, and the requisite to ultimate objectivity, is the faith that, beyond our wishes and predilections, there is an order in the universe which, though but dimly perceived, is yet amenable to rational interpretation and a rational value analysis.

One further aspect of the problem of objectivity deserves consideration. Ever since Max Weber spoke of "ethical neutrality" as a prerequisite for the social sciences it has been argued that one of the requirements of scientific objectivity is that, as scientist, the social scientist refrain from passing moral judgment on the facts he studies. In an obvious sense this requirement is fundamental and must be fulfilled. But does objectivity demand complete detachment under all circumstances?

Surely, the demand for objectivity does not mean that we must tolerate all opinions on a subject as deserving equal recognition. Some opinions deserve no recognition at all because they are warranted neither by the facts in the case nor by logical proof or critical analysis. Objectivity here requires that we repudiate these opinions, for it commits us to the demonstrable, the factual, the true; and in this sense objectivity entails its own bias, if such we wish to call it.

Moreover, objectivity requires "being detached, impersonal, unprejudiced" only in the sense of not permitting one's feelings, desires, and prejudices to abrogate or to flout principles which are themselves the criteria of objectivity; it does not require that one tolerate in a detached manner every infraction of basic valuations and/or established principles. In order to clarify this point, let us consider two specific problems: to wit, the problem of racial equality in the United States, and the problem of naturalistic reductionism in the social sciences.

It is Weber's thesis, if I understand him correctly, that the social scientist may attempt to get at the facts but that he ought to refrain from making value judgments pertaining to those facts. "Ethical neutrality" demands that the investigator merely record what he observes. It seems to me, however, that the problem is not as simple as that, for even the collecting of facts, as we have seen, can be carried on only within a value framework which the scientist accepts, and among the "facts" are the value commitments of the group under investigation. The so-called race problem is a problem only because of a contradiction inherent in the subject matter under study—the contradiction, namely, between the value commitment of the group and the actual behavior of members of the group. Merely to study the behavior of the members does not even reveal the problem. Objectivity here requires that the value commitments of the group be included, along with the facts of behavior, in the data relevant to the study.

In the case of the "race problem" in the United States, an appropriate value commitment of the group is provided by the Declaration of Independence: "We hold these truths to be self-evident, that all men are created equal, that they are endowed by their Creator with certain unalienable Rights, that among these are Life, Liberty and the pursuit of Happiness. That to secure these rights, Governments are instituted among Men, deriving their just powers from the consent of the governed." Of course, we may not accept this creed as our own value commitment—in which case we may encounter no race problem; but if we, as a nation, do accept it, as interpreted in recent decisions of our Supreme Court, then we have a value premise from which to evaluate without emotional bias all relevant facts of individual and group behavior. Indeed, the principle of self-consistency requires that we do make such an evaluation. In other words, objectivity requires that we record not only the facts of observation but also the value commitments with which these facts may or may not be in harmony. If there is a discrepancy between the facts of behavior and the professed value commitments, then objectivity requires not that we omit all reference to the commitments but that we point up the discrepancy, even if doing so should entail a moral condemnation of the observed practices and facts.

If it be argued that the men who wrote the Declaration of Independence did not interpret it as we do today, such an argument raises a problem, not about our valuations within the accepted value framework, but one pertaining to the framework itself; and this is clearly a shift in the argument. As Hitler and others have demonstrated again and again, it is perfectly possible to deny that all men are equal or that they are endowed with certain inalienable rights, and that therefore racial minorities should not receive equal treatment. But this is like refusing to accept the premises of Euclidean geometry and then to maintain that the Pythagorean theorem does not hold. We are confusing the issues. The crux of the matter is the basic value commitment. The problem of objectivity is most acute at this point, for value commitments change as man's hopes and aspirations change, and, in any case, it is the task of philosophy, not of the social sciences, to clarify and to justify whatever value premises we ought to accept.

This task of philosophy is not an easy one. Its full magnitude dawns upon us when we realize that even the natural sciences operate within a framework of principles, and that they are legitimately objective only to the extent to which that framework finds ultimate justification. It is at this point, also, that the problem of naturalistic reductionism arises.

The basic framework of the physical sciences includes the assumption that reality is a matter-energy pattern in space-time which is determined in its structure and governed in its functioning by the principle of the conservation of matter-energy, the principle of the conservation of momentum, Carnot's principle and its systemic complement, and the principle of entropy, as well as by some form of Hamilton's principle of least action. The history of modern science reveals the slow process, involving checks and counter-checks, which has led to the general acceptance of these broad principles as basic—the justification of their acceptance being the tremendous success in predicting and controlling nature which scientists have achieved.

It must be noted, however, that the principles pertain, and can pertain, only to *physical* reality. If this limitation is disregarded, and if the principles are set forth as determining or governing the whole of reality, serious difficulties (the difficulties inherent in naturalistic reductionism) arise, for there are aspects of human existence—such as consciousness, perception, insight, and logical reasoning as well as valuations and aesthetic appreciations and the moral *ought*—which are hardly amenable to an interpretation in terms of physics and chemistry, or in terms of physiology, for that matter. To refuse to admit in the light of such facts that there are aspects of reality which lie outside the framework of the broad principles of the physical sciences is but to reveal a prejudice in favor of the physical sciences and to betray a lack of objectivity in the most profound sense possible.

What is true in the case of the physical sciences is equally true, of course, in the case of all partial approaches to reality which masquerade as the whole. They lack that objectivity which is synonymous with "being detached, impersonal, unprejudiced." If it now be argued that to insist upon the whole of reality as the ultimate criterion of objectivity is itself but a prejudice, then it can readily be shown that the argument misses the point; for we do not prejudge an approach or an attitude or a belief by insisting that it remain within its own framework of principles and valuations, limited though they may be. This applies also to the valuational framework within which the basic problem of racial minorities arises. The difficulty is to find a framework of principles broad enough to include the whole of reality. It is at this point that the problem of objectivity as a quality or character of being objective merges into the problem of objectivity as the problem of objective reality. The search for principles adequate for the realization of this objectivity is again the task—and the most profound task—of philosophy.

NOTES

1. This is so because substitution of 1, 2, or 3 for n_1, and of n (or one of its indicated specific values 2, 3, 4, 5, 6, . . .) will yield, respectively, the Lyman or Balmer or Paschen series.

2. In this equation, π is the ratio of circumference to diameter of the electronic orbits, μ represents the total mass of the atom, Z is the atomic number, ε represents the electric charge, and h is Planck's constant, which ties the whole model to a quantum-mechanical rather than a Newtonian interpretation. It must be noted that in this equation nothing is being said about spectral lines. What the equation does give us is an energy differential within the Bohr model of the atom, and the various series of spectral lines are "explained" in the sense that they are now understood as observational manifestations of the assumed energy differentials within the atom.

3. These equations are necessary for the transformation of time references from a stationary frame of reference to one which is in rectilinear motion with respect to it.

BIBLIOGRAPHY

ADAMS, BROOKS. *The Law of Civilization and Decay.* New York: Alfred A. Knopf, Inc., 1943; first edition, 1896.

GOLDENWEISER, ALEXANDER. "The Concept of Causality in the Physical and Social Sciences," *American Sociological Review,* III (1938), 624-36.

HALL, EVERETT W. *Modern Science and Human Values.* Princeton: D. Van Nostrand Company, Inc., 1956.

HART, HORNELL. "Atomic Cultural Lag: I The Value Frame," *Sociology and Social Research,* XXXII (1948), 768-75.

KAUFMANN, FELIX. *Methodology of the Social Sciences.* New York: Oxford University Press, 1944.

LADD, JOHN. *The Structure of a Moral Code.* Cambridge: Harvard University Press, 1957.

LUNDBERG, GEORGE A. *Foundations of Sociology.* New York: The Macmillan Company, 1939.

MALINOWSKI, BRONISLAW. *A Scientific Theory of Culture and Other Essays.* Chapel Hill: University of North Carolina Press, 1944.

MERTON, ROBERT K. *Social Theory and Social Structure.* Glencoe, Ill.: The Free Press, 1949.

PARSONS, TALCOTT. *Essays in Sociological Theory.* Glencoe, Ill.: The Free Press, 1949.

RICKERT, HEINDRICH. *Die Grenzen der Naturwiss enschaftlichen Begriffsbildung,* 5th edition. Tubingen: J. C. B. Mohr, 1929.

WEBER, MAX. *Gesammelte Aufsatze zur Wissenschaftslehre.* Tübingen: J. C. B. Mohr, 1922.

WERKMEISTER, W. H. *A Philosophy of Science.* New York: Harper and Brothers, 1940.

———. *The Basis and Structure of Knowledge.* New York: Harper and Brothers, 1948.

———. "An Epistemological Basis for Quantum Physics," *Philosophy of Science,* XVIII (1950), 1-25.

———. "Normative Propositions and the Ideal of an Integrated and Closed System," *Philosophy of Science,* XVIII (1951), 124-31.

———. "Prolegomena to Value Theory," *Philosophy and Phenomenological Research,* XIV (1954), 293-308.

16

Sociological Science and the
Problem of Values

PAUL HANLY FURFEY

The Catholic University of America

There are three ways in which a sociologist *qua* sociologist may be concerned with values. (1) He may choose values as subject matter for sociological research. Thus, through his field studies, he may discover that members of community X assign a high value to the possession of wealth or a low value to a certain minority group. There seems to be no question among sociologists as to the legitimacy of using values in this way.[1] (2) He may introduce certain statements of value as postulates into his own sociological system. For example, the author of a criminology textbook may assume, perhaps tacitly, the value postulate that crime is undesirable and ought to be suppressed. There has been a controversy of long standing among sociologists about the legitimacy of value postulates. However, the subject will not be pursued further in the present paper.[2] (3) Finally, he may assign values to sociology itself, to some particular approach to sociology or school of sociological thought, or to some specific application of sociology in the world of practical affairs. It is with values and value statements of this third type that the present paper is exclusively concerned.

In the interest of logical clarity it is important to note that statements about the third type of values mentioned above do not belong within the content of sociology. Sociology is a science which deals with society, with the real world of men and events; its statements concern facts pertaining to this world. On the other hand, a statement such as "Sociology is a useful aid to social planning," is not a statement about society, but a statement about sociology itself, assigning a particular value to sociology. In order to discuss such statements systematically, it is convenient to define a separate science which we shall call *metasociology* whose function it shall be to furnish "the methodological presuppositions necessary for carrying out sociological research, constructing sociological systems, and criticizing such research and such systems after they have been completed." [3] It is easy to see why the science of metasociology is logically necessary. If sociology is a science, it must not be constructed at haphazard but in accordance with certain definite rules. These rules must be developed systematically so that they can be known and applied with assurance. The orderly development and application of a system of such rules may reasonably be considered the function of a separate science, namely, metasociology. Modern mathematicians speak of "metamathematics," a science which develops the logical foundations of mathematics; sociologists need metasociology for a parallel reason.

It is not the purpose of the present paper to discuss metasociology as a whole, but only that part of metasociology that has to do with values. The discussion will concern the judgments that sociologists make about their science (metasociological value judgments) and statements embodying these judgments (metasociological value statements). It is this paper's thesis that metasociological value judgments play a very important role in determining the content of sociology. In other words, logical considerations alone are not sufficient to explain why some propositions about society are accepted into the content of scientific sociology whereas others are rejected. The process of acceptance and rejection involves not only logic, but also certain value judgments which lie beyond the scope of the logic of science. All this is unavoidable. Since it is unavoidable, this paper will argue, metasociological value judgments should be made explicitly rather than implicitly, systematically rather than unsystematically, and in accordance with definite principles rather than at haphazard.

METASOCIOLOGICAL VALUE JUDGMENTS AND THE CONTENT OF SOCIOLOGY

We assume without discussion the metasociological postulate that sociology is a science. Actually, this is a value statement. It means that *qua* sociologists we prefer to discuss society scientifically rather than in some alternative way.

Each particular science has as its subject matter some specific segment or aspect of reality; and, moreover, it deals with this subject matter in a specific manner which we designate as "scientific." Therefore, no proposition can be accepted as forming part of the content of a given science unless it (1) is *relevant* to that science, and (2) possesses *scientific quality*. Thus, we reject from sociology the proposition, "Under standard conditions mercury boils at 357°C.," because the fact which it states is not *relevant* to the field of sociology; and we reject the proposition, "All crime is due to biological inheritance," because it cannot be verified and therefore lacks *scientific quality*.

If the science of sociology is to be developed systematically and not haphazardly, there must be definite procedures for making decisions as to relevance and scientific quality. This implies the recognition of definite *criteria of relevance* and *criteria of scientific quality* on which the decisions are to be based. It is the business of metasociology to develop and apply such criteria. In the following sections, the two types of criteria will be separately examined, and it will be shown that neither type can be developed or applied without the use of metasociological value judgments. From this, it will follow that the content of sociology is conditioned, at least in part, by the particular sets of metasociological values that sociologists prefer.

Criteria of Relevance

Sociologists differ a good deal among themselves about the exact area of reality which their science discusses. This follows clearly enough from the definitions of sociology which they have given. Consider, for example, the following, chosen almost at random:

Sociology is the science of the social process.[4]

Sociology is . . . the science of statesmen and organizers, that is, of *social technicians.*[5]

Sociology is nothing other than social psychology.[6]

[Sociology] seeks to formulate natural laws and generalization in regard to human nature and society that are of universal validity.[7]

Sociology is a scientific study of society. It aims to become a complete scientific description and history of society, and as nearly as possible a complete explanation of society in terms of simpler phenomena.[8]

Clearly, such divergent definitions reflect real differences of viewpoint as to the scope of sociology. However, it is unnecessary to labor the point. Disputes as to the exact area to be covered by the science have bedeviled sociology from its early period down to the present. To express the same fact in other languages, sociologists have never agreed very well on the proper criteria of relevance for their science.

The important point in the present connection is that it is impossible

to argue that one set of relevance criteria is true and another false, that
one is right and another wrong. All one can do is to argue that one set
is preferable because it is more practical or more illuminating or possessed in a greater degree of some other desirable quality. In other words,
the choice among alternative sets of criteria is determined by metasociological value judgments. The definition of sociology and its scope cannot
be predetermined by logic. Within broad limits one may choose arbitrarily one's own criteria for deciding what sort of propositions should
be accepted as relevant to sociology and what ones must be excluded as
irrelevant.

It is clear that the content of sociology is directly affected by the
choice among divergent sets of relevance criteria. Thus, referring to the
definitions quoted above, one sees that Giddings' definition logically
implies a sociology weighted with history, that Palante's definition implies one with a dominant psychological orientation, and that Neurath's
definition implies one exclusively oriented toward practice. Of course,
sociologists do not always follow out in their writings all the logical implications of their verbal definitions; but the fact remains that their sociological systems often differ very markedly among themselves and present
their readers with quite differing pictures of societal reality.

There is scope for value judgments not only in the choice of relevance criteria, but also in the application of these criteria after they
have been chosen. For example, take Reuter's definition which was
quoted above. He considers the content of sociology to be "natural laws
and generalization in regard to human nature and society that are of
universal validity." Obviously this is a large order. All human activity
is grist for the sociologist's mill. He must begin somewhere. He must
arbitrarily choose the segment of human activity which seems most
promising for the beginning of his research. Until sociologists shall have
had time to study everything that human beings do in society, our sociological systems will be based on data gathered here and there at points
arbitrarily selected. We get partial pictures of society as a result, and
the character of these partial pictures depends on sociologists' value
judgments, their choices of subjects for research.

When he selects subjects for research, a sociologist's choices are
likely to be affected by the availability of material. For example, convicted criminals safely confined in prisons and jails are very much more
available for study than criminals at large. As a result, criminological
research deals almost exclusively with the former. Thus, criminology
becomes the science of convicted criminals, rather than of criminals in
general. City dwellers are more available than isolated rural residents;
it is easier to establish contact with the educated than with the unedu-
cated; and college sophomores are always at the mercy of the instructor

seeking subjects for research. Therefore, the observations about society ✓ which one reads in sociology textbooks are not actually observations about society in general, but rather observations about the particular segments of modern American society which happen to be most available for research.

Sociologists tend to be much more ready to choose dramatic and exciting subjects for research and discussion than dull and prosaic ones. Race riots and lynchings attract the student of intergroup relations much more than the uneventful symbiosis of Negroes and whites in some peaceful little town. Students of family life have much to say about the emotional tensions between husbands and wives that bring couples to a counseling center, but less to say about the calm family lives of well-matched couples. Corps of psychiatrists, psychologists, and social workers study our juvenile delinquents, and sociologists find their results very interesting; but who studies the very average little boy who grows up to be a very average and very inoffensive clerk?

The choice of one sort of material for research and discussion rather than another sort need not necessarily lead to a false picture of society, but it can lead to a very partial and incomplete one. Moreover, if the reader of sociological literature forgets that the picture *is* incomplete, he may very easily be misled. Thus, when he reads statements about the average intelligence of prison inmates, he may forget that these are the criminals who got caught and that the criminals who got away may be considerably more intelligent. In the present state of knowledge, no sociologist can give a really complete account of human society. His account is necessarily one-sided; and its particular variety of one-sidedness depends on the set of relevance criteria which the sociologist chooses for himself, and on the way he interprets and applies these criteria. Thus, ultimately, the picture of society which a sociologist presents to his readers depends on a series of metasociological value judgments. Within broad limits, it is arbitrary. It is a matter of free choice.

Ⓓ Criteria of Scientific Quality

The ordinary process of scientific research may be summarized as follows: (1) The scientist gathers a mass of carefully verified facts concerning some phenomenon or group of phenomena. (2) He conceives, as a hypothesis, some generalization which will account for all these facts. (3) From his hypothesis he deduces certain consequences about hitherto unexamined phenomena; then he turns to these phenomena and studies them to see whether they actually occur in the way his hypothesis predicts. (4) Finally, he makes a decision as to whether or not his hypothesis should be accepted as a verified generalization of his science.

In the physical and biological sciences, there are cases in which the process of research can be carried out approximately as outlined above without uncertainty and without significant use of value judgments. No one can seriously doubt that the linear coefficient of expansion for iron is approximately 0.000012 per degree centigrade or that scurvy is a deficiency disease due to lack of ascorbic acid in the diet. However, in the light of rigorous logic, there are certain difficulties in the process, and in many actual cases these difficulties are serious from a practical standpoint.

The chief source of logical difficulty in the research process outlined above is the fact that it can involve what is called "the fallacy of the consequent." Consider the argument:

> If hypothesis X is true, then consequences x, y, and z will follow.
> But x, y, and z do follow.
> Therefore hypothesis X is true.

Obviously, the argument does not really prove that X is true; it merely proves that X can explain x, y, and z. However, there may exist some alternative hypothesis Y which can also explain them. Moreover, when a wider range of phenomena is examined, some fact w may turn up which can be explained by Y but not by X. For X to be verified convincingly it would be necessary to argue:

> If, *and only if*, hypothesis X is true, x, y, and z will follow.
> But x, y, and z do follow.
> Therefore X is true.

In other words, for X to be convincingly verified, it must not only explain all the known facts, but it must be known to be the *only* hypothesis which can explain them.

In practice, it is usually very difficult to exclude all alternative hypotheses and to state with certainty that X is the only possible generalization that can conceivably explain the known facts. Normally, scientists do not claim this sort of verification for their generalizations. Normally, they are satisfied to claim that they explain the *known* facts and that they explain them *reasonably well*. The cautious scientist hesitates to predict that no new facts, at present unknown, will ever force modification of his generalizations; and he hesitates, also, to claim that even the known facts are accounted for with rigorously perfect accuracy. Scientists, assaying the scientific quality of their generalizations, are inclined to settle for something less than perfection!

If the scientist is willing to accept hypotheses even though their acceptance is not imposed by rigorous logic, then obviously he is exercising a certain freedom of choice. Acceptance is not imposed by logic,

but the scientist nevertheless does accept the hypothesis because he
judges it useful or illuminating or suggestive or otherwise advantageous
to do so. A value judgment, not strict logic, is the immediate ground
for acceptance. As Rudner has very well said:

Now I take it that no analysis of what constitutes the method of science
would be satisfactory unless it comprised some assertion to the effect that
the scientist as scientist accepts or rejects hypotheses. But if this is so then
clearly the scientist as scientist does make value judgments. For, since no
scientific hypothesis is ever completely verified, in accepting a hypothesis the
scientist must make the decision that the evidence is *sufficiently* strong or
that the probability is *sufficiently* high to warrant the acceptance of the
hypothesis.[9]

It is no answer to this argument to claim that scientists do not accept or
reject hypotheses outright, but merely assign them a certain degree of
probability.[10] To decide that a hypothesis is "probable" involves the
same sort of arbitrariness as to decide that it is "acceptable." Also, one
must remember that, even before making this decision, the scientist
must make a number of preliminary decisions as to "what makes a relevant observation, what controls should be applied in taking observations,
how many observations ought to be made, what 'model' to use as a
framework for observations, and so on." [11]

Thus far we have been discussing only one criterion for the acceptance of scientific hypotheses, namely, agreement with the facts. There
are, however, other legitimate criteria which are used constantly by scientists in making value judgments about scientific quality. Thus, they
may prefer to accept a very succinct and simple generalization which
sums up the known facts reasonably well, rather than a very complicated generalization which represents them somewhat more accurately.
Again, a broad generalization that fits a very wide range of facts fairly
well may be accepted in preference to a narrow one that explains fewer
facts with superior accuracy. Sometimes a hypothesis may prove acceptable because it pictures the facts in a concrete way that appeals to the
imagination; doubtless this was one of the reasons that made the Bohr
atom popular. Sometimes scientists accept a theory because it promises
to be "fertile," that is, to be able to suggest still further theories. All in
all, it is evident that "scientific quality" is not a simple thing. Acceptance of a hypothesis is seldom imposed forcibly by the facts. Normally,
acceptance depends on a series of delicate value judgments.[12]

If even in the physical sciences value judgments condition the acceptance of generalizations, surely this is much more the case in the
social sciences and specifically in sociology. Sociologists labor under
very special difficulties. Very seldom, aside from trivial cases, is the
evidence so clear that it imposes assent. There are many reasons for

this state of affairs—reasons with which every sociologist is familiar. The sociologist's material lacks the homogeneity which facilitates generalization in the physical sciences. If one specimen of lead melts at 327°C., the physicist can assume that another specimen will melt at the same temperature; but a sociologist dares not assume that social stratification in Riverside, California, is similar to social stratification in Portland, Maine. It is wise to assume that every social situation is unique until it is proved otherwise. Again, the sociologist seldom has accurate measurements available; usually, he must fall back on descriptive epithets in contrast to the physicist with his incredibly sensitive measuring devices. Worst of all, the sociologist is constantly haunted by the complexity of social causation. In sociology, simple explanations almost always turn out to be untenable. Seldom, if ever, in the social sciences, will one find the simple sort of functional relationship which connects, for example, the volume, pressure, and temperature of a gas.[13]

One might argue that under the circumstances the only honest thing for the sociologist to do is to forgo generalizing, to confine himself to the collection of facts and hope that a future generation of sociologists may be able to use these facts for the discovery of laws. From the standpoint of abstract logic, this course might be advisable. However, the sociologist lives in a real world where practical decisions must be made, a world in which his advice is constantly sought. Juvenile delinquency is a pressing problem everywhere. Law-enforcement officials must do *something* about it. Even though the sociologist has no comprehensive theory which explains delinquency satisfactorily, he is nevertheless one of those best qualified to suggest a plausible working hypothesis on which a practical program of delinquency control may be based. Under the circumstances, *the sociologist ought to suggest plausible hypotheses concerning delinquency even though they cannot be satisfactorily validated.* The italicized words, of course, are a metasociological value statement. The statement assigns a positive value to the making of less-than-certain sociological generalizations in a certain important area. Probably most sociologists would agree with this value statement, and with other value statements about generalizations in other socially significant areas. In other words, sociologists deliberately choose, for reasons that seem to them sufficient, to adopt relatively lax criteria of scientific quality. They consciously compromise a bit with the ideals of scientific rigor; for they tend to believe that, in our real world, shaky but plausible generalizations about society are better than none at all. If the sociologist set his criteria of scientific quality at too high a level, he would not dare to generalize at all. Setting his standards a bit lower, he can proffer generalizations which, though definitely imperfect, are yet the best available and definitely superior to the ignorant and preju-diced opinions of the man in the street.

FACTORS CONDITIONING METASOCIOLOGICAL VALUE JUDGMENTS

It seems clear that metasociological value judgments condition the content of sociology; but what factors condition these value judgments themselves? This is a question of transcendent importance. If we could answer it, we could trace sociology back to its roots and explain why it is that current systems of sociology are as they are, and not otherwise. We would then be able to understand why we sociologists have chosen to picture society as we actually have pictured it. Then we would be able to criticize sociological systems much, much more realistically than is at present possible.

It is unfortunate that very little empirical research has been carried out in this vitally important area. Something has been written on bias and prejudice; but next to nothing has appeared on the value judgments of the fair-minded and unprejudiced scientist.[14] Such a scientist must inevitably make some value decisions—for reasons hereinbefore men-tioned. Presumably, he does not make them by pure chance. Presum-ably definite motives underlie his choices; yet we are still much in the dark as to what these motives are. However, since the subject is of such extraordinary importance, we shall proceed to review the available in-formation, such as it is. In making this review, it will be convenient to distinguish psychological and social factors and to treat them separately. Obviously, the two sorts overlap; yet, imperfect as it is, the division is convenient for purposes of exposition.

Psychological Factors

Every sociologist is aware that each of his colleagues has his own personal and characteristic approach to the science. It is hard to find two who have precisely the same research interests or two who, being faced with the same problem, would go about solving it in exactly the same way. Face to face with a mass of field data, half a dozen sociolo-gists might well give half a dozen somewhat different interpretations. There are qualities inherent in the individual sociologist which make his research peculiarly his own; for his value choices are not identical with those of others.

Kubie, on the basis of many psychiatrically oriented interviews with scientists, believes that unrecognized neurotic forces in the scientist's own life can be very important in his choice of a profession and can influence the specific manner in which he carries on his research.[15] Instead of being a disinterested search for truth, his investigations may be simply the overt working out of hidden conflicts.

The very choice of sociology as a profession, rather than some alternative, probably reflects a particular type of personality. Becker and Carper interviewed samples of graduate students in philosophy, physiology, and mechanical engineering and found rather striking differences in their ideals, attitudes, and conceptions of their roles in the larger society.[16] It is doubtless true, though empirical evidence is lacking, that students who have chosen sociology as a career differ significantly from other graduate students. It would not be surprising to find, for example, that they have a more intense social idealism. Sociologists wear a protective covering of cold scientific objectivity; but, underneath, a good many of them are social crusaders.

It is hard to classify the ways in which sociologists differ among themselves; but surely one difference must be in their intellectual flexibility. There is the man who holds inflexibly to the system of sociology he studied in graduate school; and there is the man who is always happily devising new theories, the man whose sociology is always in flux. The former's value judgments assign high values to what is tried, tested, and traditional; the latter's value judgments favor what is up to date, on the principle that the progress of science renders last year's sociology antiquated. There exists some psychological research on mental set (*Einstellung*), the inability to abandon a method that has proved itself inappropriate.[17] Although no such research has been carried out on sociologists as such, it seems a fair presumption that they, too, differ in their mental flexibility, their freedom from mental set, their ability to discard familiar mental habits at the appropriate time.

Shaffer has published some research on fundamental attitudes of psychologists, and his findings may be relevant to sociologists as well.[18] He distinguished the *intuitive* attitude—characterized by "the preference for knowing by immediate and direct processes without intervening steps of formal interpretation"—and the *objective* attitude of the scientist who wants the "raw stuff of experience" to be quantified and ordered in neat columns of numerical data which will yield measures of central tendency and variances. After studying a sample of American psychologists, Shaffer concluded that their position on an intuitive-objective attitude scale was closely related to the training they had received and the work they had done, but was not significantly related to "any investigated datum antecedent to entrance in professional training." In other words, it was professional experience, rather than home or social background, that determined the psychologists' attitudes. Fisher and Fisher, however, investigated a closely similar problem with a somewhat different result.[19] They gave a group of 51 graduate students in psychology and a control group of 51 undergraduates a test of intuitive-objective attitude much like Shaffer's and also a test for level of personal anxiety. Their results showed that "the intuitively oriented subjects manifest a higher level of anxiety than those subjects who are objectively oriented." Thus, Fisher and Fisher produced some support for Kubie's thesis that deep-lying conflicts can affect one's scientific attitudes.

Social Factors

Scientific research is a social activity. A particular piece of research may be carried out either by an individual or a team. However, even when a researcher works on his project alone, he consciously builds on the previous work of his colleagues and he knows that they will inevitably pass judgment on his work when it is done. Their judgment is important. Unless they approve, the researcher will find it hard to continue; media of publication will be closed to him, grants-in-aid will not be forthcoming, and promotion will be slow for him within the scientific hierarchy. Then beyond the circle of his colleagues, the scientist is conscious of the larger society. If society disapproves, science itself will languish from lack of support. Research is thus carried on in the midst of social pressures, some subtle, some not so subtle; consciously or unconsciously, the scientist must somehow adjust himself to these pressures if he is to carry on his work.

One very subtle, but very pervasive, social pressure comes from what has been called "the climate of opinion." In every age, certain principles are accepted as self-evident; certain types of evidence are accepted unquestioningly as convincing. Yet that which is taken for granted in one age may seem not only questionable, but positively bizarre in another. It is often difficult to understand sympathetically the reasonings of a long-ago period. In his delightful book, *The Heavenly City of the Eighteenth-Century Philosophers*,[20] Carl L. Becker imagines the soul of Dante summoned up for an interview about the League of Nations, a live topic when Becker wrote. Dante responds with words he actually used in his *De monarchia*. To most modern readers, the words would simply not make sense. Yet Dante was a great intellect, and an influential man in his day. The trouble is not with Dante—or with ourselves. The trouble is that we live in different climates of opinion, and communication between these climates is difficult.

An important group of writers has recognized these facts and sys-

tematized them under the name of *Wissenssoziologie,* awkwardly translated as "sociology of knowledge." Not all writers of the school agree in
detail, but the essence of their theory is that thinkers are deeply influenced by the climates of opinion in which they live. The scientist may
feel that his writings merely reflect objective reality and that his methods
allow no scope for the workings of subjective bias; nevertheless, the pervasive effect of the climate of opinion may influence his work far more
than he suspects.[21]

It is unfortunate that there has been relatively little empirical research to support the viewpoint of the *Wissenssoziologie* school. However, some isolated bits of evidence are available. Sorokin, for instance,
has tried to measure quantitatively the fluctuations in popularity of different systems of truth and knowledge, century by century, since 600
B.C.[22] It is interesting to see how such systems as empiricism, rationalism,
or mysticism ebb and flow. Such systems show vast differences in popularity with the passage of time. What this means is that criteria of truth
accepted in one century are rejected in another. Men living at different
times are convinced by different arguments. Evidence that seems to us
overwhelming would have seemed unimportant to men living five hundred years ago, and may seem unimportant to men living five hundred
years hence. This does not mean, of course, that there exist no objectively valid criteria of truth; but it does mean that men of different centuries disagree as to what these criteria are. This is the central contention
of *Wissenssoziologie.*

Even in the physical sciences, our habitual thoughtways may incline
us to interpret the evidence in one particular way and to overlook alternative interpretations. Thus, Eddington remarks that our ingrained habits
of thought are such "that we shall not rest satisfied until we are able to
represent all physical phenomena as an interplay of a vast number of
structural units intrinsically alike," although "there is nothing in the external world which dictates this analysis into similar units." [23] The sociologist, whose material is vastly more complex and confusing than the
physicist's, has a correspondingly greater leeway for imposing his own
preferred interpretation on it.

Anthropologists have successfully demonstrated again and again the
pervasive influence of culture on the individual. A child born into a certain culture acquires a certain language, learns certain food habits, adopts
a certain manner of dress, and learns to regulate his behavior in accordance with certain folkways and traditional attitudes. This learning goes
on, for the most part, unconsciously. The child does not choose these
particular culture elements because they seem attractive to him. He
adopts them because they are the only ones he has ever heard of; no
alternatives exist for him. Thus, if he is born into a tribe where noble

lineage is the chief ground for social prestige, he simply takes it for granted as true that a certain type of ancestry renders a man superior, and that it is intrinsically more important than wealth or martial valor or intellectual cleverness or any other mark of distinction. If he thinks of the matter at all, he soon convinces himself that his own tribal viewpoint is "natural" and that an alternative viewpoint of another tribe is "queer" or "bizarre."

More recently sociologists have begun to realize that the cultural phenomena noted by anthropologists among primitive tribes are repeated in a fashion among civilized peoples. The modern educated man with his newspaper, his radio, and his proneness to travel is not as culturally isolated as a tribesman living in some remote island; yet to a certain extent and in his own way he may share the latter's cultural narrowness. Even a college graduate may feel that his own nation is intrinsically superior to other nations, that his own social class is intrinsically superior to other social classes, and that his own viewpoint on politics, economics, and things in general is unquestionably the only correct one. Such narrow beliefs and attitudes are reinforced by group support if one moves habitually among men of similar background. After all, men are men everywhere, and cultural influences react on the individual not altogether dissimilarly in New Guinea and in New York.

Sociologists, too, are subject to cultural conditioning. Many of them come to graduate school from a certain type of home background.[24] At least all have been to college and all share certain interests which have attracted them to sociology. A graduate student in a sociological department is a particular sort of person. He is not simply an average American, picked at random out of the crowd. In the graduate school, the selective process is continued. Faculties are self-perpetuating; new members are selected by old members.

The university replenishes its teaching staff from among those students who conform most closely to prevailing standards. The best students are those who do best what their teachers do. For the unconformer, the innovator, the challenger, there is neither tolerance nor support.[25]

Thus, a certain cultural continuity, linking academic generation to academic generation, is assured.

The sociologist who has passed through this selective process, who has received his doctorate and who has obtained a job as a sociologist on a university faculty or elsewhere, finds himself a member of a definite group, namely, the professional sociologists of the country. As such, he joins societies, subscribes to journals, attends meetings, and develops pleasant interpersonal relations with his sociological colleagues. It is very important to him to remain a member in good standing within the group;

his bread and butter may depend on it. If he conforms to the mores and thoughtways of the group, he may be in line for desirable appointments and continued promotions. If he gets a reputation for being erratic, he may be shunted aside to live his life in exile in an undesirable post in some obscure college. It is quite normal for any group to develop social controls to keep its members in line, and groups of scientists do not differ strikingly from other groups in this respect.[26]

One need not imagine that the social control which sociologists as a group exert on individual sociologists is sinister or selfish. Sociologists use pressure to urge one another in the direction of social and scientific ideals to which they are sincerely and unselfishly devoted. By and large, they are ideals which the present writer accepts, and which the reader would quite probably also accept. The point of the present paper is not that group influences on individual sociologists are baleful and deplorable, but merely that they exist, that they significantly influence metasociological value judgments, and that they thus help to determine the content of sociology.

Sociologists tend to be relatively homogeneous in their social philosophy. This homogeneity was illustrated by a study of the value postulates stated or implied in the first five issues of *Social Problems,* the official journal of the Society for the Study of Social Problems.[27] It was found that 63 per cent of all the articles contained some value postulates. Moreover, these value postulates tended to be consistent with one another, to reflect, that is to say, a particular point of view.

Taken together, these value postulates constituted a fairly comprehensive fragment of social philosophy. It was not a complete social philosophy, of course—the sample was too small for that—but it was nevertheless a social philosophy whose general character was clearly discernible.[28]

Generally speaking, the viewpoint expressed in the value postulates of the writers was what one might call "humanitarianism." It was a philosophy which placed a good deal of stress on the dignity of the human person and strongly asserted the right of each man to pursue happiness in his own way. It was a reasonable, tolerant, and kindly philosophy, religiously neutral, and tending to be independent of tradition. The fact that social pathologists tend to share such a philosophy may be accepted as redounding to their credit. It reveals them as kindly, tolerant, understanding persons. Yet, from the standpoint of sheer, rigorous, scientific logic, if ostensibly empirical statements are influenced by a particular philosophical viewpoint, then they are biased statements. We may sympathize with the social pathologists' bias, but bias it nevertheless is!

A couple of concrete examples may illustrate how the humanitarian philosophy may condition the acceptance of sociological generalizations.[29]

Consider first the treatment of the subject of minority groups. The humanitarian philosophy, with its constant sympathy for the underdog, tends to interpret intergroup relations from the standpoint of minority-group members. Certainly most of us would agree that in majority-minority group relations abstract justice is mostly on the side of the minority group. However, one might question whether the empirical evidence justifies the one-sided picture that sociologists present.

None of the theories now current, or any of the factual studies, finds the cause of prejudice in the minority group itself. This is amazing when it is considered that the everyday explanation for prejudice always locates the causes in the minority group. Despite the tremendous diversity among the theories, all of them are in direct opposition to the man-in-the-street's conception of prejudice.[30]

Of course, it is not immediately evident that sociologists are not justified in placing *all* the blame for bad intergroup relations on the majority group. Perhaps the sociologists are *completely* right and the man in the street is *completely* wrong. Yet such a conclusion is a bit suspect. Experience shows that in interhuman relations the fault is seldom completely on one side. It seems that one may reasonably suspect that the fact that both the social pathologists' theories and their factual studies find the causes for intergroup friction entirely on the side of the majority group in all cases may not be due entirely to the objective evidence, but may be due at least in part to a humanitarian philosophy which inclines the social pathologists both to collect and to interpret their facts in a certain specific way.

The sociological treatment of crime and delinquency furnishes another example. Here again, sociologists interpret their data in accordance with the humanitarian philosophy.

Not all writers give exactly the same explanation, but all their accounts do have one striking characteristic in common. All of them tend to shift the blame from the offender himself. A poor home environment may be invoked to explain one case. Bad adjustment in school may be used to explain another. In a third instance the causation may be found deep in the offender's unconscious. . . . Seldom is it admitted that the offender decided freely and in cold blood to commit the crime.[31]

In this case, also, it is not obvious that the sociological view of crime is incorrect. Conceivably, it may be entirely justified. Yet it is worth noting that among those who disagree sharply with sociologists are a good many experienced police officers, judges, and attorneys who are familiar with criminals and their ways. It is worth noting, also, that sociological theories of crime and delinquency have not scored particularly brilliantly on the pragmatic test when they have been applied by law-enforcement agencies. In this area, sociology can point to no success even very remotely comparable to the success of modern medicine in, say, the eradication of yellow fever wherever public-health measures have been vigorously applied.

In an earlier section of this paper, it was shown that value judgments are inevitably involved in the selection and application both of relevance criteria and of criteria of scientific quality for sociology. In other words, it was shown that the acceptance and rejection of propositions by sociologists did not depend entirely on logic, but were conditions, within broad limits, by value choices made by the sociologists themselves. In the present section the attempt has been made to explain why sociologists make the particular value choices which they actually do make. Doubtless the explanation lies partly in the sociologists' individual personality characteristics; each man has his own particular scale of values, his own particular preferences. Yet probably a far greater role is played by group influences. Sociologists do not exist as isolated individuals; they form a group. The sociological group exerts social control over its members. Like other groups, this group too develops common attitudes and common standards from which the deviant individual departs at his peril. As an illustration, it was shown that at least those sociologists who write on social problems share a common social philosophy which may be described as humanitarianism. Suggestive evidence was offered to show how this humanitarianism may influence sociological treatments of the minority-group problems and of the crime problem. One may reasonably suspect that group influences play no small part in shaping the course of American sociology.

STANDARDS FOR METASOCIOLOGICAL VALUE JUDGMENTS

Metasociological value judgments should be derived from definite principles and they should be embodied in explicit value statements. The alert reader will recognize the foregoing sentence as a value statement, and indeed a value statement about metasociology itself. It asserts that certain parts of metasociology should be developed in a certain way, namely, explicitly and on the basis of definite principles. The statement might appropriately be called a "meta-metasociological value statement" because it bears the same relation to metasociology that metasociological value statements bear to sociology.

The value statement of the last paragraph is asserted with some confidence on the basis of human intellectual experience. This experience has shown that we reason more efficiently when both our statements and the ground for our statements are set down explicitly; then they may be examined, reviewed, criticized, and, if necessary, revised. On this basis it seems desirable that metasociologists should set down their value statements explicitly, both those concerning relevance criteria and those concerning criteria of scientific quality, and also that they should set down their reasons for accepting these particular value statements rather than alternative ones. This seems a better procedure than to allow oneself to be influenced by unconscious neurotic forces or by unrecognized group influences.

What the meta-metasociological value statement made above implies concretely will now be discussed, first, as regards the explicitness of value statements and, secondly, as regards their derivation from definite principles.

The Explicitness of Value Satements

It was asserted above that metasociological value judgments should be embodied in explicit value statements. It is currently rather common practice to be explicit about one's relevance criteria. That is to say, writers of systematic treatises on sociology commonly discuss their concept of sociology and quite usually give a formal definition of the science. Thus, the reader can learn what these writers judge to be relevant to sociology as they conceive it. Writers are much less likely to be explicit about their criteria of scientific quality. Most of them at least pay lip service to the abstract ideal of science and perhaps contrast scientific sociology favorably with prescientific speculation about society. Few, however, express their criteria of scientific quality in operational terms. If they were really operationally explicit about their criteria, it would be possible for the reader to apply these criteria to any dubious statement about society and decide unambiguously whether the statement possessed sufficient scientific quality to merit inclusion within the science of sociology. Anyone familiar with the literature will readily recognize that this degree of explicitness is extraordinarily rare among writers on sociological topics. Their value judgments as to the qualities that a truly scientific statement must have are very likely to remain implicit.

The Derivation of Value Statements from Definite Principles

The purpose of the present discussion is exclusively to argue that it is desirable to derive value statements from definite principles and to illustrate what this derivation would involve. It is certainly not the purpose to suggest what these definite principles should be; to attempt to treat the latter topic, even cursorily, would take us too far afield.

The topic will be discussed first as it concerns relevance criteria. The thesis is that it would be desirable for writers not only to set down their concept of the scope of sociology, but also to explain why they judge it preferable to alternative concepts. An example of the contrary procedure is given in the following passage:

Inasmuch as in the present system the dynamic aspects of social relations receive most attention, as they must in any system that is based upon actual observation of interhuman behavior, we may say that scientific sociology concentrates upon actions of approach and avoidance; *tertium in sociologia non datur.*[32]

The authors of this passage present their concept of sociology as though it were the only acceptable one. They seem to be utterly unconscious of the fact that, in choosing their concept, they are merely making a value judgment, merely expressing a preference. Since they do not realize that they are making a value judgment, they naturally do not attempt to justify their preference in the light of reasonable principles.

There are many types of principles that might be invoked to justify one's preference for one set of relevance criteria rather than another, or, equivalently, for one definition of sociology rather than some alternative definition. Thus, one might argue that a good definition should follow the trend of existing definitions because it would be confusing to define sociology in some completely novel and unprecedented way. One might argue that a good definition should not be too inclusive; for, if sociology covers too wide a territory, it must necessarily be superficial. One might argue that a good definition should not be too narrow, either; for a narrow sociology would tend to give a partial and one-sided view of society. These are merely examples of the many principles that can be used as major premises from which to derive relevance criteria for sociology. It is not the purpose of this discussion to comment on the validity of any of these principles. The point of our argument is only that it is better to invoke principles of some sort to justify one's concept of sociology than merely to assert one's concept dogmatically.[33]

So much for relevance criteria; now for criteria of scientific quality. The subject is a tough one and here we can do little more than indicate its scope. The criteria that one chooses will depend on whether one considers sociology to be a pure or an applied science. Most sociologists will state without hesitation that it is a pure science; but they will add that it has important applications. The current opinion seems to be, therefore, that sociology is essentially a pure science, but that it also partakes to some extent of the nature of an applied science.

An applied science exists as a means to an end, as an aid to the accomplishment of some further purpose. To the extent that sociology is an applied science, it exists, presumably, to aid the amelioration of society. A proposition of sociology as an applied science therefore has scientific quality if it can be shown that the proposition is practically helpful in the amelioration of society, on the same principle that a proposition qualifies as a valid proposition of the science of agronomy if it can be shown to be helpful in the practical production of field crops. Criteria of scientific quality applicable to sociology as an applied science would have to be developed on such principles.

In so far as sociology is a pure science, it exists precisely to yield knowledge for its own sake; it is pursued because it helps the student understand society better, gives him a deeper insight into societal phenomena. The metasociologist has the task of making value judgments about the sort of propositions which serve this end efficiently, and then embodying these judgments in value statements about scientific quality. Obviously, the ideal scientific proposition is one known with complete certainty. However, it is often hard to attain complete certainty in propositions about society, and the metasociologist must decide what degree of probability he will tolerate. If he sets his standards too low, his sociology will contain much that is false; if he sets them too high, his sociology becomes meager in content. Obviously, the metasociologist must make difficult decisions.

An ideal scientific statement is very general, like the "laws" of physics. We all know how hard it is to discover important generalizations about society which are universal in their application. We are forced to be content with generalizations of more limited scope, say, those applicable to a particular time and region. Thus, the metasociologist is forced to compromise once more with his scientific ideal and content himself with a limited sort of generalization; but how far shall he compromise? Sociology must not be reduced to a mere list of singular facts. Here, again, is a delicate problem about which the metasociologist has to make value judgments.

There are many other qualities of ideal scientific propositions. Such propositions should be *explanatory;* they should not merely state *that* something occurs, but also *why* it occurs; in other words, they should reveal causal relationships. An ideal scientific proposition should be relatively *simple*. If it is so complex that it is practically unintelligible, it will be no great help in understanding the phenomenon it attempts to describe.

The metasociologist has the task of reviewing all the attributes that endow a proposition with scientific quality and deciding how many of these he can demand for the propositions of sociology. Then he must translate his criteria of scientific quality into practical procedural rules for sociological research, so that the criteria will not remain on a theoretical level, but will be available in such a form that they may be applied in the day-by-day operations of the working sociologist. Only then will the latter know what to look for. Only then will he be able to decide with assurance what is acceptable as genuinely scientific sociology and what is not acceptable.

SUMMARY

This paper has defended the following three propositions: (1) It is impossible to develop the science of sociology without making certain value judgments about the scope of the science and about the qualities that propositions must have if they are to be considered sufficiently scientific to be admissible into scientific sociology. (2) Currently, such decisions are very often made implicitly and without full awareness, very often in response to unconscious neurotic urges or unrecognized group pressures. (3) It is desirable that value judgments of the sort discussed, value judgments affecting the content of sociology, should be made consciously on the basis of definite principles and should be embodied in explicit value statements.

NOTES

1. "It is widely asserted by sociologists, and denied by none, so far as the present writer has discovered, that ethical valuations, ideals, approvals and disapprovals, since they are socially conditioned, and since they influence social behavior and social change, enter in very important ways into the subject matter of sociology, are a proper concern of scientific sociology, and indeed cannot be ignored by the sociologist." Hornell Hart, "Value-Judgments in Sociology," *American Sociological Review,* 3 (December, 1938), pp. 862-67.

2. See Paul H. Furfey, *The Scope and Method of Sociology; a Metasociological Treatise* (New York: Harper & Brothers, 1953), pp. 217-25, for the present author's position on this issue.

3. Furfey, *Scope and Method, op. cit.,* p. 8.

4. Albion W. Small, *General Sociology* (Chicago: University of Chicago Press, 1905), p. 35.

5. "Soziologie ist . . . die Wissenschaft der Staatsmänner und Organisatorem, das ist der *Gesellschaftstechniker.*" Otto Neurath, *Empirische Soziologie* (New York: Springer Publishing Company, Inc., 1931), p. 17.

6. "La Sociologie n'est autre chose que la Psychologie sociale." G. Palante, *Précis de sociologie* (6th ed., Paris: Alcan, 1921), p. 3.

7. Edward B. Reuter, *Handbook of Sociology* (New York: Dryden Press), p. 157.

8. Franklin H. Giddings, *Inductive Sociology* (New York: The Macmillan Company, 1901), p. 7.

9. Richard Rudner, "The Scientist *Qua* Scientist Makes Value Judgments," *Philosophy of Science,* 20 (January, 1953), pp. 1-6.

10. Richard C. Jeffrey, "Valuation and Acceptance of Scientific Hypotheses," *Philosophy of Science,* 23 (July, 1956), pp. 237-46.

11. C. West Churchman, "Science and Decision Making," *ibid.,* pp. 247-49.

12. For a valuable discussion of the topic of this paragraph, see Philipp G. Frank, "The Variety of Reasons for the Acceptance of Scientific Theories," *Scientific Monthly,* 79 (September, 1954), pp. 139-45.

13. On generalizing in the social sciences, see Kyung D. Har, *Social Laws* (Chapel Hill: University of North Carolina Press, 1930), and Robert Brown, "Explanation by Laws in Social Science," *Philosophy of Science,* 21 (January, 1954), pp. 25-32.

14. For a bibliography of the literature on bias and prejudice, see Furfey, *Scope and Method, op. cit.,* p. 176.

15. L. S. Kubie, "Some Unsolved Problems of the Scientific Career," *American Scientist,* 41 (October, 1953), pp. 596-613. See also Rollo Handy, "Personality Factors and Intellectual Production," *Philosophy of Science,* 23 (October, 1956), pp. 325-32.

16. Howard S. Becker and John Carper, "The Elements of Identification with an Occupation," *American Sociological Review,* 21 (June, 1956), pp. 341-48.

17. See especially A. S. Luchins, "Mechanization in Problem Solving: the Effect of Einstellung," *Psychological Monographs,* Vol. 54, No. 6, 1942.

18. Laurance F. Shaffer, "Of Whose Reality I Cannot Doubt," *American Psychologist,* 8 (November, 1953), pp. 608-23.

19. Seymour Fisher and Rhoda Fisher, "Relationship Between Personal Insecurity and Attitude Toward Psychological Methodology," *American Psychologist,* 10 (September, 1955), pp. 538-40.

20. New Haven: Yale University Press, 1932.

21. The classical source is Karl Mannheim, *Ideologie und Utopia* (Bonn: Cohen, 1929), translated as *Ideology and Utopia* (New York: Harcourt, Brace and Company, 1936). See also the same author's article "Wissenssoziologie" in Alfred Vierkandt, ed., *Handwörterbuch der Soziologie* (Stuttgart: Enke, 1939). See also the chapter on "The Sociology of Knowledge" by Merton in Georges Gurvitch and Wilbert E. Moore, eds., *Twentieth Century Sociology* (New York: Philosophical Library, 1945), pp. 366-405.

22. Pitirim A. Sorokin, *Social and Cultural Dynamics* (4 vols., New York: American Book Company, 1937–41). See particularly the graph in Vol. 2, p. 32.

23. A. S. Eddington, *The Philosophy of Physical Science* (New York: The Macmillan Company, 1939), p. 125.

24. C. Wright Mills, "The Professional Ideology of Social Pathologists," *American Journal of Sociology,* 49 (September, 1943), pp. 164-80, shows that this is true of the authors of social-problems textbooks.

25. Eli Ginzberg, "Social Science and the Established Order," *Science,* 107 (June 11, 1948), pp. 607-11.

26. See Furfey, "The Sociologist and Scientific Objectivity," *American Catholic Sociological Review,* 6 (March, 1945), pp. 3-12, for a further development of this topic.

27. Furfey, "The Social Philosophy of Social Pathologists," *Social Problems,* 2 (October, 1954), pp. 71-75.

28. *Ibid.,* p. 71.

29. Furfey, "The Humanitarian Philosophy and the Acceptance of Sociological Generalizations," *American Catholic Sociological Review,* 15 (June, 1955), pp. 117-22.

30. Arnold Rose and Caroline Rose, *America Divided* (New York: Alfred A. Knopf, Inc., 1948), p. 304.

31. Furfey, "The Humanitarian Philosophy and the Acceptance of Sociological Generalizations," p. 120.

32. Leopold von Wiese, *Systematic Sociology,* adapted and amplified by Howard Becker (New York: John Wiley & Sons, Inc., 1932), p. 38.

33. For an extended discussion of principles determining relevance criteria for sociology, see Furfey, *Scope and Method, op. cit.,* chapters 5 and 6.

BIBLIOGRAPHY

CHURCHMAN, C. WEST. *Elements of Logic and Formal Science.* Philadelphia: Lippincott, 1940.

———. *Theory of Experimental Inference.* New York: The Macmillan Company, 1948.

FRANK, PHILIPP G. "The Variety of Reasons for the Acceptance of Scientific Theories," *Scientific Monthly,* 79 (September, 1954), pp. 139-45.

FURFEY, PAUL H. *The Scope and Method of Sociology; a Metasociological Treatise.* New York: Harper & Brothers, 1953.

———. "The Social Philosophy of Social Pathologists," *Social Problems,* 2 (October, 1954), pp. 71-75.

HAR, KYUNG D. *Social Laws.* Chapel Hill: University of North Carolina Press, 1930.

LUNDBERG, GEORGE A. *Foundations of Sociology.* New York: The Macmillan Company, 1939.

NORTHROP, F. S. C. *The Logic of the Sciences and the Humanities.* New York: The Macmillan Company, 1947.

PORTERFIELD, AUSTIN L. *Creative Factors in Scientific Research.* Durham, N.C.: Duke University Press, 1941, part I, "Cultural Factors in Science."

WOODGER, J. H. "The Technique of Theory Construction," *International Encyclopedia of Unified Science,* Vol. 2, No. 5. Chicago: University of Chicago Press, 1939.

17

Theory Construction in Sociology;
A Methodological Inquiry

LLEWELLYN GROSS
University of Buffalo

All discussions of sociological theories and all proposals for constructing such theories must contend with the largely indisputable fact that as yet there are no laws of social behavior in the exact sense in which there are laws of physical behavior. But the general acceptance of this fact does not mean that sociologists are in agreement on how the fact is to be explained. Some hold that laws of social behavior will be discovered when precise methods of measurement are available. Others hold that precise methods of measurement will never be obtained because of an essential indeterminacy that precludes anything more than plausible relationships among social events.

One group of sociologists advocates the use of natural-science assumptions and procedures but in doing so ignores the thought that their achievements are no more than extremely crude imitations of what the natural scientist has done. So far this group has established no fundamental measurements, no empirically based mathematical constants, and no crucial experiments. Thus, they can offer no laws of social behavior that will permit of precise predictions. A second group of sociologists favors procedures that are observationally accurate and phrasable as general patterns of social relationships. They rely heavily on insight, contextual interpretation, and other informal devices for gaining acceptance but overlook the thought that their conclusions are often subjective and therefore beyond the ken of scientific method. The first group is guided

by the faith that a science of social behavior is possible, a faith that is
sustained despite the absence of any well-confirmed law of social behavior. The second group is guided by the faith that carefully interpreted
descriptions of social events will provide greater understanding than any
attempt to imitate the methods of natural science.

Unfortunately, the unescapable actualities of the present state of
affairs are such that no one has found a cosmopolitan principle of justification, be it metaphysical or methodological, which would enable the
student to choose between these two points of view. If the student prefers, he can argue that since we now have sciences of physics, chemistry,
and biology we can eventually expect to have a science of sociology. But
this kind of argument from historical analogy is no more convincing than
its opposite. He might just as well argue that since there has never been
a science of social behavior there never will be. Moreover, if the presence
of universal laws is taken as a criterion of science and the Heisenberg
principle is regarded as an insurmountable obstacle to the attainment of
such laws, then not even physics is a fully developed science. The utiliza-
tions of methods to maximize probable associations among variables become the bases for judging whether or not a subject is scientific. And
then the door is open for interpreting any subject that uses methods designed to report some form of order and regularity as basically scientific.

Despite the common observation that there are no firm answers to
questions about the proper methods and goals of sociology, each contender of one or the other viewpoint holds fast to his prejudices and pro-
clivities. Each is sure that he is working in the right direction and believes
he has good reasons for disparaging the other's achievements. Each sticks
to the narrow groove of his chosen specialty, preferring neither to know
nor to understand those who would pursue a different course. This is
indeed a paradox. Granting the large measure of uncertainty that sur-
rounds the most thoughtful of human endeavors, it is a source of wonder
that so few professional sociologists have searched for fresh alternatives.
With so little substantial knowledge, why haven't more sociologists attempted to combine the perspectives and resources of both approaches?
No doubt there are cultural and psychological obstacles, as well as methodological ones, to account for this situation. Some sort of combined
approach is bound to contain hybrid elements that are objectionable to
those who take one or the other of the positions previously mentioned.
Without well-established cultural precedents and a supporting body of
co-workers, the scholar who would extend the margins of competing approaches by introducing elements from each that are foreign to the other
must be prepared to work against the academic tides. Yet, such a course
appears at present to be the only intelligible departure to the deep-rooted

division that now separates natural scientists from some social scientists and sociologists from one another.

Since the kind of "unification" we have in mind can take several forms and can be expressed in terms of several types of compromises, a reasonably detailed attempt to spell out the direction of our own efforts is in order. This attempt will take as its principal points of departure certain apparent agreements among philosophers of science regarding the meaning of key terms in the conceptual apparatus of science. Throughout our exposition, we will strive to be both elementary and nontechnical, avoiding whenever possible the numerous side issues and areas of dispute that tend to encumber the more specialized discussions of the experts. The exposition will be necessarily brief and incomplete, since a full treatment of the innumerable issues involved would introduce a complexity easily capable of paralyzing any attempt to find new order in the data of sociology. After stating in summary form the main criteria of lawlike statements in science, we will suggest several procedures for theory construction that appear to be of pragmatic value to sociology. Emphasis on pragmatic procedures is justified by the observation that although sociologists often write in an uncompromising idiom and express an uncompromising attitude they are frequently forced to compromise on workable methods.

THE CONCEPT OF EXPLANATION IN NATURAL SCIENCE

In common usage, explanation consists of an answer to the question of why certain phenomena (objects or events) occur. By contrast, the minimum essentials of scientific explanation seem to require specifically (1) a class of general statements that have the form of universal regularities, (2) a class of descriptive statements that refer to particular antecedent conditions, and (3) a class of descriptive statements that refer to particular consequent conditions. The subsumption of "hypotheses" of type (2) under "laws" of type (1) permits of "predictions" of type (3). When statements of type (3) are verified by direct observation statements of types (1) and (2) are said jointly to explain them. Thus, by bringing certain events, occurrences, or states of affairs "under a law" or showing them to be particular instances of a universal regularity, other events, occurrences, or states of affairs are predicted and in this way explained. In some cases, the states of affairs to be predicted are themselves restricted generalizations or limited laws. These may in turn be explained by bringing them under generalizations or laws of wider scope.[1]

Let us illustrate the pattern of explanation by reference to the statement, "All socialized persons are acculturated." Assuming this statement expresses an unexceptional regularity and also that the antecedent statement, "Jones is a socialized person" is true, we can logically assert the consequent "Jones is acculturated." Explanation of the statement "Jones is acculturated" follows as a logical deduction from the conjunction of the two statements, "All socialized persons are acculturated" and "Jones is a socialized person." Similarly, an explanation of the statement "All college graduates are acculturated" can be provided by establishing the truth of the antecedent statement, "All college graduates are socialized persons" and subsuming it under the general law, "All socialized persons are acculturated."

On closer analysis, the structure of the explanatory process is found to be based on the following considerations:

(1) The concept of scientific law is construed to apply to empirically true statements only. It is said that if the concept were applied to highly confirmable statements we would have a relativized concept of law, one subject to the changes of new evidence. Thus, what would be a law on the basis of a given body of information might no longer be a law if the factual truth of that body of information were altered. Admission of the possibility that existing uniformities could be altered amounts to a denial that such uniformities are regular or universal.

(2) The empirical phenomena to which scientific laws refer extend beyond the empirical evidence upon which they are established. Law statements must be nonlimited in scope unless they are derived from some more inclusive law that possesses this characteristic. That is to say, any statement which refers to a finite number of objects or events, all of which have been clearly identified, is not a law. To have predictive power, laws must refer to instances which, though presumed to be finite, have not been empirically examined in their entirety.

(3) Scientific laws do not refer to or designate particular objects or events that are restricted by spatiotemporal location or specialized circumstances except when such laws are deducible from more inclusive laws that do not possess these characteristics. The specific degree, shape, or unique quality of a particular object or event must not be represented in the law invoked to explain it.

(4) In addition to these criteria of scientific laws, there are a number of considerations that pertain to the specific circumstances under which antecedent conditions (hypotheses) and consequent conditions (predictions) can be utilized in the explanatory process. It is said that the particular conditions subsumed under laws must be referable to a definite range of observational sentences. Observational sentences may be directly verifiable, indirectly verifiable, or verifiable "in principle." The latter kinds of sentences are those which would be obtained if certain

technical resources could be utilized to test adequately the events to which they refer. Both the direct and indirect verification of observational sentences are determined by perceptual discriminations, some of which require the assignment of numerical values to objects and events in a restricted spatiotemporal region. Broadly considered and in elliptical language, the verification of observational sentences depends upon semantic rules and co-ordinating definitions, or laws of pointer-coincidence, in terms of which specific operational procedures are interpreted.

The preceding criteria imply that statements of scientific laws are universal in form. They hold regardless of outside influences or conditions, and for this reason pertain to all instances representing a general form or quality. They are meant to symbolize a constant conjunction of characteristics that are capable of repeated exemplification in concrete objects and events, but are not themselves concrete objects or events. They can be constructed by replacing correlations between concrete qualities with values of variables that are expressible as timeless mathematical functions of one another. When mathematical functions are used as laws of explanation, the class of particular statements subsumed under these laws are represented as variables to which specific values can be assigned. From the specific values of a so-called independent variable and the constant of proportionality, the specific values of a so-called dependent variable can be predicted.

THE PROBLEM OF EXPLANATION IN SOCIOLOGY

We have noted that scientific laws refer to regularities among events that are presumed to be repeated without exception. Unfortunately, this degree of regularity has not yet been found for social events. Social events, it appears, are tied together occasionally or frequently, but never invariably. Their associations do not have that essential quality of near certainty that characterizes the laws of natural science. For this reason, sociologists have devoted the larger portions of their efforts to the collection, classification, and correlation of statistical data. But without fundamental measurement, depending as it does upon units that are equal and additive, such correlations have not provided major advances in the scientific explanation of social phenomena. In this light, the assumption that interfering influences are isolated or controlled when variables are correlated within an experimental design is no more justified than the assumption that social phenomena can be explained by a chain of conditional sentences resembling the structure of natural laws. Both the process of designing experiments, in which irrelevant variables are presumed to be isolated, and the process of constructing explanatory schemes, in which supplementary laws are presumed to account for deviations from regularity, are predicated on the belief that the sociologist may legitimately simulate the procedures of natural science. Both proceed from the nonfactual premise that the best way to find order in social behavior is to work "as if" the data before them were amenable to devices that resemble those used in natural science.

In accepting this broad premise, we must recognize that special limitations apply to the observational sentences that would be eligible for subsumption under "social laws." To comply fully with the requirements of explanation as previously described, observational sentences would have to be true for all appropriate times and places. Usually, however, such sentences are accurate only for certain periods in the past, present, or future, or they are verifiable for a given place or area—in "Centerville," parts of one country rather than another, for this social strata rather than that, etc. Sometimes their range of application is so indefinite that it is easy to make the mistake of believing that a particular statement is subsumable under a more general one or, as the case may be, deducible from it, when in truth it is really an instance of something else. Suppose we wish to subsume the statement, "All children are socialized persons" under the lawlike statement, "All socialized persons are acculturated." Are we going to use "age" or "maturity" or some criteria of "humanness" as the range of application for "children"? If we use "age" as a clearer mode of designation, where do we draw the line between those to be included and those to be excluded? Exactly when is a child no longer an infant and not yet an adult? And, if this question is unambiguously settled, are all individuals in the chosen age range "socialized" even though they are idiots, delinquents, schizophrenics, or ferals? Of course, we can say that all except the latter groups are socialized, but this way of handling the difficulty does no more than transfer the problem of adequate designation to the more difficult one of deciding who are or are not idiots, delinquents, schizophrenics, and ferals. Despite such problems, and this one is simpler than most in sociology, we do make decisions and are willing to proceed as though they had some measure of scientific utility. Either implicitly or explicitly we mean to stipulate, sometimes quite arbitrarily, that certain observational sentences do refer to particular kinds of phenomena. At best, such stipulations may be regarded as "inference proposals" or conceptual strategies in accordance with which social events can be chronicled, compared, and colligated.

A second limitation confronting the sociologist relates to the manner in which he usually connects observational concepts to lawlike concepts. In many cases, the sociologist summarizes under one heading a variety of diverse circumstances, states these circumstances as a regular association, and frames them in the form of an explanatory statement. For example, he defines "middle class" by occupational and educational status, life chances, or patterns of consumption, and represents these diverse circumstances by a statement that is cast in the universal form. Now, if we think of a universal statement as expressing a regularity of a given form, this representation is not adequate. It is not a case of the enumeration or characterization of instances all of which belong to an unambiguous logical class or relation, and for this reason does not permit of the deduction of observational sentences from general uniformities. That is to say, from the diverse circumstances mentioned above, so many nonspecific kinds of behavior follow that precise prediction is impossible.

③ A third limitation stems from the fact that any relationship between characteristics that contain identical elements has problematic status as a scientific law. From one viewpoint, two variables that are joined by universal association are conceivably of independent status; we can imagine that they could occur separately in the sense that we are not always compelled to think of the two as conjoined in every possible context. In this notion of scientific law, definitional relationships between terms that are merely nominalistic must be avoided, since such terms are meant to refer to identical phenomena. From a different viewpoint, however, variables related through explicit mathematical functions sometimes perform the same role as certain nominalistic definitions in theory, even when these functional relationships are actually regarded as universal laws. These two viewpoints pose the problem of setting criteria for distinguishing relationships which are lawlike or "real" from those which are primarily nominalistic and for assessing the role such relationships play in a system of theoretical statements. Take, for instance, our simplified statement, "All socialized persons are acculturated." Although we treated this sentence as lawlike, its major terms have a degree of unclarity suggestive of the possibility that socialized and acculturated persons may refer to one and the same range of phenomena. If we say that a socialized person is an individual who acquires group beliefs and customs and the latter are a part of culture, the concepts of socialization and acculturation are linked through identical elements of meaning and therefore possess the qualities of a nominalistic definition.

The problem of how definitions enter into the process of theory construction is closely related to the problem of how would-be laws or principles of inference are to be effected in sociology. Too many studies of correlations among social events are assumed apodictically to apply to a range of events that are clear and definite. Sociologists readily identify the assumption that their events are structured with the assumption that they can specify the form of these structures. Thus, they do not consider issues that bear on questions of whether or not their provisional uniformities refer to events that are temporarily continuous or discontinuous, or assert associations that are primarily those of regular precedences, simultaneities, or sequences. Again, little thought is given to questions of whether or not these uniformities refer to events that have spatial contact or contiguity. As we have stated, such distinctions do not usually play a part in the formulation of universal laws. But, for sociologists, distinctions of this kind may serve as useful reference points or frameworks in terms of which general (boundary) as well as specific (initial) conditions can be approximated. From distinctions of this kind, considerations concerning the scope of social uniformities and the extent to which certain conditions can be manipulated and controlled are brought into clearer focus.

Despite these difficulties, the adoption of a lawlike framework is often all that the sociologist can do. Since he cannot provide uniformities of a given form, he must attempt to impose some kind of form on the presumed uniformities with which he deals. He must substitute practical utility in inference for mathematical exactitude, investigatory rules of behavior for logical necessity and scientific rigor.

We have pointed out that sociological uniformities are either too narrowly or too broadly conceived to fulfill the strictest requirements of science. They either subsume localized conditions that lack general extension to an unrestricted region of space and time or they presuppose a multitude of unspecified conditions that are prohibitive of precise predictions of accompanying events. We can only conclude that the present state of sociological science is such that the linkage of concepts in the explanatory process is loosely ordered and for this reason must often be based on extralogical considerations. If qualities similar to what sociologists sometimes call "plausibility," "insight," and "illumination" seem required to bridge obvious gaps of vagueness and ambiguity, the construction of sociological theories which simulate those of natural science should then be of value. Even though simulated theories of this type prove to be inconclusive, they may be highly suggestive as temporary scaffoldings for later examination and criticism. By placing on trial an arrangement of sentences, many of which have varying degrees of intersubjective or consensual validity, we are in strategic position to increase our knowledge of methodological problems.

THE PROBLEM OF METHODOLOGICAL CRITERIA

The proposal that sociologists explore the possibility of developing criteria of theory construction that resemble those found in methodological analyses of natural science should not be construed as excluding other modes of understanding or other procedural policies. The suggestion that some such approach as the one proposed herein would preclude the possibility of making positive advances within the idiomatic language of ordinary scientific expression is far from our intention. Well-written discourses of the latter type often prove to be highly rewarding from an intellectual standpoint. The present situation is rather more like the following: First, sociology is usually presented in either the professional *1.* idiom of ordinary language or as limited empirical correlations of social data. Second, from the perspective of neopositivist methodology, both *2.* ordinary language and limited empirical correlations of social data do not meet criteria of scientific adequacy. Third, from the perspective of *3.* this same methodology certain crucial problems such as the nature of inductive inference, the character of scientific confirmation, and the role of counter-factual conditionals (if-then statements) remain partially un- *4.* resolved. Fourth, from the viewpoint of the actual behavior of the working natural scientist many of the problems posed by neopositivist methodologists are ignored without appearing to prejudice the outcomes of their research. It is a well-known fact, for instance, that natural scientists construct and test theories and obtain highly useful results without benefit of methodological analyses as the philosopher of science interprets these words. Given these four perspectives, any sociologist who wishes to formulate new criteria of theory construction will have to contend with the seemingly contradictory fact that both the least developed and the most developed of the sciences—sociology and physics—are working without benefit of extensive methodological analyses. In this many-sided context, any one of several choices may be reasonable. Our current preference is to look for independent methodological criteria when pragmatic expediency dictates, but, when such criteria seem inaccessible, our preference is to proceed as if one could produce theories that simulate in intelligible ways those that have been successful in ordering natural phenomena.

In constructing a tentative scheme or format for sociological theory, we will introduce a number of considerations which amount to distinct compromises of the explanatory process that supposedly characterizes the natural sciences. We shall, to begin with, adapt a flexible interpreta- *1.* tion of conditional sentences. We will assume that any explanatory statement can be expressed as a conditional sentence or hypothesis if there is some basis in evidence or customary sociological thinking for believing that its presence as a circumstance would contribute to the probability of its consequence. This means that the linkage between conditional hypotheses and their consequences may vary all the way from approximations of necessary implications as found in scientific laws to approximations of what are here called "decisional" implications. The latter constitute proposed rules of reasoning that are sociologically justified when they provide grounds for professional communication. As such, they are procedural contrivances in terms of which empirical events are conceptually ordered and prepared for critical examination.

2   Secondly, we will express our sociological generalizations in the categorical form as a reminder that they are admitted to have evidential grounding in a restricted region of observations. Despite the common use of both large and small sample statistics, verification of the relevance of statistical parameters for establishing unrestricted generalizations remains a task for the future. This does not mean that such generalizations cannot be easily restated as conditional sentences, with functions analogously similar to laws of uniformity in natural science. A fuller discussion of our use of "conditional sentence" and "generalization" will be presented somewhat later in the paper.

3   A third major compromise concerns the manner in which our sociological hypotheses, generalizations, and consequences are selected. Whereas we attempt to delete from the idiom of professional discourse many superfluous and redundant words, we do retain those logically unnecessary terms that seem responsive to customary usage, including those types of peripheral meanings that are familiarly found in the writings of sociologists. To achieve generality and avoid discursiveness, we will ignore the minor details of description available in the more adequate observational reports. To maintain awareness of specialized contexts and useful kinds of extralinguistic meanings, we will adopt a lenient view of logical cogency. This means acceptance of logically incomplete schematizations and, when necessary, heuristic devices that offer no more than programmatic clues to future lines of inquiry. Admitting that tests of logical validity are often inapplicable or inconclusive, we shall nonetheless hold the rules of logic in mind; whenever possible, we will attempt to explain logically what we are saying while we are saying it. By observing these principles, we hope to escape the kind of ambiguity that is nurtured by the inclusion of irrelevant words in scientific writing. To be sure, we will still find it convenient to interpret some of our words ambiguously. For, like other sociologists, we must recognize that ambiguity is inherent in most applied abstraction; that we can sometimes have a definite sense for a word without being able to say it refers to one thing rather than another. As a result, we will have to sacrifice some degree of precision and elegance in logical formulation. But what we lose in the latter respect we hope to gain in ease of understanding and intellectual satisfaction.

The sociological theorist who can bear the uncertainties imposed by conceptually unfinished schematizations may achieve some measure of the rigor common to logical discourse and of the adequacy found in sound empirical research. Of greater significance, he may find himself in strategic position to arbitrate differences between theorists and empiricists. When the conclusions of empirical research are subject to dispute, the theorist is often asked to render a decision. When theory itself is rocked with controversy, resolution is sought in empirical research. Who now can be of assistance when both theory and empirical research become infirm? Will it not be the student who has attempted to steer a middle course between the two? But whoever attempts to bring theory and empirical research together will have to invent methods for making inferences more exact without sacrificing observational pertinence. This is the central assumption of our preliminary inquiry. The method proposed by this inquiry attempts to integrate a cumulative body of empirical observations with successively higher orders of conditional sentences, each of which possesses increasingly greater degrees of adequacy and coherence. In applying this method we have chosen to utilize the content and underlying data of E. H. Sutherland's widely read volume, *White Collar Crime*.[2] As a pioneering study based on sustained knowledge of group behavior it appears eminently suited to provide a sound empirical foundation for the present venture.

PROBLEMATIC SITUATIONS

The incipient beginnings of theory construction may arise at any time or place in which there is at least one intelligently responsive individual confronted by a problematic situation.[3] The concept "problematic situation" suggests, among other things, the clear commitment by some observer to the desirability of transforming presumptive knowledge about a situation into either *explanatory* or *instrumental knowledge* of that situation.[4] The desire for *explanatory knowledge* is founded on the value judgment that testable knowledge of the actual occurrence and conjunction of certain events should be obtained. The desire for *instrumental knowledge* is founded on the value judgment that testable knowledge of how to control (produce, alter, or eliminate) certain events should be obtained. The character of the two kinds of value judgments determines the appropriateness of any such procedures as are tried and adapted. If *explanatory knowledge* is sought, the "simple form" of conditional sentence can be used as a prototype. This form states that certain phenomena behave in certain ways under certain conditions. If *instrumental knowledge* is sought, the more "complex forms" of the conditional sentence can be used as a prototype. These forms state that certain phenomena behave in certain ways under certain conditions *when certain acts or operations are performed upon them or introduced within them*.[5] In the light of Sutherland's adverseness toward interpreting the purpose of his book, *White Collar Crime,* as a suggestion of "what ought to be done," [6] this essay will be confined to an examination of the simple form of conditional sentence.

To delineate the scope and constituents of his problematic situation, Sutherland undoubtedly found it necessary to "experiment" with a number of conceptual schemes and, during the process, to break away from intellectual habits of long academic standing. The perspectives of earlier criminologists led them to conceive of the problematic situation of crime in terms of the ingredient of punishment. As a consequence, cases which Sutherland labels "white collar crime" were excluded from consideration. Sutherland contended that for purposes of a theory of criminal behavior the issue of punishment per se was irrelevant. By substituting the notion of *punishability* for punishment, he was able to include such new categories of cases as acts in violation of antitrust and N. L. R. laws. By taking account of the influence of "variations in administrative procedure," he was able to relate categories of cases that earlier criminologists had set apart and treated as different orders of phenomena. Thus, Sutherland appears to have made a deliberate effort to expand the boundaries of the criminological problem, as previously understood, to the point where they would include certain "essential but superficially dissimilar instances." [7] The result was a redefinition of the problematic situation in accordance with the new knowledge ascertained from a reconstructed analysis of it. [8]

In pursuing their objectives, both Sutherland and his predecessors utilized certain "summarizing" words and statements of relatively high abstraction to designate categories of criminological cases. In Sutherland's study, the summarizing words "ordinary crime" are, by definition, co-ordinate with murder, assault, burglary, robbery, sex offenses, and public intoxication. The latter categories are in turn co-ordinate with empirical sentences descriptive of observations made on boys and girls, frontier and city peoples, slum and nonslum residents, immigrant and nonimmigrant groups apart from their respective states of prosperity. [9] The co-ordination of categories of cases that fall within the scope of successive orders of summarizing words permits of an increasingly discriminate designation of problematic instances to the point where no relevant ingredient is overlooked. In principle, Sutherland contended that any criminological theory which omits the preceding categories of cases, as does the theory which places primary emphasis upon poverty, fails to deal with all the relevant instances of its problematic situation.

CONDITIONAL SENTENCES AND PROBLEMATIC
SITUATIONS

We have seen how summarizing words and co-ordinating definitions (or definitions by equivalent statement) can be used to specify
the range of cases or instances included within the scope of a problematic situation. But specification and clarification of instances is only
a beginning step. For purposes of explanation, the major terms (e.g.,
white collar crime) used in designating the scope of a problematic situation can be effectively expressed in sentences of the conditional form.
We indicated earlier that conditional sentences state that certain phenomena behave in certain ways under certain conditions. In logical
usage, a conditional sentence is an instance of any hypothetical proposition that may be expressed in the form, "If *A* is *B*, then *A* is *C*" or
"If *A* is *B*, then *C* is *D*." Thus, the assertion of the consequence "*A*
is *C*" is based on whatever rational grounds are available for asserting
the antecedent. The antecedent asserts that "*A* is *C*" only under certain
conditions; in the above case, specifically that "*A* is *B*." It does not
mean to assert that other conditions may not account for the consequence "*A* is *C*." When other conditions are known and not usually
taken for granted, it is assumed that they too should be made explicit
and definite. In this way, a chain of conditional clauses may be constructed. If such a chain can be shown to interlock so that every clause
is both a condition and consequence for every other, then a scientific
system becomes possible. In the miniature system above, this requirement would be met if we could prove the truth of the sentences, "When
A is *B*, then *A* is *C*" and "When *A* is *C*, then *A* is *B*."

The conditional sentence therefore makes explicit the requirement
that there be grounds for an assertion even though not all of these
grounds may be stated. It suggests a more essential and durable kind
of relationship between occurrences or events than is connoted by our
use of the term "generalization." In our usage, a generalization will
refer to the kind of categorical proposition that describes what has been
actually observed and enumerated under limited circumstances: to relationships between objects and events that happen to appear together.
This meaning of "generalization" will serve as a reminder that sociological statements are based on observations of a definite number of
objects or events at a particular time and place and have limited application.

To say that a conditional relationship is more durable or essential
than a generalization amounts to saying that it *could* hold anywhere
and at any time by virtue of the "very nature" or fixed structure of

natural phenomena. To say that the possession of one characteristic requires or necessitates the possession of another characteristic implies that what is true of all observed objects or events will be true of all as yet unobserved objects or events. Thus the actual function of a conditional sentence is to go beyond the individual qualities or characteristics of things, each of which is separately observed, to a general type or universal class. Of indefinite extent, this general type or universal class supposedly constitutes a system of relationships that are invariant. Objects and events are no longer particular individuals possessing specific characteristics or qualities that have observational locus, but representations of a type which is describable by generic qualities alone.

Just as our use of the word "generalization" will serve to remind us of the limitations of empirical studies in sociology, so the phrase "conditional sentence" will suggest the aims and potentialities of a simulated natural science of sociology. In methodological accounts of natural science, conditional sentences of the type described above are often fictionized and thus contrary to or different from the actual way in which events are found to be related. It is often said, for instance, that *if* a particular thing possessed a given quality *then* it would possess some other quality even when no cases have been observed of that particular thing possessing the given quality. In view of the indeterminate character of conditional sentences, the absence of clear criteria for assessing them, and our objective of constructing theories that have some of the appurtenances of natural science, we shall adopt a pragmatic view of the role of such sentences. Until the precise meanings of conditional sentences have been resolved by analytic philosophers, the sociologist is at liberty to use them in whatever way seems most congenial for his purposes.

It is undoubtedly true that in sociological usage conditional sentences do not express relationships of either logical implication or universal regularity. They do appear to be regarded as highly probable hypotheses possessing some degree of extra-inductive or counter-factual validity. When viewed as "conditional hypotheses" they rest upon empirical generalizations which are in turn assumed to possess high probability. Such generalizations, it seems, are usually meant to express the association of one class of attributes or variables with another class of attributes or variables. Evidence for this interpretation is seen in the common-sense expression, "If white collar criminals attempt to increase their gains, then they will attempt to secure price uniformities *because* gains are increased when price uniformities are secured." Here the "because phrase" is the simple generalization through which the particular consequence is inferable from the conditional hypothesis.

With these distinctions in mind, there seems to be no more appropriate point of departure for our analysis than Sutherland's own definition:

White collar crime may be defined approximately as a crime committed by a person of respectability and high social status in the course of his occupation.[10]

In its present form, this passage cannot fulfill the role of a conditional hypothesis capable of integrating lower-level hypotheses and empirical generalizations. For theoretical purposes, it will be useful to transform the passage, as an indicative statement, into a statement of the conditional form, and to interpret its constituent concepts in such a way as to make each of them as explicit and determinate as possible. The latter objective may be accomplished by examining the connotations of the larger context in which the passage falls, and then introducing substitute or additional concepts and phrases when advantageous.

We submit the following as the best of a number of attempted reformulations of the passage in question:

Hypothesis *A* . . . (If) White collar criminals are people of high social status and power who consistently use the most expedient means available to maximize their possession of scarce goods.[11]

The most noticeable variations of this passage from the earlier one include the substitution of "criminals" for "crime"; of "power" for "respectability"; and of the phrase, "to maximize their possession of scarce goods," for "course of occupation." To these changes, we have added the largely implicit notion of a hierarchy of expedient means. In its new form, the statement comes close to being a kind of compound hypothesis (complex of interdependent hypotheses) which may serve in the capacity of antecedent "if clauses" for explaining consequential "then clauses" (lower order hypotheses and generalizations).

In the following analysis, all generalizations linking antecedent "if clauses" to consequential "then clauses" are assumed to be true on the basis of Sutherland's data. They are introduced here as illustrations of the kind of structural ordering that can be made explicit when logical cogency and empirical confirmation are sought.[12] In conjunction with generalizations resembling those listed below, "if clauses" can be said to offer plausible explanations for "then caluses." In addition, the analysis attempts to show how certain higher level consequences may be taken to function as hypotheses for sentences obtaining on successively lower levels of abstraction.

By remaining largely within Sutherland's framework, the probable truth of hypothesis *A* can be viewed as dependent upon the truth of generalizations of the following type which stand in the relationship of *evidence* to it:

Generalization 1 linking . . . . . (And)   The most expedient means for maxi-
A with *B*.   mizing scarce goods are acts which
    establish price uniformity and price
    discrimination.

Consequence *B* . . . . (Then)   White collar criminals act to establish
    price uniformity and price discrimina-
    tion.[13]

Generalization 2 linking. . . . . (And)   The most expedient means for maxi-
A with *C*.   mizing scarce goods are acts which
    annihilate competitors (when price
    uniformity and price discrimination
    are not available).

Consequence *C* . . . . (Then)   White collar criminals act to annihi-
    late competitors.[14]

Hypothesis *A* and . . . . (If)
Generalization 2.

Generalization 3 linking . . . . . (And)   The most expedient means for anni-
A and 2 with *D*.   hilating competitors are acts which re-
    duce their sales and increase their
    costs.

Consequence *D* . . . . (Then)   White collar criminals act to reduce
    competitors' sales and increase their
    costs.[15]

Consequences *B* and *C* . . . . (If)

Generalization 4 linking . . . . . (And)   The most expedient means for estab-
B and *C* with *E*.   lishing price uniformity and price dis-
    crimination and for annihilating com-
    petitors are private systems of justice.

Consequence *E* . . . . (Then)   White collar criminals act to establish
    private systems of justice.[16]

Consequence *E* . . . . (If)

Generalization 5 linking . . . . . (And)   The most expedient means for estab-
E with *F*.   lishing private systems of justice are
    policies of regimentation, bureauc-
    racy, and snooping.

Consequence *F* . . . . (Then)   White collar criminals act to estab-
    lish policies of regimentation, bu-
    reaucy, and snooping.[17]

This sample analysis of the manner in which hypotheses and consequences may be linked through the use of empirical generalizations
is based upon Sutherland's discussion of "Restraint of Trade," the first
chapter in *White Collar Crime*. The same general type of analysis,
omitted because of space limitations, can be applied to other chapters

in this book—those treating of "Rebates," "Patents," "Trademarks and Copyrights," "Misrepresentations and Advertising," "Unfair Labor Practices," "Financial Manipulations" and "War Crimes." [18]

RESTATEMENT OF SUTHERLAND'S HYPOTHESES

The hypotheses that Sutherland develops for explaining his data are those of "differential association" and "social disorganization."

According to the hypothesis of differential association, "Criminal behavior is learned in association with those who define such behavior favorably and in isolation from those who define it unfavorably, and that a person in an appropriate situation engages in such criminal behavior if, and only if, the weight of the favorable definitions exceeds the weight of the unfavorable definitions." [19]

Viewed in its larger context the hypothesis of differential association seems to imply the following:

1. Those who learn criminal behavior associate with people who define criminal behavior in a favorable way. (The theory does not treat of differences in response among persons who assume the role of either exemplars or imitators of criminal behavior.) [20]

2. Favorable and unfavorable definitions can be objectively apportioned, i.e., some reliable estimate can be made of their qualitative strength if not of their quantitative value. (There is no indication of whether weight is to be determined by the frequency, number, type, or intensity of association.) [21]

3. Situations vary in appropriateness for criminal behavior and reliable estimates can be made of this. (There is no explicit indication of the criteria to be used in defining an appropriate criminal situation, though such criteria may possibly be inferred from the author's context.)

It is apparent from this tentative analysis that Sutherland's terms and definitions are amenable to more rigorous formulation. If it were our main intention to substantiate his theory of criminal behavior, it would be proper at this point to implement these terms and definitions by supplying specific content for each of them. It will be sufficient for present purposes, however, to indicate that though the term "association" is not explicitly defined one may gather from the use to which Sutherland puts it in his case materials that it refers to more than social contact or physical proximity. The term appears to include direct exemplification and indoctrination of definitions favorable to crime and even coercion of behavior on the part of groups of persons whose status is at least equal to and probably superior to that of their newly inducted members.[22]

Turning to social disorganization, Sutherland finds that it "may be either of two types: anomic or the lack of standards which direct the behavior of members of a society in general or in specific areas of behavior; or the organization within a society of groups which are in conflict with reference to specific practices." [23] The author recognizes that precise definitions of his concepts are wanting and that they cannot be tested for validity. However, he does present a quasi-historical analysis of the conditions upon which the concepts are seen to depend. Like the hypothesis of differential association, these conditions can be shaped into something approximating an explicit analytical scheme. The following conditions seem to be the ones upon which Sutherland based his hypothesis of social disorganization: (1) Complexity, technicality, and unobservability of business behavior by inexperienced citizens; (2) survival within society of the ideology of free competition and enterprise as regulators of business; (3) lack of consensus on the part of the public and the government regarding the value of social planning for the whole of society; (4) lack of organization on the part of the public and the government for the enforcement of laws designed to regulate business; (5) consensus on the part of businessmen regarding the value of social planning in the interest of businessmen; (6) organization on the part of the public and the government for defining specific acts of business organizations as illegal; (7) organization by businessmen for the violation of laws designed to regulate business in the interests of the whole of society.

Conditions number 2 and 5 are extracted from Sutherland's discussion of the effect of free competition and enterprise on the developing system of private collectivism and government regulation of business. These conditions, together with condition number 1, suggest the presence of anomie or lack of standards within society. Likewise, the joint occurrence of conditions number 3 and 6 on the one hand, and conditions number 4 and 7 on the other hand, suggest the presence of differential social organization or conflict of standards within society.

AN EXPLANATORY SCHEME FOR CRIME

Having extracted the main ingredients from Sutherland's "hypotheses" of differential association and social disorganization, certain building blocks are available for constructing a tentative explanatory scheme or "theoretical model." If the hypotheses of the scheme proposed herein prove to be reasonably adequate, they will incorporate many of the ingredients of Sutherland's hypotheses, explain most forms of crime, including "ordinary crime," and will enable the criminologist to predict or to forecast reliably the types of criminal behavior that can be expected in problematically relevant situations.

For each hypothesis, the conditional prefix (If) is assumed.

Scheme I

Hypothesis 1. *In society X upper- and lower-status groups place primary value on the acquisition of scarce goods.*

This hypothesis provides a definite focus for Sutherland's emphasis upon the ideology of free competition and enterprise (condition No. 2) as a factor in crime. It defines the starting point in "locating those factors which, being common to crimes of the rich and the poor, are more significant for a general theory of criminal behavior." [24]

Hypothesis 2. *In society X upper- and lower-status groups possess respectively greater and lesser amounts of scarce goods.*

This hypothesis respecifies one of Sutherland's distinctions between white collar crime and ordinary crime, viz., differences in status and respectability. (Cf. Sutherland's definition of white collar crime.)

Hypothesis 3. *In society X upper- and lower-status groups separately associate to enlarge their means of acquiring scarce goods.*

This hypothesis defines the condition of anomie within which differential association and conflict of standards give rise to definitions favorable to criminal behavior. (Cf. our restatement of Sutherland's "conditions" for anomie and conflict of standards in society.)

Hypothesis 4. *In society X upper- and lower-status groups separately seek to enact laws which enlarge their means of acquiring scarce goods.*

This hypothesis defines the principal area in which conflict of standards occurs. It is derived in part from a reinterpretation of conditions number 5 and 6.

Hypothesis 5. *In society X upper- and lower-status groups possess respectively greater and lesser degrees of power to violate laws which restrict their means of acquiring scarce goods.*

This hypothesis is supported in part by condition number 7 and Sutherland's statement that "persons of the upper socioeconomic class are more powerful politically and financially and escape arrest and conviction to a greater extent than persons who lack such power, even when equally guilty of crimes." [25]

Generalization 1. (And) *The greater the amount of scarce goods possessed by a group, the greater its success in acquiring new increments of scarce goods.*

Consequence 1. (Then) *Upper-status groups have greater success than lower-status groups in acquiring new increments of scarce goods.* (By hypothesis 2 and generalization 1)

Generalization 2. (And) *When groups separately associate to enlarge their means of acquiring scarce goods, each finds it expedient to oppose the means used by the other to acquire scarce goods.*

Consequence 2. (Then) *Upper- and lower-status groups find it expedient to oppose the means used by the other to acquire scarce goods.* (By hypothesis 3 and generalization 2)

Generalization 3. (And) *The higher the social status of a group, the more successful it is in enacting laws which enlarge its means of acquiring scarce goods.*

Consequence 3. (Then) *Upper-status groups are more successful than lower-status groups in enacting laws which enlarge their means of acquiring scarce goods.* (By hypothesis 4 and generalization 3)

Generalization 4. (And) *The greater a group's power to violate laws which restrict its means of acquiring scare goods, the more frequently it violates such laws.*

Consequence 4. (Then) *Upper-status groups more frequently violate laws which restrict their means of acquiring scarce goods than do lower-status groups.* (By hypothesis 5 and generalization 4)

Definition 1. *White collar crimes are legal violations committed by upper-status groups.*

Definition 2. *White collar criminals are members of upper-status groups.*

Definition 3. *Ordinary crimes are legal violations committed by lower-status groups.*

Definition 4. *Ordinary criminals are members of lower-status groups.*

Definition 5. *The power to violate laws is synonymous with the power to escape punishment.*

Consequence 5. (Then) *Both ordinary and white collar crimes are legal violations committed by groups that place primary value on the acquisition of scarce goods.* (By hypothesis 1 and definitions 1 and 3)

Consequence 6. (Then) *White collar crimes are legal violations committed by groups possessing greater amounts of scarce goods.* (By hypothesis 2 and definition 1)

Consequence 7. (Then) *Ordinary crimes are legal violations committed by groups possessing lesser amounts of scarce goods.* (By hypothesis 2 and definition 3)

Consequence 8. (Then) *White collar criminals have greater success than ordinary criminals in acquiring new increments of scarce goods.* (By consequence 1 and definition 2)

Consequence 9. (Then) *Both white collar and ordinary criminals find it expedient to oppose the means used by each other to acquire scarce goods.* (By consequence 2 and definitions 2 and 4)

Consequence 10. (Then) *White collar criminals are more successful than ordinary criminals in enacting laws which enlarge their means of acquiring scarce goods.* (By consequence 3 and definitions 2 and 4)

Consequence 11. (Then) *White collar criminals more frequently violate laws which restrict their means of acquiring scarce goods than do ordinary criminals.* (By consequence 4 and definitions 2 and 4)

Consequence 12. (Then) *White collar criminals have greater power to escape punishment than ordinary criminals.* (By hypothesis 5 and definitions 2 and 5)

The preceding consequences are among those which follow from one or another combination of the scheme's hypotheses, generalizations, and definitions. By tampering more liberally with Sutherland's language and paying less attention to the continuity of our hypotheses with those of his, we could construct a somewhat more elegant scheme than the one presented. With greater liberty to introduce new ideas, it is likely that other conceivable arrangements of sentences would prove more useful for theory construction. Consider, for example, a possible relationship between hypotheses 2 and 5. Hypothesis 5 could be deduced as a consequence of both hypothesis 2 and the generalization, "Any group that possesses greater amounts of scarce goods possesses greater degrees of power to violate laws." Similarly, if the generalization "Whenever groups associate to enlarge their means of acquiring scarce goods, they seek to enact laws for this purpose" is admissible, then hypothesis 4 can be deduced as a consequence of this generalization and hypothesis 5.

It should be noted again that the consequences of this type of scheme can perform the role of hypotheses in the deduction of new consequences. Take as an important illustration consequence 2. If we accept this consequence and the generalization that "Restraint of trade is a means used by upper-status groups to acquire scarce goods," then we can further conclude that "lower-status groups will find it expedient to oppose restraint of trade." In this way, numerous conclusions, including those taken from Sutherland's chapter on "Restraint of Trade," can be derived by linking appropriate empirical generalizations to hypotheses expressible within the scheme. Such a procedure tests the scheme's fruitfulness, and when, in addition, independent data can be shown to offer direct verification, confidence in its adequacy is increased. In this connection, a recent study by Aubert is worth mentioning. Aubert stresses the desirability of handling crime and punishment "as two aspects of a group process or two links in a specific type of social interaction"; of knowing "the location and scope of the groups supporting the legislation, the function it serves in those groups, and the social norms it is based upon." He states, moreover, that crimes are frequently committed by persons who give each other social support and that white collar criminals are usually a group with considerable economic and political power.[26] These assumptions are in close consistency with those found in our scheme. The only apparent divergence between our scheme and his stems from the latter's emphasis upon the ambivalent attitudes held by businessmen and legislators, a point similar to the one suggested as a proposed hypothesis in the following paragraph.

The hypotheses of Scheme I constitute a system of (socio-) logically related sentences. They are structured in such a way as to resemble the broader requirements of a postulate system. These requirements consist of a class of classes (a society of groups); of class properties (amounts of status, power, scarce goods) and of a number of relational variables. On the negative side, it must be emphasized that such hypotheses merely simulate the postulates found in a fully axiomatized scientific theory, where content is of lesser concern. We have provided no specification of the range of instances or values subsumable under them, and we can offer no demonstration of the presence of universal associations among them. At best, they may be regarded as uniformities of exceedingly limited scope. Were our hypotheses purely formal—more like postulates— we would want to apply tests of completeness, independence, and consistency—the alleged criteria of rigorous systems. To approximate *completeness,* certain statements that are but implicit in the present formulation would have to be made explicit. For instance, since there are no statements in the above scheme to account for the intuitive notion that both high- and low-status groups may support the enactment of the *same* laws, one or more additional hypotheses could be developed from the following assumption:

In society X, laws of type L are supported by both upper- and lower-status groups because they are believed by each to limit the power of the other to enlarge its means of acquiring scarce goods.

The introduction of additional hypotheses and definitions would not, of course, guarantee the completeness of the scheme. In some cases, further additions may even be a hindrance from the standpoint of the scheme's fruitfulness. To approximate *independence,* the present scheme would have to be revised. From this scheme, numerous deductions would have to be made to provide reasonable assurance that no single hypothesis could be derived as a logical consequence from the others. A broad range of deductions would, at the same time, uncover any contradictory elements within the scheme and thereby tend to establish its *consistency.*

It is possible that our hypotheses could be simplified or rephrased without sacrificing logical cogency or empirical significance. No doubt, they could be expressed in shorter form, though with less total economy, by presenting them in sentences comprised of simpler subject and predicate terms. We could, moreover, add a number of definitions to the theoretical scheme. For example, something like "Scarce goods are goods with demand-supply ratios in excess of unity." Co-ordinating definitions of the latter kind pointing toward lower levels of abstraction are helpful in clarifying ambiguous points of empirical application.[27] It is likely also that explicit definitions of the concepts "status groups," "scarce goods," and particularly "power" in a metalanguage which has its conceptual origin outside of our theoretical scheme would be of aid to both novice and critic.[28] However, this more complete, not to say finished, formulation, would *at the present stage of inquiry* create a premature sense of exactness, an attitude of certainty hardly warranted by the available data in social science. Perhaps the concept of "power" *should* possess a measure of ambiguity sufficient to allow of the rapid realignment of theoretical frameworks to new discoveries in empirical phenomena. The definition of any term, then, could be justifiably omitted when more than one of its meanings is conceivable within the scheme of interrelated statements constituting a theoretical system and at least one of its meanings is known and understood by the professional reader.

DEDUCTION OF HYPOTHESES FROM SCHEME I

Sutherland indicates that the usual interpretation of crime "includes the ordinary violations of the penal code, such as murder, assault, burglary, robbery, larceny, sex offenses, and public intoxication" [29] and further insists that the customary explanations of criminal behavior "which take their data from poverty and the conditions related to it are inadequate and invalid," the main reason being that they "do not consistently fit the data of criminal behavior." [30] Briefly stated, this data includes differences in percentage of boys and girls adjudged delinquent; the lower rates of delinquency and adult crime among frontier groups and certain groups residing in slum areas (e.g., Chinese colonies); the relatively lower rate of crime among peasants as compared to immigrant groups living in American cities; and the lack of significant association between depressions and crime rates.[31]

The crucial question then becomes: Will the theory of Scheme I provide a more adequate explanation of the data of criminal behavior than the "theory of poverty"? Let us explore this possibility. The theory states, among other things, that crime occurs when upper- and lower-status groups place primary value on the acquisition of scarce goods and when there is separate association by each group to enlarge their own and oppose the other's means of acquiring such goods. It may be inferred from these hypotheses that whenever any two groups differ in the degree to which they possess the characteristics designated by them such groups will differ in their rates of criminal behavior. Now it is a matter of common observation that the institutional roles of males and females are not the same. Since females are often dependent for financial support and leadership upon males, they are not strongly motivated toward the acquisition of scarce goods. Moreover, they do not separately associate to oppose males or other females in accordance with varying degrees of power. Hence, we would expect the crime rate of females to be low. In a similar vein, the lower rates of crime among frontier groups may be explainable in terms of any one or all of the hypotheses in our constructed scheme. Among frontier groups we do find appreciable degrees of agreement on the primary value of scarce goods. Nevertheless, marked differences in possession of scarce goods are lacking; association among opposition groups is infrequent; and there is reluctance to enact laws defining criminal behavior. When we turn to Chinese colonists and other immigrant groups in America, we find that their behavior is governed by communal norms that emphasize intragroup solidarity rather than the acquisition of scarce goods as a primary value. Finally, the absence of a significant association between crime rates and depressions may be explained by the possibility that the hypotheses emphasized by our scheme are as a group neither more nor less operative in one economic period than in another.

The informal hypotheses of the preceding paragraph can be presented in the same quasi-logical way that we presented Sutherland's materials on restraint of trade. But before offering a specific illustration we must again remind the reader that the mode of expression chosen to state these hypotheses represents a linguistic compromise. In style of formulation, our expressions fall somewhere between the precision of formal language and the fluidity of ordinary discourse. Moreover, since the hypotheses of our scheme are loosely organized, appropriate empirical generalizations may approximate the scheme in varying degrees. This means that all deductions of consequences are necessarily exploratory and tentative. Assuming, then, that the following specialized hypotheses and underlying generalizations rest upon factual observations and provide adequate empirical content for our general hypotheses, we may conclude that the crime rate of females is low:

From Hypothesis 1. (If) In female society, upper- and lower-status groups do not place primary value on the acquisition of scarce goods.

Linking Generalization. (And) Whenever upper- and lower-status groups do not place primary value on the acquisition of scarce goods, the crime rate is low.

From Hypothesis 3. (If) In female society, upper- and lower-status groups do not separately associate to enlarge their means of acquiring scarce goods.

Linking Generalization. (And) Whenever upper- and lower-status groups do not separately associate to enlarge their means of acquiring scarce goods, the crime rate is low.

From Hypothesis 4. (If) In female society, upper- and lower-status groups do not separately seek to enact laws which enlarge their means of acquiring scarce goods.

Linking Generalization. (And) Whenever upper- and lower-status groups do not separately seek to enact laws which enlarge their means of acquiring scarce goods, the crime rate is low.

(Then) In female society the crime rate is low.[32]

In the preceding scheme, hypotheses 1, 3 and 4 alone are used as a basis for deducing the "low" criminality of women. Hypotheses 2 and 5 appear to be applicable and consistent with the occurrence of crime. To apply the hypotheses as a group, we must assume that each hypothesis presents a range of probabilities favorable to the occurrence of crime and such probabilities are additive. On this assumption, any subgroup that fails to conform with several of the general hypotheses stated in Scheme I will have a low rate of crime. To prove the latter, one would of course have to establish a range of probable values for each specialized hypothesis and for the phrase "low rate of crime," and then be able to demonstrate that the two sets of values are commensurate.

Although the generalizations utilized in deriving the above conclusion have not been widely confirmed, their methodological value need not be impugned. Using the above scheme as a point of departure, three procedures are suggested as possible strategies for research. These include (a) the specification of a particular group whose crime rate is to be explained, (b) the formulation of specialized hypotheses about this group which are subsumable under the more comprehensive hypotheses of Scheme I, and (c) the empirical confirmation or infirmation of these specialized hypotheses, either by directly reducing them to observation sentences or by indirectly deriving them from generalizations which rest upon observation sentences.[33]

More complete knowledge concerning the adequacy of Scheme I must await serious efforts to test the deducibility of all "lower-level" hypotheses and empirical generalizations relevant to crime. We examine but two classes of seemingly relevant instances. First, can certain business firms, which failed to engage in black-market violations during the war, be accounted for within the scope of Scheme I? Second, can this scheme explain the behavior of single individuals who violated black-market regulations without benefit of differential association or organized planning? Clinard, for instance, suggests "that *some*, but by no means all, persons tended to accept or reject black-market opportunities according to their basic personality make-up." [34]

The *desirability* of including noncriminal business firms within the range of application of our scheme can hardly be disputed. But from a liberal viewpoint any *requirement* of this kind would be too demanding. For purposes of initial exploration, it is sufficient to assume that the general hypotheses of our scheme define the particular types of cases that may be legitimately subsumed under them—in the present instance, groups of individuals who associate to acquire scarce goods by criminal means. If, then, careful analysis should reveal that noncriminal business firms possess characteristics unrelated to these general hypotheses, we would have plausible reasons for regarding such firms as beyond the scope of our scheme.

Similarly, for "individual" violators: If they could be shown to fall within the scope of Scheme I, it would have greater universality. However, before this step could be taken the scheme's hypotheses would have to be formulated in such a way as to include the behavior of all members of society, since it has been shown elsewhere that probably everyone has at one time or another committed a criminal act.[35] Eventually, then, we would want to include all nonviolators as well as all violators. Perhaps the latter possibility is what Sutherland intended to suggest when he wrote: "The processes which result in systematic criminal behavior are fundamentally the same in form as the processes which result in systematic lawful behavior." [36]

AN ALTERNATIVE SCHEME

The following scheme contains explicit hypotheses for explaining both the behavior of noncriminal business firms and of individual violators by way of intervening variables. The reader should take special note of the open meaning of the word "group." Here it *may* refer to an aggregate of individuals in which differential association is absent. The scheme is incomplete since the necessary supporting generalizations are not supplied. The phrase "If in society X" is assumed as a conditional for each hypothesis.

Theoretical Scheme II

Hypothesis 1. *Groups A, B, and C possess relatively major, medium, and minor amounts of scarce goods.*

Hypothesis 2. *Groups A, B, and C seek to maximize their possession of scarce goods.*

Definition 1. *Reward is a net increase in the possession of scarce goods.*

Definition 2. *Punishment is a net decrease in the possession of scarce goods.*

Hypothesis 3. *Groups A, B, and C use whatever means are expedient for maximizing their rewards or minimizing their punishments.*

Definition 3. *Variables r, s, t, . . . are conditions favoring insufficient certainty of punishment for law violation.*

Definition 4. *Variables x, y, z, . . . are conditions favoring insufficient effectiveness of punishment for law violation.*

Hypothesis 4. *Variables r, s, t, . . . favorable to insufficient certainty of punishment include opportunities to escape arrest and conviction by influencing legal functionaries; to violate trust without detection; to buy expert legal protection, etc.*

Hypothesis 5. *Variables x, y, z, . . . favorable to insufficient effectiveness of punishment include high incidence of poverty, unemployment and disease; of inadequate housing and recreational facilities; of personal and family disorganization, etc.*

Hypothesis 6. *When variables r, s, t, . . . or x, y, z, . . . obtain, law violation is an expedient means for maximizing rewards.*

Hypothesis 7. *Variables r, s, t, . . . and x, y, z, . . . are, respectively, functions of the initial possession of major and minor amounts of scarce goods.*

Consequence 1. *Groups A and C are law-violating.*

Consequence 2. *Group B is not law-violating.*

Consequence 3. *For groups A and C law violation is an expedient means for maximizing rewards.*

Consequence 4. *For group B law violation is not an expedient means for maximizing rewards.*

In general, many of the same strictures and limitations that apply to Scheme I apply to Scheme II. Nevertheless, a comparison of the two schemes in respect to their more apparent similarities and differences may be instructive.

The first two hypotheses of Schemes I and II closely resemble one another. The hypotheses of the latter are, however, more precisely stated, as can be seen by directly comparing the corresponding sentences of each scheme. Scheme II poses a trichotomy of groups rather than a dichotomy, as in Scheme I. It provides for a degree of societal differentiation sufficient to explain noncriminal behavior as well as criminal behavior. In Scheme II, white collar and ordinary crimes are not defined as such, though quite obviously these concepts are equivalent to law violations by groups *A* and *C,* respectively, and could be so indicated by simple definition. In Scheme I, the concepts of white collar and ordinary crimes are introduced via definitions of key phrases contained in the hypotheses; in Scheme II they are equivalent to certain expressions found in the consequences of the scheme. This difference in the analytic location of the two concepts is probably inconsequential for sociology so long as they are an integral part of each scheme and relevant problematic situations are not obscured.

Taken as a whole, the hypotheses of Schemes I and II state implicitly that the possession of major and minor amounts of scarce goods contributes toward law violation, and law violation (in turn) contributes toward the maximization of major and minor amounts of scarce goods. All that is needed to close the circle "formally" is the derivation of an explicit sentence stating that the *maximization* of major or minor amounts of scarce goods is equivalent to the *possession* of major or minor amounts of such goods. In circular relationships of this kind, system closure is approximated and the appearance of infinite regress is lessened. However, structural rigidity is increased and it is more difficult to incorporate newly discovered empirical processes. Examination of the two schemes will reveal that Scheme I comes nearer to a dynamic formulation than does Scheme II. The larger portion of definitional content in the latter fosters precision at the cost of flexibility.

Hypotheses 4 and 5 in Scheme II are offered as suggestive summarizations of the kinds of intervening variables which may be found to explain the behavior of individual violators. They differ, in some respects, from the type of intervening variables found in psychology, since they are less demonstratively functional and more directly testable.

CONCLUSION

The process of theory building is viewed as springing from a matrix of one or more problematic situations that require resolution. A useful theory will, accordingly, contain generalized categories that are conceptual counterparts of those problematically relevant distinctions which can be drawn from empirical phenomena.

We have attempted to show how the scope and categories of a problematic situation can be defined by the use of summarizing terms, co-ordinating definitions, and conditional sentences. For illustrative purposes, the terms and sentences of Sutherland's *White Collar Crime* were analyzed, restated, articulated, and subsequently elaborated in the form of a theoretical scheme. Within the framework of this scheme, certain questions of methodological significance were posed and explored. Emphasis was placed on quasi-logical analysis of the scheme's adequacy in the light of general knowledge concerning the character of the confirmatory process. On the assumption that certain types of relevant data could not be explained, a second scheme was proposed. Comparison of the two schemes in terms of their distinctive characteristics served to clarify the strengths and weaknesses of each.

The present endeavor rests upon the assumption that particular aspects of sociological theory may be fruitfully reconstructed along lines that represent analogical approximations of positivistic methods in the natural sciences. In principle, such an endeavor is no different from what has come to be acceptable procedure in thousands of studies where fundamental measurement is simulated. Although fundamental measurement can be found nowhere in sociology, many of its professionals continue to work as if they could in fact achieve it. The establishment of fundamental measurement and universal generalizations or laws are part and parcel of essentially the same process. Without risk-taking attempts to bring them about, a mature science of sociology may never come into being.

NOTES

1. For an introductory treatment of scientific explanation and related concepts, see Carl G. Hempel, "The Function of General Laws in History," *The Journal of Philosophy,* 39 (Jan., 1942), pp. 35-48; Monroe C. Beardsley, *Practical Logic* (New York: Prentice-Hall, Inc., 1950); John Hospers, *An*

Introduction to Philosophical Analysis (New York: Prentice-Hall, Inc., 1953); Arthur Pap, *Elements of Analytic Philosophy* (New York: The Macmillan Company, 1949). For a more advanced treatment, see Richard B. Braithwaite, *Scientific Explanation* (Cambridge: Cambridge University Press, 1955); Herbert Feigl and May Brodbeck, eds., *Readings in the Philosophy of Science* (New York: Appleton-Century-Crofts, Inc., 1953). In the latter volume, the essays by Hempel and Oppenheim, Kneale, Beck, Nagel, Abel, and Watkins are especially useful. For an analysis distinctly different from the one presented above, see the recent papers by Israel Scheffler, "Explanation, Prediction and Abstraction," *The British Journal for the Philosophy of Science,* 7 (Feb., 1957), pp. 293-310, and Nicholas Rescher, "On Prediction and Explanation," same *Journal* (February, 1958), pp. 281-91.

2. Edwin H. Sutherland, *White Collar Crime* (New York: Dryden Press, 1949). Unless otherwise indicated, all page references will be from this volume.

3. Our concept of "problematic situation" is a modification of Dewey's. Dewey writes, "Inquiry is the controlled or directed transformation of an indeterminate situation into one that is so determinate in its constituent distinctions and relations as to convert the elements of the original situation into a unified whole. . . . The unsettled or indeterminate situation might have been called a *problematic* situation. This name would have been, however, proleptic and anticipatory. The indeterminate situation becomes problematic in the very process of being subjected to inquiry." John Dewey, *Logic, The Theory of Inquiry* (New York: Henry Holt and Company, Inc., 1938), pp. 104-5, 107.

4. The term "instrumental," though unavoidably ambiguous, is the best I can come up with. Scientific usage of this term varies so much that a rather lengthy analysis would be necessary to achieve greater contextual clarification.

5. These forms of the conditional sentence will be discussed in a later essay.

6. Sutherland, *op. cit.,* p. 88. However, certain passages in *White Collar Crime* suggest that Sutherland would, in fact, admit of the presence of conditions that *should not* be allowed to occur, viz., "violation of trust and therefore creation of distrust" (p. 13) or whatever "undermines our traditional institutions" (p. 88) or "destroys the system of free enterprise and competition" (p. 110).

7. Contrariwise, it is conceivable that future exponents of "ordinary" crime may succeed in reducing Sutherland's conceptual boundaries to the point where they will exclude certain "unessential but superficially similar instances." Note, for example, E. W. Burgess' "Comment" on Frank E. Hartung, "White Collar Offences in the Wholesale Meat Industry in Detroit," *American Journal of Sociology,* 56 (July, 1950), pp. 32-33: "The point, then, is not to consider all violators of statutes, ordinances, and regulations as a homogeneous group. The differences are far greater than the resemblances between the automobilist who exceeds the speed limit, the OPA violator, and the burglar. Legally, they all violate a law or regulation and are subject to a penalty. Sociologically, they are different, and it is the differences that are significant."

8. Cf. Robert K. Merton, *Social Theory and Social Structure* (Glencoe, Ill.: Free Press, 1957), pp. 90-92.

9. Sutherland, *op. cit.,* p. 7.

10. *Ibid.,* p. 9.

11. For "ordinary crime" this statement may be altered to read: "Ordinary criminals are people of low social status and power, etc."

12. Apropos of this endeavor consider the question raised by Samuel A. Stouffer, in his presidential address before the American Sociological Society: "Are the times now ripe for making sociology cumulative by advancing 'If then' ideas which can be proven wrong if they are wrong or right if they are right?" Samuel A. Stouffer, "Measurement in Sociology," *American Sociological Review,* 18 (Dec., 1953), p. 597.

13. This consequence is based on empirical generalizations discussed by Sutherland under methods of securing uniform prices (*op. cit.,* p. 68 ff.) and types of price discrimination (*ibid.,* p. 80 ff.). The empirical generalizations upon which subsequent consequences are based can usually be found by examining those pages which follow immediately after the page number cited for each consequence.

14. *Ibid.,* p. 76.

15. *Ibid.,* pp. 76-77.

16. *Ibid.,* p. 78.

17. *Ibid.,* pp. 78-79

18. We stated earlier that the linkage of hypotheses and consequences through empirical generalizations is suggested as one procedure that seems to be most in accord with the limited, probabilistic nature of scientific statements in sociology. To appraise the present attempt and its shortcomings further, compare our usage with that version of the logic of science that confines explanatory statements to particular antecedents. In our usage, the role of generalizations, hypotheses, and consequences is analogously similar to the role of universal, explanatory, and predictive statements in the logic of natural science. The latter may be described as follows:

(1) Universal statement: "For all X's, if X is A then X is B"
(2) Explanatory statement: "X is an instance of A"
(3) Predictive statement: "X is an instance of B"

The logical form of these statements becomes evident when (1) is taken as the major premise, (2) as the minor premise, and (3) as the conclusion. If (1) and (2) are assumed then (3) can be logically deduced. If (1) is established as a universal law and (2) asserted as a fact, then (3) can be logically deduced as a fact. This does not mean that the factual occurrence of (3) is logically necessary but only that the predictive *statement* follows logically from (1) and (2) taken as premises. Whether or not (3) proves to be a fact depends upon some empirical test (confirmation, verification, or "truth"). When the universal statement expresses a relationship of equivalence, as it properly should, viz., "X is A if, and only if, X is B," then the assertion of (1) and (3) permits of the logical derivation of (2). From a universal statement and its relevant predictive statement, one can derive the relevant explanatory statement.

19. *Ibid.,* p. 234.

20. Cf. Walter C. Reckless, *The Etiology of Delinquent and Criminal Behavior* (New York: Social Science Research Council, 1943), p. 62.

21. However, in his *Principles of Criminology* (New York: J. B. Lippincott Company, 1939), p. 6, Sutherland writes, "The chance that a person will participate in systematic criminal behavior is determined roughly by the frequency and consistency of his contacts with the patterns of criminal behavior."

22. For Sutherland's informal "predictions" and "confirmations" of the hypothesis of differential association, see his *White Collar Crime,* pp. 243-53.

23. *Ibid.,* pp. 253-54.

24. *Ibid.,* p. 10.

25. *Ibid.,* p. 8.

26. Concerning the latter point V, Aubert writes: "It seems justified to interpret the growing number of legally defined crimes in this area as a symptom of a slow change in Norwegian social structure, where two partly competing social hierarchies, each with its own marks of distinction, are existing peacefully side by side. Of these, the labor movement and the government agencies it controls represent the ascendant hierarchy, while the business group and its fringes represent the descendant hierarchy. It seems that the definition of new legal crimes of the white-collar brand has served an important social function by giving the ascendant group a feeling of possessing the economic power corresponding to its political supremacy. We do, on the other hand, find traces of resistance to implementation in the social structure in general and in the enforcement machinery." "White Collar Crime and Social Structure," *American Journal of Sociology,* 58 (Nov., 1952), p. 269.

27. From either a positivistic or pragmatic standpoint, additional meaning could be attached to our hypotheses by reducing them to pairs of sentences which specify the experimentally sufficient conditions within which a particular result can be expected to occur or not occur. Thus, the meaning of our hypothesis, "In society X upper- and lower-status groups place primary value on the acquisition of scarce goods," is reducible to sentences like this: "If groups of people possessing specified characteristics a_1 a_2 a_3 are presented with the opportunity to choose between scarce goods and lawful action they will choose scarce goods." Or, "If groups of people possessing specified characteristics b_1 b_2 b_3 are presented with the opportunity to choose between scarce goods and lawful action they will not choose scarce goods." Vague conditions and results may be respecified by other pairs of reduction sentences until one arrives at the point where a satisfactory degree of precision is achieved. By adapting this procedure, one may hope to determine, for any hypothesis, what constitutes pertinent observations and relevant confirmations.

28. Although the aforementioned concepts are not explicitly defined by the context of terms constituting our scheme, this limitation need not be fatal for sociology. Primitive terms analogously similar to these do occur and must occur in all scientific schemes. Moreover, when required, any

word may be defined in a language analytically outside of the scheme in question.

29. Edwin H. Sutherland, *White Collar Crime* (New York: Dryden Press, 1949), p. 3.

30. *Ibid.,* p. 6.

31. *Ibid.,* p. 7.

32. This type of polar scheme occurs frequently in science. But to interpret its hypotheses as a denial of the hypotheses of some co-ordinate scheme is tantamount to the deduction of false consequences from false premises, to engaging in what is called "the fallacy of denying the antecedent." Since false premises may give rise to true consequences, we are logically justified in drawing the consequence "the crime rate of females is low" only if we are justified in construing the hypotheses regarding absence of association to acquire scarce goods, etc., as true sentences of a polar scheme that obtains in its own right.

33. We have not attempted to confirm the above hypotheses by deriving quasilogical consequences that can be tested by direct observation. It might be argued, however, that the three particular hypotheses subsumed under hypotheses 1, 2 and 4 of Scheme I can be supported by a host of empirical studies: (1) The fact that women offenders are more often motivated by sex repression, envy, jealousy, and vengeance, and that their preferred victims are infants, children, husbands, and lovers, suggests that they do not place primary value upon the acquisition of scarce goods. (2) The relatively high criminal liability of females in domestic and personal service and of female shoppers in department stores, as contrasted with female factory workers, suggests that they do not associate to acquire scarce goods. (3) The fact that culture encourages indirection, conceit, and concealment in the commission of crimes and forces females into the roles of instigators, decoys, and watchers, rather than direct perpetrators of crime, suggests that they do not themselves seek to enact laws for acquiring scarce goods. Examine the *data* in Otto Pollak, *The Criminality of Women* (Philadelphia: University of Pennsylvania Press, 1950).

34. M. B. Clinard mentions in particular "egocentricity, emotional insecurity or feelings of personal inadequacy, negative attitudes toward other persons in general, the relative importance of status symbols of money as compared with nationalism, and relative lack of importance of one's personal, family, or business reputations." *The Black Market* (New York: Rinehart & Company, Inc., 1952), p. 310.

35. See James S. Wallerstein and Clement J. Wyle, "Our Law-Abiding Law Breakers," *Probation,* 26 (April, 1947), pp. 107-112.

36. Edwin H. Sutherland, *Principles of Criminology* (New York: J. B. Lippincott Company, 1939), p. 4.

BIBLIOGRAPHY

BEARDSLEY, MONROE C. *Practical Logic.* New York: Prentice-Hall, Inc., 1950.

BRAITHWAITE, RICHARD B. *Scientific Explanation.* Cambridge: Cambridge University Press, 1955.

CHURCHMAN, C. WEST, and ACKOFF, RUSSELL L. *Methods of Inquiry.* St. Louis: Educational Publishers, 1950.

FEIGL, HERBERT, and BRODBECK, MAY (eds.). *Readings in the Philosophy of Science.* New York: Appleton-Century-Crofts, Inc., 1953.

FRANK, PHILIPP G. (ed.). *The Validation of Scientific Theories.* Boston: Beacon Press, Inc., 1954.

GOODMAN, NELSON. *Fact, Fiction and Forecast.* Cambridge: Harvard University Press, 1955.

HEMPEL, CARL G. *Fundamentals of Concept Formation in Empirical Science.* Chicago: University of Chicago Press, 1952.

HOSPERS, JOHN. *An Introduction to Philosophical Analysis.* New York: Prentice-Hall, Inc., 1953.

MARX, MELVIN H. (ed.). *Psychological Theory.* New York: The Macmillan Company, 1951.

LEWIS, CLARENCE I. *An Analysis of Knowledge and Valuation.* La Salle, Ill.: Open Court Publishing Company, 1946.

NORTHROP, F. S. C. *The Logic of the Sciences and the Humanities.* New York: The Macmillan Company, 1947.

REICHENBACH, HANS. *Nomological Statements and Admissible Operations.* Amsterdam: North-Holland Publishing Co., 1954.

STRAWSON, P. F. *Introduction to Logical Theory.* John Wiley and Sons, Inc., 1952.

IX

SOCIOLOGY OF KNOWLEDGE

18

The Sociology of Knowledge and Sociological Theory

The paper which follows is a very personal paper. It is not, however, a private, idiosyncratic venture but, on the contrary, an experiment in communication—with myself and with those whom I hope to draw into the experiment. You and I will be participating in a joint venture. We shall start on this venture in an expository mood; but as we proceed, we shall find ourselves in a more pleading mood, and there will be points in our journey where we may attain unexpected balances between exposition and rhetoric.

We shall visit much longer with the sociology of knowledge and sociology than with sociological theory, to which we shall come only at the end of our journey. When we look back then, our itinerary should lie clearly traced on the map which we shall realize to have used for our trip.

We start, naturally, from home, with the familiar. We begin with a standard review of the sociology of knowledge. We ask for information and shall receive it. We ask:

In memory of Karl Mannheim.

I am deeply indebted particularly to John W. Bennett and Llewellyn Gross, but also to Aron Gurwitsch, Paul Kecskemeti, Anthony Nemetz, Talcott Parsons, Alfred Schutz, and Melvin Seeman for critical readings of earlier drafts of this paper and for pertinent comments. Unfortunately, I have not been able to act on all of them. K.H.W.

I. "WHAT IS THE SOCIOLOGY OF KNOWLEDGE?"

And we are told, or we remember, that it takes only a slight acquaintance with the subject to suspect or know that the term "sociology of knowledge" is a misnomer, namely, a translation of the German *"Wissenssoziologie."* *"Wissen,"* however, is broader than "knowledge." [1] "Knowledge" usually refers to scientific or positive knowledge alone. *"Wissen,"* on the other hand, is at least noncommittal on the inclusion of other kinds of knowledge as well. And as to *"Soziologie,"* it is closer to "social philosophy" and thus broader than is "sociology," which, particularly in its American usage, is more closely linked to a natural-science model. And indeed, efforts carried on in the name of the sociology of knowledge, no matter in what language, have been concerned less with scientific knowledge than with outlooks, world views, concepts, and categories of thought. Furthermore, these efforts have been made less in a self-conscious sociological perspective than in the moods of philosophy of history, epistemology, or philosophical anthropology.

The two immediate antecedents of the sociology of knowledge are Marxism [2] and Durkheimian sociology. Marxism gave it its critical, often debunking outlook and the basis of that outlook in a philosophy of history. Durkheimian sociology gave it its interest in the relations between forms of primitive social organization and forms or categories of thought. What is usually referred to as "sociology of knowledge" itself is the *Wissenssoziologie* [3] which flourished in Germany in the 1920's and was predominantly Marxist or anti-Marxist. After 1933 and since, it has led a precarious transplanted existence, mainly in the United States, although since the end of World War II it has also been revived in Germany.[4]

The two outstanding representatives of *Wissenssoziologie* were Max Scheler (1874–1928) and Karl Mannheim (1893–1947); its two signal publications, Scheler's "Problems of a Sociology of Knowledge" (1924) and Mannheim's *Ideology and Utopia* (1929).[5] Scheler was critical of the Marxist tradition. A philosopher of phenomenologist inclination, he tried to incorporate the sociology of knowledge into a philosophical anthropology. Mannheim, on the other hand, was rooted in the Marxist tradition. He took the Marxian concept of ideology more broadly than it had been before, but in doing so, he ran into epistemological difficulties which he failed to resolve. No matter how different Scheler and Mannheim, they were alike in hardly being influenced by Durkheim and his school. As far as the sociology of knowledge is concerned, Durkheimian sociology has had its greatest effect, outside of France, in the United States, where the sociology of knowledge, nevertheless, was introduced chiefly through the English edition of Mannheim's book in the 1930's.[6]

In the United States, movements theoretically similar to the sociology of knowledge had existed for roughly half a century. Historically, however, and thus in their general intellectual significance, these movements —pragmatism, social behaviorism, instrumentalism [7]—were different. Pragmatism, social behaviorism, instrumentalism are, among other things, distillates of a more general and pervasive American outlook: practical, amelioristic, future-oriented.[8] American students of the sociology of knowledge have combined these American orientations with German and French orientations. Among the results of their efforts are the most orderly survey of important philosophical problems of the field yet achieved; [9] the most succinct summary of its sociological research problems; [10] and the most concise sketch of its background and its American relations.[11]

One way of characterizing the writings that have been produced in the name of the sociology of knowledge in general and of *Wissenssoziologie* in particular is to call them "more speculative and theoretical than empirical" and to consider them in need of systematization into a general sociology of intellectual-emotional behavior,[12] intellectual life,[13] mental productions,[14] the mind,[15] or gnosio-sociology [16] (to mention some of the few attempts at improving on the term "sociology of knowledge"). Such systematizing, however, would have to be preceded by making inventories of considerable bodies of knowledge and theory which, though accumulated outside the "sociology of knowledge," nevertheless bear on its central problem, the relations between society and intellectual life. They lie scattered in the social sciences, the humanities, and certain biological sciences. Such inventories would have to cover,

in the *social sciences,* in addition to general sociological findings and to more specialized findings, . . . above all, social psychology in a very broad sense . . . , cultural anthropology, particularly linguistics with its various subdivisions, the study of "culture and personality," and the study of culture itself; in the *humanities,* social and cultural history, literary criticism, historical linguistics, and . . . methodological and empirical aspects of philosophy . . . ; and, finally, in the *biological sciences,* whatever throws light upon the biological dimensions of intellectual behavior (that is, especially the field of human genetics). All these are sources of knowledge relevant to the problem of the relations between society and intellectual life. To assemble and dovetail them, obviously is a tremendous task, but also, it would seem, a tremendous challenge.[17]

We might continue with the answer to our question, "What is the sociology of knowledge?," by additional observations, such as these: Despite its predominantly "speculative and theoretical" character, the sociology of knowledge has produced some outstanding empirical investigations by, among others, Merton, Kohn-Bramstedt, Mannheim, and Zilsel.[18] It has given us useful (though not too widely used) concepts—e.g., Mannheim's typology of interpretations [19] or Znaniecki's of "men of knowledge." [20] It has had a continuing effect, "as a latent frame of reference," [21] in other disciplines. Some of its American students, both sociologists [22] and philosophers,[23] have later in their careers turned to work in other areas; the selection of this work, however, or the approaches to it, have probably been influenced by their previous preoccupation with the sociology of knowledge, and they may yet return to such preoccupation since their careers are still going on.

The foregoing answer to our question, "What is the sociology of knowledge?," is what we referred to as a standard review of the field. Now we are going a step further. We shall take such a step when we realize, first, that in our question and in the answer to it we paid no attention to the persons who did the asking and answering; and, second, that not to have done so is a very serious omission, which we now must try to make good. Let us attempt to identify these persons—first as types of men, and then (beginning in Section III) historically, that is, in respect to their place and time.

II. OUTSIDERS AND PARTICIPANTS

We did say something about the types of men who inquired into the sociology of knowledge and who expounded it by referring to them as seeking and receiving information. They were outsiders to the sociology of knowledge. They talked from the standpoint of some more or less unarticulated version of the contemporary academic tradition in social science. Not only were they not among the developers of the sociology of knowledge: they betrayed no awareness of the fact that to ask and be given information about an intellectual endeavor is one thing; but that to develop it, participate in it, be on the inside, insiders, is quite another. It involves a much greater risk.

In our asking and answering, there was no risk. There was no risk of participation—such that the two activities of asking and answering and the two roles of asker and answerer might have fused and been transformed into one joint venture. The outcome of such a venture would not have been certain; the kind of its outcome, in fact, quite unforeseeable. Yet the sociology of knowledge, like any intellectual endeavor worth its salt, has had its participants; it would not have come into being without them. Unlike the asker and answerer of the question with which we started on our journey, these participants were startled, puzzled, bewildered, and troubled by novel problems. Of them, Karl Mannheim perhaps was the one who took the greatest chances of getting confused and stymied, who accepted the fewest among the received notions at his disposal, who staked the most of himself—who was the most unconditional participant. This may be gathered, even more palpably perhaps than from his published writings, from a letter written (15 April 1946) to the author in response to a critical analysis of Mannheim's work by members of a seminar on the sociology of knowledge. Mannheim wrote:

> . . . If there are contradictions and inconsistencies in my paper this is, I think, not so much due to the fact that I overlooked them but because I make a point of developing a theme to its end even if it contradicts some other statements. I use this method because I think that in this marginal field of human knowledge we should not conceal inconsistencies, so to speak covering up the wounds, but our duty is to show the sore spots in human thinking at its present stage.
>
> In a simple empirical investigation or straightforward logical argument, contradictions are mistakes; but when the task is to show that our whole thought system in its various parts leads to inconsistencies, these inconsistencies are the thorn in the flesh from which we have to start.
>
> The inconsistencies in our whole outlook, which in my presentation only become more visible, are due to the fact that we have two approaches which move on a different plane [*sic*].
>
> On the one hand, our most advanced empirical investigations, especially those which come from history, psychology, and sociology, show that the human mind with its whole categorical apparatus is a dynamic entity. Whereas our predominent epistemology derives from an age, the hidden desire and ideal of which was stability, the traditional epistemology still thinks of concepts as reflecting eternal ideas. The premium is put on absoluteness and supertemporaneousness and accordingly, no other knowledge and truth can be conceived. . . . (than) the static one. . . .
>
> Now, whereas one part of our progressive insight convinces us that language and logic are also a part of culture which, in its turn—most people will agree on that—is different with different tribes and in different epochs and therefore nothing can be stated but in relation to a frame of reference; the other part of our intellectual orientation through its traditional epistemology cannot put up with this insight. The latter is reluctant to accept this because it failed to build into its theory the fact of the essential perspectivism of human knowledge.
>
> To use a simple analogy, what happens is that in our empirical investigation we become aware of the fact that we are observing the world from a moving staircase, from a dynamic platform, and, therefore, the image of the world changes with the changing frames of reference which various cultures create. On the other hand, epistemology still only knows of a static platform where one doesn't become aware of the possibility of various perspectives and, from this angle, it tries to deny the existence and the right of such dynamic thinking. There is a culture lag between our empirical insight into the nature of knowing and the premises upon which the traditional idealist epistemology is built. Instead of perspectivism, the out-of-date epistemology wants to set up a veto against the emerging new insights, according to which man can only see the world in perspective, and there is no view which is absolute in the sense that it represents the thing in itself beyond perspective.
>
> In the world of visual objects, we acknowledge that completely. That

you can only see various perspectives of a house and there is no view among them which is absolutely the house and in spite of that there is knowing because the various perspectives are not arbitrary. The one can be understood from the other. What we, without any difficulty, admit for the apperception of the visual world, we ought to admit for knowledge in general.

I hope this is intelligible and it at least convinces you and your seminar that if there are contradictions they are not due to my shortsightedness but to the fact that I want to break through the old epistemology radically but have not succeeded yet fully. But the latter is not one man's work. I think our whole generation will have to work on it as nothing is more obvious than that we transcended in every field the idea that man's mind is equal to an absolute Ratio in favour of a theory that we think on the basis of changing frames of reference, the elaboration of which is one of the most exciting tasks of the near future. . . .[24]

Mannheim's letter has been quoted exclusively as the document of an insider and will be commented on in this respect alone. It suggests that for the insider, problems of the sociology of knowledge—leading toward it or issuing from it—are more or less faithful formulations of his craving for an ordered world, are, in this sense, existential problems for him. In the case of Mannheim in particular, most of the work he did (not only that explicitly devoted to the sociology of knowledge) could be characterized as a "diagnosis of our time" (the title he gave one of his books): for him, existential problems were above all historical problems. They were the questions: "Where have we come from?" "Where are we?" "What, therefore, must we do?" Though never as explicit on the matter as some might have desired him to be, Mannheim appears to have held that if we know who we are, we know what we must do.

This is a very old proposition. We do well to realize, however, that it is incompatible with the much newer, though almost all-pervasive, total separation between the Is and the Ought. For more than two millennia men had been saying that our existence itself, our "Is," is normative, that it includes the "Ought"; hence that if we recognize ourselves we know what we must do. What is new, now, about this Socratic position is the place and time of its rediscovery—of, perhaps, its fermenting.

We have only touched lightly on the place and time of the outsider who inquires into the sociology of knowledge. All we have said is that he seeks information, raising his question on the basis of some more or less unarticulated version of the contemporary academic tradition in social science—in which he has grown up but which he has hardly examined. Mannheim's example suggests an additional distinction between outsider and insider. It is that, unlike the outsider, the insider finds that he cannot inquire into the sociology of knowledge short of examining this tradition, and that examining this tradition includes exploring his place and time. We shall now attempt to visualize such an exploration.

III. ON OUR PLACE AND TIME

We begin with the place and the time: the West, now. This will include something on the Western tradition, too; and later we shall examine some features of our tradition in sociology particularly (Section VI and ff.). In our inspection of place and time, we limit ourselves to three interrelated aspects: (1) the administered nature of our lives; (2) "the world as underdeveloped"; and (3) "one-world-and-cultural-relativism."

(1) The part of the social structure which administers our lives is bureaucracy, "the type of organization designed to accomplish large-scale administrative tasks by systematically co-ordinating the work of many individuals." [25] This part is so important that much of our outlook and conduct is the outlook and conduct of the administered life: not spontaneous interaction, but control, and the fear of its failing. If this is so, the reason may be that we have not come to terms with secularization and rationalization,[26] but that, rather, we are ambivalent toward them. On this, we shall have more to say below (Section VIII). Now, we put the matter by stating that we find ourselves having to pay for the recession of objective reason.[27] What do we mean by this?

"Objective" must be distinguished from "subjective" reason. Subjective reason is part of our mental equipment. It is our faculty of thinking, notably that of adapting means to ends.[28] Objective reason is the rational order of the cosmos (nature, society, history), which also contains *us*. This order is normative, teleological; it includes ends. Yet when we employ our subjective reason in a manner which lets us forget objective reason, we lose our very capacity of assessing ends. One effect of this forgetting and this loss is that ends turn sour, and we may declare them to be matters of taste, irrational.[29] Is and Ought have become divorced. Once this divorce has occurred, all our efforts to derive Ought from Is are vain.[30]

The last sentence expresses a logically correct proposition. Its empirical applications, however—such as doubt and worry over the Ought or attempts at obtaining it from the Is—are so frequent that they may be said to characterize our contemporary consciousness.[31] To recognize the recession of objective reason may help us understand another phenomenon of our time, the simultaneous spurt in science and technology and the emergence of totalitarianism. It may come to appear less paradoxical that this period of unprecedented rise in the standard of living, of democratization, of decreasing superstition, of proliferating alternatives should also be the period, not only of totalitarianism, but also of Western feelings that traditional ideals have lost significance, and the goal of a higher standard of living has become a barren one.

The administered nature of our lives has been hinted at in many expressions—e.g., "brave new world," "1984," "other-directedness" (David Riesman), "escape from freedom" (Erich Fromm). But it could be that the contrasts or solutions, such as Riesman's "autonomy" or Fromm's "productive personality," [32] will be confined to the status of alternatives in addition to those already available, thus contributing to their proliferation. As long as almost ninety years ago, Dostoevsky wrote:

In those days people seem to have been animated by one idea, but now they are much more nervous, more developed, more sensitive—they seem to be animated by two or three ideas at a time—modern man is more diffuse and, I assure you, it is this that prevents him from being such a complete human being as they were in those days. [33]

(2) We in the West have not, perhaps not yet, recognized the objectively rational status of man's desire to be free from hunger, sickness, fear, ignorance. We have not recognized that from this desire we might develop the world. Instead, we tend to single out some areas of it as needing a push in the direction of Western "development." On this view, the current notion of "underdeveloped" peoples or countries appears as a distortion of what should read "the world as underdeveloped." [34] It is a corrupted text, the corrupting element being a Western projection. *We* are underdeveloped, as witness our helpless, administered lives, our helplessness in front of totalitarianism, the climax of administeredness, of derationalization and, at the same time, detraditionalization, of a-historicity and, at the same time, a-morality.

No matter how much our projectionism is attenuated—not least by the spontaneous understanding and puzzlement of social scientists, among them some of those active in "underdeveloped countries" [35]—we are glad, nevertheless, and understandably so, to repress our own dilemma. We tend to hold on to the essentially nineteenth-century dichotomies of sacred, folk, traditional *vs.* secular, urban, rational societies (cf. Section VIII below), believing ourselves to belong to the latter, with which we want to christen and dominate the nascent one world. Instead, we might cling to such nonprojective ideas as that the science and technology we have mastered under the very guide of subjective reason and its stubborn insistence on control (and in only precarious relation with objective reason), if deliberately applied to our economies, can reduce hunger and sickness faster than they have been; that return to trust in objective reason can increase knowledge and alleviate fear; [36] and that, acting on these insights, we may help reason in its "cunning," recognizing in our very befuddlement a reminder of objective reason and of the relation of objective to subjective reason.

(3) Such "help to reason" may be help to us in this time when one of the most palpable meanings of "one world" is the feeling of global claustrophobia. On the one hand, our science and technology have made our destruction feasible and thus a possibility. On the other hand, our social science in particular (especially cultural anthropology) has so overwhelmed us with a range of cultures which are strange and yet human—and, being human, ours—that we are terrified and confused. We may feel relief when we can transcend our terror and confusion by transforming them into questions such as these: What can we do with our own ways of life? How can we reinterpret our traditions so that we can all live together, not by compromise, but by being truer to ourselves? In the light or mood of such questions, the idea of "one world and cultural relativism" may impress us as a democratized version of the idea of the brotherhood of man and the immortality of the soul. If developments under the sway of subjective reason have "disenchanted" us to the point of being haunted by our own disappearance, we may revive by insisting that these developments, despite world wars, death camps, atom bombs, genocide, and the administered life, are a phase of secularization and rationalization whose "enchantment" we have yet to discover. We may revive if we realize that this phase challenges us to re-invent ourselves so that we learn how we can *live* in one world. We must get hold of our *trans*cultural selves after we have been so fascinated by cultural relativism, by our cultural unselves.

Without postulating a transcultural human nature, we could not account for the possibility of understanding between two persons of different cultures [37]—but this means between any two persons, including between myself today and yesterday, here and in another place. The pursuit of understanding others and ourselves evinces faith in their dignity and our dignity, in the dignity of man. It is incompatible with condescension, toward "underdeveloped" man and "ourselves" alike, and perpetually challenges us to keep to the fine line between the belief of being in grace and the sin of pride. In the pursuit of understanding, it is of secondary importance whether by our "transcultural selves" we mean a supracultural core or residue, biological or spiritual, and whether, accordingly, we engage in the investigation of the physiological processes of thought, or of intellectual history, or of the "sociology of knowledge." In all these endeavors, we further our understanding by the awareness that we are embracing both transcultural human nature and human culture, both man, or human nature, and unique cultures; and must be wary lest we confuse the first with the second or the second with the first— biology with learning, acquired with innate traits, nature with nurture, environment with heredity, or "supervenient" with "primal" categories.[38]

IV. METHODOLOGICAL, VOLITIONAL, AND METAPHYSICAL PREMISES OF THE SOCIOLOGY OF KNOWLEDGE: ITS DUALISM AND NATURALISM

We may seem to have strayed from the sociology of knowledge. Actually, we are in the process of becoming insiders, of participating in it. For that matter, it has just been mentioned, in the course of reflections on our time. It was listed among various endeavors in the pursuit of understanding; it was also referred to, by implication, in the warning not to take "supervenient" for "primal" categories (and vice versa): this distinction has been proposed by Arthur Child in an attempt at solving one of the crucial philosophical problems of the sociology of knowledge, precisely that of the categories of thought. It is now necessary to show that the connection between the sociology of knowledge and our time is not casual, that it can be analyzed, and that it can be argued to be of a determinable kind and importance.

In his first explicit paper on the subject (1925),[39] Karl Mannheim examined four "ultimate, fundamental factors" which constitute the "problem constellation" of the sociology of knowledge. These are (1) the "self-transcendence" or "self-relativization of thought," that is, the possibility of not taking thought at its face value; (2) "the emergence of the 'unmasking' turn of mind" (or "debunking"); (3) the transcendence of thought toward the historical and social sphere, which is hypostatized as the "ontological absolute" or emerges as "a new system of reference"; in other words, the understanding of thought as "the expression of" or "in relation to" history and society; and (4) the social relativization of the "totality" of the "mental world," not only of *some* thoughts. Without these four factors, Mannheim held, the historical emergence of the sociology of knowledge is unthinkable; but once in existence, these factors make for a constellation which "necessarily" gives "rise to [its] problems." [40] More succinctly, the sociology of knowledge tackles the question of what happens if intellectual processes and products are unmasked as the expression of, or in relation to, social-historical circumstance—if intellectual life as such is so unmasked. And the sociology of knowledge must come to terms with this question because this is precisely what has actually happened. It has to come to terms with what it itself has realized to have happened in the modern world. It must transform a new and shattering experience into a problem.

This does not mean that the theoretical distillate of this historical experience depends for its emergence exclusively on that experience. Theoretical preoccupations with the sociology of knowledge are at least as old as Xenophanes of Colophon (sixth century B.C.) and Sextus Empiricus (A.D. third century), to mention only two [41] of many theoretically relevant writers throughout the ages. But, as in the case of the "American predecessors," their general intellectual significance is different from that of the historically conscious sociology of knowledge.

Mannheim's previously quoted letter, written more than twenty years after the paper just now referred to, shows that even then he was still struggling with the problem of intellectual-life-unmasked; that problem had not lost its humbling magnitude. Already the early source presents him engaged in a diagnosis of our time: he asks where we have come from, where we are, what, therefore, we must do; and he looks for an answer in the exploration of the modern (Western) consciousness.

Such a concept of consciousness is Hegelian-Marxian. Possibly for this reason, it is absent from American preoccupations with the sociology of knowledge. Even the few American comments on the very time and place in which the sociology of knowledge arose do not imply it, let alone explicitly use it. Those by Louis Wirth and Robert K. Merton may serve as illustrations.

Wirth describes that time and place, our period, as one of increasing secularization. As such, it has come to question "norms and truths which were once believed to be absolute," and to recognize that thought itself is disturbing because "capable of unsettling routines, disorganizing habits, breaking up customs, undermining faiths, and generating skepticism." Certain "facts" of the social life may not be investigated because this would impinge on vested interests. Mannheim, says Wirth, has gone beyond this insight into the reflection of interest "in all thought, including that part of it which is called science." Mannheim has tried "to trace out the specific connection between actual interest groups in society and the ideas and modes of thought which they espoused." [42]

Thus Wirth, in the course of his attempt at locating our time historically, in effect praises Mannheim as a modern representative of the Enlightenment, particularly of the Enlightenment theory of interests. We saw, however, that Mannheim himself, even before publishing the book to which Wirth wrote the introduction just quoted, had no longer operated with such a theory but with the social relativization of the "totality of the mental world." And as to the Enlightenment itself, Mannheim had argued in the earlier paper that it was a phase in the development of the modern consciousness which we have left far behind. It was a phase endowing Reason with autonomy and thus "least likely to effect a relativization of thought." Rather, it pointed "in the opposite direction, that is, toward an absolute self-hypostatization of Reason." [43]

Merton remarks that, in an era of increasing social conflict and distrust, inquiry into the validity of ideas tends to shift toward preoccupation with their origin. "Thought becomes functionalized; it is interpreted in terms of its psychological or economic or social or racial sources and functions": witness not only the sociology of knowledge but also "psycho-analysis, Marxism, semanticism, propaganda analysis, Paretanism, and, to some extent, functional analysis." [44] Merton no more than Wirth operates with a conception of history in which the notion of a consciousness either commensurate with or reflective of a period is a constitutive element.

The exploration of our time and place undertaken in the preceding section suggests the hope of an understanding which presupposes the acceptance of the dualism of man and his unique cultures. An analysis of recurring problems of the sociology of knowledge undertaken elsewhere [45] has shown the same dualism as one of the metaphysical premises of the sociology of knowledge—and naturalism as the other. As this is explained, it will become evident that naturalism, too, is a presupposition of the understanding in which we have found the hope of transcending our time.

Besides metaphysical, there are two other kinds of premises: methodological and volitional. The distinctions among the three may be made as follows: A *methodological premise* is a proposition accepted because of its usefulness as a guide to inquiry. A *volitional premise* is an affect or desire which animates the researcher. A *metaphysical premise* is a proposition concerning the nature of reality.

Among the *methodological premises* of the sociology of knowledge are the propositions that the scientific validity of intellectual phenomena has nothing to do with their origin; that intellectual phenomena have logical, as well as social, aspects. The corresponding *volitional premises* of the sociology of knowledge are the desires for unimpeachable validity, on the one hand, and social relevance, on the other. They are the desires for maximum "intrinsic" interpretation, which illuminates, among others, the logical aspects of intellectual phenomena, and for maximum "extrinsic" interpretation, which illuminates, among others, their social aspects. The nature of these wishes presupposes a certain conception of reality, which is expressed in the *metaphysical premises* of the sociology of knowledge. Accordingly, reality is both relative (socially, culturally, historically, biologically, etc.) and absolute, that is, itself, true, irrespective of relativity. It follows that the appropriate approach to reality likewise is dual: both the most thorough extrinsic interpretation of phenomena (as instances of laws) and their most thorough intrinsic interpretation (in their own terms) which are possible on any given occasion at any time.

The first of these metaphysical premises (concerning reality) predicates ontological dualism; the second (concerning the interpretation of this reality) espouses naturalism, understood as continuity of analysis.[46] It should now be clear (as has been anticipated) that naturalism, in this sense, also is a metaphysical premise of the understanding which resulted as a hope from the analysis of our time and place. This analysis implied that the inquiry into the nature of man and culture, and into their mutual relations and boundaries, would never be completed.

V. SCIENTIFIC *VS.* EXISTENTIAL TRUTH

It is important to realize that methodological problems, including those of testing methodological premises, on the one hand, and volitional and metaphysical problems, with the corresponding inclusion, on the other, have different criteria of confirmation or truth. For methodological problems, the criterion of truth is pragmatic in relation to a given inquiry or type of inquiry; in this sense, it is a "means" criterion. For volitional and metaphysical problems, the criterion is agreement with the result of the most rigorously imaginable intrasubjective "dialectical" examination of one's most important experiences: it is an "end" criterion.[47]

The truth sought in the solution of methodological problems may be called *stipulative,* in the sense that the predicate "true" is stipulated as suitable to the investigatory purpose in hand (or to the class of investigatory purposes of which the one in hand is an instance). It may also be called *hypothetical,* in the sense that it is contingent on the validation of a given hypothesis which is being examined in respect to its truth; or in the more compelling sense that even if validated, hypotheses remain hypotheses, namely propositions which can be validated only within the hypothetical methodological, pragmatic, scientific attitude— that attitude for which metaphysical propositions (concerning the nature of reality) are irrelevant. Finally, this truth may be called *propositional,* in the sense that it is predicated only (or predominantly [48]) of propositions. It is clear that this stipulative, hypothetical, propositional truth, which is the truth sought in the solution of methodological problems, also is the truth sought in the solution of scientific problems. This is widely, if not generally, recognized by philosophers of science and of value. It implies that science makes no claims about the nature of (ultimate) reality; it is not concerned with this reality. We shall refer to this stipulative, hypothetical, propositional truth as *"scientific* truth."

The truth sought in the solution of volitional and metaphysical problems may, in accordance with the definition given above, be called experiential or *existential.* From a sociological standpoint, the seeker after scientific truth who commits an error risks his technical well-being, including, if he is a scientist, his professional reputation. By contrast, the seeker after existential truth risks his life and the world. Concerning both he may die in greater error than he would if he had "surrendered" [49] more fully, consciously, and intelligently to them.

Paul Kecskemeti has illuminated the nature of Mannheim's sociology of knowledge by arguing that Mannheim in effect distinguished between two kinds of truth, which are closely related to scientific and existential truth, respectively. These are the "Aristotelian concept of truth as 'speaking the truth,'" or "the truth of propositions . . ."; and truth as "one's response to reality," "the existential concept of truth as 'being in truth.'" We should remember, Kecskemeti writes, that truth has been conceived in these two ways throughout the history of philosophy. For the first, "truth" is predicative of sentences; it

has nothing to do with the things of the world as they exist in themselves. According to the other definition, 'truth' is first and foremost an attribute of *existence,* and only secondarily of *discourse.* One *is* or *is not* in the Truth; and one's possession of Truth depends on being in communion with a reality which 'is' or embodies truth.[50]

VI. SOCIAL NOMINALISM *VS.* SOCIAL REALISM

This reality, for Mannheim (for the early Mannheim, as we shall see later in this section), was history. The positing of history, or of anything else, as "real," is not for the scientist to do. He pursues scientific truth, and in so doing ignores metaphysical questions. In other words, the scientific attitude "brackets"—to use the language of phenomenology—the ontological quest. To the extent, however, that a given science or scientist deviates from the type, there may be metaphysical premises which have their influence on the selection and formulation of problems, on the interpretation of findings, etc. Mannheim is by no means alone, or even an exception, in such deviation. Thus, it has been said of American sociology as a whole that it is characterized by "voluntaristic nominalism," that is, by

the assumption that the structure of all social groups is the consequence of the aggregate of its separate, component individuals and that social phenomena ultimately derive from the motivations of these knowing, feeling, and willing individuals.

American sociology, therefore, is unsympathetic to any social determinism.

A sociology of knowledge, for instance, which maintains a strict causal relationship between a specific form of social existence or class position

and knowledge is unlikely to gain many adherents among American sociologists. . . . neither Durkheim's notion of society as an entity *sui generis*
nor Marx's interpretation of social stratification in terms of economic relations and consequent class consciousness has been accepted in American
sociology in spite of widespread familiarity with these ideas.[51]

Not being pure, that is, self-conscious, self-critical, self-correcting,
neither American nor European sociology wholly rejects its own metaphysical inclinations. As sciences, they should withhold an "accent of
reality," whereas, in fact, they bestow it, although each of them bestows
it on a different sphere. American sociology places it on the individual,
withdrawing it from society. We may refer to this by saying that American sociology represents individual realism (and social nominalism, to
paraphrase the term "voluntaristic nominalism"). European sociology
places it on society or history, withdrawing it from the individual. It
represents social realism (individual nominalism).

Social realism is related to historical realism. This relation has
been shown by Ernest Manheim in respect to Karl Mannheim's career.
The later stages of this career, Manheim observes, show increasing
interest in psychology, which "is inherent in Mannheim's adoption of
the nominalist theory of groups, the view that groups have no reality
of their own beyond the existence of their individual members." (This
is, of course, the characteristically American conception of sociology.)
And this turning toward "social nominalism" also explains Mannheim's
*"abandonment of the doctrine which asserts the primacy of the his-
torical frame of reference."* As Ernest Manheim points out, it is only
in what has been called "individual realism," that is,

when the individual becomes the ultimate term of reference of sociological
constructs (as is typically the case in American sociology) that questions of motivation can have meaning for the analysis of social action.
Sociological concepts formed on the level of the group are impervious to
psychology.[52]

Thus we can formulate a further contrast: American sociology is characterized by psychological realism (social nominalism); European sociology, by social realism (psychological nominalism).

It is perhaps unnecessary to point out that these are no more than
broad characterizations. For a fuller description (surely not to be undertaken here), qualifications must be entered. Also, there are exceptions.
For instance, much recent American work in bureaucracy and social
stratification leans more toward social realism; and on the other hand,
there is a strong interest in psychology, verging on psychological realism,
in as different European writers as Tarde, LeBon, and some of Simmel.
It is also possible to make relevant distinctions on the American scene
according to individual and typical sociologists, institutions, and levels

(textbook *vs.* monograph, for instance). On the whole, nevertheless, American sociology has from almost the beginning been more deeply involved with ("social") psychology ("interests," "social forces," "instincts," "needs," "attitudes," etc.) than with society or history, whereas the opposite tends to describe European sociology.

Ernst Grünwald's distinction of the "psychological theory" and the "historical theory" as the "roots" or forerunners of the sociology of knowledge suggests the pertinence of this discussion for the sociology of knowledge itself. The "psychological theory," including its conceptions of truth and falsehood, is based on a theory of human nature; the "historical theory," with the same inclusion, on a theory of history.[53] Without detailing names, tendencies, and movements, it is clear that the sociology of knowledge, although the German variant more than the French, is in the "historical" rather than the "psychological" tradition. Along with much European sociology—to add a last generalization— the sociology of knowledge operates with a concept of existential truth, sometimes at the cost of inadequate attention to the concept of scientific truth. This last contrast gives credence to the often-heard derogatory designation of European sociology generally as "philosophical," "metaphysical," "speculative," "armchair," etc., and, on the other hand, to the European comments that in American sociology "reliability has been won by surrendering theoretic relevance." [54]

A summary presentation of the characteristics of American and European sociology that have been suggested may be useful (Table 1):

TABLE 1.

METAPHYSICAL TENDENCIES OF AMERICAN AND EUROPEAN SOCIOLOGY

American Sociology	European Sociology (and Sociology of Knowledge)
Scientific Truth	Existential Truth
Individual-Psychological Realism	Social-Historical Realism
Social-Historical Nominalism	Individual-Psychological Nominalism

VII. CONNECTIONS BETWEEN THE SOCIOLOGY OF KNOWLEDGE AND OUR TIME

At the beginning of our inquiry into the premises of the sociology of knowledge (Section IV), we spoke of the need for showing the nature of the connection between it and our time. The intervening discussion was necessary before we could hope to meet this need. In the present section we shall try to do so. It may help to recall the course of our argument thus far. In recalling it, we shall rephrase it in the light of the gains we have made.

We began by asking, "What is the sociology of knowledge?"—a question raised and answered by an outsider requesting and receiving scientific knowledge. The central concern of the insider, who then was introduced, emerged as the concern to recognize himself and his fellow-men in their common time and place in order to know what to do. This—our—time and place appeared to us as characterized by the administered nature of our lives, by "the world as underdeveloped," and by "one-world-and-cultural-relativism," with understanding as the hope of transcending this time, and dualism—and, as we saw later, naturalism—as the metaphysical premises of such understanding. These also were seen as the metaphysical premises, related to its methodological and volitional premises, of the sociology of knowledge. We may now make explicit those implications of the subsequent steps of our inquiry which are relevant to the task of showing that the connection between the sociology of knowledge and our time can be analyzed and can be argued to be of a determinable kind and importance.

These steps dealt with the distinction between scientific and existential truth and with the preponderant association of the former with individual-psychological realism (social nominalism) and of the latter with social-historical realism (individual nominalism). Social-historical realism and existential truth, we suggested, characterize the sociology of knowledge, and one indication of this is its notion of historical consciousness. We had earlier remarked on the absence of this notion from the American preoccupation with the sociology of knowledge and had illustrated this absence by Wirth's and Merton's observations on the time in which the sociology of knowledge arose.

The connection between the sociology of knowledge and our time thus appears as follows: (1) To speak of such a connection makes sense only if the concept "our time" itself makes sense. And it does this only on a historical (social-historical-realist) view, rather than a psychological (individual-psychological-realist) one. (2) Once such a view is adopted, the sociology of knowledge can be seen as one of several articulations [55] of the consciousness of our time, an articulation which, as it becomes conscious of being such, contributes to the transcendence of this consciousness. The sociology of knowledge thus emerges as the reaffirmation or, better, re-invention of the Socratic position, on the occasion of its insight into its own time and place. (3) In becoming conscious of being an articulation of the consciousness of our time—in becoming conscious of its methodological, volitional, and metaphysical premises in their historical relevance—the sociology of knowledge appears as a revision of our way of . . . looking at ourselves and the world, of our attitude toward the world, of our interpretation of it. It "defines" a new "situation" . . . and prior to this self-realization of the sociology of knowledge the situation was merely new, profoundly fascinating and profoundly threatening. The sociology of knowledge, therefore, may be called an elucidation of a new experience man has had and is still having. Through it, man adapts himself to living in one world, and through it he transcends cultural relativism toward the view of himself as dual and inexhaustibly challenging his own exploration.[56]

Or, in words used earlier, the sociology of knowledge transforms a new and shattering experience into a problem.

VIII. NINETEENTH- AND TWENTIETH-CENTURY CIVILIZATIONAL-HISTORICAL DICHOTOMIES, MODERN AMERICAN SOCIOLOGY, AND THE SOCIOLOGY OF KNOWLEDGE

In the exploration of our time and place, "the world as underdeveloped" appeared as a correction of the notion of "underdeveloped countries," that is, of the tendency to project our own underdevelopment on non-Western peoples. In that connection, we commented on some civilizational-historical dichotomies as attempts at coming to terms with the emerging one world. We now wish to apply our subsequent distinction between scientific and existential truth to a reinterpretation of these dichotomies so that differences and relations between the sociology of knowledge and American sociology may be brought out further.

Henry Maine's contrast between societies based on status and societies based on contract; Herbert Spencer's military and industrial societies; Ferdinand Tönnies' *Gemeinschaft* and *Gesellschaft;* Emile Durkheim's societies characterized by mechanical and those characterized by organic solidarity; Max Weber's distinction between traditionalism and rationalism; Howard Becker's sacred and secular societies; Ralph Linton's ascribed and achieved status (and "universals" and "alternatives"); Robert Redfield's folk and urban societies; and Godfrey and Monica Wilson's primitive and civilized,[57] to mention only some of the dichotomies articulated during the last hundred years, are not only what they were predominantly intended by their authors to be, namely scientific hypotheses submitted for confirmation or falsification by subsequent research. They also claim existential truth:

For decades, the pictures of primitive character brought back by anthropologists, no matter how well intended, were used by the denizens of Western industrialized civilization, either to preen themselves on their progress or to damn their cities, machines, or customs by reference to a constructed preliterate Eden—all, of course, under the guidance of such supposedly scientific terms as "fo":. society," *"Gemeinschaft,"* "sacred society," and other such phrases.[58]

In our words, the existential element in these dichotomies is the mixture of faith and doubt that liberalism, increasing rationalization, reasonableness, progress are indeed true. The faith probably is more plausible than the doubt, but we must recall that some of the dichotomists did express their worries. Thus, Durkheim was disturbed by anomie, Weber by bureaucratization, Mannheim by the preponderance of functional over substantial rationality—and Durkheim looked to social reorganization through professional groups; Weber expressed his belief in prophecy; Mannheim, in ecstasy.[59] The appearance of these dichotomies and their authors' attitudes toward them thus tell the later story of liberalism (more spontaneously or, one might say, in a more clinical sense than do Nietzsche, Spengler, or Toynbee) as the doubt concerning the existential truth of the liberal historical interpretation and the scientific truth of its historical account.[60] The dichotomists (or other Westerners) have not succeeded either in writing a scientifically more accurate history or in revising liberalism toward greater historical adequacy. Instead, we have been overwhelmed by totalitarianism—among other things an alternative, antiliberal interpretation of the historical moment—and have experienced and witnessed the helplessness of liberalism confronted with it.[61]

Reinhard Bendix has shown that certain trends in the development of the Western image of man from Bacon through the Enlightenment to Marx, Nietzsche, and Freud represent an increasing "distrust of reason." [62] The last four centuries, especially the last hundred years, have thrown man ever more back on himself, unmasking ideas, beliefs, customs, and traditions as unreliable and unworthy crutches, as ideologies (Marx) or sublimations (Freud).

There arose, therefore, the question, "what, then, is man?" It was being asked by the same analysts who had stripped man to the necessity of (again) asking it, as well as by many others, from Descartes through Kierkegaard to the contemporary existentialists, phenomenologists, and various theologians. But this question intruded during the same period in which science and technology developed and (especially in its later phases) the standard of living rose to levels never reached before. These developments themselves thus appeared tempting as the very answers. The question, "What is man?," therefore, had to be asked in a whisper, in an embarrassed whisper—as a lover asks his beloved in the din of a factory, a cafeteria, a movie house, and (particularly in the twentieth century) the roar of world wars, an atom-bomb explosion, a concentration camp. Science, technology, prosperity, and disaster seem to

have kept our self-inspection in a balance between the desire for it
and its postponement as long as the automobile and the screen were
there for us to escape with; and as long as the war, which had to be
fought, urged us to tell who we are by asking science and ignoring
history, ourselves. Witness scientism, infatuation with methodology in
general, and more particularly such phenomena as formal literary criticism, philosophical analysis, structural linguistics, and the strong ritual-
istic element in social relations.[63]

These are some historical problems to which modern sociology,
specifically, might address itself. Instead, it appears to be preoccupied,
in America possibly more than elsewhere, with rather ahistorical formal
"structural" relations and processes and with improving itself as a specialty in such preoccupation. To say this is not to suggest that sociology
should not be a generalizing science. Rather it is to argue that sociology would facilitate its task of being a generalizing science if it recognized its need for a historical theory of society, no matter how crude
it might be to begin with.[64] If sociology wants to be historically relevant,
it cannot reject its commitment to historical realism and abide its psychological realism which no longer is historically adequate. For even
a generalizing science, *if it is a social science,* starts with the historical
situation; it may deny it but it cannot escape it. In this respect, social
science cannot be entirely true to the pure type of science which
"brackets" the ontological quest.[65]

The sociology of knowledge escapes this difficulty of modern American sociology by its historical realism and its much more openly recognized connection with the quest for existential truth. It is alien to the
formalism of our time and in this sense, and by contrast, substantive [66];
it is "applied" theory, in the service of changing the world, whether in
the sense of Marx (specifically the *Theses on Feuerbach*) or Durkheim.
Both Marx and Durkheim preceded the modern bifurcation of the world
into Is and Ought, a bifurcation which has been shared and pushed by
contemporary social science. Marx, much more than Durkheim, was
one of the "strippers" of modern man, but his historical focus kept the
Is and Ought together. Durkheim, like Max Weber, is a figure of transition in the sense that in their actual researches both keep Is and Ought
together while in their explicit methodological writings they separate
them (Weber more pointedly and passionately than Durkheim).[67] In
the United States, the form secularization took in Marx (by way of
Hegel and Feuerbach) appears to be an unmanageable alternative to
American liberalism.[68] The other, the separation of Is and Ought, is
intimately connected with the phenomena discussed in our exploration
of the contemporary Western scene and with those mentioned in the
next to the last paragraph above. In American sociology, this separa-

tion is of recent date, probably the 1920's. It had not yet appeared in Cooley's *Social Process* (1918); Lundberg-Anderson-Bain's *Trends in American Sociology* (1929) was a milestone in its articulation and acceptance. Already ten years later, Robert S. Lynd manifested discontent with it in *Knowledge for What?*

IX. MERTON'S COMPARISON BETWEEN THE SOCIOLOGY OF KNOWLEDGE AND MASS COMMUNICATIONS

And now let us consider that comparison between European and American sociology which is most pertinent here: Merton's juxtaposition of the European sociology of knowledge and that recent branch of American sociology, research into mass communications, which seems most closely related to it.

Although the sociology of knowledge and "mass communications," Merton observes, have, on the whole, developed independently from one another, they may be regarded "as two species of that genus of research which is concerned with the interplay between social structure and communications." [69] The numerous contrasting aspects of these two "species" may be presented in tabular form (Table 2):

TABLE 2.

MERTON'S COMPARISON BETWEEN THE SOCIOLOGY OF KNOWLEDGE AND MASS COMMUNICATIONS

Aspects	Sociology of Knowledge (European)	Mass Communications (American)
Subject matter and definition of problems	Knowledge Bodies of systematically connected facts or ideas Total structure of knowledge available to a few	Information Isolated fragments of information available to masses of people
Data and facts	Historical Long-range Impressions of mass opinion set down by a few observers as facts Chief question: "why" Chief concern: problem, even if speculation is the best that can be done Studies and findings are important, even if empirically questionable	Contemporary Short-range Collection of facts Chief question: "what" Chief concern: securing adequate empirical data, even if the problem gets lost Studies and findings may be trivial but are empirically rigorous

Table 2 (*Continued*)

Merton's Comparison Between the Sociology of Knowledge
and Mass Communications

Aspects	Sociology of Knowledge (European)	Mass Communications (American)
Research techniques and procedures	Limited to the authentication of documents	A considerable array of various techniques
	Reliability is no problem	Reliability is an important problem
	A tradition in and from the history of different interpretations of the same data; a humanities background	No such tradition and background
	Cumulative nature of findings not stressed	Cumulative nature of findings is stressed
	No audience research because the chief question is the "why" or "how come" of the intellectual phenomena investigated	Emphasis on audience research because the chief question is the "what" or "what impact" of the intellectual phenomena investigated
	Impetus behind the studies is academic	Impetus behind the studies is practical (market and military research, propaganda, etc.) [70]
Social organization of research	Lone wolf No organizational pressure toward reliability	Team Organizational pressure toward reliability
Social origins of investigators (tentative)	Investigators are marginal to different social systems and perceive diverse intellectual perspectives of different groups	Investigators are mobile within an economic or social system and get data needed by those who operate organizations, seek markets, and control many people

It is hardly necessary to insist that Merton's description of the sociology of knowledge and the study of mass communications largely agrees with that of the sociology of knowledge and American sociology, respectively, presented in this paper. (It is true, of course, that each of the two efforts has commented on aspects ignored by the other; most obviously, the present essay has left out of consideration the last two of Merton's five categories, the social organization of research and the social origins of investigators.) Translating Merton's characterizations which touch most closely on our enterprise into the language of the latter, we obtain the following propositions: (1) As to subject matter and definition of problems, the sociology of knowledge examines intellectual life as a whole, whereas mass communications takes it for granted such as it finds it and explores features of it which unexamined traditions have made problematical (cf. the last entry under "Research techniques and procedures" in the "Mass Communications" column of Table 2); the former is practiced in a philosophical-anthropological and historical sense, the latter in an unsystematically contemporary one. (2) As to data and facts, the sociology of knowledge is guided by concern with history, existential truth, causality, the nature of knowledge and of intersubjectivity itself, whereas mass communications strives to register the pulse of opinion with scientifically unimpeachable methods. (3) As to research techniques and procedures, for the sociology of knowledge these are secondary, whereas for mass communications they tend to be primary, self-consummatory, and self-proliferating; the former is in the service of "culture," the latter, of "civilization." [71]

Aside from these all too abbreviated comments on the content of Merton's and the present characterizations, a word must be said about the difference between their respective volitional premises and criteria of truth. Merton wishes to establish true propositions concerning similarities and differences between the sociology of knowledge and communications research. He operates with the scientific conception of truth, in line with the scientific approach and, more specifically, with his effort to "codify" extant theory and research. By contrast, what has been said in the preceding pages has affirmed the historical and perspective in which it was stated, as well as the effort to arrive at existential truth. To put it differently, Merton's chief concern is "what" (a characteristic of the right-hand column in Table 2); mine, "why" or "how come" (a characteristic of the left-hand column). Merton's analysis, and the translation of some of his own hopes stated in the text on which Table 2 is based, teaches us gaps in the attention to scientific problems, to be filled by scientific propositions, whereas the European column shows gaps in the attention to existential problems, to be filled by existentially true propositions.

It should be noted, however, that what has just been said claims to be true in the scientific sense of the term. Its "attitude" is the same as that of Merton's analysis. What it talks about, however, is different, namely existential truth, on which Merton, as behooves the scientist.

including the social scientist, is silent. To discuss the nature of truth, as is widely recognized, is not the scientist's but the philosopher's concern. It is also widely recognized that it is important to distinguish between talking about one's own views of truth, which is considered a philosophical enterprise, and about somebody else's, which is accepted as a legitimate scientific enterprise. In expounding my own views of truth in the present paper, I have sometimes talked as a philosopher (in the philosophical "attitude"); in commenting on Merton's, I have talked as a scientist. Social science, in contrast to natural science, is concerned, no matter how indirectly, with human beings, that is, fellow men. At least *at this time* (which I have tried to characterize)—and we have no other—social science has to start, I have argued, with this time, with the historical situation. In order to grasp the historical situation and communicate the process of grasping it, as this process has been going on in the making of this paper, I had to suspend ("bracket") the safety which comes from limitation to scientific truth and open myself ("surrender") to existential truth. In the present paragraph, on the occasion of commenting on Merton's paradigm, I have returned to the scientific attitude.

X. THE SOCIOLOGY OF KNOWLEDGE AND SOCIOLOGICAL THEORY

By now, the reader may long have forgotten the title of this paper—or its first sentence. Actually, however, the whole paper has dealt with the relation between the sociology of knowledge and sociological theory, as a concluding summary and explication of what it has to say about this will show.

First, let us list some of the things it has nothing to say about. (1) It has nothing to say about the relation between the sociology of knowledge and sociological theory such as might be disclosed by an analysis of the work of sociologists of knowledge and sociological theorists. (2) It has no recommendation to make concerning the way in which a scientific study is carried out. (3) It offers no list of scientific problems to be investigated under the program of a sociology of knowledge such as it conceives of—in the present context, this is too large a topic.[72] (4) It urges no particular definition of "sociological theory."

At this point we must make an observation about "sociological theory," which will lead us to the more positive statements we have to submit. It is that, with only one exception that I know of,[73] the relatively few extant definitions of the term "sociological theory"—to the extent that they go beyond elevating a casual collection of colloquial referents to definitional status—are much more specific about its formal features [74]—what its structure is like or how it is constructed—than about its content, or what it is *about*. It is almost as if sociology, in relation to which they try to define "theory," *had* no specific content. This suggests that these conceptions of "theory" do not regard the subject matter of sociology, human beings, of sufficient theoretical dignity to incorporate it into a definition of "sociological theory." It is a further indication of their corresponding conceptions of sociology.

This observation concerning "sociological theory" is the major reason why the present paper has proceeded as it has. Thus, it has had to say much more about modern American sociology in general than about sociological theory or particular theories. Modern sociology and sociological theory are so intimately connected that a historical analysis has appeared to be a more adequate tool for identifying them than a systematic analysis would have been. A systematic analysis could easily fall prey to the temptation to take sociology and sociological theory at their face value. It is hoped, however, that this paper may help clear the ground for such an analysis.

If we put positively what the last three paragraphs have said in the negative, we can now formulate what this paper does have to say about the relations between the sociology of knowledge and sociological theory. (1) The analysis of the sociology of knowledge in the context of our time appears to make it incumbent on sociological theory to define itself, either in a way which is adequate to the subject matter of sociology and to the historical occasion of such a definition, or such as to disprove the relevance of this double requirement of adequacy. (2) The extant, overwhelmingly social-historically nominalistic sociological theory appears to make it incumbent on the sociology of knowledge (reinspect the "unfavorable" items in the left-hand column of Table 2) to clarify its status in reference to scientific *vs.* existential truth, science *vs.* history, and science *vs.* philosophy. As it is, the sociology of knowledge is two things. One, particularly in America, is dead. The other is not yet—it is a heap of fragments and shoots waiting to be given form and life. Dead is the excitement attendant on the appearance of Mannheim's *Ideology and Utopia*—it would be good if this paper had managed to show that that excitement had a greater claim than that of a fad, that there is hope of recalling its origin in the confrontation of sociology with history, existential truth, philosophy. Not yet alive are two potentialities of the sociology of knowledge. The first is the codification of the great mass of relevant research into a more viable sociology of intellectual life. The other, different, even though causally related, is the injection of more self-conscious humanness and historicity, and thus greater scientific relevance, into contemporary sociology.

NOTES

1. Jacques J. Maquet (*Sociologie de la connaissance: sa structure et ses rapports avec la philosophie de la connaissance; étude critique des systèmes de Karl Mannheim et de Pitirim A. Sorokin* [Louvain: Institut de Recherches Economiques et Sociales; E. Nauwalaerts, éditeur, 1949], p. 19; *The Sociology of Knowledge: Its Structure and Its Relation to the Philosophy of Knowledge: A Critical Analysis of the Systems of Karl Mannheim and Pitirim A. Sorokin*, transl. by John F. Locke [Boston: Beacon Press, Inc., 1951], p. 3) claims that *"connaissance"* in *"sociologie de la connaissance"* and "knowledge" in "sociology of knowledge" have "greater denotations" than *"wissen"* which, "taken as a whole, means science, whereas 'knowledge' includes at one and the same time the simple act of presenting an object to the mind . . . and the act of thinking which reaches a complete understanding of this object." This "greater denotation" refers to the fact that the German term connotes a higher claim to certainty than the French and English terms do (to which latter corresponds the German *"kennen,"* not *"erkennen,"* as Maquet writes). By the criterion of the relation of knower to known, however, *"wissen"* is broader than "knowledge" inasmuch as it refers not only to the scientist and his scientific knowledge but also to philosopher, artist, mystic, religious person, etc., and their respective kinds of knowledge. For "commonsense" questions concerning the meanings of these terms, this is the more expected criterion. It thus appears to be less misleading to say that *"wissen"* has a "broader" meaning than "knowledge" does.

2. Along with historicism (cf. T. B. Bottomore, "Some Reflections on the Sociology of Knowledge," *British Journal of Sociology,* VII [March, 1956], pp. 52-58, esp. 52) and Nietzsche, leading to Freud and Pareto and the "related current" of positivism (Ratzenhofer, Gumplowicz, Oppenheimer, Jerusalem: cf. Karl Mannheim, "The Sociology of Knowledge" [1931], *Ideology and Utopia: An Introduction to the Sociology of Knowledge,* transl. by Louis Wirth and Edward Shils [New York: Harcourt, Brace and Company, 1936], pp. 278-79). For the history of the sociology of knowledge and a critique of the major ideas advanced by its various factions, see Ernst Grünwald, *Das Problem der Soziologie des Wissens: Versuch einer kritischen Darstellung der wissenssoziologischen Theorien* (Wien-Leipzig: Wilhelm Braümuller, 1934). For the significance of Marxism, see Robert K. Merton, "The Sociology of Knowledge," in Georges Gurvitch and Wilbert E. Moore, eds., *Twentieth Century Sociology* (New York: Philosophical Library, 1945), Chapter XIII, *passim* (reprinted in Merton, *Social Theory and Social Structure: Toward the Codification of Theory and Research* [Glencoe, Ill.: Free Press, 1949], Chapter VIII; revised and enlarged edition [*ibid.,* 1957], Chapter XII). For a collection of relevant texts by Marx himself, some of them previously untranslated, see Karl Marx, *Selected Writings in Sociology and Social Philosophy,* ed. with an introduction and notes by T. B. Bottomore and Maximilien Rubel (London: Watts, 1956), including the editors' introduction.

3. This term is a coinage of the early 1920's. It was subsequently taken over in translation. For French, Dutch, and Italian versions, see Maquet, *The Sociology of Knowledge, loc. cit.,* p. 261, n. 1.

4. E.g., Hans-Joachim Lieber, *Wissen und Gesellschaft: Die Probleme der Wissenssoziologie* (Tübingen: Max Niemeyer, 1952); Mannheim, *Ideologie und Utopie* (3rd enlarged edition, Frankfurt/Main: G. Schulte-Bulmke, 1952).

5. Max Scheler, "Probleme einer Soziologie des Wissens," in Scheler, ed., *Versuche zu einer Soziologie des Wissens* (München und Leipzig: Duncker und Humblot, 1924), pp. 5-146; enlarged under the same title in Scheler, *Die Wissensformen und die Gesellschaft* (Leipzig: Der neue Geist Verlag, 1926), pp. 1-229; Mannheim, *Ideologie und Utopie* (Bonn: Friedrich Cohen, 1929).

6. Mannheim, *Ideology and Utopia, loc. cit.*

7. Louis Wirth, "Preface" to Mannheim, *op. cit.,* esp. pp. xvii-xxiii (reprinted in Wirth, *Community Life and Social Policy,* ed. by Elizabeth Wirth Marvick and Albert J. Reiss, Jr. [Chicago: University of Chicago Press, 1956], esp. pp. 40-45).

8. There probably is an affinity, on the other hand, between the "sociology of knowledge" and a European outlook. A good deal of what we shall have to say later in this paper will evince, and bears on, this affinity, although we shall not analyze it explicitly.

9. Arthur Child, *The Problems of the Sociology of Knowledge: A Critical and Philosophical Study* (unpublished Ph.D. dissertation, Berkeley: University of California, 1938). Five of the eight chapters of this dissertation have been published in revised form: "The Theoretical Possibility of the Sociology of Knowledge," *Ethics,* LI (July, 1941), pp. 392-418 (henceforth referred to as "Possibility"); "The Existential Determination of Thought," *ibid.,* LII (January, 1942), pp. 153-85; "The Problem of Imputation in the Sociology of Knowledge," *ibid.,* LI (January, 1941), pp. 200-219 ("Imputation"); "The Problem of Imputation Resolved," *ibid.,* LIV (January, 1944), pp. 96-109; "The Problem of Truth in the Sociology of Knowledge," *ibid.,* LVIII (October, 1947), pp. 18-34 ("Truth"); "On the Theory of the Categories," *Philosophy and Phenomenological Research,* VII (December, 1946), pp. 316-35 ("Categories").

10. Merton, "The Sociology of Knowledge," *loc. cit.*

11. Wirth, *op. cit.* Cf. also Franz Adler, "The Sociology of Knowledge since 1918," *Midwest Sociologist,* XVII (Spring, 1955), pp. 3 ff.

12. Kurt H. Wolff, "A Preliminay Inquiry into the Sociology of Knowledge from the Standpoint of the Study of Man," *Scritti di sociologia e politica in onore di Luigi Sturzo* (Bologna: Nicola Zanichelli, 1953), Vol. III, p. 586 ("Inquiry").

13. Louis Wirth, quoted in Howard W. Odum, *American Sociology: The Story of Sociology in the United States through 1950* (New York: Longmans, Green & Co., Inc., 1951) p. 231.

14. In his "Paradigm for the Sociology of Knowledge," Merton (*op. cit.,* p. 372 [reprinted, *op. cit.,* pp. 221-22; rev. ed., pp. 460-61]) uses "mental

productions" without, however, advocating "sociology of mental productions" as a substitute for "sociology of knowledge."

15. Karl Mannheim, *Essays on the Sociology of Culture*, ed., by Ernest Manheim in co-operation with Paul Kecskemeti (New York: Oxford University Press, 1956), Part 1, "Towards the Sociology of the Mind; an Introduction."

16. Gerard DeGre, "The Sociology of Knowledge and the Problem of Truth," *Journal of the History of Ideas*, II (January, 1941), p. 110.

17. Wolff, "Inquiry," p. 587. Also cf. Franz Adler, "The Range of Sociology of Knowledge," in Howard Becker and Alvin Boskoff, eds., *Modern Sociological Theory in Continuity and Change* (New York: Dryden Press, 1957), Chapter 13. An attempt at assembling relevant materials, though in a rather haphazard and exceedingly incomplete manner, is my *The Sociology of Knowledge: A Preliminary Bibliography* ([Columbus: Ohio State University, Department of Sociology and Anthropology, 1945 [mimeographed]; "Additions" [1951]). Despite its serious shortcomings and its preliminary character, it is more comprehensive than others, among which Mannheim's (*Ideology and Utopia, loc. cit.*, pp. 281-304, augmented in the 1952 German edition of *Ideologie und Utopie, loc. cit.*, pp. 269-91) is the most important. For a very comprehensive, indispensable, and only slightly overlapping bibliography on the sociology of literature, see Hugh Dalziel Duncan, *Language and Literature in Society: A Sociological Essay on Theory and Method in the Interpretation of Linguistic Symbols, with a Bibliographical Guide to the Sociology of Literature* (Chicago: University of Chicago Press, 1953), pp. 143-214.

18. E. g., Robert K. Merton, "Science, Technology and Society in Seventeenth-Century England," *Osiris*, 4 (1938), pp. 360-632; Ernest Kohn-Bramstedt, *Aristocracy and the Middle-Classes in Germany: Social Types in German Literature, 1830–1900* (London: P. S. King, 1937); Karl Mannheim, "Historicism" (1924), in *Essays on the Sociology of Knowledge*, Paul Kecskemeti, ed. (London: Routledge and Kegan Paul, 1952), pp. 84-133; "Conservative Thought" (1927), in *Essays on Sociology and Social Psychology*, Paul Kecskemeti, ed. (New York: Oxford University Press, 1953), pp. 74-164; Edgar Zilsel, "The Sociological Roots of Science," *American Journal of Sociology*, XLVII (January, 1942), pp. 544-62.

19. Karl Mannheim, "Ideologische und soziologische Interpretation der geistigen Gebilde," *Jahrbuch für Soziologie*, 2 (1926), pp. 424-40 (a mimeographed translation is available on request).

20. Florian Znaniecki, *The Social Role of the Man of Knowledge* (New York: Columbia University Press, 1940).

21. Leo P. Chall, "The Sociology of Knowledge," in Joseph S. Roucek, ed., *Contemporary Sociology* (New York: Philosophical Library, 1958), p. 289.

22. For Robert K. Merton, cf. his chronological bibliography in *Social Theory and Social Structure, loc. cit.*, pp. 409-12. In regard to C. Wright Mills, compare his early work in the sociology of knowledge (e.g., "Methodological Consequences of the Sociology of Knowledge," *American Journal of Sociology*, XLVI [November, 1940], pp. 316-30) with his later books

on labor leaders, white-collar workers, and the "power elite." Gerard DeGre *(op. cit.* and *Society and Ideology: An Inquiry into the Sociology of Science* [Garden City, N. Y.: Doubleday, 1955]; this study, however, shows that DeGre has not abandoned his interest in the sociology of knowledge proper—see esp. pp. 34-37). Frank E. Hartung, on the other hand, has continued to publish from time to time in the field since 1944 (e.g., "The Sociology of Positivism," *Science and Society,* 8 [Fall, 1944], pp. 328-41; "Problems of the Sociology of Knowledge," *Philosophy of Science,* 19 [January, 1952], pp. 17-32). For Howard Becker and Pitirim A. Sorokin, the sociology of knowledge has never been central—cf. Becker and Helmut Otto Dahlke, "Max Scheler's Sociology of Knowledge," *Philosophy and Phenomenological Research,* II (March, 1942), pp. 309-22; Sorokin, *Social and Cultural Dynamics,* Vol. II, *Fluctuation of Systems of Truth, Ethics, and Law* (New York: American Book Company, 1937), "a treatise in *Wissenssoziologie,* considered in its basic forms and principles" *(ibid.,* p. vii); Sorokin has been treated as a sociologist of knowledge by Merton, "The Sociology and Knowledge," *loc cit.,* and Maquet, *op. cit.*

23. Arthur Child, following his extended work in the sociology of knowledge, has turned to problems of philosophy of history; his "Moral Judgment in History," *Ethics,* LXI (July, 1951), pp. 297-308, is a connecting link. Virgil G. Hinshaw, Jr., has moved from the sociology of knowledge, especially the critique of Mannheim's epistemological claims ("The Epistemological Relevance of Mannheim's Sociology of Knowledge," *Journal of Philosophy,* XL [4 February 1943], pp. 57-72 ["Relevance"]), to epistemology ("Basic Propositions in Lewis's Analysis of Knowledge," *ibid.,* XLVI [31 March 1949], pp. 176-84) and philosophy of science ("Levels of Analysis," *Philosophy and Phenomenological Research,* XI [December, 1950], pp. 213-20). Thelma Z. Lavine ("Sociological Analysis of Cognitive Forms," *Journal of Philosophy,* XXXIX [18 June 1942], pp. 342-56) has subsequently undertaken studies in the history of epistemology ("Knowledge as Interpretation: An Historical Survey," *Philosophy and Phenomenological Research,* X [June, 1950], pp. 526-40, and XI [September, 1950], pp. 88-103).

24. The purpose of this essay is not, of course, a critique of Mannheim's conceptions. They have received abundant and incisive examination. To mention only the more painstaking analyses in English (except for the first), in chronological order: Alexander von Schelting, *Max Weber's Wissenschaftslehre; das logische Problem der historischen Kulturerkenntnis; die Grenzen der Soziologie des Wissens* (Tübingen: J. C. B. Mohr, 1934), pp. 94-100, 117-67, and his review of Mannheim's *Ideologie und Utopie, American Sociological Review,* 1 (August, 1936), pp. 664-74; Hans Speier, review of Mannheim's *Ideology and Utopia, American Journal of Sociology,* XLIII (July, 1937), pp. 155-66; Maurice Mandelbaum, *The Problem of Historical Knowledge: An Answer to Relativism* (New York: Liveright Publishing Corporation, 1938), pp. 67-82; Child, "Imputation," pp. 204-07, "Possibility," pp. 410-11, "Truth," pp. 20-21; Robert K. Merton, "Karl Mannheim and the Sociology of Knowledge," *Journal of Liberal Religion,* 2 (Winter, 1941), pp. 125-47 (reprinted in *Social Theory and Social Structure, loc. cit.,* Chapter IX; rev. ed., Chapter XIII); Hinshaw, "Relevance"; Maquet, *op. cit.,* esp. Chapters 3 and 5.

25. Peter M. Blau, *Bureaucracy in Modern Society* (New York: Random House, 1956), p. 14.

26. On "secularization," see Max Weber, "The Protestant Sects and the Spirit of Capitalism" (1906), *From Max Weber: Essays in Sociology,* transl. ed., and with an introd. by H. H. Gerth and C. Wright Mills (New York: Oxford University Press, 1946), p. 307; Talcott Parsons, *The Structure of Social Action* (New York: McGraw-Hill Book Company, Inc., 1937), pp. 685-86; and, one of the most searching recent analyses, Hannah Arendt, "History and Immortality," *Partisan Review,* XXIV (Winter, 1957), esp. pp. 16-22. On "rationalization," see *From Max Weber, loc. cit.,* "Introduction," pp. 51-52.

27. Max Horkheimer, *Eclipse of Reason* (New York: Oxford University Press, 1947), pp. 3-4 and *passim.* Here the discussion of "value judgments" in social science is relevant. See especially Max Weber, *On the Methodology of the Social Sciences,* transl. and ed. by Edward A. Shils and Henry A. Finch (Glencoe, Ill.: Free Press, 1949); Felix Kaufmann, *Methodology of the Social Sciences* (New York: Oxford University Press, 1944), Chapters IX and XV; Leo Strauss, *Natural Right and History* (Chicago: University of Chicago Press, 1953), Chapter II; Dwight Macdonald, *The Root Is Man: Two Essays in Politics* (Alhambra, Cal.: Cunningham Press, 1953), "Scientific Method and Value Judgment," pp. 36-39; Joseph Wood Krutch, *Man the Measure* (1953, 1954) (New York: Grosset and Dunlap, Inc., n. d.), esp. Chapter 4.

28. Despite terminological appearance possibly to the contrary, "subjective reason" is much closer to Mannheim's "functional" than to his "substantial rationality" (the unclarity in which he left the latter concept itself evinces the loss of objective rationality): Karl Mannheim, *Man and Society in an Age of Reconstruction* (1935) (New York: Harcourt, Brace and Company, 1940), pp. 52-60.

29. This experience probably is exhibited more poignantly by Max Weber than by any other social scientist. See, e.g., Weber, " 'Objectivity' in Social Science and Social Policy" (1904), *On the Methodology of the Social Sciences, loc. cit.,* pp. 52-57; "The Meaning of 'Ethical Neutrality' in Sociology and Economics" (1913, 1917), *ibid.,* pp. 11-15, 18-21; "Science as a Vocation" (1918), *From Max Weber, loc. cit.,* pp. 148, 152-53. Leo Strauss, *op. cit.,* has clearly described and criticized Weber's position.

30. On futile attempts at deriving Ought from Is, that is, on the "naturalistic fallacy," cf. Eliseo Vivas, *The Moral Life and the Ethical Life* (Chicago: University of Chicago Press, 1950), Part I, "Animadversions upon Naturalistic Moral Philosophies," *passim,* esp. pp. 81-82.

31. In an important, if not the essential respect, Erich Kahler's *The Tower and the Abyss: An Inquiry into the Transformation of the Individual* (New York: George Braziller, 1957) is a history of contemporary consciousness.

32. David Riesman, in collaboration with Reuel Denney and Nathan Glazier, *The Lonely Crowd: A Study of the Changing American Character* (New Haven: Yale University Press, 1950), Part III, "Autonomy," esp. pp. 287-88 (Anchor Book edition, 1953, p. 278); Erich Fromm, *Man for*

Himself: An Inquiry into the Psychology of Ethics (New York, Toronto: Rinehart & Co., Inc., 1947), pp. 82-107.

33. Fëdor Dostoevsky, *The Idiot* (1869), transl. with an introd. by David Magarshack (Penguin Books, Inc., 1955), p. 563.

34. Cf. my "The World as Underdeveloped," *Atti del Congresso internazionale di studio sul problema delle aree arretrate* (Milan: Dott. A. Giuffre, 1955), Vol. III, *Communicazioni,* pp. 505-08.

35. The literary record of these social scientists is impressive and important. Cf. e.g., Edward H. Spicer, ed., *Human Problems in Technological Change: A Case Book* (New York: Russell Sage Foundation, 1952), *Human Organization,* official journal of the Society for Applied Anthropology; the increasing attention to relevant problems in several social-science periodicals, especially in anthropology and sociology, including certain issues of the *Annals of the American Academy of Political and Social Science,* such as Vol. 305, "Agrarian Societies in Transition" (May, 1956). For representative statements on problems of "applied anthropology," see *Anthropology Today: An Encyclopedic Inventory,* prepared under the chairmanship of A. L. Kroeber (Chicago: University of Chicago Press, 1953), "Problems of Application," pp. 741-894; Sol Tax, Loren C. Eisely, Irving Rouse, and Carl F. Voegelin, eds., *An Appraisal of Anthropology Today (ibid.,* 1953), Chapters X and XI; William L. Thomas, Jr., ed., *Yearbook of Anthropology—1955* (New York: Wenner-Gren Foundation for Anthropological Research, 1955), Parts Four and Five, *passim;* the symposium on applied anthropology at the 1957 meetings of the American Anthropological Association (*Human Organization,* 17, 1 [Spring, 1958], "Values in Action: A Symposium," pp. 2-26). Also note the very recent collaboration of several social sciences, including history and economics, on common problems (in contrast to the more accustomed "interdisciplinary" work among sociologists, anthropologists, psychologists, psychiatrists, and psychoanalysts)—see esp. Mirra Komarovsky, ed., *Common Frontiers of the Social Sciences* (Glencoe, Ill.: Free Press and Falcon's Wing Press, 1957), and Karl Polanyi, Conrad Arensberg, and Harry Pearson, eds., *Trade and Market in the Early Empires (ibid.,* 1957). Here also belongs Robert Redfield's qualification of the folk-urban dichotomy by his emphasis on the distinction between "great" and "little" traditions—see esp. his *Peasant Society and Culture: An Anthropological Approach to Civilization* (Chicago: University of Chicago Press, 1956). This qualification appears of particular significance when the folk-urban dichotomy is seen alongside other civilizational and historical dichotomies (cf. Section VIII below) in their function as attempts at coming to terms with the emerging "one world." A more specific correction of the outlook represented in them (according to which earlier or non-Western societies are characterized by sacredness, status, ascription, etc.) is constituted by the discovery of the significance of kinship relations in societies characterized by secularization, contract, achievement, etc. Cf., e.g., Talcott Parsons, "The Kinship System of the Contemporary United States" (1943), *Essays in Sociological Theory, Pure and Applied* (Glencoe, Ill.: Free Press, 1949), Chapter XI (rev. ed. [*ibid.,* 1954], Chapter IX), Michael Young and Peter Willmott, *Family and Kinship in East London (ibid.,* 1957), and Leo A. Despres, "A Function of Bilateral Kinship Patterns in a New England Industry," *Human Organization,* 17, 2 (Summer, 1958), pp. 15-22.

36. This dialectic between subjective and objective reason parallels Herbert Marcuse's between the "performance" (reality) principle and the pleasure principle: *Eros and Civilization: A Philosophical Inquiry into Freud* (Boston: Beacon Press, Inc., 1955). Space limitations forbid an examination of Marcuse's thesis.

37. This is a proposition more pointed to than explicitly made by some of the students of the most spontaneous, unconscious, varied part of culture, namely language. See especially the work of Dorothy D. Lee (particularly "Conceptual Implications of an Indian Language," *Philosophy of Science,* 5 [January, 1938], pp. 89-102; "A Primitive System of Values," *ibid.,* 7 [July, 1940], pp. 355-78; "Lineal and Non-Lineal Codifications of Reality" [1950], *Explorations,* 7 [March, 1957], pp. 30-45, where she says: "If reality itself were not absolute, then true communication of course would be impossible. My own position is that there is an absolute reality, and that communication is possible" [p. 30]) and Benjamin Lee Whorf (particularly "A Linguistic Consideration of Thinking in Primitive Communities" [1936?], "Languages and Logic" [1941], and "Language, Mind, and Reality" [1941], all reprinted in *Language, Thought, and Reality: Selected Writings of Benjamin Lee Whorf,* ed., and with an introduction by John B. Carroll ([Cambridge, Mass., and New York: Technology Press of Massachusetts Institute of Technology and John Wiley & Sons, Inc., 1956]).

38. This distinction is developed by Child ("Categories") and expounded in my "The Unique and the General: Toward a Philosophy of Sociology," *Philosophy and Science,* 15 (July, 1948), pp. 203-204, and more fully, "Inquiry," pp. 595-600).

39. Karl Mannheim, "The Problem of a Sociology of Knowledge," Chapter IV, pp. 134-90, in *Essays on the Sociology of Knowledge, loc. cit.;* cf. pp. 136-44.

40. *Ibid.,* p. 136. While the first, third, and fourth factors can be accounted for "in terms of the immanent development of ideas," the second, the "unmasking turn of mind," must be understood "in terms of real, social developments" which resulted in the rise of the "oppositional science of sociology" from Humanism and Enlightenment with their "main task," the "disintegration of the monarchy" and the clergy (cf. *ibid.,* pp. 139-40). And now that we are "increasingly aware of the fact that *all* thinking of a social group is determined by its existence, we find less and less room for the exercise of 'unmasking,' and the latter undergoes a process of sublimation which turns it into a mere operation of determining the functional role of any thought whatever" (*ibid.,* p. 144).

41. My attention to whom has been called by Professor Alfred Schutz, as I herewith gratefully acknowledge.

42. Cf. Wirth, *op. cit.,* pp. xiii, xvii, xxiii.

43. Mannheim, *op. cit.,* p. 139.

44. Merton, *Social Theory and Social Structure,* rev. ed., pp. 457, 458. Cf. also H. Otto Dahlke, "The Sociology of Knowledge," in Harry Elmer Barnes, Howard Becker, and Frances Bennett Becker, eds., *Contemporary Social Theory* (New York and London: Appleton-Century, 1940), pp. 64-65.

45. Wolff, "Inquiry."

46. In John Dewey's sense, as developed by Thelma Z. Lavine ("Naturalism and the Sociological Analysis of Knowledge," in Yervant H. Krikorian, ed., *Naturalism and the Human Spirit* [New York: Columbia University Press, 1944], p. 184).

47. Wolff, "Inquiry," p. 612.

48. Predominantly, if (in addition to propositions) truth is also considered predicable of definitions. It can be so considered if a cognitive function of the operational character of definitions is emphasized: in this case, "definition" borders on hypothesis. It cannot be, if a definition is considered to be an analytical proposition and nothing else: in this case, it has no truth dimension while of course the *use* of the definition (in methodology or research) does, namely that of stipulative (hypothetical, propositional) truth.

49. On the concept of "surrender," see my "Before and After Sociology," *Transactions of the Third World Congress of Sociology*, Vol. VII, pp. 151-52, and more fully, *Loma Culture Change: An Introduction to the Study of Man* (Columbus: Ohio State University, 1952 [mimeographed]) "Introduction," pp. 22 ff.—It is a not irrelevant, further characterization of our time that one should be led to ask, in a footnote, whether the concern here exhibited with existential truth won't alienate professional colleagues; or, hyperbolically, whether, in trying to save my life and the world, I am not risking the loss of my profession.

50. Paul Kecskemeti, "Introduction," Chapter I in Mannheim, *Essays on the Sociology of Knowledge, loc. cit.*, pp. 15, 31. The difference between scientific and existential truth corresponds, in a way that cannot be discussed here, to that between mathematical and "inner" time (*durée*); on the latter, see, e.g., Alfred Schuetz, "On Multiple Realities," *Philosophy and Phenomenological Research*, V (June, 1945), pp. 538-42; Pitirim A. Sorokin, *Sociocultural Causalty, Space, Time* (Durham, N. C.: Duke University Press, 1943), Chapter IV; Igor Stravinsky, *Poetics of Music in the Form of Six Lessons* (1939–40) (New York: Vintage Books, 1956), pp. 31-34.

51. Roscoe C. Hinkle, Jr., and Gisela J. Hinkle, *The Development of Modern Sociology: Its Nature and Growth in the United States* (Garden City, N.Y.: Doubleday & Company, Inc., 1954), pp. vii, 73, 74.

52. Ernest Manheim, "Introduction" to Karl Mannheim, *Essays on the Sociology of Culture, loc. cit.*, p. 5 (original italics).

53. Cf. Grünwald, *op. cit.*, Chapter I. (This important work has not been adequately appreciated in this country. Aside from a few citations there is only, as far as I know, Child's analysis of Grünwald's own position [in several of Child's papers on the sociology of knowledge cited in n. 8 above] and a very brief exposition of parts of it in Adler, "The Range of Sociology of Knowledge," *loc. cit.*, pp. 412-13.) A more detailed presentation and critique of Grünwald's discussion of the "psychological" and "historical" theories, while relevant and highly interesting, exceeds the scope of this paper. The central significance of his own position on the sociology of knowledge, however, must be registered. This position is what might be called "interpretational relativism": according to Grünwald, the sociology of knowledge is only one among many equally valid or invalid interpretations of intellectual phenomena. (It has also, and rightly, been designated

as "postulational skepticism": Child, "Possibility," p. 404; Wolff, "Inquiry," pp. 592-93, esp. n. 21.) If we ask how it is possible that a number of interpretations can be entertained, that is, if we inquire into the basis of interpretational relativism, we find that interpreter and interpretandum emerge as relatively unanalyzable presuppositions or "givens," that is, we find the dualism of reality as relative and absolute—the same dualism we came upon as a metaphysical premise of the sociology of knowledge. If this dualism is in turn posited as, in some sense, optional, the burden of proof rests on the exploration of this positing, wherewith the continuity of analysis is made both possible and mandatory: this consideration vindicates the continuity of analysis (naturalism), the second metaphysical premise of the sociology of knowledge.

54. Merton, *Social Theory and Social Structure*, rev. ed., p. 449.

55. Many examples of such articulations are given and analyzed in Kahler, *op. cit.*, Chapters Four and Five.

56. Wolff, "Inquiry," p. 618.

57. Godfrey and Monica Wilson, *The Analysis of Social Change on the Basis of Observations in Central Africa* (Cambridge: University Press, 1945). For a convenient conspectus of many such dichotomies (and trichotomies), see Howard Becker, *Through Values to Social Interpretation* (Durham, N.C.: Duke University Press, 1950), pp. 258-61.

58. David Riesman, "Some Observations on the Study of American Character," *Psychiatry*, 15 (August, 1952), p. 333.

59. Emile Durkheim, *The Division of Labor in Society* (1893), transl. by George Simpson (Glencoe, Ill.: Free Press, 1947), Preface to the second edition (1902), "Some Notes on Occupational Groups," and, particularly, *Professional Ethics and Civic Morals* (1890's) transl. by Cornelia Brookfield (London: Routledge & Kegan Paul, 1957), esp. Chapters I-III; Max Weber, "Science as a Vocation," *loc. cit.*, esp. p. 153; ". . . the decisive state of affairs: the prophet . . . simply does not exist"; Karl Mannheim, *Essays on the Sociology of Culture, loc. cit.*, "The Problem of Ecstasy" (in "The Democratization of Culture" [1933]), the argument of which the translator, Paul Kecskemeti, characterizes (*ibid.*, p. 239, n. 1) as the "necessity to transcend the purely pragmatist and positivist approach"; Mannheim himself writes: "We inherited from our past another need: that of severing from time to time *all* connection with life and with the contingencies of our existence. We shall designate this ideal by the term 'ecstasy'" (*ibid.*, p. 240).

60. Related to these civilizational-historical dichotomies is that between "culture" and "civilization," independently formulated by Alfred Weber and Robert M. MacIver. (Cf. Alfred Weber, "Der soziologische Kulturbegriff" [1912], *Ideen zur Staats- und Kultursoziologie* [Karlsruhe: G. Braun, 1927], pp. 31-47; *Kulturgeschichte als Kultursoziologie* [Leiden: A. W. Sijthoff, 1935], pp. 9-10, 421. MacIver has discussed the distinction in numerous places, from Community [London: Macmillan, 1917], pp. 179-80, to MacIver and Charles H. Page, *Society* [New York: Rinehart & Co., Inc., 1949], pp. 446, 486-87, 498-506. Also cf. Robert K. Merton, "Civilization and Culture," *Sociology and Social Research*, 21 [November-December, 1936], pp. 103-13, and Howard Becker, *op. cit.*, pp. 165-68.) In reference to the concerns of the present paper, this distinction has a twofold significance. (1) It is a formulation of a dualism which parallels, within culture

itself, that between what here has been called "transcultural human nature" and "human culture." (2) It is an attempt at preserving historical continuity (through "culture") and, at the same time, independence from it ("civilization")—at preserving, that is, both the absolute and the relative in man (cf. the last quotation in Section VII above).

61. Its most dramatic expression probably is the confusion of Soviet communism with a historically more adequate version of liberalism and the shock, if not despair, on the realization of this confusion. Cf. such works as Arthur Koestler, Ignazio Silone, Richard Wright, Andre Gidé, Louis Fischer, and Stephen Spender, *The God That Failed* (New York: Bantam Books, 1952).

62. Reinhard Bendix, *Social Science and the Distrust of Reason* (Berkeley and Los Angeles: University of California Press, 1951). Cf. also Institut für Sozialforschung, *Soziologische Exkurse, nach Vorträgen und Diskussionen* (Frankfurt am Main: Europäische Verlagsanstalt, 1956), Chapter XII, "Ideologie." Both this chapter and Bendix, *op. cit.*, draw heavily on Hans Barth, *Wahrheit und Ideologie* (Zurich: Manesse Verlag, 1945). Chapter I of the Frankfurt volume ("Begriff der Soziologie") is an impressive description of the fate of social thought, beginning with Plato, in its shift toward sociology (Comte), and of the development of sociology itself to the present time. Among the various but rare critiques of modern sociology, this and Bendix's are important. In this context, special attention should also be called to C. Wright Mills, " 'The Power Elite': Comment on Criticism," *Dissent*, IV (Winter, 1957), pp. 22-34.

63. Portrayed more in fiction than in social science; but see C. Wright Mills, *White Collar: The American Middle Classes* (New York: Oxford University Press, 1951), esp. Part Three, and William H. Whyte, Jr., *The Organization Man* (New York: Simon and Schuster, Inc., 1956), esp. Parts VI and VII.

64. Cf. my "Before and After Sociology," *loc. cit.*, p. 153, "Sociology and History; Theory and Practice" (presented at the 1958 meetings of the American Sociological Society), and John W. Bennett and Kurt H. Wolff, "Toward Communication between Sociology and Anthropology," William L. Thomas, Jr., ed., *Yearbook of Anthropology—1955, loc. cit.*, p. 330 (reprinted in William L. Thomas, Jr., ed., *Current Anthropology: A Supplement to Anthropology Today* [Chicago: University of Chicago Press, 1956] same pagination).

65. This, on the surface of it, would appear to contradict Alfred Schuetz's characterization of "the world of scientific theory" (in his "On Multiple Realities," *loc. cit.*, pp. 563-75) but actually seems a consequence of affirming his proposition "that sociality and communication can [only] be realized within . . . the world of everyday life which is the paramount reality" (*ibid.*, p. 575). Space limitations make it impossible to enter into a discussion of this important, if not crucial, question of the philosophy of science.

66. This meaning of "substantive," in contrast to "formalistic," is obviously different from H. Otto Dahlke's (*op. cit., passim,* e.g., p. 86) or from Mannheim's "empirical" (*Ideology and Utopia, loc. cit.,* pp. 239 ff.), both of which contrast with "epistemological."

67. Compare, e.g., Durkheim's *Rules of Sociological Method* (1895) or "The Determination of Moral Facts" (1906), Chapter II in *Sociology and Philosophy,* transl. by D. F. Pocock, with an introduction by J. G. Peristiany (Glencoe, Ill.: Free Press, 1953), with his worry about anomie (cf. n. 59 above); or Weber's *Methodology of the Social Sciences, loc. cit.,* with e.g., his *Protestant Ethic,* and, on the discrepancy between Weber's methodological prescriptions for practice and his practice itself, Leo Strauss, *op. cit.* (I am not acquainted with a corresponding analysis of Durkheim's work. Cf., however, some relevant observations in my "The Challenge of Durkheim and Simmel," *The American Journal of Sociology,* LXIII (May, 1958), pp. 590-593.

68. In respect to American sociology, cf. the Hinkles' remark quoted above. On the unrivaled position of liberalism in American political and social thought, cf. Louis Hartz, *The Liberal Tradition in America: An Interpretation of American Political Thought Since the Revolution* (New York: Harcourt, Brace and Company, 1955).

69. Merton, *Social Theory and Social Structure,* Part III, "The Sociology of Knowledge and Mass Communications," rev. ed., pp. 439-55. The quotation is from p. 439.

70. "Such dynamic categories, with little direct bearing on commercial interests, as 'false consciousness' . . . have as yet played little part in the description of audiences" (*ibid.,* pp. 451-52). Merton asks whether communications research may one day become "independent of its social origins," which question "is itself a problem of interest for the sociology of science," and whether the development of social science might not parallel that of the physical sciences in the seventeenth century, when the impetus, too, came not so much from the universities as from the new scientific societies (*ibid.,* pp. 452-53).

71. Cf. n. 60 above.

72. For divers items from such a list, see my "The Sociology of Knowledge: Emphasis on an Empirical Attitude," *Philosophy of Science,* 10 (April, 1943), pp. 122-23. Also cf. notes 17 and 18 above.

73. Alfred Schutz, "Concept and Theory Formation in the Social Sciences," *Journal of Philosophy,* LI (29 April 1954), pp. 257-73, esp. 271-72, and "Common-Sense and Scientific Interpretation of Human Action," *Philosophy and Phenomenological Research,* XIV (September, 1953), pp. 1-38, esp. 26-37 (reprinted [abridged] in Lewis A. Coser and Bernard Rosenberg, eds., *Sociological Theory: A Book of Readings* [New York: The Macmillan Company, 1957], pp. 233-46, esp. 240-46). From Schutz's conception of social-scientific theory it is illuminating to go to scientific theory in general; see, e.g., Morris R. Cohen and Ernest Nagel, *An Introduction to Logic and Scientific Method* (New York: Harcourt, Brace and Company, 1934), pp. 397-99, and Philipp Frank, *Foundations of Physics* (Chicago: University of Chicago Press, 1946 [International Encyclopedia of Unified Science, Vol. 1, No. 7]), pp. 3-11.

74. E.g., Talcott Parsons, *The Structure of Social Action, loc. cit.,* p. 24; Nicholas S. Timasheff, *Sociological Theory: Its Nature and Growth* (Garden City, N.Y.: Doubleday & Company, Inc., 1955), pp. 9-10; Merton, *op. cit.,* rev. ed., pp. 96-97.

19

Operationalism and Social Research

GIDEON SJOBERG

University of Texas

This paper seeks to analyze operationalism via the sociology-of-knowledge approach and thereby to clarify a number of methodological issues surrounding its use in sociology. But has not enough been said on the subject of operationalism? Should we not get on with theorizing and data gathering and bury the methodological controversies? So argue numerous physical scientists and philosophers of science who, because of these conflicts, view social science with a jaundiced eye. But there is good reason for the social scientists' concern with methodological questions: it is methodology which provides one prime justification for the view that the social sciences are scientific in nature.

Operationalism is not a dead issue. The term is still variously interpreted by social scientists, including sociologists. It is so loosely bandied about that it requires critical evaluation. Some writers assume it is sufficient merely to state that this or that term is operationally defined and the issue of a concept's scientific status is automatically settled. Operationalism—whether this refers to "physical" or to "mental" operations—is in fact used to rationalize a variety of scientific activities. A re-evaluation of it seems all the more pressing if we examine current trends of thought on the role of operationalism in scientific activity. Bridgman, the foremost exponent of operationalist thought, simply confounds the situation by disavowing some of his earlier work and charging that basically his approach is not really understood. At one point

603

in a recent article, he states: ". . . I feel that I have created a Franken-stein, which has certainly got away from me." [1] Sociologists should be wary lest they find themselves espousing uncritically positions which are being re-examined by other members of the intellectual community.

This essay has two main sections. First, the theoretical issues under-lying operationalism and its role in the social sciences, sociology in particular, are briefly surveyed to provide background for the paper's central discussion. The problem "What is operationalism?" is consid-ered. Here the meaning of "physical" as opposed to "mental" oper-ationalism is clarified. Next, some of the controversies surrounding physical operationalism are brought to light through examination of the question, "Is rigid operationalism in sociology feasible or possible?" Much could be said concerning the philosophical presuppositions of operationalism. The views of philosophers necessarily form part of our discussion of issues which have preoccupied sociologists for almost three decades. But the metaphysical underpinnings of operationalism will receive only brief and indirect treatment, for Benjamin has recently considered these in detail and with considerable acumen.[2] And a recent symposium in the *Scientific Monthly* [3] adds much to our understanding of the controversies currently engaging social and scientific philosophers.

Second, the bulk of the paper analyzes those facets of modern social systems which encourage the development of operationalism in social science as well as others prejudicial to it. An effort is made, through the admittedly deviant perspective of the sociology of knowledge, to contribute positively to an understanding of the role of operationalism in social science inquiry. Few sociologists set the contemporary re-searcher into societal context and examine how he responds to pres-sures emanating from the scientific community and the total social order. Yet, it will be argued herein that the sociology of knowledge, applied as a method, can clarify existing controversies over operational-ism and pinpoint some of the advantages and disadvantages of the operationalist approach. In so far as the author is able to determine, this is the first attempt at such an undertaking.

This essay is directed primarily to the sociologist. But sociology overlaps other fields, requiring us to draw upon pertinent studies in allied disciplines. The results should impart to the paper a great degree of generality.

CONTROVERSIES SURROUNDING OPERATIONALISM IN SOCIOLOGY

Operationalism, as we have noted, is encircled by several contro-versies that cannot be ignored. The first issue at hand is:

1. What Is Operationalism?

Sociologists frequently cite Bridgman's original definition of operationalism in *The Logic of Modern Physics* as the classic formulation of this concept.[4] But Benjamin has recently documented in considerable detail the fluctuations in Bridgman's thought patterns over the years.[5] Some of these revisions seem to have resulted from the many severe criticisms leveled against Bridgman's original definition. It would appear that scientists should be able to settle on a definition of operationalism which is precise, comprehensible, and acceptable to large numbers of their own group—but such has not yet been attained.

Although Bridgman has modified his position a number of times, his classic statement, which has set the pace for the development of operationalism in sociology and for the ensuing controversies, is nevertheless a logical starting point for discussion and this concept herein. Bridgman writes: [6]

In general, we mean by any concept nothing more than a set of operations; *the concept is synonymous with the corresponding set of operations.* If the concept is physical, as of length, the operations are actual physical operations, namely, those by which length is measured; or if the concept is mental, as of mathematical continuity, the operations are mental operations, namely those by which we determine whether a given aggregate of magnitudes is continuous. It is not intended to imply that there is a hard and fast division between physical and mental concepts, or that one kind of concept does not always contain an element of the other; this classification of concept is not important for our future considerations.

Although Bridgman dismisses the problem of the relation of physical to mental operations, this question is still very much alive in sociological literature. The advocates of operationalism in sociology have taken physical operations to be clearly superior to the mental forms. The representatives of neopositivism—e.g., Lundberg, Chapin, and Bain, as well as their many followers among empirical researchers—have championed physical operationalism. They have viewed verbal theories and definitions in sociology with considerable skepticism. Chapin in 1939 observed that verbal definitions are cheap, and he strongly urged that they be dispensed with as soon as possible in sociology.[7] For him, verbal definitions were only the initial step in social research. In many respects this is the most extreme theoretical statement of operationalism in sociological literature. In a recent work, Chapin retreats somewhat from his position and concedes that verbal definitions—or verbal theory—will always form part of sociology.[8] But he still views as eminently preferable the delineation of sociological concepts through "physical" operations. Lundberg maintains a similar position. In a recent article, he writes: "If you can do scientific research (of the kind scientists recognize and value) without quantitative procedures and operational definitions, go ahead." [9] But it is evident from his subsequent discussion that he believes "true" scientists will recognize and value only that type of research which emphasizes operationalism.

But we still have not defined what sociologists mean by "physical operationalism." One approach would be to list the varying usages of the concept. But it is preferable to set forth in summary fashion the meaning physical operationalism has acquired in sociological literature, not just for theoreticians but for empirical researchers as well. The latter, as a matter of fact, have often given a more definite meaning to physical operationalism—freeing it of some of the qualifications which theoreticians tend to introduce.

Physical operationalism is at times loosely associated by its adherents with empiricism. More specifically it is equated with explicit, clear-cut research operations which can be standardized and are capable of duplication by social researchers working independently. As Lundberg [10] would have it, the recipe for a cake defines the cake. Thus, carefully defined sampling procedures, controlled observation, and quantification and experimentation are at times employed interchangeably with physical operationalism. In its ideal form, physical operationalism has been identified most closely with social measurement. The works of Chapin,[11] Lundberg,[12] and Zetterberg,[13] recent texts in research methods, and numerous empirical studies do just this. Chapin operationally defines social status through a social status scale. Lundberg continually advances the notion that an IQ is what an IQ test measures. And the Rileys *et al.* consider scales as providing "empirical representations of certain sociological concepts," [14] a viewpoint in keeping with the tradition of physical operationalism. This identification of rigid operationalism with measurement is implicit in Bridgman's original definition cited above and has been perpetuated in sociology by the neopositivists, the behaviorists, and the pragmatists. In this paper "rigid" or "physical" operationalism refers to the efforts to define concepts or to seek "empirical" or "numerical" representations of social phenomena through a well-defined set of research operations, measurement in particular.

Physical operationalism has gained wide acceptance in sociology. It has provided the stimulus for the development and application of measurement tools such as Bogardus' social distance scale, Thurstone's social attitude scale, Guttman's scalogram analysis, Lazarsfeld's qualitative measurement technique, and perhaps even Moreno's sociometric analysis. In this paper, the term "measurement" denotes not only interval and ratio scales but also less powerful techniques such as ordinal (or even nominal) scales. Stevens and Coombs have shown that the ordinal scale logically can be considered as a kind of measurement device.[15] It involves simply the ranking of attributes—e.g., in geology the hardness of rocks. Ordinal scales are particularly important for current sociological research; they form the basis of Guttman's and Lazarsfeld's measurement techniques.

Although rigid operationalism has numerous adherents in sociology, especially among empirical researchers, another school of thought gives priority to mental operations. Most of the "conceptualist" sociologists implicitly adhere to this position, although few employ the terminology of operationalism. Levy,[16] however, does speak of defining concepts operationally in the broadest meaning of the term. Furthermore, many philosophers have carefully distinguished between physical and mental operationalism. Hempel [17] speaks of "symbolic operations," which he identifies with *logical thought*. Benjamin [18] refers to "generalized operationism" and has sought to categorize the various types of "mental" operations.

This schism between physical and mental operationalism suggests that the former has not been completely accepted—a fact which leads us to the question:

2. Is Rigid Operationalism in Sociology Feasible or Possible?

During the 1930's and to some extent in the 1940's when the controversies over physical operationalism were at their height, critiques and rebuttals flowed fast from the pens of sociologists. There were, for example, essays by Alpert and Adler, the latter objecting to the inherent circularity of the rigid operationalists' arguments.[19] Some other issues, however, appear more pertinent to this discussion.

First, those sociologists who espouse a rationalistic or even idealistic philosophical position implicitly oppose rigid operationalism and implicitly accept mental operationalism. The very nature of their approach precludes acceptance of certain features of rigid operationalism—for them an extreme form of empiricism. They admit the need for observation and data collection but consider empirical investigation to be realizable only within a theoretical frame of reference. Many adherents of the conceptualist approach—Talcott Parsons,[20] despite the various positivistic elements in his approach, might be classed in this group—believe that to a degree order can be imposed upon reality through theory. This group might utilize rigid operationalism to a limited extent in hypotheses testing but would never concede to physical operationalism a central role in sociological theory and research, as the proponents of rigid operationalism are wont to do. They do accept the view that a set of "research operations" defines the concept—that, for example, the operations performed through Guttman's scalogram analysis can define an "attitude universe," or that a social-status scale can satisfactorily define social status.

Second, some of the opponents of physical operationalism have challenged its feasibility and utility on the grounds that social data, differing rather markedly from physical data, cannot be comprehended through the traditional procedures of physical or natural science.[21] These sociologists have argued that social data are inherently too heterogeneous and complex to be examined operationally: such would involve an oversimplification of reality. They have observed that sociology can never develop precise and well-defined concepts: the best that can be achieved are "sensitizing" concepts. This does not imply that concepts cannot be modified through research findings, but rather that these concepts are loosely structured, for this is the nature of social reality. Sociologists who argue that the social and physical worlds are distinct believe that the methods of the physical sciences are often inapplicable to social data and that this information must instead be obtained through procedures such as *verstehen*—which involves introspection and "taking the role of the other."

The rigid operationalists counter these points by insisting that physical and social phenomena are not inherently disparate, that they are amenable to similar analytic procedures. They concede that their concepts do not embrace all of reality, and argue that oversimplification is a concomitant of the scientific method. The rigid operationalists, moreover, question the need for the subjectivist approach: they believe that one does not have to experience naziism in order to analyze and understand the development of Hitlerism.

A third controversy stems from the fact that the rigid operationalists, as strict empiricists, devote little attention to the whys and wherefores of selecting problems for study. From the contention that a set of operations defines the concept they leap to the conclusion that a problem to be significant must be treated operationally (and perhaps even that a problem treated operationally is therefore significant). Perhaps no one has stated this position quite this boldly, but some writers approach it. Thus Ogburn[22] in his article, "Some Observations on Sociological Research," argues that a good project is in effect one which is researchable through highly developed instruments and procedures.

The tendency of physical operationalists to select problems for study simply on the basis of researchability is illustrated by a conversation I witnessed between two colleagues of mine. X was propounding a sociological problem, primarily theoretical in nature, which he was pursuing in the field of social control. *Y* listened attentively and after some reflection insisted the question should be put to the test in a small group laboratory. It was evident from *Y*'s observations that he equated a problem's significance with its amenability to experimental and operational treatment. As *X* walked away he turned to me and remarked: "Just how does *Y* propose to test theories on the spread of communism in Asia, or measure its effect, in a small group laboratory?"

There are, then, social scientists who believe that physical operationalism must transcend the boundaries of its own logic in choosing research problems, that it is highly negligent in not weighing the possible ultimate significance of day-by-day research for social-science theory. Moreover, there are social scientists who would select problems on an entirely different basis. They argue that it is the social scientist's duty to provide leadership for the politicians and the citizenry as a whole, that this consideration should override all others in the scientist's quest for knowledge.

Discussion of these issues has not only provided further background on the nature of operationalism but has shown that though rigid operationalism receives wide acceptance it is viewed with a skepticism in a number of quarters. The succeeding sections of this essay will examine the role of rigid operationalism in terms of the sociology of knowledge. This should go far toward setting operationalism in proper perspective. The controversies already considered will be observed in a new light and others brought to notice. We shall see that the social system functionally demands rigid operationalism despite the limitations of this approach. On the other hand, the ristrictions imposed upon operationalism by the very social order which sustains it lend support directly and indirectly to some of the criticisms of operationalism outlined above. We now turn to the central problem of the paper.

SOCIAL FORCES AND OPERATIONALISM IN SOCIAL RESEARCH

Before examining the effects of the social system upon operationalism, it seems advisable to review the sociology-of-knowledge orientation which we shall employ to gain perspective on the methodology of operationalism. Sociology-of-knowledge theory has generated considerable debate in sociology and in such related disciplines as social philosophy. Mannheim [23] introduced a number of complex intellectual issues when he sought to establish the basis of knowledge in society as primarily a product of the actor's role in the system. Too close an adherence to Mannheim's position presents a dilemma for the social scientist. This is: How is it possible to gain generalizable, universal knowledge if this knowledge is merely a reflection of the intellectual's own culture or of his position in the social system? Mannheim suggested that a way out of this predicament was possible for the "free-floating" intellectual—that person who is able to transcend his cultural milieu, particularly his class position in it. But his formulation is only a partial solution.

If we are to avoid the more dangerous epistemological pitfalls implicit in Mannheim's sociology-of-knowledge perspective, his approach must be applied simply as a "method"—not as a means for arriving at "truth" per se. Our argument is essentially that only through evaluation of the sociologist's, or other social scientist's relationship to the present-day social system with its particular functional demands can we gain a comparative perspective on current methodology, including operationalism, which is of immediate concern to sociology. Contemporary sociologists when evaluating social scientists of the past are prone to view these men as products of their culture and historical period. But these same sociologists are reluctant to concede that they too are caught in the web of demands imposed by their own primary group, by the norms of science, and especially by the broader society in which they live. It is admittedly difficult to view one's role detachedly, yet much is to be gained thereby.

The sociologist who studies a social system is in a significantly different position from the physical scientist. Unlike the latter, he cannot as readily remove himself from his subject matter. Although this point has been made by numerous writers, methodologists still tend to view the social scientist as existing apart from his subject matter, the social order. A perusal of texts on methods—those by Goode and Hatt, Jahoda *et al.,* and Young, to mention only a few [24]—reveals the general disregard for the impact of the sociocultural system upon the investigator, upon his techniques, and upon his mode of analysis. Although considering the researcher as removed from his social system—i.e., as if functioning in a vacuum—may prove in some instances a useful analytic device, it is decidedly unrealistic and distorts many aspects of the real world in which the social scientist must necessarily function. The rigid operationalist may object to being recast against the background of society, but the empirical evidence in support of this step is overwhelming.

Our concern is with determining the relationship of the social scientist to his subject matter. If he views himself in the mirror of the sociology of knowledge, he can to a degree overcome the limits set upon his research and theory by elements of the sociocultural system (not just the class system, which was Mannheim's concern). The exponents and critics of the sociology of knowledge alike have failed to view this approach as a means by which the scientist can to a degree avoid lapsing into "historicism." If the sociologist employs it as a method, he is not necessarily being antirationalistic, a charge commonly leveled against sociologists of knowledge. Rather, by viewing sociology in comparative perspective he is able to attain a greater degree of rationality than he would otherwise. Mannheim did not conceive of the sociology of knowledge as a tool by which the scientist sees his own theory and research in comparative and historical perspective, thereby acquiring a better understanding of his own thought patterns. Yet, implicitly, Mannheim's "free-floating" intellectual transcends his culture-boundedness to the extent that he reflects upon his role in the system. No "escape" is ever complete, but efforts must be made to counteract the tendency toward ethnocentrism which precludes any generality in sociology.

Now to examine how the social system drives the sociologist to employ a rigid form of operationalism; after that we shall treat in some detail the counter forces which impede the use of rigid operational techniques.

1. The Strains Toward Operationalism

A number of social pressures converge to sustain and encourage a physical-operationalist perspective in sociology. The prestige attached to the natural sciences has been one factor which has induced the flowering of operationalism in social science. The physical scientist, largely because of his ability to predict the "behavior" of natural phenomena and satisfactorily resolve problems of a "practical" nature, has in recent decades gained status ascendancy within the intellectual community. For he has been able to construct "gadgets" which really work and which can easily be appreciated by the layman. The industrial-urban society supports the natural sciences generously and is in turn buttressed by them. Without natural and physical scientists, modern societies could hardly advance or even survive. The natural scientist has, then, been accorded high status. This is true not only for theoretical scientists but, in the United States, for technicians in particular. Social scientists, like other actors in the system, desire social recognition. Just as in a class system, where those lower in rank emulate persons with higher status and power, so too the social scientist, and the sociologist is no exception, seeks to pattern himself after the natural scientist. On the surface it appears that the physical scientist's success has been predicated upon his instruments. Why not, therefore, adopt instrumentation in the social sciences as well?

When Bridgman set forth the notion that operationalism was the key to the success of the physical sciences, he offered the social scientist (especially the sociologist) a convenient device by which to transform himself into a "true" scientist. Here was an opportunity to effect real identification in the methodology of the social and physical sciences despite the apparent differences in their data. Many social scientists have felt that adoption of a rigid operationalist approach was one procedure by which they could rid themselves once and for all of the stigma of subjectivism. Rigid operationalism calls for precision, objectivity, and reproducibility of research results: social science has been deficient in all of these scientific ideals. Thus, with similar social phenomena being interpreted in diverse fashions, consensus has been the exception rather than the rule. This problem, many social scientists reasoned, could be resolved through the methodology of operationalism. The result is that social scientists of various theoretical persuasions—the neopositivists, the pragmatists, and the behaviorists—have, whatever their differences, come to champion rigid operationalism as a means of reshaping the social sciences after the model of the physical sciences, which have been so obviously successful in prediction and analysis.

If we examine the existential bases of operationalism we see even more compelling reasons than the prestige of the physical sciences inducing the sociologist to acceptance of rigid operationalism. These involve the specific functional requirements of modern social structures.

Sociologists are becoming increasingly aware of the bureaucratizing process and its impact on American society. But what about the influence of the "organizational revolution" upon the sociologist? The modern sociologist, unlike his predecessors, is being actively sought by officials in government, business, and education for counsel and assistance in resolving numerous practical, everyday problems. And he gains tangible financial rewards from these activities. Merton and Lerner [25] have suggested that the need for solutions to immediate, work-a-day issues in the realm of social relations has strongly affected the sociologist's status and role. Sociologists are no longer seeking to remake society, as did Small, Ross, and other "belligerents" of their time, or even those of the depression era who were oriented toward social work. Instead, sociology, and social science in general, seems much more concerned with reinforcing certain values and beliefs in the social system. Coser [26] has remarked that this trend, by emphasizing social statics rather than social dynamics, has influenced sociological theory per se. More than this—and something which is not quite so apparent—the tendency to integrate the social scientist into the contemporary organizational structure has affected the whole of methodology in social science. All of this has special relevance for the proliferation of operationalism and for an evaluation of its proper role in science. Now to unravel these relationships.

The question must be posed: What is there about contemporary American bureaucracy, or industrial-urban bureaucratic structure in general, which induces the development of so-called operational or instrumental procedures? We are primarily concerned with operations such as social measurement. Writers on bureaucracy in Europe and America have with few exceptions conceived of this structure in light of the Weberian ideal type.[27] Not only is this system highly "rational" but it is typified by office holders who seek to maintain a universalistic, impersonal, and objective orientation toward one another and toward outsiders, particularly their "clientele." There is a functional need for procedures which will permit the development of these norms. Special instruments are required to rationalize and justify the "decision-making" process, e.g., the hiring and promotion of personnel. And these techniques must be objective and capable of standardization. Those who apply these instruments should arrive at similar results and interpretations. Moreover, these methods ideally should be sufficiently complex and "mysterious" so that the intricacies of the bureaucratic process will not become known to the general public—i.e., outsiders. Merton [28] has observed that bureaucratic systems allow discussion of their over-all policies but not of their day-by-day procedures of administration. Concerning the latter, secrecy is required to protect the system from excessive criticisms by the general public, who might object if they understood the workings of the system. We can therefore conclude that rigid operationalism as we have defined it assists the bureaucrat in the attainment of his goals and thus contributes to the effective functioning of a rationally oriented bureaucratic system.

We need to be more specific in our observation that social scientists with their physical-operationalist orientation have come to serve a distinct function in modern bureaucracies. Businesses require systematic studies of marketing patterns. Governmental agencies are in continual need of standardized procedures to be used, for example, in setting up a cost-of-living index or delineating slum housing. But this is only the beginning. Witness the pressing need of educational organizations for measurement instruments by which to evaluate personnel within the system as well as to "select" students for college entrance on both the graduate and undergraduate levels. (The Binet test—the forerunner of so many modern techniques—was developed in order to assist the City of Paris in rooting out "unqualified" students who were felt to constitute a special burden to the educational system and consequently to society in general.) Measurement instruments are presently employed also by the armed forces, industry, and government agencies for selecting personnel and evaluating the latter's performance. The proliferation of measurement devices in psychology (perhaps the most highly developed of the social sciences in this respect) is in answer to the demands of these various bureaucracies. This can be discerned from a perusal of such publications as the *Journal of Applied Psychology*. So, too, many of the advances in sociology seem correlated with the sociologist's increased activities in government, military, or business organizations, especially during and after World War II.

By way of contrast, many bureaucratic structures in preindustrial societies—e.g., those found even today in the Middle East—do not conform to the ideal organizational model set forth by Weber. Here universalism is not a desired norm in dealing with employees or with clientele. Instead personnel are selected and often advanced according to the particularistic criteria of kinship and friendship ties. No real need for precise operational instruments exists for the structure to achieve its goals; these would in fact run counter to the values and norms governing the functioning of this type of social structure.

One significant point about many rigid operational procedures in modern society is that they tend to develop and proliferate even in the face of their questionable predictive value. This is *not* to imply that some are not useful predictive instruments. On the other hand, that so many are found wanting in this respect, even for a single culture, cannot be ignored.

In the field of education, researchers have consumed considerable time and energy seeking to develop tests which can serve as accurate predictive instruments of, for example, success in college. Up to now, the results have by no means been completely satisfactory. For as Bloom and DeV. Heyns have observed, educators have in recent decades strained "every effort to raise the correlation between the initial measures and later achievement measures beyond the usual correlation of $+.50$." [29] Jenson's study is illustrative of this problem.[30] He correlated the results of various tests (e.g., the Miller Analogy Test) administered to students in the first semester of graduate study at the University of Pittsburgh with the later performance of these individuals in graduate work. Not only did the predictive worth (or validity) of the tests appear to vary considerably among subject-matter fields, e.g., chemistry and education, but in general the predictions based on the examinations correlated poorly—many of them lower than $+.50$—with the demonstrated academic success of the students (judged by grade averages). Implicit in Jenson's study is that when subject-matter fields are considered separately the tests' predictive worth increases. Moreover, it has been observed that as these "aptitude" tests are adjusted to a school's particular characteristics their predictive value improves.[31] These last-mentioned patterns tend to support our contention that operationalists often come to concern themselves with particulars.

The justification for the various instruments used to define "operationally" the aptitude of students does not rest solely upon their predictive validity. (Note that the question of their cross-cultural predictive utility—something far more difficult to achieve—has not been raised.) One fundamental rationale for their use stems from the requirements of bureaucratic structures. It can be argued that these tests are "better than nothing," for they demonstrate a modicum of predictive utility, particularly when the alternative is recourse to personal ties and other particularistic criteria in the selection of students. For example, a state university, to carry out its aims in modern society, requires certain objective, impersonal, universalistic standards by which to process large numbers of students, and it must follow a course of action which can be justified to the general public. One means of avoiding criticisms is to make the techniques of administration sufficiently complex and obscure and then to claim that they are "scientific," a highly valued criterion in our society.

College entrance examinations are not the only widely used evaluative tools with low predictive utility. Numerous tests are being developed nowadays to assist organizations in judging the "aptitude" of potential personnel in particular occupations. A number of studies suggest that many of these tests have rather low predictive validity. A situation described by Whyte in his book, *The Organization Man,* is pertinent here. Whyte administered a test used by business organizations for selecting "executive talent" to a number of corporation presidents, some middle-management men, and also a group of prominent scientists. Although Whyte admittedly dealt with a small N, it is of interest that the top corporation executives fared poorly on the very tests which were supposedly designed to identify persons with executive ability.[32]

The fact is that numerous facets of contemporary bureaucratic structures call for the ranking of people. In certain situations multidimensional data—i.e., that which is quite complex and heterogeneous—must be reduced to a single dimension if the organization is to function adequately. And when, theoretically, order does not prevail in the real world, such must frequently be imposed. Take, for example, the realm of teaching. Here it seems fair to assert that various dimensions to this skill exist whether this be on the precollege or the university level. Even college professors disagree among themselves as to what constitutes good teaching. Nevertheless, in many instances people are advanced or held back on the basis of their performance in this area. Rank ordering is imposed upon them, and in the process contradictory evidence is ignored. A similar situation appears with respect to the ranking of students according to "intelligence" or other criteria. Order must be achieved even if it is but a "social fiction." Coombs is one of the few measurement theorists or supporters of operationalism who has demonstrated awareness of the social bases of social measurement.[33] He seems to recognize that measurement instruments are being employed because society demands it, even when the assumptions underlying their use are not properly met.

The argument must not be pressed so far as to imply that order does not exist in the real world. We have dramatized our position because of the propensity of physical operationalists—strong supporters of measurement that they are—to ignore the existential foundations of their approach. Sociologists in particular should recognize their own role in creating and rationalizing an organizational system and even at times in serving as key technicians in it. This pattern is not necessarily undesirable. As scientists, we may not wish to go as far as William Whyte, who satirized this process in contemporary society in his treatise on the "universal card," wherein he observes that the ultimate would consist of recording on a single card the results of a battery of tests—Warner's ISC Status Scale (regarding one's parents), the Wechsler-Bellevue Intelligence Scale, etc.[34] All pertinent information would thus be readily available to companies in selecting their personnel, and a man's success in a particular role theoretically could be predicted from the data on the universal card—a company could select a man for a specified position simply by running the cards through a sorter. In a sense, Whyte shows that the "operational viewpoint" contravenes a number of traditional values in American society emphasizing the individual or, more precisely, the evaluation of each person as an individual. He develops this further in his book, *The Organization Man*,[35] wherein he shows that the operationalists (although not labeled as such) are instrumental in advancing the notion of conformity in contemporary organizational structures. Although the issues he raised will not be pursued, Whyte has performed a service by setting forth some of the ideological implications of rigid operationalism.

In this paper we are primarily concerned with methodological (rather than ideological) issues as they are revealed through a sociology-of-knowledge orientation. We have seen how physical operationalism conveniently serves the needs of contemporary bureaucratic structures. It continues to be employed despite the fact that its predictive worth or validity is often open to serious question. To review other facets of this problem we now turn to the curbs imposed by the social system upon the application of physical operationalism.

2. Social Forces Restricting Physical Operationalism

Numerous constraints upon social science in general and the use of rigid operationalism in particular are in evidence. There are the obvious pressures from religionists and some intellectuals who challenge the right of social science to exist, questioning the assumption that any society can be studied scientifically. Of necessity, the romantic and intuitionist schools in philosophy historically have opposed the social sciences and are firmly committed to resisting a rigid form of operationalism. We earlier noted the theoretical objections to physical operationalism by social scientists themselves. Here, however, we shall examine strictures of a much more concrete and practical nature.

It may seem self-contradictory that social systems which require operational procedures at the same time inhibit the development of these; yet the empirical evidence supports this fact. Preliminary efforts to treat this issue have neglected to explore its many implications. Sociologists are loath to discuss in print the barriers they encounter in social research even though they express awareness of these in informal conversations. Aside from the various ethical and moral considerations involved in social research—recently discussed by Kolb and Fichter and Edward Gross [36]—we see elements of the institutional matrix, especially social power, impinging upon the researcher. These actually restrict the kinds of materials which can be collected and the manner in which they may be analyzed and written up. These patterns are most perceptible when sociologists attempt to carry out research on a comparative basis. The possibility of a sociologist investigating the social structures of contemporary China or the Soviet Union, particularly their power system, in a systematic, first-hand fashion at the present time is extremely slight. Aside from the materials made available by the system itself in the form of publications, or garnered by non-social scientists such as foreign newspapermen, who collect their data under noncontrolled observational conditions, the only recourse is to use marginal informants who have left the system. The point is that in many societies no carefully designed research project providing data comparable to those obtained through studies in the United States could be realized. Random sampling, well-designed questionnaires, and social measurement techniques simply cannot be applied in a number of instances. Yet, systematic data from these societies might be critical for the verification or rejection of sociological theories. Rigid operationalists cannot continue to ignore these facts.

Deviations from ideal research designs are common even on the American scene, because of barriers erected against social research by the institutional structure. Many research procedures, which in practice are idealized by the rigid operationalists, become inapplicable in certain situations. Kish indirectly brought this question into the open, though this perhaps was not his intent, when he observed that most statistical tests applied by sociologists rest on the assumption that the sampling units are drawn independently in a random manner, but in actual practice this assumption is often not met. He states: "Simple random selection of human populations is a rare phenomenon. . . ." [37] Nevertheless, as Kish emphasizes, probability statistics are constantly being applied even in the face of this situation. There is, then, real doubt as to the *significance* of the results of much sociological research. In some cases, the universe is unspecified, and simple random selection is not even approximated; yet despite this, probability statistics such as chi square are employed to justify the results, at times without any qualifications being attached.

Kish, among others, tends to attribute the departures from random sampling designs primarily to financial impediments. But this is an oversimplification: societal restrictions can be quite significant. The American social system, though it offers researchers considerably more freedom than many other societies, nevertheless contains some highly sensitive "nerve centers" wherein social investigation cannot be conducted without great difficulty. For example, random sampling is often of limited value when studying the power structure of large-scale organizations— e.g., it may overlook key individuals, or if these are selected they may choose not to respond. Kinsey's report on the sexual behavior of Americans deviates from the ideal research design,[38] inasmuch as the values of a number of subsystems in our society do not tolerate open discussion of sexual matters.

How does all of this relate to physical operationalism? Most operationalists implicitly assume that it is possible to carry out a well-defined and specified set of research operations. But such is not always the case. Thus, if social measurement is to be applied, the difficulties attendant upon data collection should not be disregarded. A building is no more substantial than its foundation. In many types of social research, if random sampling cannot effectively be employed the physical operationalist is unable to select his respondents in a systematic fashion and thereby is hindered in his efforts to generalize from a group to its universe. The generalizability of the results obtained from Guttman's scalogram analysis depends in large measure not only upon how the respondents are selected but also upon the method of choosing the items in the scale.[39] Thus, we can conclude that in the area of social measurement the institutional matrix, especially the factor of social power, reinforces the tendency of operationalists to deal with particulars, for they cannot rigorously generalize beyond a narrowly conceived "universe," i.e., if they hold to the logic of their assumptions.

The institutional structure circumscribes the application of operational procedures in areas other than random sampling. Note the recent negative reactions against the "behavioral scientists" from the University of Chicago Law School who sought to examine jury trials by tape recording the deliberations of federal juries.[40] These social scientists were in effect subjecting to scrutiny a key value in American society: namely that individuals as jury members can rationally judge their peers. As a consequence of this action a number of restrictions were imposed which now clearly restrict the tape recording of federal-jury deliberations. This in turn sets limits on the application of formalized operational procedures in analyzing the federal-jury system. In fact, the social scientist must be satisfied with evidence of a highly inferential nature.

Physical operationalists not only suffer disabilities in collecting and analyzing social research data, but they encounter barriers in the publication of their findings. Those operationalists seeking to emulate the laboratory experiments of the physical sciences have before them the ideal model of the reproducibility of social research. But restrictions in the shape of informal censorship can at times act to prevent this. Hunter in his study of the power structure of a southern city utilized sociometric techniques to aid him in delineating the power system of the community. Yet, he was forced to conceal the identity of the individuals he studied— members of the power group would hardly have co-operated otherwise.[41] This instance, actually mild in nature (one author of a community study told me that he even changed the sex of his informants to conceal their identity), illustrates the near impossibility of applying independent checks in certain instances. This is not to challenge the results of Hunter's or similar empirical studies, but simply to call to notice the ever-present restrictions upon the use of well-defined research operations. Actually, viewed more broadly, there may be functional limits to the amount and kinds of research which can be undertaken in a social system (a problem which has not been explored by sociologists), for social research tends to expose a system's machinations, thereby threatening the position of the power groups in the system.

Turning from the limitations imposed by the institutional structure, especially insofar as social power can be wielded against social researchers, we note that the differential functional requirements of social systems or subsystems also limit the utility of physical operationalism. This point requires elaboration. Sociologists in their research are often forced to rely upon data collected by nonsociologists. For example, many business and governmental organizations do not necessarily amass data with an eye to the needs and interests of the social scientist, but rather with a view to the requirements of the system in question. The materials of the U. S. Census, utilized by a variety of social scientists, are a case in point. Numerous aspects of the process by which these data are collected are unique to the American scene. The result is that such a scheme as the Shevky-Williams-Bell technique of urban analysis,[42] which has received considerable acclaim in sociology, is in its present form closely linked to a number of unique cultural configurations in American society which preclude its application in other social orders.

The technique of social-area analysis is based upon a system of social measurement originally proposed by Lazarsfeld. Here census tracts of a city are ranked in attribute space—i.e., a space with three dimensions constructed from indexes of social rank, urbanization, and segregation. It is significant that the indexes are dependent upon data collected by the U. S. Bureau of the Census. Thus, that pertaining to social rank is constructed from information concerning occupation and education (and rent in the earlier applications of this method). The index of urbanization is based upon fertility, women in the labor force, and the number of single-family dwelling units. Theoretically, the Shevky-Williams-Bell measurement device enables the sociologist to rank census tracts in an urban community with respect to the degree of their urbanization and segregation, and also to determine which have greater or fewer persons in various social strata; this in turn makes it possible to compare urban communities in terms of their degree of urbanization, segregation, etc.

But why concern ourselves with all this detail? The reason is that the Shevky-Williams-Bell measurement tool has been implicitly referred to by at least one writer as a cross-cultural procedure.[43] To be sure, the authors themselves are relatively cautious in their claims. However, many sociologists overlook the shortcomings of this approach, valuable though it may be. Like so many systems of measurement in the social sciences, it relies upon categories which are unique to almost a single cultural nexus, the United States, and then perhaps for a single time period. To apply social area analysis in a comparative sense, it is essential to have access to similar types of data. For example, to compare different time periods in the United States assumes stability in the census categories and in the data-collecting methods. But twenty years from now the U. S. Census Bureau may, because of political exigencies, do away with the present census tract classification. Then what? And how can social-area analysis be applied to other cultures if comparable census-tract data are unattainable? Such societies as India, Nigeria, China, or Afghanistan—which incidentally contain some large urban centers—do not have census tracts. Nor if any were developed is it likely that the data would be classified in such a fashion that the indexes constructed for social rank, urbanization, and segregation would be equivalent to those employed by Shevky, Williams, and Bell.

Throughout this section we have stressed the fact that social forces tend to drive operationalists to preoccupation with particulars. This actually compounds a problem stemming from the striking variability among social systems—that it is extremely difficult to achieve comparisons when highly empiricistic categories are employed. And the latter are continually being used by operationalists as they seek to enhance the reliability of their tools. For example, Chapin's scale for operationally delineating or defining social status relies heavily upon empirical traits which are unique to the American status system. In a recent revision of this scale, attention is given to such possessions as hardwood floors, windows with drapes, television sets, etc.[44] But some of these items simply do not exist in certain sociocultural systems. These facts have clear-cut implications for any evaluation of the operationalist viewpoint.

CONCLUSIONS

It is now time to take stock, to see where we have gone and to evaluate the role of physical operationalism in social science, especially sociology. The main purpose of this paper has been to examine physical operationalism from a sociology-of-knowledge perspective and thereby to gain some new insights into the methodological controversies which are plaguing the social sciences.

One fact seems clear. Social forces are propelling social scientists toward the use of the operationalist orientation despite any theoretical objections which may be raised against it. Key among these pressures are the requirements of modern bureaucracies. Irrevocably, it seems to me, numerous social scientists will come to serve as technicians in order to further the objectives of large-scale social organizations and to aid in carrying out the ideal norms of the system. There seems to be no letup in the demands for added instrumentation in government, education, and the armed forces. Often, these operational tools are being employed even though their predictive worth, or validity, is open to serious question.[45] Although this pattern seems most highly developed in the United States, it is prevalent in other industrial-urban systems as well. Protestations against the instrument-makers may be voiced from time to time by "alienated" intellectuals, who are concerned with the moral implications of the rigid operationalist approach, but rigid operationalism will continue with us.

Actually the physical operationalist viewpoint has not only articulated well with the needs of modern bureaucracies but it has contributed to the progress of science. Physical operationalism has been helpful in emphasizing the need for empirically testing hypotheses, for clarity in the definition of concepts, and for a precise delineation of the steps necessary in ideal research operations. Scientific research should be standardized so that the operations performed by one sociologist can be duplicated by others wherever possible. That the rigid operationalists have been highly valuable in formalizing the research process can hardly be doubted. The research reports which have appeared in the journals in the 1950's seem far superior to those of the 1920's in that they are more likely to make explicit their hypotheses and research designs.

But the limitations of physical operationalism cannot be disregarded. In this paper, considerable effort has been expended to show that social systems impose numerous restrictions upon the employment of rigid operationalism—especially as a device for gaining generalized or valid cross-cultural knowledge.[46] In his search for reliability, the operationalist emphasizes particulars and sacrifices generality.[47] This seems advantageous for meeting the particular requirements of some bureaucracies, but it hardly fulfills the demands of a generalizing science. The rigid operationalists have amassed some worth-while data, but if they are to give meaning to their findings, they must extend beyond the confines of their own system. The arguments the conceptualists or mental operationalists level against the empiricistic physical operationalists take on added significance if the barriers to research encountered by the physical operationalists are fully perceived. To be sure, Lundberg, among others, dismisses the problem of generalizability as nonsignificant. He argues that in the physical sciences the "laboratory culture" sets even greater limits upon the scientist's ability to generalize.[48] Lundberg rightly observes that all scientific laws are "if-statements": if such and such holds true, then such and such will result. But he has pressed his analogy to the breaking point. The assumption that the physical and social sciences are basically similar can be pushed too far. It is my own belief that in terms of abstract methodology the two disciplines have much in common. But certain major divergencies in the nature of the data in the natural and social sciences cannot be minimized. For one thing, it appears to be far more difficult to apply standardized research procedures in the social sciences (especially on a cross-cultural basis) than in the physical sciences. Moreover, the physical operationalists tend to disregard the fact that it is considerably more difficult to isolate invariant reference points or universal categories for social systems than for natural systems. The variability of human behavior among societies throughout the world forces social scientists to consideration of the question: "What is being measured?" Otherwise, they will be comparing apples and oranges.

Sociologists who are concerned with cross-cultural generalizations are driven to high-level conceptualizations as a means of achieving a common base of comparison of one system with another. Such can hardly be attained through the extreme empiricism of physical operationalism. For example, to examine the relationships between technology and social class in several cultures one must have a conception of technology and a conception of class common to all the cultures involved. However, the invariant points of reference concerning social class cannot be identified through operational procedures such as Chapin's social-status scale, which utilizes criteria some of which are typically characteristic of American culture. Thus, physical operationalists who wish to transcend particulars also resort to mental operations: this, in fact, is quite apparent in sociological literature.

To be sure, the conclusions of the conceptualists in sociology are easy targets of criticism, principally because of their highly abstruse nature. For example, the efforts to isolate key invariant reference points or universal categories for all cultures—by Kluckhohn, Parsons, and von Neumann and Morgenstern [49]—are vulnerable to the charge of abstruseness. Even though Parsons, for example, seeks to fit his universal categories—i.e., pattern variables—into a logically systematic theory, he is not always explicit as to how one employs these in testing hypotheses, with the result that many researchers see little significance in them. A balance between theory and research on a cross-cultural plane is difficult to achieve.

All of this implies that the schism between the physical operationalists (with their concern for particulars) and the generalizers is likely to be maintained in sociology for a long time to come. For one thing, bureaucracies will continue to demand information in areas which are of special interest to them and not necessarily advantageous to social science (although the aims of bureaucracy and of science do at times overlap). It appears that for decades to come the evidence for most cross-cultural generalizations will be of a highly inferential type. Yet, "tenable" hypotheses over which arguments arise are withal better than nothing. Even in such a field as demography, where mountains of empirical data exist, the sociologist must use indirect methods of verification—for one thing, censuses classify their materials quite dissimilarly. There is a need for reliance upon mental operations to provide plausible explanations for the data which are collected—by rigid operationalists and others—but which on a strictly empirical level are not comparable. Theorists must resort, for example, to ideal-type constructions to order and render comparable data amassed under conditions not conducive to standardization. It must be stressed that the writer does not devalue rigor—he in fact champions it—yet generality should not always be sacrificed for rigor's sake. The fact is that when sociologists attempt to generalize, not only cross-culturally but also within their social system, they must rely upon the mental operational procedures which the physical operationalists view with disfavor.

A final point concerns research procedures in the social sciences. If amenability to the methods of rigid operationalism is the principal criterion for selecting research projects (as some researchers assume), a number of key issues in the social sciences, sociology included, will go unexamined. For as we have indicated, many segments of social systems do not permit the ready use of some of the precise techniques which rigid operationalists idealize. Application of rigorous procedures wherever possible is a worthy goal. Yet, these should not be allowed to dictate the choice of the project. To resolve this dilemma sociologists might revise some of their research procedures and techniques to conform to the special difficulties they encounter. I have argued elsewhere that for comparative study sociologists need to place greater reliance upon the negative case method than they have in the past.[50] And even in data collection social scientists need to work out rationalizations for techniques which will permit them to amass relevant empirical materials on power structures and the like.[51] This would provide the social scientist interested in fundamental scientific and social issues a better basis upon which to accept or reject hypotheses. Moreover, sociologists need to exert some caution in applying "rigorous" techniques in situations where these are not applicable. For although in many respects the natural and social sciences have the same abstract logical structure, the sociologist must still face up realistically to the many special problems he encounters.

NOTES

1. P. W. Bridgman, "Remarks on the Present State of Operationalism," *Scientific Monthly,* 79 (October, 1954), p. 224.

2. A. Cornelius Benjamin, *Operationism* (Springfield, Ill.: Charles C. Thomas, 1955).

3. *Scientific Monthly,* 79 (October, 1954).

4. P. W. Bridgman, *The Logic of Modern Physics* (New York: The Macmillan Company, 1948).

5. Benjamin, *op. cit.,* chaps. 2 and 3.

6. Bridgman, *The Logic of Modern Physics, op. cit.,* pp. 5-6.

7. F. Stuart Chapin, "Definition of Definitions of Concepts," *Social Forces,* 18 (December, 1939), p. 155.

8. F. Stuart Chapin, *Experimental Designs in Sociological Research* (rev. ed., New York: Harper & Brothers, 1955), p. 155.

9. George Lundberg, "The Natural Science Trend in Sociology," *American Journal of Sociology,* 61 (November, 1955), p. 193.

10. George Lundberg, Clarence C. Schrag, and Otto N. Larsen, *Sociology* (New York: Harper & Brothers, 1954), p. 34.

11. Chapin, "Definition of Definitions of Concepts," *op. cit.,* pp. 153-60.

12. Lundberg, "The Natural Science Trend in Sociology," *op. cit.,* pp. 191-202.

13. Hans L. Zetterberg, *On Theory and Verification in Sociology* (New York: Tressler Press, 1954).

14. Matilda White Riley, John W. Riley, Jr., and Jackson Toby, *Sociological Studies in Scale Analysis* (New Brunswick: Rutgers University Press, 1954), p. 7.

15. S. S. Stevens, "Mathematics, Measurement, and Psychophysics," in S. S. Stevens, ed., *Handbook of Experimental Psychology* (New York: John Wiley & Sons, Inc., 1951), pp. 1-49; Clyde H. Coombs, "Theory and Methods of Social Measurement," in Leon Festinger and Daniel Katz, eds., *Research Methods in the Behavioral Sciences* (New York: Dryden Press, 1953), pp. 471-535.

16. Marion J. Levy, Jr., *The Structure of Society* (Princeton: Princeton University Press, 1952), p. 226.

17. Carl G. Hempel, "A Logical Appraisal of Operationism," *Scientific Monthly,* 79 (October, 1954), pp. 215-20.

18. Benjamin, *op. cit.*

19. Harry Alpert, "Operational Definitions in Sociology," *American Sociological Review,* 3 (December, 1938), pp. 855-61; Franz Adler, "Operational Definitions in Sociology," *American Journal of Sociology,* 52 (March, 1947), pp. 438-44.

20. Talcott Parsons, "The Role of Theory in Social Research," *American Sociological Review,* 3 (February, 1938), pp. 13-20.

21. A number of writers could be cited here. For a recent statement of this position, see, e.g., Herbert Blumer, "What Is Wrong with Social Theory?" *American Sociological Review,* 19 (February, 1954), pp. 3-10.

22. William Fielding Ogburn, "Some Observations on Sociological Research," *Social Forces,* 34 (October, 1955), pp. 10-18.

23. Karl Mannheim, *Ideology and Utopia,* trans. by Louis Wirth and Edward Shils (New York: Harcourt, Brace and Company, 1936).

24. William J. Goode and Paul K. Hatt, *Methods in Social Research* (New York: McGraw-Hill Book Co., Inc., 1952); Marie Jahoda, Morton Deutsch, and Stuart W. Cook, eds., *Research Methods in Social Relations* (New York: Dryden Press, 1951); Pauline V. Young, *Scientific Social Surveys and Research* (3d ed., Englewood Cliffs, N.J.: Prentice-Hall, Inc., 1956).

25. Robert K. Merton and Daniel Lerner, "Social Scientists and Research Policy," in Daniel Lerner and Harold D. Lasswell, *The Policy Sciences* (Stanford: Stanford University Press, 1951), pp. 282-307.

26. Lewis A. Coser, *The Functions of Social Conflict* (Glencoe, Ill.: Free Press, 1956), pp. 26 ff.

27. Max Weber, *The Theory of Social and Economic Organization,* trans. by A. M. Henderson and Talcott Parsons (New York: Oxford University Press, 1947), pp. 329 ff.

28. Robert K. Merton, *Social Theory and Social Structure* (Glencoe, Ill.: Free Press, 1949), p. 153.

29. Benjamin S. Bloom and I. DeV. Heyns, "Development and Applications of Tests of Educational Achievement," *Review of Educational Research,*

26 (February, 1956), p. 76. For a general critique of intelligence tests, see Pitirim A. Sorokin, *Fads and Foibles in Modern Sociology* (Chicago: Henry Regnery Company, 1956), chap. 5. Unfortunately, Sorokin does not analyze the societal reasons for their existence, nor are his comments always dispassionate.

30. Ralph E. Jenson, "Predicting Scholastic Achievement of First-Year Graduate Students," *Educational and Psychological Measurement*, 13 (Summer, 1953), pp. 322-29.

31. Edwin R. Henry, "Predicting Success in College and University," in Douglas H. Fryer and Edwin R. Henry, eds., *Handbook of Applied Psychology*, II (New York: Rinehart & Co., Inc., 1950), p. 451.

32. William H. Whyte, Jr., *The Organization Man* (New York: Simon and Schuster, Inc., 1956), pp. 198-99.

33. Coombs, *op. cit.*, p. 487.

34. Otis Binet Stanford (pseud. for William H. Whyte, Jr.), "The Case for the Universal Card," *Fortune*, 49 (April, 1954), pp. 137, 229, 230, 232.

35. Whyte, *op. cit.*

36. Joseph H. Fichter and William L. Kolb, "Ethical Limitations on Sociological Reporting," *American Sociological Review*, 18 (October, 1953), pp. 544-50; Edward Gross, "Social Science Techniques: A Problem of Power and Responsibility," *Scientific Monthly*, 83 (November, 1956), pp. 242-47.

37. Leslie Kish, "Confidence Intervals for Clustered Samples," *American Sociological Review*, 22 (April, 1957), p. 154. Also note the comments in the Appendix to his article, p. 165.

38. William G. Cochran, Frederick Mosteller, and John W. Tukey, *Statistical Problems of the Kinsey Report* (Washington, D.C.: American Statistical Association, 1954).

39. On this last-mentioned point, see, e.g., F. James Davis, Robert Hagedorn, and J. Robert Larson, "Scaling Problems in a Study of Conceptions of Air Force Leader Roles," *Public Opinion Quarterly*, 18 (Fall, 1954), p. 286.

40. "Why Eavesdropping on Juries," *U. S. News & World Report*, 39 (October 21, 1955), pp. 28, 30-32.

41. Floyd Hunter, *Community Power Structure* (Chapel Hill: University of North Carolina Press, 1953), p. 24. For an example of another study in which the persons, places, and times in the narrative were concealed, see: Leon Festinger, Henry W. Riecken, and Stanley Schachter, *When Prophecy Fails* (Minneapolis: University of Minnesota Press, 1956).

42. Eshref Shevky and Marilyn Williams, *The Social Areas of Los Angeles* (Berkeley: University of California Press, 1949) and Eshref Shevky and Wendell Bell, *Social Area Analysis* (Stanford: Stanford University Press, 1955).

43. Robert C. Tryon, *Identification of Social Areas by Cluster Analysis*, University of California Publications in Psychology, VIII (Berkeley: University of California Press, 1955), p. 30.

44. Young, *op. cit.*, pp. 343-45.

45. Some problems exist here which cannot be explored. It appears that if our system were to become static the predictive worth of these instruments would greatly increase. Yet, if real stability occurred, would there be a need for predictive tools?

46. For a philosophical critique of operationalism relating to this problem, see: Benjamin, *op. cit.*

47. Here the writer's discussion is influenced by Roger Nett, "System Building in Sociology—A Methodological Analysis," *Social Forces,* 31 (October, 1952), pp. 25-30.

48. George A. Lundberg, "Alleged Obstacles to Social Science," *Scientific Monthly,* 70 (May, 1950), p. 300.

49. Florence Kluckhohn, "Dominant and Substitute Profiles of Cultural Orientations: Their Significance for the Analysis of Social Stratification," *Social Forces,* 28 (May, 1950), pp. 376-93; Talcott Parsons, *The Social System* (Glencoe, Ill.: Free Press, 1951); John von Neumann and Oskar Morgenstern, *Theory of Games and Economic Behavior* (2d ed., Princeton: Princeton University Press, 1947).

50. Gideon Sjoberg, "The Comparative Method in the Social Sciences," *Philosophy of Science,* 22 (April, 1955), pp. 106-17. Actually, a special study needs to be devoted to examining the relationships of the "negative case method" and rigorous research procedures.

51. This has been attempted on a modest scale in my forthcoming article, "The Interviewee as a Marginal Man," *Southwestern Social Science Quarterly.*

INDEX

The Library of Congress has catalogued this book as follows:

Gross, Llewellyn, *ed.*
   Symposium on sociological theory. New York and Evanston,
Harper & Row, Publishers, Incorporated
[1959]

   642 p. illus. 24 cm.

   1. Sociology.   I. Title.

HM24.G75   301.082   59–8402 ‡

Library of Congress